ANNUAL EDIT

Human Sexualities 12/13
Thirty-Fourth Edition

EDITOR

Bobby Hutchison
Stanford University

Bobby Hutchison is currently a Fellow in Human Rights Education at Stanford University. He is also a Professor of Psychology and Human Sexualities at Modesto Junior College. He graduated from the University of California at Santa Barbara with degrees in psychology and sociology. He also has an academic background in the biological sciences and French language and literature, having completed the equivalent of a major in French. Focusing on gender and sexualities during his graduate studies, Professor Hutchison has taught sex and gender courses at a variety of institutions, from community colleges to public and private universities. He has published numerous articles, essays and reviews in psychology, sociology, education, and history journals.

Professor Hutchison conducts trainings on adolescent psychosexual development, sexual risk-taking, lesbian/gay/bisexual/transgender youth, teen pregnancy, and sexually transmitted infections. His work with foster and adoptive families has been recognized by awards from the local county board of supervisors and child welfare agency. Through his work on campus, in the community, and with *Annual Editions,* Professor Hutchison is committed to promoting the application of academic theory and scientific research in everyday life. In addition to serving as editor for *Annual Editions: Human Sexualities,* Professor Hutchison is also the editor of *Annual Editions: Gender.*

ANNUAL EDITIONS: HUMAN SEXUALITIES, THIRTY-FOURTH EDITION

Published by McGraw-Hill, a business unit of The McGraw-Hill Companies, Inc., 1221 Avenue of the Americas, New York, NY 10020. Copyright © 2013 by The McGraw-Hill Companies, Inc. All rights reserved. Printed in the United States of America. Previous edition(s) © 2012, 2011, and 2010. No part of this publication may be reproduced or distributed in any form or by any means, or stored in a database or retrieval system, without the prior written consent of The McGraw-Hill Companies, Inc., including, but not limited to, in any network or other electronic storage or transmission, or broadcast for distance learning.

Some ancillaries, including electronic and print components, may not be available to customers outside the United States.

This book is printed on acid-free paper.

Annual Editions® is a registered trademark of the McGraw-Hill Companies, Inc.
Annual Editions is published by the **Contemporary Learning Series** group within the McGraw-Hill Higher Education division.

2 3 4 5 6 7 8 9 0 QVS/QVS 1 0 9 8 7 6 5 4 3

MHID: 0-07-805117-7
ISBN: 978-0-07-805117-3
ISSN: 1091-9961 (print)
ISSN: 2158-4079 (online)

Managing Editor: *Larry Loeppke*
Senior Developmental Editor: *Jade Benedict*
Senior Permissions Coordinator: *Lenny J. Behnke*
Marketing Specialist: *Alice Link*
Project Manager: *Connie Oertel*
Design Coordinator: *Margarite Reynolds*
Cover Graphics: *Studio Montage, St. Louis, Missouri*
Buyer: *Susan K. Culbertson*
Media Project Manager: *Sridevi Palani*

Compositor: Laserwords Private Limited
Cover Image: ©Dave and Les Jacobs/Blend Images LLC (inset); Corbis Photography/ Veer (background)

www.mhhe.com

Editors/Academic Advisory Board

Members of the Academic Advisory Board are instrumental in the final selection of articles for each edition of ANNUAL EDITIONS. Their review of articles for content, level, and appropriateness provides critical direction to the editors and staff. We think that you will find their careful consideration well reflected in this volume.

ANNUAL EDITIONS: Human Sexuality 12/13
34th Edition

EDITOR

Bobby Hutchison
Modesto Junior College

ACADEMIC ADVISORY BOARD MEMBERS

Editors/Academic Advisory Board continued

Preface

In publishing ANNUAL EDITIONS we recognize the enormous role played by the magazines, newspapers, and journals of the public press in providing current, first-rate educational information in a broad spectrum of interest areas. Many of these articles are appropriate for students, researchers, and professionals seeking accurate, current material to help bridge the gap between principles and theories and the real world. These articles, however, become more useful for study when those of lasting value are carefully collected, organized, indexed, and reproduced in a low-cost format, which provides easy and permanent access when the material is needed. That is the role played by ANNUAL EDITIONS.

Sex lies at the root of life and we can never learn to reverence life until we know how to understand sex.

Many editions of this book have opened with the above quote from Havelock Ellis, a late nineteenth-century sexologist. Sex researchers and educators today persist in the belief that an accurate understanding of sex and sexualities is essential to fully appreciate the human condition. It is one piece of a bigger puzzle. But it is an essential piece. This perspective, which is at the very heart of this book, is reflected as a continuing tradition. The original purpose and core values of this book have never changed. With the passage of time, however, some things have changed.

Perhaps nowhere can we find more change and diversity than in the sexual landscape of the world today. Globalization and technology have brought in new possibilities for more complex human connections. In the more than three decades of this book's publication, vast changes have occurred in the study of human sexualities, and in society as a whole. Human sexuality has come into its own as an interdisciplinary field within academia. When this book was first published, there were few academic programs for students seriously interested in studying sex. Today, there are undergraduate majors and minors in human sexuality studies as well as dedicated graduate programs. Related areas of inquiry such as women's studies, lesbian/gay/bisexual/transgender studies, and ethnic studies have thrived. What was once an area of inquiry that drew suspicion among "serious" scholars is now a flourishing academic field with its own journals, conferences, and degree programs. Sex researchers from diverse academic perspectives make rich and lasting contributions to their own disciplines such as biology, psychology, sociology, anthropology, education, nursing, public health, and medicine, to name just a few.

The multidisciplinary nature of sex education and research is reflected throughout this book. As of the last edition, the title of this book was updated from the original (and singular) *Human Sexuality* to the plural *Human Sexualities*. This is a subtle change, but one that is important. The rich diversity in the field as well as the diverse lives of those we study are reflected in the title: *Human Sexualities.* We have a better understanding today of the incredible range of not only sexual behaviors but also identities, experiences, perspectives, voices, and social worlds. There is also an ever-increasing understanding of the importance of a range of biological processes on sexual development and behavior. What we once talked about in the singular (as if it were a unified, single, easily identified phenomenon) has often now become plural. Today, we speak of heterosexualities, homosexualities, and bisexualities. This reflects greater evidence that there are multiple developmental pathways to who we are. In sum, the title of this book is reflective of the diversity of the world today and the people we study, as well as the richness and variety of perspectives in a multidisciplinary, dynamic area of inquiry.

Each article included in this volume was selected to relate to current sexuality textbooks as well as to important trends in research and teaching today. The organization of this volume is intended to provide the reader the greatest flexibility possible, making this book the most useful, dynamic, ancillary text of human sexuality on the market.

The articles are organized by topic in the *Topic Guide.* Two new learning features have been added to this edition to aid you in your study and expand critical thinking about each article topic. Located at the beginning of each unit, *Learning Outcomes* outline the key concepts that you should focus on as you are reading the material. *Critical Thinking* questions, located at the end of each article, allow you to test your understanding of key concepts. The up-to-date *Internet References* can be used to explore the many topics presented in this book. You may be surprised by what you will learn about human sexualities just from doing a little bit of browsing on some of these sites.

Appreciation and thanks go to Jade Benedict, Senior Developmental Editor, responsible for this volume. Jade has been wonderful to work with on this project. I would also like to thank both Larry Loeppke, Managing Editor, and Debra Henricks, Senior Developmental Editor, who worked with this book through numerous editions at McGraw-Hill. They have all been incredibly supportive of this book.

I want to thank previous academic editors of *Annual Editions: Human Sexuality.* When I was an undergraduate in my first human sexuality course, we were assigned *Annual Editions: Human Sexuality.* I got hooked on studying sex, in part because of *Annual Editions.* I never could have guessed, as I read that book, that I would one day take over the editing and writing responsibilities of that very text. There may be a student reading this who will one day be at the helm of *Annual Editions: Human Sexualities.*

Much gratitude and thanks go to Janice and John Baldwin, my professors who inspired and taught me when I was an undergraduate at the University of California at Santa Barbara. I am very fortunate to be joined by them on this volume as they serve as consulting editors.

I want to thank my friends and colleagues at Stanford University where I am currently a scholar and fellow in human rights. Our many collaborations and the projects we are currently working on have influenced this edition of this book in numerous ways.

I am most thankful to my amazing daughters, Anaïs and Elise, who are my biggest inspiration. Being a parent, I find that I care even more about each of the topics we cover in human sexuality. Everything in life, including this course, takes on so much more meaning than I ever thought possible.

Finally, many thanks to those who have submitted articles for this anthology or reviewed articles from previous editions. The many updates and changes in this new edition are a direct result of readers' input. Students and professors have told us what they think, and we have responded accordingly. Because of that feedback, this is one of the most useful and up-to-date books available today. We very much look forward to hearing from you and receiving your feedback.

Bobby Hutchison
Editor

The Annual Editions Series

VOLUMES AVAILABLE

Adolescent Psychology
Aging
American Foreign Policy
American Government
Anthropology
Archaeology
Assessment and Evaluation
Business Ethics
Child Growth and Development
Comparative Politics
Criminal Justice
Developing World
Drugs, Society, and Behavior
Dying, Death, and Bereavement
Early Childhood Education
Economics
Educating Children with Exceptionalities
Education
Educational Psychology
Entrepreneurship
Environment
The Family
Gender
Geography
Global Issues
Health
Homeland Security

Human Development
Human Resources
Human Sexualities
International Business
Management
Marketing
Mass Media
Microbiology
Multicultural Education
Nursing
Nutrition
Physical Anthropology
Psychology
Race and Ethnic Relations
Social Problems
Sociology
State and Local Government
Sustainability
Technologies, Social Media, and Society
United States History, Volume 1
United States History, Volume 2
Urban Society
Violence and Terrorism
Western Civilization, Volume 1
World History, Volume 1
World History, Volume 2
World Politics

Contents

Unit 1
Social and Cultural Foundations

The concepts in bold italics are developed in the article. For further expansion, please refer to the Topic Guide.

Unit 2
Biological Foundations

The concepts in bold italics are developed in the article. For further expansion, please refer to the Topic Guide.

UNIT 3
Sexualities, Education, and Development

The concepts in bold italics are developed in the article. For further expansion, please refer to the Topic Guide.

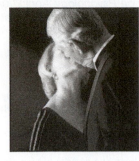

UNIT 4
Intimacies and Relationships

Unit 5
Gender and Sexual Diversity

The concepts in bold italics are developed in the article. For further expansion, please refer to the Topic Guide.

Unit 6
Sexual Health and Well-Being

Unit Overview

The concepts in bold italics are developed in the article. For further expansion, please refer to the Topic Guide.

Unit 7
Sexualities and Social Issues

The concepts in bold italics are developed in the article. For further expansion, please refer to the Topic Guide.

The concepts in bold italics are developed in the article. For further expansion, please refer to the Topic Guide.

Correlation Guide

The *Annual Editions* series provides students with convenient, inexpensive access to current, carefully selected articles from the public press. **Annual Editions: Human Sexualities 12/13** is an easy-to-use reader that presents articles on important topics such as *biology, gender, health,* and many more. For more information on *Annual Editions* and other *McGraw-Hill Contemporary Learning Series* titles, visit www.mhhe.com/cls.

This convenient guide matches the units in **Annual Editions: Human Sexualities 12/13** with the corresponding chapters in three of our best-selling McGraw-Hill Human Sexuality textbooks by Kelly, Yarber, and Miller.

Annual Editions: Human Sexualities 12/13	Sexuality Today, 10e by Kelly	Human Sexuality: Diversity in Contemporary America, 8e by Yarber et al.	Intimate Relationships, 6e by Miller
Unit 1: Social and Cultural Foundations	**Chapter 1:** Cultural, Historical, and Research Perspectives on Sexuality **Chapter 5:** Developmental and Social Perspectives on Gender	**Chapter 1:** Perspectives on Human Sexuality **Chapter 2:** Studying Human Sexuality	**Chapter 1:** The Building Blocks of Relationships
Unit 2: Biological Foundations	**Chapter 2:** Female Sexual Anatomy and Physiology **Chapter 3:** Male Sexual Anatomy and Physiology	**Chapter 3:** Female Sexual Anatomy, Physiology, and Response **Chapter 4:** Male Sexual Anatomy, Physiology, and Response	**Chapter 3:** Attraction
Unit 3: Sexualities, Education, and Development	**Chapter 4:** Human Sexual Arousal and Response **Chapter 5:** Developmental and Social Perspectives on Gender **Chapter 6:** Sexuality in Infancy, Childhood, and Adolescence	**Chapter 5:** Gender and Gender Roles **Chapter 6:** Sexuality in Childhood and Adolescence	**Chapter 9:** Sexuality
Unit 4: Intimacies and Relationships	**Chapter 7:** Adult Sexuality and Relationships **Chapter 9:** Sexuality, Communication, and Relationships	**Chapter 7:** Sexuality in Adulthood **Chapter 8:** Love and Communication in Intimate Relationships	**Chapter 6:** Interdependency **Chapter 7:** Friendship **Chapter 8:** Love **Chapter 9:** Sexuality
Unit 5: Gender and Sexual Diversity	**Chapter 13:** Same-Gender Orientation and Behavior **Chapter 14:** The Spectrum of Human Sexual Behavior	**Chapter 5:** Gender and Gender Roles	**Chapter 1:** The Building Blocks of Relationships
Unit 6: Sexual Health and Well-Being	**Chapter 17:** Sexually Transmitted Diseases, HIV/AIDS, and Sexual Decisions	**Chapter 13:** The Sexual Body in Health and Illness **Chapter 14:** Sexual Function Difficulties, Dissatisfaction, Enhancement, and Therapy **Chapter 15:** Sexually Transmitted Infections	**Chapter 9:** Sexuality
Unit 7: Sexualities and Social Issues	**Chapter 14:** The Spectrum of Human Sexual Behavior **Chapter 15:** Sex, Art, the Media, and the Law	**Chapter 9:** Sexual Expression **Chapter 10:** Variations in Sexual Behavior	**Chapter 9:** Sexuality **Chapter 14:** Maintaining and Repairing Relationships

Topic Guide

This topic guide suggests how the selections in this book relate to the subjects covered in your course. You may want to use the topics listed on these pages to search the Web more easily.

On the following pages a number of websites have been gathered specifically for this book. They are arranged to reflect the units of this Annual Editions reader. You can link to these sites by going to www.mhhe.com/cls

All the articles that relate to each topic are listed below the bold-faced term.

Abortion
47. Flower Grandma's Secret

Adulthood, later
8. Sexual Behavior in the United States: Results from a National Probability Sample of Men and Women Ages 14–94
12. A Man's Shelf Life
22. No Kids, No Grief: The Case against Having Kids
24. An Affair to Remember

Adulthood, middle
8. Sexual Behavior in the United States: Results from a National Probability Sample of Men and Women Ages 14–94
12. A Man's Shelf Life
22. No Kids, No Grief: The Case against Having Kids

Adulthood, young
8. Sexual Behavior in the United States: Results from a National Probability Sample of Men and Women Ages 14–94
12. A Man's Shelf Life
19. Teenage Fatherhood and Involvement in Delinquent Behavior
20. Truth and Consequences at Pregnancy High
21. Religiosity and Teen Birth Rate in the United States

Anatomy, male and female
15. The Orgasmic Mind

Biology
9. Starting the Good Life in the Womb
11. Effects of Prenatal Social Stress on Offspring Development: Pathology or Adaptation?
12. A Man's Shelf Life
14. Scents and Sensibility
15. The Orgasmic Mind
33. Gender Bender

Culture
1. Breastfeeding Is Not Obscene
2. Rise of the Desperate House Husband
3. Gendercide
4. Death by Gender
5. Evulvalution: The Portrayal of Women's External Genitalia and Physique Across Time and the Current Barbie Doll Ideals
6. Female Power
7. Estranged Spouses Increasingly Waiting out Downturn to Divorce
10. Women in Developing Countries 300 Times More Likely to Die in Childbirth
27. Where Is Marriage Going?

Desire
14. Scents and Sensibility
15. The Orgasmic Mind
16. Women's Vibrator Use in Sexual Partnerships: Results from a Nationally Representative Survey in the United States

Ethical issues
3. Gendercide
4. Death by Gender

10. Women in Developing Countries 300 Times More Likely to Die in Childbirth
24. An Affair to Remember
28. Contributing to the Debate over Same-Sex Marriage
29. The Polygamists
31. Women's Rights as Human Rights: The Promotion of Human Rights as a Counter-Culture
37. Finding the Switch
38. Children of Lesbian and Gay Parents
39. New Mammogram Guidelines Raise Questions
44. Rationing Antiretroviral Therapy in Africa—Treating Too Few, Too Late
45. HIV Plan B
47. Flower Grandma's Secret
48. Porn Panic!
49. Does Proximity to Schools Tempt Former Sex Offenders?
50. The Face of Domestic Violence
51. Options for Reporting Sexual Violence: Developments over the Past Decade
53. Male Rape Myths: The Role of Gender, Violence, and Sexism

Female sexualities
5. Evulvalution: The Portrayal of Women's External Genitalia and Physique Across Time and the Current Barbie Doll Ideals
8. Sexual Behavior in the United States: Results from a National Probability Sample of Men and Women Ages 14–94
13. Pubic Hair Removal among Women in the United States: Prevalence, Methods, and Characteristics
14. Scents and Sensibility
15. The Orgasmic Mind
16. Women's Vibrator Use in Sexual Partnerships: Results from a Nationally Representative Survey in the United States
24. An Affair to Remember
30. Kinky Sex Makes for Happy People
42. Condom Use Rates in a National Probability Sample of Males and Females Ages 14 to 94 in the United States

Gender
4. Death by Gender
10. Women in Developing Countries 300 Times More Likely to Die in Childbirth
19. Teenage Fatherhood and Involvement in Delinquent Behavior
23. Role Reversal
31. Women's Rights as Human Rights: The Promotion of Human Rights as a Counter-Culture,
32. The End of Men
33. Gender Bender
34. Goodbye to Girlhood
35. (Rethinking) Gender
36. Progress and Politics in the Intersex Rights Movement: Feminist Theory in Action

Health
10. Women in Developing Countries 300 Times More Likely to Die in Childbirth
39. New Mammogram Guidelines Raise Questions
40. Health Behaviors, Prostate Cancer, and Masculinities: A Life Course Perspective
41. Body Dissatisfaction in Adolescent Females and Males: Risk and Resilience
42. Condom Use Rates in a National Probability Sample of Males and Females Ages 14 to 94 in the United States

Internet References

The following Internet sites have been selected to support the articles found in this reader. These sites were available at the time of publication. However, because websites often change their structure and content, the information listed may no longer be available. We invite you to visit www.mhhe.com/cls for easy access to these sites.

Annual Editions: Human Sexualities 12/13

General Sources

The Kinsey Institute for Research in Sex, Gender, and Reproduction
www.indiana.edu/~kinsey

This is the official website for Indiana University's Kinsey Institute. This website will be helpful to anyone interested in the scientific study of sex. Check out its latest news and events section as well as resources. Find out about the history of this important research institute.

National Institutes of Health (NIH)
www.nih.gov

Consult this site for links to extensive health information and scientific resources. The NIH is one of eight health agencies of the Public Health Service, which in turn is part of the U.S. Department of Health and Human Services.

SexInfo
www.soc.ucsb.edu/sexinfo

SexInfo is based at the University of California at Santa Barbara. The site is run by advanced human sexuality students under the supervision of two UCSB sexuality professors. All aspects of sex and sexuality are covered on this website with great articles and Q&As.

SIECUS
www.siecus.org

Visit the Sexuality Information and Education Council of the United States (SIECUS) home page to learn about the organization, to find news of its educational programs and activities, and to access links to resources in sexuality education.

The Society for the Scientific Study of Sexuality
www.sexscience.org

SSSS is a professional association of sex researchers from many different scientific disciplines. According to its website, they are "[t]he oldest professional society dedicated to the advancement of knowledge about sexuality." Have a look at its ethics statement as well as the various kinds of publications it sponsors.

World Health Organization: Sexual Health
www.who.int/topics/sexual_health/en

The World Health Organization (WHO) maintains this website to provide educational information on the organization's sexual health activities and programs. This is a great resource for facts, statistics, reports, and educational materials on sexual health around the world.

UNIT 1: Social and Cultural Foundations

Department of State: Human Rights
www.state.gov/g/drl/hr

The U.S. State Department's web page for human rights includes country reports, fact sheets, reports on discrimination and violations of human rights, plus the latest news covering human rights issues from around the world.

SocioSite: Feminism and Women's Issues
www.sociosite.net/topics/women.php

Visit the University of Amsterdam's "Social Science Information System" to gain insights into a number of issues that affect both men and women. It provides biographies of women in history, an international network for women in the workplace, links to family and children's issues, and much more.

Women's Human Rights Resources
www.law-lib.utoronto.ca/Diana

This list of international women's human rights websites provides interesting resources on marriage and the family; rights of girls; sexual orientation; slavery, trafficking, and prostitution; and violence against women.

UNIT 2: Biological Foundations

Ask NOAH about Pregnancy: Fertility & Infertility
www.noah-health.org/en/search/health.html

New York Online Access to Health (NOAH) seeks to provide relevant, timely, and unbiased health information for consumers. You will find extensive links to a variety of resources about infertility treatments and issues at this interesting website.

Childbirth.Org
www.childbirth.org

This interactive site about childbirth options is from an organization that aims to educate consumers to know their options and provide themselves with the best possible care to ensure healthy pregnancies and deliveries. The site and its links address a myriad of topics, from episiotomy to water birth.

Infertility Resources
www.ihr.com/infertility/index.html

This site includes links to the Oregon Health Sciences University Fertility Program and the Center for Reproductive Growth in Nashville, Tennessee. Ethical, legal, financial, psychological, and social issues are discussed.

Planned Parenthood
www.plannedparenthood.org

Visit this well-known organization's home page for links to information on the various kinds of contraceptives and pregnancy prevention options (including outercourse and abstinence) as well as discussions of other topics related to sexuality and reproduction.

UNIT 3: Sexualities, Education, and Development

American Association of Retired Persons (AARP)
www.aarp.org

The AARP, a major advocacy group for older people, includes among its many resources suggested readings and Internet links to organizations that deal with the health and social issues that may affect one's sexuality as one ages.

Internet References

National Institute on Aging (NIA)
www.nih.gov/nia

The NIA, one of the institutes of the National Institutes of Health, presents this home page to lead you to a variety of resources on health and lifestyle issues that are of interest to people as they grow older.

SIECUS
www.siecus.org

Visit the Sexuality Information and Education Council of the United States (SIECUS) home page to learn about the organization, to find news of its educational programs and activities, and to access links to resources in sexuality education.

World Association for Sexology
www.tc.umn.edu/nlhome/m201/colem001/was/wasindex.htm

The World Association for Sexology works to further the understanding and development of sexology throughout the world. Access this site to explore a number of issues and links related to sexuality throughout the lifespan.

UNIT 4: Intimacies and Relationships

American Psychological Association
www.apa.org/topics/divorce/index.aspx

By exploring the APA's resources (and this one on marriage and divorce in particular) you will be able to find links to an abundance of articles and other information related to interpersonal relationships throughout the life span.

Bonobos Sex and Society
http://songweaver.com/info/bonobos.html

This site, accessed through Carnegie Mellon University, includes an article explaining how a primate's behavior challenges traditional assumptions about males, females, and relationships.

Go Ask Alice
www.goaskalice.columbia.edu

This interactive site provided by Healthwise, a division of Columbia University Health Services, includes discussion and insight into a number of personal issues of interest to college-age people—and those younger and older. Many questions about physical and emotional health and well-being in the modern world are answered.

SexInfo: Love and Relationships
www.soc.ucsb.edu/sexinfo/category/love-relationships

The Love and Relationships section of the SexInfo website provides students and the general public with an excellent overview of relationship issues, including communication and building effective relationships.

UNIT 5: Gender and Sexual Diversity

The Gay, Lesbian, and Straight Education Network
www.glsen.org

The Gay, Lesbian, and Straight Education Network (GLSEN) provides resources for teachers, parents, and students. They promote safe school environments for all students regardless of sexual orientation.

The Intersex Society of North America (ISNA)
www.isna.org

ISNA maintains this resource for anyone interested in the issue of intersex conditions. Physicians, therapists, parents, intersexed individuals and many others will want to learn more about the problems caused by stigma and lack of knowledge for people who are born intersexed.

Parents, Families, and Friends of Lesbians and Gays
www.pflag.org

This is the site of PFLAG: Parents, Families and Friends of Lesbians and Gays. Information and downloadable pamphlets with information and support on a variety of topics including "coming out" can be found here.

SocioSite: Feminism and Women's Issues
www.sociosite.net/topics/women.php

Visit the University of Amsterdam's "Social Science Information System" to gain insights into a number of issues that affect both men and women. It provides biographies of women in history, an international network for women in the workplace, links to family and children's issues, and much more.

Women's Human Rights Resources
www.law-lib.utoronto.ca/Diana

This list of international women's human rights websites provides interesting resources on marriage and the family; rights of girls; sexual orientation; slavery, trafficking, and prostitution; and violence against women.

UNIT 6: Sexual Health and Well-Being

The Body: The Complete HIV/AIDS Resource
www.thebody.com

On this site you can find essential basics about HIV disease, learn about treatments, exchange information in forums, and gain insight from experts.

The Johns Hopkins University HIV Guide
www.hopkins-aids.edu

This is an educational site, including a Q&A forum for patients and clinicians run by Johns Hopkins University's Professor Joel Gallant, an internationally recognized expert on HIV disease and Editor in Chief of the *HIV Guide*.

National Cancer Institute: Breast Cancer
www.cancer.gov/cancertopics/types/breast

The National Institutes of Health (NIH) National Cancer Institute runs this Breast Cancer website. Find out more about breast cancer and treatment options here. This site includes information on both male and female breast cancer.

National Cancer Institute: Ovarian Cancer
www.cancer.gov/cancertopics/types/ovarian

The National Institutes of Health (NIH) National Cancer Institute runs this Ovarian Cancer website. Find out more about ovarian cancer and treatment options here. This site includes a wide range of information on ovarian cancer.

National Cancer Institute: Testicular Cancer
www.cancer.gov/cancertopics/types/testicular

The National Institutes of Health (NIH) National Cancer Institute runs this Testicular Cancer website. Find out more about testicular cancer and treatment options here. This site includes a wide range of information on testicular cancer.

SexInfo: Sexually Transmitted Infections
www.soc.ucsb.edu/sexinfo/category/sexually-transmitted-infections

The Sexually Transmitted Infections section of the SexInfo website provides students and the general public with essential information on various kinds of STIs. There is also an excellent discussion of STIs and communication issues, including sharing sexual histories with a new partner. This is not to be missed!

Internet References

World Health Organization: Sexual Health

www.who.int/topics/sexual_health/en

The World Health Organization (WHO) maintains this website to provide educational information on the organization's sexual health activities and programs. This is a great resource for facts, statistics, reports, and educational materials on sexual health around the world.

UNIT 7: Sexualities and Social Issues

Child Exploitation and Obscenity Section (CEOS)/U.S. Department of Justice

www.usdoj.gov/criminal/ceos/trafficking.html

This site introduces the reader to essential information about trafficking and sex tourism. There are links to sex trafficking of minors and child prostitution FAQs in addition to other resources at this site.

The Child Rights Information Network (CRIN)

www.crin.org

The Child Rights Information Network (CRIN) is a global network that disseminates information about the Convention on the Rights of the Child and child rights among nongovernmental organizations (NGOs), United Nations agencies, intergovernmental organizations (IGOs), educational institutions, and other child rights experts.

Planned Parenthood

www.plannedparenthood.org

Planned Parenthood has an "Abortion Issues" section to provide information on reproductive rights.

Rape, Abuse, and Incest National Network (RAINN)

www.rainn.org

RAINN is committed to providing "anti-sexual assault" information and education. Learn about rape, incest, and other kinds of sexual victimization as well as what you can do to make a difference. There are a variety of resources, including RAINN's 2008 Back-To-School Tips for Students.

UNIT 1

Social and Cultural Foundations

Unit Selections

1. **Breastfeeding Is Not Obscene,** Catherine Marshall
2. **Rise of the Desperate House Husband,** Gaby Hinsliff
3. **Gendercide,** *The Economist*
4. **Death by Gender,** Cynthia Fuchs Epstein
5. **E*vulv*alution: The Portrayal of Women's External Genitalia and Physique Across Time and the Current Barbie Doll Ideals,** Vanessa R. Schick, Brandi N. Rima, and Sarah K. Calabrese
6. **Female Power,** *The Economist*
7. **Estranged Spouses Increasingly Waiting out Downturn to Divorce,** Donna St. George
8. **Sexual Behavior in the United States: Results from a National Probability Sample of Men and Women Ages 14–94, Debby Herbenick,** et al.

Learning Outcomes

After reading this Unit, you will be able to:

- Describe how female breasts are viewed in our culture.

- Explain how the way in which we define breastfeeding culturally can impact the experience and benefits of breastfeeding.

- Describe how broad social changes have resulted in a reversal of roles for some couples.

- Explain the social significance of these changes in relation to long-term trends.

- Discuss the extent of female infanticide within a global context.

- Assess to what extent female infanticide is a social problem and the effectiveness of any potential solutions.

- Describe what is meant by "evulvalution."

- Discuss how and in which arenas women have become more empowered.

- Discuss recent economic trends as they have impacted couples continuing to remain legally married.

- Explain the influence of economic and financial influences at the societal level on the individual's social, emotional, and psychological well-being.

- Describe the characteristics of sexual behaviors among men and women in the United States today.

Student Website
www.mhhe.com/cls

Internet References

Department of State: Human Rights
www.state.gov/g/drl/hr

SocioSite: Feminism and Women's Issues
www.sociosite.net/topics/women.php

Women's Human Rights Resources
www.law-lib.utoronto.ca/Diana

Human sexuality is a dynamic and complex force that involves psychological, sociocultural, and physiological facets. Our sexualities include our biological, psychological, and social selves. However strong the influence of biology, we learn what it means to be sexual and to behave sexually within the structure and parameters of the era in which we live, through our families, social groups, the media, and the society as a whole. By studying different cultures and times, we see more clearly the interplay between the biological, psychological, and sociocultural factors influencing sexualities. With a strong sociocultural foundation, we are better equipped to understand the individual within the broader generational and societal contexts.

Anthropological and historical evidence indicate that there is remarkable variation in human sexualities across cultures and times. Indeed, people of different civilizations during various historical periods have engaged in an amazing variety of sexual behaviors. What is common here and now wasn't always so. There seems to be a strong temptation to think that how we do things in our culture is simply the "natural" way to do things. Cross-cultural and historical studies call that assumption about what we consider "natural" very much into question.

For several centuries, Western civilization, especially Western European and, in turn, American cultures, has been characterized by an "antisex ethic." Antisex belief systems include a variety of negative views and expectations about sex and sexualities, including denial, fear, restriction, and the detachment of sexual feelings and behavior from the wholeness of personhood or humanity. Indeed, it has only been in the last 50 years that the antisex proscriptions against knowing or learning about sex have lost their stranglehold. More and more, people can find accurate information about their sexual health, sexual functioning, and birth control without fear of social disapproval or even eternal damnation. For sex educators, this is a cause for celebration. As with many things, there's also another side to the coin. Access to accurate information about sex is not available uniformly around the world. While we may live in a global economy, where technology and travel have created new opportunities and challenges, there is still incredible repression and suppression of human (often female) sexualities in the world. In some societies today, women and sexual minorities sometimes pay with their lives for expressing who they are. It would be hard to overstate the magnitude of the unspeakable human rights violations occurring right this very minute around the world. Sexuality is often a focus for some of the most extreme forms of social control.

Societies can and do change. Political, economic, and scientific/technological changes have created new possibilities for the expression of human sexualities. The industrial revolution provided new opportunities for people to move away from home-based modes of production and economies. Some

© Jose Luis Pelaez, Inc/Getty Images

people were freed from the social and family constraints that were necessary for survival. Moving to large population centers, selling one's labor, and living independently became increasingly possible. Within our society, there have been important shifts in the past few decades that have impacted sexualities and relationships. The liberation of women from the kitchen and their participation in the workforce meant that women were no longer required to stay in abusive or unfulfilling relationships. Changes in the legality and availability of birth control and abortion, the reconsideration of democratic values of individual freedom and the pursuit of happiness, demographic shifts in age groups, the growth of the mass media, and the ushering in of the computer age have all influenced the expression of human sexualities in very complex ways. Some changes in the sexual landscape have simply been unintended and unanticipated by-products of technological and/or historical shifts. Some changes have been hard fought and won by social groups. In the United States, these groups include the earliest feminists, the suffragettes, civil rights organizers, and lesbian/gay/bisexual and transgender activists. So-called sodomy laws suffered a serious defeat with a 2003 ruling by the U.S. Supreme Court. Same-sex marriage is now legal in all of Canada, European countries such as Spain and Norway, and in Connecticut, Iowa, Massachusetts, New Hampshire, New York, Vermont, Washington, D.C.

Many interest groups continue to work for social change in various areas related to our study of human sexualities. Intersexed people have organized and are pushing for greater understanding and rights for intersexed children. Their goal is to educate parents and doctors in order to protect intersexed children's bodies from irreversible surgeries before they are able to consent. Others have organized to protest routine circumcision of boys. International groups have formed in order to fight against female circumcision and genital infibulation. These are just a few examples. But they illustrate the range of issues, from the past to the present, that surround the social and cultural contexts of human sexualities.

This unit highlights a number of social and cultural influences in order to show the incredible variations and interesting connections in our values, practices, and experiences of human sexualities. In studying these, readers are challenged to adopt a very broad perspective through which their examination of today's sexualities, and their experiences of their own sexualities, can be more meaningful. By examining various social, cultural, and historical influences, we are better equipped to avoid a return to a reliance on a fear-based "anti-sex ethic," while striving to evaluate the impact and value of the social changes that have so profoundly affected sexualities today.

Breastfeeding Is Not Obscene

CATHERINE MARSHALL

Breasts are everywhere these days. They saturate our media in guises both trivial and sombre. Whether grotesquely augmented, stricken with cancer or tumbling unbidden from the frocks of soccer wives, breasts guarantee rapt attention and ongoing debate.

But never are these appendages more hotly debated than when they are being used according to their very purpose and design—that is, for the nourishment of babies.

Although the west's growing technological sophistication is inversely proportionate to its tolerance for organic activities such as breastfeeding, the negative attitudes are hardly new. History is littered with wet nurses to whom this distasteful activity was outsourced and modern mothers who dispensed with the biological process altogether in favour of Nestle's magical infant formula.

Buoyed by groups like the World Health Organisation, breastfeeding is creeping back into the public square, but western newborns still enter a world riven with dissent over their right to a ready meal.

It was refreshing to see the lactating Mexican actress and UNICEF ambassador Salma Hayek instinctively suckle a malnourished Sierra Leonean baby while visiting that country earlier this year. Hayek told reporters it was a compassionate act for a dying child, and that it came naturally to her to reach out to this baby when her own milk supply was plentiful. It was also an attempt to diminish the stigma of breastfeeding.

Not since Rose of Sharon breastfed a dying man in John Steinbeck's *The Grapes of Wrath* had breasts been used to commit such a revolutionary act. This Hollywood sex symbol wasn't just sharing her milk with a stranger's baby; she was doing so under the full public gaze.

How could it possibly be, then, that just last month in culturally diverse and thoroughly modern Australia a mother was asked by a flight attendant to conceal her breastfeeding activity from the puritanical eyes of fellow travellers? And that as recently as 2007 the NSW state government was forced to pass legislation making it illegal to discriminate against women breastfeeding in public?

Opinions around this issue are violently split between the supporters who believe babies should be allowed to feed wherever they please and the detractors who accuse nursing mothers of indecent exposure.

Could this really be happening in the same laissez-faire society where, not long before Kevin Rudd became Prime Minister, he was praised as being 'red-blooded' for visiting a New York strip club? Where young women flaunt their cleavages on city streets and semi-naked models stare out from the covers of men's magazines in service stations and news agencies across the country? Where prostitutes advertise their ware on the classified pages of suburban family newspapers?

Or, to put it more bluntly: is female nakedness culturally acceptable only when it is aimed exclusively at the arousal and satisfaction of men?

The reaction from some quarters to the Salma Hayek story seems to reinforce this hypothesis. As a presenter on the American talk show *The Young Turks* remarked, 'I wanted to be turned on by her breasts, but in that context I just couldn't do it.'

Of course, the reverse is true in traditional societies, where women tend to dress conservatively and the natural function of breasts is well-respected. In the many years I breastfed my own children, it never occurred to me that I might offend anyone. The fact that I lived in Africa contributed, no doubt, to the ease with which I was able to conduct this ritual.

In Africa, breasts exist primarily as vessels of nourishment rather than as sexual objects. Women breastfeed their children on trains, buses and taxis, in restaurants and on park benches, in church and at work. Mostly they do so discreetly, but it's hardly newsworthy when they don't.

Using these African mamas as role models, I fed my babies on demand, regardless of where we happened to be at the time. The only person to object was a friend's mother, who believed vehemently that breasts were for sex, not babies. As if the two were somehow mutually exclusive.

And herein, perhaps, lies the absurd conundrum facing Australian women, who live in a strangely dichotomous society which tolerates them lying topless on the beach but chokes on its collective latte when they expose their nursing bras. In its typically prurient way, Western culture has co-opted breasts and sexualised them so thoroughly that their basic function is no longer accommodated.

This primordial act, upon which every other mammal relies for survival, has been twisted from its nurturing premise into an act of awful obscenity.

Sadly, society's fixation on the 'perversion' of public breastfeeding obscures the inordinate benefits that flow from it: breast milk improves infants' health and intellectual outcomes and decreases their carbon footprints; its production results in elevated levels of oxytocin within the nursing mother's brain, contributing to her emotional equilibrium, and decreases her risk of developing ovarian and breast cancer.

Almost a decade into the new century, it's a disgrace that women are still made to feel uncomfortable while using their breasts to nourish their babies. Breastfeeding is neither primitive nor obscene; it is an act of love and generosity, a forward-thinking deposit into society's depleted bank account.

Critical Thinking

1. What social significance do the female breasts have in our culture?

2. How do social and cultural definitions of breastfeeding impact the experience and outcomes of breastfeeding?

Rise of the Desperate House Husband

Gaby Hinsliff

There were two fathers this week at our tiny Oxfordshire playgroup. One dad among all the mothers, mumbling valiantly through the more obscure nursery songs in the manner of John Redwood tackling the Welsh anthem, is de rigueur for modern toddler gatherings. But two? Two means solidarity, a masculine presence subtly altering the chemistry in a roomful of women. They ended up happily talking football while washing up the Play-Doh cutters.

For both sexes, such blurred gender lines should be welcome. One of the biggest shocks of my maternity leave was navigating the overwhelmingly female world of those at home with small children: after a career spent in testosterone-soaked newsrooms, I found all that warm fuzziness confusing. Men used to living and working with women might equally find an all-male office weirdly retro now.

But suddenly these divides have started to crumble at great speed. A recession that has pummelled traditionally male industries—construction, finance, manufacturing—while sparing the female-dominated public sector (at least until the spending cuts start) is quietly redrawing family lives. This recession has driven men back home and some women into work.

In Canada, the number of women in employment recently overtook the number of men for the first time. Women in the US may pass the same milestone soon, having reached 49.9 percent of the workforce. Although such progress looks breathtaking, it is less a female surge than a case of men falling back. But it has profound implications: four in ten American working mothers are now their family's main breadwinner, while the number of US female professionals whose husbands don't work has risen by 28 per cent in the past five years.

After the Mancession

In Britain, the pace of change is slower—over 46 per cent of the workforce is now female, up from 45 per cent in 2007—but there are still a lot of men who suddenly have time for playgroup. In every quarter since last spring, redundancies hit men proportionally harder than women. Employers report part-time women asking for more hours because a partner's income is at risk. And a surprising 7 per cent of mothers with three children now have more than one (usually low-paid) job. Research from the Family Commission, a study of roughly 1,000 families, led by the charity 4 Children, has shown a rising trend for house husbands.

The rise of the female breadwinner/male homemaker model seems a logical outcome of a "mancession". It happened during the Great Depression, too—the percentage of working women in the US rose between 1930 and 1940, despite immense social disapproval of women "stealing" male jobs. Then, as now, need simply trumped other considerations for many couples: typically "female" clerical or sales jobs survived the slump better than "male" roles, and were thus easier to get. The trend continued into wartime as female employees replaced men away at the front.

Without a war, the gender power shift could quickly go into reverse when the recovery begins (or public-service jobs start being axed). But if it isn't a temporary blip, how might that affect both professional and domestic life? Does she who earns the pay cheque call the shots? Should he who changes nappies get custody of the children after a divorce? Some men, post-recovery, may not automatically pick up where they left off. Treasury officials predict a permanently smaller future economy, with some manufacturing jobs migrating overseas and a shrunken City. Many new jobs will be graduate-only, favouring girls, who now outnumber boys at university.

Other questions arise for fathers pushed into temporary part-time working as an alternative to redundancy. When recovery comes, might some who can afford it, having got used to seeing more of their children, seek permanently shorter hours? Similarly, some mothers forced into upshifting their careers will discover they don't want to stop when the crisis is over.

Status Anxiety

Office culture has already been greatly feminised over the past 40 years, both superficially—girlie calendars stripped from garage walls, tights machines installed in the House of Commons—and more profoundly, with a new emphasis on "soft" skills and parental rights. The critical mass of working women has started to change the culture, but has proved weaker on structural inequalities such as the pay gap. Canadian women still earn 74 cents on average for every man-dollar. A female-dominated workforce counts for little if most of those women remain stuck in low-status jobs.

And becoming the breadwinner in a crisis may be a bittersweet experience. Many working mothers will simply be relieved they can still support their family if a partner loses his job, others genuinely liberated by doing so. But some will be torn between suddenly needing to make more money and still wanting more time with their children. And while it may make financial sense for an unemployed father to mind the children, emotions are less easily directed. Where house husbands are reluctant, and working mothers guilty or jealous, resentment quickly follows. Evolution in family structure is a sensitive business and changes that are hard to debate calmly in public—as recent near-hysteria at Westminster over the future of marriage has shown—can be even harder to negotiate within a stressed home.

But we are entering a new year and, perhaps, a new decade characterised by uncertainty and change. It will bring opportunities as well as conflicts. Like it or not, the recession is reshaping our domestic landscape. Time to consider seriously how that should look.

Critical Thinking

1. What social shifts have caused role reversals for some couples?
2. Explain the changes in male and female roles in relation to economic influences.
3. What is the impact of role reversals on intimate relationships and family dynamics?

GABY HINSLIFF is former political editor of the *Observer*, newstatesman .com/writers/gaby_hinsliff.

Gendercide

Killed, aborted or neglected, at least 100m girls have disappeared—and the number is rising.

Imagine you are one half of a young couple expecting your first child in a fast-growing, poor country. You are part of the new middle class; your income is rising; you want a small family. But traditional *mores* hold sway around you, most important in the preference for sons over daughters. Perhaps hard physical labour is still needed for the family to make its living. Perhaps only sons may inherit land. Perhaps a daughter is deemed to join another family on marriage and you want someone to care for you when you are old. Perhaps she needs a dowry.

Now imagine that you have had an ultrasound scan; it costs $12, but you can afford that. The scan says the unborn child is a girl. You yourself would prefer a boy; the rest of your family clamours for one. You would never dream of killing a baby daughter, as they do out in the villages. But an abortion seems different. What do you do?

For millions of couples, the answer is: abort the daughter, try for a son. In China and northern India more than 120 boys are being born for every 100 girls. Nature dictates that slightly more males are born than females to offset boys' greater susceptibility to infant disease. But nothing on this scale.

For those who oppose abortion, this is mass murder. For those such as this newspaper, who think abortion should be "safe, legal and rare" (to use Bill Clinton's phrase), a lot depends on the circumstances, but the cumulative consequence for societies of such individual actions is catastrophic. China alone stands to have as many unmarried young men—"bare branches", as they are known—as the entire population of young men in America. In any country rootless young males spell trouble; in Asian societies, where marriage and children are the recognised routes into society, single men are almost like outlaws. Crime rates, bride trafficking, sexual violence, even female suicide rates are all rising and will rise further as the lopsided generations reach their maturity.

It is no exaggeration to call this gendercide. Women are missing in the millions—aborted, killed, neglected to death. In 1990 an Indian economist, Amartya Sen, put the number at 100m; the toll is higher now. The crumb of comfort is that countries can mitigate the hurt, and that one, South Korea, has shown the worst can be avoided. Others need to learn from it if they are to stop the carnage.

The Dearth and Death of Little Sisters

Most people know China and northern India have unnaturally large numbers of boys. But few appreciate how bad the problem is, or that it is rising. In China the imbalance between the sexes was 108 boys to 100 girls for the generation born in the late 1980s; for the generation of the early 2000s, it was 124 to 100. In some Chinese provinces the ratio is an unprecedented 130 to 100. The destruction is worst in China but has spread far beyond. Other East Asian countries, including Taiwan and Singapore, former communist states in the western Balkans and the Caucasus, and even sections of America's population (Chinese- and Japanese-Americans, for example): all these have distorted sex ratios. Gendercide exists on almost every continent. It affects rich and poor; educated and illiterate; Hindu, Muslim, Confucian and Christian alike.

Wealth does not stop it. Taiwan and Singapore have open, rich economies. Within China and India the areas with the worst sex ratios are the richest, best-educated ones. And China's one-child policy can only be part of the problem, given that so many other countries are affected.

In fact the destruction of baby girls is a product of three forces: the ancient preference for sons; a modern desire for smaller families; and ultrasound scanning and other technologies that identify the sex of a fetus. In societies where four or six children were common, a boy would almost certainly come along eventually; son preference did not need to exist at the expense of daughters. But now couples want two children—or, as in China, are allowed only one—they will sacrifice unborn daughters to their pursuit of a son. That is why sex ratios are most distorted in the modern, open parts of China and India. It is also why ratios are more skewed after the first child: parents may accept a daughter first time round but will do anything to ensure their next—and probably last—child is a boy. The boy-girl ratio is above 200 for a third child in some places.

How to Stop Half the Sky Crashing Down

Baby girls are thus victims of a malign combination of ancient prejudice and modern preferences for small families. Only one country has managed to change this pattern. In the 1990s

South Korea had a sex ratio almost as skewed as China's. Now, it is heading towards normality. It has achieved this not deliberately, but because the culture changed. Female education, anti-discrimination suits and equal-rights rulings made son preference seem old-fashioned and unnecessary. The forces of modernity first exacerbated prejudice—then overwhelmed it.

But this happened when South Korea was rich. If China or India—with incomes one-quarter and one-tenth Korea's levels—wait until they are as wealthy, many generations will pass. To speed up change, they need to take actions that are in their own interests anyway. Most obviously China should scrap the one-child policy. The country's leaders will resist this because they fear population growth; they also dismiss Western concerns about human rights. But the one-child limit is no longer needed to reduce fertility (if it ever was: other East Asian countries reduced the pressure on the population as much as China). And it massively distorts the country's sex ratio, with devastating results. President Hu Jintao says that creating "a harmonious society" is his guiding principle; it cannot be achieved while a policy so profoundly perverts family life.

And all countries need to raise the value of girls. They should encourage female education; abolish laws and customs that prevent daughters inheriting property; make examples of hospitals and clinics with impossible sex ratios; get women engaged in public life—using everything from television newsreaders to women traffic police. Mao Zedong said "women hold up half the sky." The world needs to do more to prevent a gendercide that will have the sky crashing down.

Critical Thinking

1. Why is there such an imbalance between the numbers of male and female infants worldwide?
2. Why do some countries have a bigger problem with female infanticide?
3. What are the impacts of female infanticide at both the individual and societal levels?

Death by Gender

CYNTHIA FUCHS EPSTEIN

Finally, the atrocity of gendercide—the murder and mutilation of victims selected by sex—is getting prominent attention in the press. Through feminist online activism, but more prominently through the efforts of *New York Times* columnist Nicholas Kristof (in his new book *Half the Sky,* written with his wife, Sheryl WuDunn, and in his *New York Times* column), a socially embedded and systematic assault on women and girls in much of the world has been brought to public consciousness. The crimes at issue range from the killing of girls and women—often by their fathers, brothers, or male cousins, acting for the "honor" of the family—to the trafficking of women as sex slaves and to their forced recruitment as suicide bombers.

I will focus in this article on honor killing because the act is so vile. Further, the concept is difficult to dislodge. The notion of "honor" is at the core of many conflicts within and between societies all over the world, although it has been substantially reduced in the West. But, notions of honor underpin the marriage system in the tribal societies that are common in the Middle East and many parts of Africa. The most important connections between tribes are based on kinship and marriage, and value in the marriage market depends on female "virtue"—so girls and women must be tightly controlled to assure the "purity" of these social connections. Girls' families won't invest emotionally in them because they typically leave their birth families while very young and are brought into their husband's families as outsiders whose purpose is to bear children and take care of elderly family members. Without personal or social resources, they often are forced to be the servants or slaves of men in their birth families and then again in the families they enter by marriage. In "honor societies," which are characteristic of much of the developing world, girls and women are denied the protections that outside affiliations and affection might provide. Deviation from the rules imposed by male authorities may label a female as "contaminated" and elicit harsh sanctions. At its most serious, contamination is decreed when a women or girl is believed to have sought or had a sexual connection outside marriage—whether she acts from a desire to choose her own mate or is a victim of rape. Whether it has occurred within or outside the family, sexual contamination may be punished by murder. Thus, in some societies, the murder of girls and woman is justified by perceived social and moral infractions, and women are held in strict segregation to guard against these possibilities.

The belief that women are symbolic bearers of the honor of the clan or tribe is widely held, most often in Muslim countries but in others as well. And although Islamic law, or sharia, does not mandate honor killing as a punishment, it is practiced in many Islamic communities, openly so in some of them. It can be found also in some other groups, such as the Sikhs. There are lesser violations of honor for which girls and women are sometimes killed, like failing to comply with restrictive dress codes—wearing makeup or taking off the head scarf or hijab, for example—or for dating or merely appearing with unrelated boys or men in public. (According to the Al Arabia Web site, a Saudi father killed his daughter for chatting with a man on Facebook.) Trying to escape an arranged marriage is another important violation of traditional family norms that may merit death—as in the case of a young British woman who was stabbed to death by her father in London in 2002 when her family heard a love song dedicated to her on the radio and suspected that she had a boyfriend she had chosen for herself. A similar report comes from Turkey.

Women who protest forced marriage and abusive husbands can become targets of honor killings. And women and girls who have been raped can be doomed to death at the hands of a kinsman—or be forced to kill themselves to shield the rapist, if he himself is a kinsman, from punishment by the civil authorities. The dishonor of rape is so great that it can be used for political purposes. In January 2009, an Iraqi woman, Samira Ahmed Jassim, confessed to organizing the rapes of more than eighty women so that their shame would make them susceptible to recruitment as suicide bombers by al Qaeda. Twenty-eight of the women were said to have carried out suicide attacks.

The Turkish Human Rights Directorate reported in 2008 that in Istanbul alone there is one honor killing every week; more than one thousand occurred there in the preceding five years. UNICEF reported that in the Gaza Strip and the West Bank, according to 1999 figures, two-thirds of all murders were probably honor killings. In 2003, anthropologist/journalist James Emery of the Metropolitan State College of Denver stated that in the Palestinian communities of the West Bank, Gaza Strip, Israel, and Jordan, dishonored women were executed in their homes, in open fields, and occasionally in public before cheering crowds. Honor killings, Emery reported, account for virtually all recorded murders of Palestinian women. Although there are attempts by organizations such as the Women's Affairs

Technical Committee (WATC) and other NGOs to provide education and practical services to protect and assist women, they have had little success so far.

Death because of gender is arguably a leading cause of female homicide in many societies, but gendercide occurs in other ways: in 1990 the Nobel laureate Amartya Sen wrote in the *New York Review of Books* that more than one hundred million women were missing from the world as a result of sex-selective abortion and ill treatment. No doubt, the number has increased as girls continue to be selectively pruned in such places as India and Pakistan—not only by the poor who undernourish their girl babies but also by members of the middle class who use sonograms to determine the sex of a fetus and then abort the females. The truth is that gender is regarded as a birth defect in much of the world, and this fact is neither analyzed nor addressed.

The officially reported estimates of the numbers of women who die in honor killings range from five thousand to ten thousand a year. (The UN Population Fund has estimated the total at five thousand a year, and that figure was reported by the secretary-general to the UN General Assembly in 2006.) But these numbers underestimate the actual toll because most honor murders are recorded as suicides or accidental deaths—or are not recorded at all. And the reports cannot begin to describe the terror girls and women must feel when they know that any aberrant behavior might provoke their fathers or close kin to kill them. Commentators in the West who suggest that women freely choose to conform to restrictions on their behavior and dress are not sensitive to the lurking threat of deadly punishment for violations of the codes. It is ludicrous to suggest that Islamic women decide for themselves to wear restrictive clothing and head coverings, given the possible consequences of not doing so.

Surprisingly, the support for honor killings is not limited to tribal societies but exists also among individuals living in traditional communities in modern societies. Even there, women who "go astray" and violate the bonds of marriage or assume individual identities often face physical assault. A poll by the BBC's Asia network, for example, found that one in ten young British Asians believe that honor killings can be justified. And in a poll of five hundred Hindus, Sikhs, Christians, and Muslims reported in 2009 by the online Women's E-news, one-tenth said they would condone the murder of someone who "disrespected" their family's honor.

Honor killings are not identified as a critically important instance of women's degraded status in many societies, and the practice is rarely condemned by the educated and sophisticated members of the societies in which the killings occur— nor by the social activists or leaders of the "free world." Nicholas Cohen, a writer for *Standpoint* magazine, asks why the outrage against apartheid does not extend to the women who are segregated and locked in their own homes, forced into arranged marriages, or raped and stoned. Why, he asks, do the societies that tolerate such practices not face irate Western boycotts or demonstrations in front of their embassy buildings?

It is clear, however, that the practice and the reasoning behind it will be difficult to erase. The protection of women's honor is an important part of the symbolic glue of kin groups that are, in many societies, the essential political bodies that maintain social order. Sociologists like Roger Friedland and Mounira Charrad have argued that control over women and marriage ensures that tribal groups can fully regulate the relationships between clans. (This is not so different from the marriages negotiated between the royal houses and aristocratic families of many countries in the West up to the early twentieth century.) Young women have to have unsullied reputations, and of course, they have to be virgins. Offering the bloodied sheets of the marital bed to relatives of the bride and groom is still necessary in many countries of the world.

Friedland has criticized the lack of awareness by political scientists (to say nothing of the media experts) who attempt to understand societies such as Afghanistan and Pakistan without attending to the tribal alliances created by marriages engineered by tribal elders. The obedience of women (actually girls, because these marriages are typically of underage children) is essential, and so the discipline over them is intense. Charrad, a sociologist studying the tribal foundations of the former French colonies of Algeria, Morocco, and Tunisia, similarly points to the political importance of tribal alliances created through the exchange of women.

Of course, men also are affected by these exchanges, but the men stay in their families of origin and it is the exchanged women who are forced to leave their places of birth and childhood. Because girls are married off early and torn from their families, they are powerless in the new environments to which they come as strangers. They are virtual slaves in the women's quarters of their new families.

Why do some women and girls internalize these views of honor and defend the very practices that enslave them? Why do we hear accounts of mothers who hold down their daughters as their husbands plunge knives into them or who observe the stoning that kills them? Or who insist that their daughters be circumcised when they know the pain and future discomfort this practice will bring?

Taken as child brides into the homes of their husbands, the only power these women have comes later in life as the mothers of sons who may, or may not, support them—and as the mothers of daughters, whom they can help to control but can't protect. They have learned the costs of deviance, and they teach those costs to, and even impose them on, their daughters. The resistance to the education of girls in Afghanistan, by the Taliban and also, sometimes, by their own parents, is now well known, but girls' education is poor in many other regions where their "honor" is the most important thing about them— as in Pakistan, for example, and parts of India.

Are things getting better? Attempts by international human rights associations and women's rights organizations to impose penalties for honor killings have recently been undercut at the UN. According to ESCR-FEM, the online listserv for Women's Economic, Social and Cultural Rights, the UN Human Rights Council adopted a resolution in 2009 "promoting human rights and fundamental freedoms through a better understanding of *traditional* values of humankind. . ." [emphasis added]. The vote was twenty-six in favor, fifteen against, with six abstentions.

The resolution was proposed by Russia and supported by the Arab League and the Organization of the Islamic Conference, a grouping of fifty-seven UN member states. Human Rights organizations across the globe strongly opposed it, declaring that its passage would set a destructive precedent by affirming a concept ("traditional values") often used to legitimize human rights abuses. The nongovernmental Cairo Institution for Human Rights Studies issued a statement expressing deep concern over the text. It declared that "such a concept has been used in the Arab region to justify treating women as second class citizens, female genital mutilation, honor crimes, child marriage, and other practices that clearly contradict international human rights standards."

There are a number of organizations devoted to improving the conditions of girls' and women's lives in the countries where those lives are most at risk. They include the International Initiative on Maternal Mortality and Human Rights and the Association for Women's Rights in Development, the Center for Women's Global Leadership, and the International Women's Rights Action Watch–Asia Pacific. Some organizations devoted to improving the situation of women are connected to agencies of the United Nations. It is more than thirty years since 90 percent of the member countries of the United Nations signed on to the Convention on the Elimination of all forms of Discrimination Against Women, which proclaimed that women's rights are human rights. But many of the signatories are countries in which the worst practices are carried out against women. Ironically, the United States has not signed.

What is to be done? We know that individuals' hearts and minds are difficult to change, but we also know that with proper incentives and political will they can sometimes change swiftly. Perhaps it is time for world leaders to insist on basic standards of human rights as a precondition for full commercial and diplomatic relations regardless of a country's religion or traditional culture. And perhaps it is also time for the resurgence of a woman's movement in the United States that will connect with the fledgling women's movements in countries of the Global South to form an alliance that will act politically to insist that women's and girls' rights be on the agenda of every international meeting.

Critical Thinking

1. What is the purpose of honor killings?
2. Why would some women defend honor killings?
3. Other than murder, how else does death by gender occur?

CYNTHIA FUCHS EPSTEIN is Distinguished Professor of Sociology at The Graduate Center of the City University of New York. Among her books are *Woman's Place*, *Women in Law*, and *Deceptive Distinctions*.

From *Dissent*, Spring 2010, pp. 54–57. Copyright © 2005 by Foundation for Study of Independent Ideas, Inc. Reprinted by permission of University of Pennsylvania Press. www.dissentmagazine.org

E*vulva*lution: The Portrayal of Women's External Genitalia and Physique Across Time and the Current Barbie Doll Ideals

Media images of the female body commonly represent reigning appearance ideals of the era in which they are published. To date, limited documentation of the genital appearance ideals in mainstream media exists. Analysis 1 sought to describe genital appearance ideals (i.e., mons pubis and labia majora visibility, labia minora size and color, and pubic hair style) and general physique ideals (i.e., hip, waist, and bust size, height, weight, and body mass index [BMI]) across time based on 647 *Playboy Magazine* centerfolds published between 1953 and 2007. Analysis 2 focused exclusively on the genital appearance ideals embodied by models in 185 *Playboy* photographs published between 2007 and 2008. Taken together, results suggest the perpetuation of a "Barbie Doll" ideal characterized by a low BMI, narrow hips, a prominent bust, and hairless, undefined genitalia resembling those of a prepubescent female.

VANESSA R. SCHICK, BRANDI N. RIMA, AND SARAH K. CALABRESE

Media depictions of the female body commonly inform women's conceptions of the societal ideal, serving as the gold standard for self-evaluation. Over time, the chasm between the average woman's body and the ideal portrayed within media images has widened, with thinness becoming a hallmark of *Playboy Magazine* centerfold models, Miss America pageant winners, and fashion models alike (Byrd-Bredbenner, Murray, & Schlussel, 2005; Owen & Laurel-Seller, 2000; Spitzer, Henderson, & Zivian, 1999). Other anthropometric features of media models have also been criticized for being incongruent with the natural female form and unattainable for the majority of the female population (e.g., Byrd-Bredbenner et al., 2005).

Previous literature has documented the destructive impact that exposure to these publicized images has on women's satisfaction with their body and overall appearance, as well as the risks posed to their mental and physical health. Multiple experimental studies manipulating women's duration of exposure to media images exemplifying the thin ideal have documented the link between media exposure and body dissatisfaction (for a review, see Groesz, Levine, & Murmen, 2002). Neither body mass index (BMI) nor objectified body consciousness was found to moderate this relationship within a college sample, suggesting that women may be vulnerable to the harmful effects of media exposure irrespective of their physical appearance or tendency to self-objectify (Hamilton, Mintz,

& Kashubeck-West, 2007). In addition to fostering poor body image, media exposure has been linked to multiple negative health outcomes, including depression (Bessenoff, 2006) and disordered eating symptomatology (Harrison & Cantor, 1997).

Although all media depictions of the female body have the potential to affect women's perceptions of their own physical appearance, sexually explicit media images may be particularly influential in determining women's perceptions of their genital appearance. In recent years, the Internet and other technologies have facilitated access to pornographic films and photographs, and female viewing of such imagery has become increasingly mainstream (Braun & Tiefer, in press). However, the images projected through these media commonly misrepresent the female genitalia in their naturally occurring form as a result of digital modification of the images or surgical modification of their subjects (Green, 2005). Further, the taboo surrounding direct display or discussion of the female genitalia has yet to be extinguished (Braun, 1999). As compared to other aspects of physical appearance, women have limited access to sources of information about genital appearance other than the media, including visual exposure to other women's genitalia and factual resources (Blank, 1993; Dodson, 1996). Thus, women's conception of the average or typical appearance of female genitalia may be rooted largely in media images, which may be detrimental to women's genital perceptions to the extent that such media images exhibit a restricted or unrealistic range of genital appearances.

To our knowledge, no existent research to date has systematically characterized the female genital prototype displayed in mainstream U.S. media, with the exception of a single study documenting a tendency to obscure the female genitalia or portray them as a smooth curve between magazine models' thighs, without any extrusions or indentations (Bramwell, 2002). However, the sample of photographs from which this conclusion was drawn was derived from glossy women's magazines and was largely comprised of photos in which women's pubic area was clothed. Further research is warranted to characterize the genital prototypes displayed in sexually explicit magazines, a media source that is likely to be a more powerful determinant of the genital ideals women develop, given the nudity of the models exhibited. In addition, a more comprehensive approach to characterizing genital appearance is needed to address multiple aesthetic features (e.g., size, shape, and color) of the individual components of the genitalia.

The purpose of this research was to replicate and extend previous work by examining the portrayal of women's external genitalia as well as aspects of their general physique within *Playboy Magazine,* a sexually explicit magazine that targets a heterosexual male audience. The first of the two content analyses (Analysis 1) was conducted to characterize the genital appearance ideals and more general body ideals exhibited by *Playboy Magazine* centerfolds and their evolution across time between 1953 and 2007. The second content analysis (Analysis 2) was performed to examine recent trends in *Playboy Magazine*'s portrayal of the female genitalia in greater detail, focusing exclusively on issues published in 2007 and 2008 and including all published photographs in which models' montes pubis were visible.

Analysis 1

The initial content analysis was exploratory in nature, seeking to characterize the evolution of the genital appearance ideals exhibited by *Playboy Magazine* centerfolds from 1953 to 2007. Specific features studied included mons pubis and labia majora visibility, labia minora size, labia minora color, and pubic hair style. A second goal of Analysis 1 was to examine the evolution of general physique ideals portrayed by centerfolds across this 54-year period, including hip size, waist size, bust size, height, weight, and BMI.

Method

Sample. The sample was composed of 647 centerfolds from *Playboy Magazine,* a mainstream heterosexual men's magazine featuring photographs of nude women. *Playboy Magazine* was chosen due to (a) its widespread circulation and popularity and (b) the sexual explicitness of its pictorial content. We chose to analyze only the centerfold[1] from each issue, as opposed to including other published photographs within the magazine. The centerfold is likely the most commonly viewed photograph in the magazine given its three-page, fold-out format. Further, the centerfold model is considered to be the most physically attractive model of the month and is therefore most likely to embody reigning appearance ideals. The images were obtained via an online subscription to the magazine, which enabled coders to utilize a zoom feature to maximize accuracy. The centerfolds from all monthly issues published before November 2007, beginning with the first issue (December 1953), were included.

Categories and coding. The year of publication was recorded for each centerfold. In addition, the appearance of each centerfold model's external genitalia and general physique was coded. Specifically, each centerfold was coded based on the following criteria.

Mons pubis visibility. Mons pubis visibility was dichotomized as 0 = invisible mons pubis (e.g., obscured by clothing or position) or 1 = visible mons pubis, and was coded according to whether the model's mons pubis could be seen in the photograph.

Pubic hair visibility. Pubic hair style was treated as a continuous variable ranging from 1 (*fully visible*) to 3 (*invisible*), and was only coded for the subset of centerfolds in which the model's mons pubis was visible. Coding options were as follows: 1 = pubic hair is visible and appears unaltered, 2 = pubic hair is visible but appears to have been partially removed (e.g., by shaving or waxing), or 3 = pubic hair appears to have been completely removed (i.e., no pubic hair is visible).

Labia majora visibility. Labia majora visibility was dichotomized as 0 = invisible labia majora (e.g., obscured by clothing or position) or 1 = visible labia majora, and was coded according to whether the model's labia majora could be seen in the photograph.

Labia minora size. Labia minora size was treated as a continuous variable ranging from 1 (*invisible*) to 3 (*prominent*), and was only coded for the subset of centerfolds in which the model's labia majora were visible. Coding options were as follows: 1 = labia minora are not visible, 2 = labia minora are visible and do not protrude beyond the labia majora, or 3 = labia minora are visible and protrude beyond the labia majora.

Labia minora color. The labia minora color variable concerned the color of the model's labia minora, and was only coded for the subset of centerfolds in which the model's labia minora were visible. Coding categories were as follows: 1 = labia minora are a shade of pink or light red, or 2 = labia minora are a color other than pink or light red (e.g., purple or black).

General physique. Body measurements pertaining to the centerfold model's general physique were published in most issues of the magazine. When available, the model's bust size (in inches), waist size (in inches), hip size (in inches), height (in inches), and weight (in pounds) were coded. In addition, the model's BMI was calculated and coded based on published height and weight measurements using the following formula: weight (pounds)/[height (inches)]^2 × 703 (Centers for Disease Control, 2008).

Interrater reliability. We developed and tested a coding manual for variables related to the appearance of centerfold models' external genitalia. Two independent, blind raters were trained to conduct a content analysis of the centerfolds in *Playboy Magazine* using the coding manual. Raters were female undergraduate students of unknown sexual orientation. Since rater characteristics have the potential to bias coding, measures were taken to maximize objectivity. Detailed criteria were provided for each coding category, including example images for pubic hair visibility and labia minora size. In addition, raters were unaware of the objectives and hypotheses of the study and blind to the date of publication for each centerfold. During training, each rater coded a random selection of non-centerfold photographs of nude women published in *Playboy Magazine* in order to establish interrater reliability.

In the actual content analysis of the centerfolds, both raters independently coded a subset of 446, overlapping on 38% (*n* = 245) of the full sample. Cohen's kappa, a conservative measure (Perreault & Leigh, 1989), was calculated to assess interrater reliability. A Cohen's kappa coefficient of .77 was obtained, indicating acceptable agreement (Banerjee, Capozzoli, McSweeney, & Sinha, 1999). To address coding discrepancies, the three primary researchers independently coded items on which the trained raters disagreed, and a final code for each item was established when two out of the three researchers reached agreement.

Results and Discussion

Independent samples *t* tests showed an increase in the visibility of the centerfold models' montes pubis, *t* = 27.59, *p* < .001; and an increase in the visibility of their labia majora, *t* = 20.18, *p* < .001, over time (in years). Among the subset of centerfolds in which the model's mons pubis was visible (*n* = 328), pubic hair became less visible (i.e., shaved, waxed, or otherwise modified from its natural presentation) as years increased (*r* = .70, *p* < .001; see Figure 1). The limited number of centerfolds exhibiting labia majora (*n* = 16) precluded statistical analysis of change in labia minora size over time, as labia minora size could not be evaluated for those centerfolds in which the labia majora were not visible.

Consistent with Bramwell's (2002) notion of "invisible labia," a noticeable tendency to minimize the appearance of the labia minora or portray them as absent altogether was observed within the subset of centerfolds with visible labia majora. Specifically, the labia minora were completely invisible in 14 of the 16 centerfolds showing labia majora; instead, only the line demarcating the division of the labia majora (i.e., the labia line) was apparent. Further, none of the centerfolds portrayed prominent labia minora (i.e., labia minora protruding beyond the labia majora). No variation in labia minora color was observed; labia minora were unanimously portrayed as pink or light red among the few centerfolds in which they were visible.

A series of Pearson product–moment correlations was run in order to assess changes in the models' general physique across time. As seen in Table 1, as time (in years) increased, the

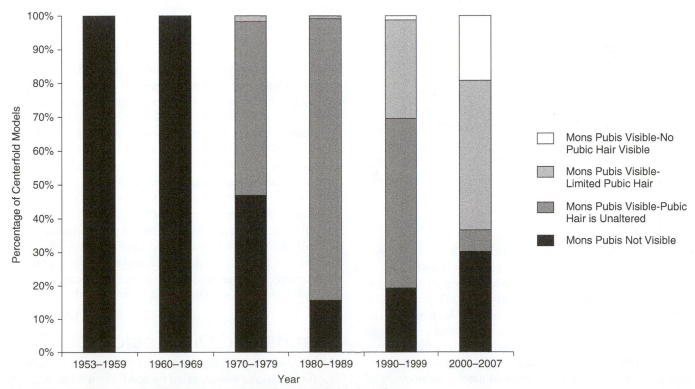

Figure 1 Public hair style among playboy centerfold models by decade.

Table 1 Intercorrelations Between Magazine Publication Year and Centerfold Models' Physical Characteristics

Variable	1	2	3	4	5	6	7	8
1. Year of publication	—	−.190***	.170***	.010	−.280***	.320***	.100**	.700***
2. Body mass index	—	—	−.610***	.460***	.370***	.180***	.240***	.090
3. Height	—	—	—	.065	−.210***	.030	−.050	.030
4. Weight	—	—	—	—	.500***	.500***	.360***	−.060
5. Hip size	—	—	—	—	—	.320***	.300***	.080
6. Waist size	—	—	—	—	—	—	.240***	.150**
7. Bust size	—	—	—	—	—	—	—	.270***
8. Pubic hair style	—	—	—	—	—	—	—	—

*$p < .05$. **$p < .01$. ***$p < .001$.

models were characterized by smaller hips ($r = −.28$, $p < .001$) and a lower BMI ($r = −.19$, $p < .001$), the latter of which is attributable to the models' height increasing while their weight remained constant. In contrast, bust size of the models ($r = .10$, $p < .01$) increased over the years.

These findings suggest that the overall body ideal is shifting farther away from a natural female form, calling for women to exhibit ectomorphic body types and sizeable busts simultaneously—a combination that is difficult to attain without taking extreme and potentially dangerous measures (e.g., undergoing cosmetic surgery). Results pertaining to pubic hair visibility and labia minora size and color suggested similarly unnatural genital appearance ideals (e.g., hairlessness and invisible labia minora). However, the latter conclusion required further investigation and empirical support given the limited number of centerfolds in which the model's mons pubis and labia majora were visible. Since labia majora visibility was more prevalent in recent issues of *Playboy Magazine* relative to earlier ones, a finding consistent with previous reports of increasing sexual explicitness among photographs published in *Playboy Magazine* over time (e.g., Bogaert & Turkovich, 1993), a second content analysis was conducted that focused exclusively on photographs published between 2007 and 2008. Rather than restricting the sample to centerfolds, all photographs in which models' montes pubis were visible were analyzed, allowing for a more comprehensive understanding of the genital ideals presented by *Playboy Magazine*.

Analysis 2

Analysis 2 was designed to investigate recent trends in *Playboy Magazine*'s portrayal of the female genitalia in greater depth by describing the genital appearance ideals depicted in a wide range of photographs published between 2007 and 2008 in which models' montes pubis were visible. In keeping with the finding in Analysis 1 that the appearance of centerfold models' genitalia was becoming increasingly deviant from a natural female appearance, we hypothesized that pubic hair would appear partially or completely removed among the majority of the sample in Analysis 2. In addition, based on observations made during Analysis 1, we hypothesized that labia minora would be undetectable among the majority of the sample in which labia majora were visible, and would be a shade of pink or light red when visible.

Method

Sample. The sample was composed of photographs from all monthly issues of *Playboy Magazine* published between May 2007 and April 2008, obtained via an online subscription. All photographs in which the model's mons pubis was visible (i.e., not concealed by clothing or the model's positioning; $N = 185$) were coded.

Categories and coding. All categories used in Analysis 1 that pertained to genital appearance, with the exception of mons pubis visibility (per the inclusion criterion requiring that the models' montes pubis be visible), were included in Analysis 2.

Interrater reliability. The same coding manual developed for Analysis 1 was employed in Analysis 2. Two female undergraduate raters underwent training to conduct a content analysis of the pictures in *Playboy Magazine* using the coding manual. To establish interrater agreement during training, each rater coded a random selection of non-centerfold photographs of nude women published in *Playboy Magazine* prior to 2007.

In the actual content analysis, raters independently coded a subset of 122 centerfolds, overlapping on 32% ($n = 59$) of the full sample. A Cohen's kappa coefficient of .77 was obtained, indicating acceptable agreement between raters (Banerjee et al., 1999). As in Analysis 1, raters were blind to the hypotheses and objectives of the study. To resolve coding discrepancies between the two raters, the three primary researchers independently coded discrepant items and used the code agreed on by the majority.

Results and Discussion

The representation of the female genitalia in recent issues of *Playboy Magazine* was assessed by conducting frequency analyses of pubic hair visibility, labia minora size, and labia minora color across photographs that displayed the model's mons pubis. Pubic hair was visible and appeared unaltered in 18.9% of the pictures ($n = 35$), visible but altered in 19.5% of the pictures ($n = 36$), and altered to the point of being invisible in 61.2% of the pictures ($n = 112$). Two of the photographs (1.1%) were not coded because the pictures could not be conclusively categorized for various reasons (e.g., dark shadowing). Of the 183 photographs that clearly depicted the model's mons pubis, 60.5% obscured the labia majora so that the appearance of the labia minora could not be determined. Of those photographs ($n = 73$) in which the labia majora were visible, 82.2% ($n = 60$) depicted the labia minora as absent, with only the labia line visible, 15.1% ($n = 11$) depicted the labia minora as present but contained within labia majora, and 2.7% ($n = 2$) depicted the labia minora as present and protruding beyond the labia majora. Overall, labia minora were visible in only 7.0% ($n = 13$) of the full sample of photographs, and were a color other than pink or light red in only a single photograph.

Thus, findings from Analysis 2 corroborated and extended results of Analysis 1, indicating that the growing trend observed among centerfolds for both pubic hair and labia minora to be minimized was upheld across other types of photographs recently published in *Playboy Magazine*.

General Discussion

In sum, findings from Analysis 1 indicated that minimal pubic hair, invisible labia minora, narrow hips, and a low BMI are becoming increasingly common among centerfold models, and findings from Analysis 2 confirmed that an unnatural genital appearance has become normative among centerfold models and other models alike in recent years. Taken together, these prototyped characteristics for women's genital appearance and overall physique in many ways emulate those of a Barbie doll, an American icon that has been described as an image of perfection, the definition of physical beauty (Kuther & McDonald, 2004), and the ideal sought by heterosexual men for their female partners (Cunningham, 1993).

The Barbie-like slenderness and narrow hips (Norton, Olds, Olive, & Dank, 1996) increasingly exemplified by *Playboy Magazine* centerfold models are consistent with previous research documenting the glorification of thinness among women within the media (e.g., Byrd-Bredbenner et al., 2005; Owen & Laurel-Seller, 2000). Correspondingly, young men have reported low body weight and narrow hips to be attractive and desirable attributes for female romantic partners to possess (Singh & Young, 1995).

There is a striking parallel between Barbie dolls and *Playboy Magazine* models in terms of their portrayal of female sexuality. Despite Barbie's designation as a sexual icon, her sexual anatomy is incomplete; while featuring a prominent bosom, she lacks any semblance of genitalia. In light of her inaccurate representation of the female body, she has been criticized as being a "simulacrum of a human being, a sad grotesquerie" (Cunningham, 1993, p. 81). However, it appears that this same distortion of female sexuality has reemerged in human form: The images presented in *Playboy Magazine* also emphasize

breasts but mask or minimize genitalia, presenting them in a hairless, prepubescent form. Thus, the warped perception of the adult female body that young girls may acquire via exposure to Barbie dolls may be reinforced later in life via exposure to images in *Playboy Magazine*.

The juvenile ideals exhibited for women's genitalia match existing social constructions of women's sexuality according to which women's sex drive is absent and their sexual demeanor is subdued. Such a portrayal contradicts the natural appearance of a sexually mature woman's genitalia, particularly during sexual arousal given the swelling that occurs (Blackledge, 2004). Accordingly, the modern idealization of diminutive labia minora may be rooted in historical attributions of elongated labia minora to sexual promiscuity (Manderson, 2004). Historically, elongated labia have also been tied to marginalized groups of women including Black (e.g., Sarah Bartmann, also known as "Venus Hottentot") and homosexual women (Gillman, 1985; Terry & Urla, 1995). Thus, the presentation of the genitalia of Barbie dolls and *Playboy* models alike may represent a natural progression from longstanding social constructions surrounding female sexual anatomy and female sexual behavior.

Playboy Magazine models' bust size is ever increasing, creating even more of a paradox next to their amorphous, underemphasized genitalia. The idealization of larger breasts has been supported in recent decades by research documenting males' preference for larger breasts (e.g., Singh & Young, 1995), as well as females' desire for their breasts to be larger and their belief that males prefer larger breasts (Thompson & Tantleff, 1992). Furthermore, both sexes associate negative attributes (e.g., depression or loneliness) with smaller breast sizes and positive attributes (e.g., popularity and confidence) with larger breast sizes (Thompson & Tantleff, 1992).

Taken together, the disproportionate physical features exemplified by *Playboy Magazine* models may perpetuate the Barbie doll ideals that are unmatched by the majority of women in the general population. Glorification of this combination of features lacks an evolutionary basis, as some aspects (e.g., a BMI at anorexic levels) are contraindicated for survival and reproduction. Nonetheless, as these ideals are increasingly embraced, women's physical deviation from the prototype may become especially salient to them and cause significant body image disturbance. Moreover, with some population norms shifting in the opposite direction of *Playboy* ideals (e.g., increasing BMI; Spitzer et al., 1999), more women are likely to be affected and greater discrepancies in appearance are likely to be perceived.

Women may be particularly prone to developing distorted impressions of their genitalia as a result of exposure to media images, as evidenced by previous experimental research demonstrating the malleability of women's perceptions about their genital appearance. Schick, Calabrese, and Rima (2008) found that women exposed to a set of images of vulvas pre-labiaplasty subsequently judged their own labia minora to be significantly smaller, as compared to women exposed to a set of images of the same vulvas post-labiaplasty (i.e., with surgically reduced labia minora) or a set of images of *Playboy* centerfold models' vulvas. Further, prelabiaplasty images were rated as significantly less attractive than the images shown in the other two conditions, consistent with Braun and Tiefer's (in press) report that a "tucked-in look" is one aspect of the prototypical genital appearance that is promoted by pornographic imagery and, consequently, sought and desired by women. Given women's vulnerability to developing distorted perceptions of their own genital appearance, the unnatural genital ideals upheld by *Playboy Magazine* may encourage unhealthy self-comparisons and be particularly detrimental to their self-image.

Although considerable variation in the appearance of labia minora among women has been documented (Blank, 1993; Lloyd, Crouch, Minto, Liao, & Creighton, 2005), a highly restricted range of labia minora appearances was found in the images presented by *Playboy Magazine.* The labia minora were depicted as absent in the vast majority of photographs, even when the labia majora were visible. Moreover, the reported proportion of photos in which labia minora were present may be an overestimate of the actual proportion of photos in which labia minora are seen in print versions of the magazine. Whereas the Internet version of the magazine enables viewers to magnify images, a feature heavily utilized during data collection in both analyses, fine details, such as a glimpse of labia minora peaking out from the labia majora, may be missed during the viewing of photographs in print. The apparent homogeneity of the images of labia minora presented in *Playboy Magazine* may not only lead women to view their own genitalia as differing from the ideal, but may also lead them to view their genitalia as differing from the majority, evoking significant concern about the normality of their genital appearance. As Braun and Tiefer (in press) stated, "Women's perceptions and experiences of their genitalia are far from straightforward, positive, or even neutral. . . . Numerous concerns, often related to appearance, are expressed by women, and 'many women nurture fearful fantasies about the abnormality of their genitals' (Laws, 1987, p. 9)" (p. 5).

Media images may not only contribute to concerns about genital appearance, but may also affect women's sexual health via the body modifications they encourage. According to a 2001 excerpt from *Shine Magazine* (as cited in Braun, 2005), "A lot of women bring in *Playboy,* show me pictures of vaginas and say, 'I want to look like this'" (p. 413). Women who undergo cosmetic genital surgery in an attempt to more accurately fit media ideals put themselves at risk for reduced physical sensation (Liao & Creighton, 2007), among other complications. Even seemingly more feasible and benign physical changes may confer negative health repercussions; for instance, shaving pubic hair increases the likelihood of spreading sexually transmitted infections (Palefsky & Handley, 2002). Thus, the unnatural ideals presented in *Playboy Magazine* can have far-reaching implications for women's physical self-image as well as their sexual health.

The safety and well-being of younger members of the female population may also be affected by the prepubescent ideals promoted by *Playboy Magazine.* By sexualizing childlike physical characteristics, *Playboy* photographs have the potential to condition readers to experience sexual arousal in response to viewing or fantasizing about girls and young women. In addition, repeated masturbation to these pornographic images is likely to reinforce and enhance any formed associations. Moreover, the "childlification" of *Playboy* models may lead readers to not only regard children and adolescents as sexual objects, but to justify treating them as such and desensitize them to any internal inhibitions surrounding pedophilia (Russell & Purcell, 2006). Disturbingly, in addition to depicting models in a childlike form, *Playboy Magazine* often includes childhood photographs of its centerfold models within their individual pictorials, further intensifying the connection between children and sexuality presented to its readers.

The body ideals espoused by *Playboy Magazine* are widely recognized and endorsed among males and females living in the United States. With national circulation exceeding three million copies per month (see Playboy Cyber Club, 2008; www.playboy.com), *Playboy Magazine* has become well established as a sexually explicit media force over the past five decades. Although the magazine predominantly targets a heterosexual male audience, over 19.3% of subscription-holders are female (Simmons Choices III, 2006), suggesting that many women actively seek this publication out and regularly view its depictions of the female body. Countless more women are likely to encounter these published images, although perhaps on a less frequent basis, as approximately 32% of undergraduate women report having viewed sexually explicit magazines at some point in their lifetime (Schick, Rima, & Calabrese, 2009).

Not only does *Playboy Magazine* have the potential to directly impact women's conceptions of appearance ideals via the images it presents, but it also could impact them indirectly via *Playboy*'s male readership, who may impart the ideals to women. Previous work has documented the influence of male sexual partners on women's body image (e.g., Grogan, 1999). Thus, irrespective of the frequency with which women actually view the magazine, the physical characteristics exemplified by *Playboy* models may impact their self-evaluation by setting cultural standards for attractiveness that are adopted and reinforced by significant others and society in general.

Limitations and Concluding Remarks

Findings of this study provide key insight regarding the physical ideals promoted within *Playboy Magazine.* However, the extent to which women are actually viewing the magazine and internalizing these norms is uncertain at present. Although statistics suggest that hundreds of thousands of women subscribe to the magazine, these women's motivation for purchasing the magazine (e.g., because of same-sex attraction, as a basis for self-comparison, or as a gift to male partners) and the frequency and nature of their perusal of the imagery contained within remain unknown. These contextual factors surrounding women's exposure to *Playboy Magazine* images are likely to modulate the effect of such exposure on women's perceptions of their own genitals. Regardless, any amount of exposure to these media representations of the female body, whether actively sought out or unintentionally absorbed, is likely to have some bearing on women's conceptions of the physical prototype.

However, *Playboy Magazine* is not the sole media source informing such conceptions. Although findings of this study are informative with regard to the genital and general physique ideals portrayed by *Playboy Magazine,* ideals espoused by other sexually explicit media cannot be assumed to be identical. It is possible that the presentation of women's bodies in other media may be more diverse or embody different ideals depending on numerous other factors (e.g., economic and technological resources or target audience). Future research examining the presentation of the female genitalia and general physique in other magazines and alternative types of media (e.g., pornographic videos) would be beneficial in developing a broader conceptualization of the appearance ideals upheld in mainstream society and the associated pressures faced by its female members.

In addition, *Playboy Magazine* and other sexually explicit media may not be the sole source of information shaping women's conception of appearance norms and ideals. It is possible that some women may be turning elsewhere for more healthy self-comparisons. For instance, some women may be able to overcome the cultural taboo associated with genital discussion and exhibition to locate more realistic genital referents (e.g., friends or female partners). Alternatively, women may possess personal characteristics (e.g., high body esteem) or receive external messages about their bodies (e.g., positive feedback from sexual partners) that mitigate the potentially harmful effects of exposure to media images such as those presented in *Playboy Magazine.* Further research is warranted to identify additional factors influencing women's physical self-evaluation, as well as protective factors that could buffer any negative effects of exposure to unrealistic media imagery.

Importantly, the perceived relevance of the ideals presented in *Playboy Magazine* may vary according to women's racial and ethnic background, socioeconomic status, and sexual orientation, particularly given the apparent homogeneity of the models featured. Past research has documented differences in body attitudes and ideals across demographic categories, including race (e.g., Harris, Walters, & Waschull, 1991) and social class (Wardle & Marsland, 1990). Accordingly, for some female viewers, the ideals embodied by *Playboy* models may not represent the ideals embraced by their predominant culture, which may enable these women to more comfortably reject such ideals. However, other research indicates that women belonging to racial, sexual, and socioeconomic minority groups are not impervious to mainstream cultural values and experience similar pressures to conform to reigning body ideals as does the majority (Grogan, 1999), suggesting that *Playboy* imagery may in fact affect a diverse audience.

This study provides compelling evidence for a shift in the genital appearance ideals endorsed across five decades. However, some of the trends observed over time may alternatively reflect advancements in technology and medicine as opposed to shifting ideals. It is possible that the digital enhancement techniques and surgical procedures that have become available more recently have enabled models to more closely approximate ideals that were always prevalent. Nonetheless, whether the current ideals presented in *Playboy Magazine* are novel or longstanding, the fact remains that they comprise a narrow and skewed representation of the female body and have the potential to foster significant body image disturbance among female viewers.

An important next step will be to investigate women's reactions to viewing *Playboy* photographs, particularly in terms of its impact on genital perceptions. Although the general body image literature suggests that women's body image is likely to suffer from exposure to representations of the female body that deviate from population norms (Groesz et al., 2002), further research is needed to confirm that this exposure effect applies to genital perceptions as well. In addition to studying cognitive and emotional aspects of media exposure effects, future research is needed to explore the behavioral repercussions of exposure to *Playboy* photographs and other pornographic materials; the prepubescent appearance of women's genitalia typically portrayed within this media may encourage body modifications such as shaving and female genital cosmetic surgery. Finally, alternative media images representing a natural and diverse range of adult female bodies, including sexually mature genitalia, need to be introduced to combat present ideals and empower women to feel good about their physical appearance.

Note

1. Since a three-page centerfold format was not included in issues of *Playboy Magazine* published before March of 1956, the featured Playmate photograph was substituted for the centerfold in our sample for issues published between December 1953 and February 1956.

References

Banerjee, M., Capozzoli, M., McSweeney, L., & Sinha, D. (1999). Beyond kappa: A review of interrater agreement measures. *The Canadian Journal of Statistics, 27,* 3–23.

Bessenoff, G. R. (2006). Can the media affect us? Social comparison, self-discrepancy, and the thin ideal. *Psychology of Women Quarterly, 30,* 239–251.

Blackledge, C. (2004). *The story of V: A natural history of female sexuality.* New Brunswick, NJ: Rutgers University Press.

Blank, J. (1993). *Femalia.* San Francisco, CA: Down There Press.

Bogaert, A. F., & Turkovich, D. A. (1993). A content analysis of Playboy centerfolds from 1953 through 1990: Changes in explicitness, objectification, and model's age. *Journal of Sex Research, 30,* 135–139.

Bramwell, R. (2002). Invisible labia: The representation of female external genitals in women's magazines. *Sexual and Relationship Therapy, 17,* 187–190.

Braun, V. (1999). Breaking a taboo? Talking and laughing about the vagina. *Feminism & Psychology, 9,* 367–372.

Braun, V. (2005). In search of (better) sexual pleasure: Female genital "cosmetic" surgery. *Sexualities, 8,* 407–424.

Braun, V., & Tiefer, L. (in press). The "designer vagina" and the pathologisation of female genital diversity: Interventions for change. *Radical Psychology.*

Byrd-Bredbenner, C., Murray, J., & Schlussel, Y. R. (2005). Temporal changes in anthropometric measurements of idealized females and young women in general. *Women & Health, 41,* 13–30.

Centers for Disease Control and Prevention. (2008). *Healthy weight.* Retrieved October 10, 2008, from www.cdc.gov/nccdphp/dnpa/healthyweight/index.htm.

Cunningham, K. (1993). Barbie doll culture and the American waistland. *Symbolic Interaction, 16,* 79–83.

Dodson, B. (1996). *Sex for one: The joy of selfloving.* New York: Three Rivers Press.

Gillman, S. L. (1985). *Difference and pathology: Stereotypes of sexuality, race, and madness.* Ithaca, NY: Cornell University Press.

Green, F. J. (2005). From cliterodectomies to "designer vaginas": The medical construction of heteronormative female bodies and sexuality through female genital cutting. *Sexualities, Evolution and Gender, 7*(2), 153–187.

Groesz, L. M., Levine, M. P., & Murmen, S. K. (2002). The effect of experimental presentation of thin media images on body satisfaction: A meta-analytic review. *International Journal of Eating Disorders, 31,* 1–16.

Grogan, S. (1999). *Body image: Understanding body dissatisfaction in men, women, and children.* London: Routledge.

Hamilton, E. A., Mintz, L., & Kashubeck-West, S. (2007). Predictors of media effects of body dissatisfaction in European American women. *Sex Roles, 56,* 397–402.

Harris, M. B., Walters, L. C., & Waschull, S. (1991). Gender and ethnic differences in obesity-related behaviors and attitudes in a college sample. *Journal of Applied Social Psychology, 21,* 1545–1566.

Harrison, K., & Cantor, J. (1997). The relationship between media consumption and eating disorders. *Journal of Communication, 47,* 40–67.

Kuther, T. L., & McDonald, E. (2004). Early adolescents' experiences with, and views of, Barbie. *Adolescence, 39,* 39–51.

Liao, L. M., & Creighton, S. M. (2007). Requests for cosmetic genitoplasty: How should healthcare providers respond? *British Medical Journal, 334,* 1090–1092.

Lloyd, J., Crouch, N. S., Minto, C. L., Liao, L., & Creighton, S. M. (2005). Female genital appearance: "normality" unfolds. *British Journal of Obstetrics and Gynecology, 112,* 643–646.

Manderson, L. (2004). Local rites and body politics: Tensions between cultural diversity and human rights. *International Feminist Journal of Politics, 6,* 285–307.

Norton, K. I., Olds, S. T., Olive, S., & Dank, S. (1996). Ken and Barbie at life size. *Sex Roles, 34,* 287–294.

Owen, P. R., & Laurel-Seller, E. (2000). Weight and shape ideals: Thin is dangerously in. *Journal of Applied Social Psychology, 30,* 979–990.

Palefsky, J., & Handley, J. (2002). *What your doctor may not tell you about HPV and abnormal pap smears: Get the facts on this dangerous virus—Protect your health and your life!* New York: Warner Books.

Perreault, W. D., & Leigh, L. E. (1989). Reliability of nominal data based on qualitative judgments. *Journal of Marketing Research, 26,* 135–148.

Playboy Cyber Club. (2008). Retrieved September 2007–April 2008, from www.playboy.com.

Russell, D. E. H., & Purcell, N. J. (2006). Exposure to pornography as a cause of child sexual victimization. In N. E. Dowd, D. G. Singer, & R. F. Wilson (Eds.), *Handbook of children, culture, and violence* (pp. 59–85). Thousand Oaks, CA: Sage.

Schick, V. R., Calabrese, S. K., & Rima, B. N. (2008, November). *Does (labia) size really matter? The distorting impact of exposure to unrealistic labia minora images on women's perceived labia size: Implications for genital discontent and sexuality.* Poster presented at the annual meeting of the Society for the Scientific Study of Sexuality, San Juan, Puerto Rico.

Schick, V. R., Rima, B. N., & Calabrese, S. K. (2009, March). *Recreating a genital aesthetic: Public representations of female genitalia 35 years after Betty Dodson's slideshow.* Paper presented at the annual convention of The Association for Women in Psychology, Newport, Rhode Island.

Simmons Choices III. (2006). Retrieved February 12, 2009, from Simmons Choices III database.

Singh, D., & Young, R. K. (1995). Body weight, waist-to-hip ratio, breasts, and hips: Role in judgments of female attractiveness and desirability for relationships. *Ethology and Sociobiology, 16,* 483–507.

Spitzer, B. L., Henderson, K. A., & Zivian, M. T. (1999). Gender differences in population versus media body sizes: A comparison over four decades. *Sex Roles, 40,* 545–565.

Terry, J., & Urla, J. (1995). *Deviant bodies.* Bloomington, IN: Indiana University Press.

Thompson, J. K., & Tantleff, S. (1992). Female and male ratings of upper torso: Actual, ideal, and stereotypical conceptions. *Journal of Social Behavior and Personality, 7,* 345–354.

Wardle, J., & Marsland, L. (1990). Adolescent concerns about weight and eating: A social–developmental perspective. *Journal of Psychosomatic Research, 34,* 377–391.

Critical Thinking

1. Define the "Barbie Doll ideal."

2. What is the impact of the representation of female genitalia in centerfolds on the "Barbie Doll ideal"?

3. How does the "Barbie Doll ideal" impact men and women today?

An earlier version of this article was presented at the 9th Congress of the European Federation of Sexology in Rome, Italy, April, 2008. We are thankful to Katie Armstrong, Brittany Novak, and Diana Pierszchala for their assistance with data coding. We are also grateful for Alyssa Zucker's help and guidance throughout various stages of the research process.

Correspondence should be addressed to **VANESSA R. SCHICK,** Center for Sexual Health Promotion, Indiana University, HPER Building 116, Bloomington, IN 47405. E-mail: vschick@gwu.edu.

Female Power

THE ECONOMIST

Across the rich world more women are working than ever before. Coping with this change will be one of the great challenges of the coming decades.

The economic empowerment of women across the rich world is one of the most remarkable revolutions of the past 50 years. It is remarkable because of the extent of the change: millions of people who were once dependent on men have taken control of their own economic fates. It is remarkable also because it has produced so little friction: a change that affects the most intimate aspects of people's identities has been widely welcomed by men as well as women. Dramatic social change seldom takes such a benign form.

Yet even benign change can come with a sting in its tail. Social arrangements have not caught up with economic changes. Many children have paid a price for the rise of the two-income household. Many women—and indeed many men—feel that they are caught in an ever-tightening tangle of commitments. If the empowerment of women was one of the great changes of the past 50 years, dealing with its social consequences will be one of the great challenges of the next 50.

At the end of her campaign to become America's first female president in 2008, Hillary Clinton remarked that her 18m votes in the Democratic Party's primaries represented 18m cracks in the glass ceiling. In the market for jobs rather than votes the ceiling is being cracked every day. Women now make up almost half of American workers (49.9% in October). They run some of the world's best companies, such as PepsiCo, Archer Daniels Midland and W.L. Gore. They earn almost 60% of university degrees in America and Europe.

Progress has not been uniform, of course. In Italy and Japan, employment rates for men are more than 20 percentage points higher than those for women. Although Italy's female employment rate has risen markedly in the past decade, it is still below 50%, and more than 20 percentage points below those of Denmark and Sweden. Women earn substantially less than men on average and are severely under-represented at the top of organisations.

The change is dramatic nevertheless. A generation ago working women performed menial jobs and were routinely subjected to casual sexism—as "Mad Men", a television drama about advertising executives in the early 1960s, demonstrates brilliantly. Today women make up the majority of professional workers in many countries (51% in the United States, for example) and casual sexism is for losers. Even holdouts such as the Mediterranean countries are changing rapidly. In Spain, the proportion of young women in the labour force has now reached American levels. The glass is much nearer to being half full than half empty.

What explains this revolution? Politics have clearly played a part. Feminists such as Betty Friedan have demonised domestic slavery and lambasted discrimination. Governments have passed equal-rights acts. Female politicians such as Margaret Thatcher and Mrs Clinton have taught younger women that anything is possible. But politics is only part of the answer: such discordant figures as Ms Friedan and Lady Thatcher have been borne aloft by subterranean economic and technological forces.

The rich world has seen a growing demand for women's labour. When brute strength mattered more than brains, men had an inherent advantage. Now that brainpower has triumphed the two sexes are more evenly matched. The feminisation of the workforce has been driven by the relentless rise of the service sector (where women can compete as well as men) and the equally relentless decline of manufacturing (where they could not). The landmark book in the rise of feminism was arguably not Ms Friedan's "The Feminine Mystique" but Daniel Bell's "The Coming of Post-Industrial Society".

Demand has been matched by supply: women are increasingly willing and able to work outside the home. The vacuum cleaner has played its part. Improved technology reduced the amount of time needed for the traditional female work of cleaning and cooking. But the most important innovation has been the contraceptive pill. The spread of the pill has not only allowed women to get married later. It has also increased their incentives to invest time and effort in acquiring skills, particularly slow-burning skills that are hard to learn and take many years to pay off. The knowledge that they would not have to drop out of, say, law school to have a baby made law school more attractive.

The expansion of higher education has also boosted job prospects for women, improving their value on the job market and shifting their role models from stay-at-home mothers to successful professional women. The best-educated women have always been more likely than other women to work, even after having children. In 1963, 62% of college-educated women in the United States were in the labour force, compared with

46% of those with a high school diploma. Today 80% of American women with a college education are in the labour force compared with 67% of those with a high school diploma and 47% of those without one.

This growing cohort of university-educated women is also educated in more marketable subjects. In 1966, 40% of American women who received a BA specialised in education in college; 2% specialised in business and management. The figures are now 12% and 50%. Women only continue to lag seriously behind men in a handful of subjects, such as engineering and computer sciences, where they earned about one-fifth of degrees in 2006.

One of the most surprising things about this revolution is how little overt celebration it has engendered. Most people welcome the change. A recent Rockefeller Foundation/Time survey found that three-quarters of Americans regarded it as a positive development. Nine men out of ten said they were comfortable with women earning more than them. But few are cheering. This is partly because young women take their opportunities for granted. It is partly because for many women work represents economic necessity rather than liberation. The rich world's growing army of single mothers have little choice but to work. A growing proportion of married women have also discovered that the only way they can preserve their households' living standards is to join their husbands in the labour market. In America, families with stay-at-home wives have the same inflation-adjusted income as similar families did in the early 1970s. But the biggest reason is that the revolution has brought plenty of problems in its wake.

Production versus Reproduction

One obvious problem is that women's rising aspirations have not been fulfilled. They have been encouraged to climb onto the occupational ladder only to discover that the middle rungs are dominated by men and the upper rungs are out of reach. Only 2% of the bosses of Fortune 500 companies and five of those in the FTSE 100 stockmarket index are women. Women make up less than 13% of board members in America. The upper ranks of management consultancies and banks are dominated by men. In America and Britain, the typical full-time female worker earns only about 80% as much as the typical male.

This no doubt owes something to prejudice. But the biggest reason why women remain frustrated is more profound: many women are forced to choose between motherhood and careers. Childless women in corporate America earn almost as much as men. Mothers with partners earn less and single mothers much less. The cost of motherhood is particularly steep for fast-track women. Traditionally "female" jobs such as teaching mix well with motherhood because wages do not rise much with experience and hours are relatively light. But at successful firms wages rise steeply and schedules are demanding. Future bosses are expected to have worked in several departments and countries. Professional-services firms have an up-or-out system which rewards the most dedicated with lucrative partnerships. The reason for the income gap may thus be the opposite

of prejudice. It is that women are judged by exactly the same standards as men.

This Hobson's choice is imposing a high cost on both individuals and society. Many professional women reject motherhood entirely: in Switzerland 40% of them are childless. Others delay child-bearing for so long that they are forced into the arms of the booming fertility industry. The female drop-out rate from the most competitive professions represents a loss to collective investment in talent. A study of graduates of the University of Chicago's Booth School of Business by Marianne Bertrand and her colleagues found that, ten years after graduating, about half of the female MBAs who had chosen to have children remained in the labour force. It also leaves many former high-flyers frustrated. Another American study, this time of women who left work to have children, found that all but 7% of them wanted to return to work. Only 74% managed to return, and just 40% returned to full-time jobs.

Even well-off parents worry that they spend too little time with their children, thanks to crowded schedules and the ever-buzzing BlackBerry. For poorer parents, juggling the twin demands of work and child-rearing can be a nightmare. Child care eats a terrifying proportion of the family budget, and many childminders are untrained. But quitting work to look after the children can mean financial disaster. British children brought up in two-parent families where only one parent works are almost three times more likely to be poor than children with two parents at work.

A survey for the Children's Society, a British charity, found that 60% of parents agreed that "nowadays parents aren't able to spend enough time with their children". In a similar survey in America, 74% of parents said that they did not have enough time for their children. Nor does the problem disappear as children get older. In most countries schools finish early in the afternoon. In America they close down for two months in the summer. Only a few places—Denmark, Sweden and, to a lesser extent, France and Quebec—provide comprehensive systems of after-school care.

Different countries have adopted different solutions to the problem of combining work and parenthood. Some stress the importance of very young children spending time with their mothers. Austria, the Czech Republic, Finland and Hungary provide up to three years of paid leave for mothers. Germany has introduced a "parent's salary", or Elterngeld, to encourage mothers to stay at home. (The legislation was championed by a minister for women who has seven children.) Other countries put more emphasis on preschool education. New Zealand and the Nordic countries are particularly keen on getting women back to work and children into kindergartens. Britain, Germany, Japan, Switzerland and, above all, the Netherlands are keen on mothers working part-time. Others, such as the Czech Republic, Greece, Finland, Hungary, Portugal and South Korea, make little room for part-time work for women. The Scandinavian countries, particularly Iceland, have added a further wrinkle by increasing incentives for fathers to spend more time caring for their children.

The world's biggest economy has adopted an idiosyncratic approach. America provides no statutory paid leave for mothers and only 12 weeks unpaid. At least 145 countries provide paid sick leave. America allows only unpaid absence for serious family illness. America's public spending on family support is low by OECD standards. It spends only 0.5% of its GDP on public support for child care compared with 1.3% in France and 2.7% in Denmark.

It is difficult to evaluate the relative merits of these various arrangements. Different systems can produce similar results: anti-statist America has roughly the same proportion of children in kindergartens as statist Finland. Different systems have different faults. Sweden is not quite the paragon that its fans imagine, despite its family-friendly employment policies. Only 1.5% of senior managers are women, compared with 11% in America. Three-quarters of Swedish women work in the public sector; three-quarters of men work in the private sector. But there is evidence that America and Britain, the countries that combine high female employment with reluctance to involve the state in child care, serve their children especially poorly. A report by UNICEF in 2007 on children in rich countries found that America and Britain had some of the lowest scores for "well-being".

A Woman's World

The trend towards more women working is almost certain to continue. In the European Union, women have filled 6m of the 8m new jobs created since 2000. In America, three out of four people thrown out of work since the recession began are men; the female unemployment rate is 8.6%, against 11.2% for men. The Bureau of Labour Statistics calculates that women make up more than two-thirds of employees in ten of the 15 job categories likely to grow fastest in the next few years. By 2011, there will be 2.6m more women than men studying in American universities.

Women will also be the beneficiaries of the growing "war for talent". The combination of an ageing workforce and a more skill-dependent economy means that countries will have to make better use of their female populations. Goldman Sachs calculates that, leaving all other things equal, increasing women's participation in the labour market to male levels will boost GDP by 21% in Italy, 19% in Spain, 16% in Japan, 9% in America, France and Germany, and 8% in Britain.

The corporate world is doing ever more to address the loss of female talent and the difficulty of combining work with child care. Many elite companies are rethinking their promotion practices. Addleshaw Goddard, a law firm, has created the role of legal director as an alternative to partnerships for women who want to combine work and motherhood. Ernst & Young and other accounting firms have increased their efforts to maintain connections with women who take time off to have children and then ease them back into work.

Home-working is increasingly fashionable. More than 90% of companies in Germany and Sweden allow flexible working. A growing number of firms are learning to divide the working week in new ways—judging staff on annual rather than weekly hours, allowing them to work nine days a fortnight, letting them come in early or late and allowing husbands and wives to share jobs. Almost half of Sun Microsystems's employees work at home or from nearby satellite offices. Raytheon, a maker of missile systems, allows workers every other Friday off to take care of family business, if they make up the hours on other days.

Companies are even rethinking the structure of careers, as people live and work longer. Barclays is one of many firms that allow five years' unpaid leave. John Lewis offers a six-month paid sabbatical to people who have been in the company for 25 years. Companies are allowing people to phase their retirement. Child-bearing years will thus make up a smaller proportion of women's potential working lives. Spells out of the labour force will become less a mark of female exceptionalism.

Faster change is likely as women exploit their economic power. Many talented women are already hopping off the corporate treadmill to form companies that better meet their needs. In the past decade, the number of privately owned companies started by women in America has increased twice as fast as the number owned by men. Women-owned companies employ more people than the largest 500 companies combined. Eden McCallum and Axiom Legal have applied a network model to their respective fields of management consultancy and legal services: network members work when it suits them and the companies use their scale to make sure that clients have their problems dealt with immediately.

Governments are also trying to adjust to the new world. Germany now has 1,600 schools where the day lasts until mid-afternoon. Some of the most popular American charter schools offer longer school days and shorter summer holidays.

But so far even the combination of public- and private-sector initiatives has only gone so far to deal with the problem. The children of poorer working mothers are the least likely to benefit from female-friendly companies. Millions of families still struggle with insufficient child-care facilities and a school day that bears no relationship to their working lives. The West will be struggling to cope with the social consequences of women's economic empowerment for many years to come.

Critical Thinking

1. What factors are contributing to women being offered corporate board positions at a very low rate compared to men?

Estranged Spouses Increasingly Waiting out Downturn to Divorce

Donna St. George

In the Great Recession, breaking up is hard to do.

With housing values depressed and jobs disappearing, divorce has become a luxury beyond the reach of some couples. There is often not enough money to pay for separate households or to hire lawyers, fight over children and go to court.

What has always been painful is now desperate and confounding, with a growing number of couples deciding to wait out the economic storm while others take new approaches—such as living together as they separate.

"I have lots of files sitting in the drawer, where people can't move forward," says David Goldberg, a divorce lawyer and mediator in Gaithersburg. He has been working in family law for 44 years and says he has never seen a time like this one.

Lately, he said, "I have a lot of clients who have ended up in bankruptcy."

The difficulties of divorce in the downturn are familiar to Paulene Foster, a 42-year-old federal worker from Olney, who says her precarious finances forced her to wait a year. If that wasn't enough, she also shared a house with her estranged husband—him in the basement, her upstairs. Strapped months went by as the couple were saddled with a suburban townhouse that would not sell.

"It was a mess," Foster said.

Her divorce, filed last month with a $105 check after going to a *self-help law clinic* in Montgomery County, comes as the national rate of failed marriages has declined slightly—not necessarily because divorce-minded couples are happier than before but, some experts suggest, because they don't have the money to call it quits.

At one Woodbridge law firm, 20 to 25 percent of clients seeking a divorce live under the same roof as their estranged spouse to save money as they await court action.

Other couples say they are stymied by the grim reality that they owe more on the family home than they could get if they sold it.

How do they start over if debt is all that's left to divide?

Heather Hostetter, who has a divorce practice in Bethesda, said that many couples used to divorce with enough equity in a house so that both spouses could re-create lives not so different from their old ones.

"It used to be you could go own another home," she said. "Maybe it's a little smaller, maybe it's not in the same neighborhood.

"Now you see people who go from homeowners to renters."

Divorce and Bankruptcy

Facing harsher circumstances, Marissa Fuller, who works in child care in Fairfax City, says her husband's job loss and then his underemployment had an accumulating impact. They had relationship troubles. They fell short on bills month after month. She tired of begging utility companies to turn back on the family's water and electricity.

In January, she filed both for bankruptcy and divorce, sure that the economic tension and the discord that came with it took a toll. "That really made the marriage crumble," she said. Fuller found housing through a nonprofit program and is saving for her own apartment, but she says the math of providing for two children on her salary seems nearly impossible.

Experts say that divorce claims slightly more than 40 percent of marriages. *Rates calculated by the National Marriage Project* show a modest decline in divorce during 2008, the first year of the recession, when 838,000 cases were granted in 44 states—at a time when growing economic strain might have produced a spike in divorce. A year earlier, 856,000 divorces were finalized. Scores of studies show a link between tough times and divorce.

W. Bradford Wilcox, director of the National Marriage Project at the University of Virginia, says some families are pulling together amid the economic turmoil, and others that want to split up are postponing until they see a rebound in the economy and in home values. A divorce can cost as little as $100 on a do-it-yourself basis with little in dispute and $10,000 to $20,000—or more—for a divorce that ends up in court.

Still, dividing into two households can prove the more daunting task—the same income being used to cover an extra housing payment, extra utility bills, separate groceries. This can be tricky when a home has no equity or line of credit to draw from.

In Manassas, lawyer Kirk Wilder says that in some cases, the house is so void of value that neither party wants to be stuck with it. "It used to be, 'Well, I want the house,' " he said. "Now it's, 'You take the house.' That's a huge change."

The economics of breaking up are a little better in the District and parts of Northern Virginia, where spouses can live in the same house during the required separation period, as long as they share little more than the space around them. No sex. No meals. No togetherness.

"They don't do each other's laundry, they don't eat together, they don't go to the kids' soccer game together," says Pat Hammond, a lawyer in Prince William County who advises clients with increasing frequency about how to get divorced without moving out of the house. "If they live in a three-bedroom townhouse, and they have four kids, it ain't going to work."

A Place to Sleep

Steve Halbert, an Arlington County resident who divorced in 2008, attests to the difficulty of the proposition.

His wife lived in one bedroom; he lived in another. He tried to work as much as possible to stay out of the house. "If you're in the same room, then a fight is waiting to happen," he said. For all of the struggle, his mortgage is still upside down 18 months later—and he still does not have a way to refinance his house and clear his ex-wife's name from the mortgage loan.

Halbert, a commercial real estate appraiser, says he earns half of what he did in the boom days and now pays alimony. "There used to be a lot of disposable income," he said, "and now it's, 'Be glad you have a place to sleep.' "

Prince William lawyer Larry Fabian says perhaps a quarter of his clients live together while they seek a divorce, which was almost unheard of five or so years ago. "It's really difficult," he says of their experiences. "It's pretty much the worst of all worlds."

Then again, some would say it is even harder in Maryland, which requires a full year of separate residences for mutual and voluntary divorce. That requirement is economically difficult for some; impossible for others.

Jesslyn Haskins, 42, a nurse and mother of three in Upper Marlboro, says a judge threw out her divorce case because she and her ex-husband had shared the same house during their separation. She says she then left, moving in with friends and ultimately getting an apartment, as relations grew more bitter and the mortgage went unpaid. Now divorced, she says she lives in the house and pays the mortgage but is in jeopardy of foreclosure because of missed back payments.

The National Marriage Project's Wilcox says working-class couples, who already have high rates of divorce, are especially vulnerable to a recession-related breakup because they are hit harder by unemployment, which is a significant predictor of divorce. Men, in particular, see themselves as breadwinners and are prone to feelings of worthlessness and depression during lengthy periods without a job, Wilcox says. "We would predict this recession is having a pretty big impact on working-class couples," he says.

In terms of divorce, the recession bears similarities to the Great Depression, says Johns Hopkins University sociologist Andrew Cherlin, noting that in the 1930s, divorce rates fell amid the worst of the economic crisis, only to rise as the country recovered. "Troubled economic times breed troubled marriages," he says. "But whether those marriages end in divorce right away is another thing."

Cherlin said the recession has probably created "a backlog of unhappy married couples who would like to get a divorce soon but can't afford it," and he predicted a surge in cases during the first several recovery years. "The longer this severe economic downturn continues," he said, "the larger the backlog will be."

Critical Thinking

1. What economic trends have impacted the decision to stay married vs. divorce for many couples?
2. How have social problems such as the housing market collapse and economic downturns impacted the relationship decisions people make?
3. What strategies have couples devised to deal with new challenges brought on by changes in global economic forces?

Sexual Behavior in the United States: Results from a National Probability Sample of Men and Women Ages 14–94

DEBBY HERBENICK, PhD, MPH ET AL.

Introduction

Sexual health emerged during the past decade as a key unifying concept addressing clinical and public health issues as diverse as unintended pregnancy among adolescents, sexually transmitted infections (STI) among young adults, and sexual dysfunctions among older adults. In 2002, the World Health Organization (WHO) described sexual health as ". . . a state of physical, emotional, mental and social well-being related to sexuality; it is not merely the absence of disease, dysfunction or infirmity. Sexual health requires a positive and respectful approach to sexuality and sexual responses, as well as the possibility of having pleasurable and safe sexual experiences, free of coercion, discrimination and violence."

Nationally representative up-to-date data about human sexual behavior are required to fully translate the WHO definition into public health policy and practice and to provide physicians with a suitable basis for understanding sexuality through the life course. Relatively recent national surveys (e.g., the National Survey of Family Growth [NSFG], the Youth Risk Behavior Survey, and the National Social Life, Health, and Aging Project [NSHAP]) had limited age ranges and explored a narrow range of sexual behaviors. The most recent nationally representative survey of adult sexual behavior in the United States, conducted in 1992, was limited to adults aged 18 to 60.

Much has changed since 1992 that may have influenced sexual behavior in the United States. Previously less common sexual behaviors such as oral and anal sex appear to have become more widely practiced. Changes in oral–genital behaviors may be linked to increased rates of genital infections by Type 1 herpes simplex viruses and to increased rates of oropharyngeal cancer linked to human papilloma virus infections. The Internet has influenced sexual knowledge, norms, and behaviors. A vaccine for prevention of cancers associated with sexually transmitted human papilloma virus infections has been marketed amid concern about its influence on sexual behaviors. Since 1997, over $1.5 billion of federal funding for abstinence-only sexuality education has been in place although with equivocal evidence of efficacy. Since 1998, oral medications to treat erectile dysfunction have been available; more than 6 million outpatient prescriptions were written for sildenafil in the 6 months following approval by the United States Food and Drug Administration. Attitudes toward same-sex relationships have changed, with same-sex marriage and civil unions now legally recognized in several U.S. states. As such, there is a need for nationally representative data that adequately captures contemporary American sexual behavior given these many social and historical changes.

Aims

The purpose of this study, the National Survey of Sexual Health and Behavior (NSSHB), was to assess solo and partnered sexual behaviors in a national probability sample of men and women ages 14–94 years and to thus provide a comprehensive snapshot of American sexual behavior over a wide range of the sexual life course.

Methods
Data Collection

During March–May 2009, NSSHB data were collected using a population-based cross-sectional survey of adolescents and adults in the United States via research panels of Knowledge Networks (Menlo Park, CA, USA). Research panels accessed through Knowledge Networks are based on a national probability sample established using both random digit dialing (RDD) and an address-based sampling (ABS) frame. ABS involves the probability sampling of a frame of residential addresses in the United States derived from the U.S. Postal Service's Delivery Sequence File, a system that contains detailed information on every mail deliverable address in the United States. Collectively, the sampling frame from which participants are recruited covers approximately 98 percent of all U.S. households. Randomly selected addresses are recruited to the research panel through a series of mailings and subsequently by telephone follow-ups to nonresponders when possible. To further correct sources of sampling and nonsampling error, study samples are corrected with a post-stratification adjustment using demographic distributions from the most recent data available from the Current Population Survey (CPS), the monthly population survey conducted by the U.S. Bureau of the Census considered to be the standard for measuring demographic and other trends in the United States. These adjustments result in a panel base weight that was employed in a probability proportional to size (PPS) selection method for establishing the samples for this study. Population specific distributions for this study were based upon the December 2008 CPS.

Once the sample frame was established, all individuals within that frame received a recruitment message from Knowledge Networks that provided a brief description of the NSSHB and invited them to participate. Adolescent recruitment included obtaining consent from a parent (or legal guardian) and, if provided, subsequently from the adolescent. A total of 2,172 parents (or legal guardians) reviewed a study description, including the survey, and 62 percent (N = 1,347) consented for their child to be invited to participate. Of 1,347 adolescents contacted electronically, 831 responded, with 99.0 percent (N = 820) consenting to participate. An electronic recruitment message was sent to 9,600 potential adult participants, of whom 6,182 (64 percent) responded, with 82 percent (N = 5,045) consenting to participate. All study protocols were approved by the Institutional Review Board of the primary authors' academic institution.

All data were collected by Knowledge Networks via the Internet; participants in a given Knowledge Networks panel were provided with access to the Internet and hardware if needed. Multiple researchers have used Knowledge Networks for multiple health-related studies, substantiating the validity of such methods for obtaining data from nationally representative samples of the U.S. population.

Main Outcome Measures

Some participant characteristics were previously collected by Knowledge Networks for purposes of sample stratification and for sample adjustments using post-stratification data weights. These measures included gender, age, race (black, Hispanic, white, other), U.S. geographic region (Midwest, North, South, West), and sexual orientation (heterosexual/straight, homosexual/gay/lesbian, bisexual, asexual, other). Household income included an adult's reported household income; for adolescents household income was reported by their parent or guardian. Additionally, level of educational attainment and marital status were collected from adult participants.

Participants were asked to report whether or not they had engaged in certain solo and partnered sexual behaviors and, if so, how recently each behavior had occurred (never, within the past month, within the past year, more than 1 year ago), consistent with other nationally representative studies of sexual behaviors.

Measures of oral sex were specific to the participant's role and partner's sex (receiving from male, receiving from female, giving to female, giving to male). Also assessed were receptive (men and women) and insertive (men only) anal intercourse.

Analyses

The proportions of participants reporting histories of participating in each sexual behavior are reported based upon whether that behavior occurred within the past month, past year, or at some other point during one's lifetime. For each percentage of individuals reporting a history of participating in a behavior during the specified periods of time, corresponding 95 percent confidence intervals using the Adjusted Wald method, were calculated and are presented by age group. During analyses, post-stratification data weights were applied to reduce variance and minimize bias caused by nonsampling error. Distributions for age, race, gender, Hispanic ethnicity, education, and U.S. census region were used in post-stratification adjustments. These distributions were based upon the December 2008 CPS.

Results

A total of 5,865 individuals (2,936 men, 2,929 women) ages 14 to 94 years participated.

Men's Sexual Behaviors
Masturbation

Solo masturbation was reported with the most consistency, as 27.9 percent to 68.6 percent of men in each age group reported masturbation during the past month. The majority of men in all age groups reported masturbation during the past year with the exception of the 14- to 15-year-old and 70+ age groups. Solo masturbation (past month and past year) was more commonly reported than most partnered sexual behaviors for ages 14 through 24 years and among those aged 50 years or older.

Vaginal Intercourse

Although most men in the 18- to 19-year-old age group had experienced vaginal intercourse, it was not a fixed aspect of every man's experience. For example, although about 85 percent of men in their 20s and 30s reported engaging in vaginal intercourse in the previous year, this proportion decreased to 73.6 percent among men in their 40s and to 57.9 percent among men in their 50s. For men ages 25 to 49 years, vaginal intercourse was more common than other sexual behaviors.

Partnered Noncoital Behaviors

Partnered noncoital behaviors were reported by at least some men in all age groups. Although a minority of those ages 14–15 years had ever engaged in partnered masturbation (5.7 percent) or received oral sex from a female (13.0 percent), among the 16- to 17-year-old cohort, approximately one-fifth reported having engaged in partnered masturbation and one-third having received oral sex from a female partner. The highest proportions who reported having engaged in recent (past month) partnered masturbation and who reported oral sex with a woman (giving and receiving) were between 25 and 49 years.

Anal Intercourse

Insertive anal intercourse was less common than other partnered behaviors but was not rare, being reported in the past year by more than 5 percent of 16- to 19-year olds, 10.8 percent of those ages 20–24 years, greater than 20 percent of those 25–49 years and 11.3 percent of men in their fifties. More than 40 percent of men ages 25–59 years reported ever having engaged in insertive anal intercourse during their lifetime.

Same-Sex Sexual Behavior

Sexual activity between men was relatively uncommon. Among men ages 18 to 59, 4.8 percent to 8.4 percent reported having received oral sex from another man in the previous year. However, 13.8 percent of men ages 40–49 years and 14.9 percent ages 50–59 years reported such lifetime behavior. A total of 4.3 percent to 8.0 percent of men aged 18–59 years reported having performed oral sex on another man in the previous year; however, more than 10 percent of men in the 18–19, 40–49, and

50–59 age groups reported having ever engaged in this behavior. Receptive penile-anal intercourse was the least common behavior reported (less than 6 percent of men in any age group in the past year). Lifetime receptive anal intercourse was most prevalent among 20- to 24-year olds (10.8 percent) and those aged 40–49 and 50–59 years (8.5 percent and 9.5 percent, respectively).

Women's Sexual Behaviors

Masturbation

Solo masturbation was reported by more than 20 percent of women in all age groups during the past month and by more than 40 percent of all women within the past year, with the exception of those over 70 years. A greater proportion of those ages 14 to 17 reported lifetime solo masturbation compared with any other sexual behavior.

Vaginal Intercourse

Beginning with women ages 18–19 years (26.0 percent of women reported solo masturbation and 4.3.1percent reported vaginal intercourse during the previous month), vaginal intercourse was the sexual behavior that more women in all age groups reported as having occurred during the past month compared with all other sexual behaviors assessed. Beginning in the cohort in their thirties, increasing proportions of women reported having had no vaginal intercourse during the previous year; this was the case for approximately one-fourth of women ages 30–39, nearly 1/3 of women 40–49, one-half of women ages 50–59, and ultimately nearly four-fifths of women ages 70 years and older.

Partnered Noncoital Behaviors

Masturbation with a partner during the previous month and year was most commonly reported by women ages 16 through 49 and most women between the ages of 25–49 reported this behavior in their lifetime. Approximately 10 percent of 14- to 15-year-old women and 23.5 percent of 16- to 17-year-old women reported receiving oral sex from a male partner in the previous year. More than half of women in the age groups between 18 and 49 had received oral sex from a male partner in the previous year as had 34.2 percent of females ages 50–59 and 24.8 percent of females ages 60–69 years.

A total of 11.8 percent of 14- to 15-year-old women and 22.4 percent of 16- to 17-year-old women reported having given oral sex to a male partner in the past year. Also, most women in the age groups between 18 and 49 years reported having given oral sex to a man in the past year. Oral-genital sex given to male partners during the previous month was rarely reported by women in the 70+ age group in the past year (6.8 percent) though 42.7 percent had done so in their lifetime.

Anal Intercourse

A total of 4 percent or less of 14- to 17-year-old women and those aged 50 or older reported anal intercourse in the previous year. However, 18.0 percent of 18- to 19-year-old females and more than 20 percent of those between the ages of 20 and 39 reported anal sex in the past year. Lifetime anal sex was reported by 40 percent or more of women ages 20–49 years, and by about 30 percent or more of women ages 50–69 years.

Same-Sex Sexual Behavior

Sexual activity between women was relatively uncommon. Fewer than 5 percent of women in most age groups reported having received oral sex in the past year from a female partner, with the exception of the 8.5 percent of women ages 20–24 who reported having performed oral sex on a woman in the past year. A total of 2.0 percent to 9.2 percent of those ages 16 to 49 years reported having given oral sex to another woman in the past year.

Discussion

These findings provide a detailed picture of solo and partnered sexual behavior through a lifespan, showing that one's sexual repertoire varies across different age cohorts, with masturbation relatively more common in young and older individuals and vaginal intercourse being more common than other sexual behaviors from early to late adulthood. Partnered noncoital sexual behaviors (oral and anal sex) also appear to be well established aspects of a contemporary sexual repertoire in the United States. The baseline rates of behavior established by the analyses provided in this report will be helpful to sexuality educators who develop, implement, and evaluate programs that seek to improve societal knowledge related to the prevalence of sexual behaviors and to sexual health clinicians whose work to improve sexual health among the population often requires such rates of behavior.

Although the largest proportion of adults reported vaginal intercourse during the past month throughout most of the reproductive year age cohorts, the reproductive years are not marked exclusively by potentially procreative sex. Sizable proportions of individuals ages 18 and 49 years reported solo masturbation, partnered masturbation, oral sex, and anal sex during the previous year, a common time frame between wellness visits, particularly for women.

Data about sexual activity in the previous year inform clinicians about the proportions of patients who are likely to have engaged in various sexual behaviors since their last clinical exam and who may benefit from annual, detailed sexual history taking. Also, the lack of sexual behavior experienced by some groups has clinical relevance. For example, the decreasing proportion of men in their forties engaging in vaginal intercourse may reflect, at least in part, a growing incidence of erectile dysfunction that may be related to cardiovascular disease or diabetes. Similarly, the decreasing proportion of sexual activity among women as they age may, for some, reflect pain with vaginal intercourse (caused by vaginal dryness), lower libido, or other sexual health concerns.

Also related to important clinical concerns, the rates of behavior established in this report may be helpful to those dedicated to reducing rates of human immunodeficiency virus, STIs, and unintended pregnancy. The rates of these sexual health challenges do provide a rationale for continued surveillance of sexual behaviors among both adults and adolescents in order to inform health-related policy and practice. However, given the purpose of this particular report, the analyses presented do not consider the situational or partner-related variables that influence the extent to which a sexual behavior poses the potential for negative impacts to sexual health, and those using these data to substantiate public health programs should consider the lack of context that underlies the rates presented here. The NSSHB did collect such variables, and additional in-depth analyses from the NSSHB are presented in multiple other reports that provide rates of condom use for both adolescents and adults, and those that consider the situational characteristics and potential health consequences of recent sexual events among both adolescents and adults, including reports focused specifically on the aging population and ethnic minorities.

Although not longitudinal, a strength of this study, compared with other studies that have focused on more narrow age ranges, is that a developmental trajectory of sexual expression is apparent. A minority of 14- to 17-year-old adolescents report engaging in partnered sexual activity with sharply raised proportions of partnered sexual behavior reported among 18- to 24-year olds. Although partnered sexual activity remains common throughout the 20s, 30s, and 40s, there is a clear decline in partnered activity for both genders in their 50s and 60s and a sharper decline as individuals reach age 70. The latter echoes findings from the recent NSHAP, which found substantial declines in sexual activity among individuals aged 74 or older in association with partner loss and health problems. Of course, differences in sexual behavior between various age groups are likely to be influenced not only by development throughout the life course but also by cohort effects that reflect socialization related to sexuality.

Compared with the 1992 National Health and Social Life Survey (NHSLS), in this present study more men and women have engaged in oral sex and a significantly greater proportion have engaged in anal sex. The larger proportions of those who had engaged in anal sex were not limited to the youngest cohorts. Most participants in all adult (18+) age groups had engaged in oral sex with the exception of females in the 70+ age group, of whom slightly less than half had done so. Anal sex was reported by sizable proportions of adults ages 20 to 49 and twice the proportion of 18- to 19-year-old females reported lifetime receptive anal sex (20.0 percent) as the proportion of 18- to 19-year-old males who reported lifetime insertive anal sex (9.7 percent). These proportions were twice as large for each gender in the 20- to 24-year-old cohort.

Neither the NHSLS nor the NSHAP included questions about mutual masturbation or the gender of respondents' oral sex partners. As such, it is not known to what extent mutual masturbation, or same-sex vs. other-sex oral sex behaviors, may have changed over time. Little is known about same-sex behaviors from nationally representative studies, as none—including ours—have oversampled those who identify as homosexual or bisexual, leaving the numbers too few for adequate statistical analysis. However, findings reflect those from the NHSLS and from the Kinsey interview data in that a greater number of males and females have engaged in same-sex sexual behaviors than identify as homosexual or bisexual.

The current study is only the second nationally representative study of sexual behavior of adults living in the United States and the first to include such an expansive range of ages. Although Alfred Kinsey and his team reported data from adults about their sexual lives from childhood through older age, sampling was not nationally representative, people married at younger ages, the life expectancy was lower when data were collected (late 1930s to early 1950s) and older age was experienced in clinically different ways that likely impacted sexuality. The social changes occurring since both of the large-scale studies of sexual behavior have been significant and up-to-date data about human sexual behavior among different age groups is important.

Depending on the country and time period in which sexual behavior has been studied, previous studies of sexual behavior in the United States and in other countries have recruited participants and collected data via in-person interviews, computer-assisted interviews, questionnaires, RDD phone interviews, computer-assisted telephone interviewing, intercept methods, or door-to-door sampling. In our study, by recruiting participants and collecting data over the Internet, respondents may have felt more comfortable reporting taboo sexual behaviors compared with the NHSLS data, which were collected via in-person interviews.

In addition, while some studies have focused on only men, only women, or a more narrow age range we sampled both women and men from adolescence through old age, resulting in a sample of individuals that spanned eight decades of age. However, a limitation of the present study is that, like the NHSLS and NSHAP, the sample was likely only accessible to those who were living in the community and so is not representative of all adults, particularly older adults, who are more likely to be hospitalized or living in long term care facilities.

A limitation of the study is that nationally representative survey data often obscures data points of minority groups, such as those who identify as gay, lesbian or bisexual. Certainly a proportion of those individuals who did not engage in sexual behaviors between women and men (such as vaginal intercourse) were likely to be gay or lesbian. The present data cannot therefore be generalized to gay, lesbian, or bisexual individuals and more detailed analyses are needed to illuminate the sexual behaviors of these individuals. Like other studies of sexual behavior, this study may have been subject to self-selection. Although the sampling procedures ensured a lack of differences on key sociodemographic characteristics between those who chose to participate and those who refused, sexual behavior data are not available on nonresponders, and it is therefore not possible to assess the extent to which participants were different from those who either did not respond to the recruitment messages or those who responded and chose not to participate. However, the proportion of those who responded and chose to participate was slightly higher than the participation rate of the eligible, contacted individuals in the NHSLS who were recruited through in-person recruitment efforts at their homes.

Although statistical differences between men's and women's reports of sexual behaviors were not assessed for this particular paper, the data demonstrate that, for all age cohorts, recent (past month and past year) masturbation was strikingly more prevalent among men than women. Similarly, with the exception of the 25- to 29-year-old age cohort, more men reported vaginal intercourse in the past month and more men reported vaginal intercourse in the past year in advanced age, likely caused by the greater number of available female partners. Compared with men's reports of insertive anal intercourse, more women in the 18- to 19-year-old age cohort reported receptive anal intercourse, which may be an artifact of having the small number of individuals in this age group or the result of younger women partnering with older men. More detailed data related to the sexual behavior of women and men in this sample can be found in other reports that have examined gender-specific behaviors and that collectively offer in-depth analyses that provide for comparisons across genders.

Conclusions

In summary, findings provide medical and public health professionals with up-to-date information about solo and partnered sexual behaviors throughout the life course. Such information should assist both educators and clinicians in their efforts to increase knowledge about contemporary sexual behaviors and provide a valuable context that can be useful particularly to health professionals during sexual history taking and during discussion with patients about sexual problems and dysfunctions.

Critical Thinking

1. What societal influences are contributing to the diversity in solo and partnered sexual behaviors?

UNIT 2
Biological Foundations

Unit Selections

9. **Starting the Good Life in the Womb,** W. Allan Walker, and Courtney Humphries
10. **Women in Developing Countries 300 Times More Likely to Die in Childbirth,** Sarah Boseley
11. **Effects of Prenatal Social Stress on Offspring Development: Pathology or Adaptation?,** Sylvia Kaiser, and Norbert Sachser
12. **A Man's Shelf Life,** Mark Teich
13. **Pubic Hair Removal among Women in the United States: Prevalence, Methods, and Characteristics,** Debby Herbenick et al.
14. **Scents and Sensibility,** Elizabeth Svoboda
15. **The Orgasmic Mind,** Martin Portner
16. **Women's Vibrator Use in Romantic Relationships: Results from a Nationally Representative Survey in the United States,** Debby Herbenick et al.

Learning Outcomes

After reading this Unit, you will be able to:

- Describe how women's choices while pregnant can have life-long consequences for the baby.

- Explain how prenatal influences impact a developing fetus.

- Describe how prenatal social stress impacts fetal development.

- Explain the long-term impact of prenatal social stress on the organism.

- Discuss the biological reproductive challenges men face as they age.

- Assess the male contribution to birth defects.

- Describe the prevalence, methods and characteristics of female pubic hair removal in the United States.

- Discuss the physiological components of arousal and orgasm.

- Discuss the cognitive and affective aspects involved in arousal and orgasm.

- Explain the role of the brain in desire, arousal, and orgasm.

- Discuss the uses and roles of vibrators within the context of intimate relationships.

Student Website
www.mhhe.com/cls

Internet References

Ask NOAH About Pregnancy: Fertility & Infertility
www.noah-health.org/en/search/health.html
Childbirth.Org
www.childbirth.org
Infertility Resources
www.ihr.com/infertility/index.html
Planned Parenthood
www.plannedparenthood.org

Whereas Unit 1 focused on Social and Cultural Foundations, this unit explores the biological influences on our sexual development and functioning. As we have learned, knowledge of social and cultural processes that impact sexualities provide us with part of the picture in our attempt to understand sexualities. Another essential part of the picture, explored here in this unit, is biology.

We are biological beings with the capacity for a range of sexual behaviors, as well as for reproduction. Even though most people have the capacity for sexual reproduction, infertility issues are common in today's society. There are far too many aspects of sexual biology that many people simply do not know enough about. Most of us have an incomplete understanding of how our bodies work. This is especially true of our bodily responses and functioning during sexual activity. Efforts to develop a healthy sexual awareness may be severely hindered by misconceptions and the lack of quality information about anatomy and physiology.

Part A of this unit explores reproductive capacities . This section directs attention to the development of a clearer understanding and appreciation of the workings of biological processes in relation to human reproduction. While human reproduction is as old as humanity, many things in today's society are changing at an amazing pace. New technologies have had a major impact on reproductive capacities. Women in their 60s, and even 70s, have given birth recently. Major news media outlets reported that a 70-year-old woman had given birth to twins. Reporters noted that she was old enough to be her children's great-grandmother. At the same time, other women struggle with the pain and stress of infertility with few options, if any, available to them. Still others remain "childless by choice."

Lesbian, gay, and transgender people are becoming parents in larger numbers than ever before. Many gay people have had biological children through heterosexual marriages, before "coming out." Some gay men and lesbians opt for pregnancy through artificial insemination, co-parenting as friends or as (nonsexual) gay family units. Lesbians can opt to have biological children using known or anonymous sperm donors. Gay men are increasingly having biological children through traditional or gestational surrogates. Recently, a transgender man was able to give birth to a biological child because he had chosen to keep his uterus. Lesbian, gay, and transgender people adopt children through private adoption agencies, some specializing in gay families, as well as from public agencies through the foster care system. Choices abound, and the world is getting more and more diverse.

© Sigrid Olsson/PhotoAlto/Corbis

New technologies and reproductive options have affected the "how" of reproduction, but personal, social, and cultural forces have also affected the "who," the "when," and the "when not." Unplanned pregnancies and parenthood in the United States and worldwide continue to present significant, sometimes devastating problems for parents, children, families, and society. Topics explored here, in Unit 2, link to topics such as parenthood, contraception, and abortion in the units that follow.

Given that reproduction is such an important theme in our look at biology, it should come as no surprise that in this unit we consider the impact of the prenatal environment on the developing fetus. It is important to understand how choices that are made during pregnancy can have a lasting impact on the child. Today, child protective services struggle with the impact of amphetamines, heroin, and cocaine among other nonprescription drugs on substance exposed newborns. Should taking "meth" during pregnancy be considered abuse and neglect of the fetus? Should the child be removed and placed into protective custody? What are the lifelong consequences for behavior and learning for someone who was substance exposed in utero? These are a few of the issues that confront us as a society today. Matters of biology can quickly become social issues of urgent importance. As you read through the articles in this section, you will be able to see more clearly that matters of sexual biology and behavior go well beyond the biological realm. The articles included hint at some of the psychological, social, and cultural origins and consequences of sexual behaviors as well.

Starting the Good Life in the Womb

Pregnant women who eat right, watch their weight and stay active can actually improve their unborn babies' chances of growing into healthy adults.

W. Allan Walker, MD, and Courtney Humphries

Most pregnant women know they can hurt their babies by smoking, drinking alcohol and taking drugs that can cause birth defects. But they also may be able to "program" the baby in the womb to be a healthier adult. New research suggests that mothers-to-be can reduce the risk of their babies developing obesity, high blood pressure, heart disease and diabetes by monitoring their own diet, exercise and weight.

The science behind this is relatively new and still somewhat controversial. In the late 1980s, a British physician and epidemiologist named David Barker noticed that a group of Englishmen who were born small had a higher incidence of heart disease. Studies showed that rates of obesity, high blood pressure and diabetes—illnesses that often are associated with heart disease—are higher in men born small. Barker proposed that poor nutrition in the womb may have "programmed" the men to develop illness 50 years or more later.

The "Barker Hypothesis" is still hotly debated, but it is gaining acceptance as the evidence builds. Because organs develop at different times, it appears that the effects of too little food during pregnancy vary by trimester. One example comes from study of the Dutch Hunger Winter, a brief but severe famine that occurred during World War II. Pregnant women who didn't get enough to eat in their first trimester had babies who were more likely to develop heart disease. If they were in their second trimester, their babies were at risk for kidney disease. A poor diet in the last three months led to babies who had problems with insulin regulation, a precursor of diabetes.

More-recent research has focused on the negative effects of too much food during pregnancy. Women who gain excessive weight during pregnancy are more likely to have babies who are born large for their age and who become overweight in childhood. A recent study from the National Birth Defect Prevention Study found that obesity in pregnancy also increases a baby's risk for birth defects, including those of the spinal cord, heart and limbs.

A mother's nutrition and exercise patterns during pregnancy influence the long-term health of the baby by shaping her baby's metabolism. "Metabolism" includes everything that allows your body to turn food into energy—from the organ systems that process food and waste to the energy-producing chemical reactions that take place inside every cell. It is the collective engine that keeps you alive.

A mother's body may influence her baby's metabolism on many levels: the way organs develop, how appetite signals get released in the brain, how genes are activated, even the metabolic chemistry inside the baby's cells. Research now shows that the environment of the womb helps determine how a baby's metabolism is put together, or "programs" it for later health. The science of fetal programming is still new; it will be a long time before we have all the answers, since these health effects emerge over a lifetime. But several principles already are clear for a pregnant woman.

The first is to get healthy before pregnancy. Weighing too little or too much not only hampers fertility but can set the stage for metabolic problems in pregnancy. Doctors used to think of body fat as nothing more than inert insulation, but they know now that fat is an active tissue that releases hormones and plays a key role in keeping the metabolism running. Women should also eat a balanced diet and take prenatal vitamins before pregnancy to ensure that their bodies provide a good environment from the beginning.

The amount of weight gain is also critical. Women who gain too little weight during pregnancy are more likely to give birth to small babies, while women who gain too much weight are likely to have large babies. Paradoxically, both situations can predispose a child to metabolic disease. The weight gain should come slowly at first—about two to eight pounds in the first trimester, and one pound per week after that for normal-weight women. Obese women (with a body-mass index, or BMI, higher than 29) should gain no more than 15 pounds.

Pregnancy Pounds

Putting on too much or too little weight during pregnancy can predispose the baby to metabolic disorders. The right amount to gain:

Body-mass index (BMI) before pregnancy	Recommended weight gain
Less than 19.8 (underweight)	28–40 lb.
19.8–25 (normal weight)	25–35
26–29 (overweight)	15–25
Greater than 29 (obese)	No more than 15

Source: "Programming Your Baby for a Healthy Life" by W. Allan Walker, MD, and Courtney Humphries.

During pregnancy, women are already more susceptible to metabolic problems such as gestational diabetes and preeclampsia (high blood pressure), so choosing foods that help your metabolism run smoothly is important. Eating whole grains and foods rich in protein and fiber while avoiding foods high in sugar can help even out rises and falls in blood sugar. Pregnant women should eat about 300 extra calories per day while they're pregnant. But, as always, the quality of the calories matters even more. It's important to eat a diet rich in nutrients, since a lack of specific nutrients in the womb can hamper a baby's long-term health. A clear example is folic acid, without which the brain and spinal cord do not develop properly. But new research is uncovering other nutrients that may have subtler but long-lasting effects on health.

Studies suggest that women could benefit from taking omega-3 fatty-acid supplements, particularly those containing docosahexaenoic acid (DHA, for short), a type of fat that has been shown to help prevent prematurity and contribute to healthy brain development. A recent study found that women with more vitamin D in their bodies have children with stronger bones; adequate vitamin D is also needed for organ development.

Women may have different nutrient needs because of genetic differences, but to be safe every woman should take a daily prenatal vitamin before and during pregnancy. But supplements, whether in the form of a pill, a fortified shake or energy bar, don't replace the nutrients found in fruits, vegetables, low-fat meats, whole grains and other foods.

The energy you expend is as important as what you take in. Regular activity helps keep a woman's metabolism running smoothly and offsets problems of pregnancy like varicose veins, leg cramps and lower back pain. Pregnant women should avoid high-impact activities, especially late in their pregnancies.

All this may sound daunting, but most of the changes are simple ones that will improve a mother's long-term health as well as her children's.

Critical Thinking

1. How do the choices women make while pregnant impact the developing fetus?
2. How do prenatal choices impact the baby long-term?

W. ALLAN WALKER MD, the Conrad Taff Professor of Pediatrics at Harvard Medical School, and **COURTNEY HUMPHRIES**, a science writer, have written "The Harvard Medical School Guide to Healthy Eating During Pregnancy." For more information, go to www.health.harvard.edu/newsweek.

Women in Developing Countries 300 Times More Likely to Die in Childbirth

UN report reveals 500,000 women in developing world die each year as a result of pregnancy.

SARAH BOSELEY

Women in the world's least developed countries are 300 times more likely to die during childbirth or because of their pregnancy than those in the UK and other similarly developed countries, a UN report says today.

The death toll is more than half a million women a year, according to Unicef, the UN children's emergency fund. Some 70,000 who die are girls and young women aged 15 to 19. Although it is the subject of one of the millennium development goals, the death toll is not going down.

The reasons are multiple, according to Unicef's annual state of the world's children report on maternal and newborn health. "The root cause may lie in women's disadvantaged position in many countries and cultures and in the lack of attention to, and accountability for, women's rights," it says.

"Saving the lives of mothers and their newborns requires more than just medical intervention," said Ann Veneman, Unicef's executive director. "Educating girls is pivotal to improving maternal and neonatal health and also benefits families and societies."

Women die as a result of infection and of haemorrhage. Some have obstructed labour and cannot get a caesarean section. Others die of preventable complications.

Both mothers and babies are vulnerable in the weeks after birth, the report points out. They need post-natal visits, proper hygiene and counselling about the danger signs for themselves and their baby.

Many developing countries have succeeded in reducing the death rate for children under five, but have failed to make much progress on mothers. Niger and Malawi, for example, cut under-five deaths by nearly half between 1990 and 2007.

In the developing world, a woman has a one-in-76 risk of dying because of pregnancy or childbirth in her lifetime. In developed countries, that risk is only one in 8,000.

Having a child in a developing country is one of the most severe health risks for women. For every woman who dies, another 20 suffer illness or injury, which can be permanent.

The 10 countries with the highest risk of maternal death, says Unicef, are Niger, Afghanistan, Sierra Leone, Chad, Angola, Liberia, Somalia, the Democratic Republic of Congo, Guinea-Bissau and Mali.

Deaths of newborns have also received too little attention, the report says. A child born in one of the least developed countries is nearly 14 times more likely to die within the first 28 days of life than one in an industrialised country such as the UK.

Critical Thinking

1. What actions could reduce the risk of illness or injury for women during childbirth? How about after childbirth?
2. What role does education play in preventing illness or injury?

Effects of Prenatal Social Stress on Offspring Development
Pathology or Adaptation?

SYLVIA KAISER, AND NORBERT SACHSER

Ontogeny is the development of an individual from the moment the egg is fertilized until death. Most research on *behavioral* ontogeny has focused on the early postnatal phase, probably because socialization and learning processes are thought to play their most important role during this time. However, there is growing evidence that environmental influences before birth also have impact on the individual's development later in life (de Weerth, Buitelaar, & Mulder, 2005). In particular, stressors acting on the mother during pregnancy can have distinct and long-term effects on behavior, reproductive functions, and the immune, neuroendocrine and autonomic systems of her offspring (de Kloet, Sibug, Helmerhorst, & Schmidt, 2005).

In most experimental studies on the effects of prenatal stress, pregnant female animals have been subjected to nonsocial stressors (e.g., bright light, restraint). Interpretation of these studies is difficult, because such artifical stressors typically do not occur in those animals' natural environments (Kaiser & Sachser, 2005). In their natural habitats, animals have to cope with a variety of stressors that depend on their ecological niche. They have to adjust to the physical environment (e.g., weather) and to the biotic world that surrounds them (e.g., predators, food shortage). A major part of an individual's biotic environment consists of other members of the same species, which can be defined as that individual's "social world." In fact, a majority of human and animal daily expectations, motivations, and behaviors are directed toward encounters with conspecifics. On the one hand, this social world can support welfare and health (e.g., through the effects of social support). On the other hand, it can result in severe stress, eventually leading to disease and even death (e.g., in the case of social defeat, social instability, or crowding; von Holst, 1998). Thus, the social environment represents a very influential stressor, which, during pregnancy, can be crucial for the development of the offspring (Kaiser & Sachser, 2005).

Effects of the Prenatal Social Environment on Offspring Development and Behavior
Animal Studies

The most comprehensive insights from studies of nonhuman animals regarding prenatal social influences on offspring development have been derived from studies in guinea pigs (Kaiser & Sachser, 2005). For example, when compared to daughters whose mothers had lived in a stable social environment during pregnancy (that is, group composition was kept constant, with one male and five females), female guinea pigs whose mothers had lived in an unstable social environment (every third day, two females from different groups were exchanged) showed conspicuous behavioral masculinization (e.g., displaying high levels of male-typical courtship behavior) later in life, increased testosterone concentrations, and a male-typical distribution pattern of androgen receptors in parts of the limbic system (Kaiser, Kruijver, Swaab, & Sachser, 2003). Compared to male guinea pigs whose mothers had lived in a stable social environment, those whose mothers had lived in an unstable social environment during pregnancy showed behavioral infantilization (e.g., displaying behavioral patterns usually shown only by very young male guinea pigs, such as sitting in close bodily contact), delayed development of the adrenocortical system, and down-regulation of androgen receptor expression in the limbic system (Kaiser, Kruijver, Straub, Sachser, & Swaab, 2003).

Studies of prenatal social influences on offspring development have been conducted only in a few other species (e.g., mice, rats, squirrel monkeys). Although a variety of different social stressors have been applied in these experiments (e.g., crowding, social confrontation, changing group membership), a common characteristic of all approaches is the induction of social instability. In general, under such conditions, the number of interactions with conspecifics increases and the predictability and controllability of social encounters dramatically decline. Interestingly, modern stress research shows that, in animals as well as in humans, situations of uncertainty or unpredictability are a major source of stress responses (von Holst, 1998).

When all experimental studies on prenatal social stress are compared, some general conclusions can be drawn: Female offspring show a masculinization of behavior, endocrine state, and brain development. Male offspring show a less pronounced expression of male-typical traits (e.g., demasculinization, feminization) and/or a delay in development. In addition, there are some indications that both sexes might have a more or less severe impairment of reproductive functions (cf., Kaiser & Sachser, 2005).

Human Studies

The long-lasting effects of prenatal stress on offspring are also well known in humans: Children of mothers who were stressed during pregnancy develop higher risk of different diseases (including cardiovascular illness and diabetes) and may experience physical and cognitive developmental delays (e.g., Huizink, Mulder, & Buitelaar, 2004; Wadhwa, 2005). However, only limited data concerning the effects of *social* stressors during pregnancy on human offspring later in life are available. Those few studies, however, point to distinct effects on behavioral and physiological development. For instance, family discord during pregnancy leads to behavioral disturbances in children, and such children are more likely to develop psychopathological disorders such as autism (Ward, 1990; unfortunately, it is not mentioned whether this finding is controlled for postnatal effects). Similarly, moderate to severe stressors combined with low levels of social support during pregnancy reduce children's head circumference at birth, pointing to the effects of prenatal stress on brain development (Glynn & Sandman, 2006). Children whose mothers experienced high levels of daily hassles and pregnancy-specific anxiety show lower mental and motor developmental scores at 8 months of age after correcting for postnatal stress (Buitelaar, Huizink, Mulder, Robles de Medina, & Visser, 2003).

Effects of Prenatal Social Stress: Pathology or Adaptation?

Researchers typically interpret the characteristic traits of individuals who were exposed to adverse environmental stimuli (stressors) during pregnancy as deviations from some standard considered optimal, and phenotypic differences in offspring are frequently called pathological. Alternatively, and in accordance with current evolutionary theory, these traits might also represent adaptive maternal effects; that is, the offspring's fitness is enhanced by maternal adjustments to the current environmental conditions.

Adaptation through maternal effects—that is, control and/ or modulation of the offspring's phenotype—has become a key concept in modern evolutionary biology (see, e.g., Groothuis,

Müller, von Engelhardt, Carere, & Eising, 2005; Mousseau & Fox, 1998) and numerous studies to reveal the mechanism underlying these phenomena are currently underway. Particular maternal hormonal responses to environmental stimuli represent a potential tool by which development of offspring can be influenced. Indeed, in different bird species, mothers' deposition of androgens into the yolk of their eggs varies with environmental factors or social conditions, and experimental studies have shown effects of enhanced androgen levels on offspring traits such as competitiveness or growth (Groothuis, Müller, von Engelhardt, Carere, & Eising, 2005). Results of two recent studies in wild spotted hyenas and guinea pigs suggest that prenatal androgen exposure can adaptively influence offspring phenotype (in terms of aggression, sexual behavior, and testosterone responsiveness to social challenge) regularly in mammals as well (Dloniak, French, & Holekamp, 2006; Kemme, Kaiser, & Sachser, 2007). If such traits result in enhancement of fitness parameters such as social dominance or reproductive benefits, we can speak of an adaptive phenotype.

Possible Benefits of Altered Phenotypes

The questions arise: What is the benefit of being a masculinized daughter? And what is the benefit for sons who show less pronounced expression of male-typical traits and/or a delay in development?

Consider the case of fluctuations in the density of natural populations of mammals. Under high-density conditions, social instability is a common trait, whereas low population densities are characterized by stable social situations (von Holst, 1998). Hence, different pregnant females may experience very different degrees of social stability in their natural habitats. If a pregnant female living in a high-density population has the possibility of preprogramming her daughters in such a way that they will gain maximum reproductive success in that high-density situation, it would seem reasonable for her to masculinize them in order to make them more robust and/ or more competitive. These and other masculine traits facilitate the attainment of dominant social positions, which in turn help to defend important resources such as food and shelter (which are scarce in high-density situations) more efficiently. However, frequently a characteristic feature of masculinized females is impairment of reproductive function later in life (Kaiser & Sachser, 2005). Thus, under high-density conditions, there is likely to be a trade-off between the benefits of a behaviorally and endocrinologically masculinized phenotype and the costs of decreased reproductive success. Although decreased reproductive success might seem inconsistent with the idea of enhanced fitness, under such conditions, masculinized females might fare better than nonmasculinized females; the latter may often fail to reproduce at all because of lower social status that prevents access to resources necessary for reproduction. Under low-density conditions, however, sufficient resources are available and competitive abilities are less important. Under such conditions, it would seem more beneficial to invest time and energy in reproductive effort rather than to build and maintain a male-typical phenotype for defending resources. Thus, under low-density conditions, reproductive success would be higher in nonmasculinized females than in masculinized ones (Kaiser & Sachser, 2005).

The argument is similar for sons. Around the time of sexual maturity, they can find themselves in different situations. Consider a low-density condition with only a few males of the same age and some females present. In such a situation, the best strategy to maximize reproductive success would be to fight for the access to a copulation partner, because usually the winners will mate. Under such conditions, mothers will maximize their own fitness if they program their sons prenatally in a way that maximizes the timely expression of male-typical traits. In contrast, when animals live at high densities in large, age-graded populations, a different situation exists: Under such conditions, in many species, high-ranking (alpha) males almost exclusively sire all the offspring. Remarkably, males usually do not attain an alpha position until well beyond the age of sexual maturity (e.g., mandrills; Setchell, Charpentier, & Wickings, 2005). A male born in a high-density population should avoid agonistic encounters at too early an age, because this will not result in reproductive success. By neither signaling sexual interest in females nor displaying other signs of sexual maturity, a pubescent male is less likely to be attacked by the alpha males. This strategy should change, however, around the time of social maturity in order to attain the alpha position that is required for reproductive success. Thus, under conditions of high density, mothers may provide their sons with a more adaptive reproductive strategy by programming them prenatally in a way that delays development and/or diminishes expression of male-typical traits until social maturity is attained (Kaiser & Sachser, 2005).

Currently, much experimental animal research is being conducted to test such hypotheses on the adaptive value of prenatal maternal programming (Dloniak, French, & Holekamp, 2006; Kemme, Kaiser, & Sachser, 2007).

Human Studies

Similar arguments for the adaptive value of the response to prenatal-stress effects in humans have been put forward. For example, Bateson et al., (2004) hypothesize that a period of starvation during pregnancy tells the developing fetus that food is probably going to be scarce in the future. Babies of such mothers often show small body weight and correspondingly modified metabolism. These traits are not necessarily pathological, inasmuch as they help the baby to cope with environments of low food availability. The proposed mechanism for these persistent effects into adulthood involves alteration in set points for various aspects of basic metabolism (e.g., glucoregulation, adiposity, and blood pressure; Roseboom, de Rooij, & Painter, 2006).

For ethical reasons, in humans it is not feasible to experimentally manipulate hormonal levels during early development or exposure to stress in pregnant mothers. Nevertheless, good evidence that the behavioral phenotype of daughters can be shaped by prenatal androgens does exist. For example, girls with congenital adrenal hyperplasia (an autosomal recessive disorder that causes elevated adrenal androgens) are exposed to elevated androgen concentrations during fetal development, and this results in a masculinized phenotype—revealed, for example, by increased rough-and-tumble play (Hines, 2006). Other evidence shows that androgen levels in women can be affected by environmental situations: Testosterone concentrations increase, for example, in periods of high-intensity exercise (Bergeron et al., 1991). We therefore propose that androgen concentrations in pregnant women may change as a result of environmental factors and that these changed androgen concentrations may influence fetal central-nervous-system differentiation during early development, thereby shaping the behavioral phenotype of the offspring later in life. Whether or not this specific phenotype represents an adaptive adjustment to the environmental conditions under which the mother has lived during pregnancy remains to be determined.

Conclusion

Studies of animals and humans clearly show that severe stressors acting upon a pregnant female can have profoundly negative effects on the later development and health of her offspring. In such cases, prenatal stress results in pathology and no discussion about adaptive function seems appropriate. Recent experimental animal studies of prenatal stress, when considered from an evolutionary perspective, draw attention to an additional hypothesis: that variation in behavioral phenotype brought about by prenatal stressors may represent an adaptation to the prevailing environmental situation. From this point of view, deviations from the behavioral and physiological standard, such as masculinized daughters and infantilized sons, should not be regarded as pathological but may rather be seen as representing adaptations to the offspring's likely environment. It is timely and exciting to test whether some of the individual variation among members of our species might not reflect the action of similar, and perhaps now vestigial, processes. Accordingly the central hypothesis is this: We share the same mechanisms with nonhuman mammals that allow infants to be preadapted to the world their mothers live in during pregnancy. In particular, we assume that the environment in which a pregnant woman lives affects her endocrine state, which in turn influences fetal brain development, thereby adapting the infant's behavior and physiology to cope successfully with the challenges of the environmental niche of the mother. If so, children of mothers who have lived in a stable social situation during pregnancy will cope better with conditions of social stability later in life than will children whose mothers have lived under unstable social conditions. However, children whose mothers have lived under unstable social conditions during pregnancy might cope better with conditions of social instability later in life than might children of mothers who have lived in stable social situations. Future studies are required to test these hypotheses.

Recommended Reading

Bateson, P., Barker, D., Clutton-Brock, T., Deb, D., D'Udine, B., Foley, R.A., et al., (2004). Developmental plasticity and human health. *Nature, 430,* 419–421. Discusses developmental plasticity and human health in more details than the current article.

Champagne, F.A., & Curley, J.P. (2005). How social experiences influence the brain. *Current Opinion in Neurobiology, 15,* 704–709. A clearly written, user-friendly, and relatively comprehensive review for readers who wish to expand their knowledge on influences of social experiences on brain development.

de Kloet, E.R., Sibug, R.M., Helmerhorst, F.M., & Schmidt, M. (2005). (See References). A clearly written, user-friendly, and relatively comprehensive review for readers who wish to expand their knowledge on long-lasting effects of early stress on brain programming.

Dufty, A.M., Jr., Clobert, J., & Moller, A.P. (2002). Hormones, developmental plasticity and adaptation. *Trends in Ecology & Evolution, 17,* 190–196. A clearly written, user-friendly, and relatively comprehensive review for readers who wish to expand their knowledge on developmental plasticity and adaptation.

Kaiser, S., & Sachser, N. (2005). (See References). A comprehensive, highly accessible overview of what is known about mechanisms and function of the effects of prenatal social stress.

References

Bateson, P., Barker, D., Clutton-Brock, T., Deb, D., D'Udine, B., Foley, R.A., (2004). Developmental plasticity and human health. *Nature, 430,* 419–421.

Bergeron, M.E., Maresh, C.M., Kraemer, W.J., Abraham, A., Conroy, B., & Gabaree, C. (1991). Tennis: A physiological profile during match play. *International Journal of Sports Medicine, 12,* 474–479.

Buitelaar, J.K., Huizink, A.C., Mulder, E.J., Robles de Medina, P.G., & Visser, G.H.A. (2003). Prenatal stress and cognitive development and temperament in infants. *Neurobiology of Aging, 24,* S53–S60.

de Kloet, E.R., Sibug, R.M., Helmerhorst, F.M., & Schmidt, M. (2005). Stress, genes and the mechanism of programming the brain for later life. *Neuroscience and Biobehavioral Reviews, 29,* 271–281.

de Weerth, C., Buitelaar, J.K., & Mulder, E.J.H. (Eds.). (2005). Prenatal programming of behaviour, physiology and cognition. *Neuroscience and Biobehavioral Reviews, 29,* 207–384.

Dloniak, S.M., French, J.A., & Holekamp, K.E. (2006). Rank-related maternal effects of androgens on behaviour in wild spotted hyaenas. *Nature, 449,* 1190–1193.

Glynn, L.M., & Sandman, C.A. (2006). The influence of prenatal stress and adverse birth outcome on human cognitive and neurological development. *International Review of Research in Mental Retardation, 32,* 109–129.

Groothuis, T.G.G., Müller, W., von Engelhardt, N., Carere, C., & Eising, C. (2005). Maternal hormones as a tool to adjust offspring phenotype in avian species. *Neuroscience and Biobehavioral Reviews, 29,* 329–352.

Hines, M. (2006). Prenatal testosterone and gender-related behaviour. *European Journal of Endocrinology, 155,* S115–S121.

Huizink, A.C., Mulder, E.J.H., & Buitelaar, J.K. (2004). Prenatal stress and risk for psychopathology: Specific effects or induction of general susceptibility? *Psychological Bulletin, 130,* 115–142.

Kaiser, S., Kruijver, F.P.M., Straub, R.H., Sachser, N., & Swaab, D.F. (2003). Early social stress in male guinea pigs changes social behaviour, and autonomic and neuroendocrine functions. *Journal of Neuroendocrinology, 15,* 761–769.

Kaiser, S., Kruijver, F.P.M., Swaab, D.F., & Sachser, N. (2003). Early social stress in female guinea pigs induces a masculinization of adult behavior and corresponding changes in brain and neuroendocrine function. *Behavioral Brain Research, 144,* 199–210.

Kaiser, S., & Sachser, N. (2005). The effects of prenatal social stress on behaviour: Mechanisms and function. *Neuroscience and Biobehavioral Reviews, 29,* 283–294.

Kemme, K., Kaiser, S., & Sachser, N. (2007). Prenatal maternal programming determines testosterone response during social challenge. *Hormones and Behavior, 51,* 387–394.

Mousseau, T.A., & Fox, C.W. (1998). The adaptive significance of maternal effects. *Trends in Ecology and Evolution, 13,* 403–407.

Roseboom, T., de Rooij, S., & Painter, R. (2006). The Dutch famine and its long-term consequences for adult health. *Early Human Development, 82,* 485–491.

Setchell, J.M., Charpentier, M., & Wickings, E.J. (2005). Sexual selection and reproductive careers in mandrills (*Mandrillus sphinx*). *Behavioral Ecology and Sociobiology, 58,* 474–485.

von Holst, D. (1998). The concept of stress and its relevance for animal behavior. *Advances of the Study of Behavior, 27,* 1–131.

Wadhwa, P.D. (2005). Psychoneuroendocrine processes in human pregnancy influence fetal development and health. *Psychoneuroendocrinology, 30,* 724–743.

Ward, A.J. (1990). A comparison and analysis of the presence of family problems during pregnancy of mothers of "autistic" children and mothers of normal children. *Child Psychiatry and Human Development, 20,* 279–288.

Critical Thinking

1. How does prenatal social stress impact the fetus?
2. Explain the biological changes in the fetus brought about by prenatal social stress.
3. What is the impact of prenatal social stress on the well-being of the fetus?

Address correspondence to **Sylvia Kaiser,** Department of Behavioral Biology, University of Muenster, Badestrasse 13, D-48149 Muenster, Germany; e-mail: kaisesy@uni-muenster.de.

From *Current Directions in Psychological Science,* April 2009, pp. 118–121. Copyright © 2009 by the Association for Psychological Science. Reprinted by permission of Sage Publications via Rightslink.

A Man's Shelf Life

As men age, their fertility decreases and the health risks to their unborn offspring skyrocket. But men who attend to their health can slow down the reproductive clock.

MARK TEICH

Women have long understood that general fitness and age are both critical to conceiving a healthy child. But their partners often feel absolved of such concerns; men tend to think they can drink, carouse, smoke like coal trains, and conceive whenever they want, with no impact on fertility or their future offspring. Would that it were so.

"Everybody was familiar with the concept of women's biological clock, but when we introduced 'male' to the equation, the reaction was 'What are you talking about? Men can have children at *any* age,'" recalls urologist Harry Fisch, director of the Male Reproductive Center at Columbia Presbyterian Hospital in New York City and author of *The Male Biological Clock*. "It became a social issue. Men do not like to be told they have a problem."

Nonetheless, a virtual tidal wave of recent research has made it irrefutable: Not only does male fertility decrease decade by decade, especially after age 35, but aging sperm can be a significant and sometimes the *only* cause of severe health and developmental problems in offspring, including autism, schizophrenia, and cancer. The older the father, the higher the risk. But what's truly noteworthy is not that infertility increases with age—to some degree, we've known that all along—but rather that older men who can still conceive may have such damaged sperm that they put their offspring at risk for many types of disorders and disabilities.

"Men thought they were getting off scot free, and they weren't. The birth defects caused by male aging are significant conditions that can cause a burden to families and society," says Ethylin Wang Jabs, professor of pediatric genetics at Johns Hopkins University and leader of a recent study showing the link between aging paternity and certain facial deformities in offspring. "We now know that men and women alike could be increasing the risk of infertility or birth defects by waiting too long to have children." In other words, by looking for perfection in your life before you conceive, there's a very real chance you'll have less perfect kids."

By looking for perfection in your life before you conceive, there's a very real chance you'll have less perfect kids.

In the past several years, studies worldwide have found that with each passing decade of their lives and with each insult they inflict on their bodies, men's fertility decreases, while genetic risk to offspring slowly mounts. The range of findings is staggering: Several studies have shown that the older the man, the more fragmented the DNA in his ejaculated sperm, resulting in greater risk for infertility, miscarriage or birth defects. Investigations out of Israel, Europe, and the United States have shown that non-verbal (performance) intelligence may decline *exclusively* due to greater paternal age; that up to a third of all cases of schizophrenia are linked to increasing paternal age; and that men 40 and older are nearly six times more likely to have offspring with autism than men under age 30. Other research shows that the risk of breast and prostate cancer in offspring increases with paternal age.

Fisch has found that when both parents are over 35, paternal aging may be responsible for as many as half of all cases of Down syndrome, formerly thought to be inherited from the mother. And recent studies show that half a dozen or more rare but serious birth defects appear to be inherited exclusively from the father, including Apert syndrome, Crouzon syndrome, and Pfeiffer syndrome (all characterized by facial abnormalities and the premature fusion of skull bones) as well as achondroplasia (the most common form of dwarfism).

Male versus Female Mutations

Scientists have long known that advanced paternal age (like increased maternal age) played *some* role in fertility problems and birth defects. Yet because the reports mainly involved children who died before birth or who had extremely rare disorders, no one really rang the alarm. Now, with new studies linking the father's age to relatively frequent, serious conditions like autism, schizophrenia, and Down syndrome, the landscape is shifting.

If you want to father a child after age 40, get in the best shape of your life.

Women have unfairly borne the brunt of the blame for birth defects. When the conditions were familial, passed on through chromosomal lineage, women were somehow widely believed culpable, even though such defects can be traced to either partner. "But what we're finding now is that in humans as well as in other mammals, when there's a *new* genetic change—called 'de novo or sporadic point mutation'—it almost always happens in the male parent," says Dolores Malaspina, chair of psychiatry at New York University Medical Center. And these de novo mutations increase in frequency with the age of the male parent.

These mutations could reflect the differences in male and female reproduction, notes Jabs. By the time females reach their teen years, their eggs have already been formed—just one new egg matures each month. Men, on the other hand, produce millions of sperm cells every time they ejaculate. After each ejaculation, they must literally *replicate* those cells, and each replication multiplies the chance for a DNA "copy error"—a genetic chink in the sperm DNA. The more ejaculations a man produces, the greater the chance for chinks to arise, leading to increased point mutation and thus increased infertility and birth defects. While a woman's reproductive capacity halts more or less abruptly after all her eggs have been used up somewhere in their forties or fifties, men experience a longer, more gradual winnowing and disintegration. "We believe that something in men's DNA replication machinery keeps becoming less efficient and less accurate with age, and the problems accumulate," says Jabs.

A Chilling Finding

The biggest news—the father's role in brain disorders—has come to light largely because of research from Israel, where birth records routinely include the age of the male parent. The first unsettling finding linked paternal age and schizophrenia.

"In our first study, looking at every pregnancy in Jerusalem from 1964 to 1976, we found that increased age in the father predicted increased cases of schizophrenia in the children," explains Malaspina, who was on the team doing the work. "In our second study we found that when the cases arose from new mutations—not familial inheritance—it almost always could be traced to the genetics of the father. Somewhere between a quarter and a third of the cases could be explained *only* by the age of the father—a threefold risk linked to fathers older than 50 compared with those in their 20s." Studies in Sweden and California produced almost identical results.

Male Health: The Long Shot

From puberty on, reproductive health and the viability of sperm continue to evolve.

Teens

Until age 13 or 14, sperm is not fully formed, increasing the risk of infertility or birth defects. Sperm may be extremely healthy in older teens, who are famous for their potency. But risky teen behavior may put sperm at risk.

20s

These are prime years for male reproduction. Men have the maximum amount of mature sperm cells and the least DNA damage. The risk of producing birth defects or causing other problems in offspring is as low as it ever will be.

30s

Testosterone levels start to decline at age 30, bringing a decrease in potency. By 32–34, fertility begins to fall. Men who are 35 or older are twice as likely to be infertile as men under age 25. The mid-thirties also bring a significant increase in sperm DNA damage and thus an increased risk of producing birth defects. One in 99 fathers ages 30–35 sire children with schizophrenia versus one in 141 for fathers under age 25.

40s

Type 2 diabetes and metabolic syndrome, involving pre-diabetes symptoms and cardiovascular risk factors, start to occur more often in men. Both disorders are strongly associated with below normal levels of testosterone, lowering potency. Erectile dysfunction (ED) starts to be a problem in a number of men. The risk of schizophrenia doubles in children of fathers in their late forties compared with children of fathers under age 25. Men 40 and older are nearly six times more likely to have offspring with autism than men younger than 30.

50s

Erectile dysfunction increases for many men. By age 50, the DNA cells that create sperm have gone through more than 800 rounds of division and replication, vastly decreasing the quality of sperm and increasing the chances of mutation and birth defects. The risk of schizophrenia almost triples for children of fathers 50 and older; one in 47 fathers sires a child with the condition.

60s

At the age of 60, 85 percent of sperm is clinically abnormal, something researchers attribute to normal aging.

The autism findings are even more disturbing: Men 40 and older in the Israeli study were almost six times as likely to have offspring with autism than men under 30. Some researchers believe that older fathers may hold a clue to the vast upsurge in autism cases in the past decade. "With older and older couples having children—in the past two years, for the first time, more babies are being born to women over age 30 than under age 30, and on average, male partners tend to be older than female partners—it's very feasible that paternal age is a major predictor of autism," asserts Fisch.

Minor Damage Is the Worst Kind

Perhaps the creepiest aspect of the new findings is that a little genetic damage in men's sperm may actually be worse than a lot of damage. "When we started doing the research, our first concern was fertility, and these new studies do show that fertility may be compromised by DNA damage. But that's not the most important thing" declares Charles Muller, lab director of the Male Fertility Clinic at the University of Washington in Seattle.

The greater threat to offspring is the less flagrant DNA damage that gets passed on. Experts like Muller believe that a substantial amount of the damage is caused by free radicals—the destructive, highly reactive particles produced by our body's energy factories, the mitochondria, as we metabolize oxygen. "One of the scariest things we're finding is that sperm DNA is damaged by even *low* levels of free radicals. Whereas high levels of damage lead to infertility, miscarriages, or spontaneous abortions, low levels chew up the DNA but the sperm can still fertilize," Muller states.

Complicating matters, sperm is incapable of repairing itself; Muller and his colleague Narendra P. Singh find that as men age, natural processes such as apoptosis—in which damaged cells naturally commit suicide to protect the body—become increasingly less efficient and less able to eliminate damaged DNA. Resulting defects may not show up until offspring are adults and it's too late to trace the cause. Damage may then be passed from one generation to the next.

"In short, the biggest genetic threat to society may not be infertility but fertile old men," says University of Wisconsin in Madison geneticist James F. Crow.

The Playing Field Levels

The new findings have profound implications for any potential parent. Women may increasingly feel they share the onus of potential infertility and birth defects with men. Older women, focused though they are on their own reproductive timetable, may increasingly view their partner's age with a wary eye. When both parents are aging, the risks to offspring multiply. "If women are under age 35, the father's age may not matter that much, but if the mother is over 35, advanced male age can be a real problem," says Jabs.

For men, the findings may be, above all, a clarion call to take better care of themselves. "This should make men reconsider their role and responsibility in childbearing," says Barbara Willet, of the Best Start childhood resource center in Ontario, Canada. "Aging in men is an important issue, but *health* is the key issue. It's as if we're suddenly aware that men who want to be fathers need to be healthy, too."

One key is testosterone, necessary for the maturation of sperm. "If you have less testosterone, you have worse sperm."

Protecting the Family Jewels

Anything that hurts a man's health hurts his sperm. The good news: preserving your reproductive potential will also keep you healthy.

- **Protect Your Heart**—"What's bad for your heart is bad for your penis," says Columbia's Harry Fisch. Erections depend on arterial flow from the heart, and when that's reduced or blockage occurs, erectile dysfunction (ED) is often close behind. Get an annual physical including heart checkup and cholesterol test once you reach your 30s. If your cholesterol is high, cholesterol-lowering medicine may help.
- **Stay Active**—"If you're trying to have a child in your 30s, 40s, or 50s, getting into the best shape of your life will give you the highest testosterone level possible," says Fisch.
- **Watch Your Weight**—Potbellies and excessive waist size are often telltale signs of heart disease. They also generate heat that can reach the testicles, decreasing the testosterone in sperm. In general, the bigger the belly, the lower the testosterone. Eat a balanced, low-fat diet, and reduce your calorie intake.
- **Take Antioxidants**—such as vitamin C or E, since they may help battle free radicals that play a part in breakdown of sperm DNA.
- **Don't Smoke, Drink to Excess, or Abuse Drugs**—All of these behaviors accelerate DNA breakdown in sperm and put the heart and other organs at risk.
- **Avoid Hot Baths, Jacuzzis, and Hot Tubs**—All can reduce sperm counts for three to six months.
- **Keep Laptops on the Desk**—Balancing laptops on the lap raises the scrotum's temperature, say SUNY Stony Brook urologists.
- **See a Urologist**—if you are over 40, have toxic exposure, or have tried to conceive for a year. Sperm content and testosterone levels can both be evaluated. ED can be treated. You can also ask your doctor to refer you to a lab that tests DNA fragmentation in sperm.
- **Have Varicoceles Removed**—The urologist should always look for engorgements of the veins in scrotums, which can begin as early as adolescence. Almost 40 percent of infertile men have them. By trapping the blood flow in the scrotum, they can cook and choke the sperm, leading to risk of infertility. This is easily reversible.

Testosterone naturally starts to decline in the 30s, but also varies based on factors from weight to heart health. "Fat cells in a potbelly overheat the testes and break testosterone down; clogged arteries break it down. Whatever hurts your heart, hurts your penis," Fisch states.

Men typically don't think about their health, and we need to get them to. If you're drinking or smoking, if you're working in toxic environments with pesticides, X-rays, solvents, or ionizing radiation, these things affect you as well as women, and will ultimately affect the children you conceive.

Alarming though the findings may be to some, researchers have a clear directive: "Don't panic." "The research is still fresh" says Crow, "and more needs to be done before we start making sweeping recommendations like urging people to have children younger, or telling men to freeze their sperm after their 20s. I don't advocate asking the general public to change at this point, because while some of these mutations cause very severe effects, in the totality of things that can go wrong, this is not that large a part of the picture."

Freezing sperm may sometimes be the way to go. While frozen sperm may not be quite as potent as when it is fresh, it is not a proven problem. Since the turn of the last century, sperm of domestic animals has been frozen safely for as long as 75 years, says Muller. And frozen sperm is used routinely in humans for artificial insemination. Pregnancy rates and childbirth are right up there with regularly conceived birth, and there is no substantial DNA breakdown. If you're going to get a vasectomy, join the Army, or go through cancer therapy, "I'd advise you to freeze your sperm beforehand," Muller says.

Some men don't have to worry. Their sperm is fine in their 70s.

Most men can steer a gentler course just by watching their health. "Despite the new research, there's still a big difference between the female and the male biological clock," says Muller. "When the female's alarm goes off at the end, that's it. For men, the battery slowly winds down. Yes, chances of problems increase as the years pass, but some men have significant DNA damage at 35, while others go on forever—their sperm is fine in their 70s."

Men can't rewind their biological clocks, but they can slow them down, Fisch agrees. Just remember, once you're in your 40s, you're past your maintenance-free years—you have to take care of yourself. "If you want children from then on," he advises, "get into the best shape of your life."

Critical Thinking

1. What are some of the reproductive challenges men face as they age?
2. What biological changes can bring about reproductive challenges for men as they age?
3. What is the impact of the male's biological contribution to birth defects?

MARK TEICH is a health writer based in Connecticut.

Pubic Hair Removal among Women in the United States: Prevalence, Methods, and Characteristics

Debra Herbenick, PhD, MPH et al.

Introduction

Women's total removal of their pubic hair has been referred to as "genital hairlessness" and described as a "new norm" for women in the United States that has occurred over the past decade, with possible clinical implications [1, 2]. However, as pubic hair styles and removal practices have rarely been documented, it is questionable to what extent women's total removal of their pubic hair is either new or normative. From artistic renderings of nude women, limited scientific literature, and survey data, it is clear that the extent to which women have removed or groomed their pubic hair has varied by historical time and place [2–5]. For example, art and artifacts suggest that women in ancient Egypt and classical Greece may have removed some or all of their pubic hair (in Greece, by plucking or singeing with a lamp) and that groomed pubic hair may have been considered a feature of women's sexual attractiveness [3]. Removal of significant amounts of pubic hair among women in India have been documented as well [6, 7]. Similarly, nude women depicted in some Italian Renaissance art have no pubic hair, whereas nude women depicted in some Northern Renaissance and Gothic art are depicted with pubic hair—a difference that may be of artistic significance or may reflect women's actual pubic hair styles of the time [4].

Although the absence of pubic hair depicted on women in art has, at times, been suggested to result from men's fear of female genitals or from suppression of female sexuality, other researchers have presented alternative explanations for female genital hairlessness [3, 5]. These explanations include that the models themselves may have removed their pubic hair either because they lived in a warm climate or because artistic models in some cultures were often courtesans, who may have removed their hair even if other women in the culture did not [5]. It has also been suggested that an absence of pubic hair on female nudes might be due to an artistic view of the era that presented smooth, unbroken "snakelike" lines—such as those of the hairless vulva—as more aesthetically appealing than short, scattered or broken lines, such as those that would have been necessary to depict pubic hair [5].

Findings from a 1968 survey of women in a nudist club in Australia suggest that 10 percent removed all of their pubic hair, 50 percent trimmed their pubic hair and the rest did nothing to their pubic hair [8]. In addition, a recent content analysis of *Playboy* centerfolds from issues dated December 1953 through October 2007 demonstrated that a far greater proportion of centerfolds in issues dated 2000–2007 had little or no pubic hair [9]. However, as with nude figures rendered in art from earlier centuries, it is unclear to what extent the *Playboy* centerfolds' pubic hair styles reflect or influence the pubic hair styles of contemporary women.

Given these variations in pubic hair styles over time, it may be more accurate to state that, rather than female genital hairlessness being a "new norm," in the past decade or so, an increasing number of women in the United States, the United Kingdom, and Australia appear to be removing all of their pubic hair—with potential benefits (e.g., reduced risk of pubic lice) and clinical risks (e.g., genital cuts, irritation, or infection) noted [2,10–12]. However, as neither the prevalence nor the extent of pubic hair removal was previously well documented, it is difficult to know when pubic hair styles changed, why they changed or how many more contemporary women may be removing all of their pubic hair compared to women in earlier generations.

Much of what is known about recent trends in women's pubic hair removal are derived from anecdotal reports by physicians and mainstream media reports or depictions of total removal of pubic hair (such as by Brazilian waxing techniques) [10,11,13–15]. However, such sources may give a false impression of the prevalence of female genital hairlessness or may influence women to engage in such hair removal practices.

One study of 235 female undergraduate students in Australia found that approximately 22 percent were currently in the practice of removing all of their pubic hair and that total removers were more likely to use waxing than shaving [15]. Furthermore, those who removed all of their hair were younger, on average, than partial removers, and more likely to endorse doing so for reasons related to sexual attractiveness, femininity, and self-enhancement rather than social norms. Another survey of more than 600 women in the United Kingdom found removal of pubic hair to be more common among women who were 50 years of age or younger [16].

Although anecdotal reports suggest that pubic hair removal is common, the extent to which women in the United States remove their pubic hair has not been studied. Also, limited research exists on pubic hair removal among women of a wide range of ages. The purpose of this study was to assess pubic hair removal behavior among sexually active women in the United States and to examine the extent to which pubic hair removal methods are related to demographic, relational, and sexual characteristics, including female sexual function.

Methods

The Institutional Review Board at the author's institution approved all protocols associated with this study.

Recruitment

Data from this study are from a larger study related to women's lubricant use. During winter 2008, e-mail recruitment messages were sent to colleagues, community and campus organizations, and health-related listservs. The messages invited adult women (age 18+) to visit a study website to learn more about an Internet-based study about lubricant use. The study website provided detailed information about the study and participant eligibility. To be eligible, individuals had to be at least 18 years old, female, living in the United States, and sexually active alone or with a partner. "Sexually active" was defined as masturbating and/or being the receptive partner in vaginal or anal sex at least four times, on average, in a typical month at the time of the study.

Interested individuals were asked to complete online questions (based on the above criteria) to determine their eligibility. If eligible, participants read and electronically signed a statement of informed consent that they could print and retain. The data presented here are from the baseline portion of the study that consisted of a cross-sectional Internet-based survey that took 10–20 minutes to complete.

Main Outcome Measures

Participants completed a baseline questionnaire that included items related to their demographics (e.g., age, education, race/ethnicity, relationship status, sexual orientation), health history and behaviors (e.g., age at menarche, whether they had a gynecological exam in the previous year, whether they had looked closely at or examined their genitals in the previous month), and whether they had received cunnilingus in the previous 4 weeks. As the sample was part of a larger study about lubricants and sexual activity, participants were asked about a wider range of sexual behaviors; however, it was cunnilingus that was hypothesized by the authors to be positively related to pubic hair removal behaviors.

Participants were also asked approximately how many times they had removed some or all of their pubic hair during the previous month (response choices ranged from 0 to 10 times, with "More than 10 times" as a choice that represented the highest frequency) through shaving or waxing, as well as the frequency of laser hair reduction and electrolysis use over the previous month.

In addition, participants completed the Female Genital Self-Image Scale (FGSIS), a reliable and valid 7-item scale that assesses how women feel about their genitals, with a higher score indicating more positive genital self-image [17].

Participants also completed the Female Sexual Function Index (FSFI), a 19-item questionnaire with demonstrated reliability and validity [18–20]. The FSFI provides scores for the domains of desire, arousal, lubrication, satisfaction, orgasm, and pain during sex, with higher scores indicating more positive sexual function (and on the pain domain, a higher score indicates no or less pain). The FSFI also results in a total score representing overall sexual function.

Analyses

Analyses were performed using SPSS 17.0 (SPSS Inc., Chicago, IL, USA). Descriptive statistics were used to report sample characteristics and the proportion of women who had removed some or all of their pubic hair in each of five age groups (18–24, 25–29, 30–39, 40–49, 50–68 years). As pubic hair removal behaviors have been suggested to be a newer phenomenon, it was decided that the data would be most informative if examined by age cohorts.

Next, women were categorized into groups based on the frequency and totality of their pubic hair removal. Those who reported having removed all of their pubic hair by waxing at least once in the past month, or from shaving more than 10 times in the past month were categorized as "typically hair-free." Women were categorized as "some total removal" if they reported having shaved all of their pubic hair 10 or fewer times during the past month but did not report total removal through waxing in the past month.

Those who reported waxing or shaving some of their pubic hair in the past month, or who reported having had electrolysis or laser hair reduction during the past month, but no total removal, were categorized as having "partial removal." Those who reported no removal using the listed techniques (waxing, shaving, electrolysis, or laser) were categorized as "no removal."

Once categorized, chi-square analyses and analysis of variance or covariance (using Tukey's test of honestly significant difference or Bonferroni post hoc tests) was used to examine differences between the groups.

Results
Participants

A total of 2,451 women completed the study. Participants largely reported being heterosexual, partnered, and white/Caucasian). Participants ranged in age from 18 to 68 years (mean = 32.69, median = 31.0, standard deviation = 9.17).

Prevalence and Extent of Pubic Hair Removal

The prevalence and extent of pubic hair removal varied by age. In the 18–24-year-old age group, the largest proportion of women engaged in some total removal (38.0%), the second largest proportion engaged in partial removal (29.1%), and about one-fifth were typically hair-free over the previous month (20.6%). It was less common for women in this age group to engage in no removal at all during the previous month.

Among women aged 25–39 years, the largest proportion of women engaged in partial removal followed by some total removal, no removal, and being typically hair-free (which was least common). Women in the 40–49-year-old age group also most commonly engaged in partial removal of their pubic hair, although more than a quarter of them did not engage in any hair removal behaviors over the previous month. Some total removal and being typically hair-free were less common.

The largest proportion of women in the 50+ age group had not engaged in any of the listed hair removal behaviors over the previous month (51.7%). More than a third had engaged in partial removal (37.1%). About one-tenth engaged in some total removal, while being typically hair-free was rare (2.1%).

Characteristics of Women Based on Pubic Hair Removal Behaviors

Women who were typically hair-free in the previous month were significantly younger than women in all other categories ($\chi^2 = 28.74$). Those who engaged in some total removal were significantly younger ($\chi^2 = 29.54$) than those who had engaged in partial ($\chi^2 = 33.67$) or no removal ($\chi^2 = 36.74$). There were no significant age differences between the latter two groups. In addition, a significantly greater proportion of women who identified as bisexual were typically hair-free over the previous month (18.0%) as compared to those who identified as heterosexual (10.8%) or lesbian (9.4%). The greatest proportion of women in each of the sexual orientation groups were partial removers.

Also, a greater proportion of women who were partnered (but not married) were categorized as typically hair-free or as having engaged in some total removal over the previous month. Women who were currently sexually active with someone other than a monogamous partner were the most likely to remove their pubic hair, while those who were not sexually active with a partner more often reported no pubic hair removal.

Pubic Hair Behaviors in Relation to Health Behaviors

Women who were typically hair-free or who had removed all of their pubic hair at least once during the previous month (some total removers) were more likely to have looked closely at their genitals during the previous month but were no more or less likely to have had a gynecological exam than partial or no removers.

Pubic Hair Behaviors in Relation to Sexual Behaviors

Typically hair-free women and those who had removed all of their pubic hair at least once during the previous month (some total removers) were also more likely to have received cunnilingus in the previous 4 weeks. However, because that could be an artifact of a partnered relationship status or of younger age, which is conflated with more frequent sex overall, we controlled for these variables in a multivariate model. When included in this model, pubic hair still emerged as a significant predictor. Despite reported differences in sexual behavior, pubic hair patterns were unrelated to the participant's reported human immunodeficiency virus and sexually transmitted infections diagnoses within the year ($P < 0.05$).

Pubic Hair Behaviors and Female Genital Self-image

The FGSIS had sufficient reliability in this sample (Cronbach's alpha = 0.87). Women who were typically hair-free or sometimes hair-free during the previous month scored significantly higher on the FGSIS after controlling for age, sexual orientation, and sexual relationship status, indicating more positive genital self-image, as compared to those who had not removed any or all of their pubic hair in the previous month.

Pubic Hair Behaviors and Female Sexual Function

The reliability for the FSFI in this sample was acceptable ($\alpha = 0.90$). After controlling for age, sexual orientation, and sexual relationship status, all FSFI subscales significantly varied based upon the participant's pubic hair patterns with the exception of the orgasm subscale. Overall, participants in the some total removal and typically hair-free groups tended to report significantly higher scores on the FSFI than their counterparts in the no removal and partial removal groups.

Discussion

Findings from this study of more than 2,400 women suggest that women's pubic hair removal behaviors are more variable than they are sometimes described. The data demonstrate that women who are sexually active (alone or with a partner) engage in varied pubic hair removal behaviors that include a range of frequencies and extents of shaving, waxing, and, less commonly, electrolysis and laser hair reduction. However, women who removed all of their pubic hair were generally younger, more likely to engage in cunnilingus and scored higher on measures of female genital self-image and sexual function, even after controlling for other variables.

These data are particularly relevant for those whose practice is centered on sexual medicine or gynecology, who may be the healthcare providers who are most likely to view women's genitals and to be asked questions, by their patients, about pubic hair removal practices. Women may have questions, based on what they have heard from friends or partners or read in the media, about which removal practices are normal or whether there may be any advantage to pubic hair removal in terms of health or the experience of sex. These data are among the few scientific findings to address such questions.

It has been said that having no pubic hair is normative [1,10,14]; however, findings from this study suggest that there is no one dominant pubic hair style. Given the growth rate of hair and women's often sporadic hair removal, there is likely great diversity in the amount of pubic hair that women have at any given time. After all, pubic hair is in a constant state of growth, which suggests that pubic hair "style" may be a malleable concept.

Although more than half of women in the 18–24 age group had removed all of their pubic hair at least once during the previous month, only one-fifth were considered "typically hair-free" as defined in this study (a proportion that was strikingly similar to the Australian study that found that 22 percent of undergraduate students removed all of their pubic hair). Being hair-free was less common with each older age group, suggesting either that total hair removal is, indeed, a newer phenomenon or that it may reflect a phase that women grow out of with age, developmental life stage, or the progression of their romantic relationships. As the current study provides only cross-sectional data, a longitudinal design would be better suited to address such a question as might an interview study that asks women about their shifting pubic hair removal behaviors over the course of their lives.

That a greater proportion of bisexual-identified women removed all of their pubic hair as compared to heterosexual women and lesbian women is worth noting. This adds to existing research that has reported other behavioral differences among bisexual identified women including a greater proportion of bisexual women who have masturbated in the previous month or who have used a vibrator [21].

This study had several strengths. Recruitment messages did not include language related to pubic hair or removal techniques; thus, the sample was unlikely to self-select on such variables. In addition, more than 2,400 women were surveyed, making this study—to our knowledge—the largest study of pubic hair removal techniques conducted thus far. Furthermore, women ages 18 to 68 participated in the study, which allowed for comparisons across five age cohorts.

That said, the present study did not assess women's reasons for pubic hair removal, although other researchers have done so [22]. If pubic hair removal sometimes occurs in anticipation of having sex (which it may be as pubic hair removal was sporadic for most women), then it begs the question of the extent to which women's sexual behavior is planned or considered ahead of time, whether in or outside of a relationship context. If women plan to remove their pubic hair in anticipation of a date or possible sexual encounter, perhaps pubic hair grooming reflects or even influences how women's sexual decision making can occur well before she is in an immediate sexual situation with a potential sexual partner. Future research might consider how often women groom their pubic hair in anticipation of sex and how often women avoid or decline sex if they feel that their pubic hair is not well groomed. Also, although pubic hair removal was associated with FSFI and FGSIS scores, the direction of these relationships is unclear. Thus,

future research might consider whether more positive sexual function (or positive genital self-image) influences pubic hair grooming behaviors or whether women who remove their pubic hair have more positive sexual function (or genital self-image). Regarding the former, it may be that women who choose to remove their pubic hair are more easily aroused or have greater desire for sex, or that during periods of time when women exhibit greater interest in sex, they may groom their pubic hair in ways that excite them or that they hope may excite a partner. Too, modulating pubic hair may allow greater sensitivity of vulvar skin. Alternatively, it may be that women's partners are more attracted to or attentive to vulvar or clitoral stimulation, or more interested in performing cunnilingus, when there is less hair, or it may reflect the myriad ways in which women's genitals and their body image relate to sexual function and experience [23, 24].

Women in the younger age groups tended to engage in more pubic hair removal behaviors, which likely reflects cohort effects (specifically, that when older women were growing up and/or became sexually active, there were fewer salons that offered pubic hair removal, particularly total removal, and less media discussion of these behaviors). It may reflect that younger women tend to have more frequent sex and also, perhaps, more occasions of unexpected sex. Younger women may groom more regularly in anticipation of sex as they are less likely to have a regular sex partner, and thus may find themselves wanting to be prepared in case that a sexual opportunity presents itself.

A limitation of the study is that the use of depilatory creams was not assessed, and thus, women who use depilatory creams (but no other methods) to remove some or all of their pubic hair may have been miscategorized. Trimming was also not assessed; therefore, the length of hair is not known. In addition, it is not known how much pubic hair was removed by laser or electrolysis; as such, the small number of women who used these methods may also have been miscategorized. Also, women may experience different rates of hair regrowth which may mean that some women who were perceived to be "typically hair-free" were perhaps not, even if they had waxed all of their pubic hair off in the previous month. Alternatively, women who removed their hair only sometimes, but who experience a slow rate of hair regrowth, may have been miscategorized as having some hair. As the error of these possible categorizations could flow in either direction, any error because of this should even out. We also did not assess adverse outcomes of pubic hair grooming nor did we assess removal behaviors among women who did not meet our study's definition of being "sexually active" alone or with a partner. Finally, probability methods of sampling were not used for recruitment, and thus, participants are not representative of, nor can they be generalized to, the greater population of women in the United States.

This study provides important insights into the diversity of pubic hair removal techniques among women in the United States. Although several reports from clinicians have suggested that a large number of women remove much or all of their pubic hair, it may be the case that women groom specifically in advance of gynecological visits, thus altering the perceptions of clinicians about the proportion of women who regularly remove all of their pubic hair.

Conclusions

Although women's total pubic hair removal has been described as a "new norm," findings from this study suggest that pubic hair styles are diverse and that it is more common than not for women to have at least some pubic hair on their genitals. In addition, it was found that total pubic hair removal was associated with younger age, being partnered (rather than single or married), having looked closely at one's own genitals in the previous month, cunnilingus in the past month, more positive sexual functioning scores, and a more positive genital self-image.

References

1. Labre MP. The Brazilian wax: New hairless norm for women? J Commun Inq 2002;26:113–32.
2. Ramsey S, Sweeney C, Fraser M, Oades G. Pubic hair and sexuality: A review. J Sex Med 2009;6:2102–10.
3. Kilmer M. Genital phobia and depilation. J Hell Stud 1982;102:104–12.
4. Hollander A. The clothed image: Picture and performance. New Lit Hist 1971;2:477–93.
5. Endres J. Diderot, Hogart and the aesthetics of depilation. Eighteenth Century Stud 2004;38:17–38.
6. Hershman P. Hair, sex and dirt. Man 1974;9:274–98.
7. Madnani N. Managing vulvar pruritis in Mumbai, India. Presented at the XVIII World Congress of the International Society for the Study of Vulvovaginal Disease. 2006. Queenstown, New Zealand.
8. Edwards A, Gilbert K, Skinner J. Some like it hot: The beach as a cultural dimension. Oxford: Meyer & Meyer Sport (UK); 2003.
9. Schick V. Evulvalution: The portrayal of women's external genitalia and physique across time and the current Barbie doll ideals. J Sex Res 2010;47:1–9.
10. Armstrong NR, Wilson JD. Did the "Brazilian" kill the pubic louse? Sex Trans Infect 2006;82:265–6.
11. Dendle C, Mulvey S, Pyrlis F, Grayson L, Johnson PDR. Severe complications of a "Brazilian" bikini wax. Clin Infect Dis 2007;45:29–31.
12. Olsen EA. Methods of hair removal. J Am Acad Dermatol 1999;40:143–55.
13. Fitzpatrick M. Brazilian bikini wax and the designer vagina. Br J Gen Pract 2007;57:1005.
14. Yakas L. Femininity, sexuality and body hair: The female body hair(less) ideal. Focus Anthropology 2009;VIII: 1–18. Available at www.focusanthro.org/archive/2008.2009/yakas_0809.pdf (Accessed June 20, 2010).
15. Tiggemann M, Hodgson S. The hairlessness norm extended: Reasons for and predictors of women's body hair removal at different body sites. Sex Roles 2008;59:889–97.
16. Toerin K, Wilkinson S, Choi PYL. Body hair removal: The "mundane" production of normative femininity. Sex Roles 2005;52:399–406.
17. Herbenick D, Reece M. Development and validation of the female genital self-image scale. J Sex Med 2010;7:1822–30. (early view).
18. Rosen R, Brown C, Heiman J, Leiblum S, Meston C, Shabsigh R, Ferguson D, D'Agostino R. The Female Sexual Function Index (FSFI): A multidimensional self-report instrument for the assessment of female sexual function. J Sex Marital Ther 2000;26:191–208.
19. Wiegel M, Meston C, Rosen R. The Female Sexual Function Index (FSFI): Cross-validation and development of clinical cutoff scores. J Sex Marital Ther 2005;31:1–20.
20. Witting K, Santtila P, Jern P, Varjonen M, Wager I, Hoglund M, Johansson A, Vikstrom N, Sandnabba N. Evaluation of the Female Sexual Function Index in a population based sample from Finland. Arch Sex Behav 2008;37:912–24.
21. Herbenick D, Reece M, Sanders SA, Dodge B, Ghassemi A, Fortenberry JD. Women's vibrator use in sexual partnerships: Results from a nationally representative survey in the United States. J Sex Marital Ther 2010;36:49–65.
22. Toerin M, Wilkinson S. Exploring the depilation norm: A qualitative questionnaire study of women's body hair removal. Qual Res Psychol 2004;1:69–92.
23. Lowenstein L, Gamble T, Sanses TV, van Raalte H, Carberry C, Jakus S, Pham T, Nguyen A, Hoskey K, Kenton K. Changes in sexual function after treatment for prolapse are related to the improvement in body image perception. J Sex Med 2009;7:1023–8.
24. Lowenstein L, Gamble T, Sanses TV, van Raalte H, Carberry C, Jakus S, Kambiss S, McAchran S, Pham T, Aschkenazi S, Hoskey K, Kenton K, Fellow's Pelvic Research Network. Sexual function is related to body image perception in women with pelvic organ prolapse. J Sex Med 2009;6: 2286–91.

Critical Thinking

1. What cultural forces are influencing this behavior?
2. Can media consumption impact self-image?

Scents and Sensibility

"Sexual chemistry" is more than just a way of talking about heated attraction. Subtle chemical keys actually help determine who we fall for. But here comes news that our lifestyles may unwittingly undermine our natural sex appeal.

ELIZABETH SVOBODA

Psychologists Rachel Herz and Estelle Campenni were just getting to know each other, swapping stories about their lives over coffee, when Campenni confided something unexpected: She was living proof, she said, of love at first smell. "I knew I would marry my husband the minute I smelled him," she told Herz. "I've always been into smell, but this was different; he really smelled good to me. His scent made me feel safe and at the same time turned on—and I'm talking about his real body smell, not cologne or soap. I'd never felt like that from a man's smell before. We've been married for eight years now and have three kids, and his smell is always very sexy to me."

Everyone knows what it's like to be powerfully affected by a partner's smell—witness men who bury their noses in their wives' hair and women who can't stop sniffing their boyfriends' T-shirts. And couples have long testified to the ways scent-based chemistry affects their relationships. "One of the most common things women tell marriage counselors is, 'I can't stand his smell,'" says Herz, the author of *The Scent of Desire*.

Sexual attraction remains one of life's biggest mysteries. We might say we go for partners who are tall and thin, love to cook, or have a mania for exercise, but when push comes to shove, studies show, the people we actually end up with possess few of the traits we claim to want. Some researchers think scent could be the hidden cosmological constant in the sexual universe, the missing factor that explains who we end up with. It may even explain why we feel "chemistry"—or "sparks" or "electricity"—with one person and not with another.

Physical attraction itself may literally be based on smell. We discount the importance of scent-centric communication only because it operates on such a subtle level. "This is not something that jumps out at you, like smelling a good steak cooking on the grill," says Randy Thornhill, an evolutionary psychologist at the University of New Mexico. "But the scent capability is there, and it's not surprising to find smell capacity in the context of sexual behavior." As a result, we may find ourselves drawn to the counter attendant at the local drugstore, but have no idea why—or, conversely, find ourselves put off by potential dating partners even though they seem perfect on paper.

Though we may remain partially oblivious to scent signals we're sending and receiving, new research suggests that we not only come equipped to choose a romantic partner who smells good to us, but that this choice has profound biological implications. As we act out the complex rituals of courtship, many of them inscribed deep in our brain, scent-based cues help us zero in on optimal partners—the ones most likely to stay faithful to us and to create healthy children with us.

At first blush, the idea of scent-based attraction might seem hypothetical and ephemeral, but when we unknowingly interfere with the transmission of subtle olfactory messages operating below the level of conscious awareness, the results can be both concrete and devastating. When we disregard what our noses tell us, we can find ourselves mired in partnerships that breed sexual discontent, infertility, and even—in extreme cases—unhealthy offspring.

The Scent of Desire

When you're turned on by your partner's scent, taking a deep whiff of his chest or the back of her neck feels like taking a powerful drug—it's an instant flume ride to bliss, however momentary. Research has shown that we use scent-based signaling mechanisms to suss out compatibility. Claus Wedekind, a biologist at the University of Lausanne in Switzerland, created Exhibit A of this evidence by giving 44 men new T-shirts and instructing them to wear the shirts for two straight nights. To ensure that the sweat collecting on the shirts would remain "odor-neutral," he supplied the men with scent-free soap and aftershave.

After the men were allowed to change, 49 women sniffed the shirts and specified which odors they found most attractive. Far more often than chance would predict, the women preferred the smell of T-shirts worn by men who were immunologically dissimilar to them. The difference lay in the sequence of more than 100 immune system genes known as the MHC, or major histocompatibility complex. These genes code for proteins that help the immune system recognize pathogens. The smell of their favorite shirts also reminded the women of their past and current boyfriends, suggesting that MHC does indeed influence women's dating decisions in real life.

I knew I would marry my husband the minute I first smelled him. His body scent made me feel safe and turned on.

Women's preference for MHC-distinct mates makes perfect sense from a biological point of view. Ever since ancestral times, partners whose immune systems are different have produced offspring who are more disease-resistant. With more immune genes expressed, kids are buffered against a wider variety of pathogens and toxins.

But that doesn't mean women prefer men whose MHC genes are most different from theirs, as University of Chicago evolutionary biologist Martha McClintock found when she performed a T-shirt study similar to Wedekind's. Women are not attracted to the smell of men with whom they had no MHC genes in common. "This might be a case where you're protecting yourself against a mate who's too similar or too dissimilar, but there's a middle range where you're OK," McClintock says.

Women consistently outperform men in smell sensitivity tests, and they also make greater time and energy sacrifices on their children's behalf than men do—in addition to bearing offspring, they look after them most of the time. These factors may explain why women are more discriminating in sniffing out MHC compatibility.

Men are sensitive to smell as well, but because women shoulder a greater reproductive burden, and are therefore choosier about potential mates, researchers are not surprised to find that women are also more discriminating in sniffing out MHC compatibility.

Unlike, say, blood types, MHC gene complements differ so much from one person to the next that there's no obvious way

Follow Your Nose

How to Put Your Nose to Work in Choosing a Partner—or Evaluating an Existing One

Think twice about opting for the pill if you're seeking a long-term partner. The first few weeks of a relationship are critical to assessing compatibility, so make sure your nose is up to the task.

Try a fragrance-free week. Eliminate factors that could throw your nostrils off. Have your partner set aside scented shower gels in favor of fragrance-free soap, nix the cologne, and use only unscented deodorant.

Keep smell's importance in context. If you sometimes find your partner's scent off-putting, don't panic; it doesn't necessarily mean fertility issues are in your future. Connections between MHC compatibility and conception problems have yet to be confirmed in large-scale population studies, so don't plunk down big bucks for MHC testing at this point.

to reliably predict who's MHC-compatible with whom. Skin color, for instance, isn't much help, since groups of people living in different areas of the world might happen to evolve genetic resistance to some of the same germs. "People of different ethnicities can have similar profiles, so race is not a good predictor of MHC dissimilarity," Thornhill says.

And because people's MHC profiles are as distinct as fingerprints—there are thousands of possible gene combinations—a potential sex partner who smells good to one woman may completely repel another. "There's no Brad Pitt of smell," Herz says. "Body odor is an external manifestation of the immune system, and the smells we think are attractive come from the people who are most genetically compatible with us." Much of what we vaguely call "sexual chemistry," she adds, is likely a direct result of this scent-based compatibility.

Typically, our noses steer us in the right direction when it comes to picking a reproductively compatible partner. But what if they fail us and we wind up with a mate whose MHC profile is too similar to our own? Carol Ober, a geneticist at the University of Chicago, explored this question in her studies of members of the Hutterite religious clan, an Amish-like closed society that consists of some 40,000 members and extends through the rural Midwest. Hutterites marry only other members of their clan, so the variety in their gene pool is relatively low. Within these imposed limits, Hutterite women nevertheless manage to find partners who are MHC-distinct from them most of the time.

The few couples with a high degree of MHC similarity, however, suffered higher rates of miscarriage and experienced longer intervals between pregnancies, indicating more difficulty conceiving. Some scientists speculate that miscarriages may be the body's way of curtailing investment in a child who isn't likely to have a strong immune system anyway.

What's more, among heterosexual couples, similar MHC profiles spell relational difficulty, Christine Garver-Apgar, a psychologist at the University of New Mexico, has found. "As the proportion of MHC alleles increased, women's sexual responsiveness to their partners decreased, and their number of sex partners outside the relationship increased," Garver-Apgar reports. The number of MHC genes couples shared corresponded directly with the likelihood that they would cheat on one another; if a man and woman had 50 percent of their MHC alleles in common, the woman had a 50 percent chance of sleeping with another man behind her partner's back.

The Divorce Pill?

Women generally prefer the smell of men whose MHC gene complements are different from theirs, setting the stage for the best biological match. But Wedekind's T-shirt study revealed one notable exception to this rule: women on the birth-control pill. When the pill users among his subjects sniffed the array of pre-worn T-shirts, they preferred the scent of men whose MHC profiles were similar to theirs—the opposite of their pill-free counterparts.

This dramatic reversal of smell preferences may reflect the pill's mechanism of action: it prevents the ovaries from releasing an egg, fooling the body into thinking it's pregnant. And since pregnancy is such a vulnerable state, it seems to activate a preference for kin, who are genetically similar to us and likely to serve as protectors. "When pregnant rodent females are exposed to strange males, they can spontaneously abort," Herz says. "The same may be true for human females." What's more, some women report a deficit in sex drive when they take the pill, a possible consequence of its pregnancy-mimicking function.

The tendency to favor mates with similar MHC genes could potentially hamper the durability of pill users' relationships in the long term. While Herz shies away from dubbing hormonal birth control "the divorce pill," as a few media outlets have done in response to her theories, she does think the pill jumbles women's smell preferences. "It's like picking your cousins as marriage partners," Herz says. "It constitutes a biological error." As a result, explains Charles Wysocki, a psychobiologist at Florida State University, when such a couple decides to have children and the woman stops taking birth control, she may find herself less attracted to her mate for reasons she doesn't quite understand. "On a subconscious level, her brain is realizing a mistake was made—she married the wrong guy," he says.

"Some couples' fertility problems may be related to the pill-induced flip-flop in MHC preferences," Garver-Apgar adds. No one has yet collected data to indicate whether the pill has created a large-scale problem in compatibility. Still, Herz recommends that women seeking a long-term partner consider alternative birth control methods, at least until they get to know their potential significant other well and are sure they like the way he smells. "If you're looking for a man to be the father of your child," she says, "go off the pill before you start your search."

If you were on the pill when you met your current partner, the situation is more complicated. Once a relationship has progressed to long-term commitment, says Herz, a woman's perception of her partner's smell is so intertwined with her emotional reaction to him that it could be difficult for her to assess his scent as if he were a stranger. "If she's in love, he could smell like a garbage can and she'd still be attracted to him."

Crossed Signals

The pill subverts a woman's ability to sniff out a compatible mate by causing her to misinterpret the scent messages she receives. But it may warp olfactory communication channels in the other direction as well, distorting the signals she sends—and making her seem less appealing to men, an irony given that women typically take the pill to boost their appeal in a partner's eyes.

Geoffrey Miller, an evolutionary psychologist at the University of New Mexico and author of *The Mating Mind*, noticed the pill's connection to waning male desire while studying a group of exotic dancers—women whose livelihoods depend on how sexually appealing they are to male customers. Non-pill-using dancers made about 50 percent more in tips than dancers on oral contraceptives. In other words, women who were on the pill were only about two-thirds as sexy as women who weren't.

Why were the pill-takers in the study so much less attractive to men? "Women are probably doing something unconsciously,

Solving the Mystery of Gaydar

The Ability to Discern Sexual Orientation May Be Based on Scent

Everyone knows someone with impeccable "gaydar," the seemingly telepathic ability to tell whether someone is gay or straight. New research is robbing gaydar of its sixth-sense mystique, revealing that some people literally have the power to sniff out another person's sexual orientation—and that the ability is strongly rooted in biology.

When Charles Wysocki, a geneticist at the University of Pennsylvania's Monell Chemical Senses Center, asked volunteers to sniff underarm sweat from donors of a variety of genders and sexual orientations, some clear patterns began to emerge. Gay men strongly preferred the odor of other gay men, lesbians gravitated toward the smell of other lesbians, and straight women rated the odor of straight men higher than that of gay men. Each group, in short, preferred the smell of their first-choice mates, indicating a scent-based ability to assess sexual orientation. Another study confirmed that gay men and lesbians can recognize and identify the odor of others who share their sexual preference. This kind of scent-based gaydar enables gays to pinpoint potential partners instantly.

Researchers at Karolinska University in Sweden have added to Wysocki's findings, identifying a potential reason why gay men find the smell of other males so enticing. They found that androstenone, a steroid compound men secrete in their sweat, excited brain areas that control sexual behavior in gay men but left the brains of straight men unaffected. This suggests the chemical may be an integral part of the scent-driven signaling mechanism that attracts gay men to each other.

and men are responding to it unconsciously," says Miller. "We just don't know whether it has to do with a shift in their psychology, their tone of voice, or if it's more physical, as in the kind of pheromones they're putting out."

The biggest earners in Miller's study were non-pill-using dancers at the time of ovulation. Other studies have shown that men rate women as smelling best when they are at the most fertile point of their menstrual cycles, suggesting that women give off scent-based signals that broadcast their level of fecundity. "The pill might be producing cues that a woman is in the early stage of pregnancy, which would not tend to elicit a lot of male sexual interest," Miller says. "It makes sense for men to be sensitive to that and for them not to feel the same chemistry with the woman."

Drowning in Fragrance

The pill isn't the only way we might confound sexual chemistry. Every day, far more people may be subverting their quest for love with soap and bottled fragrances. In ancestral times, smelling ripe was just a fact of life, absent hot showers and shampoo.

This held true well into the 19th century, when the miasma of body odor in Parisian streets grew so thick that it was dubbed "The Great Stink of 1880." Back when a person's scent could waft across a room, a mere handshake could provide valuable information about attraction.

The need to smell our mates—and the difficulty in doing so over the sensory din of modern perfumes and colognes—may drive the sexual disinhibition of modern society.

Since the 20th-century hygiene revolution and the rise of the personal-care industry, however, companies have pitched deodorants, perfumes, and colognes to consumers as the epitome of sex appeal. But instead of furthering our quest to find the perfect mate, such products may actually derail it, say researchers, by masking our true scent and making it difficult for prospects to assess compatibility. "Humans abuse body smell signals by hiding them, masking them, putting on deodorant," says Devendra Singh, a psychologist at the University of Texas. "The noise-to-signal ratio was much better in primitive society."

Miller argues that modern hygiene may be such an impediment to sexual signaling that it could explain why so many people in our culture get so physical so fast. "Hunter-gatherers didn't have to do a lot of kissing, because they could smell each other pretty clearly from a few feet away," Miller says. "With all the showering, scents, and soap, we have to get our noses and mouths really up close to people to get a good idea of their biochemistry. People are more motivated to do a lot more kissing and petting, to do that assessment before they have sex." In other words, the need to smell our mates—and the comparative difficulty of doing so in today's environment of perfumes and colognes—may actually be driving the sexual disinhibition of modern society.

Other scientists counter that odor detection is a bit subtler. For one thing, it's possible we select store-bought scents to complement our natural odorprints, rather than mask them entirely: One study found that people with similar MHC profiles tend to go for the same colognes. And Garver-Apgar points out that in spending hours together each day, partners have ample opportunity to experience each other sans artificial scents. "Once you're in a close enough relationship," she says, "you're going to get a real whiff at some point."

Scents and Sensibility

There's no way to know whether couples who shell out thousands of dollars to fertility clinics—and those who struggle to make a relationship work because "the chemistry just isn't there"—suffer MHC incompatibility. We might never know, since a multitude of factors contributes to every reproductive and romantic outcome. But we can, at least, be cognizant of the importance of natural scent.

"Scent can be a deal breaker if it's not right, just like someone being too stupid or unkind or short," says Miller. Nevertheless, smell isn't the be-all and end-all of attraction, but one of a constellation of important factors. Armed with knowledge of how scent-based attraction operates, we have some power to decide how much priority we want to accord it. Is it more important to be with the partner who smells amazing and with whom you have great chemistry, or with the one who may not attract you quite as much on a physical level but is honest and reliable?

"People tend to treat this as an either-or situation: Either we're completely driven by pheromones, like moths, or we're completely in charge of our own destiny," University of Chicago psychologist McClintock says. "But it's not a wild idea that both factors are involved." While people like Estelle Campenni have reaped untold benefits by trusting their scent impressions, it's ultimately up to us how highly we value what our noses tell us.

Critical Thinking

1. What role does scent play in the process of physical attraction?
2. What impact can biological processes outside the conscious awareness of the individual have on sexual attraction?
3. How is actual physical "chemistry" related to sexual attraction?

ELIZABETH SVOBODA contributes regularly to *The New York Times, Discover,* and *Popular Science.* She lives in San Jose, California.

The Orgasmic Mind

Achieving sexual climax requires a complex conspiracy of sensory and psychological signals—and the eventual silencing of critical brain areas.

MARTIN PORTNER

S
he did not often have such strong emotions. But she suddenly felt powerless against her passion and the desire to throw herself into the arms of the cousin whom she saw at a family funeral. "It can only be because of that patch," said Marianne, a participant in a multinational trial of a testosterone patch designed to treat hypoactive sexual desire disorder, in which a woman is devoid of libido. Testosterone, a hormone ordinarily produced by the ovaries, is linked to female sexual function, and the women in this 2005 study had undergone operations to remove their ovaries.

After 12 weeks of the trial, Marianne had felt her sexual desire return. Touching herself unleashed erotic sensations and vivid sexual fantasies. Eventually she could make love to her husband again and experienced an orgasm for the first time in almost three years. But that improvement was not because of testosterone, it turned out. Marianne was among the half of the women who had received a placebo patch—with no testosterone in it at all.

Marianne's experience underlines the complexity of sexual arousal. Far from being a simple issue of hormones, sexual desire and orgasm are subject to various influences on the brain and nervous system, which controls the sex glands and genitals. And many of those influences are environmental. Recent research, for example, shows that visual stimuli spur sexual stirrings in women, as they do in men. Marianne's desire may have been invigorated by conversations or thoughts about sex she had as a result of taking part in the trial. Such stimuli may help relieve inhibitions or simply whet a person's appetite for sex.

Achieving orgasm, brain-imaging studies show, involves more than heightened arousal. It requires a release of inhibitions and control in which the brain's center of vigilance shuts down in males; in females, various areas of the brain involved in controlling thoughts and emotions become silent. The brain's pleasure centers tend to light up brightly in the brain scans of both sexes, especially in those of males. The reward system creates an incentive to seek more sexual encounters, with clear benefits for the survival of the species. When the drive for sex dissipates, as it did with Marianne, people can reignite the spark with tactics that target the mind.

Fast Facts
Principles of Pleasure

1. Sexual desire and orgasm are subject to various influences on the brain and nervous system, which controls the sex glands and genitals.
2. The ingredients of desire may differ for men and women, but researchers have revealed some surprising similarities. For example, visual stimuli spur sexual stirrings in women, as they do in men.
3. Achieving orgasm, brain imaging studies show, involves more than heightened arousal. It requires a release of inhibitions engineered by shutdown of the brain's center of vigilance in both sexes and a widespread neural power failure in females.

Sex in Circles

Biologists identified sex hormones such as estrogen and testosterone in the 1920s and 1930s, and the first studies of human sexuality appeared in the 1940s. In 1948 biologist Alfred Kinsey of Indiana University introduced his first report on human sexual practices, *Sexual Behavior in the Human Male,* which was followed, in 1953, by *Sexual Behavior in the Human Female.* These highly controversial books opened up a new dialogue about human sexuality. They not only broached topics—such as masturbation, homosexuality and orgasm—that many people considered taboo but also revealed the surprising frequency with which people were coupling and engaging in sexual relations of countless varieties.

Kinsey thus debuted sex as a science, paving the way for others to dig below statistics into the realm of biology. In 1966 gynecologist William Masters and psychologist Virginia Johnson—who originally hailed from Washington University before founding their own research institute in St. Louis—described for the first time the sexual response cycle (how the body responds to sexual stimulation), based on observations of

382 women and 312 men undergoing some 10,000 such cycles. The cycle begins with excitation, as blood rushes to the penis in men, and as the clitoris, vulva and vagina enlarge and grow moist in women. Gradually, people reach a plateau, in which they are fully aroused but not yet at orgasm. After reaching orgasm, they enter the resolution phase, in which the tissues return to the preexcitation stage.

In the 1970s psychiatrist Helen Singer Kaplan of the Human Sexuality Program at Weill Medical College of Cornell University added a critical element to this cycle—desire—based on her experience as a sex therapist. In her three-stage model, desire precedes sexual excitation, which is then followed by orgasm. Because desire is mainly psychological, Kaplan emphasized the importance of the mind in the sexual experience and the destructive forces of anxiety, defensiveness and failure of communication.

In the late 1980s gynecologist Rosemary Basson of the University of British Columbia proposed a more circular sexual cycle, which, despite the term, had been described as a largely linear progression in previous work. Basson suggested that desire might both lead to genital stimulation and be invigorated by it. Countering the idea that orgasm is the pinnacle of the experience, she placed it as a mere spot on the circle, asserting that a person could feel sexually satisfied at any of the stages leading up to an orgasm, which thus does not have to be the ultimate goal of sexual activity.

Dissecting Desire

Given the importance of desire in this cycle, researchers have long wanted to identify its key ingredients. Conventional wisdom casts the male triggers in simplistic sensory terms, with tactile and visual stimuli being particularly enticing. Men are drawn to visual erotica, explaining the lure of magazines such as *Playboy*. Meanwhile female desire is supposedly fueled by a richer cognitive and emotional texture. "Women experience desire as a result of the context in which they are inserted—whether they feel comfortable with themselves and the partner, feel safe and perceive a true bond with the partner," opines urologist Jennifer Berman of the Female Sexual Medicine Center at the University of California, Los Angeles.

Yet sexual imagery devoid of emotional connections can arouse women just as it can men, a 2007 study shows. Psychologist Meredith Chivers of the Center for Addiction and Mental Health in Toronto and her colleagues gauged the degree of sexual arousal in about 100 women and men, both homosexual and heterosexual, while they watched erotic film clips. The clips depicted same-sex intercourse, solitary masturbation or nude exercise—performed by men and women—as well as male-female intercourse and mating between bonobos (close ape relatives of the chimpanzee).

The researchers found that although nude exercise genitally aroused all the onlookers the least and intercourse excited them the most, the type of actor was more important for the men than for the women. Heterosexual women's level of arousal increased along with the intensity of the sexual activity largely irrespective of who or what was engaged in it. In fact, these women were geni-

tally excited by male and female actors equally and also responded physically to bonobo copulation. (Gay women, however, were more particular; they did not react sexually to men masturbating or exercising naked.)

The men, by contrast, were physically titillated mainly by their preferred category of sexual partner—that is, females for straight men and males for gay men—and were not excited by bonobo copulation. The results, the researchers say, suggest that women are not only aroused by a variety of types of sexual imagery but are more flexible than men in their sexual interests and preferences.

When it comes to orgasm, simple sensations as well as higher-level mental processes probably also play a role in both sexes. Although Kinsey characterized orgasm in purely physical terms, psychologist Barry R. Komisaruk of Rutgers University has defined the experience as more multifaceted. In their book *The Science of Orgasm* (Johns Hopkins University Press, 2006), Komisaruk, endocrinologist Carlos Beyer-Flores of the Tlaxcala Laboratory in Mexico and Rutgers sexologist Beverly Whipple describe orgasm as maximal excitation generated by a gradual summing of responses from the body's sensory receptors, combined with complex cognitive and emotional forces. Similarly, psychologist Kent Berridge of the University of Michigan at Ann Arbor has described sexual pleasure as a kind of "gloss" that the brain's emotional hub, the limbic system, applies over the primary sensations.

The relative weights of sensory and emotional influences on orgasm may differ between the sexes, perhaps because of its diverging evolutionary origins. Orgasm in men is directly tied to reproduction through ejaculation, whereas female orgasm has a less obvious evolutionary role. Orgasm in a woman might physically aid in the retention of sperm, or it may play a subtler social function, such as facilitating bonding with her mate. If female orgasm evolved primarily for social reasons, it might elicit more complex thoughts and feelings in women than it does in men.

Simple sensations and more complex mental processes probably contribute to orgasm in both sexes.

Forgetting Fear

But does it? Researchers are trying to crack this riddle by probing changes in brain activity during orgasm in both men and women. Neuroscientist Gert Holstege of the University of Groningen in the Netherlands and his colleagues attempted to solve the male side of the equation by asking the female partners of 11 men to stimulate their partner's penis until he ejaculated while they scanned his brain using positron-emission tomography (PET). During ejaculation, the researchers saw extraordinary activation of the ventral tegmental area (VTA), a major hub of the brain's reward circuitry; the intensity of this response is comparable to that induced by heroin. "Because ejaculation introduces sperm into the female reproductive tract, it would be critical for reproduction of the species to favor ejaculation as a most rewarding behavior," the researchers wrote in 2003 in *The Journal of Neuroscience*.

The scientists also saw heightened activity in brain regions involved in memory-related imagery and in vision itself, perhaps because the volunteers used visual imagery to hasten orgasm. The anterior part of the cerebellum also switched into high gear. The cerebellum has long been labeled the coordinator of motor behaviors but has more recently revealed its role in emotional processing. Thus, the cerebellum could be the seat of the emotional components of orgasm in men, perhaps helping to coordinate those emotions with planned behaviors. The amygdala, the brain's center of vigilance and sometimes fear, showed a decline in activity at ejaculation, a probable sign of decreasing vigilance during sexual performance.

To find out whether orgasm looks similar in the female brain, Holstege's team asked the male partners of 12 women to stimulate their partner's clitoris—the site whose excitation most easily leads to orgasm—until she climaxed, again inside a PET scanner. Not surprisingly, the team reported in 2006, clitoral stimulation by itself led to activation in areas of the brain involved in receiving and perceiving sensory signals from that part of the body and in describing a body sensation—for instance, labeling it "sexual."

When a woman reached orgasm, something unexpected happened: much of her brain went silent.

But when a woman reached orgasm, something unexpected happened: much of her brain went silent. Some of the most muted neurons sat in the left lateral orbitofrontal cortex, which may govern self-control over basic desires such as sex. Decreased activity there, the researchers suggest, might correspond to a release of tension and inhibition. The scientists also saw a dip in excitation in the dorsomedial prefrontal cortex, which has an apparent role in moral reasoning and social judgment—a change that may be tied to a suspension of judgment and reflection.

Brain activity fell in the amygdala, too, suggesting a depression of vigilance similar to that seen in men, who generally showed far less deactivation in their brain during orgasm than their female counterparts did. "Fear and anxiety need to be avoided at all costs if a woman wishes to have an orgasm; we knew that, but now we can see it happening in the depths of the brain," Holstege says. He went so far as to declare at the 2005 meeting of the European Society for Human Reproduction and Development: "At the moment of orgasm, women do not have any emotional feelings."

But that lack of emotion may not apply to all orgasms in women. Komisaruk, Whipple and their colleagues studied the patterns of brain activation that occur during orgasm in five women with spinal cord injuries that left them without sensation in their lower extremities. These women were able to achieve a "deep," or nonclitoral, orgasm through mechanical stimulation

Domestic Bliss

Is the pursuit of sexual gratification vital to the health of an established relationship? In her book *Mating in Captivity* (HarperCollins, 2006), New York–based psychotherapist Esther Perel emphasizes the importance of eroticism and orgasm in a marriage. She chronicles the typical dissolution of a couple's sex life when the love bond becomes politically correct and excessively domesticated. To avoid sexual staleness, Perel advocates unusual strategies such as cultivating separateness—developing different interests and groups of friends from those of your partner, for example—instead of closeness, as a way of making your partner more mysterious and exciting. She also suggests looking for creative ways to let fantasy and even a little craziness thrive within the confines of a long-term relationship.

Other psychologists, however, advise against placing too much emphasis on orgasm in a mature relationship. In her book *Peace Between the Sheets* (Frog Books, 2003), couples therapist Marnia Robinson suggests that the journey to orgasm renders us prisoners to dopamine, a neurotransmitter secreted in the brain's reward centers. After all, dopamine underlies other addictive behaviors, from gambling to drug abuse. In Robinson's view, partners should mutually unite in pleasure, without the sexual relationship necessarily having to be crowned by orgasm.

—M.P.

(using a laboratory device) of the vagina and cervix. But contrary to Holstege's results, Komisaruk's team found that orgasm was accompanied by a general activation of the limbic system, the brain's seat of emotion.

Among the activated limbic regions were the amygdala and the hypothalamus, which produces oxytocin, the putative love and bonding hormone whose levels jump fourfold at orgasm. The researchers also found heightened activity in the nucleus accumbens, a critical part of the brain's reward circuitry that may mediate orgasmic pleasure in women. In addition, they saw unusual activity in the anterior cingulate cortex and the insula, two brain areas that Rutgers anthropologist Helen Fisher has found come to life during the later stages of love relationships. Such activity may connect a female's sexual pleasure with the emotional bond she feels with her partner.

Pleasure Pill?

Disentangling the connections between orgasm, reproduction and love may someday yield better medications and psychotherapies for sexual problems. As Marianne's case illustrates, the answer is usually not as simple as a hormone boost. Instead her improvement was probably the result of the activation or inactivation of relevant parts of her brain by social triggers she encountered while participating in an experiment whose purpose centered on female sexual arousal. Indeed, many sex therapies revolve around opening the mind to new ways of thinking about sex or about your sexual partner [see box].

Companies are also working on medications that act on the nervous system to stimulate desire. One such experimental compound is a peptide called bremelanotide, which is under development by Palatin Technologies in Cranbury, N.J. It blocks certain receptors in the brain that are involved in regulating basic drives such as eating and sex. In human studies bremelanotide has prompted spontaneous erections in men and boosted sexual arousal and desire in women, but the U.S. Food and Drug Administration has held up its progress out of concern over side effects such as rising blood pressure.

Continued scientific dissection of the experience of orgasm may lead to new pharmaceutical and psychological avenues for enhancing the experience. Yet overanalyzing this moment of intense pleasure might also put a damper on the fun. That is what the science tells us anyway.

Further Readings

Brain Activation during Human Male Ejaculation. Gert Holstege et al., in *Journal of Neuroscience,* vol. 23, no. 27, pages 9185–9193; October 8, 2003.

Brain Activation during Vaginocervical Self-Stimulation and Orgasm in Women with Complete Spinal Cord Injury: FMRI Evidence of Mediation by the Vagus Nerves. Barry R. Komisaruk et al., in *Brain Research,* vol. 1024, nos. 1–2, pages 77–88; October 2004.

Testosterone Patch Increases Sexual Activity and Desire in Surgically Menopausal Women with Hypoactive Sexual Desire. James Simon et al., in *Journal of Clinical Endocrinology & Metabolism,* vol. 90, no. 9, pages 5226–5233; September 2005.

Regional Cerebral Blood Flow Changes Associated with Clitorally Induced Orgasm in Healthy Women. Janniko R. Georgiadis et al., in *European Journal of Neuroscience,* vol. 24, no. 11, pages 3305–3316; December 2006.

Critical Thinking

1. What is the role of the brain with respect to arousal and desire?
2. Discuss sexual arousal and orgasm from a biological perspective.

MARTIN PORTNER is a neurologist living in Brazil. He is author of *Inteligência Sexual* (*Sexual Intelligence,* Editora Gente, 1999). He lectures and leads workshops on the brain and creativity.

Women's Vibrator Use in Sexual Partnerships: Results from a Nationally Representative Survey in the United States

DEBRA HERBENICK ET AL.

Vibrators may be recommended as adjunct therapy for the treatment of anorgasmia, hypoactive desire disorder, and persistent sexual arousal syndrome, as well as for sexual enhancement and pleasure (Leiblum & Nathan, 2002; LoPiccolo & Lobitz, 1972; Phillips, 2000). Although some women may use vibrators exclusively during solitary masturbation, it is likely that—due to clinicians' recommendations, personal exploration, or requests from a partner—some women may use their vibrator with a sexual partner. In a recent study of vulvar vibration therapy for vulvar pain, 44 percent of participants reported that their partner assisted with treatment (Zolnoun, Lamvu, & Steege, 2008).

Kinsey, Pomeroy, Martin, and Gebhard (1953) and Hite (1976) noted that women's use of vibrators was rare; however, as vibrators have become more widely available through adult bookstores, in-home sex toy parties, the internet, and retail stores, vibrator use has become increasingly common (Curtis, 2004; Leiblum, 2001; Loe, 1999; Reece, Herbenick, & Sherwood-Puzzello, 2004). However, few studies have explored partnered use of vibrators or the relational context in which vibrators are used.

In a convenience sample of women who had made purchases from a sex toy catalog, Davis, Blank, Lin and Bonillas (1996) found that 80 percent of the lesbian women, 71 percent of the bisexual women, and 73 percent of the heterosexual women respondents had used a vibrator with a partner and about 10 percent of the women surveyed indicated that their partner had a negative or "unenthusiastic" response to their vibrator use. More recently, a report of nationally representative survey data in the United States indicated that approximately 40 percent of women who currently used vibrators had used a vibrator with a partner and that about 90 percent of women who had used sexual aids were comfortable telling their partner (Berman Center, 2004).

Understanding partner dynamics related to vibrator use is important because some women have concerns about how

their partner will feel about their solitary use of vibrators or about the proposition of partnered use of vibrators. These concerns may hinder a woman's or couple's acceptance or use of vibrators, whether for clinical reasons or for private sexual exploration. In fact, women's concerns about introducing sex toys to their relationship partner have been found to be reflected in the types of questions that women ask at in-home sex toy parties (Fisher, Herbenick, Reece, Satinsky, & Fischtein, in press).

Partnered use of vibrators may vary based on a woman's sexual orientation or the gender of her partner, as may a woman's perceptions of her partner's attitudes toward solitary or coupled vibrator use. As such, it is important to examine partnered use in the context of sexual orientation. Data about partnered vibrator use can inform women and their partners about what is common among other couples and provide context for the use of vibrators during partnered sex.

Few scientific studies have examined women's partnered vibrator use and its correlates in a nationally representative sample. In an earlier analysis of data from the study reported here, we found that 37.3 percent of women had used a vibrator during intercourse with a partner and 40.9 percent had used a vibrator during sex play or foreplay with a partner (Herbenick, Reece, Sanders, Dodge, Ghassemi, & Fortenberry, 2009). However, in that study we did not examine characteristics of partnered vibrator use or partnered use by sexual orientation. The purpose of this current study was to document the prevalence of their vibrator use with a partner, among a nationally representative sample of women in the United States, and their reasons for using a vibrator, points of access to vibrators, relationships between vibrator use and sexual function, their partner's knowledge of and perceived liking of their vibrator use, and associations between women's assessment of their partners' perceptions of vibrator use and their sexual satisfaction.

Methods

In April 2008, data were collected from a population-based, cross-sectional survey of 2056 women aged 18–60 years in the United States via an existing research panel from Knowledge Networks (Menlo Park, CA). Knowledge Networks has established research panels based on random digit dialing methods which provided a nonzero probability selection of U.S. households with a telephone that are statistically adjusted monthly, based on updates from the U.S. Census Bureau. All data are collected by Knowledge Networks via the Internet; all participants in a given Knowledge Networks panel are provided with access to the Internet and hardware if needed. Several studies have used Knowledge Networks data collection for health-related research, providing support for the validity of such methods for obtaining nationally representative data from the U.S. population (Baker, Wagner, Singer, & Bundorf, 2003; Heiss, McFadden, & Winter, 2006; Holman, Silver, Poulin, Andersen, Gil-Rivas, & McIntosh, 2008; Silver, Holman, McIntosh, Poulin, & Gil-Rivas, 2002; Knowledge Networks, 2003).

A total of 3800 women panel members were invited to participate in the study which was described as being about sexual enhancement products. These individuals received up to three e-mail invitations or reminders and one telephone reminder. Of those invited to participate, 2338 women (61.5 percent) responded to the recruitment message, with 2056 women (87.9 percent) consenting to participate. This resulted in a response rate of 54.1 percent.

During analyses, post-stratification data weights were used to reduce variance and minimize bias due to nonsampling error. Distributions for age, race, gender, Hispanic ethnicity, education, and U.S. census region were used in the post-stratification adjustment. All study protocols were approved by the Institutional Review Board of the authors' academic institution and were in accordance with the Helsinki Declaration of 1975, revised 1983.

Measures

Participants completed items related to socio-demographics, health status, sexual behaviors and vibrator use, sexual function, and vibrator use. Socio-demographic measures included those related to age, gender, education, ethnicity, sexual orientation, geographic location, relationship status, gender of one's partner, household income, and having children at home.

Sexual behavior was assessed through questions about partnered sexual activities and self-masturbation during the 4 weeks prior to the study. Participants were asked to indicate whether they had used vibrators, lubricants, or nonvibrating dildos during the past month, past year, and lifetime. They were also asked for these time periods whether they had used vibrators while masturbating alone, during foreplay with a partner, and during sexual intercourse with a partner.

Women were grouped into two categories based on their vibrator use—Ever Users (those who reported having ever used a vibrator during masturbation or partnered sexual activities) and Never Users (those who reported never having used

a vibrator). Women who had used vibrators were asked how they had obtained vibrators in the past, as well as their reasons for beginning to use a vibrator. The latter question included an open-ended response option if their reason for using a vibrator was not listed. Regardless of vibrator use history, all participants were asked to rate their level of comfort using a vibrator alone and with a partner. Also, women were asked whether their partner knew that they used a vibrator and, if so, to what extent did their partner like or dislike the fact that they used a vibrator. If their partner did not know that they used a vibrator, they were asked why their partner did not know.

Sexual satisfaction was assessed through administration of the Female Sexual Function Index (FSFI), a 19-item measure with established reliability, validity, and temporal stability that is commonly used to assess the sexual function domains of desire, arousal, lubrication, pain, orgasm, and satisfaction (Rosen et al., 2000; Ter Kuile, Brauer, & Laan, 2006; Verit & Verit, 2007; Wiegel, Meston, & Rosen, 2005; Witting et al., 2008). The satisfaction sub-scale of the FSFI is comprised of the following three items: (1) Over the past 4 weeks, how satisfied have you been with the amount of emotional closeness during sexual activity between you and your partner? (2) Over the past 4 weeks, how satisfied have you been with your sexual relationship with your partner? and (3) Over the past 4 weeks, how satisfied have you been with your overall sexual life? Response choices include very satisfied, moderately satisfied, about equally satisfied and dissatisfied, moderately dissatisfied, and very dissatisfied. Satisfaction subscale scores range from 0.8 to 6 with a higher score indicating greater satisfaction.

Statistical Analysis

SPSS version 16.0 (Chicago, IL) was used for analyses. Descriptive statistics were used to report sample characteristics as well as the proportion of women who had, within each sexual orientation group, masturbated, used vibrators, lubricant, or dildos and who had obtained vibrators from various sources. Descriptive statistics were also used to report women's reasons for beginning to use vibrators, their comfort using vibrators alone or with a partner, and their perceptions of their partner's knowledge and liking of their vibrator use. Due to the highly uneven group sizes, statistical comparisons were not made between sexual orientation groups. However, findings are presented separately for each group within the tables.

To assess the reliability of the FSFI subscales for this sample, a cronbach's alpha was calculated. Within each sexual orientation group, analysis of covariance (ANCOVA) was used to examine the relationship between ever having used a vibrator and scores on the FSFI, with age as a covariate given that age is known to be related to sexual function. In addition, a new variable was created that differentiated whether a woman's partner (a) knew and somewhat or strongly liked that she used a vibrator or (b) did not know or knew but somewhat or strongly disliked it. Using this new variable, and within each sexual orientation group, ANCOVA was used to examine the relationship between a woman's partner's knowledge and perceptions of their liking the participants' vibrator use and participants' scores on the FSFI satisfaction subscale with age as a covariate.

Results
Participants

Of the 2056 women who completed the survey, 2051 reported a sexual orientation and were included in orientation-specific analyses. Of these, 94.1 percent (n = 1929) identified as heterosexual, 1.8 percent (n = 37) as homosexual/lesbian, and 3.4 percent (n = 70) as bisexual. A total of 15 women identified their sexual orientation as "other," 11 of whom indicated that they were in a relationship with a man. These 11 individuals are included only in analyses of the total sample.

Sexual orientation identification was highly consistent with the gender of participants' partners. Among those women who were in relationships, 99.4 percent of heterosexual-identified women were in a relationship with a man and 100 percent of lesbians were in a relationship with another woman. Nearly all (93.5 percent) bisexual women had a male relationship partner. Consequently, these three sexual orientation categories rather than the gender of participants' current partner were used to stratify the sample.

Masturbation

Approximately one-fifth of women in the total sample reported masturbating at least once per week during the previous 4 weeks, with bisexual women being most likely to report frequent masturbation. Nearly half (47.4 percent) of heterosexual women and the majority of lesbian and bisexual women had masturbated during the previous month.

Use of Sexual Enhancement Products

A total of 62.0 percent of women in the total sample had ever used lubricant during sexual activities and one out of four had done so during the previous month; this rate of "ever use" ranged from 61.4 percent to 81.6 percent depending on sexual orientation. While about one-quarter of heterosexual and lesbian women had used lubricant during the previous month, 40.5 percent of bisexual women had done so.

Although solitary and partnered vibrator use was common among heterosexual women, the vast majority of lesbian and bisexual women reported having used vibrators in these contexts. A total of 51.2 percent (n = 968) of heterosexual, 70.6 percent (n = 26) of lesbian, and 79.7 percent (n = 55) of bisexual women had ever used a vibrator (whether alone or with a partner); these participants are termed "Ever Users" in subsequent analyses related to vibrator use.

The use of a nonvibrating dildo was also common with nearly one-third of women in the total sample reporting having ever used a dildo for sexual stimulation and 9.3 percent having done so in the past month. Again, dildo use—while common among heterosexual women—was more common among lesbian and bisexual women.

Access Points

The most common way that women of all sexual orientation groups had accessed vibrators was by purchasing one for themselves (61.1 percent of Ever Users). The same proportion of lesbian Ever Users (78.8 percent) who had bought a vibrator for themselves had also bought one for a sexual partner. In fact, heterosexual women rarely indicated that they had bought a vibrator for a sexual partner (9.7 percent), something that 1 out of 4 bisexual women had done. For heterosexual and bisexual Ever Users, the second most common means of acquiring a vibrator was from a sexual partner (42 percent heterosexual women, 38.1 percent bisexual women), which was also frequent among lesbians (36.3 percent). The least common access point listed, 7.1 percent of Ever Users had been given a vibrator by a family member.

Reasons for Use

Most women indicated that they had begun using vibrators "for fun" or curiosity. Approximately one-third of Ever Users reported having begun vibrator use to make it easier to orgasm or to "spice up" their sex life. About a quarter did so for partner-related reasons: either because they didn't have a partner at the time (25.3 percent of the total sample) or because their partner wanted them to (27.6 percent)—the latter being more commonly reported by heterosexual women. Lesbian women—strikingly more often than heterosexual or bisexual women—indicated that they first started using vibrators to make it easier for their partner to have an orgasm (25.1 percent among lesbians versus 1.5 percent of heterosexual women and 2.4 percent of bisexual women).

Less than 5 percent of Ever Users indicated that they started using vibrators for reasons other than those listed. A total of 45 women provided reasons including that their spouse had been deployed, they had a high sex drive, they didn't like having sex with their partner, they had concerns about the safety of having sex with a partner, their partner was not able to have sex, they were in a "sexless marriage," to heal from sexual abuse, because they had been given one by a partner or friend, or because their partner wouldn't have sex with them while they were pregnant.

Comfort Using Vibrators

The vast majority of Ever Users indicated that they felt "somewhat" or "very" comfortable using a vibrator alone (85.0 percent) or with a partner (69.6 percent). Among Never Users, about one-quarter of heterosexual and lesbian Never Users indicated that they would feel comfortable using a vibrator alone as did more than one-half of the bisexual Never Users. Although one-fifth of Never Users indicated that they would feel comfortable using a vibrator with a partner. This was largely found among heterosexual and bisexual identified women. None of the lesbian Never Users indicated a significant level of comfort using a vibrator with a partner, although 62.5 percent did indicate that they would feel "a little" comfortable.

Partner Knowledge and Perceived Liking of Vibrator Use

The vast majority of heterosexual (85.9 percent) and bisexual (89.7 percent) Ever Users and all of the lesbian Ever Users indicated that their partners knew that they used a vibrator. Similarly, most Ever Users (80.1 percent heterosexual, 100 percent lesbian, and 64.0 percent bisexual women) felt that their partners somewhat or strongly liked the fact that they used a vibrator.

A total of 43 women provided reasons that their partner did not know they used a vibrator. These included that they did not feel comfortable telling their partner; concerns about hurting their partner's feelings, insulting him or making him feel inadequate; or feeling embarrassed to tell their partner. One woman indicated that her male partner was "oblivious and celibate."

Several women indicated that their male partner had previously made comments that knowing that she masturbated or used sex toys would "question his manhood" or "make him feel less of a man"; others expressed their own concerns that their partner would feel jealous or threatened. Another woman indicated that she was dating someone with whom she was not sexually active. Quite a few women said their partner didn't know because they hadn't told them, but they did not necessarily provide any additional information. Some said that they didn't feel it was important to tell their partner or that they used it privately. One woman wrote:

> I don't know, because he feels that he is all I need. . .maybe because I haven't tried to tell him because I like using it on myself just for me. . . it's my me time without him. . . he satisfies me completely but I like my vibrator because it feels good.

Expressions of anticipated positive reactions from a partner were rare. One woman indicated that although she hadn't yet told her partner that she used a vibrator, she thought he would "think it's hot."

Vibrator Use and Sexual Function

Ever Users in the total sample scored significantly higher than Never Users on all FSFI domains with the exception of the FSFI satisfaction subscale and the total score. Reliability analyses in this sample demonstrated sufficient reliability (0.80 to 0.98) for each subscale and the total score and within each sexual orientation group.

When analyzed separately by sexual orientation, heterosexual Ever Users scored significantly higher on the FSFI desire subscale compared to Never Users, $F(1,1917) = 97.3, p < .001$. There were no significant differences for lesbian or bisexual women.

Heterosexual Ever Users scored significantly higher on the FSFI arousal subscale compared to Never Users, $F(1,1910) = 185.0, p < .001$, as did bisexual Ever Users, $F(1,65) = 13.2, p < .002$. Scores for lesbian vibrator user groups were not significantly different.

On the FSFI lubrication subscale, heterosexual Ever Users scored significantly higher than Never Users, $F(1,1891) = 148.6, p < .001$ as did bisexual Ever Users, $F(1,65) = 5.4, p < .03$. No significant differences were found between lesbian users groups.

Lesbian Ever Users scored significantly higher on the FSFI orgasm subscale compared to Never Users, $F(1,28) = 15.07, p < .002$. There were significant differences between heterosexual or bisexual user groups.

On the FSFI satisfaction subscale, lesbian Ever Users scored significantly higher than Never Users, $F(1,26) = 7.4, p < .02$. No significant differences were found among heterosexual or bisexual user groups.

Heterosexual Ever Users scored significantly higher on the FSFI pain subscale compared to Never Users, $F(1,1898) = 52.1, p < .001$, with no significant differences found among lesbian or bisexual women.

On the FSFI Total Score, no significant differences were found between user groups within any of the three sexual orientation categories.

Sexual Satisfaction and Partner Knowledge/Perceived Liking of Vibrator Use

The FSFI satisfaction subscale exhibited strong reliability in this sample (Cronbach's alpha was calculated at 0.92 for the total sample, 0.92 among heterosexual women, 0.94 among lesbians, and 0.88 among bisexual women). After controlling for age, partner knowledge and perceived liking of vibrator use was a significant predictor of sexual satisfaction for heterosexual women, $F(1,343) = 10.04, p < .01$, omega squared = .03, as well as for bisexual women, $F(1,33) = 13.58, p < .01$, omega squared = .26. As all lesbian women indicated that their partner knew about and liked their vibrator use, it was not possible to conduct a similar analysis among lesbians.

Discussion

In a nationally representative study of women aged 18 to 60, the purpose of this study was to document the prevalence of women's vibrator use with a partner and the relational and contextual factors associated with partnered vibrator use. This study was the first to examine partnered vibrator use among heterosexual, lesbian, and bisexual women in a nationally representative sample and to assess sexual function as it relates to vibrator use among women of varied sexual orientations.

Results of this study demonstrate that partnered vibrator use is common among heterosexual, lesbian, and bisexual women, as is the use of other sexual enhancement products such as lubricants and dildos. Although a large proportion of women reported having received a vibrator from another person (usually a sexual partner), the most common way that women accessed vibrators reflected a sense of female agency as the majority of women who had previously used vibrators had bought one for themselves and about 12 percent had purchased one for a sexual partner.

Although vibrators are commonly recommended to women and their partners as adjunct therapy for sexual problems— and indeed, about one-third of women cited ease of orgasm as a reason for use—the reasons that women most often cited for beginning to use vibrators were related to sexual pleasure, enhancement, and recreation. In addition, considering the difficulty with which many individuals discuss sexuality, sexual health professionals may find it encouraging that nearly one-fifth of Ever Users had begun using a vibrator as a result of hearing from their friends that they are fun to use. In fact, even women who had never used vibrators expressed an openness and comfort using vibrators—alone or with a partner—in considerable numbers, which may be useful for clinicians to keep in mind when determining whether they should recommend the use of vibrators to individuals or couples who are vibrator naïve.

In addition, although concerns are often expressed about introducing a vibrator into a partnered relationship, data from this study overwhelmingly demonstrate that women's partners—whether male or female—are perceived as feeling positively toward their partner's vibrator use. The vast majority of women who used vibrators indicated that their partner knew and, in most cases, liked that they used a vibrator. A few voiced concerns that male partners might have a negative reaction if they knew about their vibrator use. Perhaps as vibrators have become more commonplace in popular culture and more available to women and men, they have become more widely accepted within women's sexual relationships and for both clinical and enhancement purposes.

Although women of all sexual orientations who had used vibrators had significantly more positive sexual function than women who had not, the relationship of vibrator use to sexual function was markedly different by sexual orientation. Heterosexual women who had used vibrators had significantly more positive sexual function on the desire, arousal, lubrication, and pain subscales, whereas lesbian Ever Users' scores were significantly greater only for the orgasm and satisfaction subscales. Whether this is related to reasons for using vibrators (lesbian women also more often indicated starting to use vibrators for their own or a partner's orgasm or for fun) or other reasons is unclear.

Also of importance is the significant relationship between partner knowledge and liking of women's vibrator use and women's satisfaction. It may be that being able to communicate openly and feel that one's sexual interests and pleasures are accepted by one's partner enhances satisfaction. In addition, it may be that only in a satisfying relationship do some women feel comfortable enough to disclose information about their sexual interests, fantasies, or private masturbation. Certainly this relationship warrants further study, particularly as it is not just the ability to disclose one's vibrator use—but the dynamic experience of feeling that one's sexuality is accepted or liked by one's partner—that was related to satisfaction.

Strengths and Limitations

There were several strengths to this study. Nationally representative sampling techniques were used as were data weights in order to calculate population estimates of vibrator use behavior. In addition, the ability to include open-ended response options provided a more thorough understanding of women's reasons for using vibrators, as well as why their partner did not know that they used a vibrator. The fact that the panel members were accustomed to providing data confidentially to Knowledge Networks perhaps assuaged any concerns about providing information to the research team about their intimate relationships and sexual behavior.

A limitation of the study is that, given that lesbian and bisexual women are a sexual minority in the United States, there were relatively few women in the sample who identified as such. Thus it is difficult to draw comparisons between sexual orientation groups in regard to vibrator use and the small subsample sizes may limit a representation of diversity among lesbian and bisexual women with respect to vibrators. Future research might examine vibrator use with oversampling of sexual minorities. Also, given that the survey was conducted over the internet, this study faced the same limitations as others that use survey-based techniques in that participants were not able to ask questions about items that they wished to clarify.

Implications

These data have several important implications. Clinically, sexual health professionals may find it useful to provide data to their patients and clients about the prevalence of partnered vibrator use and the fact that most women report that their partners like that they use a vibrator. Such knowledge may help some women to feel more positive or reassured about using a vibrator in a therapeutic manner or for sexual enhancement. In addition, educating clients about the finding that most women begin using vibrators for reasons of pleasure or enjoyment—but that a significant proportion use them for ease of orgasm—may help to ease perceived stigma associated with vibrator use as well as that associated with women's difficulty experiencing orgasm. Knowing that each is a common experience may help some women to feel less alone.

In addition, findings from this study underscore the important association between satisfaction and openness within one's relationship, a theme that warrants attention in both clinical settings and in research. Related are the concerns that some women have about telling their male partner about their vibrator use, such as concerns about offending or hurting their partner, or making him feel less masculine. For some couples, gendered norms related to sexual pleasure and agency are salient and may need to be attended to with care.

These data also have important implications for further research. They highlight, for example, the markedly different patterns of sexual behavior and attitudes that researchers have previously noted among bisexual, as compared to heterosexual or lesbian, women and the need to be attentive to these potential differences when categorizing women in research or clinical applications (Sanders, Graham, & Milhausen, 2008). These data also serve as important benchmarks in the current state of knowledge of women's use of vibrators and sexual enhancement products at a time when the sexual enhancement industry has been growing exponentially. Namely, they demonstrate that vibrator use is common among sexual partners, that most women's partners know about their vibrator use (and appear to like it), and that couple dynamics in regard to women being able to be open about their sexual interests—and feel accepted for them—is associated with higher rates of satisfaction.

REFERENCES

Baker, L., Wagner, T. H., Singer, S., & Bundorf, M. K. (2003). Use of the Internet and e-mail for health care information: Results from a national survey. *Journal of the American Medical Association, 289,* 2400–2406.

Berman Center. (2004). *The health benefits of sexual aids and devices: A comprehensive study of their relationship to satisfaction and quality of life.*

Curtis, D. (2004). Commodities and sexual subjectivities: a look at capitalism and its desires. *Cultural Anthropology, 19,* 95–121.

Davis, C. M., Blank, J., Lin, H.-Y., & Bonillas, C. (1996). Characteristics of vibrator use among women. *Journal of Sex Research, 33,* 313–320.

Fisher, C., Herbenick, D., Reece, M., Satinsky, S., & Fischtein, D. (in press). Exploring sexuality education opportunities at in-home sex toy parties in the United States. *Sex Education.*

Heiss, F., McFadden, D., & Winter, J. (2006). Who failed to enroll in Medicare Part D, and why? Early results. *Health Affairs (Millwood), 25,* 344–354.

Herbenick, D., Reece, M., Sanders, S. A., Dodge, B., Ghassemi, A., & Fortenberry, J. D. (2009). Prevalence and characteristics of vibrator use by women in the United States: Results from a nationality representative study. *Journal of Sexual Medicine, 6,* 1857–1866.

Hite, S. (1976). *The Hite Report.* New York: Macmillan.

Holman, E. A., Silver, R. C., Poulin, M., Andersen, J., Gil-Rivas, V., & McIntosh, D. N. (2008). Terrorism, acute stress, and cardiovascular health: A 3-year national study following the September 11th attacks. *Archives of General Psychiatry, 65,* 73–80.

Kinsey, A. C., Pomeroy, W. B., Martin, C. E., & Gebhard, P. H. (1953). *Sexual behavior in the human female.* Philadelphia: Saunders.

Knowledge Networks. (2003). *Validity of the survey of health and Internet and Knowledge Network's panel and sampling.* Stanford, CA: Stanford University.

Leiblum, S. (2001). Women, sex and the internet. *Sexual and Relationship Therapy, 16,* 389–404.

Leiblum, S., & Nathan, S. (2002). Persistent sexual arousal syndrome in women: a not uncommon but little recognized complaint. *Sexual and Relationship Therapy, 17,* 191–198.

Loe, M. (1999). Feminism for sale: Case study of a pro-sex feminist business. *Gender & Society, 13,* 705–732.

LoPiccolo, J., & Lobitz, C. (1972). The role of masturbation in the treatment of orgasmic dysfunction. *Archives of Sexual Behavior, 2,* 163–171.

Phillips, N. A. (2000). Female sexual dysfunction: Evaluation and treatment. *American Family Physician, 62,* 127–136.

Reece, M., Herbenick, D., & Sherwood-Puzzello, C. (2004). Sexual health promotion and adult retail stores. *Journal of Sex Research, 41,* 173–180.

Rosen, R., Brown, C., Heiman, J., Leiblum, S., Meston, C., Shabsigh, R., et al., (2000). The Female Sexual Function Index (FSFI): a multidimensional self-report instrument for the assessment of female sexual function. *Journal of Sex and Marital Therapy, 26,* 191–208.

Sanders, S., Graham, C., & Milhausen, R. (2008). Bisexual women differ from lesbian and heterosexual women on several sexuality measures. *Sexualities, 17,* S157–S158.

Silver, R. C., Holman, E. A., McIntosh, D. N., Poulin, M., & Gil-Rivas, V. (2002). Nationwide longitudinal study of psychological responses to September 11. *Journal of the American Medical Association, 288,* 1235.

Ter Kuile, M. M., Brauer, M., & Laan, E. (2006). The Female Sexual Function Index (FSFI) and the Female Sexual Distress Scale (FSDS): Psychometric properties within a Dutch population. *Journal of Sex and Marital Therapy, 32,* 289–304.

Verit, F. F., & Verit, A. (2007). Validation of the female sexual function index in women with chronic pelvic pain. *Journal of Sexual Medicine, 4,* 1635–1641.

Wiegel, M., Meston, C., & Rosen, R. (2005). The Female Sexual Function Index (FSFI): Cross-validation and development of clinical cutoff scores. *Journal of Sex and Marital Therapy, 31,* 1–20.

Witting, K., Santtila, P., Jern, P., Varjonen, M., Wager, I., Hoglund, M., et al., (2008). Evaluation of the Female Sexual Function Index in a population based sample from Finland. *Archives of Sexual Behavior, 37,* 912–924.

Zolnoun, D., Lamvu, G., & Steege, J. (2008). Patient perceptions of vulvar vibration therapy for refractory vulvar pain. *Sexual and Relationship Therapy, 23,* 1–9.

Address correspondence to Debra Herbenick, PhD, MPH, Center for Sexual Health Promotion, Indiana University, Bloomington, IN 47405. E-mail: debby@indiana.edu

UNIT 3

Sexualities, Education, and Development

Unit Selections

Learning Outcomes

After reading this Unit, you will be able to:

- Describe the impact a human sexuality course can have on an individual.
- Explain how the Soc 152A Human Sexuality course became a campus institution at the University of California-Santa Barbara.
- Discuss how non-classroom-based sex education may be used to increase knowledge and empower participants.
- Describe how teenage fatherhood and delinquent behavior are linked.
- Explain the impact of teenage fatherhood on adolescent males' development and life course.
- Discuss the negative impact of teenage motherhood on adolescent females' development and life course.
- Discuss the social and cultural factors that may lead young women to want to have children as teenagers.
- Describe the relationship between teen birth rate and religiosity in the United States.
- Explain how researchers used publicly available data to understand the relationships among variables such as religiosity, income, birth rates, and abortion.
- Discuss the challenges that parents in general often face.
- Discuss the case against having children—are there compelling reasons some people should consider as they weigh whether to have children?
- Describe the potential impacts of gender role reversals as they relate to the worlds of work, childcare, and family life.
- Discuss the challenges that elderly people who live in institutional settings may face as they seek emotional and physical intimacy with another person.
- Assess how prevailing social and cultural beliefs about sex and the elderly can impact opportunities for intimate relationships in later life.

Student Website

www.mhhe.com/cls

Internet References

American Association of Retired Persons (AARP)
www.aarp.org
National Institute on Aging (NIA)
www.nih.gov/nia

SIECUS
www.siecus.org
World Association for Sexology
www.tc.umn.edu/nlhome/m201/colem001/was/wasindex.htm

Individual sexual development is a lifelong process that begins before we are born and continues until the day we die. Contrary to once popular ideas about this process, there are no latent periods in childhood or old age during which the individual is not a sexual being. Research into cognitive, social, and emotional development, however, reveals real differences through various life stages. This section devotes attention to different stages of life in relation to our close relationships, our identities, and our sexualities.

As children gain self-awareness, they naturally explore their own bodies, masturbate, display curiosity about the bodies of others, and show interest in the bodies of the people closest to them, such as their parents. Exploration and curiosity are important and healthy aspects of human development, yet adults sometimes make their children feel ashamed of being sexual or for showing interest in the human body. When adults impose their own personal feelings upon a child's innocuous explorations into sexuality, fail to communicate with children about this essential aspect of human life, or behave toward children in sexually inappropriate ways, long-term damage can occur. This can hinder full acceptance and enjoyment of one's sexuality later in life. The harm that has been done to someone as a child can further impact others—intimate partners and one's own children. The damage can go far beyond that of the hurt child.

Adolescence, the social stage accompanying puberty, and the transition to adulthood, proves to be a very stressful period of life for many individuals, as they attempt to develop an adult identity and forge relationships with others. This is especially true for far too many lesbian, gay, bisexual, and transgender adolescents. Extreme self-awareness, especially at this age, is not at all uncommon. During this period, young people of all sexual orientations may feel as though they are living in a fishbowl, as if everyone around them is examining their every action and reaction.

Partly because of the physical capacity of adolescents for reproduction, sexuality tends to be heavily censured by parents and society at this stage of life. Young people are living in increasingly complicated worlds. Prevailing societal messages are powerful, conflicting, and highly confusing. How do young people even start to make sense of the simultaneous messages of "Just Say No" and "Just Do It" to which they are constantly exposed? Mixed messages come from so many sources, including ads portraying adolescent bodies provocatively, and partially undressed images in "romance" novels, television shows, music videos, movies, and increasingly sexualized teenage "boy" and "girl" singers and actors. The Internet, with an endless supply of chat rooms and social networking websites, is another potential source of influence.

The media both influence and provide a reflection of individual and societal attitudes that place tremendous emphasis on sexual attractiveness (especially for females)

© Corbis Royalty Free

and sexual competency (especially for males). The physical, emotional, and cultural pressures described in the preceding paragraphs combine to create confusion and anxiety in young adults about whether they are "normal." Information through education and assurances from adults can alleviate these stresses and facilitate positive and responsible sexuality. This is especially possible where there is trust and willingness to communicate across generations.

Sexuality finally becomes socially validated in adulthood, at least within heterosexual marriage. Whether we are young or old, gay or straight, bisexual, intersexed, or transsexual, we have a lot more in common than many people realize. Regardless of our age, we all need accurate information about sex. Even as adults, we make social comparisons of various kinds, continuing to try to figure out where and how we fit into the world around us. We rely on the feedback we get from others and information on how others perceive us to actually tell us about ourselves. Peers provide some of that information. Some of it we get from our families. Perhaps much more of that information than we realize comes from the media.

Adult sexualities can be a source of joy, pain, validation, confusion, and so many other things both positive and negative. Many people seek fulfillment through their relationships. Keeping a relationship strong requires hard work and the commitment of both partners. Routine, boredom, stress, financial pressures, work, parenting responsibilities, and lack of effective communication can exact heavy tolls on the quantity and quality of sexual interactions. Sexual misinformation, myths, and unanswered questions—especially about changes in sexual arousal, response, and functioning—can also undermine or hinder intimacy and sexual fulfillment in the middle years.

Sexuality in late adulthood has been misunderstood (and underestimated) because of the prevailing misconception that only young and attractive people are sexual. Such an attitude has contributed significantly to the apparent decline in sexual interest and activity as one grows older. However, as population demographics have shifted and the baby boomer generation has aged, these beliefs and attitudes have begun to change.

Physiological changes in the aging process are not, in and of themselves, detrimental to sexual expression. A life history of experiences, good health, and growth can make sexual expression in the later years a most rewarding and fulfilling experience. Today's aging population is becoming more vocal in letting their children and grandchildren know that as we age we don't grow out of sex and that, in fact, it can get better with age.

At UC Santa Barbara, Sex as a Matter of Course

Sex as a matter of course; Professors John and Janice Baldwin, married 41 years, are trusted voices on love at UC Santa Barbara.

LARRY GORDON

How well should people know each other before they have sex?

In the biggest classroom at UC Santa Barbara, sociology professors John and Janice Baldwin are reeling off survey results showing that male and female students are almost equally willing to sleep with someone they love. But the hall erupts in knowing laughter as a gender gap emerges: Men, the long-married couple reports, remain eager for sex through descending categories of friendship and casual acquaintance. Women don't.

By the time Janice Baldwin gets to the statistic on sex between strangers, the din from the 600 students is so loud, they can hardly hear her announce that 37% of men would have sex with a person they had just met, compared with only 7% of women.

"So you can see, males are a little more likely to go to bed with somebody they don't know very well," Baldwin says dryly.

"Or at all," she adds, to guffaws.

By turns humorous and deadly serious, "Sociology of Human Sexuality" has been an institution at the beachside campus for more than two decades. So have the Baldwins, unflappable sixty-somethings who are trusted voices on love and lovemaking for thousands of current and former UC Santa Barbara students.

Today's undergraduates have easy access to X-rated Internet sites, and many have watched television gurus dissect troubled marriages. But there are often gaps in their knowledge of biology and sexual behavior, the result of squeamish parents and less-than-candid high school health teachers.

The Baldwins step in with data about orgasm, birth control and infertility—and, implicitly, with their own example of a 41-year marriage that seems to work well.

"We don't feel we are the sex king and queen of the world," Janice Baldwin, 63, said recently in the cramped office the couple share, their desks touching. "So this is not about us. It's about the students, and we are privileged to get to teach a class that can help them avoid the downsides of sex and increase the positives."

John Baldwin, 68, said he and his wife do not aim to be role models. "We are not trying to teach them to be like us," he said. "But we are going to be talking about relationships, and a lot of them want relationships. Even though there is a lot of casual sex, they want to find somebody special. . . . So we are little hope signals."

Students say the class is fun, eye-opening and altogether useful. Clearly, many of them pay attention: Lectures on sexually transmitted infections can trigger a stampede to the campus health center.

Adam Milholland, 21, a geography major from Lompoc, Calif., said his high school health class stressed abstinence. So he appreciates the candor and scope of the Baldwins' course. "This class teaches you stuff that is important to your life," he said.

The couple's aura of nonjudgmental experience helps. "It's kind of cool to have teachers who know what they're talking about and who have been through it," Milholland said. "They've probably had their problems, but they're still happy together. You can tell by how they interact with each other and support each other."

"Sociology of Human Sexuality" is among the longest-running and most popular classes ever at UC Santa Barbara, according to the registrar. The couple have received various honors, most recently in 2003, when John Baldwin was given the campus award for distinguished teaching; the citation noted his sensitivity in a field that could be a "minefield for the careless." (His wife, a senior part-time lecturer, could not share the award, which is for tenured and tenure-track faculty only.)

Both Baldwins grew up in Ohio families that avoided talking about sex. Janice's mother never told her about menstruation. John's early sex education consisted of his father holding him up to a garage window to watch two dogs mate.

John started at Johns Hopkins University as a pre-med undergraduate and stayed for a doctorate in sociology. Janice earned a bachelor's degree at Ohio State University and, much later, a sociology doctorate from UC Santa Barbara. They met on a blind date in Florida, where he was doing research and she was attending summer school.

After marrying, they traveled for several years in the jungles of Latin America while he researched the behavior of squirrel monkeys. There, they witnessed the human suffering caused by overpopulation and lack of birth control. The experience influenced Janice to volunteer for Planned Parenthood when they returned to Santa Barbara in the early '70s.

John Baldwin worked his way up the UC academic ladder to full professor of sociology. When a sexuality course taught by graduate students was about to end, the couple picked up the torch, diving into research that concentrated on human, not monkey, behavior.

Martha Kempner, communications vice president of the nonprofit Sexuality Information and Education Council of the United States, said many colleges offer similar courses, but she knew of no other taught by a married couple. "Having role models is a really interesting addition," Kempner said.

Slim and athletic-looking, the Baldwins often wear jeans and boots to class. Standing on opposite sides of the stage during their three-times-a-week lectures, they take charge of the campus' enormous Campbell Hall like cheery radio announcers.

As large screens display *New Yorker* magazine cartoons about love alongside scientific charts about birth control, the pair speak without notes, often alternating sentence by sentence.

Occasionally, they converge at center stage for role play. In a class about the life cycles of romance, they impersonate a young couple in an awkward first meeting.

"Hey, aren't you in my history class?" John says, using a trite pickup line that resonates with his audience.

As the discussion turns to keeping love alive after infatuation fades, the professors demonstrate exercises in compliments. Janice tells John how kind and caring he is, and the class lets out a collective "Aaawww." They also act out the kind of bickering they urge couples to avoid, with Janice telling John she is "so sick" of him wearing the same jeans.

Students say they watch for signs of actual discord. If the Baldwins cut each other off, there are worried whispers about a possible tiff.

"They do skits onstage and do little flirty things, so you can obviously tell they have a good relationship. But there is still some kind of mystery behind them," said Serena Winters, 20, a communications major from Huntington Beach who leads study sessions for the class.

The Baldwins are tight-lipped about their own lives, except to say that they have no children, were never married to anyone else and spend their free time hiking. They say it is fine for students to abstain from sex, but they also give off the vibe of supportive parents who think it's all right for young people to be sexually active as long as they keep it safe.

When students express public—or more often, private—befuddlement about anatomy and arousal, John Baldwin, unperturbed, hands out pertinent illustrations the way a geology teacher might distribute seismic fault maps. He and his wife have noted that as newlyweds, they too were uncertain about the proper names and locations of some key parts.

Although their introductory classes are too large to allow much give-and-take with students, the Baldwins hold smaller sections for advanced students, including one this spring with just 16 in a small conference room.

There, the couple led students through topics from assigned readings, including the effect of testosterone on male violence and the popularity of cosmetic surgery. The professors acted as moderators, engaging students in a lively discussion on the morality of outing closeted gay politicians and celebrities.

"When is it right?" John Baldwin asked. "When is it an invasion of privacy?"

The professors are careful to handle controversial topics such as abortion and birth control in an even-handed manner, even though fliers about emergency contraception and referrals to Planned Parenthood are posted on their office walls. Over the years, a handful of students have complained to administrators about topics they found offensive, such as oral sex, but no material has been dropped.

Many topics in the course demand forthrightness as well as sensitivity. In a lecture about abortion dating to ancient Greece, the Baldwins advised students to look away if images were too upsetting. The screens showed photos of aborted fetuses and of the bodies of women who died after botched illegal abortions.

The topic that seems to upset students most, the Baldwins say, is parental sex. Year after year, the class breaks into groans at images of mature couples in nude embraces.

"They . . . don't like to think about their parents having sex," Janice Baldwin said.

A public website linked to the course, www.SexInfo OnLine.com, is explicit but not prurient. It answers such questions as "Is masturbation dangerous?" (Answer: No.) and provides information about emergency contraception, along with 50 ideas for great dates.

T he Baldwins' periodic surveys of undergraduates' sex lives generate lively discussions—and perhaps relief for the celibate at a campus that *Playboy* magazine often ranks high on its list of top party schools.

In the couple's most recent survey, from 2007, about 75% of respondents said they had engaged in vaginal intercourse. The rest said they were virgins by that definition, although some had had oral sex.

The survey also found that promiscuity on the campus peaked in the late '80s, before awareness of AIDS. In 1988, 38% of the school's sexually active undergraduates said they had had at least one sexual encounter with a person they had known one day or less; by 2007, that figure had dropped to 26%.

Professor Maria Charles, vice chair of UC Santa Barbara's sociology department, said she took the Baldwins' class as an undergraduate and is not surprised that enrollment remains high.

"It's very research-based. It's not their personal opinions and value judgments," Charles said. Yet, she added, students are drawn to the Baldwins as parental figures who speak about sex in the context of "a healthy, loving relationship."

That may explain why the couple, who say they have no thoughts of retirement, keep receiving the ultimate compliment from former students: invitations to weddings.

"We try to transmit an ethos of non-embarrassment, and I think students have felt comfortable around us for a long time, which is nice," John Baldwin said. "They keep us young."

Critical Thinking

1. Describe the human sexuality course taught by the husband-wife team at UC Santa Barbara.

2. What impact has this course had on the Santa Barbara campus?

3. What key factors have been essential to the success of this course at UC Santa Barbara?

Exploring Sexuality Education Opportunities at In-Home Sex-Toy Parties in the United States

CHRISTOPHER FISHER ET AL.

Introduction

Sexuality education in the United States has had a varied and complex history. The earliest documented form of sex education in public schools took on a question-and-answer format with medical professionals in the early 1900s (Moran 2000). Despite initial failings, World War I brought sex and the need for education around it firmly into the American purview through training of armed forces going overseas; the primary focus at the time was on prevention of syphilis and gonorrhea transmission (D'Emilio and Freedman 1997; Moran 2000). By the 1950s, sex education was quickly becoming a staple of American high schools and beginning to be included in middle school curricula (Irvine 2002; Luker 2006). In the late 1970s, the question no longer was whether sexuality education should be included in public school curricula, but what the contents of that curriculum should be (Irvine 2002; Luker 2006). Today, the content debate continues with the primary contenders being abstinence-only sexuality education and comprehensive sexuality education (Fisher 2009; Irvine 2002; Luker 2006).

With sex education debates primarily focused on public secondary schools in the United States, relatively little attention has been given to adult sexuality education outside of college courses or clinic populations or the potential venues for delivery of such information. Recently, researchers have begun to empirically study non-school venues and their potential as sites for providing adults with sex education. Previous research has shown that the adult retail industry, and stores in particular, may provide adults with access to sexuality information (Herbenick and Reece 2006; Reece, Herbenick, and Sherwood-Puzzello 2004; Reece et al., 2005).

It is likely that there are other venues within or facets of the adult retail industry that may serve as resources for adult sexuality information or education. These may include adult retail web sites, adult product packaging, and in-home sex-toy parties. The purpose of this study was to explore in-home sex-toy parties—gatherings that are typically held in women's homes, typically facilitated by other women, and for the purpose of selling sexual enhancement products—as a potential venue for the delivery of adult sexuality education.

Methods

The data for this study were part of a larger project that surveyed in-home sex-toy party consultants (Herbenick, Reece, and Hollub 2009), all of whom are female and worked for a large company with a predominantly US presence. The cross-sectional, online survey along with all study materials and procedures were approved by the Institutional Review Board at Indiana University.

Measures

The measures for this study included basic demographic variables and three open-ended questions. Descriptive demographics included age, geographic location, relationship status, race/ethnicity, sexual orientation, level of education, length of time working as a consultant, and average attendance of parties. The open-ended questions asked: 'What are the three most common questions about sexuality or sexuality-related products that women have asked you at parties during the past three months?' Three text boxes provided space for respondents to type the three most common questions. While each text box was labeled in order one, two and three, the question was not designed to determine the frequency of questions asked of a consultant. In other words, the response entered in the first text box may not have necessarily been more frequently asked of the responding consultant than the questions entered in text boxes two and three.

Data collection

Data were collected online during December 2005 and January 2006. Participants received recruitment messages via two emails and one telephone call over a two-week time frame. These calls and emails came directly from the company using standard avenues of within-company communication. The email contained an Internet link to a university-hosted website where women could learn more about the study, read an approved study information sheet and decide whether or not to participate in the study.

After survey completion, consultants had the option to supply their email address, which was not linked to the survey data, for the chance to win one of 10 $50 gift cards to a large, nationwide retailer. At the close of the study, a research assistant randomly drew 10 emails from the list of entries. The 10 women were emailed for name and mailing address to receive the gift card. Contact information was not connected to survey data, and emails were promptly deleted upon delivery of the gift cards.

Analysis

Demographic data were analyzed using standard statistical frequencies. A modified grounded theory approach was employed in the analysis of the 'questions asked' entered by each participant.

Traditional grounded theory approaches require that data analysis should be carried out concurrent with data collection (Charmaz 2004; Glaser and Strauss 1967). However, due to the mixed-methods approach of the survey (Creswell 2003), it was not possible to conduct recurring analysis and subsequently modify the data collection processes to account for emerging themes (Charmaz 2004). The modified approach more closely followed post-data collection procedures as detailed by Charmaz (2004).

Statements entered by participants indicating the most commonly asked questions at the in-home sex-toy parties that they had facilitated in the previous three months were compiled into a single list. The lead author and two graduate-level research assistants read through all statements. Following a grounded theory approach, each person individually read the collection of statements and made notes on the types of themes that emerged from the data. Sample statements representative of emerging themes were identified. Using an iterative process (Charmaz 2004),

each coder read through all statements at least three times with referral back to, and revision of, noted themes. Upon completion, all three analysts met to discuss identified emergent themes and came to consensus on the final themes to be used for coding.

Another meeting to discuss themes was held between the lead author, coders and the primary project leads. The project leads (second and third authors) had extensive working knowledge of the company contracting with the in-home sex-toy party consultants as well as a long-standing collaborative relationship with the company. This insider knowledge of the company provided an added lens with which to dialogue about the emergent themes. The investigators maintain detailed agreements with this company that clearly articulate the mechanisms that help to ensure the scientific integrity of all projects while simultaneously providing for the direct translation of research findings in ways that can help the company to better refine its training programs for facilitators to ensure that medically accurate information is included in trainings. The final descriptions of the coding themes were enriched during the consensus process of the meeting.

Three graduate-level students used the final coding themes to independently categorize all statements of questions asked provided by the participants. Initial coding agreement between the three coders was 78% (number of statements that received the same code from all three coders divided by the total number of statements). A meeting was held to discuss and categorize statements with discordant coding. The result was 100% consensus on the categorization of all statements into one of the coding themes.

A set of meetings followed completion of the categorization of questions asked. The authors met to discuss statements for each code. A dialogic, iterative process was utilized to bring meaning to and find patterns in statements within each category. The resulting subthemes within each category were then tied back to participant statements that were illustrative of the identified meaning.

Finally, to assess the potential for in-home sex-toy parties as sites for sexuality education, we compared coded themes with the Sexuality Information and Education Council of the United States (SIECUS) guidelines, which detail the recommended components of comprehensive sexuality education. The main areas to be covered in a high-school sex education (12th Grade), according to SIECUS, include: human development; relationships; personal skills; sexual behavior; sexual health; and society and culture (SIECUS 2004). Exemplar questions from each coded theme were matched to the various components outlined by SIECUS to illustrate potential teachable moments, opportunities where a situation or conversation is conducive to education related to that moment, at in-home sex-toy parties.

Results
Participants
During the data collection phase of the study, approximately 5000 consultants (all female) worked in association with the company from which participants were recruited. A total of 1197 completed surveys were submitted, resulting in a response rate of approximately 23.9%. A total of 3159 questions most frequently asked of consultants at in-home sex-toy parties were reported.

The age of participants was broad (range = 18 - 75 years) with an average age of 32.7 years (SD = 8.2). The sample geographically represented a majority of the United States. Most women were either married ($n = 711$, 59.4%) or in a committed relationship ($n = 192$, 16.0%). The majority of consultants had children ($n = 884$, 73.9%). Consultants were well educated, with most ($n = 914$, 76.3%) having had some college, a bachelor's degree, or an advanced degree. The overwhelming majority of consultants identified as heterosexual/straight ($n = 1095$, 91.6%) and identified as White/Caucasian ($n = 1013$, 85.2%). The length of time spent working as a consultant ranged from one month to 15 years.

Coded Themes
The nine coded themes were partner/relationship, product-related questions (not including lubricants), sexual function questions, orgasm questions, questions about artificial lubricants, sex behavior questions, general sexuality questions, job-related questions, and medical-related questions.

Partner/relationship Questions
Consultants responding to the survey indicated questions asked of them that related to consumers' relationships and their partner ($n = 238$, 7.6%). Three main themes emerged under this domain: skills, enhancing the sexual relationship, and perceptions and influences. Skills questions specifically focused on communication and sex-related techniques. At the core of these questions was a desire to learn how to communicate one's needs to a partner. Technique questions typically related to seeking information about 'how to' do something with a partner. Other questions related to relationship enhancement. 'How can I enrich my sex life with my partner?' and 'How can I get more foreplay?' suggest some consumers' desires for an expanded sexual repertoire within their relationships, and not necessarily advice on how to fix a sexual relationship. Finally, questions related to partner perceptions of

sex toys and the toy's influence on a relationship came through in this theme. As reported by consultants, consumers expressed concerns about what their partner would think of a sex toy as well as asked questions about how a new sex toy might influence the relationship, for better ('Do these really enhance your relationship?') or worse ('Will using my vibrator with my lover turn him off?').

Product-related Questions (Not Including Lubricants)
Not surprisingly, a high proportion of questions asked of consultants at the in-home parties ($n = 1398$, 44.4%) revolved around the products they were selling. Product-related questions fell into themes of recommendations (not based on personal experience as detailed above), questions of safety, and how to use a product.

Recommendation questions looked to address, through the use of products, issues related to sexual function, enhancement of one's sexual experience, or dyadic use. However, what was not working was not the only approach; questions also sought product recommendations, but from a position of wanting to 'enhance' sexual activity. Many questions around recommendations sought information on which products were most popular (e.g. 'What is your top seller?' and 'What is the most common toy?'). Finally, many questions asking for recommendations for selecting an appropriate product focused on what the partner might like.

Product safety was also of concern for consumers. In particular, many questions indicated an anxiety about infections. Safety also included questions on contextual use of products. Many women were also concerned with longitudinal effects of sex toy use such as possible loss of sensation.

Many product questions sought clarification on how to use or maintain a sex toy or how a particular product worked. Some women asked more specific questions about use of toys with condoms, which may have potentially also been about safety. Maintenance of products was also brought up in terms of how to care for them.

Sexual Function Questions
There were some questions reported regarding sexual functioning ($n = 276$, 8.8%). Three themes were identified. First were questions looking for information on increasing sexual satisfaction. Many women sought out advice related to helping their male partner to 'last longer'. The assumption by the research team, based on personal experiences in couples and family counseling and teaching college-level human sexuality courses, was that implicit in questions of making a male partner last longer was a sense of the partner not being able to delay orgasm

long enough to sexually satisfy their female partner. Second were questions asked about increasing desire. Finally, some consultants reported receiving questions about minimizing discomfort or addressing concerns of genital or sexual pain. For questions categorized as potentially indicating discomfort issues, pain was not directly mentioned (e.g. 'I'm not wet enough, what can I do?'). However, there were quite a few questions that reflected concerns about what to do for a painful condition experienced during sexual activity. Several consultants responded to the survey indicating that one of the most commonly asked questions of them was 'What can you do about painful intercourse?'

Orgasm Questions

Questions about orgasms ($n = 172$, 5.5%) focused on understanding what an orgasm is and the types women may experience, techniques for having an orgasm, and norms surrounding female orgasms. Many consultants reported that women had asked them about what they had heard were different types of orgasms (e.g. vaginal, clitoral, G-spot). Others simply wanted to know 'How do I know what kind of orgasms I have?' or 'How will I know if I achieve orgasm?' Other questions focused on techniques for experiencing the various types of orgasms or increasing the intensity of orgasms.

Questions about Artificial Lubricants

Because there were a significant number of consultants who reported questions specifically about artificial lubricants ($n = 237$, 7.5%), a type of product sold by the company, these questions were coded in a separate theme. Similar to product-related questions, there were several questions about recommendations for the most popular lubricant or most appropriate for a given behavior (e.g. anal sex, vaginal sex, masturbation). Also similar to product-related questions, technical questions about lubricants focused on safety, compatibility with safer-sex devices, and expiration dates. Finally, questions about use of lubricants as normal came out in the data (e.g. 'Should everyone use lubricants?').

Sex Behavior Questions

Sex behavior questions ($n = 166$, 5.3%) were any questions that focused on specific sexual behaviors. A large number of behaviors were mentioned, including masturbation (alone and with a partner), oral sex, vaginal sex, and anal sex. Questions in this theme centered on avoiding pain, increasing pleasure, and skills questions. For most pain questions, the focus was on anal sex (e.g. 'Anal sex—how to make it hurt less?'). Pleasure questions often focused on orgasms. Such questions, unlike more general questions on orgasm, sought behavioral advice on how to increase pleasure. Finally, more general skills questions not necessarily about pleasure focused on specific behavioral guidance (e.g. 'How can I make him orgasm faster?').

General Sexuality Questions

General sexuality questions ($n = 398$, 12.6%) was a catch-all category for questions that did not fit well into other themes. Many centered on values and feelings related to sexuality such as 'How do I get over being embarrassed?' Others asked questions regarding sexual orientation and gender norms. Finally, many women were looking for definitions of what was 'normal' such as 'Is it "okay" to want to fantasize about another man while having sex with my husband?'

Other general sexuality questions were more anatomically-centered. Questions about the G-spot indicated a primarily pleasure-centered line of questioning. For example, 'Where is the G-spot—how can I find it?!' was interpreted as an interest in learning more about an area commonly described as related to pleasure. Questions about the male prostate and perineum were also prevalent. Anatomy questions also drew on safety issues: 'How safe is anal sex?' brings into question the anatomical design of the anus and rectum, and how (and if) it can be sexually navigated safely.

Job-related Questions

A number of questions reported were related to the consultant's job ($n = 199$, 6.3%). Several questions were associated with company policies regarding warranties, return policies, and more general operational questions. Other questions in this category focused on recommendations of the consultants. Likewise, some questions asked about more personal experiences related to the job. These types of questions are typical questions a sales associate at any general retail establishment might get, such as questions related to income or job satisfaction. However, questions about the absence of men at the parties or 'Do you think of this as raunchy or nasty?' brought up more general notions of social norms related to the jobs in which consultants were engaged.

Medical-related Questions

Medical-related questions comprised the smallest category among the themes ($n = 62$, 2%). These questions specifically mentioned a medical procedure or diagnosis. Some were related to the efficacy of a product given a specific medical situation such as surgery (e.g. hysterectomy). These questions also tended to seek advice for improving function. One consultant reported on being asked by women who had had breast reductions whether a certain product would help to address a loss of sensation post surgery. Other similar questions about the changing nature of sexual functioning during menopause or the postpartum period inquired about interactions between associated pharmacological treatments and products being sold. Finally, the safety of products, given particular conditions such as diabetes, was brought up.

Relations Between Questions and SIECUS Guidelines for Comprehensive Sex Education

The potential for sexuality education at in-home sex-toy parties may exist. A review of the guidelines for comprehensive sexuality education published by SIECUS (2004) in tandem with questions asked of consultants at these events demonstrates this possibility. [SIECUS] presents the six key concepts and their respective topical areas, which focus on high-school-aged adolescents (ages 15–18). Next to each topic is an exemplar quote of a question reported by consultants. These questions illustrate teachable moments, points in a conversation where a consultant might move beyond the quick answer and provide additional sexuality education to event participants.

Discussion

This study sought to describe the types of questions consultants received at in-home sex-toy parties, a subset of the adult retail industry targeting women, in order to assess the viability of such venues as another avenue for adult sexuality education. Considering that few, if any, models of adult sexuality education within the context of adult retail venues exist (Herbenick and Reece 2006; Reece et al., 2005; Reece, Herbenick, and Sherwood-Puzzello 2004), and the call for sex-positive interventions (Di Mauro 1997; Reece and Dodge 2004), the comprehensive sexuality education model offered by SIECUS (2004) was utilized to ascertain the potential for teachable moments at these events.

Many of the questions were similar to questions one might encounter in a general college human sexuality course covering such topics as anatomy/physiology, orgasm, and sexual function. A common theme noted by the research team throughout several of the coded categories was norms surrounding sexuality; another topic typically addressed in a formal sexuality education setting. For example, normative notions of when and how a woman should have an orgasm were evident in many questions. Several questions indicated that, for women attending these parties, having an orgasm was normative. Questions regarding what were the most popular or most common products could be read to indicate a desire

to use sexual aides that are more mainstream, more normal. At the same time, some consumers appeared to hold a normative belief that sex toys were bad or hurtful in that they could damage the body. Still others challenged normative ways of being (sexually) for women; historically, women have often been seen as passive participants in sexual activity, whose pleasure was not a primary goal, and therefore physical pain was to be endured silently. Several consumers in this study not only acknowledged physical pain during sex, but were actively seeking solutions from the consultant and the products she offered.

While many of the questions asked of consultants provide an entry point into deeper conversations about sexuality, not all topics described by SIECUS had teachable moment questions associated with them. Topics of body image, gender identity, religion, the media, and the arts could be further discussed with regards to societal norms and the diversity that exists within our culture. The one topic for which we could not identify a teachable moment question was abortion, although, based on the array of questions related to medical procedures (e.g. hysterectomies, mastectomies) received by consultants, it is conceivable that such a topic could easily present itself. Further, we asked consultants to list the most frequently asked questions; almost certainly, not all questions asked of consultants were represented in the data.

The SIECUS guideline for personal skills includes a communication component. Communication skills may be the most salient piece of sexuality education for in-home sex-toy parties. The opportunity to practice asking questions and discussing sexuality-related topics, both for consultants and consumers, is evident in that nearly all consultants surveyed reported questions asked of them at the parties they facilitated. The chance to discuss sex in a safe, non-judgmental environment may allow consumers and consultants to improve communication skills that can be carried into their personal relationships.

Based on the diverse questions reported by consultants, it is feasible that in-home sex-toy parties provide a ripe opportunity to provide sexual information to adult women in the United States and opportunities to practice sexual communication. However, it should be noted that these participants all work with one in-home sex-toy party company, which provides these services. It is possible that women (or men) who work with other similar companies may experience questions or sexual topics differently. Also, in-home parties should not be seen as a catch-all approach to adult sexuality education. There may be unique characteristics of the women who attend these parties that are not generalizable to the larger population. As such, in different populations, the teachable moments described here may be experienced differently, if at all. All participants (consultants and consumers) in this study were women.

Addressing the specific needs of the adult male population was not an option in this study. The company involved in this project only engages women in their parties as a means to minimize discomfort that may be experienced in a mixed gender setting. The company also primarily markets itself to heterosexuals; women of differing sexual orientations and the questions they may ask may not have been well represented in this sample. Other venues should be explored to address the sexuality education needs of adults not attending such events. Finally, this study did not address the needs of specific subsets of women (e.g. younger vs older) as the questions asked were reported by consultants, not the consumers themselves; thus, there is no indication as to which questions were posed by younger or older women, women with certain health conditions, or women from certain racial/ethnic groups. Given that questions were provided by a rather homogeneous set of party facilitators, and that the demographic characteristics of the women asking the questions over time were unknown, we did not provide an analysis of the extent to which the participants' demographic characteristics were associated with the types of questions reported.

It may be reasonable to assume that consultants encounter a wide range of diversity at the parties they facilitate. As such, it may be important to provide training to consultants that enables them to deliver on teachable moments with a language and style that is appropriate and acceptable for women of differing backgrounds (e.g. ethnicity, race and age).

The results of this study suggest that consultants who facilitate in-home sex-toy parties report being asked a number of diverse questions related to sexuality. These questions provide an opportunity to move beyond selling a product and extend the sexuality education of a portion of the US adult population by providing teachable moments. There are currently very few non-clinical settings in which adult women can ask questions about sex. It may be that having an opportunity to gain such information in a home setting alleviates anxieties around questions about sex and sexuality that one might experience in a clinical venue. Further, it is possible that not only the consumers in attendance at the parties could benefit from these teachable moments, but their partners, friends, and families may also benefit from the potential dissemination of accurate, non-judgmental sex information. Sexual health professionals also stand to benefit as they may be able to increase their capacity to respond to the types of questions asked at in-home sex-toy parties. Sexuality education and sexual health advocates may need to consider partnering with the operators of the companies who provide in-home sex-toy party services to equip their employees with the knowledge and skills to identify and take advantage of these educational moments.

The teachable moments reported in this study may provide in-home sex-toy party consultants the opportunity to expand the sexual knowledge of all women who participate in these events. It is likely that many of these questions are posed in a public forum during the consultants' presentation and are then responded to in public. This may afford women an opportunity to hear questions related to sexuality they had never contemplated. It is in this moment that we believe a true teachable moment occurs; properly equipped with knowledge and skills, the consultant can facilitate a discussion that could lead to increased sexual knowledge and awareness for all. As a result of this study, other projects are under development to provide consultants of in-home sex-toy parties, and others who may be in a similar position, a deeper knowledge of the many facets of human sexuality. Consultants, armed with knowledge and training on how to take advantage of teachable moments, may be better able to help improve the sexual health and well-being of the women they serve.

Given that the in-home sex-toy party industry has grown rapidly over the past few years, and is currently reaching millions of women who turn to such events for information and products, researchers can play an important role through their attempts to understand the nature of these parties and document the extent to which women are benefitting from the opportunity to enhance their understanding of sexuality-related issues. These academic—corporate partnerships, when implemented in a manner that simultaneously seek to conduct research that adheres to strict standards of scientific integrity, while also pursuing the direct translation of research findings to the corporation that guide their training efforts and other educational endeavors, can be helpful to our mutual pursuit of improving the sexual health of women.

References

Charmaz, K. 2004. Grounded theory. In *Approaches to qualitative research: A reader on theory and practice,* ed. S. Nagy Hess-Biber and P. Leavy, 496–521. New York: Oxford University Press.

Creswell, J.W. 2003. *Research design: Qualitative, quantitative, and mixed methods approaches.* 2nd ed. Thousand Oaks, CA: Sage.

D'Emilio, J., and E.B. Freedman. 1997. *Intimate matters: A history of sexuality in America.* Chicago: The University of Chicago Press.

Di Mauro, D. 1997. Sexuality research in the United States. In *Researching sexual behavior,* ed. J. Bancroft, 3–8. Bloomington: Indiana University Press.

Fisher, C.M. 2009. Queer youth experiences with abstinence-only until marriage sexuality education: 'I can't get married so where does that leave me?'. *Journal of LGBT Youth* 6, no. 1: 61–79.

Glaser, B., and A. Strauss. 1967. *The discovery of grounded theory.* New York: Aldine de Gruyter.

Herbenick, D., and M. Reece. 2006. Sex education in adult retail stores: Positioning consumers' questions as teachable moments. *American Journal of Sexuality Education* 2, no. 1: 57–75.

Herbenick, D., M. Reece, and A. Hollub. 2009. Inside the ordering room: Characteristics of women's in-home sex toy parties, facilitators, and sexual communication. *Sexual Health* 6, no. 4: 318–327.

Irvine, J. 2002. *Talk about sex: The battles over sex education in the United States.* Berkeley: University of California Press.

Luker, K. 2006. *When sex goes to school: Warring views on sex—and sex educaton—since the sixties.* 1st ed. New York: W.W. Norton & Company.

Moran, J.P. 2000. *Teaching sex: The shaping of adolescence in the 20th century.* Cambridge, MA: Harvard University Press.

Reece, M., and B. Dodge. 2004. A study in sexual health applying the principles of community-based participatory research. *Archives of Sexual Behavior* 33, no. 3: 235–47.

Reece, M., D. Herbenick, E. Shachman, and C. Sherwood-Puzzello. 2005. The U.S. adult retail industry: A viable partner for HIV and STD prevention? *Health Education Monograph* 22, no. 3: 29–35.

Reece, M., D. Herbenick, and C. Sherwood-Puzzello. 2004. Sexual health promotion and adult retail stores. *Journal of Sex Research* 41, no. 2: 173–80.

SIECUS. 2004. *Guidelines for comprehensive sexuality education.* 3rd ed. Washington, DC: SIECUS.

Teenage Fatherhood and Involvement in Delinquent Behavior

TERENCE P. THORNBERRY, PhD, CAROLYN A. SMITH, PhD, AND SUSAN EHRHARD, MA

The human life course is composed of a set of behavioral trajectories in domains such as family, education, and work (Elder, 1997). In the domain of family formation, for example, a person's trajectory might be described as being in the following states: single, married, divorced, remarried, and widowed. Movement along these trajectories is characterized by elements of both continuity and change. Continuity refers to remaining in a certain state over time (such as being married) while change refers to transitions to a new state (such as getting divorced).

The life course is expected to unfold in a set of culturally normative, age-graded stages. In American society, for example, the culturally accepted sequence is for an individual to complete his or her high school education prior to beginning employment careers and getting married, and all the former, especially marriage, are expected to preceed parenthood. Despite these expectations, there is, in fact, a great deal of "disorder" in the life course (Rindfuss, Swicegood, & Rosenfeld, 1987). That is, many life-course transitions are out of order (i.e., parenthood before marriage) and/or off-time (i.e., either too early or too late).

A basic premise of the life-course perspective is that off-time transitions, especially precocious transitions that occur before the person is developmentally prepared for them, are likely to be disruptive to the individual and to those around the individual. Precocious transitions are often associated with social and psychological deficits and with involvement in other problem behaviors. Precocious transitions may also lead to additional problems at later developmental stages. This paper focuses on one type of precocious transition—teenage fatherhood—and investigates whether it is related to various indicators of deviant behavior.

the father and child, that are similar to those observed for teen mothers (Lerman & Ooms, 1993). These consequences include reduced educational attainment, greater financial hardship, and less stable marriage patterns for the teen parent, along with poorer health, educationally, and behavioral outcomes among children born to teen parents (Furstenberg, Brooks-Gunn, & Morgan, 1987; Hayes, 1987; Irwin & Shafer, 1992; Lerman & Ooms, 1993). Given these negative consequences, both to the young father and his offspring, it is important to understand the processes that lead some young men to become teen fathers while others delay becoming fathers until more developmentally normative ages.

One possibility is that becoming a teen father is part of a more general deviant lifestyle. If so, we would expect teen fatherhood to be associated with involvement in other problem behaviors, such as delinquency and drug use. There is some evidence for this hypothesis; teen fathering has been found to be associated with such problem behaviors as delinquency, substance use, and disruptive school behavior (Elster, Lamb, & Tavare, 1987; Ketterlinus, Lamb, Nitz, & Elster, 1992; Resnick, Chambliss, & Blum, 1993; Thornberry, Smith, & Howard, 1997). Some researchers suggest a common problem behavior syndrome underlying all these behaviors (Jessor & Jessor, 1977), a view consistent with Anderson's ethnographic data (1993). In the remainder of this paper, we explore the link between teen fatherhood and other problem behaviors, addressing two core questions:

1. Are earlier delinquency, drug use, and related behaviors risk factors for becoming a teen father?
2. Does teen fatherhood increase the risk of involvement in deviant behavior during early adulthood?

Teen Fatherhood

Until recently, the study of teen parenthood has focused almost exclusively on becoming a teen mother, and relatively little attention has been paid to teenage fatherhood (Parke & Neville, 1987; Smollar & Ooms, 1988). Nevertheless, teen fatherhood appears to be associated with negative consequences, both to

Research Methods

We examine these questions using data from the Rochester Youth Development Study, a multi-wave panel study in which adolescents and their primary caretakers (mainly mothers) have been interviewed since 1988. A representative sample from the population of all seventh- and eighth-grade students enrolled in the Rochester public schools during the 1987–1988 academic year was selected for the study. Male adolescents and students living in census tracts with high adult arrest rates were oversampled based on the premise that they were more likely than other youth to be at risk for antisocial behavior, the main concern of the original study. Of the 1,000 students ultimately selected, 73% were male and 27% were female.

Because the chances of selection into the panel are known, the sample can be weighted to represent all Rochester public school students, and statistical weights are used here. The study conducted 12 interviews with the sample members, initially at 6-month intervals and later at annual intervals. This analysis is based on the 615 men in the study who were interviewed in Wave 11, when their average age was 21. Twenty percent of these individuals are White, 63% are African American, and 17% are Hispanic. The interviews, which lasted between 60 and 90 minutes, were conducted in private, face-to-face settings with the exception of a small number of respondents who had moved away from the Northeast and were interviewed by telephone. Overall, 84% (615/729) of the total male sample was interviewed at Wave 11. Due to missing data generated by cumulating data across interview waves, the number of cases included in the models for the analysis varies from 551 to 611. There is no evidence of differential subject loss [see Thornberry, Bjerregaard, & Miles (1993), and Krohn & Thornberry (1999) for detailed discussions of sampling and data collection methods].

Measurement of Teen Fatherhood

In Wave 11, respondents were asked to identify all of their biological children, including the name, birth date, and primary caregiver of each child. If the respondent fathered a child before his 20th birthday, he is designated a teen father. The validity of the respondent's self-reported paternity is suggested by the 95% agreement with the report provided by the respondent's parent in their interview at Wave 11.

Problem Behavior Variables

In predicting teen fatherhood, we examine the effects of delinquent beliefs, gang membership, and three forms of delinquent behavior. These measures are based on data from early waves of the study, generally between Waves 2–5, covering ages 13.5 to 15.5, on average. As such, these indicators of problem behaviors precede the age at which fatherhood began for this sample, and they can be considered true risk factors for teen fatherhood.

Delinquent beliefs asks the respondent how wrong it is to engage in each of eight delinquent acts, with responses ranging from "not wrong at all" to "very wrong." The measure used here is a dichotomous variable denoting whether the respondent was above or below the median value on the scale. Gang membership is a self-reported measure of whether or not the respondent reported being a member of a street gang (see Thornberry, Krohn, Lizotte, Smith, & Tobin, 2003).

Three variables are used to measure deviant behavior: drug use, which is an index of the respondent's use of 10 different substances; general offending, which is an index based on 32 items reflecting all types of delinquency; and violent offending, which is based on 6 items measuring violent crimes. For the risk factor analysis, all three indices are based on self-reported data and are trichotomized to indicate no offending, low levels of offending (below the median frequency), and high levels of offending (above the median).

These three indicators of offending are also measured during early adulthood (ages 20–22) in order to determine the effects of teen fatherhood on deviant behavior later in life. At this stage, they are simple dichotomies indicating offending versus non-offending.

Results

We present the results in three sections. The first examines the prevalence of teen fatherhood, and the second examines whether delinquency and related behaviors are significant risk factors for becoming a teen father. The final section focuses on whether the young men who became teen fathers, as opposed to those who did not, are more likely to engage in criminal behavior during early adulthood.

Prevalence of Teen Fatherhood

In the Rochester sample, 28% of the male respondents reported fathering a child before age 20. The age distribution at which they became fathers is presented in Figure 1. Seven subjects (1%) became fathers at age 15, truly a precocious transition. The rate of fatherhood increased sharply from that point on. At 16, 3% of the sample became fathers; at 17, 6% did; and at both 18 and 19 years of age, 9% entered the ranks of the young fathers.

Risk Factors

The link between delinquent behavior and becoming a teen father is evident from the results presented in Figure 2. One-third (34%) of the high-level delinquents during early adolescence fathered a child before age 20, as compared to 21% of the low-level delinquents and only 13% of the non-delinquents.

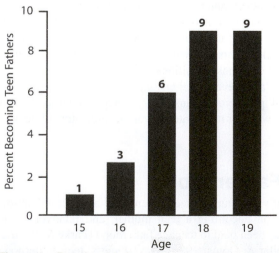

Figure 1 Relationship between age and teenage fatherhood.

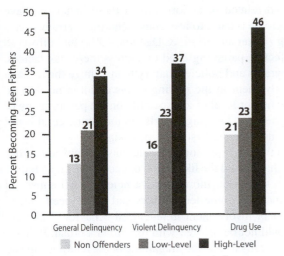

Figure 2 Relationship between early delinquent behavior and teenage fatherhood.

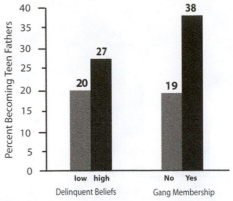

Figure 3 Relationship between delinquent beliefs and teenage fatherhood and between gang members and teenage fathers.

The same dose-response relationship can be seen for violent behavior: the prevalence of teen fatherhood increases from 16%, to 23%, to 37% across the three groups. The pattern is a little different for drug use. The prevalence of teen fatherhood for the non-users and the low-level users is about the same, 21% and 23% respectively, but the rate for the high-level drug users is substantially higher, 46%. All three of these relationships are statistically significant.

In Figure 3 we present bivariate results for two variables closely related to delinquency, holding delinquent beliefs and being a member of a street gang. Both relationships are statistically significant. Younger adolescents who have higher levels of pro-delinquent beliefs are more likely (27%) to become teen fathers than those who do not (20%). Finally, gang members are more likely (38%) to become teen fathers than non-members (19%).

To this point, we have simply investigated bivariate associations, that is, the link between delinquency, say, and teen fatherhood, without holding the effect of other potential explanatory variables constant. In a fuller investigation of this issue, Thornberry et al., (1997) examined these relationships when the following variables were controlled: race/ethnicity, neighborhood poverty and disorganization, parent's education and age at first birth, family poverty level, recent life stress, family social support, parent's expectations for son to attend college, CAT reading achievement, early onset of sexual intercourse, and depression. When this was done, delinquent beliefs were no longer significantly related to teen fatherhood, but gang membership remained a significant and sizeable predictor of becoming a teen father. These two variables—delinquent beliefs and gang membership—were then added to the above list of controls when early adolescent delinquency, drug use, and violence were considered. General delinquency was no longer significantly related to the risk of teen fatherhood, but drug use and violent behavior were (figure not included).

Overall, it appears that early problem behaviors are a risk factor for teen fatherhood. This appears to be the case especially for the more serious forms of these behaviors—violence, high-level drug use, and gang membership.

Later Consequences

The final issue we investigate is whether becoming a teen father is associated with higher rates of criminal involvement during early adulthood, ages 20–22. The results are presented in Figure 4. Teen fathers, as compared to males who delayed the onset of parenthood until after age 20, are not significantly more likely to be involved in general offending or in violent offending during their early 20s. However, there is a significant bivariate relationship between teen fatherhood and later drug use. Of the teen fathers, 66% report some involvement with drug use as compared to 47% of those who delayed fatherhood. This relationship is not statistically significant once adolescent drug use is held constant (results not shown), however. The latter finding indicates that early adult drug use is more a reflection of continuing use than a later consequence of becoming a teen father.

Conclusion

This article investigated the relationship between teenage fatherhood and involvement in delinquency and related behaviors. Based on data from the Rochester Youth Development Study, it appears that an earlier pattern of problem behaviors significantly increases the risk of later becoming a teen father. This relationship is evident bivariately for the five indicators used in this analysis. Also, three of the relationships—violence, drug use, and gang membership—remain significant when the impact of a host of other important risk factors is held constant.

While earlier involvement in deviant behavior and a deviant lifestyle is related to the odds of becoming a teen father, teen fatherhood is not significantly related to later involvement in criminal conduct. At least during their early 20s, teen fathers are not more likely than those who delayed parenthood to be involved in general offending or in violent crime. They are more likely to use drugs, although that relationship is not maintained once prior drug use is controlled.

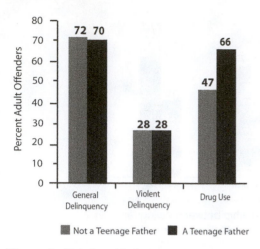

Figure 4 Relationship between teenage fatherhood and adult offending.

There is a clear link between teen fatherhood and earlier involvement in other deviant behaviors. Two kinds of explanations have been suggested for these effects. The first is that adolescent males immersed in a deviant lifestyle have many opportunities to develop a set of values and behaviors conducive to risky, adult-like adventures, some involving conquest and domination over others, including young women. This notion is supported by some ethnographic research (Anderson, 1993) and some gang studies (for example, Covey, Menard, & Franzese, 1992). Second, research has also documented that about one-fifth of teenage males feel that impregnating a young woman would make them feel "more like a man" (Marsiglio, 1993). There may be so few avenues for positive identity formation, particularly among poor adolescents and adolescents of color, that having a child is no deterrent to potential goals. Involvement in deviant behaviors, including early fatherhood, may at best be a means of achieving adult status and positive recognition or at least a means of making a mark in a world where even survival is in doubt (Burton, 1995).

Implications

It seems evident that becoming a teen father is not an isolated event in the lives of these young men. It is systematically related to involvement in a deviant lifestyle and, in a broader analysis of these data (Thornberry et al., 1997), to a variety of other deficits. These results have a number of implications for prevention programs designed to delay the transition to fatherhood and to improve the lot of these young men and their offspring. First, these programs need to be prepared to deal with this constellation of behavior problems and how teen fatherhood is intertwined with them. Focusing simply on reducing teenage fatherhood, absent a consideration of the broader context in which it occurs, may not be very effective. Second, prevention programs should include, or at least be prepared to provide access to, services to reduce involvement in antisocial behaviors for these adolescent males. Third, programs to improve the parenting skills of these young fathers need to take into account their higher level of involvement in delinquency,

drug use, and related behaviors. All of these behaviors have been shown to be related to less consistent, more erratic styles of parenting (Patterson, Reid, & Dishion, 1992) and efforts to improve effective parenting need to address these risk factors. Finally, programs and policies that try to maximize the teenage father's involvement in the rearing of his children need to be aware of the higher level of antisociality on the part of many of these young fathers. Insuring that risk to the young child is not elevated seems to be the first order of business.

Although there is a pronounced relationship between earlier antisocial behavior and the likelihood of becoming a teen father, we end on a somewhat more positive note. Not all antisocial adolescent males become teen fathers and not all teen fathers have a career of involvement in antisocial behavior. This relationship should not be painted with too broad a brush. Policies need to realistically assess the magnitude of the relationship and realistically take it into account when working with these men and their children.

References

Anderson, E. (1993). Sex codes and family life among poor inner-city youths. In R.I. Lerman & T.J. Ooms (Eds.), *Young Unwed Fathers: Changing Roles and Emerging Policies* (pp. 74–98). Philadelphia: Temple University Press.

Burton, L.M. (1995). Family structure and nonmarital fertility: Perspectives from ethnographic research. In K.A. Moore (Ed.), *Report to Congress on Out-of-Wedlock Childbearing* (pp. 147–166). Hyattsville, MD: U.S. Department of Health and Human Services.

Covey, H.C., Menard, S., & Franzese, R.J. (1992). *Juvenile Gangs.* Springfield, IL: Charles C. Thomas.

Elder, G.H., Jr. (1997). The life course and human development. In W. Damon (Ed.-in-Chief) & R.M. Lerner (Ed.), *Handbook of Child Psychology, vol. 1: Theoretical Models of Human Development* (pp. 939–991). New York: Wiley.

Elster, A.B., Lamb, M.E., & Tavare, J. (1987). Association between behavioral and school problems and fatherhood in a national sample of adolescent fathers. *Journal of Pediatrics, 111,* 932–936.

Furstenberg, F.F., Brooks-Gunn, J., & Morgan, S.P. (1987). *Adolescent Mothers in Later Life.* New York: Cambridge University Press.

Hayes, C.D. (1987). *Risking the Future: Adolescent Sexuality, Pregnancy and Childbearing* (vol. 1). Washington, DC: National Academy Press.

Irwin, C.E., Jr., & Shafer, M.A. (1992). Adolescent sexuality: Negative outcomes of a normative behavior. In D.E. Rodgers & E. Ginzberg (Eds.), *Adolescents at Risk: Medical and Social Perspectives* (pp. 35–79). Boulder, CO: Westview Press.

Jessor, R., & Jessor, S.L. (1977). *Problem Behavior and Psychosocial Development.* New York: Academic Press.

Ketterlinus, R.D., Lamb, M.E., Nitz, K., & Elster, A.B. (1992). Adolescent nonsexual and sex-related problem behaviors. *Journal of Adolescent Research, 7,* 431–456.

Krohn, M.D., & Thornberry, T.P. (1999). Retention of minority populations in panel studies of drug use. *Drugs & Society, 14,* 185–207.

Lerman, R.I., & Ooms, T.J. (1993). Introduction: Evolution of unwed fatherhood as a policy issue. In R.I. Lerman & T.J. Ooms (Eds.),

Young Unwed Fathers: Changing Roles and Emerging Policies (pp. 1–26). Philadelphia: Temple University Press.

Marsiglio, W. (1993). Contemporary scholarship on fathers: Culture, identity, and conduct. *Journal of Family Issues, 14,* 484–509.

Parke, R.D., & Neville, B. (1987). Teenage fatherhood. In S.L. Hofferth & C.D. Hayes (Eds.), *Risking the Future: Adolescent Sexuality, Pregnancy, and Childbearing, vol. 2* (pp. 145–173). Washington, DC: National Academy Press.

Patterson, G.R., Reid, J.B., & Dishion, T.J. (1992). *Antisocial Boys.* Eugene, OR: Castalia Publishing Company.

Resnick, M.D., Chambliss, S.A., & Blum, R.W. (1993). Health and risk behaviors of urban adolescent males involved in pregnancy. *Families in Society, 74,* 366–374.

Rindfuss, R.R., Swicegood, C.G., & Rosenfeld, R. (1987). Disorder in the life course: How common and does it matter? *American Sociological Review, 52,* 785–801.

Smollar, J., & Ooms, T. (1988). *Young Unwed Fathers: Research Review, Policy Dilemmas, and Options: Summary Report.* U.S. Department of Health and Human Services, Washington, DC: U.S. Government Printing Office.

Thornberry, T.P., Bjerregaard, B. & Miles, W. (1993). The consequences of respondent attrition in panel studies: A simulation based on the Rochester Youth Development Study. *Journal of Quantitative Criminology, 9,* 127–158.

Thornberry, T.P., Krohn, M.D., Lizotte, A.J., Smith, C.A., & Tobin, K. (2003). *Gangs and Delinquency in Developmental Perspective.* New York: Cambridge University Press.

Thornberry, T.P., Smith, C.A., & Howard, G.J. (1997). Risk factors for teenage fatherhood. *Journal of Marriage and the Family, 59,* 505–522.

Critical Thinking

1. How are teenage fatherhood and delinquent behavior linked?

2. What is the impact of teenage fatherhood on the adolescent male's life course?

3. What developmental issues or concerns do teenage fathers face that are particular to their situation?

TERENCE P. THORNBERRY, PhD, is Director of the Research Program on Problem Behavior at the Institute of Behavioral Science and Professor of Sociology, University of Colorado. He is the Principal Investigator of the Rochester Youth Development Study, an ongoing panel study begun in 1986 to examine the causes and consequences of delinquency, drug use, and other forms of antisocial behavior. Professor Thornberry is an author of *Gangs and Delinquency in Developmental Perspective* and an editor of *Taking Stock of Delinquency: An Overview of Findings from Contemporary Longitudinal Studies.* CAROLYN A. SMITH, PhD, is Professor in the School of Social Welfare, University at Albany. She holds an MSW from the University of Michigan, and a PhD from the School of Criminal Justice at the University at Albany. She has international social work practice experience in child and family mental health, and in delinquency intervention. Her primary research interest is in the family etiology of delinquency and other problem behaviors, and most recently the impact of child maltreatment on the life course. SUSAN EHRHARD holds an MA in Criminal Justice and is currently a doctoral student at the School of Criminal Justice, University at Albany, as well as a Research Assistant for the Rochester Youth Development Study. Her research interests include the sociology of crime, restorative justice, and capital punishment.

Truth and Consequences at Pregnancy High

The education of a teenage mother.

ALEX MORRIS

Before the sun has risen over the Bronx River, an alarm chimes in 17-year-old Grace Padilla's bedroom. Sliding from the lower bunk, she pads to the bathroom, flips on the light, brushes her teeth, then gathers up her hair into a short ponytail, which she wraps with a long row of black extensions and knots into a tight bun. She's quick and efficient, with none of the preening one might expect of a high-school junior. At 6:30 A.M., she goes back into the bedroom to wake her 2-year-old daughter.

Along with her grandparents, her mother, her sister, and her child, Grace lives in a small two-bedroom apartment on the second floor of a nondescript brick building in Hunts Point, where nearly half the residents live below the poverty line and roughly 15 percent of girls ages 15 to 19 become pregnant each year. It's the highest teen-pregnancy rate in the city, more than twice the national average.

"Lilah, wake up," Grace whispers, leaning in close. Lilah bats her mother away with a tiny hand and nestles up closer to Grace's own mother, Mayra, who had moments before returned home from her night shift as a cashier at a local food-distribution center and slipped, exhausted, into Grace's place in the bed.

"Come on, let's go get dressed," Grace pleads, pulling her daughter from under the covers as Lilah begins crying, flailing her arms and legs.

"Come *on,*" Grace begs. She fights to keep her mounting frustration in check and then counts down the seconds before she'll make Lilah go stand against the wall, her usual form of punishment. "Five . . . four . . . three . . . two . . . one."

The threat is enough. Lilah's body goes slack, her screaming dissipates to a whimper. Grace is able to wrestle her into the clothes she'd laid out beforehand. But the child's screams have woken Grace's grandparents, who are now in the galley kitchen, arguing in Spanish. Her grandfather has Alzheimer's. He accidentally makes decaffeinated coffee, which infuriates his wife.

At 7:20, Grace smoothes a tiny hat over Lilah's curls, bundles her into a coat, then jostles schoolbooks into a bag. In the empty lot across the street, a rooster starts to crow.

When Grace arrives at Jane Addams High School for Academics and Careers, she joins the daily parade of mothers—pushing strollers, grasping the chubby fists of toddlers, perching bundled babies on cocked hips—making their way to basement room B17, the headquarters of the school's Living for the Young Family Through Education (LYFE) center. Run by the Department of Education, the LYFE program operates in 38 schools in the five boroughs, teaching parenting skills and providing on-site day care to teen parents who are full-time students in New York City's public schools. Jane Addams hosts one of the most active branches in the city, with sixteen mothers currently in the program.

While the students sign in on a clipboard, social worker Ana C. Martínez flits among them with her checklist of concerns. Is this baby eating enough? (Yes.) Does that one still have a cough? (No.) When will the heat be turned back on in one young mother's apartment? (Uncertain.) If it isn't soon, has she considered going to a shelter? (She has.)

"How's the baby?" Martínez asks Grace.

"She's fine," Grace answers.

Satisfied, Martínez turns her attention to Lilah. "Can I get a hug?"

"No," the child replies coyly, pretending to hide behind her mother's legs.

"Pretty please?"

Lilah finally concedes, jumping into the woman's arms.

Martínez laughs. "We have to play that game every morning, don't we?"

The girls cluster around a table laid out with bagels and jam, which Martínez serves every morning, both to entice her charges to be at school on time and also to make sure they get enough to eat ("Some don't at home," she clucks). She admits that the LYFE program, which serves 500 families and costs taxpayers about $13 million a year, has its naysayers, people who think that it makes life too easy for the mothers and diverts money from students who've made more responsible choices.

"But the reality is, teens are having kids, and we've got to work with them," she says. "They're entitled to an education."

Grace greets Jasmine Reyes—a soft-spoken senior whose 2-year-old daughter, Jayleen, is Lilah's best friend in day care—before going over to peer at Nelsy Valerio's infant. When Iruma Moré enters the room with her 8-month-old daughter, Dymia, Grace beelines for the baby, unwrapping her from a pile of blankets.

"Dymia, Dymia, *Dy-mi-a*," she chants, bouncing the child on her lap. "She's so little," Grace marvels wistfully.

Iruma giggles. "I try to feed her all the time," she says, as she drops into a chair next to a locker crammed full of diapers. Though all four of Iruma's older sisters were teen mothers, she didn't know her school had day care until her sophomore year. "I started seeing the mothers coming in with their babies and stuff, and I always used to wonder where they take them," she says. One day, she looked through a doorway and it was like peering into a magic cupboard—a roomful of babies with soft skin and fine hair. Iruma thought she might like to have one of her own. By her junior year, she was pregnant. "I wasn't using nothing, no protection, so I mean, I knew it was gonna come sooner or later."

The nursery is a clown's paradise, brightly painted and well outfitted with funds donated by makeup artist Bobbi Brown. (In addition to the traditional high-school curriculum, Jane Addams teaches a number of vocations, including cosmetology, which Grace is studying.) Grace and Iruma each commandeer a crib and begin to strip down their daughters to their underwear, so that a caretaker can check the children for marks. Then the mothers fill out a form about when their child last ate, the child's mood, how the baby has been sleeping. Just before the bell rings for second period, they leave the nursery and head upstairs to school. For the next seven hours, they'll get to be kids again themselves.

Grace got pregnant in January 2006, less than a month after her 14th birthday and soon after she lost her virginity to a 15-year-old boy from the neighborhood named Nikko Vega. He was the only person she'd slept with, or even wanted to. After he broke up with a girlfriend ("A ho," Grace sniffs), she began cutting her eighth-grade classes to meet him at his apartment. Even then, she had full curves and a round and inviting face. She was normally sweet, but if pressed, she could fire off a string of expletives so fast the words blurred together. Nikko liked that about her. One day, the two of them found themselves playing more than Nintendo, and they just let it happen.

"It was heat-of-the-moment stuff," Grace says of having sex for the first time. Getting pregnant wasn't even on her mind. But it was on Nikko's: "A couple of hours after, I was thinking, like, *Damn*." He eventually asked Grace if she should go on birth control, but they knew that would make her mom suspicious. They decided to take their chances, though it bothered Nikko to be so reckless. "A lot of people I knew had kids young, and I didn't want to be one of them," he admits. He had hoped to go to college on a football scholarship,

had even made a pact with his friends to put off fatherhood. "Like, ever since we were younger, we all spoke about, 'No kids.' All of us."

Grace got pregnant at 14. She told Nikko that she wanted to keep the baby and that she was happy, "in a sad sort of way."

"It didn't work," Grace says archly. "Everybody he grew up with has a kid now."

Grace didn't know she was pregnant for months. She didn't get morning sickness, headaches, or cramps. She still did step dancing, played football after school, rode roller coasters when her mom took her to a theme park, fit into her regular clothes. She hadn't been having her period long enough for its absence to be a major cause for concern. When she went to a neighborhood clinic to get tested, just in case, and the results came back positive, she was shocked. "I didn't really know what to do," she says. "I didn't know what to ask. I was just like, 'What?'"

When she told Nikko, he walked away without saying a word, but a couple of hours later, he returned, driven back by the hang-dog devotion he has for Grace and by fear of her disapproval. She told him that she wanted to keep the baby and that she was happy about the decision, "in a sad sort of way." She loved babies, but she wasn't sure what she was getting into. To the extent that he could be there for her, an extent that even he understood to be meager, Nikko said he was onboard.

It took Grace a month to work up the nerve to tell her mother. When Mayra came home from work one day, Grace, her older sister, Samantha, and her cousin were sitting in front of the building waiting for her "like there was a funeral." In the elevator ride up to the apartment, Mayra looked from one girl to the next. "Which one of you is pregnant?" she asked. She thought Samantha would answer, but when she didn't, the realization set in that it was her younger daughter who was in trouble.

"How could you?" Mayra screamed, standing in their living room, shaking with anger. "How could you? You see our situation, you see what I have on my plate. How could you be so selfish?"

Grace ran to her bedroom, sobbing. Mayra stayed in the living room, sobbing. Mayra's own mother walked in the door and demanded to know what was going on.

"Your granddaughter," Mayra wailed, "your *14-year-old* granddaughter decided you needed to see a great-grandkid."

"Oh my God," the old woman said. "*¡Ay, Dios mío! ¡Ay, Dios mío, ayúdenos!*"

For a month, Mayra cried every day. Having gotten married at 16 and had Samantha at 17, she was loath to become a grandmother at 36. She had asked Grace repeatedly if she had started having sex, and the girl had always denied it. Between her parents and her own children, the apartment was already overcrowded, and money stretched thin. She threatened to send Grace to live with her father, who had left the family a decade ago. For years, they hadn't been able to track him down. Now he had a new family in Philadelphia, and Grace had been in cautious contact. But when they called to tell him about the pregnancy, he made it clear that she wasn't welcome. Grace hasn't spoken to him since.

Mayra was surprised to find herself seriously considering abortion as an option. The South Bronx has a high birthrate in part because in this largely Hispanic and Catholic community, the idea of terminating a pregnancy meets with such intense disapproval. Her mother told her that she would not be able to live under the same roof if they went through with it, but Mayra didn't see how Grace could manage to raise a child, nor did she want to put her daughter through the difficulty of labor only to give the baby away. Grace guessed that she was about four months along and agreed to visit an abortion clinic. The sonogram showed that the baby was due in ten weeks.

"Ten weeks?" Mayra asked. "This is a 14-year-old who's been to theme parks, eaten junk food the whole time, had no prenatal care. Ten weeks? I don't know what this baby's gonna be like."

The nurse nodded sympathetically, but there was nothing to be done. "There's nowhere in this country where they'll do that abortion at seven months."

Mayra set about preparing for the baby. She arranged for Grace to be enrolled in Jane Addams, the closest school that had a LYFE program. She put a call out to friends and family for a crib, a stroller, secondhand baby clothes. She started making doctors appointments, pleading her daughter's way into clinics that didn't have openings until after the baby was due. Grace looked so young when she brought her in, no one could believe she was the one who was pregnant.

Grace's water broke in the hallway of Jane Addams the second week of her freshman year, a full month before her due date. Thinking she had wet her pants, she called her mother from a bathroom stall.

"Um, I want to go home," she said when Mayra picked up.

"Why? What happened?"

"My pants are all wet."

"What do you mean your pants are all wet? Did a car splash you or something?"

"No. Like, they're all wet. Like, I went into the bathroom, and they're all wet."

"Oh my God," Mayra cut in. "Your water broke. Oh my God! You're gonna have this baby in that school!"

When Grace arrived at Albert Einstein hospital, she was having contractions. Her mother stepped outside to calm her nerves with a cigarette, and Grace took the moment alone to ask her doctor if it was possible that she might die in childbirth. He reassured her that the chances were infinitesimally slim. "He sugarcoated it," she says. "He was a nice guy."

By the time Nikko arrived the following afternoon, Grace was in the throes of "the worst pain I ever felt in my life," she says, gasping just at the thought. She refused to allow him in the room. "I was in so much pain I really just wanted to kill him. I said, 'I advise security, doctors, nurses, everybody on this floor, if that man reaches this room, it's gonna be chaos, because this is all his fault.'"

On Sunday, September 17, 2006, at 2:55 A.M., Delilah Joli Vega was born, alert and healthy.

At the McDonald's on Prospect Avenue, teenagers crowd the counter, munching fries and competing for attention, the boys with their hooded sweatshirts pulled down low over their eyes, the girls in tight jeans and baby tees, nameplate jewelry shimmering, hair ruthlessly slicked back into high ponytails. As Iruma orders a pile of cheeseburgers and two Happy Meals, Grace and Jasmine drag high chairs up to the table and settle in with Nikko. The conversation is no different from that at any other table in the place, except for the constant interruption. There's drama going down on Grace's block—"Dumbass Samantha was talking about, 'Oh, if Sasha did punch A. J. in the face, it wasn't cause A. J. hit her, it was over Killah . . .'"—but she can't focus on the story with Lilah sending golden arcs of boxed apple juice into the air.

"Lilah, you're spilling the juice," Grace points out. "You're. Spilling. The. Juice."

Jayleen, Jasmine's daughter, looks over at Lilah, then squeezes her own juice box with vigor.

"You must want to get smacked," Grace tells her, raising her eyebrows before turning to the girl's mother. "I been telling you about that, Jasmine."

"Later, later," Jasmine pleads, not in the mood for a parenting lesson. But the fact is the mothers often act as a check on one another, imparting what parenting wisdom they have, holding one another to a certain standard. Grace, particularly, prides herself on her parenting skills. She's observant. She's strict. Her mother, Mayra, taught her how to take care of Lilah but refused to do the tasks for her. Grace was the one who changed Lilah's diapers, fed her, got up in the middle of the night when she cried. "She's not Baby Alive, is she?" Mayra would ask. "There's no off-button on her."

Having teenage parents does mean that Lilah is prone to mimic teenage behavior. "Her attitude is serious," says Grace. "She'll be like, 'Mind your business.' Mind *my* business? You better be talking to the milkman! I love her, but sometimes I just want to bop her on her head." But the good manners Lilah displays in front of company—if not always at home—testify to Grace's efforts.

Even now, as Lilah eyes the chicken nuggets that Iruma has been tearing into bite-size chunks for Dymia, she doesn't reach out and take one. "Hee dat icken, Mommy?" she asks politely.

"I see that chicken," Grace answers. "But you asked for a burger, so now you're gonna eat a burger."

"She didn't ask for a burger. You said she wanted a burger," Jasmine points out. "You're mad mean."

Grace shrugs off the comment, as a girl from their school pauses on her way past their table.

"Hey! What's up, baby?" she coos at Dymia before turning to Iruma. "She's getting so big. Oh my God!"

Iruma pushes her glasses up on her nose and smiles contentedly. "Yeah, she getting big."

"Oh my God, you're so cute!" The girl stares at Dymia, shaking her head in amazement.

In the South Bronx, the stigma of having a child at a young age is remarkably absent, not just because teen parenthood has long been pervasive but also because the family structure is such that children often grow up raising younger siblings, nieces, and nephews. Adding a child of their own into the mix doesn't seem like it will change much in terms of daily routine, but it does feel like a rite of passage, a one-way ticket to adulthood. Motherhood cements a girl's fertility, her femininity. Louder than any clingy top or painted lip, it broadcasts that now she's a woman. And for some girls, that's appealing. When *The Tyra Banks Show* did an online survey of 10,000 girls across the country, one-fifth of them said they wanted to become teen moms. The latest Centers for Disease Control report shows a 3 percent increase in teen pregnancy in 2006 after more than a decade of decline. At Jane Addams, round bellies orbit the hallways like planets. The school doesn't keep track of pregnancies, but according to the attendance officer, one week this spring, seven girls out of a student body of about 1,500 were out of school to give birth.

The mothers watch as the girl from school continues on her way, joining a booth where a group of teenagers have piled in together, plopping on each other's laps, laughing loudly at each other's jokes. None of them have children. They seem not to have a single care. The chasm between being a parent and being a kid was difficult to intuit until it was crossed. Now Grace knows it well. When Nikko once teased her about all the fun she would have without him if she went to college, she leveled a cold stare at him and asked, "How am I gonna have fun in college with a child?"

Iruma fishes her cell phone out of a bag and presses a few buttons. Hip-hop starts to blare from the little speakers, setting a more festive mood. The moms relax. Jayleen and Lilah bounce in time to the music.

"Jayleen, you want to dance for everybody?" Jasmine asks. "You want to get on the table and dance?"

Jayleen tries to climb out of her high chair, and Jasmine lifts her up onto the bench, where she plants her feet and shakes her little bottom back and forth.

"Oh, she gotta donk, she gotta donk," Jasmine chants, as Jayleen's dance grows increasingly outrageous. The moms laugh.

Sometimes it's hard not to act their age. "You need to be adult and mature, but you're still young," says Grace. "Adults have fun all the time. They still joke, they still laugh. They can't take your kid away just because of that."

When grace gets home from school one afternoon, her grandparents have two eyes of the gas stove burning to drive away the apartment's chill. She steers Lilah away from the flame and to the refrigerator, where she allows her to choose a snack. Lilah points at a pitcher of red liquid, and Grace fixes her a bottle, waiting for Nikko to get home from the GED program he started the week before. When he does, he waves a sheet of loose-leaf paper in front of her. It's his first assignment, a short essay on why he should be a candidate for the program.

"I need to finish school for my 2-year-old daughter," he starts off in an even hand. "I need to finish school for her because she follows everything that I do, and I feel that it is time for me to step up to the plate." At the bottom of the page, his teacher has written "good ideas, good motivation" and given him a B-plus. Grace seems pleased. "Oh snap, babe. Now what are you gonna do to get an A-minus?"

She's only half-joking. Even if it is sometimes misplaced, Grace has a highly evolved sense of propriety. She expects to be treated a certain way, expects Nikko to embrace his responsibilities as a father. Her loyalties now are to Lilah, and her world is delineated: There are the players and hustlers and birds, people best avoided; then there are the "cousins" and *títís* and "brothers," people she may not be related to by blood but who do well by her and her daughter. She's not quite sure yet where Nikko falls. "He be all right," she says.

It took a long time for Mayra to accept Nikko as a de facto member of the family. It wasn't just his role in the pregnancy—she understood that Grace was equally at fault—it was his own neglectful upbringing that gave her pause. She refused to have his name listed on Lilah's birth certificate until her own mother interjected. "You're gonna leave her birth certificate just blank under father, like she doesn't know who her child's father is?" the older woman asked, horrified.

Since Lilah was born, Nikko has spent a smattering of nights in jail, mostly for getting in neighborhood fights or, as he says, "being in the wrong place at the wrong time." Because his mother did not force him to go to school, he has not a single high-school credit. When Mayra took him to family court for child support (a requirement of the LYFE program), Mayra told the judge that she didn't expect any money from Nikko, that she would prefer he get an education rather than a job now, so that he could support his child later; but the judge still awarded them $25 a month—less than the cost of a box of diapers—which Nikko's mother agreed to pay until her son turned 18. Grace and Mayra have still not seen a cent.

In the end, though, it was hard to keep blaming Nikko, a child, for what Mayra saw as his mother's failings. When he didn't have a winter coat, she bought him one. When he was hungry, she fed him. When his mother kicked him out after a fight with her boyfriend, Mayra temporarily let him stay with them. Over time, he grew on her. "I basically showed her a lot of respect," says Nikko. "A lot of butt kissing," corrects Grace. Mayra realizes that, in his capacity, he is a good father: He's present. Though other girls are still dating the fathers of their children, Nikko is the only boy who visits the LYFE center. A certificate stating that he completed LYFE's fatherhood-training program hangs in a frame over Grace's bed. "The only reason I don't press it is because this baby knows who her daddy is," says Mayra. "And she loves her daddy."

Still, both Mayra and Grace find their patience sputtering. In the three years since Grace got pregnant, Nikko hadn't held a single job or completed a single class. Mayra sees the writing on the wall. She knows that the statistics are not in Nikko and Grace's favor: Only 40 percent of teenagers who have children get their high-school diplomas, and 64 percent of children born to unmarried high-school dropouts live in poverty.

"Life isn't about you anymore," Mayra is quick to inform him. "You brought someone else into this world that you have to care for. If you're gonna be that type of person that's gonna just not do nothing—and because of that, statistics is gonna land you back in jail—you may as well say bye to them now while Lilah's small and can get over you fast. Because this baby's not visiting nobody in jail." At the beginning of this year, to make good on her word, she gave him one month to prove to her that he was in school or had landed a job. Right at the deadline, he signed up for his GED.

Sometimes Grace feels that she's leaving Nikko behind. She talks of going to college, studying business, opening her own beauty salon, getting her child out of Hunts Point, away from the "hustlers and divas." She expects that there will come a day when she alone is responsible for providing for Lilah. "You can hope, we can all hope that Nikko's gonna do something to better himself and want to be there and provide for his family," Mayra tells her. "But the fact remains, if he doesn't, he wouldn't be the first boy. You wouldn't be the first single mother."

One evening early this spring, the young family has the Padilla apartment to themselves. Mayra sleeps soundly behind the closed door of the bedroom, resting up for her night shift at eleven. Grace's grandparents are at church, her sister out with friends. At times like these, Grace likes to pretend the apartment belongs to her and Nikko, that she doesn't live with her mother and he doesn't crash at a friend's place, that they've managed to make a life for themselves and Lilah on their own.

Nikko prepares a bowl of popcorn, while Grace flips through channels on the TV, stopping at a music video she knows Lilah likes. The little girl follows along with the dance in the best rendition a 2-year-old could possibly muster, stroking her hips as they wiggle furiously and then flapping her wrists like a drag queen. When she looks behind her to make sure her parents are watching, Nikko and Grace laugh at her presumption. As parents, they share an easy rapport. She teases and prods him gently; he defers to her with a good-natured grin.

Later, there's homework to be done. Grace has a field trip tomorrow, so her load is light, but Nikko struggles to write an essay on the three branches of government. Once he finishes his GED, he's hoping to enroll in junior college. Grace pulls out her U.S. history folder, shows him a few photocopied papers, then goes into the kitchen to heat up frozen chicken patties.

After they eat, she gives Lilah a bath, crouching by the bathtub and allowing her daughter to splash around as long as she likes. "You a monkey," she says, laughing as Lilah dunks her head under the water and then shakes out her curls. "When she was a baby, the funnest part was the bath because her faces were just priceless." While Nikko heats up a bottle of chocolate milk, Grace towels Lilah off, rubs her down with lotion as the child tries to squirm out of her grasp—"She likes running around naked"—and dresses her in a diaper and footed fleece pajamas. Nikko puts his homework aside to give Lilah her bottle, stretching her out across his lap and rocking her gently. He waits until she's asleep to kiss Grace good-bye.

"Love you, babe," he says.

"Love you too."

Critical Thinking

1. What is the impact of teenage motherhood on the adolescent female's life?

2. What developmental issues or concerns do teen mothers face that are particular to their situation?

Religiosity and Teen Birth Rate in the United States

Joseph M. Strayhorn, and Jillian C. Strayhorn

Background

The children of teen mothers in the U.S., on the average, have worse outcomes in a number of ways. They score lower in school achievement tests, have a greater likelihood of repeating a grade, are rated more unfavorably by teachers while in high school, have worse physical health, are more likely to be indicated victims of abuse and neglect, have higher durations of foster care placement, and are almost three times more likely to be incarcerated during adolescence or the early 20s than the children of mothers who delayed childbearing; the daughters of teen mothers are more likely to become teen mothers themselves.[1]

In the United States, what to teach adolescents about sexuality and the prevention of teen pregnancy has been controversial. A number of sex education programs in the U.S. have been mandated to be "abstinence-only" programs, excluding the teaching of contraceptive techniques. As stated in a National Public Radio poll report, "the historical impetus for abstinence education has come from evangelical or born-again Christians. . . . Eighty-one percent of evangelical or born-again Christians believe it is morally wrong for unmarried adults to engage in sexual intercourse, compared with 33 percent of other Americans. . . . More than twice as many evangelicals as non-evangelicals (49 percent to 21 percent) believe the government should fund abstinence-only programs instead of using the money for more comprehensive sex education."[2]

Other polls have presented varying results on similar questions: A 2008 poll in Minnesota[3] reported that a significantly smaller fraction of those who described themselves as "very conservative" politically and those who were "born again" Christian supported comprehensive sex education than the corresponding fractions of more liberal and non-born-again; however, in this sample, 83.2% of the born-again Christians supported comprehensive sex education; only 51% of the politically "very conservative" supported it.

The connection between religion and attitudes toward contraception prompts investigation of the relationship between religiosity and teen pregnancy.

Some studies have suggested that greater religiosity is associated with either greater abstinence or lower teen birth rate. Hardy and Raffaelli, who analyzed data from the National Longitudinal Survey of Youth, reported that higher time one religiosity predicted a lower likelihood of first sexual intercourse between time one and time two.[4] Loury concluded that communities with larger communities of Catholics and Conservative Protestants have lower rates of teen childbearing, all other things equal.[5] This conclusion was drawn from an analysis of women from age 14–20 in 1979, taken from the National Longitudinal Study of Youth. McCree and colleagues found that African-American females with higher religiosity scores were more likely to have initiated sex at a later age, to have used a condom in the last six months, and to possess more positive attitudes toward condom use.[6] Rostosky et al., found that adolescent religiosity predicted later coital debut.[7] However, there was a significant interaction between race and religiosity: African-American adolescent males who were either more religious or had signed a virginity pledge were more likely to debut than African-American males who were less religious and/or who had not signed a pledge. Miller and Gur found, upon analyzing the National Longitudinal Study of Adolescent Health in the U.S., that frequent attendance of religious events in girls 12 to 21 years old was positively associated with a "responsible and planned use of birth control".[8] Personal conservatism, however, was associated with unprotected sex. Manlove and colleagues, upon analysis of the 1997 National Longitudinal Survey of Youth, found that in the sample as a whole, greater family religiosity was associated with "using contraceptives consistently"; however, among sexually active males, family religiosity was "directly and negatively associated with contraceptive consistency".[9]

Other studies have suggested that religiosity is associated with behaviors that could lead to a higher teen birth rate. Studer and Thornton found that among 18-year-olds, religious teenagers were less likely to use medical methods of contraception when sexually active.[10] Dodge and colleagues compared male college students in the United States and the Netherlands .[11] American men reported higher rates of inadequate contraception and unwanted pregnancy than their Dutch counterparts; religiosity and sex education were thought to explain these differences.

Rosenbaum compared adolescents who reported taking a virginity pledge with a matched sample of nonpledgers.[12] Among the matching variables was pre-pledge religiosity and attitudes toward sex and birth control. Pledgers did not differ from nonpledgers in lifetime sexual partners and age of first sex, but pledgers were less likely to have used birth control and condoms in the past year and at last sex. This research raises the possibility that moralistic attitudes toward sexuality can actually increase the likelihood of pregnancy, by discouraging contraception without successfully discouraging sexual intercourse.

Such a hypothesis is bolstered by the research of Santelli and colleagues, who calculated that 86% of the decline in adolescent pregnancies that occurred between 1995 and 2002 was attributable to improved contraceptive use.[13] Santelli and colleagues cite the example of the Netherlands, which in the 1970s went through a period of soul searching and consensus-building about the need for contraception and prevention of sexually transmitted infections in adolescents, and today has one of the lowest teen birth rates in the world.[14] If contraception is more effective than attempted abstinence in reducing birth rates, then attempts to discourage both contraception and sexual intercourse among teenagers could raise teen birth rates.

A complicating variable related to teen births and religiosity is the rate of abortions among teens. Adamczyk and Felson, after analyzing longitudinal survey data from the U.S., reported that more highly religious women are less likely to have either an abortion or an out of wedlock pregnancy.[15] Tomal, upon analyzing data from 1024 counties in 18 U.S. states, found that religious membership level was negatively related to teen abortion rates.[16]

Cahn and Carbone summarized differences in attitudes about family and sexuality between the more religious and conservative U.S. "red families," versus the less religious and more liberal "blue families".[17] These authors observed: "Within red families, abstinence outside of marriage is a moral imperative, the shotgun marriage is the preferred solution to an improvident pregnancy, and socialization into traditional gender roles is critical to marital stability." The blue model, however, "involves less control of sexuality, celebrates more egalitarian gender roles, and promotes financial independence and emotional maturity as the sine qua non of responsible parenthood. In this new model, abstinence is unrealistic, contraception is not only permissible, but morally compelled, and abortion is the necessary (and responsible) fallback." (p. 3). Cahn and Carbone mention that teen birth rates appear higher among "red" families.

The present study approaches the relationship between teen birth rate and religiosity by looking at data aggregated across states in the United States.

Methods
Data Sources

This study compiled data from publicly accessible data sets. The data on religiosity were from the U.S. Religious Landscapes Survey, published by the Pew Forum on Religion and Public Life in 2008.[18] The Pew survey was conducted in 2007, with additional subjects added in 2008; it employed telephone survey methodology with a sample of 35,957 participants. We used the results of eight questions from the survey, the responses to which were broken down by state. We transcribed the percent of respondents who endorsed the most conservative religious answer to each of the eight questions. Specifically, we entered the percentages of respondents for each state who endorsed each of the following statements:

1. Belief in a God or universal spirit: Absolutely Certain.
2. There is only one way to interpret the teachings of my religion.
3. Scripture should be taken literally, word for word.
4. How important is religion in your life: Very Important.
5. My religion is the one true faith leading to eternal life.
6. Frequency of attendance at religious services: at least once a week.
7. Frequency of prayer: at least once a day.
8. How often do you receive a definite answer to a specific prayer request: at least once a month.

In the tables published in the Religious Landscapes Survey, the percents reported were aggregated across three pairs of states and across Maryland and the District of Columbia, because the sample size from at least one member of those pairs was fairly small. We obtained from the Pew Forum staff the disaggregated data and used those numbers in our data set. The sample sizes were deemed too small in Wyoming and the District of Columbia for Pew Forum to release them, and thus these data points are missing. For Rhode Island, data were missing on two of the eight questions; we imputed these missing data points by means of regression on the remaining six questions, so that Rhode Island could be included in the data set.

In order to obtain one composite religiosity score for each state, we averaged the percents of respondents endorsing the most religious answer across the eight questions.

The rates of teen birth in the fifty U.S. states plus the District of Columbia were reported by the National Center for Health Statistics at the Centers for Disease Control and Prevention.[19] The data reported were for 2006 births, the latest available (and thus the closest possible in time to the date of the collection of the religiosity data set).

A possible confounding variable in the relationship between teen birthrate and religiosity is household income level. We obtained data on the median household income by state in the U.S. from data published by the U.S. Census

Bureau.[20] The median two year average household income for 2006–2007 for each state was entered into our database.

To account for another factor which could complicate the analysis of teen birthrate and religiosity, we estimated the abortion rate among teenagers for each state. The most recent data available on abortion rates were from 2005, published by the Center for Disease Control.[21] These rates were broken down by the states of residence of the women receiving the abortions. In order to estimate rates for abortions delivered to teens only, we multiplied the overall rates by the fraction of abortions delivered to teens for 2005, as published in the same Centers for Disease Control report; these were categorized by the state in which the abortion was delivered. Data were available for 46 states; the District of Columbia, California, Florida, Louisiana, and New Hampshire were missing from this data set. The product of the abortion rate and the fraction of abortions delivered to teens yielded an estimated rate of abortions per 1000 teenaged females.

The CDC obtains its abortion rates by surveying the Central Health Departments of the various regions. A different approach is used by the Guttmacher Institute, which surveys providers of abortions. We used the Guttmacher data for 2005 to cross check abortion rates.[22]

Data Analyses

We examined the intercorrelations among the individual religiosity questions to determine whether these were high enough to form an index score. We then formed an index score by averaging the eight religiosity items.

We examined the relationships of the variables with Pearson correlations and partial correlations, as computed by SPSS.[23] The partial correlation between a first and second variable, controlling for the third, is identical to the Pearson correlation between the residuals obtained when each of the first two is regressed upon the third—in other words, when the effect of the third variable is "removed" from each of the first two.[24] We computed 95% confidence intervals for the most important correlations and partial correlations, using the Fisher r-to-z transformation. The variance of the Fisher-transformed correlation is $1/(n-3)$ for bivariate correlations, and $1/(n-k-2)$ for partial correlations, where k is the total number of independent variables (e.g., $k = 2$ for a partial correlation with one variable controlled; $k = 3$ for two variables controlled).[24]

Results
The Justification for Forming an Index from the Pew Religion Items

We examined the 28 intercorrelations among the eight different religiosity variables reported in the Pew Survey. The minimum intercorrelation was 0.55, and the maximum was 0.96. The average intercorrelation was 0.81. Thus the intercorrelation of the religiosity items are high enough to justify making an index score by averaging the scores across the eight items.

The Correlation between Teen Birth Rate and Religiosity

For all the correlational analyses reported below, we examined the plots of residuals for the regressions with the same independent variables and with teen birth as the dependent variable. There was a slight trend toward increasing residuals with increasing values of the dependent variable; in our opinion this trend was not enough to invalidate the linear model, in view of the high correlations obtained and the linear appearance of scatter plots.

Teen birth rate correlated with our composite religiosity variable with $r = 0.73$; 95% CI (0.56, 0.84); $n = 49$; $p < 0.0005$. Thus teen birth rate is very highly correlated with religiosity at the state level, with more religious states having a higher rate of teen birth. A scatter plot of teen birth rate as a function of religiosity is presented in Figure 1.

Controlling for Income and Abortion Rate

Next we considered whether median family income for states could be a confounding variable. Income negatively correlated with teen birth rate, with $r = -0.63$, $n = 51$, $p < 0.0005$. Furthermore, income correlated negatively with religiosity, with $r = -0.66$, $n = 49$; $p < 0.0005$. Thus the direction and magnitude of correlations made income a primary candidate for a confounding variable. However, the partial correlation of teen birth rate with religion while controlling for income was 0.53; 95% CI (0.29, 0.71); $df = 46$; $p < 0.0005$. Thus the correlation between religion and teen birth remained large and highly significant, even when controlling for income. The raw religiosity scores and teen birth scores shared a little over half their variance ($R^2 = 0.53$) whereas these variables with income removed by partialing shared a little over a quarter of their variance ($R^2 = 0.28$).

The correlation between teen abortion rate and religiosity was -0.45; $n = 45$; $p = 0.002$. Thus the teen abortion rate was lower in states that were more religious. Furthermore, teen abortion rate was negatively correlated with teen birth rate, with $r = -0.26$, although this relationship failed significance at the 0.05 level ($n = 47$, $p = 0.078$). Would including abortion rate as a covariate greatly affect the correlation between teen birth and religiosity? The answer turned out to be no. The partial correlation between teen birth rate and religiosity, controlling for abortion rate, was 0.68; 95% CI (0.48, 0.81); $df = 42$; $p < 0.0005$. The partial correlation between teen birth and religiosity, controlling for both income and abortion rate, was 0.54; 95% CI (0.29, 0.72); $df = 41$; $p < 0.0005$. Thus, even after taking into account the abortion rate and controlling for income, the correlation between religiosity and teen pregnancy remained high and significant.

Table 1 presents a summary of the four correlations that summarize our findings on the relationship between teen birth and religiosity.

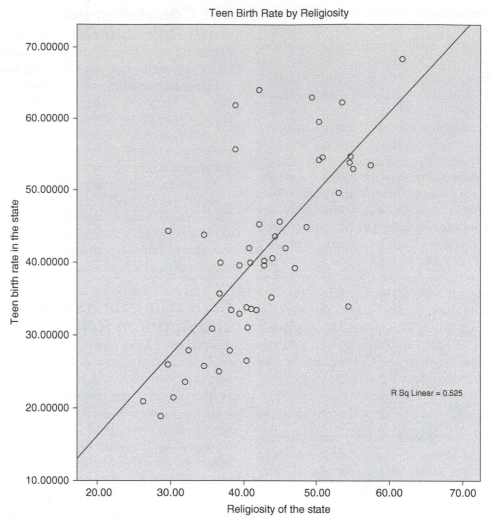

Figure 1 Scatterplot of Teen Birth Rate by Religiosity Score.

Checks for Robustness

When averaging the results of the eight items of the religiosity survey, one approach would be to first compute the z-scores for each item, and then average the z-scores. Such an approach would assign the same standard deviation to each item, so that items with higher standard deviations did not count more heavily toward the average score. When we checked this "average of standardized religiosity scores," its correlation with the average of the raw percents was 0.999 ($n = 49$, $p < 0.0005$). This result implies that the two measures are interchangeable, and that differences in standard deviations among the eight items do not appreciably influence the distribution of the average religiosity score. We used the raw percents rather than the standardized scores so that the scatterplot would be more intuitively interpretable.

Was there something about the averaging process itself that hid important information or inflated the correlation? To check this, we computed the individual correlation with teen birth rate for each of the eight religiosity items. The results are presented in Table 2.

Averaging of items probably results in a higher reliability, which would be expected to improve the correlation with teen birth; the higher reliability of the average than of the individual items is predicted by the Spearman-Brown formula.[25] However, each of the items separately reveals a reasonably high correlation with teen birth rate.

Table 1   Correlation or Partial Correlation of Teen Birth Rate with Religiosity with Various Variables Controlled

Variable(s) Controlled	None	Income	Abortion	Income and Abortion
Correlation or Partial Correlation	0.73	0.53	0.68	0.54

Table 2 Correlations of Teen Birth Rate with Individual Religiosity Items

Item	Belief God	One Interp.	Literal Scripture	Import. For Life	One True Faith	Attend Services	Frequent Prayer	Prayers Answered
Correlation	0.67	0.68	0.72	0.70	0.56	0.53	0.71	0.74

We used as the measure of religiosity the percent of respondents replying in the most religious way; how would the conclusion have been affected if we had entered the percent replying in the least religious way? Some of the questions were dichotomies, and thus the correlations for those items would have had the same magnitude with opposite sign. To check a couple of the items that were not dichotomies, we entered the percentages for the least religious response to literal interpretation of scripture and frequency of prayer, and found correlations of -0.91 and -0.90, respectively, between percent most religious and percent least religious. The correlations of teen birth with "irreligiosity" were very similar in absolute value to the correlations with religiosity for those items. The percent who prayed "seldom or never" in the states correlated at -0.67 with teen birth; the percent who felt that scripture was a "book written by men, not the word of God" correlated at -0.63 with teen birth. It appears that alternate scoring mechanisms measuring irreligiosity would yield the same conclusions and would add nothing to our results.

The Guttmacher Institute gathers data on abortion rates by contacting providers of abortions rather than central health agencies. We entered into our data set the Guttmacher abortion rate for women 15–44 for 2005; the correlation of Guttmacher abortion rate (all women) with CDC rate is 0.66 ($n = 47$, $p < 0.005$). Using the Guttmacher abortion rate rather than the CDC rate in our partial correlations made no substantive changes—for example, the partial correlation of teen birth with religiosity controlling for CDC estimated teen abortion rates was 0.68; the partial correlation controlling for Guttmacher estimated teen abortion rates (obtained by multiplying overall Guttmacher abortion rates by the fraction of abortions obtained by teens according to CDC data) was 0.65.

The variation among the fraction of teen abortion rates in different states was small enough that it made little difference for the partial correlations whether we used estimated teen abortion rates or the overall abortion rates for women in the state. The partial correlation of teen birth with religiosity, partialling out CDC abortion rates for all women was 0.69; the same partial correlation using overall rates reported by Guttmacher was 0.70. Estimated teen abortions correlated with overall abortions for the state with $r = 0.97$ for CDC rates and $r = 0.99$ for Guttmacher rates.

To what extent is the main finding reported here, i.e., the correlation between teen birth and religiosity, dependent upon any one state? Inspection of the scatterplot reveals no major outliers; two influential points appear to be those for Mississippi and Utah. Mississippi, as the state both highest in religiosity and teen birth, tends to increase the correlation; however if the correlation is recomputed without Mississippi, the correlation remains in the same region, with $r = 0.69$. Utah, which is high in religiosity but in the mid range for teen birth, tends to decrease the correlation; with Utah (but not Mississippi) eliminated the correlation between teen birth rate and religiosity would have been 0.76. For Rhode Island, we used imputation to estimate the two out of eight items that were missing; had we simply made Rhode Island a missing data point, the correlation between teen birth and religiosity would have been 0.72. Thus the magnitude of the correlation we report appears not to be greatly altered by the elimination of any one state.

Discussion

At the state level in the U.S., religiosity, as operationally defined by the eight questions of the Pew Survey, accurately predicts a high teen birth rate. The significant and high correlation continues to hold after statistically controlling for income and abortion rate.

It is a statistical maxim that higher correlations are to be found using aggregated data, for example state averages, than with individual level data. This is because some of the noise at the individual level is cancelled by the aggregation process, allowing the relationship between signals to be more clear. As stated in an introductory statistics text, "Correlations based on averages are usually too high when applied to individuals."[26] Nonetheless, the magnitude of the correlation between religiosity and teen birth rate astonished us. Teen birth is more highly correlated with some of the religiosity items than some of those items are correlated with each other. We would like to emphasize that we are not attempting to use associations between teen birth rate and religiosity, using data aggregated at the state level, to make inferences at the individual level. It would be a statistical and logical error to infer from our results, "Religious teens get pregnant more often." Such an inference would be an example of the ecological fallacy, which was explicated by Robinson in 1950[27] and reviewed by Freedman in 2001.[28] The associations we report could still be obtained if, hypothetically, religiosity in communities had an effect of discouraging contraceptive use in the whole community, including the nonreligious teens there, and only the nonreligious teens became pregnant. Or, to create a different imaginary scenario, the results could be obtained if religious parents discouraged contraceptive use in their children, but only nonreligious offspring of such religious parents got pregnant. We create these scenarios simply to illustrate that our ecological correlations do not permit statements about individuals.

We should also caution that on an individual level, certain teen pregnancies are often highly desirable, and some teen parents carry out their responsibilities exceptionally well. If it were possible to obtain good data on unplanned teen pregnancy or pregnancy by "immature" teen parents, we would use it, but we did not find such data available. Nonetheless, at the aggregate level, it is probably true that public policies or cultural practices that reduce the overall rate of teen births are, other things equal, desirable.

Our findings by themselves, of course, do not permit causal inferences. There could be unstudied confounding variables that account for the correlations we report. But if we may speculate on the most probable explanation, drawing on the other research cited above: we conjecture that conservative religious communities in the U.S. are more successful in discouraging use of contraception among their teen community members than in discouraging sexual intercourse itself.

Conclusion

At the level of states in the U.S., conservative religious beliefs predict teen birth rates highly and significantly; the correlation remains high and significant after controlling for income and estimated rates of abortion.

Competing Interests

The authors declare that they have no competing interests.

Authors' Contributions

The study was conceived by JMS, who also retrieved the data sets for the analyses. The authors shared the tasks of data entry, organization of the data, statistical analyses, and preparation of the manuscript. Both approved the final manuscript.

Acknowledgments

We are grateful to members of the Pew Forum staff for obtaining for us the disaggregated data used here, and to the reviewers of this article for thorough critical readings and helpful suggestions.

References

Hoffman SD, Maynard RA: *Kids Having Kids: Economic Costs and Social Consequences of Teen Pregnancy* 2nd edition. Washington, D.C., Urban Institute Press; 2008.

National Public Radio, Kaiser Family Foundation, Harvard University Kennedy School of Government: Sex Education in America. [www.npr.org/templates/story/story.php?storyId=1622610].

Eisenberg ME, Bernat DH, Bearinger LH, Resnick MD: Support for comprehensive sexuality education: Perspectives from parents of school-aged youth. *J Adolescent Health* 2008, 42:352–359.

Hardy SA, Raffaelli M: Adolescent religiosity and sexuality: an investigation of reciprocal influences. *Journal of Adolescents* 2003, 26:731–739.

Louri L: Teen child bearing and community religiosity. 2004 [http://ase.tufts.edu/econ]. Working Paper, Department of Economics, Tufts University.

McCree DH, Wingood GM, DiClemente R, Davies S, Harrington KF: Religiosity and risky sexual behavior in African-American adolescent females. *Journal of Adolescent Health* 2003, 33:2–8.

Rostosky SS, Regnerus MD, Wright MLC: Coital debut: the role of religiosity and sex attitudes in the add health survey. *Journal of Sex Research* 2003, 40:358–367.

Miller L, Gur M: Religiousness and sexual responsibility in adolescent girls. *Journal of Adolescent Health* 2002, 31:401–406.

Manlove J, Logan C, Moore KA, Ikramullah E: Pathways from family religiosity to adolescent sexual activity and contraceptive use. *Perspectives on Sexual and Reproductive Health* 2008, 40:105–117.

Studer M, Thornton A: Adolescent religiosity and contraceptive usage. *Journal of Marriage & the Family* 1987, 49:117–128.

Dodge B, Sandfort TGM, Yarber WL, de Wit J: Sexual health among male college students in the United States and the Netherlands. *American Journal of Health Behavior* 2005, 29:172–182.

Rosenbaum JE: Patient teenagers? A comparison of the sexual behavior of virginity pledgers and matched nonpledgers. *Pediatrics* 2009, 123:110–120.

Santelli JS, Lindberg LD, Finer LB, Singh S: Explaining recent declines in adolescent pregnancy in the United States: the contribution of abstinence and improved contraceptive use. *Am J Public Health* 2007, 97:150–156.

Santelli JS, Orr M, Lindberg LD, Diaz DC: Changing behavioral risk for pregnancy among high school students in the United States, 1991–2007. *J Adolescent Health* 2009, 45:25–32.

Adamczyk A, Felson J: Fetal positions: Unraveling the influence of religion on premarital pregnancy resolution. *Social Science Quarterly* 2008, 89:17–38.

Tomal A: The effect of religious membership on teen abortion rates. *Journal of Youth and Adolescence* 2001, 30:103–116.

Cahn N, Carbone J: Red families v. blue families (August 16, 2007). [http://ssrn.com/abstract=1008544]. GWU Legal Studies Research Paper No. 343; GWU Law School Public Law Research Paper No. 343. Available at SSRN.

Pew Forum on Religion and Public Life. U.S. Religious Landscape Survey: Religious Beliefs and Practices: Diverse and Politically Relevant. Washington, D.C.: Author; 2008.

Martin JA, Hamilton BE, Sutton PD, Ventura SJ, Menacker F, Kirmeyer S, Mathews TJ: Births: final data for 2006. In *National Vital Statistics Reports Volume 57*. Issue 7. Hyattsville, MD: National Center for Health Statistics; 2009.

U.S. Bureau of the Census: *Two-year-average median household income by state: 2004 to 2007* [www.census.gov/hhes/www/income/income07/statemhi2.xls].

Gamble SB, Strauss LT, Parker WY, Cook DA, Zane SB, Hamdan S: Abortion Surveillance—United States, 2005. *Morbidity and Mortality Weekly Report* 2008, 57:1–32.

Jones RK, Zolna MRS, Henshaw SK, Finer LB: Abortion in the United States: Incidence and access to services. *Perspectives on Sexual and Reproductive Health* 2008, 40:6–16.

SPSS, Inc: *SPSS 16.0 for Windows, release 16.0.0.* Chicago, Author 2007.

Cohen J, Cohen P: Applied multiple regression/correlation analysis for the behavioral sciences. In *Hillsdale, NJ,* Second edition. Lawrence Erlbaum Associates; 1983.

Nunnally JM: *Psychometric Theory* Second edition. New York, McGraw-Hill; 1978.

Yates DS, Moore DS, Starnes DS: *The Practice of Statistics* Second edition: New York: W.H. Freeman; 2003:230.

Robinson WS: Ecological correlations and the behavior of individuals. *American Sociological Review* 1950, 15:351–357.

Freedman DA: Ecological inference and the ecological fallacy. In *International Encyclopedia of the Social & Behavioral Sciences Volume 6.* Edited by: Smelser N, Baltes P. Philadelphia: Elsevier; 2001:4027–4030.

Critical Thinking

1. How did the researchers measure religiosity?
2. What is the relationship between teen birth rate and religiosity in the United States?
3. How does religiosity impact abortion numbers?

No Kids, No Grief
The Case against Having Kids

ANNE KINGSTON

Elaine Lui was 29 years old and had been married for a year when she and her husband, Jacek Szenowicz, decided that they didn't want children. "Before that, we didn't give it a lot of thought," says the Vancouver-based *eTalk* reporter who writes the popular celebrity gossip blog LaineyGossip.com. "It was just an assumption, 'You get married, you have kids.'" Front-line exposure to a close relative's three young children and the work they required provided a wake-up call, Lui says. "That killed it for us. We just looked at each other and said, 'We don't want them.'"

In the ensuing six years, the couple has been barraged with reasons why they should change their minds, from "Your life will have no value if you don't" to "You'll be so lonely when you get old" to Lui's favorite: "Don't you want to know what your children would look like?" "Any baby we'd have would be of mixed race," she says. "So everyone says, 'Oh, it would be so gorgeous!'" She laughs. "And I'm like, 'Wow, that's really going to make me want to change my whole life.'" It's a life the couple enjoys: they work together on her website (he handles the business side), golf together, engage in community volunteer work, and dote on their dog, Marcus.

As baby refuseniks, Lui and Szenowicz belong to a tiny but growing minority challenging the final frontier of reproductive freedom: the right to say no to children without being labelled social misfits or selfish for something they don't want.

"Are you planning to have children?" is a question Statistics Canada has asked since 1990. In 2006, 17.1 percent of women aged 30 to 34 said "no," as did 18.3 percent of men in the same category. The U.S. National Center of Health Statistics reports that the number of American women of childbearing age who define themselves as "child-free" rose sharply in the past generation: 6.2 percent of women in 2002 between the ages of 15 and 44 reported that they don't expect to have children in their lifetime, up from 4.9 percent in 1982.

Related

The 'No kids' debate continues—Writer Anne Kingston takes on the impassioned—and often cruel—reader letters about her controversial article "The case against having kids."

Still, in a pro-natalist culture that celebrates the "yummy mummy," and obsessively monitors baby bumps and the mini Jolie-Pitt entourage in magazines, saying "I don't want kids" is akin to "There's a bomb on the plane." In the past, those who chose not to have children did so quietly, observes Toronto-based poet Molly Peacock, whose 1998 memoir *Paradise, Piece by Piece* was acclaimed a breakthrough for its candid recounting of her decision not to have children. "It has been an intense and underground conversation," Peacock says, noting many childless women contacted her to say, "At last, someone is talking about what I've been living silently."

Increasingly, though, the childless by choice are vocal about it. Laura and Vincent Ciaccio are spokespeople for No Kidding!, a social club for non-parents founded in Vancouver in 1984 that now boasts more than 40 chapters in five countries. Laura, a 31-year-old attorney in New York City, refers to children as a "calling," one that she and Vincent, a PhD candidate in social psychology at Rutgers University, have decided isn't for them. "I didn't want to make such a major lifestyle change just because it was something society expected of me," she says. "Children should be something people have because they really want them."

Speaking up on the subject can elicit a smackdown. Last February, the 37-year-old British journalist Polly Vernon wrote a defiant column in the *Guardian* enumerating the reasons she didn't want children: "I'm appalled by the idea," she wrote. "Both instinctually ('Euuuw! You think I should do what to my body?') and intellectually ('And also to my career, my finances, my lifestyle and my independence?')." The response was terrifying, she reports: "Emails and letters arrived, condemning me, expressing disgust. I was denounced as bitter, selfish, un-sisterly, unnatural, evil. I'm now routinely referred to as 'baby-hating journalist Polly Vernon.'"

Lui, who observes celebrity for a living, rejects what she sees as a pernicious retrograde swing back to the '50s in which motherhood was celebrated as women's highest calling. She points to actress Jennifer Garner remaining relevant in the celebrity press simply by being photographed with her two young daughters, and to Tori Spelling reclaiming her reputation after breaking up her current husband's marriage by churning out bestsellers about motherhood. "Motherhood is the ultimate whitewash," she says. "Steal someone's husband, or be a drug addict, then become a mother and you're redeemed."

In a culture in which Jennifer Aniston's childlessness provides weekly tabloid lamentations, a female star who goes public with a decision to remain so demonstrates courage. In a recent interview in U.K. *Cosmopolitan,* the 36-year-old actress Cameron Diaz, who is childless, expressed a disinclination to have children, citing environmental reasons: "We don't need any more kids. We have plenty of people on this planet." She noted stigma still exists: "I think women are afraid to say that they don't want children because they're going to get shunned." But she also expressed optimism the tide was turning: "I have more girlfriends who don't have kids than those that do," she said.

Now the childless in North America have their most defiant advocate in a mother of two: Corinne Maier, a 45-year-old French psychotherapist whose manifesto, *No Kids: 40 Good Reasons Not to Have Children,* created a furor when published in France last year. Count on the same happening when it's released here this week. Among Maier's hard-won advice: "If you really want to be host to a parasite, get a gigolo."

The societal shift in attitudes toward childlessness is most evident in language, with the buoyant "child-free" replacing "childless," a word stigmatized for conveying a void or handicap. The childless minority has always been with us. But in the past why they didn't procreate wasn't the concern of mainstream academic study or social debate: to the extent it was even considered, it was assumed that they couldn't due to some biological reason or chose not to for negative reasons, such as having had a bad childhood themselves.

The arrival of the pill in the 1960s, which allowed women to delay childbearing, also permitted them to forgo it altogether. Support groups popped up to allow like-minded people to congregate—the first being the National Organization for Non-Parents formed in Palo Alto, Calif., in 1972.

With the advent of the "child-free" came a rethink of the reproductive imperative, formerly assumed to be hard-wired in every human brain. But as demographer David Foot, a professor of economics at the University of Toronto, points out, social factors also play a role, the most significant being female education, which was also abetted by the pill's arrival. "The higher the education a woman has, the greater likelihood that she won't have children," he says. This is consistent across cultures, he notes. The birth rate in Iran, where women go to university, is lower than that in the U.S., where census data reveals voluntarily childless women have the highest incomes compared to other women. In the U.K., 40 percent of university graduates aged 35 are childless; it has been estimated that at least 30 percent will stay that way.

Why this is happening is the subject of much theorizing: educated women delay childbearing until it's no longer an option; they refuse to pay what economists call the "motherhood premium" in which the salaries of university-educated women plateau after childbirth and then drop, while fathers' incomes are unaffected; they recognize that raising children is a sacrifice of time, money and freedom they're not willing to make; or they simply don't want to have children and are able to say no.

(The matter is complicated, Foot observes, because income level is also linked to procreation. What is known is that paying women to have children doesn't work: the only variable proven to increase the chances of women having children is to offer a supportive social network, as evident by the rising fertility rates attributed to government initiatives in Scandinavian countries and France, where generous tax breaks, incentives, and maternity- and parental-leave provisions have resulted in the birth rate rising to 2.7 per woman, the highest level in Europe.)

A growing literature on childlessness has emerged. It has been deemed a "revolution" in *The Childless Revolution: What It Means to Be Childless Today* by Madelyn Cain, herself a mother. Academic treatises such as Mardy Ireland's *Reconceiving Women: Separating Motherhood from Female Identity* attempt to diffuse stereotypes. There are also the cheerleaders, viz. Nicki Defago's *Childfree and Loving It!* And the issue has been politicized in books such as Elinor Burkett's *The Baby Boon: How Family-Friendly America Cheats the Childless,* which contends the "child-free" subsidize "breeders."

The array of narratives reveals that the choice not to have children can be as complex—or as elemental—as the desire to have them, as reflected in *Nobody's Mother: Life without Kids,* a 2004 anthology of essays by a diverse group of Canadian women, and *Nobody's Father* from the male perspective, published in 2006. Many women knew they didn't want children as children, a claim backed by research in *The Childless Revolution* that explores the notion that the impulse not to have children is genetic, like being gay. Most were clear-eyed that the choice required a new anchorage. "Children were not a way of ensuring happiness or endowing my days with meaning," the poet Lorna Crozier writes. "That hard task was mine alone." The American author Lionel Shriver, who never wanted children, writes in "Separation From Birth" that her greatest fear "was of the ambivalence itself": "Imagine bearing a child and then realizing, with this helpless, irrevocable little person squalling in its crib, that you'd made a mistake. Who really, in that instance, would pay the price?"

But no book on the subject has been more provocative or summoned more furor than Corinne Maier's *No Kids: 40 Good Reasons Not to Have Children.* It isn't the first time the Freudian analyst hit the French national nerve: her 2004 book *Hello Laziness: The Art and the Importance of Doing the Least Possible in the Workplace* pilloried the country's famously lax workplace culture. In *No Kids* she deploys an acerbic wit to dismantle the idealized depiction of parenthood perpetuated by the French state, "the fertility champion of Europe," a distinction greeted by the country's media like a sporting triumph.

Speaking from her home in Brussels, Maier says she was prompted to write *No Kids* by a conversation she had with two female friends in their 30s who told her they felt like social deviants because they didn't want children. That perception is well-founded, she writes: "To be childless is considered a defect; irrevocably judged, those who just don't want children are also the objects of pity." But Maier believes "conscientious objectors to this fertility mythology" should be rewarded, not stigmatized. "To have a kid in a rich country is not the act of a citizen," she writes. "The state should be helping those who decide not to have children: less unemployment, less congestion, fewer wars."

She admits there are times she regretted having her own children, now aged 14 and 11, a declaration that has predictably branded her a "bad mother" whose children are destined for a lifetime of therapy. (Yet she's only saying what many mothers silently think but aren't allowed to say. In 1975, Ann Landers famously asked readers: "If you had it to do over again, would you have children?" Seventy percent of respondents said "no.") Maier reports that when she had her children she was madly in love, a hostage to her hormones. She too bought into the modern parenting mythology that children could be psychic curatives. Raised as an only child, she believed children would end her feelings of loneliness. Instead, she says, their arrival created new forms of loneliness.

The professional provocateur cuts through the gauzy romanticized depiction of parenthood promoted in France, which has far less to do with love of children than "a form of nationalism to enhance our identity," she says. Maier doesn't mince words, calling labor "torture," and breastfeeding "slavery." The idea that children offer fulfillment is also dismantled: "Your kid will inevitably disappoint you" is reason No. 19 not to have them. Much of what she has to say won't be breaking news to most parents: children kill desire in a marriage and can be demanding money pits. Without them, you can keep up with your friends and enjoy your independence.

Research backs Maier's assertions. Daniel Gilbert, who holds a chair in psychology at Harvard and is the author of the 2006 best-seller *Stumbling on Happiness,* reports that childless marriages are far happier. He also reports researchers have found that people derive more satisfaction from eating, exercising, shopping, napping, or watching television than taking care of their kids: "Indeed, looking after the kids appears to be only slightly more pleasant than doing housework," he writes in *Stumbling on Happiness.*

Yet a 2007 Pew Research Center survey found people insisted that their relationships with their children are of the greatest importance to their happiness. Gilbert believes the reason people say this is because they're expected to. He puts it in clinical economic terms: the more people pay for an item, the more highly they tend to value it, and children are expensive: the latest data suggests it costs upward of $250,000 to raise one to age 18.

No Kids is less anti-child polemic, however, than scathing cultural criticism. Maier lampoons the modern family ("an inward-looking prison focused on the child") and the prevailing mindset that celebrates reproducing one's DNA as "the ultimate objective of human experience." Over-attentive focus on children saps cultural creativity, she argues: "Children are often used as an excuse for giving up on life without really trying. It takes real courage to say 'Me first.'"

Parents, not non-parents, are the selfish ones, she avers: "Every baby born in a developed country is an ecological disaster for the whole planet." She's pessimistic about these babies' future prospects, telling French women their children will be "loser babies," destined for unemployment or to become factory drones. Maier blames contraception, which allows people to opt out of parenthood, for irrevocably altering the parenting dynamic. Once, "people had children because they had them," she says. Now, every child must be a desired child, which requires of parenthood a "performance worthy of Superman or Superwoman."

And that in turn has created a backlash among the childless that is less focused on children than on modern parenting itself, what Lui refers to as the "mommy cult" and Vernon calls the "pampering cult of Bugaboo-wielding, Mumsnet-bothering dullness." Like Maier, Vernon doesn't like what parenting does to grown-ups: "Spare me the one-track conversations. Spare me the self-righteousness, the sense of entitlement . . . Spare me the pretensions of martyrdom and selflessness." There's nothing selfless about having a baby, she argues, pulling out The Planet card: "You really want to be selfless? Adopt, lover."

Shriver is less righteous about the non-parenting choice, admitting "there is something nihilistic about refusing to reproduce, selfish in the worst way." She explains: "Take individual fulfillment at the expense of parenthood to the limit, and one generation has a cracking good time, after which the entire human race, poof, vanishes from the planet." (This, in fact, is precisely the goal of the most extreme childlessness advocates out there: the Voluntary Human Extinction Movement, which says, "the hopeful alternative to the extinction of millions of species of plants and animals is the voluntary extinction of one species: *Homo sapiens . . . us.*")

Now that we're a full generation into voluntary childlessness, research is beginning to reveal the longer-term consequences. Ingrid Connidis, a sociologist at the University of Western Ontario and the author of *Family Ties and Aging,* has conducted pioneering studies among people 55 and over that distinguish between those who are childless by choice and those who are childless by circumstance. All have adapted, she says: "But the childless by choice are more content, have higher levels of well-being and are less depressed." She has also compared levels of satisfaction between the childless and parents, dividing the latter group into parents who have a good relationship with their children and those who do not. "Parents who don't have good relationships with children are not as happy as people with good relationships with their children or people who are childless by choice," she says.

Molly Peacock's husband, Michael Groden, an English professor at the University of Western Ontario, says he has no regrets about not being a parent. Now 62, he says fatherhood was never a life goal. He and Peacock, who dated as teenagers, married 16 years ago, "Reconnecting with me sort of made that a conscious thought for him," she says.

As part of his doctoral dissertation, Vincent Ciaccio is investigating why men choose to remain childless—new terrain. As with women, the reasons are all over the map, and include "betterment of relationships," "career motivations," "fear of failure as a father," "not liking kids," and "the desire to remain in their current lifestyle."

Connidis's research also explores the common concern that the childless will be lonely or bereft in old age. She found they're no less lacking in support than those with children.

"They've created their own network," she says, noting people without children are more likely to end up in a nursing home. Her conclusion: "There's no guarantee that having children will make you happy or not having them will make you sad."

Of course, the idea that parenting choices should bring happiness one way or the other has modernity written all over it. But what any happiness appears to stem from is not children or their absence but rather the ability to make the choice.

Maier, who's a brilliant contradiction of her own claim that women have to choose between motherhood and success, knows her polemic would have been ignored if she didn't have children; she would have been judged "a bitter, jealous old hag," she writes. *No Kids* puts her in a no-win position, she says with

a laugh: "People think I'm a bad mother. But if I didn't have children, people would have said I'm a person who is not happy because I don't have children."

It's an ironic Catch-22 that it takes a parent to support the choice not to become one. But somebody has to do it. As Elaine Lui points out: "Why did we fight so hard for the right to make this choice, only to have it not respected when we do?"

Critical Thinking

1. What challenges do people with children face?

2. What reasons do some people have for not having children?

3. What is the social significance of remaining child-free?

Role Reversal

Amid bruised egos, resentments and confusion, families are struggling to find their footing as they cope with the financial, emotional and who-does-the-dishes-now restructuring of their lives brought on by the recession.

SARA ECKEL

On a cold, rainy November morning, Christine Fruehwirth's 5-year-old son showed up at preschool without a coat—or even a sweater. "The sweater was dirty," says Christine's husband, John. He also had taken their 7-year-old daughter out to run errands in the ballerina pajamas she'd slept in. "I didn't know. I thought it was an outfit," John says of the wardrobe mishap, one of several that have occurred since he took over many of the household and child-care duties two years ago. That's when he lost his job as the managing director of a Washington, DC, private equity firm. To support their family of five, Christine began working part-time as a career consultant for George Washington University in addition to the career-coaching business she was already running out of their home.

Like many families coping with the turmoil brought on by the recession, the Fruehwirths have been fumbling to find their footing now that the roles of family breadwinner and household caretaker have been shuffled around. Though Christine, 40, had planned to work while her three kids were young, she was thinking one job, not two. But now she says, "Maybe this was meant to be." She's appreciating the chance to further develop her professional life. And although John is adamant that he's *not* a stay-at-home dad—he's developing a private equity company he purchased with his severance pay—he's enjoying extra time with the kids now that he's the one taking them to and from school and helping them with homework.

With job loss comes heightened anxiety, as well as recast parental and household duties, causing a major upheaval in many families. Working moms are increasingly logging extra hours in the office—and spending more time away from their children—while more men are finding themselves without an office to go to. Getting the bills paid and cutting back on nonessential spending is a strain for sure. Yet for many, the greatest challenge hasn't been financial; it's been psychological. Amid all the changes, moms and dads are trying to adjust not only to new daily schedules but also to bruised egos and growing resentments. We talked to couples about how their families are coping with this shift—and learned what they're doing to keep the peace.

Shattered Self-esteem

After Stefania Sorace Smith's husband lost his security job last May, she landed a higher-paying position in her profession, as the residential programmer at a home for mentally disabled people. But she also doubled her commuting time, and her workweek soared to 60 hours from 40—a particular strain since she's now pregnant with the couple's second child. Even with her higher salary and the part-time work her husband, Darren, has secured, the Dingman's Ferry, PA, couple has not made up the lost income. Now charged with the family's financial security, Stefania, 26, is more stressed than ever. "Bills definitely get behind," she says, adding that she sometimes plays "Russian roulette" with her checkbook by alternating which bills she pays—and which she skips—each month. At home, Darren is doing more of the basic cleaning, and he makes their 2-year-old daughter breakfast and prepares dinner for the family—but the major scrub work still falls to Stefania because he "just doesn't do it the way I want it done," she says.

For Stefania, one of the biggest disparities in this new structure is free time. She spends most of her day working and commuting. Darren—while doing handyman work and pitching in with the household chores—still spends a fair amount of time playing Flight Simulator on his computer. "This transition has been tough," he says. "I started building houses when I was twelve. I'm used to working ninety hours a week. All I ever did was work." Though he's enjoying the time he spends with his daughter, he feels unproductive. "It's difficult to go from self-sufficient to depending on someone, but we're making it work," he says. "It is what it is."

The ego blow of job loss leaves many men unable to find fulfillment in their new role. In the months after Ron Mattocks was laid off two years ago, he admits, he had a tough time transitioning from his former life as a vice president of sales for a major homebuilder to Daddy Day Care. "I was an officer in the army and then an executive in the corporate world. Suddenly, I'm packing lunches and making sure the kids have everything in their backpacks. My entire self-image pretty much got shattered," says Ron, 37, from Houston. "I had to really rethink myself, and that's been a long, discouraging process."

Feeling the Pain

The loss of a husband's job can cause severe stress as some families move into smaller homes or scramble to secure health insurance. Here, a snapshot by the numbers.

- **75%** of the jobs lost during this recession were held by men. That has made the ever-growing share of women in the workforce even larger.
- **51%** of all workers on U.S. payrolls are women, compared with 33% in 1969.
- **31%** of working moms earned as much as or more than their husbands in 2008 vs. 11% in 1967. More women are now the primary breadwinner.

He misses the external validation he got through his work—the backslapping for a job well done—and is struggling to find that same sense of confidence internally. It has helped, however, to see his wife, Ashley, gain confidence in her career. "Though I don't bring value to the family the way I used to, my role is important," he says.

Why Men Don't Do Windows

Wives should be mindful of the fact that a recently unemployed husband is in a fragile emotional state, says Ellen Ostrow, PhD, a psychologist who works with professional women reentering the workforce. "The psychological impact is enormous," she says. This is one reason many men don't automatically start picking up the scrub brush after a job loss. According to the 2008 American Time Use Survey released by the U.S. Bureau of Labor Statistics, unemployed women spend almost six hours a day on child care and household chores like cleaning and cooking, while unemployed men spend only three hours a day on such tasks— and also spend more than four hours a day watching television.

Often men with a very traditional view of gender roles will refuse to do housework, as a way to gain control, says Stephanie Coontz, who teaches history and family studies at The Evergreen State College in Olympia, WA. "They think that they have to compensate for their loss of masculinity by asserting masculine privilege in other ways."

But the reasoning may be even more subtle than that. Jeremy Adam Smith, author of *The Daddy Shift,* suggests that most men simply don't see housework and child care as a vocation that could give them a sense of identity and pride, as many women do. "For a lot of women who lose their job, a pathway presents itself," he says. "They decide, 'I'm a stay-at-home mom. My job now is to take care of the home and kids, and I'm going to be good at that.' But for many fathers, that pathway doesn't exist in any well-developed way."

Teaching the Basics

However understandable this aversion to scouring bathtubs and laying out school clothes may be, the fact remains that the work needs to be done. Kelly Sons says her marriage became

Making Mr. Mom

Do you bring home the bacon—but he refuses to fry it up in a pan? Experts say there are ways to nudge even the most reluctant husband into doing his share.

Make a plan. Rather than give him piecemeal instructions or complaints about picking up dry cleaning, sit down with him and discuss what needs to be done— and decide who should do it. "It's quite likely that the husband doesn't *know* what Mom did. Everything just sort of happened," says Professor Joan C. Williams, JD, director of the Center for WorkLife Law at the University of California, Hastings.

Give up control. He may not do the laundry or load the dishwasher the way you do, but if the work is getting done, don't nitpick. "Wives do have this tendency to regard husbands as unskilled assistants, but that's the worst thing you can do to men who have had the ego blow of being laid off," says family historian Stephanie Coontz, author of *Marriage, a History: How Love Conquered Marriage.*

Show your appreciation. It doesn't matter if the pork chops overcooked—let him know how much you appreciate coming home to a hot meal. Coontz says that most families don't show enough gratitude, which is essential for marital harmony—and why, for example, men who do more housework also have more sex. One survey found that the more housework a man did, the happier he was with his sex life.

rocky two years ago when her husband's declining auto repair business forced her to support the family. The problem wasn't the *paying* work—Kelly gets tremendous satisfaction from her freelance writing—but rather her second shift as the primary caregiver to their six children. "He assumed that I would handle everything. I was incredibly stressed out," says Kelly, 40, of Morrison, TN.

Though working mothers have long grumbled that their spouses are slackers when it comes to housework in their dual-income homes, a husband's refusal to chip in often becomes intolerable when she's suddenly working longer hours and he's home all day. Kelly's very traditional husband, James, had to be schooled in the basics—like the fact that their sons' black clothes should not be washed with the bathroom towels—but he did gradually step up. Today, he runs the household with pride. "He does most of the housework and takes care of our children and actually brags about me to his friends," says Kelly.

Getting to that point was a long, painful process, says Kelly. Her breakthrough came when she realized that instead of fighting and nagging, she needed to make him a partner in finding the solution. "I told him we needed to figure this out—together." With each would-be housework war, she stopped taking on full responsibility and instead turned to him for an answer. "If our family wanted to go to the local aquarium, I'd say, 'I can't go

The Impact on Your Kids

Studies show that a drop in family income can have a negative effect on child development, particularly when parents become depressed, disengaged or argumentative. Kids can struggle with behavioral issues, anxiety or depression. To fend off problems:

Stay positive. Shield kids from any escalating fighting. Be honest but "use language that doesn't scare them," says Joshua Coleman, PhD, cochair of the Council on Contemporary Families. Say, "It's going to work out. Dad will find another job."

Reassure them. Assure kids that it's not their fault if Mom and Dad are feeling a bit down right now. "Children tend to personalize things," Dr. Coleman says. "If they can't make a parent happy, they think there is something wrong with them."

Enlist their help. Ask if they can think of ways the family can save money—like starting a garden or cutting back on soda. "Use it as a teaching experience that can show them that crisis is a part of life and this is how we deal with it," says Dr. Coleman.

until I have this work done and the house is clean, so how is that going to happen?'"

"Watching the Michael Keaton character in the movie *Mr. Mom* struggle with his new role and then master it had a big influence on my husband."

Surprisingly, one of the most helpful influences came from an old movie. "It sounds crazy, but a lot of it had to do with *Mr. Mom*. Watching the Michael Keaton character struggle with his new role and then master it and eventually take pride in it had a big influence on James." Kelly has also made sure to recognize her husband's contribution—even though it was completely taken for granted when she was doing it. "That's what made it so hard at first. Nobody ever told me thank-you." Since James was sensitive to criticism, especially about his cooking, she always tried to find something positive to say and advises other women to do the same: "Find the good in it even if it's the worst thing you've ever eaten . . . Well, it smells good."

Making Inroads

While they may not do as much around the house as women, American men are doing substantially more than their fathers or grandfathers ever did. In 1980, 29 percent of wives reported that their husbands did absolutely no housework; 20 years later, that figure dropped to 16 percent. And today, a third of American wives report that their husbands do at least half or more of either the housework or the child care.

"The more attached a man is to the size of his paycheck, the more difficult the transition will be," says Coontz. "The good news is a lot of men have been discarding that kind of identity. They're seeing themselves less as workers and more as husbands and fathers."

Of course, it's not just men who have a hard time letting go of old roles. Many women have a difficult time seeing Dad do his job a little too well. Dara Turketsky Blaker, 42, a music educator from Coral Springs, FL, says her heart breaks when her daughter wakes up in the middle of the night and calls for Daddy. "At first it was all about Mommy, and then suddenly it wasn't."

The question remains: Once kids get used to spending more time with Dad, Mom learns to appreciate his quirky housekeeping and parents value each other's role, will it last when the economy rebounds? For the Fruehwirths, seeing how the other half lives has given them more empathy for each other. "We often laugh about it," says Christine. "I'll come home and say, 'That commute was an hour!' and he'll say, 'Yeah, I remember.' Or he'll say, 'The kids drove me crazy,' and I'll say, 'Yeah, been there.'" Whether or not roles revert back remains to be seen. But the growing empathy couples say they've experienced for one another cannot help but linger. They know firsthand that indeed the surest cure for judging another person is to walk a mile in their shoes.

Critical Thinking

1. Predict percentage of male homemaker, female breadwinner by 2015.
2. Identify factors that make a job loss psychologically traumatic.
3. Give advice for making role reversal more fulfilling for men and women.

An Affair to Remember

She was 82. He was 95. They had dementia. They fell in love. And then they started having sex.

MELINDA HENNEBERGER

Bob's family was horrified at the idea that his relationship with Dorothy might have become sexual. At his age, they wouldn't have thought it possible. But when Bob's son walked in and saw his 95-year-old father in bed with his 82-year-old girlfriend last December, incredulity turned into full-blown panic. "I didn't know where this was going to end," said the manager of the assisted-living facility where Bob and Dorothy lived. "It was pretty volatile."

Because both Bob and Dorothy suffer from dementia, the son assumed that his father didn't fully understand what was going on. And his sputtering cell phone call reporting the scene he'd happened upon would have been funny, the manager said, if the consequences hadn't been so serious. "He was going, 'She had her mouth on my dad's penis! And it's not even clean!'" Bob's son became determined to keep the two apart and asked the facility's staff to ensure that they were never left alone together.

After that, Dorothy stopped eating. She lost 21 pounds, was treated for depression, and was hospitalized for dehydration. When Bob was finally moved out of the facility in January, she sat in the window for weeks waiting for him. She doesn't do that anymore, though: "Her Alzheimer's is protecting her at this point," says her doctor, who thinks the loss might have killed her if its memory hadn't faded so mercifully fast.

But should someone have protected the couple's right to privacy—their right to have a sex life?

"We were in uncharted territory," the facility manager said—and there's a reason for that. Even the *More* magazine-reading demographic that thinks midlife is forever (and is deeply sorry to see James Naughton doing Cialis ads) seems to believe that while sex isn't only for the young, exceptions are only for the exfoliated. We're squeamish about the sex lives of the elderly—and even more so when those elderly are senile and are our parents. But as the baby boom generation ages, there are going to be many more Dorothys and Bobs—who may no longer quite recall the Summer of Love but are unlikely to accept parietal rules in the nursing home. Gerontologists highly recommend sex for the elderly because it improves mood and even overall physical function, but the legal issues are enormously complicated, as Daniel Engber explored in his 2007 article "*Naughty Nursing Homes*": Can someone with dementia give informed consent? How do caregivers balance safety and privacy concerns? When families object to a demented person being sexually active, are nursing homes responsible for chaperoning? This one botched love affair shows the incredible intensity and human cost of an issue that, as Dorothy's doctor says, we can't afford to go on ignoring.

Dorothy's daughter, who contacted me, said that, in a lucid moment, her mother asked her to publicize her predicament. "We're all going to get old, if we're lucky," said the daughter, who is a lawyer. And if we get lucky when we're old, then we need to have drawn up a sexual power of attorney before it's too late. Who controls the intimate lives of people with dementia? Unless specific provision has been made, their families do. And for Dorothy, which is her middle name, and Bob, which isn't his real name at all, that quickly became a problem.

"Who do you love?" Dorothy asked me, right after her daughter introduced us. She'd married her first—and only other—sweetheart, a grade-school classmate she'd grown up with in Boston and waited for while he flew daylight bombing raids over Germany during World War II. Together they had four children, built a business, and traveled all over the world, right up until she lost him to a heart attack 16 years ago. But she never mentions him now and doesn't like it when anyone else does, either, because how could she not remember her own husband? Her daughter visits every evening, and because Dorothy loves kids, her daughter pays the housekeeper to bring hers over every afternoon, "and she thinks they're her grandchildren, and it makes her happy."

But even showing me around her well-appointed, little apartment in the nice-smelling assisted-living facility was an exercise in frustration for Dorothy: She joked and covered, but she might as well have been guiding me through Isabella Stewart Gardner's house, because all around were tokens from her past that have lost their meaning for her. There were tiny busts of Bach and Brahms, a collection of miniature porcelain pianos, Japanese woodcuts, and some Thomas Hart Benton lithographs she picked up for a few dollars in the '40s. "These are all my favorites," she said, pointing to shelves of novels by the Brontes and books about Leonardo da Vinci and Franklin and Eleanor Roosevelt. But her expression said that she couldn't recall why she liked these volumes best, and what I think she wanted me to know is that she once was a person who could have told me. When her daughter mentioned Bob's name—Bob, who was led away in January, shouting, "What's going on? Where are you taking me?" right in front of her—it wasn't clear how much she remembered: "He came and he went, and there's nothing more to say."

So it was left to her daughter, her doctor, and the woman who runs the assisted-living facility to explain how this grown woman, who lived through the Depression and survived breast cancer, managed a home and mourned a mate, wound up being treated like a child. "Come back anytime," Dorothy told me sweetly.

Downstairs, in her bright, tidy office, I met the woman who runs the facility—one of the nicest I've seen, with tea service in the lobby and white tablecloths in a dining room that's dressed up like a restaurant. In 30 years of taking care of the elderly, she's seen plenty of couples, but none as "inspiring" or heart-breaking as Dorothy and Bob. Which is why she keeps a photo of the two of them on her desk. In the picture, Dorothy is sitting at the piano in the lobby, where she used to play and he used to sing along—with gusto, usually warbling, "I dream of Jeanie with the light brown hair," no matter what tune she was playing. She is all dolled up, wearing a jangly red bracelet and gold lamé shoes, and they are holding hands and beaming in a way that makes it impossible not to see the 18-year-olds inside them.

Before Dorothy came along, the manager said, Bob was really kind of a player and had all the women vying to sit with him on the porch. But with Dorothy, she said, "it was love." One day, the staff noticed that they were sitting together, then before long they were taking all their meals together, and over a matter of weeks, it became constant. Whenever Bob caught sight of Dorothy, he lit up "like a young stud seeing his lady for the first time." Even at 95, he'd pop out of his chair and straighten his clothes when she walked into the room. She would sit, and then he would sit. And both of them began taking far greater pride in their appearance; Dorothy went from wearing the same ratty yellow dress all the time to appearing for breakfast every morning in a different outfit, accessorized with pearls and hair combs.

Soon the relationship became sexual. At first, Dorothy's daughter and the facility manager doubted Dorothy's vivid accounts of having intercourse with Bob. But aides noticed that Bob became visibly aroused when he kissed Dorothy good night—and saw that he didn't want to leave her at her door anymore, either. (Note to James Naughton: Bob did not need what you are selling.) His overnight nurse was an obstacle to sleepovers, but the couple started spending time alone in their apartments during the day. When Bob's son became aware of these trysts, he tried to put a stop to them—in the manager's view because the son felt that old people "should be old and rock in the chair." When I called Bob's son and told him I was writing about the situation without using any names, he passed on the opportunity to explain his perspective. "I don't choose to discuss anything that involves my father," he said, and he put the phone down.

But according to the facility manager, the son was convinced that Dorothy was the aggressor in the relationship, and he worried that her advances might be hard on his father's weak heart. He wasn't the only one troubled by the physical relationship. The private-duty nurse who had been tending Bob also had strong feelings about the matter, said the manager: "At first, she thought it was cute they were together, but when it became sexual, she lost her senses" for religious reasons and asked staff members to help keep the two of them apart.

Employees wound up choosing sides—as did other residents, including some women who were apparently jealous of Dorothy's romance. And because the couple now had to sneak around to be together—for instance, cutting out when they were supposed to be in church—their intimacy became more and more open and problematic. At one point, the manager had to make Bob stop "pleasuring her" right in the lobby, where Dorothy sat with a pillow placed strategically over her lap. In all of her years of working with elderly people, the manager said, this was not only her worst professional experience but was the only one that left her feeling she had failed her patients. She had a particularly hard time staying neutral and detached, she said, because she kept thinking that "if that was my mom or dad, I'd be grateful they'd found somebody to spend the rest of their lives with."

One day when Dorothy's daughter arrived to visit, she found Bob sitting in the lobby, surrounded by a wheelchair brigade of dozing people who had been posted around him by the private-duty nurse to block Dorothy from approaching him. That's when Dorothy's daughter got the state involved and started throwing around the word *lawsuit*, which only made things worse, the manager said. "Once she started talking legal, that pushed things over the edge." The state did send someone in to try to mediate the situation—but then the mediator was diagnosed with cancer and died just five weeks later. Though the mediator's replacement tried to pick up where he had left off, she was never able to establish a rapport with Bob's son.

Finally, Bob's family decided to move him and insisted that neither he nor Dorothy be told in advance. No one in either family was there the morning Bob's nurse hustled him out the door. Later, the manager called his son and asked if there was any way Dorothy might come and visit just briefly, to say good-bye. The son thought about it for a few days and then said no, his father was already settled into his new home and was not thinking about her at all anymore. The lawyers told Dorothy's family that there was no way they could make the legal case that Bob's rights were being violated by his family, because you couldn't put people with dementia on the witness stand.

Dorothy's son-in-law, who is a doctor, suspects Bob's son of fearing for his inheritance. Bob had repeatedly proposed for all to hear and called Dorothy his wife, but his son called her something else—a "gold digger"—and refused to even discuss her family's offer to sign a prenup. According to Dorothy's daughter, Bob's son told her, "My father has outlived three wives, including the one he married in his 80s, and your mother is just one of many." But surely Bob's safety was a true concern, too, and maybe his son had religious or moral qualms? "I don't think so," the manager said. "I don't think he meant his dad any harm, but he couldn't see what his dad needed. . . . He wanted his dad to have a relationship but on his terms: You can sit together at meals, but you can't have what really makes a relationship, and be careful how much you kiss and don't retire to a private place to do what all of us do."

Though Dorothy might or might not remember what happened, "there's a sadness in her" that wasn't there before, the manager said. Bob "gave her back something she had long lost—to think she's pretty, to care about her step and her stride." She eats in her room now rather than in the dining room where she shared meals with Bob. And she no longer plays the piano. A new couple in the facility has gotten together in the last few weeks. The manager called their families in right away and was relieved to see that they were happy for their parents, and the families have been taking them on outings together. As a result of the whole experience, the manager, who is 50, recently had a different version of "the talk" with her 25-year-old daughter, instructing her never, ever to let such a thing happen to her or her husband: "I hope I get another shot at it when I'm 90 years old."

Dorothy's doctor also took their experience personally. "Can you imagine as a clinician, treating a woman who's finally found happiness and then suddenly she's not eating because she couldn't see her loved one? This was a 21st-century *Romeo and Juliet*. And let's be honest, because this man was very elderly, I got intrigued; my respects to the gentleman." His patient was happier than he could ever remember; she was playing the piano again, and even her memory had improved.

And though the doctor never laid eyes on Bob, in general, he said, the fear of sex causing heart attacks is wildly overblown: "If you've made it to age 95, I'm sorry, but having sex is not going to kill you—it's going to prolong your life. It was as if someone had removed the sheath that was covering [Dorothy], and she got to live for a while." But after the trauma of losing Bob, Dorothy's doctor came close to losing his patient, he said, adding that most people her age would not have survived the simultaneous resulting insults of depression, malnutrition, and dehydration. "We can't afford the luxury of treating people like this. . . . But we don't want to know what our parents do in bed."

Then the daughter interjected that Bob's son certainly didn't want to see them having oral sex, and the doctor proved his own point. Holding a hand up to stop her from saying any more, he told her, "I didn't need to know that." But maybe the rest of us do.

Critical Thinking

1. What challenges might elderly people who live in institutional settings face as they seek emotional and physical intimacy with another person?

2. How can prevailing social and cultural beliefs about sex and the elderly impact opportunities for intimate relationships in later life?

MELINDA HENNEBERGER is a *Slate* contributor and the author of *If They Only Listened to Us: What Women Voters Want Politicians To Hear.*

UNIT 4

Intimacies and Relationships

Unit Selections

Learning Outcomes

After reading this Unit, you will be able to:

- Describe how to improve the feeling of satisfaction in a marriage.

- Explain how people sometimes view their partner in ways that can be detrimental to the relationship.

- Describe the attributes of a successful relationship.

- Describe what factors are associated with the end of a relationship.

- Discuss the evolution of marriage within social and historical context.

- Discuss the impact of social stigma on the well-being of lesbian and gay people.

- Discuss the arguments given in favor of same-sex marriage.

- Describe the religious belief system that supports polygamy.

- Describe the experiences of woman and men in plural marriage within a fundamentalist religious community.

- Explain how sexual variations or "kink" can positively influence an individual's sexuality.

- Describe the attributes of an urban setting that may help facilitate expressions of sexual variations.

Student Website

www.mhhe.com/cls

Internet References

American Psychological Association
   www.apa.org/topics/divorce/index.aspx
Bonobos Sex and Society
   http://songweaver.com/info/bonobos.html
Go Ask Alice
   www.goaskalice.columbia.edu
SexInfo: Love and Relationships
   www.soc.ucsb.edu/sexinfo/category/love-relationships

Think for a moment about the term "sexual relationship." It denotes an important dimension of sexuality—interpersonal sexuality, or sexual interactions occurring between two (or more) individuals. For most people, interpersonal contact and relationships with others form the basis for living meaningful lives. Conversely, isolation results in loneliness and depression for most human beings. People seek intimacy. Indeed, we cultivate friendships and relationships for the warmth, affection, supportiveness, and sense of trust and loyalty that they can provide. The importance of feeling connected to others can hardly be overstated. However, as this unit demonstrates, there are various kinds of relationships, intimacies, and experiences of connectedness.

Relationships often start when they are least expected. Sitting next to someone on a bus, talking to someone at a party, sending an instant message, all of these may be the possible beginnings to a relationship. Sometimes friendships may develop into intimate (and sexual) relationships. The qualifying word in the previous sentence is "may." Today many people, single as well as married, yearn for close or emotionally intimate interpersonal relationships, but fail to find them.

Despite developments in communication and technology that have led to a sense of always being "connected," discovering how and where to find potential friends or partners is reported by many to be as difficult today (if not more so) than in the past. Fear of rejection causes some to avoid interpersonal relationships and others to present a false front or illusory self that they think is more acceptable or socially desirable. This sets the stage for a relationship that is counterproductive to genuine intimacy. For others a major dilemma may exist—the problem of balancing closeness with the preservation of individual identity in a manner that satisfies the need for both personal and interpersonal growth and integrity. In either case, partners in a relationship should be advised that the development of interpersonal awareness (the mutual recognition and knowledge of others as they really are) rests upon trust and self-disclosure—letting the other person know who you really are and how you truly feel. In American society, this has never been easy, and today some fear it may be more difficult than ever.

These considerations regarding interpersonal relationships apply equally well to achieving meaningful and satisfying sexual relationships. Three basic ingredients lay the foundation for quality sexual interaction: self-awareness, understanding and acceptance of the partner's needs and desires, and mutual efforts to accommodate both partners' needs and desires in safe and healthy ways. Without these, misunderstandings may arise, ultimately bringing anxiety, frustration, dissatisfaction, and/or resentment into the relationship. There may also be a heightened risk of sexually transmitted infections, including HIV, experiencing an unplanned pregnancy, or experiencing sexual dysfunction by one or both partners. On the other hand, experience and research show that ongoing attention to these three ingredients by intimate partners contributes not only to sexual responsibility, but also to true emotional and sexual intimacy, as well as a longer and happier life.

Being in a relationship, in search of intimacy and fulfillment, involves being vulnerable. That vulnerability carries great emotional risks. One area that is a significant source of pain for

© Ingram Publishing

many people is infidelity. Relationships and marriages can be torn apart by an "unfaithful" partner. Unfortunately, the children are often the ones who suffer the most. Although the number of married persons who have been unfaithful to their spouses may not be as high as many people may think, for those who are unfaithful, they are very unlikely to confess their unfaithfulness to their spouse/partner. If it becomes known, it is usually because the infidelity was discovered somehow, not due to a "confession."

As might already be apparent, there is much more to quality sexual relationships than our popular culture recognizes. Such relationships are not established by means of sexual techniques or beautiful bodies. Rather, it is the quality and integrity of the interaction that makes sex a celebration of our humanity and sexualities. A person-oriented (as opposed to genitally oriented) sexual awareness, coupled with an open, relaxed, even playful attitude toward exploration makes for joy and pleasure in experiencing our sexualities.

The Expectations Trap

Much of the discontent couples encounter today is really culturally inflicted, although we're conditioned to blame our partners for our unhappiness. Yet research points to ways couples can immunize themselves against unseen pressures now pulling them apart.

HARA ESTROFF MARANO

Six years, ten months, and eight days into their marriage, Sam and Melissa blew apart. Everyone was stunned, most of all the couple themselves. One day she was your basic stressed-out professional woman (and mother of a 3-year-old) carrying the major financial burden of their household. The next day she was a betrayed wife. The affair Sam disclosed detonated a caterwaul of hurt heard by every couple in their circle and her large coterie of friends and family. With speed verging on inevitability, the public knowledge of their private life commandeered the driver's seat of their own destiny. A surge of support for Melissa as the wronged woman swiftly isolated Sam emotionally and precluded deep discussion of the conditions that had long alienated him. Out of respect for the pain that his mere presence now caused, Sam decamped within days. He never moved back in.

It's not clear that the couple could have salvaged the relationship if they had tried. It wasn't just the infidelity. "We had so many background and stylistic differences," says Sam. "It was like we came from two separate cultures. We couldn't take out the garbage without a Geneva Accord." Constant negotiation was necessary, but if there was time, there was also usually too much accumulated irritation for Melissa to tolerate. And then, opening a public window on the relationship seemed to close the door on the possibility of working through the disappointments, the frustrations, the betrayal.

Within weeks, the couple was indeed in discussions—for a divorce. At least they both insisted on mediation, not litigation, and their lawyers complied. A couple of months, and some time and determination later, they had a settlement. Only now that Sam and Melissa have settled into their mostly separate lives, and their daughter appears to be doing well with abundant care from both her parents, are they catching their respective breaths—two years later.

Americans value marriage more than people do in any other culture, and it holds a central place in our dreams. Over 90 percent of young adults aspire to marriage—although fewer are actually choosing it, many opting instead for cohabitation. But no matter how you count it, Americans have the highest rate of romantic breakup in the world, says Andrew J. Cherlin, professor of sociology and public policy at Johns Hopkins. As with Sam and Melissa, marriages are discarded often before the partners know what hit them.

"By age 35, 10 percent of American women have lived with three or more husbands or domestic partners," Cherlin reports in his recent hook. *The Marriage-Go-Round: The State of Marriage and the Family in America Today.* "Children of married parents in America face a higher risk of seeing them break up than children born of unmarried parents in Sweden."

With general affluence has come a plethora of choices, including constant choices about our personal and family life. Even marriage itself is now a choice. "The result is an ongoing self-appraisal of how your personal life is going, like having a continual readout of your emotional heart rate," says Cherlin. You get used to the idea of always making choices to improve your happiness.

The constant appraisal of personal life to improve happiness creates a heightened sensitivity to problems that arise in intimate relationships.

The heightened focus on options "creates a heightened sensitivity to problems that arise in intimate relationships." And negative emotions get priority processing in our brains. "There are so many opportunities to decide that it's unsatisfactory," says Cherlin.

It would be one thing if we were living more satisfied lives than ever. But just gauging by the number of relationships wrecked every year, we're less satisfied, says Cherlin. "We're carrying over into our personal lives the fast pace of decisions and actions we have everywhere else, and that may not be for the best." More than ever, we're paying attention to the most volatile parts of our emotional makeup—the parts that are too reactive to momentary events to give meaning to life.

> **More than ever, we're paying attention to the most volatile parts of our emotional makeup—parts that are too reactive to momentary events to give meaning to life.**

Because our intimate relationships are now almost wholly vehicles for meeting our emotional needs, and with almost all our emotions invested in one relationship, we tend to look upon any unhappiness we experience—whatever the source—as a failure of a partner to satisfy our longings. Disappointment inevitably feels so *personal* we see no other possibility but to hunt for individual psychological reasons—that is, to blame our partners for our own unhappiness.

But much—perhaps most—of the discontent we now encounter in close relationships is culturally inflicted, although we rarely interpret our experience that way. Culture—the pressure to constantly monitor our happiness, the plethora of choices surreptitiously creating an expectation of perfection, the speed of everyday life—always climbs into bed with us. An accumulation of forces has made the cultural climate hostile to long-term relationships today.

Attuned to disappointment and confused about its source, we wind up discarding perfectly good relationships. People work themselves up over "the ordinary problems of marriage, for which, by the way, they usually fail to see their own contributions," says William Doherty, professor of family sciences at the University of Minnesota. "They badger their partners to change, convince themselves nothing will budge, and so work their way out of really good relationships." Doherty believes it's possible to stop the careering disappointment even when people believe a relationship is over.

It's not going to happen by putting the genie back in the bottle. It's not possible to curb the excess of options life now offers. And speed is a fixture of the ongoing technological revolution, no matter how much friction it creates in personal lives. Yet new research points to ways that actually render them irrelevant. We are, after all, the architects of our own passions.

The Purpose of Marriage

Marriage probably evolved as the best way to pool the labor of men and women to enable families to subsist and assure that children survive to independence—and data indicate it still is. But beyond the basics, the purpose of marriage has shifted constantly, says Stephanie Coontz, a historian at Washington's Evergreen State College. It helps to remember that marriage evolved in an atmosphere of scarcity, the conditions that prevailed for almost all of human history. "The earliest purpose of marriage was to make strategic alliances with

---

Case Study
Stephen and Christina

Five years into his marriage, not long after the birth of his first son, most of Stephen G.'s interactions with his wife were not pleasant. "I thought the difficulties would pass," he recalls. "My wife, Christina, got fed up faster and wanted me to leave." He was traveling frequently and finances were thin; she'd gone back to school full-time after having worked until the baby was born. "Very few needs were being met for either of us. We were either yelling or in a cold war."

They entered counseling to learn how to co-parent if they indeed separated. "It helped restore our friendship: At least we could talk civilly. That led to deeper communication—we could actually listen to each other without getting defensive. We heard that we were both hurting, both feeling the stress of new parenthood without a support system of either parents or friends. We could talk about the ways we weren't there for each other without feeling attacked. It took a lot longer for the romance to return."

Stephen, now 37, a sales representative for a pharmaceutical company in San Francisco, says it was a time of "growing up. I had to accept that I had new responsibilities. And I had to accept that my partner, now 38, is not ideal in every way although she is ideal in many ways. But her short temper is not enough of a reason to leave the relationship and our two kids. When I wish she'd be different, I have to remind myself of all the ways she is the person I want to be with. It's not something you 'get over.' You accept it."

---

other people, to turn strangers into relatives," says Coontz. "As society became more differentiated, marriage became a major mechanism for adjusting your position."

It wasn't until the 18th century that anyone thought that love might have anything to do with marriage, but love was held in check by a sense of duty. Even through the 19th century, the belief prevailed that females and males had different natures and couldn't be expected to understand each other well. Only in the 20th century did the idea take hold that men and women should be companions, that they should be passionate, and that both should get sexual and personal fulfillment from marriage.

We're still trying to figure out how to do that—and get the laundry done, too. The hassles of a negotiated and constantly renegotiated relationship—few wish a return to inequality—assure a ready source of stress or disappointment or both.

From We to Me

Our mind-set has further shifted over the past few decades, experts suggest. Today, the minute one partner is faced with dissatisfaction—feeling stressed-out or neglected, having

Case Study
Susan and Tim

Susan Pohlman, now 50, reluctantly accompanied her workaholic husband on a business trip to Italy believing it would be their last together. Back home in Los Angeles were their two teenagers, their luxurious home, their overfurnished lives—and the divorce lawyer she had contacted to end their 18-year marriage.

They were leading such parallel lives that collaboration had turned to competition, with fights over things like who spent more time with the kids and who spent more time working. But knocked off balance by the beauty of the coast near Genoa toward the end of the trip, Tim asked, out of the blue, "What if we lived here?" "The spirit of this odd day overtook me," recalls Susan. At 6 P.M. on the evening before departure, they were shown a beautiful apartment overlooking the water. Despite knowing no Italian, they signed a lease on the spot. Two months later, with their house sold, they moved with their kids to Italy for a year.

"In L.A. we were four people going in four directions. In Italy, we became completely dependent on each other. How to get a phone? How to shop for food? Also, we had no belongings. The simplicity forced us to notice the experiences of life. Often, we had no idea what we were doing. There was lots of laughing at and with each other." Susan says she "became aware of the power of adventure and of doing things together, and how they became a natural bridge to intimacy."

Both Pohlmans found Italy offered "a more appreciative lifestyle." Says Susan: "I realized the American Dream was pulling us apart. We followed the formula of owning, having, pushing each other. You have all this stuff but you're miserable because what you're really craving is interaction." Too, she says, American life is exhausting, and "exhaustion distorts your ability to judge problems."

Now back in the U.S. and living in Arizona, the Pohlmans believe they needed to remove themselves from the culture to see its distorting effects. "And we needed to participate in a paradigm shift: 'I'm not perfect, you're not perfect; let's not get hung up on our imperfections.'" But the most powerful element of their move could be reproduced anywhere, she says: "The simplicity was liberating."

a partner who isn't overly expressive or who works too hard or doesn't initiate sex very often—then the communal ideal we bring to relationships is jettisoned and an individualistic mentality asserts itself. We revert to a stingier self that has been programmed into us by the consumer culture, which has only become increasingly pervasive, the current recession notwithstanding.

Psychologically, the goal of life becomes *my* happiness. "The minute your needs are not being met then you appropriate the individualistic norm," says Doherty. This accelerating consumer mind-set is a major portal through which destructive forces gain entry and undermine conjoint life.

"Marriage is for *me*" is the way Austin, Texas, family therapist Pat Love puts it. "It's for meeting *my* needs." It's not about what *I do*, but how it makes me *feel*.

Such beliefs lead to a sense of entitlement: "I deserve better than I'm getting." Doherty sees that as the basic message of almost every advertisement in the consumer culture. You deserve more and we can provide it. You begin to think: This isn't the deal I signed up for. Or you begin to feel that you're putting into this a lot more than you're getting out. "We believe in our inalienable right to the intimate relationships of our choice," says Doherty.

In allowing such free-market values to seep into our private lives, we come to believe that a partner's job is, above all, to provide pleasure. "People do not go into relationships because they want to learn how to negotiate and master difficulties," observes Brown University psychiatrist Scott Haltzman. "They want the other person to provide pleasure." It's partner as service provider. The pleasure bond, unfortunately, is as volatile as the emotions that underlie it and as hollow and fragile as the hedonic sense of happiness.

The Expectations Trap: Perfection, Please

If there's one thing that most explicitly detracts from the enjoyment of relationships today, it's an abundance of choice. Psychologist Barry Schwartz would call it an *excess* of choice—the tyranny of abundance. We see it as a measure of our autonomy and we firmly believe that freedom of choice will lead to fulfillment Our antennae are always up for better opportunities, finds Schwartz, professor of psychology at Swarthmore College.

Just as only the best pair of jeans will do, so will only the best partner—whatever that is. "People walk starry-eyed looking not into the eyes of their romantic partner but over their romantic partner's shoulder, in case there might be somebody better walking by. This is not the road to successful long-term relationships." It does not stop with marriage. And it undermines commitment by encouraging people to keep their options open.

Like Doherty, Schwartz sees it as a consequence of a consumer society. He also sees it as a self-fulfilling phenomenon. "If you think there might be something better around the next corner, then there will be, because you're not fully committed to the relationship you've got."

It's naïve to expect relationships to feel good every minute. Every relationship has its bumps. How big a bump does it have to be before you do something about it? As Hopkins's Cherlin says, if you're constantly asking yourself whether you should leave, "there may be a day when the answer is yes. In any marriage there may be a day when the answer is yes."

One of the problems with unrestrained choice, explains Schwartz, is that it raises expectations to the breaking point.

A sense of multiple alternatives, of unlimited possibility, breeds in us the illusion that perfection exists out there, somewhere, if only we could find it. This one's sense of humor, that one's looks, another one's charisma—we come to imagine that there will be a package in which all these desirable features coexist. We search for perfection because we believe we are entitled to the best—even if perfection is an illusion foisted on us by an abundance of possibilities.

If perfection is what you expect, you will always be disappointed, says Schwartz. We become picky and unhappy. The cruel joke our psychology plays on us, of course, is that we are terrible at knowing what will satisfy us or at knowing how any experience will make us feel.

> **A sense of multiple alternatives, of unlimited possibility, breeds in us the illusion that the perfect person is out there waiting to be found.**

If the search through all possibilities weren't exhausting (and futile) enough, thinking about attractive features of the alternatives not chosen—what economists call opportunity costs—reduces the potential pleasure in whatever choice we finally do make. The more possibilities, the more opportunity costs—and the more we think about them, the more we come to regret any choice. "So, once again," says Schwartz, "a greater variety of choices actually makes us feel worse."

Ultimately, our excess of choice leads to lack of intimacy. "How is anyone going to stack up against this perfect person who's out there somewhere just waiting to be found?" asks Schwartz. "It creates doubt about this person, who seems like a good person, someone I might even be in love with—but who knows what's possible *out* there? Intimacy takes time to develop. You need to have some reason to put in the time. If you're full of doubt at the start, you're not going to put in the time."

Moreover, a focus on one's own preferences can come at the expense of those of others. As Schwartz said in his 2004 book, *The Paradox of Choice: Why More Is Less,* "most people find it extremely challenging to balance the conflicting impulses of freedom of choice on the one hand and loyalty and commitment on the other."

And yet, throughout, we are focused on the partner we want to have, not on the one we want—or need—to be. That may be the worst choice of all.

Disappointment—or Tragedy?

The heightened sensitivity to relationship problems that follows from constantly appraising our happiness encourages couples to turn disappointment into tragedy, Doherty contends.

Inevitably, images of the perfect relationship dancing in our heads collide with our sense of entitlement; "I'm entitled to the best possible marriage." The reality of disappointment becomes intolerable. "It's part of a cultural belief system that says we are entitled to everything we feel we need."

Through the alchemy of desire, wants become needs, and unfulfilled needs become personal tragedies. "A husband who isn't very expressive of his feelings can be a disappointment or a tragedy, depending on whether it's an entitlement," says Doherty. "And that's very much a cultural phenomenon." We take the everyday disappointments of relationships and treat them as intolerable, see them as demeaning—the equivalent of alcoholism, say, or abuse. "People work their way into 'I'm a tragic figure' around the ordinary problems of marriage." Such stories are so widespread, Doherty is no longer inclined to see them as reflecting an individual psychological problem, although that is how he was trained—and how he practiced for many years as an eminent family therapist. "I see it first now as a cultural phenomenon."

First Lady Michelle Obama is no stranger to the disappointment that pervades relationships today. In *Barack and Michelle: Portrait of an American Marriage,* by Christopher Anderson, she confides how she reached a "state of desperation" while working full-time, bringing in the majority of the family income, raising two daughters, and rarely seeing her husband, who was then spending most of his week away from their Chicago home as an Illinois state senator, a job she thought would lead nowhere while it paid little. "She's killing me with this constant criticism," Barack complained. "She just seems so bitter, so angry all the time." She was annoyed that he "seems to think he can just go out there and pursue his dream and leave all the heavy lifting to me."

But then she had an epiphany: She remembered the guy she fell in love with. "I figured out that I was pushing to make Barack be something I wanted him to be for me. I was depending on him to make me happy. Except it didn't have anything to do with him. I needed support. I didn't necessarily need it from Barack."

Certainly, commitment narrows choice. But it is the ability to remember you really do love someone—even though you may not be feeling it at the moment.

Commitment is the ability to sustain an investment, to honor values over momentary feelings. The irony, of course, is that while we want happiness, it isn't a moment-by-moment experience; the deepest, most enduring form of happiness is the result of sustained emotional investments in other people.

Architects of the Heart

One of the most noteworthy findings emerging from relationship research is that desire isn't just something we passively feel when everything's going right; it develops in direct response to what we do. Simply having fun together, for example, is crucial to keeping the sex drive alive.

But in the churn of daily life, we tend to give short shrift to creating positive experiences. Over time, we typically become more oriented to dampening threats and insecurities—to resolving conflict, to eliminating jealousy, to banishing problems. But the brain is wired with both a positive and negative motivational system, and satisfaction and desire demand keeping the brain's positive system well-stoked.

Even for long-term couples, spending time together in novel, interesting, or challenging activities—games, dancing, even conversation—enhances feelings of closeness, passionate love, and satisfaction with the relationship. Couples recapture the excitement of the early days of being in love. Such passion naturally feeds commitment.

From Michelle to Michelangelo

Important as it is to choose the right partner, it's probably more important to *be* the right partner. Most people are focused on changing the wrong person in the relationship; if anyone has to change in a relationship, it's you—although preferably with the help of your partner.

Important as it is to choose the right partner, it's probably more important to *be* the right partner. We focus on changing the wrong person.

Ultimately, "Marriage is an inside job," Pat Love told the 2009 Smart Marriages Conference. "It's internal to the person. You have to let it do its work." And its biggest job is helping individuals grow up. "Marriage is about getting over yourself. Happiness is not about focusing on yourself." Happiness is about holding onto your values, deciding who you are and being that person, using your particular talent, and investing in others.

Unfortunately, says Margin family therapist and *PT* blogger Susan Pease Gadoua, not enough people today are willing to do the hard work of becoming a more mature person. "They think they have a lot more choices. And they think life will be easier in another relationship. What they don't realize is that it will be the same relationship—just with a different name."

The question is not how you want your partner to change but what kind of partner and person you want to be. In the best relationships, not only are you thinking about who you want to be, but your partner is willing to help you get there. Psychologist Caryl E. Rusbult calls it the Michelangelo phenomenon. Just as Michelangelo felt the figures he created were already "in" the stones, "slumbering within the actual self is an ideal form," explains Eli Finkel, associate professor of psychology at Northwestern University and frequent Rusbult collaborator. Your partner becomes an ally in sculpting your ideal self, in bringing out the person you dream of becoming, leading you to a deep form of personal growth as well as long-term satisfaction with life and with the relationship.

It takes a partner who supports your dreams, the traits and qualities you want to develop—whether or not you've articulated them clearly or simply expressed vague yearnings.

Case Study
Patty and Rod

Patty Newbold had married "a really great guy," but by the time their 13th anniversary rolled around, she had a long list of things he needed to change to make the marriage work. At 34, she felt depressed, frantic—and guilty, as Rod was fighting a chronic disease. But she had reached a breaking point, "I read my husband my list of unmet needs and suggested a divorce," even though what she really wanted was her marriage back. "I wanted to feel loved again. But it didn't seem possible."

Newbold has had a long time to think about that list. Her husband died the next day, a freak side effect of his medications. "He was gone, but the list remained. Out of perhaps 30 needs, only one was eased by losing him. I was free now to move the drinking glasses next to the sink."

As she read through the list the morning after he died, she realized that "marriage isn't about my needs or his needs or about how well we communicate about our needs. It's about loving and being loved. *Life* is about meeting (or letting go of) my own *needs*. *Marriage* is about loving another person and receiving love in return. It suddenly became oh so clear that receiving love is something I make happen, not him." And then she was flooded with memories of all the times "I'd been offered love by this wonderful man and rejected it because I was too wrapped up in whatever need I was facing at the time."

Revitalized is "a funny word to describe a relationship in which one party is dead," she reports, "but ours was revitalized. I was completely changed, too," Everything she learned that awful day has gone into a second marriage, now well into its second decade.

"People come to reflect what their partners see in them and elicit from them," Finkel and Rusbult report in *Current Directions in Psychological Science*.

Such affirmation promotes trust in the partner and strengthens commitment. And commitment, Rusbult has found, is a key predictor of relationship durability. "It creates positive bias towards each other," says Finkel. "It feels good to achieve our goals. It's deeply satisfying and meaningful." In addition, it immunizes the relationship against potential distractions—all those "perfect" others. Finkel explains, "It motivates the derogation of alternative partners." It creates the perception—the illusion—that even the most attractive alternative partners are unappealing. Attention to them gets turned off—one of the many cognitive gymnastics we engage in to ward off doubts.

Like growth, commitment is an inside job. It's not a simple vow. Partners see each other in ways that enhance their connection and fend off threats. It fosters the perception that the relationship you're in is better than that of others. It breeds the inclination to react constructively—by accommodation—rather than destructively when a partner does something inconsiderate. It even motivates that most difficult of tasks, forgiveness for the ultimate harm of betrayal, Rusbult has shown.

It is a willingness—stemming in part from an understanding that your well-being and your partner's are linked over the long term—to depart from direct self-interest, such as erecting a grudge when you feel hurt.

The Michelangelo phenomenon gives the lie to the soul mate search. You can't find the perfect person; there is no such thing. And even if you think you could, the person he or she is today is, hopefully, not quite the person he or she wants to be 10 years down the road. You and your partner help each other become a more perfect person—perfect, that is, according to your own inner ideals. You are both, with mutual help, constantly evolving.

Critical Thinking

1. How can the perception of unhappiness in the context of a relationship influence how a person views his/her partner?

2. How can the feelings of closeness and satisfaction in a relationship be enhanced?

3. How can the pursuit of perfection impact an individual's relationship success?

Making Relationships Work

A Conversation with Psychologist

The best science we have on relationships comes from the most intense relationship of all—marriage. Here's what we know about it.

John M. Gottman

It has become common to extol the value of human relationships in the workplace. We all agree that managers need to connect deeply with followers to ensure outstanding performance, and we celebrate leaders who have the emotional intelligence to engage and inspire their people by creating bonds that are authentic and reliable. There's a large and fast-growing support industry to help us develop our "softer" relationship skills; many CEOs hire executive coaches, and libraries of self-help books detail how best to build and manage relationships on the way to the top.

Despite all the importance attached to interpersonal dynamics in the workplace, however, surprisingly little hard scientific evidence identifies what makes or breaks work relationships. We know, for instance, that the personal chemistry between a mentor and his or her protégé is critical to that relationship's success, but we don't try to work out what the magic is, at least not in any rigorous way. The absence of hard data and painstaking analysis exacts a heavy price: When relationships sour, as they easily can, there's little guidance on what you can do to patch things up. Even the best human resources officers may not know how or when to stage an intervention. If companies were more effective in helping executives handle their relationships through difficult times, they would see the company's productivity soar and find it much easier to retain leadership talent.

Good relationships aren't about clear communication—they're about small moments of attachment and intimacy.

But if there's little research on relationships at work, some is beginning to emerge on relationships at home. That's good news because the way that people manage their work relationships is closely linked to the way they manage their personal ones. People who are abusive at home, for example, are likely to be abusive at work. If you believe that—as most psychologists do—then the relevance of the work of those who study relationships at home immediately becomes obvious.

Few people can tell us more about how to maintain good personal relationships than John M. Gottman, the executive director of the Relationship Research Institute. At the institute's Family Research Laboratory—known as the Love Lab—Gottman has been studying marriage and divorce for the past 35 years. He has screened thousands of couples, interviewed them, and tracked their interactions over time. He and his colleagues use video cameras, heart monitors, and other biofeedback equipment to measure what goes on when couples experience moments of conflict and closeness. By mathematically analyzing the data, Gottman has generated hard scientific evidence on what makes good relationships.

HBR senior editor Diane Coutu went to the Seattle headquarters of the Relationship Research Institute to discuss that evidence with Gottman and to ask about the implications of his research for the work environment. As a scientist, he refuses to extrapolate beyond his research on couples to relationships in the workplace. The media have sensationalized his work, he says. However, he was willing to talk freely about what makes for good relationships in our personal lives.

Successful couples, he notes, look for ways to accentuate the positive. They try to say "yes" as often as possible. That doesn't mean good relationships have no room for conflict. On the contrary, individuals in thriving relationships embrace conflict over personality differences as a way to work them through. Gottman adds that good relationships aren't about clear communication—they're about small moments of attachment and intimacy. It takes time and work to make such moments part of the fabric of everyday life. Gottman discusses these and other nuances of his wisdom, acquired from experience and research, in this edited version of Coutu's conversation with him.

You're said to be able to predict, in a very short amount of time and with a high degree of accuracy, whether couples will stay together for the long term. How do you manage that?

Let me put it this way: If I had three hours with a couple, and if I could interview them and tape them interacting—in positive ways as well as in conflict—then I would say that I could predict a couple's success rate for staying together in the next three to five years with more than 90% accuracy. I've worked with 3,000 couples over 35 years, and the data support this claim, which have now been replicated by other scientists.

Could you train me to decide whether I should hire Dick or Jane?

I know this question has come up in the media, which have tried to sex up my work. But the reliability you see in my research has to do with studying relationships specifically. Just to predict whether an interviewee would be a good fit for a job—you couldn't do it. At least I know *I* couldn't do it. I rely on my research to be able to look at *couples*. And even with couples, I need to witness a sample interaction. The more emotional and the more realistic the situation is, the better I am at predicting with a high level of accuracy.

For instance, one test we've used for years is the "paper tower task." We give couples a bunch of materials, such as newspaper, scissors, Scotch tape, and string. We tell them to go build a paper tower that is freestanding, strong, and beautiful, and they have half an hour to do it. Then we watch the way the couples work. It's the very simple things that determine success. One time we had three Australian couples do the task. Beforehand, we had the couples talk on tape about each other and about a major conflict in their relationship that they were trying to resolve. So we had some data about how relatively happy or unhappy they were. When one couple who came across as happy started building their paper tower, the man said, "So, how are we going to do this?" The woman replied, "You know, we can fold the paper, we can turn the paper, we can make structures out of the paper." He said, "Really? Great." It took them something like ten seconds to build a tower. The wife in an unhappily married couple started by saying, "So how are we going to do this?" Her husband said, "Just a minute, can you be quiet while I figure out the design?" It didn't take much time to see that this couple would run into some difficulties down the line.

Your work depends heavily on your interviewing technique. How did you develop it?

My hero was Studs Terkel. I think he's by far the greatest interviewer ever. Bill Moyers is good. Barbara Walters is very good, too, but Terkel is amazing. In one interview, he went into a woman's attic and said to her, "Give me a tour, tell me what's up here." He had a big cigar in his mouth, but he was really interested. Acting as the tour guide, she said, "Well, I don't talk much about this doll." Terkel pointed out that it was not a new doll. "No," she said, "my first fiancé gave me this doll, before he was killed in a car accident. He was the only man I've ever loved." Surprised, Terkel remarked, "You're a grandmother; you must have married." She replied, "Yeah, and I love my husband, but just not like I loved Jack." The woman then launched into a great monologue, prompted by Terkel. We studied his tapes and based our interview technique on his approach.

What's your biggest discovery?

It sounds simple, but in fact you could capture all of my research findings with the metaphor of a saltshaker. Instead of filling it with salt, fill it with all the ways you can say yes, and that's what a good relationship is. "Yes," you say, "that is a good idea." "Yes, that's a great point, I never thought of that." "Yes, let's do that if you think it's important." You sprinkle yeses throughout your interactions—that's what a good relationship is. This is particularly important for men, whose ability to accept influence from women is really one of the most critical issues in a relationship. Marriages where the men say to their partners, "Gee, that's a good point" or "Yeah, I guess we could do that" are much more likely to succeed. In contrast, in a partnership that's troubled, the saltshaker is filled with all the ways you can say no. In violent relationships, for example, we see men responding to their wives' requests by saying, "No way," "It's just not going to happen," "You're not going to control me," or simply "Shut up." When a man is not willing to share power with his wife, our research shows, there is an 81% chance that the marriage will self-destruct.

> **When a man is not willing to share power with his wife, our research shows, there is an 81% chance that the marriage will self-destruct.**

Does that mean that there's no room for conflict in a good relationship?

Absolutely not. Having a conflict-free relationship does not mean having a happy one, and when I tell you to say yes a lot, I'm not advising simple compliance. Agreement is not the same as compliance, so if people think they're giving in all the time, then their relationships are never going to work. There are conflicts that you absolutely must have because to give in is to give up some of your personality.

Let me explain by illustrating from personal experience. My wife is very bad at just sitting still and doing nothing. A couple of years ago I gave her a book called *The Art of Doing Nothing*. She never read it. She always has to be up and about doing things. I'm not like that. I don't multitask the way she does; if I take a day off, I want it to be a day off. I want to play music; I want to have a sense of leisure. We fight about this difference all the time. She wants me to do stuff around the house, and I want her to take it easy. And it's worth fighting about this because it's an important personality difference between us. I don't want to adopt her style, and she doesn't want to adopt mine.

Another common issue in many relationships is punctuality. People have huge differences in their attitudes toward it and fight about it constantly. And they should—because unless you do, you can't arrive at an understanding of your differences, which means you can't work out how to live with them.

What else do people in relationships fight about?

I actually analyzed about 900 arguments last summer. With the help of the lab staff, I interviewed people about their fights—we saw them fighting in the lab and then outside the lab, and we talked about the issue. What we learned from measuring all these interactions is that most people fight about nothing. Their fights are not about money, or sex, or in-laws—none of that stuff. The vast majority of conflicts are about the *way* people in the relationship fight. One fight we studied was about a remote control. The couple was watching television, and the man said, "OK, let me see what's on," and started channel surfing. At one point the woman said, "Wait, leave it on that program, it's kind of interesting." He replied, "OK, but first let me see what else is on." She kept objecting until he finally said, "Fine, here!" and handed her the remote. She bristled and said, "The way you said 'fine,' that kind of hurt my feelings." He shot back with, "You've always got to have it your way." It may seem really elementary, but that's what people fight about. Unfortunately, most of these issues never get resolved at all. Most couples don't go back and say, "You know, we should really discuss that remote control issue." They don't try to repair the relationship. But repair is the sine qua non of relationships, so everybody needs to know how to process those regrettable moments.

I want to stress that good relationships are not just about knowing when to fight and how to patch things up. We also need humor, affection, playing, silliness, exploration, adventure, lust, touching—all those positive emotional things that we share with all mammals. Something that's been so hard for me to convey to the media is that trivial moments provide opportunities for profound connection. For example, if you're giving your little kid a bath and he splashes and you're impatient, you miss an opportunity to play with him. But if you splash back and you clean up later, you have some fun together and you both get really wet, laugh, and have a beautiful moment. It's ephemeral, small, even trivial—yet it builds trust and connection. In couples who divorce or who live together unhappily, such small moments of connection are rare.

We can't splash around at work. Are there equivalent ways to achieve connections there?

There are many similar things you can do in a work environment. You can go into your friend David's office and say, "How's little Harry doing?" And he might say, "You know, he really likes his new school. He's excited by it, and in fact you know what he's doing now . . . ?" The conversation might take five or ten minutes, but you've made a connection. This goes for the boss, too. A lot of times the person who's running an organization is pretty lonely, and if somebody walks into her office and doesn't talk about work but instead asks about her weekend, the message is, "Hey, I like you. I notice you independent of your position." Within organizations, people have to see each other as human beings or there will be no social glue.

What about intimate relationships at work—thumbs up or down?

That can be really problematic. Marriage researcher Shirley Glass did some terrific work on friendship in the work-place. She gave this wonderful example of a man who hadn't had sex for a long time. He and his wife had a new baby and were fighting a lot. Then after work one day, he and his coworkers went out to celebrate a really successful quarter at the company. Everybody had a good time. People eventually started to go home, but this man and a female coworker lingered. They were talking about the excellent fourth quarter earnings, and she said, "You know, George, this is the happiest I've seen you in months." Nothing untoward was happening, but he was enjoying the conversation in a way that he hadn't with his wife in a long time. So on the way home, he thought to himself, "You know, we laughed and shared a lot, and it was kind of intimate, and I should really go home and say, 'Nancy, I'm really kind of worried because I just had a conversation with a woman at work, and I felt closer to her than I've felt to you in months, and it scares the hell out of me, and we need to talk.' " But he knew exactly how his wife would react. She'd tell him to grow up and would say, "Hey, I have this baby sucking at my teats and now you're being a baby, too. I don't need this kind of crap from you, so just suck it up and get on with it. You're a new father, and quit having those conversations with that woman at work." So he decided not to share the experience with his wife because, he thought, "Nothing really happened anyway." But something did happen, and now he's got a secret. That's the beginning of betrayal.

Is there no difference between an emotional and a physical affair?

I honestly don't think so. I've seen this in my clinical work and in my research. Most affairs are not about sex at all; they're about friendship. They're about finding somebody who finds you interesting, attractive, fascinating. This can be on a physical or an emotional level—it all boils down to the same thing.

What contributes to a successful long-term relationship?

Look for the positive in each other. Robert Levenson, of the University of California at Berkeley, and I are in the 18th year of a 20-year longitudinal study in the San Francisco Bay area. We have two groups of couples who were first assessed when they were in their forties and sixties and are now, respectively, in their sixties and eighties. The surprising thing is that the longer people are together, the more the sense of kindness returns. Our research is starting to reveal that in later life your relationship becomes very much like it was during courtship. In courtship you find your new partner very charming and positive. It was all so new then. You de-emphasized the negative qualities and magnified the positive ones. In the long term, the same thing happens. You say, "She's a wonder woman. She can get us through anything." For instance, my wife and I have just moved out of the house we lived in for 14 years, and she orchestrated the entire thing. She was amazing. My genius was to sit back and say nothing. In good relationships, people savor the moments like this that they have together.

Is there such a thing as an ideal relationship?

I don't really know. Somebody I admired a long time ago was Harold Rausch, now retired, from the University of Massachusetts, who studied relationships and decided there was an optimal level of intimacy and friendship—and of conflict. He called couples who had achieved those levels "harmonious."

He said that couples who preferred some emotional distance in their relationships were psychologically brittle and not very oriented toward insight and deep understanding. Rausch identified another type of couple—those who fought a lot and were really passionate—and he said they're messed up, too.

We studied those three groups of couples as well, and our research showed that they could all be successful. The people who wanted more distant relationships and friendships valued loyalty, commitment, and dedication but weren't so interested in intimacy. Still, they could have very happy marriages. You might think, "OK, they don't fight a lot in order to avoid conflict, and maybe that's bad for the kids." It turns out that wasn't true at all. We followed the kids' emotional and intellectual development, and a distant relationship between the parents turned out to be fine for the children. Our research showed that bickering a lot can be fine, too, provided that both people in the relationship agree to it. People have different capacities for how much intimacy and passion they want and how much togetherness they want. The problem is when there's a mismatch.

Within organizations, people have to see each other as human beings or there will be no social glue.

Are the short-term factors for success in relationships different from the factors that make for long-term success?

We face this question about short- and long-term success when we study adolescents and their relationships. We don't necessarily want a 14-year-old's dating relationship to last, but we'd like it to be a positive experience, and we'd like to facilitate our kids' growth and not lead them down a negative path. Whether we look at teenagers or at older couples, it turns out again and again that respect and affection are the two most important things. Whatever your age, there are so many ways you can show respect for your partner. Express interest in the story she's telling at dinner, pay him compliments, listen to her ideas, ask him to watch a *Nova* special with you so that you can discuss it later. The possibilities abound.

What other advice emerges from your study of good relationships?

I think that men need to learn how to embrace their wives' anger. This message is particularly pertinent today because women are now being educated and empowered to achieve more economically, politically, and socially. But our culture still teaches women that when they assert themselves they are being pushy or obnoxious. Women who get angry when their goals are blocked are labeled as bitchy or rude. If men want to have a good relationship with women, they have to be sensitive to the changing dimensions of power and control in the Western world. And they have to accept the asymmetry in our relationships for the time being. The good news is that embracing your wife's anger just a little bit can go a long way toward unleashing feelings of appreciation and affection.

I had this funny experience when I sold my book *The Seven Principles for Making Marriage Work* to my publisher. I met with the head of the marketing department, a young guy who leaned back in his chair as if he were not at all impressed by any of my work. He pointed his finger at me and said, "All right, tell me one thing in the next 30 seconds that I can do to improve my marriage right now!" I told him that if I were to pick just one thing it would be to honor his wife's dreams. The guy jumped up, put on his coat, and left the room. I found out months later that he had immediately hopped on the subway to Brooklyn, where he surprised his wife, who was at home with a young baby. Her mouth dropped when he asked her what her dreams were. He told me later that she said she thought he would never ask.

What would you suggest we be on guard against in relationships?

What I call the Four Horsemen of the Apocalypse—criticism, defensiveness, stonewalling, and contempt—are the best predictors of breakup or continued misery. Readers familiar with my work will remember that I consider contempt to be the worst: It destroys relationships because it communicates disgust. You can't resolve a conflict with your partner when you're conveying the message that you're disgusted with her. Inevitably, contempt leads to greater conflict and negativity. Our research also shows that people in contemptuous relationships are more likely to suffer from infectious illnesses—flu, colds, and so on—than other people. Contempt attacks the immune system; fondness and admiration are the antidotes.

Are you in a successful relationship?

Yes, my wife and I have just celebrated our 20th wedding anniversary, but we both had disastrous first marriages. Mine failed because my first wife and I had opposite dreams. I really love children and wanted to be a father, but she wasn't so sure and that was a deal breaker. Could a therapist have saved that relationship? I don't think so. My need to be a father was too great. And I'm so glad I became a dad. It's the most important thing I've ever done.

Critical Thinking

1. What common factors contribute to the failure of a marriage?
2. How can the chances of relationship success be improved?

From *Harvard Business Review*, December 2007, pp. 45–50. Copyright © 2007 by Harvard Business School Publishing. Reprinted by permission.

Where Is Marriage Going?

Anthony Layng

It was bad enough when the divorce rate in the U.S. reached epidemic proportions and single parenting became commonplace. Now, more and more Americans are developing a tolerance for same-sex marriage. New York recognizes such marriages, and the California and Connecticut Supreme Courts struck down those states' laws banning marriage for same-sex couples, allowing them to join Massachusetts in accepting homosexual unions. Even though Californians recently voted to stop granting marriage licenses to same-sex couples, the sanctity of marriage seriously seems to be undermined and in danger of further deterioration.

Most Americans believe that marriage is an inherently sacred institution, the purpose of which is procreation and the socialization of children. That is why the idea of same-sex marriage, the prevalence of single mothers raising children, and the frailty of modern marriages are considered such a threat to "proper" marriage. Such pessimism particularly is prevalent among biblical literalists and other Christian fundamentalists who feel that any alteration of traditional marriage constitutes a moral decline, and many others agree.

However, examining the history of marriage encourages quite a different conclusion. The ethnographic study of tribal societies suggests what marriage meant to our ancestors thousands of years ago. Obviously, having children is an ancient concern, but most tribal people did not view marriage as something sacred. Many tribes had no ritual to acknowledge the start of a marriage, nothing we would equate to a wedding. Among the traditional Cheyenne, courtship involved a girl allowing a suitor to sleep with her in her parents' tepee, entering stealthfully after dark and leaving before the others in the tepee awakened. All the couple needed to do to be considered married was to have the young man sleep late enough to be discovered by her parents. Similarly, some Pacific islanders, such as the Ulithi, allowed couples to "announce" that they wished to be considered married simply by cohabiting. Coming-of-age rituals were far more common in tribal societies than weddings, and yet marriage was, with very few exceptions, the norm in all these societies.

Somehow, the belief that marriages are arranged in heaven, an extremely romantic idea, has become equated with considering marriage as sacred. Again, taking a historical perspective as provided by our knowledge of traditional societies, marriages frequently were arranged by parents or other relatives. Among the Sambia of New Guinea and the Tiwi of northern Australia, many marriages involved infant brides. In numerous warlike tribes such as the Yanomamo of Venezuela, men obtained wives by capturing them from enemy villages.

Granted, marriage in this country often is associated with religious concepts and usually initiated with a sacred ritual. Yet, from the perspective of the history of humanity, this is a rather recent development. Even newer are our present matrimonial motives. Instead of marrying to ensure that our offspring will care for us when we are too old to provide for ourselves, we now consciously limit the number of children to how many we can afford. No longer does marrying and having children provide assurance that the elderly will be cared for. Understandably, most modern couples, for a variety of reasons, choose to limit their fecundity to one or two children or remain childless. Unlike tribal people, those of us who elect to avoid marriage nevertheless may be admired and influential. However, our tribal ancestors structured their lives around marriage. Who you were, your role in society, and your prestige all largely were determined by your place in the kinship system. Whom you and your kin married could ensure or alter your status in society. One rose and fell in the social order by strategic marriage. Of course, infant marriage and marriage by capture no longer are acceptable. Arranged marriages remain legal, but are considered unsuitable. Now, it seems, the only legitimate motivation for marriage is romantic love and seeking emotional fulfillment. Marriage to enhance status still occurs, but generally is frowned upon. We are quite critical of the wealthy senior socialite who marries her young tennis instructor, or the twentysomething beauty who marries a famous elderly celebrity. Such unions are considered laughable or crass.

Tribal people married to gain prestige by having many children (hopefully, several sons) to ensure their future welfare. Additionally, given the strict sexual division of labor in these societies, at least one man and one woman were necessary components of a normal household. This had been the case since our ancestors lived as hunters and gatherers. Even in traditional agrarian societies, the labors of men and women produced very different things, and both were required for running a successful household and providing for children. Now that men and women are obtaining nearly equal educations and more and more couples are, of necessity, gainfully employed, any domestic division of labor likely is to be dictated by personal inclinations and circumstances rather than gender. No longer is the husband inevitably the breadwinner and the wife a stay-at-home mother. Marriage in the U.S. is a very flexible institution today. The nature of a marital relationship is not determined primarily by custom but is left to each couple to work out according to personal needs and preferences. It no longer necessarily involves a hierarchical arrangement between spouses. Contemporary husbands and wives frequently consider themselves to be equal partners. Even parenting has lost its imperative tie to marriage since it has become acceptable for single people to raise children today.

The nature of a marital relationship is not determined primarily by custom but is left to each couple to work out. . . .

It is under these circumstances, given how marriage has evolved to its present form, that homosexual men and women have begun to find same-sex marriage attractive. Clearly, each marriage is an ever-adapting relationship, altering over time as circumstances change. Similarly, the institution of marriage has evolved and will continue to do so. Since the earliest marriages in very primitive societies, this custom has taken various forms, always adjusting as society evolved. That process particularly is evident today because social change has been accelerating. Current legislative attempts to prohibit such change are understandable, but unsuitable and unlikely to succeed, as our technology, beliefs, and customs have a long dynamic history, and marriage is subject to the same forces of social change as the rest of our culture.

Critical Thinking

1. What societal influences are contributing to our definition of marriage?
2. Name some positive and negative outcomes from having a narrow definition of marriage.

ANTHONY LAYNG is professor emeritus of anthropology at Elmira (N.Y.) College.

Contributing to the Debate over Same-Sex Marriage

DR. GWENDOLYN PURYEAR KEITA

Among APA's primary roles is increasing and disseminating knowledge about human behavior and applying what we know about psychology to address human concerns. A recent example of our work in these areas was our filing an *amicus curie* brief, along with the California Psychological Association, the American Psychiatric Association and the National Association of Social Workers, in the California case that challenged the decision to deny marriage licenses to same-sex couples.

The court found that restricting marriage to same-sex couples violates the state constitution. In its decision, the court cited only APA's brief—one out of the 45 submitted. APA offered rigorous psychological evidence emphasizing the major impact stigma has on well-being, the benefits of marriage, and the lack of difference between lesbian and gay parents and heterosexual parents.

According to the brief:

1. Homosexuality is neither a disorder nor a disease, but rather a normal variant of human sexual orientation. The vast majority of social prejudice, discrimination and violence against lesbians, gay men and bisexuals takes a cumulative toll on the well-being of members in each of these groups. "Minority stress" is the term used by researchers to refer to the negative effects associated with the adverse social conditions experienced by those belonging to a stigmatized social group.

   As a product of sociopolitical forces, structural stigma "represents the policies of private and governmental institutions that restrict the opportunities of stigmatized groups." By legitimating and reinforcing the undesired differences of sexual minorities and by according them inferior status relative to heterosexuals, structural stigma gives rise to individual acts against them, subsequently increasing levels of stress as a result.

2. Substantial numbers of gay and lesbian couples are successful in forming stable, long-lasting, committed relationships. Empirical studies using nonrepresentative samples of gay men and lesbians show that the vast majority of participants have been involved in a committed relationship at some point in their lives. Data from the 2000 U.S. Census indicate that of the 5.5 million couples who were living together but not married, about one in nine had a same-sex partner.

3. Being married affords individuals a variety of benefits that have important implications for physical and mental health and for the quality of the relationship itself. These health benefits do not appear to result from simply being in an intimate relationship because most studies have found that married men and women generally experience better physical and mental health than their cohabitating unmarried counterparts.

4. Empirical research has consistently shown that lesbian and gay parents do not differ from heterosexuals in their parenting skills, and their children do not show any deficits compared with children raised by heterosexual parents.

In addition, if their parents are allowed to marry, the children of same-sex couples will benefit not only from the legal stability and other familial benefits that marriage provides, but also from elimination of state-sponsored stigmatization of their families.

In 2004, APA's Council of Representatives adopted two resolutions relevant to this issue, which can be found on APA's Public Interest Directorate Web pages. In the Resolution on Sexual Orientation and Marriage, it was resolved, based on empirical research concerning sexual orientation and marriage, "that the APA believes that it is unfair and discriminatory to deny same-sex couples legal access to civil marriage and to all its attendant benefits, rights, and privileges." In the Resolution on Sexual Orientation, Parents, and Children, the association recognized that "There is no scientific evidence that parenting effectiveness is related to parental sexual orientation."

Adopting these and similar resolutions and filing *amicus* briefs are but two of the many ways that APA demonstrates its steadfast commitment to providing scientific and educational resources and support to inform public discussion and a clear and objective understanding of these issues.

The full text of the California *amicus* brief can be found at www.apa.org/psyclaw/marriage.

Critical Thinking

1. How does social stigma impact the lesbian and gay community?

2. What are the arguments in favor of same sex marriage?

3. What are some of the research findings on lesbian and gay parenting?

The Polygamists

A sect that split from the Mormons allows multiple wives, expels "lost boys," and heeds a jailed prophet.

SCOTT ANDERSON

The first church members arrive at the Leroy S. Johnson Meeting House in Colorado City, Arizona, at about 6 P.M. Within a half hour the line extends out the front doors, down the side of the building, and out into the parking lot. By seven, it stretches hundreds of yards and has grown to several thousand people—the men and boys dressed in suits, the women and girls in Easter egg–hued prairie dresses.

The mourners have come for a viewing of 68-year-old Foneta Jessop, who died of a heart attack a few days ago. In the cavernous hall Foneta's sons form a receiving line at the foot of her open casket, while her husband, Merril, stands directly alongside. To the other side stand Merril's numerous other wives, all wearing matching white dresses.

Foneta was the first wife.

Colorado City is a town with special significance for those of Foneta's faith. Together with its sister community of Hildale, Utah, it is the birthplace of the Fundamentalist Church of Jesus Christ of Latter-Day Saints (FLDS), a polygamous offshoot of the Mormon Church, or LDS. Here in the '20s and '30s, a handful of polygamous families settled astride the Utah-Arizona border after the leadership of the Mormon Church became increasingly determined to shed its polygamous past and be accepted by the American mainstream. In 1935 the church gave settlement residents an ultimatum: renounce plural marriage or be excommunicated. Practically everyone refused and was cast out of the LDS.

At the memorial service for Foneta, her husband and three sons give testimonials praising her commitment to the covenant of plural marriage, but there is an undertone of family disharmony, with vague references by Merril Jessop to his troubled relationship with Foneta. No one need mention that one of Merril's wives is missing. Carolyn Jessop, his fourth wife, left the household in 2003 with her eight children and went on to write a best-selling book on her life as an FLDS member. She describes a cloistered environment and tells of a deeply unhappy Foneta, an overweight recluse who fell out of favor with her husband and slept her days away, coming out of her room only at night to eat, do laundry, and watch old Shirley Temple movies on television.

At the conclusion of the service, most of the congregation walk over to the Isaac Carling cemetery for a graveside observance. I assume the enormous turnout—mourners have come in from FLDS communities in Texas, Colorado, and British Columbia—stems from the prominent position Foneta's husband holds: Merril Jessop is an FLDS leader and the bishop of the large chapter in West Texas. But Sam Steed, a soft-spoken, 37-year-old accountant acting as my guide, explains that elaborate funerals are a regular occurrence. "Probably between 15 and 20 times a year," he says. "This one is maybe a little bigger than most, but even when a young child dies, you can expect three or four thousand people to attend. It's part of what keeps us together. It reminds us we're members of this larger community. We draw strength from each other."

Few Americans had heard of the FLDS before April 2008, when law enforcement officials conducted a raid on a remote compound in West Texas known as the Yearning for Zion Ranch. For days after, television viewers witnessed the bizarre spectacle of hundreds of children and women—all dressed in old-fashioned prairie dresses, with elaborately coiffed hair—being herded onto school buses by social workers and police officers.

That raid had been spurred by phone calls to a domestic violence shelter, purportedly from a 16-year-old girl who claimed she was being sexually and physically abused on the ranch by her middle-aged husband. What lent credibility to the calls was that the residents of YFZ Ranch were disciples of the FLDS and its "prophet," Warren Jeffs, who had been convicted in a Utah court in 2007 for officiating at the marriage of a 14-year-old girl to a church member.

The raid made for gripping television, but it soon became clear that the phone calls were a hoax. And although authorities had evidently anticipated a violent confrontation like the 1993 shoot-out at the Branch Davidian compound in Waco—SWAT teams were brought in, along with an armored personnel carrier—the arsenal at the YFZ Ranch consisted of only 33 legal firearms. A Texas appeals court later found that authorities had not met the burden of proof for the removal of the more than 400 children, and most were returned to their families within two months.

Yet after interviewing teenagers who were pregnant or had children, Texas authorities began investigating how many

118

underage girls might have been "sealed" to older men. (Plural marriages are performed within the church and are not legal.) The result: Twelve church members, including Warren Jeffs, were indicted on charges ranging from bigamy to having sex with a minor. The first defendant to stand trial, Raymond Jessop, was convicted of one charge last November. Trials of the other defendants are scheduled to take place over the coming year.

From the Bluff behind his Hildale home, Joe Jessop has a commanding view of the Arizona Strip, an undulating expanse of sagebrush and piñon-juniper woodland that stretches south of the Utah border all the way to the northern rim of the Grand Canyon, some 50 miles away. Below are the farm fields and walled compounds of Hildale and Colorado City, which Joe refers to collectively by their old name, Short Creek. "When I first came to Short Creek as a boy, there were just seven homes down there," says Joe, 88. "It was like the frontier."

Today, Short Creek is home to an estimated 6,000 FLDS members—the largest FLDS community. Joe Jessop, a brother of Merril, has contributed to that explosive growth in two very different ways. With the weathered features and spindly gait of a man who has spent his life outdoors and worked his body hard, he is the community's undisputed "water guy," a self-taught engineer who helped with the piping of water out of Maxwell Canyon back in the 1940s. He's had a hand in building the intricate network of waterlines, canals, and reservoirs that has irrigated the arid plateau in the decades since.

A highly respected member of the FLDS, Joe is also the patriarch of a family of 46 children and—at last count—239 grandchildren. "My family came to Short Creek for the same reason as everyone else," he says, "to obey the law of plural marriage, to build up the Kingdom of God. Despite everything that's been thrown our way, I'd say we've done a pretty good job."

Members of the faith describe the life that the Jessops and other founding families have built as idyllic, one in which old-fashioned devotion and neighborly cooperation are emphasized and children are raised in a wholesome environment free of television and junk food and social pressures. Critics, on the other hand, see the FLDS as an isolated cult whose members, worn down by rigid social control, display a disturbing fealty to one man, the prophet Warren Jeffs—who has claimed to be God's mouthpiece on Earth.

To spend time in Hildale and Colorado City is to come away with a more nuanced view. That view is revealed gradually, however, due to the insular nature of the community. Many of the oversize homes are tucked behind high walls, both to give children a safe place to play and to shield families from gawking Gentiles, as non-Mormons are known. Most residents avoid contact with strangers. *National Geographic* was given access to the community only on the approval of the church leadership, in consultation with the imprisoned Warren Jeffs.

In keeping with original Mormon teachings, much of the property in Hildale and Colorado City is held in trust for the church. Striving to be as self-sufficient as possible, the community grows a wide variety of fruits and vegetables, and everyone, including children, is expected to help bring in the yield. Church members also own and operate a number of large businesses, from hotels to tool and machine manufacturers. Each Saturday, men gather at the meetinghouse to go over a roster of building and maintenance projects around town in need of volunteers. In one display of solidarity, the men built a four-bedroom home, from foundation to roof shingles, in a single day.

This communal spirit continues inside the polygamous home. Although living arrangements vary—wives may occupy different wings of a house or have their own granny cottages—the women tend to carve out spheres of influence according to preference or aptitude. Although each has primary responsibility for her own children, one wife might manage the kitchen, a second act as schoolteacher (virtually all FLDS children in Hildale and Colorado City are homeschooled), and a third see to the sewing. Along with instilling a sense of sorority, this division of labor appears to mitigate jealousy.

"I know it must seem strange to outsiders," says Joyce Broadbent, a friendly woman of 44, "but from my experience, sister wives usually get along very well. Oh sure, you might be closer to one than another, or someone might get on your nerves occasionally, but that's true in any family. I've never felt any rivalry or jealousy at all."

Joyce is a rather remarkable example of this harmony. She not only accepted another wife, Marcia, into the family, but was thrilled by the addition. Marcia, who left an unhappy marriage in the 1980s, is also Joyce's biological sister. "I knew my husband was a good man," Joyce explains with a smile as she sits with Marcia and their husband, Heber. "I wanted my sister to have a chance at the same kind of happiness I had."

Not all FLDS women are quite so sanguine about plural marriage. Dorothy Emma Jessop is a spry, effervescent octogenarian who operates a naturopathic dispensary in Hildale. Sitting in her tiny shop surrounded by jars of herbal tinctures she ground and mixed herself, Dorothy admits she struggled when her husband began taking on other wives. "To be honest," she says, "I think a lot of women have a hard time with it, because it's not an easy thing to share the man you love. But I came to realize this is another test that God places before you—the sin of jealousy, of pride—and that to be a godly woman, I needed to overcome it."

What seems to help overcome it is an awareness that a woman's primary role in the FLDS is to bear and raise as many children as possible, to build up the "celestial family" that will remain together for eternity. It is not uncommon to meet FLDS women who have given birth to 10, 12, 16 children. (Joyce Broadbent is the mother of 11, and Dorothy Emma Jessop of 13.) As a result, it's easy to see why this corner of the American West is experiencing a population explosion. The 400 or so babies delivered in the Hildale health clinic every year have resulted in a median age of just under 14, in contrast with 36.6 for the entire U.S. With so many in the community tracing their lineage to a handful of the pioneering families, the same few names crop up over and over in Hildale and Colorado City, suggesting a murkier side to this fecundity: Doctors in Arizona say a severe form of a debilitating disease called fumarase deficiency, caused by a recessive gene, has become more prevalent in the community due to intermarriage.

The collision of tradition and modernity in the community can be disorienting. Despite their old-fashioned dress, most FLDS adults have cell phones and favor late-model SUVs. Although televisions are now banished, church members tend to be highly computer literate and sell a range of products, from soaps to dresses, via the Internet. When I noticed how few congregants wore glasses, I wondered aloud if perhaps a genetic predisposition for good eyesight was at work. Sam Steed laughed lightly. "No. People here are just really into laser surgery."

The principle of plural marriage was revealed to the Mormons amid much secrecy. Dark clouds hovered over the church in the early 1840s, after rumors spread that its founder, Joseph Smith, had taken up the practice of polygamy. While denying the charge in public, by 1843 Smith had shared a revelation with his closest disciples. In this "new and everlasting covenant" with God, plural wives were to be taken so that the faithful might "multiply and replenish the earth."

After Smith was assassinated by an anti-Mormon mob in Illinois, Brigham Young led believers on an epic 1,300-mile journey west to the Salt Lake Basin of present-day Utah. There the covenant was at last publicly revealed and with it, the notion that a man's righteousness before God would be measured by the size of his family; Brigham Young himself took 55 wives, who bore him 57 children.

But in 1890, faced with the seizure of church property under a federal antipolygamy law, the LDS leadership issued a manifesto announcing an end to plural marriage. That certainly didn't end the practice, and the LDS's tortured handling of the issue—some church leaders remained in plural marriages or even took on new wives after the manifesto's release—contributed to the schism between the LDS and the fundamentalists.

"The LDS issued that manifesto for political purposes, then later claimed it was a revelation," says Willie Jessop, the FLDS spokesman. "We in the fundamentalist community believe covenants are made with God and are not to be manipulated for political reasons, so that presents an enormous obstacle between us and those in the LDS mainstream."

Upholding the covenant has come at a high price. The 2008 raid on the YFZ Ranch was only the latest in a long list of official actions against polygamists—persecutions for simply adhering to their religious principles, in the eyes of church members—that are integral to the FLDS story. At various times both Utah and Arizona authorities attempted to crack down on the Short Creek community: in 1935, in 1944, and most famously, in 1953. In that raid some 200 women and children were hauled to detention centers, while 26 men were brought up on polygamy charges. In 1956 Utah authorities seized seven children of Vera Black, a Hildale plural wife, on grounds that her polygamous beliefs made her an unfit mother. Black was reunited with her children only after agreeing to renounce polygamy.

Melinda Fischer Jeffs is an articulate, outgoing woman of 37, and she gives an incredulous laugh when describing what she's read about the FLDS. "Honestly, I can't even recognize it!" the mother of three exclaims. "Most all of what appears in the media, it makes us sound like we're somehow being kept against our will."

Melinda is in a unique position to understand the conflicting views of this community. She is a plural wife to Jim Jeffs, one of the prophet's nephews and an elder in the FLDS. But she is also the daughter of Dan Fischer, a former FLDS member who has emerged as one of the church leadership's most vociferous critics. In 2008 Fischer testified before a U.S. Senate committee about alleged improprieties within the FLDS, and he now heads an organization that works with people who have been kicked out of the church or who have "escaped." When Fischer broke with the church in the 1990s, his family split apart too; today 13 of his children have left the FLDS, while Melinda and two of her half siblings have renounced their father.

"And that is not an easy thing," Melinda says softly, "obviously, because I still love my father. I pray all the time that he will see his errors—or at least, stop his attacks on us."

If there is one point on which FLDS defenders and detractors might agree, it is that most of the current troubles can be traced to when its leadership passed to the Jeffs family, in 1986. Until then, the FLDS had been a fairly loosely run group led by an avuncular man named Leroy Johnson, who relied on a group of high priests to guide the church. That ended when Rulon Jeffs took over following Johnson's death. After being declared the prophet by the community, Rulon solidified the policy of one-man rule.

Charges that a theocratic dictatorship was taking root in the Arizona Strip grew louder when, after Rulon's death in 2002, the FLDS was taken over by his 46-year-old son, Warren. Assuming the role of the prophet, Warren first married several of his father's wives—and then proceeded to wed many more women, including, according to Carolyn Jessop, eight of Merril Jessop's daughters. Although many FLDS men have multiple wives, the number of wives of those closest to the prophet can reach into the double digits. A church document called the Bishop's Record, seized during the Texas raid, shows that one of Jeffs's lieutenants, Wendell Nielsen, claims 21 wives. And although the FLDS would not disclose how many plural wives Warren Jeffs has taken (some estimate more than 80), at least one was an underage girl, according to a Texas indictment.

Although the issue of underage marriage within the church has garnered the greatest negative media attention, Dan Fischer has championed another cause, the so-called Lost Boys, who have left or been forced from the community and wound up fending for themselves on the streets of Las Vegas, Salt Lake City, and St. George, Utah. Fischer's foundation has worked with 300 such young men, a few as young as 13, over the past seven years. Fischer concedes that most of these boys were simply "discouraged out," but he cites cases where they were officially expelled, a practice he says increased under Jeffs.

Fischer attributes the exodus partly to a cold-blooded calculation by church leaders to limit male competition for the pool of marriageable young women. "If you have men marrying 20, 30, up to 80 or more women," he says, "then it comes down to biology and simple math that there will be a lot of other men who aren't going to get wives. The church says it's kicking these boys out for being disruptive influences, but if you'll notice, they rarely kick out girls."

Equally contentious has been the FLDS restoration of an early Mormon policy of transferring the wives and children of a church member to another man. Traditionally, this was done upon the death of a patriarch so that his widows might be cared for, or to rescue a woman from an abusive relationship. But critics argue that under Jeffs this "reassignment" became one more weapon to hold over the heads of those who dared step out of line.

Determining who is unworthy has been the exclusive province of the prophet. When in January 2004 Jeffs publicly ordered the expulsion of 21 men and the reassignment of their families, the community acquiesced. Jeffs's diary, also seized during the Texas raid, reveals a man who micromanaged the community's every decision, from chore assignments and housing arrangements to who married whom and which men were ousted—all directed by revelations Jeffs received as he slept. He claimed that God guided his every action, no matter how small. One diary entry reads: "The Lord directed that I go to the sun tanning salon and get sun tanned more evenly on their suntanning beds."

In 2005 a Utah court transferred control of the trust that oversees much of the land in Hildale and Colorado City from the FLDS leadership to a state-appointed fiduciary; the church is currently waging a campaign to recover control of the trust. As for Jeffs, after spending over a year on the lam avoiding legal issues in Utah—and earning a spot on the FBI's Ten Most Wanted list—he was caught and is currently serving a ten-year-to-life sentence as an accomplice to rape. He awaits trial on multiple indictments in Arizona and Texas. The 11 other church members awaiting trial in Texas include Merril Jessop, who was indicted for performing the marriage of Jeffs to an underage girl.

Yet Jeffs's smiling portrait continues to adorn the living room of almost every FLDS home. In his absence, his lieutenants have launched a fierce defense of his leadership. While conceding that underage marriages did occur in the past, Donald Richter, contributor to one of the official FLDS websites, says the practice has now been stopped. As for the Lost Boys, he argues that both the numbers involved and the reasons for the expulsions have been greatly exaggerated by the church's enemies. "This is only done in the most extreme cases," Richter says, "and never for the trivial causes they're claiming. And anyway, all religious groups have the right to expel people who won't accept their rules."

Certainly Melinda Fischer Jeffs hasn't been swayed by the ongoing controversy. "Warren is just the kindest, most loving man," she says. "The image that has been built up about him by the media and his enemies is just unrecognizable to who he really is." Like other church members, Melinda has ready answers for most of the accusations leveled against Jeffs and is especially spirited in defending the policy of reassignment.

According to her, it is almost always initiated at the request of a wife who has been abandoned or abused. This is debatable. In his diary Jeffs recounts reassigning the wives of three men, including his brother David, because God had shown him that they "couldn't exalt their ladies, had lost the confidence of God." One of his brother's wives had difficulty accepting the news and could barely bring herself to kiss her new husband. "She showed a great spirit of resistance, yet she went through with it," Jeffs records. "She needs to learn to submit to Priesthood."

Yet Melinda's defense of Jeffs underscores one of the most curious aspects of the polygamous faith: the central role of women in defending it. This is not new. In Brigham Young's day a charity rushed to Utah to establish a safe house for polygamous women seeking to escape this "white slavery"; that house sat virtually empty. Today FLDS women in the Hildale–Colorado City area have ample opportunity to "escape"—they have cell phones, they drive cars, there are no armed guards keeping them in—yet they don't.

Undoubtedly one reason is that, having been raised in this culture, they know little else. Walking away means leaving behind everything: the community, one's sense of security, even one's own family. Carolyn Jessop, the plural wife of Merril Jessop who did leave the FLDS, likens entering the outside world to "stepping out onto another planet. I was completely unprepared, because I had absolutely no life skills. Most women in the FLDS don't even know how to balance a checkbook, let alone apply for a job, so contemplating how you're going to navigate in the outside world is extremely daunting."

It would seem there's another lure for women to stay: power. The FLDS women I spoke with tended to be far more articulate and confident than the men, most of whom seemed paralyzed by bashfulness. It makes sense when one begins to grasp that women are coveted to "multiply and replenish the earth," while men are in extraordinary competition to be deemed worthy of marriage by the prophet. One way to be deemed worthy, of course, is to not rock the boat, to keep a low profile. As a result, what has all the trappings of a patriarchal culture, actually has many elements of a matriarchal one.

There are limits to that power, of course, for it is subject to the dictates of the prophet. After hearing Melinda's stout defense of Jeffs, I ask what she would do if she were reassigned.

"I'm confident that wouldn't happen," she replies uneasily.

"But what if it did?" I ask. "Would you obey?"

For the only time during our interview, Melinda grows wary. Sitting back in her chair, she gives her head a quarter turn to stare at me out of the corner of one eye.

On a sunny afternoon in March 2009, Bob Barlow, a friendly, middle-aged member of the FLDS, gives me a tour of the YFZ Ranch in West Texas. The compound consists of about 25 two-story log-cabin-style homes, and a number of workshops and factories are scattered over 1,700 acres. At the center sits a gleaming white stone temple. It is remarkable what the residents have created from the hardscrabble plain. With heavy machinery, they literally made earth out of the rocky terrain, crushing stone and mixing it with the thin topsoil. They planted orchards and gardens and lawns and were on their way to creating a self-sufficient community amid the barren landscape. All that ground to a halt after the 2008 raid.

"The families are slowly coming back now," Barlow says. "We'll come out the other side of this better and stronger than before."

I suspect he's right. So many times in the history of Mormon polygamy the outside world thought it had the movement on the ropes only to see it flourish anew. I'm reminded of this one afternoon in Colorado City when I speak with Vera Black. Now 92 and in failing health, Vera is the woman whose children were taken from her by Utah authorities in 1956 and returned only after she agreed to renounce polygamy. Within days of making that promise, she was back in Short Creek with her

children and had renewed her commitment to the everlasting covenant.

Now living with her daughter Lillian, Vera lies in a daybed as her children gather around. Those children are now in their 50s and 60s, and as they recount the story of their long-ago separation—both from their mother and their faith—several weep, as if the pain were fresh.

"I had to make that promise," Vera says, with a smile, "but I crossed my fingers while I did it."

Critical Thinking

1. How do the experiences of men and women in a fundamentalist polygamist community differ?

2. Describe the religious belief system that makes polygamist marriages possible.

From *National Geographic*, vol. 217, no. 2, February 2010, pp. 34–57. Copyright © 2010 by National Geographic Society. Reprinted by permission.

Kinky Sex Makes for Happy People

PIETA WOOLLEY

The Brentwood Town Centre food court was, during lunch time on November 6, not an obvious hub of sexuality. Diners hunched over the bolted-down tables, ingesting soft meat burritos and fried rice. Most ate alone in silence. But to sex-positive activist Jennifer Skrukwa, there was nothing flaccid about such an ordinary crowd.

"I'll bet 40 percent of the people here are kinky," she told the *Georgia Straight* in an interview at the food fair. "But do they label their kinks? Surely there's a lot of people here who like to have their nipples pinched really hard before they come. Or get scratched. Or feel the full weight of someone lying on top of them. Or have their bums spanked a couple of times a year. I'll bet there's a woman here who likes to dress up in heels and bustiers. And that man over there wearing a Betty Boop jacket, he's probably wearing red silk undies. Someone here has got his wife's panties in his pocket and sniffs them each time he goes to the washroom today.

"These people are alive with sex. But many of them are denying that they are."

Skrukwa isn't a denier, inside or out. At the food fair, she wore a turquoise lace tank, push-up bra, and black stilettos. Her lipstick was perfectly applied, her eyes popped under heavy mascara, and her long dark hair was immaculately teased and sprayed. That evening, at the Love Nest sex store across from Metrotown, she taught cock-sucking to a full house.

Vancouver wants what she is selling. The 35-year-old mom leads 170 workshops per year on subjects ranging from "butt sex and anal pleasure" to "finding and stimulating the G-spot", which features a live demonstration "where you can actually see the G-spot spurt", she said. Skrukwa claims she's hosted about 7,000 people each year since she started her business, Libido Events (*libidoevents.com*), eight years ago. On Saturday (November 24), she's throwing a 120-person sex party at 595 Hornby Street that will include: eight queen-sized beds; one bondage suspension rack; a sex room; a dance floor; a flogging station; 4,800 square feet in which to frolic; and a set of house rules.

This isn't porn or prostitution. It's grownups of diverse sexual preferences consensually and shamelessly getting their freak on. And Vancouver has become one giant sexy experiment, with Generations Y and X leading the way.

Sin City's fetish nights at Gastown's Club 23 West attract 500 naughty schoolgirls, goths, and others monthly and boast 1,085 Facebook members. Kitsilano's Art of Loving offers classes in sexual massage, kissing, how to "make her moan", and other subjects. The CY Club, Vancouver's oldest swinging club, offers "hump day" once a month. The two-year-old Club Eden, a warehouse-sized club in Delta, charges $50 for a couples membership, $90 per event, and another $100 to stay overnight. This summer, it expanded to Calgary. "Poly-amorists" (those who love more than one person) are finding each other on the Web, and UBC PhD candidate Danielle Duplassie believes their numbers may reach the thousands in B.C.

"There seems to be a trend that one person cannot meet all of another person's needs," she told the *Straight*. "There's certainly a trend to more openness."

This is just the tip. Almost every night of the month, there's some easy-to-find kinky event where consenting adults can get off.

But are *you* getting any? You, *Straight* reader, who bought into the monogamous "lifestyle", as sanctioned by society, law, the church, the synagogue, the temple, and the mosque. How much sex are you having?

In the absence of any recent, local, decently sampled research on sexual frequency, it's impossible to know just what you and your neighbours are up to. In his work, local sex therapist David McKenzie refers to *The Social Organization of Sexuality: Sexual Practices in the United States*, by Edward O. Laumann, John H. Gagnon, Robert T. Michael, and Stuart Michaels (University of Chicago Press, 1994). They found that about 10 percent of adults are sexually inactive, and about a quarter have sex a few times a year or not at all. In total, they found, 60 percent of adults are having sex a few times a month or less. Not exactly burning up the bedrooms.

Burnaby counsellor Dawn Schooler sees plenty of Generation Y and Xers who are having no sex. In fact, that's a trend that is going to worsen, she predicted to the *Straight* in a phone interview.

"There's a growing isolation," she said. "Leisure time is spent in solitary pursuits, on the Internet, iPods, video games. They don't learn to have social relationships." As for monogamous couples, she said of those she sees in her practice, they're simply too busy to have sex, thanks to work, the high cost of living, and children.

Skrukwa's answer is kink. Get kinky and get some.

"For me, it started when a partner asked me to wear high-heeled shoes in bed," she recalled. "Stilettos. So I started wearing shoes for him, and it spiralled." She tried out an S&M club. "It was not my cup of tea, but I was captivated by the idea that you can be in a space where people accept you for what you want."

Now, with a female partner of six years, a male partner of one year, and a growing business helping folks sort out their freaks, Skrukwa is at the helm of the mainstreaming of kink in Vancouver, for the sake of keeping everyone's sex life alive.

Lulu West was 29 the first time she strapped on an oversized, sparkly, clear-jelly dildo, paired it with stockings, garters, and a corset, and braved a fetish night with some girlfriends. With a one-year-old at home, she hadn't been out for a couple of years. She panicked before going.

"But after about five minutes, I loved the titillation, the dancing, the eye candy, the outfits," she told the *Straight* in an Oak Street coffee shop. "There was a really beautiful bleached-blond lady who was bending all these guys over a pool table, and they were begging her to spank them. She had a huge hickory switch, and she was laughing and having a good time, swatting them with it. At the end, she pulled out her boob and squeezed breast milk all over their bums and rubbed it in all over."

West paused and her eyes opened wide.

"And I thought, 'Wow! I'm not bored! Check this out!'"

Avoiding boredom is a big motivator for West. Now married, she still goes to fetish nights and adult play parties with permission from her husband. She's allowed to do anything except have sex with men—though she frequently has "dildo sex" with women. For her, she said, it keeps her primary relationship fresh and her work as a federal civil servant more tolerable.

"I love my husband, but everybody gets bored," she said. "Sometimes you just want to colour outside the lines. It makes you energized. You feel sexier [after a party], and you get a mood boost for days. . . . When you go out, you bring back something new, something you saw or did. And you can play with that for a while. Play with your thoughts, the things you saw. Have a fantasy."

West looked to the existing scene to freshen her sex life, but SFU student Scott Barnes simply introspected. Nine years ago, Barnes was 17 and travelling across Canada with his girlfriend. In Montreal, he met another woman. He asked his girlfriend, "If I sleep with this other woman, does that mean we have to break up?" She thought that didn't make sense. So Barnes began a two-year "freeing and liberating" sexual era in his life: lots of partners, lots of sex.

Next, he spent seven years in an almost sex-free monogamous relationship.

"Her sex drive waned so dramatically," he explained to the *Straight* in a phone interview. "For four years, we had no

sex. It really reinforced to me the reasonableness of being nonmonogamous."

Recently, he fell "madly and completely in love" with a woman. He explained to her his preference for nonmonogamy. She considered it. Tragically, he said, the same day he realized he didn't need anyone else, she broke up with him over the issue. So now he's buying flowers, trying to lure her back.

To help himself and others sort through the issues, Barnes started a Facebook group called Poly-Monogamy: An Inquiry Into Open Relationships. After heated on-line debates and private thoughts, his conclusion is, "Except for those who enshrine a coherent set of principles—like Roman Catholic or fundamentalist Muslim marriage, unless it's that strict—I think everyone wants something different out of their relationships."

That conclusion, and Barnes and West's own histories, are consistent with their demographic, according to sex counsellor McKenzie. Those under 40, he said, are far more willing to try kink and open relationships than their seniors. In the six years since McKenzie started his practice, the biggest change he's seen is the more liberal attitudes of many of his clients toward swinging.

"Sex is not the big bogeyman for them that it was for us," he told the *Straight* in a phone interview. "Generation Y saw their parents get divorced, and they don't want to divorce. At the same time, there's a deep need for variety."

Indeed, if Skrukwa is at the helm of nonmonogamy in Vancouver, Barnes and West are tossed about by the waves.

A young Barnes saw a marriage close to him disintegrate under the pressure of monogamy. The woman didn't want sex; the man did. And in the long term, their solution looked a lot like his first nonmonogamous relationship—only unhappy, and without her consent. Why, he wonders, shouldn't the man be up-front about his desire for everyone's sake?

West estimated that about a third of her friends are open to the kink scene. It's a relief after the mainstream dating scene, she said.

"I wasted a lot of time before," she said. "I used to go to the regular clubs endlessly, trying to be charming. I think people really misrepresent themselves there. Guys can rob you emotionally when they're not honest [about being nonmonogamous]. In the kink scene, you're just out there, asking for exactly what you want."

In West's experience, though, the other two-thirds of folk are too scared or unmotivated to break out of their low-sex lives. Television sucks the sex drives out of plenty of friends who don't participate in kink, she said. For others, "they're in serious 'no' mode," she relayed. For undefined reasons, West said, some refuse because of amorphous "values" or "judgments".

Monogamy is not working, according to Duplassie, the founder and director of Burnaby's Shanti Counselling Centre. Divorce is almost at 50 percent; affairs are epidemic; and those who claim to be monogamous often simply go from one partner to the next—hardly the definition of the word.

Her PhD thesis in counselling psychology addresses polyamory. She hopes that a better clinical understanding of the subject will aid counsellors in helping those with more than one partner.

Duplassie started her research when, two years ago, she found herself to be in love with two people. At a conference she attended in Ottawa, she talked about the idea of polyamory.

"My questions were shut down," she told the *Straight* during an interview at a Commercial Drive coffee shop. "They said, 'I wonder what polyamorists are running away from?' and I thought, 'Wow. That's ignorant.' I wanted to research women who can speak to that experience, without the pathological viewpoint."

What she's found so far is that there are hundreds, if not thousands, of Vancouverites who identify as polyamorous, and probably many more who consensually have more than one partner, without self-labelling. And—apart from the December 2006 issue of the U.K.-based *Sexualities* on-line journal, which was devoted to polyamory—there's very little recent academic research on nonmonogamy, Duplassie has found. Canadian laws governing marriage and benefits don't support it; universities don't study it; the pharmaceutical companies would rather medicate low sex drives than promote alternative sexual expression; and society does not yet embrace it, she said. Yet lots and lots of people are doing it, in spite of all that.

The growth of kink is good news to John Ince, the leader of the Vancouver-based Sex Party (*sexparty.ca*). Those in their 20s and 30s, he echoed, are the most sexually liberal generation. But they fall apart politically. To have a true sex-positive culture, he said, the laws must change. Censorship must be restricted; sex education should teach positive, gradual skills; public nudity should be allowed; sex work must be legalized—among many other provincial and federal changes listed in the party's on-line platform.

"It disturbs me that the most sex-positive component of the culture is the least likely to vote," he told the *Straight* on the phone. "It's a problem for the entire progressive community."

Youth in Vancouver enjoy a comparatively free sexual stage, he said, including: Wreck Beach; a thriving destination gay scene; a diverse indoor sex industry largely unhampered by police; a fetish community; and "Porn North", the emerging sex-entertainment industry.

Still, Ince said, there's a long way to go. He pointed to Surrey's recent stir over the nudists who wanted to use the Newton Wave Pool as a prime example.

For Skrukwa, though, it's not about politics. It's about the small, personal barriers holding people back from embracing sex positivity. Breaching the subject with your partner. Going to a first event. Even Vancouver's casual fashion scene is a cold shower on sexuality.

"I always have heels on," Skrukwa explained. "If you want to feel sexy, you have to do something about it. If you feel like the same old craptacular image wearing your washed-out whatevers, you're not eye candy. Sexy is as sexy does. And most men like a pair of heels."

If, as Ince says, youth are apolitical, the redefinition of what mainstream sexuality is for the 21st century depends on the personal decisions of folk like Skrukwa, West, Barnes, and Duplassie. They're voting with their feet—and minds and sexy bits—for nonmonogamy.

Critical Thinking

1. How can sexual variations (or "kink") positively influence an individual's sexuality?
2. In what ways can urban communities help facilitate expressions of sexual variations?

UNIT 5

Gender and Sexual Diversity

Unit Selections

Learning Outcomes

After reading this Unit, you will be able to:

- Discuss the importance of the Convention on the Elimination of All Forms of Discrimination against Women (CEDAW).

- Describe the interplay between nature and nurture in gender related behaviors.

- Discuss the role of genes and prenatal hormones on gender identity and gendered behaviors.

- Describe how women and girls are depicted in the media.

- Relate the media's representation of the female gender to women's and girl's health and well-being.

- Discuss the challenges faced by transgendered people in our culture today.

- Discuss the social shifts and changes that have improved the quality of life of people who are transitioning from one gender to another.

- Summarize the history of the intersex rights movement.

- Describe the relationship of the intersex rights movement to the feminist movement.

- Summarize the likely developmental pathways to a homosexual orientation.

- Discuss the influence of genetics and hormones on the development of homosexuality.

- Evaluate the impact of parental sexual orientation on child development.

- Determine if there are differences between children raised by heterosexual parents as compared to children raised by gay or lesbian parents.

Student Website

www.mhhe.com/cls

Internet References

The Gay, Lesbian, and Straight Education Network
www.glsen.org

The Intersex Society of North America (ISNA)
www.isna.org

Parents, Families, and Friends of Lesbians and Gays
www.pflag.org

SocioSite: Feminism and Women's Issues
www.sociosite.net/topics/women.php

Women's Human Rights Resources
www.law-lib.utoronto.ca/Diana

In Unit 5, we consider Gender and Sexual Diversity. We begin with Perspectives on Gender, with articles on gender. Here we explore differences between males and females. What we know from research is that although there are some interesting differences between men and women, there are many more similarities. It is important to realize that when we talk about gender differences from a research perspective, we are usually talking about differences that are "statistically significant." The actual lived experiences of individual men and women may or may not match the "statistically significant differences" reported in scientific research literature.

Perhaps the importance of gender is hard for many of us to recognize. There are so many things about gender that we take for granted. Its importance may only become apparent when a social expectation is somehow not met or when a social norm is broken. When we are born, we are born into a world of norms, expectations, and sometimes conflicting attitudes and beliefs surrounding gender. The first thing most new parents want to know, other than if the baby is healthy, is the gender of the new addition to their family. So many decisions are made, almost automatically, by the gender of the child. The color of clothes that are chosen, the color of the baby's room, the types of toys the baby is given to play with—all of this is decided for most parents at the moment they find out if their new bundle of joy is a boy or a girl. The words used to describe the little one, the interactions that the parent(s) have with their child, and how others view him or her—all of these things are determined by the label "male" or "female." If someone can't tell what gender a child is because of his or her dress, not knowing may actually cause feelings of discomfort or distress. In other words, if a baby is dressed in yellow, green, and white, some people may actually become upset that they cannot tell right away if the baby is a boy or a girl. This will almost surely lead to questions. Of course, the baby couldn't care less about all this silly gender chaos that seems to constantly swirl around him or her. Only later will these things be internalized.

In this unit, we also explore the issue of transgenderism, also often called transsexuality. For transgendered people, there is a disconnect between anatomical/biological sex and gender identity. This can produce a very complicated life situation. Hormone therapies, sex reassignment, and related surgeries are all options for transgendered people who have the resources to pursue bringing their outside appearance in line with their identity. How various states and countries deal with the legalities of changing one's sex differs significantly. In some places, the form to change one's gender is easily located at the local Department of Motor Vehicles. In other places, there may be significant obstacles.

In Part B, we explore Perspectives on Sexual Orientation. Why we humans feel, react, respond, and behave sexually can be quite complex. This is especially true regarding the issue of sexual orientation. Perhaps no other area of sexual behavior is as misunderstood. Although experts do not agree about what causes our sexual orientations—homosexuality, heterosexuality, or bisexuality—growing evidence suggests multiple possible

© Ryan McVay/Getty Images

developmental pathways for each sexual orientation. Some factors that may contribute to sexual orientation include biological factors, sociocultural influences, and free choice. While most gay people seem to report that there is no point in time when they chose to be gay, there are some who have reported that they made a conscious choice. Whether we are heterosexual, gay, lesbian, or bisexual, who we are is fixed at a very early age for most of us. For others, there may be fluidity to their sexual attractions and expression.

In the mid-1900s, biological scientist and sex researcher Alfred Kinsey introduced his seven-point continuum of sexual orientation known as the Kinsey scale. It placed exclusive heterosexual orientation at one end, exclusive homosexual orientation at the other, and identified the middle range as where most people would fall if society and culture were unprejudiced. Since Kinsey, many others have added their research findings and theories to what is known about sexual orientation, including some apparent differences in the contributions of biological, psychological, environmental, and cultural factors for males versus females. In addition, further elaboration of the "middle" range on the Kinsey scale has included some distinction between bisexuality—the attraction to males and females, and ambisexuality—representing individuals for whom gender is no more relevant than any other personal characteristic, such as height, hair color, right- or left-handedness, with respect to sexual attraction and/or orientation.

Research on sexual orientation has certainly come a long way since the time of Kinsey. Today, researchers examine many aspects of sexual orientation, from biological, to psychological, to sociocultural. Anthropological and historical evidence suggests that homosexuality has existed across cultures and times. Political scientists and sociologists have conducted research on such topics as the lesbian and gay movement, public opinion, same-sex marriage, and lesbian and gay communities, among many other interesting topics.

The birth of lesbian and gay studies has been an exciting new development in academia. This multidisciplinary area of inquiry grew out of the diverse body of research conducted (especially) since the late 1960s, on the lives of lesbian, gay, and bisexual men and women. As this research has documented, there has been significant social change over the past several decades. There are more possibilities today than ever before for lesbian, gay, bisexual, and transgendered people to fully participate as "out" citizens with greater expectations for rights truly equal to those of their heterosexual counterparts. It will be interesting to see the social, political, and legal changes that occur over the next several decades. These changes surely will have a significant impact on the lives of many people and their families. A number of issues that are likely to continue to be important well into the future are explored in this unit.

Women's Rights as Human Rights
The Promotion of Human Rights as a Counter-Culture

Zehra F. Kabasakal Arat

Human rights are rights claimed against the State and society by virtue of being a human being. However, the human rights of most people have been continuously violated all around the world. Since all civilizations have been patriarchal,[1] regardless of the overall human rights conditions maintained in a society, women have been subject to more human rights violations than men. Women constitute the poorest and the least powerful segments of their communities. They are denied equal access to education, job training, employment, leisure time, income, property, health care, public office, decision-making power and freedoms, as well as control over their own body and life.[2] Cultural norms, laws and philosophies, including those that are considered progressive and emancipatory, have usually discriminated against women.

Omission of Women

The ancient Stoics' notion of natural rights, that human beings are created with certain inalienable rights, did not encompass women. When the Christian Church leader St. Thomas Aquinas (c. 1225–1274) was exposed to ancient Greek philosophy—largely through the writings of the Muslim philosophers Avicenna (Ibn Sina, 980–1037) and Averroes (Ibn Rushd, 1126–1198) who studied ancient Greek philosophy, reconciled reason with faith and championed equality and religious tolerance—he incorporated natural rights theory into his teaching. However, he ignored Averroes' egalitarian approach that opposed the unequal treatment of sexes and considered the reduction of women's value to childbearing and rearing as detrimental to the economic advancement of society and thus causing poverty.[3] Instead, Aquinas revived Aristotle's misogynous perception of woman as "misbegotten man" and wondered why God would create woman, a defective creature, in the first production of things;[4] while other church leaders later questioned if women had souls, that is, if they were fully human.

In modern times, progressive philosophers, such as Jean-Jacques Rousseau (1712–1778), could promote political freedoms and rights, but reject the notion of equality of the sexes. The revolutionary fervour of the eighteenth century that opposed oppression led to the French Declaration of the Rights of Man and Citizen (1789). However, the articulation of human rights in this document, which continued to inspire people all over the world for centuries, could not escape sexism prevalent at the time and omitted women. Nevertheless, a few elite women, such as French playwright and essayist Olympe de Gouges (1748–1793) and English philosopher Mary Wollstonecraft (1759–1797), raised their objections and defended women's rights by issuing The Declaration of the Rights of Woman (1790) and A Vindication of the Rights of Women (1791), respectively. The collaboration of Harriet Taylor Mill (1807–1858) with her husband John Stuart Mill (1806–1873) resulted in writings that advocated women's rights and political equality.[5]

Yet, gender biases prevailed throughout the twentieth century. Even members of the Commission that drafted the 1948 Universal Declaration of Human Rights were willing to employ the word "man" in reference to the holder of the rights. When the Soviet delegate, Vladimir Koretsky, objected to using the words "all men" as "historical atavism, which preclude us from an understanding that we men are only one half of the human species", the Commission Chair, Eleanor Roosevelt, defended the wording by arguing: [in English] "When we say 'all men are brothers', we mean that all human beings are brothers and we are not differentiating between men and women."[6] Thus, the language was maintained for some time. The final draft mostly employed the gender-neutral terms of "human being," "everyone" and "person," and the Preamble included a specific reference to the "equal rights of men and women," thanks largely to the efforts of two female Commission members, Hansa Mehta of India and Minerva Bernardino of the Dominican Republic.[7]

However, the Universal Declaration and the subsequent human rights documents adopted by the United Nations and other intergovernmental organizations have continued to employ the nominative and possessive pronouns "he" and "his", in line with the established tradition and understanding that male nouns or pronouns would stand for the female ones as well. Despite their clearly and repeatedly stated anti-discrimination clauses, which specify that sex as a characteristic or status cannot be used as grounds for discrimination or for denial of human rights, documents issued by the United Nations fell short of ensuring that human rights are equally applicable to both sexes.[8] Gender gaps were visible even in the United Nations, which did not have women in high office posts, as they were concentrated in clerical and lower-paying jobs, thus maintaining occupational segregation. Starting in the 1970s, however, some significant steps towards addressing gender disparities have been taken by various intergovernmental and non-governmental organizations and government agencies.

The CEDAW: An International Treaty for Women's Rights

A very important stimulus was the UN General Assembly resolution of December 1972, declaring 1975 as the International Women's Year. In 1975, the first UN world conference on women, held in Mexico City, declared 1976 to 1985 as the United Nations Decade for Women. The intensive efforts and actions undertaken during the decade included organizing more conferences on women, the creation of specialized agencies, such as the United Nations Development Fund for Women (UNIFEM) and the UN International Research and Training Institute for the Advancement of Women (INSTRAW), elevating the Branch of the Advancement of Women to a "Division" status and putting women's rights and concerns on the agenda of other conferences and organizations. Arguably, the most important development that took place during the Decade was the preparation of the Convention on the Elimination of All Forms of Discrimination against Women (CEDAW), which was adopted by the Assembly in 1979.

CEDAW was the culmination of a long process, but was given impetus in 1973 by the UN Commission on the Status of Women (CSW). In its working paper, the Commission stated that neither the Declaration on the Elimination of Discrimination Against Women (1967) nor the legally binding human rights treaties had been effective in advancing the status of women. It also argued for a single comprehensive convention that would legally bind States to eliminate discriminatory laws, as well as de facto discrimination. With 30 articles organized in six parts, CEDAW defines "discrimination against women" in its first article: "For the purposes of the present Convention, the term 'discrimination against women' shall mean any distinction, exclusion or restriction made on the basis of sex, which has the effect or purpose of impairing or nullifying the recognition, enjoyment or exercise by women, irrespective of their marital status, on a basis of equality of men and women, of human rights and fundamental freedoms in the political, economic, social, cultural, civil or any other field."

The subsequent 15 articles of the Convention (Articles 2 to 16) specify the areas of discrimination, such as laws, legal structure, political and public life, education, employment, health care, rural environment, marriage and family, in which States parties should take measures to eliminate discrimination. The last two parts (Articles 17 to 30) refer to the administration of the implementation of the Convention. "For the purpose of considering the progress made in the implementation", Article 17 creates a Committee on the Elimination of Discrimination against Women, which functions as a monitoring and advisory agency. The Committee evaluates the periodic reports submitted by States parties, questions government delegations that present the reports, guides and advises States parties in meeting the objectives of the Convention, and issues general recommendations that help interpret the intention and scope of the Convention.

The general recommendations issued by the Committee have been important for elaborating on the provisions of the Convention and for drawing attention to some gender-specific human rights violations and the attitudes and practices that disregard the value of women. By stressing such issues as gender-based violence, unequal pay for work of equal value, undervalued and unremunerated domestic activities of women, polygamy and other marital practices that disadvantage women and violate their dignity, the general recommendations have broadened the scope of CEDAW and made it a living document. In other words, some limitations in the wording of the Convention, such as treating man as a measure by requiring States parties to ensure that women enjoy a series of rights "on equal terms with men", or failing to make explicit references to some violations that are experienced mainly by women, are redressed by CEDAW through the general recommendations.

The popularity of CEDAW, as reflected in its high rate of ratification, has been encouraging. It entered into force on 3 September 1981, less than two years after the General Assembly adopted it on 18 December 1979. According to the Office of the High Commissioner for Human Rights, as of 15 February 2008, 185 countries constituting 96 percent of UN Member States have become parties to the Convention. However, ratification, accession or succession by 78 countries (42 percent of States parties) involved declarations or reservations, which allow them to limit their treaty obligations.[9] Since more States have placed reservations on this Convention than on any other human rights treaties,[10] CEDAW appears to be "the human rights instrument least respected by its States parties".[11] Reservations can be withdrawn later; so far, 14 States parties have withdrawn their reservations and a similar number withdrew or modified theirs with regard to some provisions. However, reservations justified by the claim that the culture or religion of the country conflicts with the provisions of the Convention are not likely to be withdrawn in the near future. Such broad reservations undermine "the object and purpose" of the treaty and leave it inapplicable for all practical purposes.

Cultural or religious objections to the provisions can be challenged by two interrelated arguments: first, it should be pointed out that the United Nations human rights regime, including regional ones, are essentially counter-culture; and second, although there may be tensions between goals (e.g., the preservation of culture versus the elimination of discriminatory cultural norms) or between two or more human rights (e.g., people's right as opposed to women's rights to self-determination), the international human rights regime requires them to be resolved by upholding the principles of universality and equality in dignity.

Promotion of Human Rights as a Counter-Culture

Although recognition and respect for some rights articulated in the Universal Declaration on Human Rights can be found in the cultural references and religious texts of many communities, the traditional cultural norms and practices also include numerous discriminatory stipulations. The novelty of the Declaration and subsequent human rights documents is not only universalism—the notion that *all* people hold certain rights by virtue of being human—but is also the desire to end *all* forms of violations that have been allowed in existing cultures. In other words, international human rights follow a reactive pattern: as violations are noticed, the rights violated within prevailing cultures are enumerated in declarations and treaties to bring them under protection. In the case of women, many human rights violations and discrimination have been not only culturally permissible, but often encouraged or demanded by cultural norms. That is why CEDAW makes specific references to culture, as well as traditions and customs embodied in cultures, and emphasizes the need to change discriminatory cultural norms, values and practices.

- It stresses that "a change in the *traditional* role of men, as well as the role of women, in society and in the family is needed to achieve full equality between men and women" (Preamble);
- States Parties . . . agree . . . "to take all appropriate measures, including legislation, to modify or abolish existing laws, regulations, *customs and practices* which constitute discrimination against women" (Article 2(f));
- States Parties shall take in all fields, in particular in the political, social, economic and *cultural fields,* all appropriate measures, including legislation, to ensure the full development and advancement of women, for the purpose of guaranteeing them the exercise and enjoyment of human rights and fundamental freedoms on a basis of equality with men (Article 3);
- States Parties shall take all appropriate measures: (a) To modify the *social and cultural patterns of conduct* of men and women, with a view to achieving the elimination of *prejudices and customary and all other practices* which are based on the idea of the inferiority or the superiority of either of the sexes or on *stereotyped roles* for men and women (Article 5). (Emphasis mine.)

Tensions between Competing Rights

The universality of human rights, and especially women's rights, is often challenged by cultural relativists. Relativist arguments, especially when combined with charges of cultural imperialism, pose a major dilemma for the international human rights community. How can peoples' cultures and their right to self-determination be recognized when several aspects of those very cultures systematically violate a number of human rights? This question is particularly important for women's rights. Since all contemporary societies are patriarchies, promoting women's rights inevitably conflicts with patriarchal "cultural" values, religious norms and other hierarchical structures in all countries. Thus, following a strict rule of cultural relativism would keep women's rights "alien" virtually to all societies, and the

emancipatory aspects of the international human rights regime would be undermined and jeopardized in the name of cultural preservation.

With regard to culture and religion, we need to ask the following questions: Who speaks on behalf of the people and religion? Who *defines* the meaning of culture or *interprets* the sources of religion and develops doctrines? Cultures, of course, are neither monolithic nor static, but within each culture there are people who would benefit from making it monolithic and keeping it static. In other words, cultures are based on power structures, and by setting norms and assigning values they also perpetuate those structures. Culturally (and officially) promoted values privilege some members of society and disadvantage others, and the privileged ones would tend to use their power to sustain those values that would justify and preserve their privileged positions. Thus, without any democratization of the interpretation and decision-making processes, cultural relativism and preservation of culture end up serving only as shields protecting the privileged people.

By the same token, all religious texts and oral traditions are received in a cultural context and filtered through and fused with the prevailing cultural norms. Always open to interpretation, their messages can be subverted and mitigated by the existing power structures. Thus, religions can embody contradictory norms, which are selectively used and reinterpreted both by the privileged and those who challenge their understanding of religion and its requirements. It is needless to note that in patriarchal systems, it is the voice of the privileged men that dictates cultural and religious norms, even though women may help in their transmission and perpetuation. Egalitarian and emancipatory interpretations by women and their advocates tend to be disregarded or suppressed.

What Needs to Be Done?

Human rights are closely linked to culture, and the expansion, full recognition and protection of rights would demand the transformation of cultural norms and their material foundations. Thus, compliance with international human rights would require a shift in cultural mores, as well as political commitment. The advocacy of human rights has to involve: (1) analyzing cultural norms in terms of their conformity with human rights principles; (2) acknowledging the diversity of the interpretation of cultures and religious sources; and (3) demanding that States parties to conventions be specific about their reservations, indicating when and how they will remove their reservations.

Universalists usually attempt to advance their arguments against relativist claims by pointing out that several rights embodied in the Universal Declaration and other human rights instruments have existed and have been respected in the cultural and religious traditions of most societies. Although such assertions can be empirically supported, as already noted, the traditional cultural norms and practices also include numerous discriminatory stipulations. Thus, both aspects of cultures (egalitarian-emancipatory and discriminatory-oppressive) should be acknowledged, and all cultures analysed as to where and how they observe the principle of universality. Since human rights are about human dignity, the principle of universality means establishing the dignity of all and calls for equal treatment. Cultures therefore should be examined to identify their contradictions with regard to the principle of equality. Once revealed, the "egalitarian" aspects of cultures can be highlighted and linked to international human rights in terms of principles.[12]

Critical assessment of cultures and egalitarian interpretation of cultural sources already exist, but these alternative voices tend to be repressed at home and ignored in international debates. Nations and other members of the international human rights community have to break away from the habits of tolerating cultural discrimination in the name of respect for differences, attributing violations solely to the culture, equating culture with religion and treating cultures as monolithic and static. While there has been considerable attention on interfaith and intercommunal conflicts and domination, e.g., rights of religious and ethnic minorities, their has been no effort to address *the intra-communal differences and hegemonies.* Acknowledging the diversity within a culture and religious community by States parties and in international forums would provide support to the alternative voices and help democratize the interpretation process.

The relativist arguments and reservations placed on treaties can be countered by pointing out that international human rights norms demand such a change of customs and traditions, and what is presented as religious requirement is open to interpretation. It should be demanded of States parties that make such claims, not only to fully explain and specify their reservations, but also to stipulate a programme that would lead to their removal. The expert committee that oversees the implementation of CEDAW has already taken some action on these lines. For example, it has issued several recommendations to press States parties that placed "blanket reservations", declaring they would implement CEDAW as long as its provisions do not contradict the Islamic law *Shari'a,* to clarify their points of reservation.[13] The Committee also problematized the issue of interpretation: " . . . at its 1987 meeting, the CEDAW Committee adopted a decision requesting that the United Nations and the specialized agencies promote or undertake studies on the status of women under Islamic laws and customs, and in particular on the status and equality of women in the family, on issues such as marriage, divorce, custody and property rights and their participation in public life of the society, taking into consideration the principle of El Ijtihad (interpretation) in Islam."[14]

Not surprisingly, the States parties affected by the decision denounced it as a threat to their religious freedoms and rejected the Committee's recommendation, but the Committee has been persistent in pressing this issue. In 1994, it amended the guidelines for the preparation of reports to provide additional and specific guidelines for States parties that have entered substantial culture- and religion-based reservations. Jane Connors provides a summary:[15] "Such States should report specifically with regard to their reservations, why they consider them to be necessary, their precise effect on national law and policy, and whether they have entered similar reservations to other human rights treaties which guarantee similar rights. Such States are also required to indicate plans they might have to limit the effect of the reservations or withdraw them and, where possible, specify a timetable for withdrawing them. The Committee made particular reference to . . . [some States], indicating that the Committee considers such reservations to be incompatible with the object and purpose of the Convention and requiring a special effort from such countries who are directed to report on the effect and interpretation of their reservations."

In its persistent effort, the Committee should also encourage shadow reports, which not only include the assessments of what has not been done by the reporting State towards implementing the Convention, but which also present alternative interpretations of the culture and religious sources. Inviting such reports would equip the Committee with the information needed to effectively question States parties' justification for their reservations and allow them to recognize the diversity within their society. It would also support women and women's rights advocates by validating their *right to interpret* their cultural and religious sources.

Notes

1. Here, "civilization" is employed as a sociological term in reference to societies that achieve high levels of economic productivity, which lead to specialization of labour, social stratification and institutionalization. A curious case is the Iroquois nations. The extent of power that the Iroquois matrons had over public affairs has led many impressed observers to classify these nations as "matriarchy". Although the Iroquois matrons enjoyed some authority, they could not be chiefs or serve on the Council of Elders—the highest ruling body of the six-nation Iroquois Confederacy. Women mainly maintained a veto power and exercised an indirect influence due to their control of food and other supplies. No matriarchal society—as exact opposites of patriarchy—has been recorded in history. Although some pre-civilized societies have demonstrated more egalitarian gender relations, even in those societies the power balance has been usually tilted in favour of men. See, Rayna R. Reiter, ed., *Toward an Anthropology of Women* (New York: Monthly Review Press, 1975).

2. For current statistical information on the gender gap in many areas, see *Human Development Report 2007/2008.* (New York: Oxford University Press, 2007) tables 28–33.

3. Majid Fakhry, *Averroes: His Life, Work,* (Oxford: Oneworld Publications, 2001).

4. St. Thomas Aquinas found women to be valuable (thus created in the first production) only for their reproductive role (in procreation). See, St. Thomas Aquinas, *Summa Theologicae,* Question XCII, art. 1, "Whether Woman Should Have Been Made in the First Production of Things", available at www.newadvent.org/summa/109201.htm.

5. John Stuart Mill and Harriet Taylor Mill, *Essays on Sex Equality.* Edited with and an introductory essay by Alice S. Rossi (Chicago: University of Chicago Press, 1970).

6. Mary Ann Glendon. *A World Made New* (New York: Random House, 2001), 68.

7. Glendon, (2001): 111–112 and 162.

8. Hilary Charlesworth, "Human Rights as Men's Rights", *Women's Rights Human Rights: International Feminist*

Perspectives. Edited by Julie Peters and Andrea Wolper (New York: Routledge, 1995): 103–113.

9. Article 28 allows the ratification of the Convention with reservations, as long as they are compatible "with the object and purpose" of the Convention. Thus, States may enter reservations or "interpretive declarations" when they sign or ratify the Convention. Although "declarations" are not referred to in the text, they tend to employ a language similar to the one used in reservations and play the same role in limiting State obligations. Thus, for the purposes of this essay, declarations are treated the same as reservations.

10. Henry J. Steiner and Philip Alston, *International Human Rights in Context: Law, Politics, Morals.* Second Edition (Oxford: Oxford University Press, 2000): 180.

11. Belinda Clark, "The Vienna Convention Reservations Regime and the Convention on the Discrimination against Women." *American Journal of International Law,* 85:2 (April 1991): 281–321, 318.

12. Such a study of *The Qur'an,* the sacred text and highest authority in Islam, shows that Muslim women are granted equality with men at the spiritual level, but denied equality at the social level, and argues for the elevation of the spiritual equality recognized in the sacred text to become the standard that would be used in the reformulation of social roles. See, Zehra Arat, "Women's Rights in Islam: Revisiting Qur'anic Rights", *Human Rights: New Perspectives, New Realities.*

Edited by Peter Schwab and Adamanta Pollis, eds., (Boulder: Lynne Rienner Publishers, 2000): 69–94.

13. Michele Brandt and Jeffrey A. Kaplan, "The Tension between Women's Rights and Religious Rights: Reservations to CEDAW by Egypt, Bangladesh and Tunisia", *The Journal of Law and Religion* 12:1 (1995–96): 105–142; Connors, 1997; Clark, 1991.

14. UN Doc E/1987/SR 11.

15. Jane Connors. "The Women's Convention in the Muslim World", *Human Rights as General Norms and a State's Right to Opt Out: Reservations and Objections to Human Rights Convention.* Edited by J.P. Gardner (London: British Institute of International and Comparative Law, 1997): 85–103, 99–100.

Critical Thinking

1. How do discriminatory stipulations within religious texts impede the evolution of women's rights?

ZEHRA F. KABASAKAL ARAT is Juanita and Joseph Leff Professor of Political Science at Purchase College of the State University of New York and is Chair of the Human Rights Research Committee of the International Political Science Association. She is the author of *Human Rights Worldwide.* Some of the arguments presented here appeared in her earlier publications.

The End of Men

Earlier this year, women became the majority of the workforce for the first time in U.S. history. Most managers are now women too. And for every two men who get a college degree this year, three women will do the same. For years, women's progress has been cast as a struggle for equality. But what if equality isn't the end point? What if modern, postindustrial society is simply better suited to women? A report on the unprecedented role reversal now under way—and its vast cultural consequences.

HANNA ROSIN

In the 1970s the biologist Ronald Ericsson came up with a way to separate sperm carrying the male-producing Y chromosome from those carrying the X. He sent the two kinds of sperm swimming down a glass tube through ever-thicker albumin barriers. The sperm with the X chromosome had a larger head and a longer tail, and so, he figured, they would get bogged down in the viscous liquid. The sperm with the Y chromosome were leaner and faster and could swim down to the bottom of the tube more efficiently. Ericsson had grown up on a ranch in South Dakota, where he'd developed an Old West, cowboy swagger. The process, he said, was like "cutting out cattle at the gate." The cattle left flailing behind the gate were of course the X's, which seemed to please him. He would sometimes demonstrate the process using cartilage from a bull's penis as a pointer.

In the late 1970s, Ericsson leased the method to clinics around the U.S., calling it the first scientifically proven method for choosing the sex of a child. Instead of a lab coat, he wore cowboy boots and a cowboy hat, and doled out his version of cowboy poetry. (*People* magazine once suggested a TV mini-series based on his life called *Cowboy in the Lab.*) The right prescription for life, he would say, was "breakfast at five-thirty, on the saddle by six, no room for Mr. Limp Wrist." In 1979, he loaned out his ranch as the backdrop for the iconic "Marlboro Country" ads because he believed in the campaign's central image—"a guy riding on his horse along the river, no bureaucrats, no lawyers," he recalled when I spoke to him this spring. "He's the boss." (The photographers took some 6,500 pictures, a pictorial record of the frontier that Ericsson still takes great pride in.)

Feminists of the era did not take kindly to Ericsson and his Marlboro Man veneer. To them, the lab cowboy and his sperminator portended a dystopia of mass-produced boys. "You have to be concerned about the future of all women," Roberta Steinbacher, a nun-turned-social-psychologist, said in a 1984 *People* profile of Ericsson. "There's no question that there exists a universal preference for sons." Steinbacher went on to complain about women becoming locked in as "second-class citizens" while men continued to dominate positions of control and influence. "I think women have to ask themselves, 'Where does this stop?'" she said. "A lot of us wouldn't be here right now if these practices had been in effect years ago."

Ericsson, now 74, laughed when I read him these quotes from his old antagonist. Seldom has it been so easy to prove a dire prediction wrong. In the '90s, when Ericsson looked into the numbers for the two dozen or so clinics that use his process, he discovered, to his surprise, that couples were requesting more girls than boys, a gap that has persisted, even though Ericsson advertises the method as more effective for producing boys. In some clinics, Ericsson has said, the ratio is now as high as 2 to 1. Polling data on American sex preference is sparse, and does not show a clear preference for girls. But the picture from the doctor's office unambiguously does. A newer method for sperm selection, called MicroSort, is currently completing Food and Drug Administration clinical trials. The girl requests for that method run at about 75 percent.

Even more unsettling for Ericsson, it has become clear that in choosing the sex of the next generation, *he* is no longer the boss. "It's the women who are driving all the decisions," he says—a change the MicroSort spokespeople I met with also mentioned. At first, Ericsson says, women who called his clinics would apologize and shyly explain that they already had two boys. "Now they just call and [say] outright, 'I want a girl.' These mothers look at their lives and think their daughters will have a bright future their mother and grandmother didn't have, brighter than their sons, even, so why wouldn't you choose a girl?"

Why wouldn't you choose a girl? That such a statement should be so casually uttered by an old cowboy like Ericsson—or by anyone, for that matter—is monumental. For nearly as long as civilization has existed, patriarchy—enforced through the rights of the firstborn son—has been the organizing principle, with few exceptions. Men in ancient Greece tied off their left testicle in an effort to produce male heirs; women have killed themselves (or been killed) for failing to bear sons. In her iconic 1949 book, *The Second Sex,* the French feminist Simone de Beauvoir suggested that women so detested their own "feminine condition" that they regarded their newborn daughters with irritation and disgust. Now the centuries-old preference for sons is eroding—or even reversing. "Women of our generation want daughters precisely because we like who we are," breezes one woman in *Cookie* magazine. Even Ericsson, the stubborn old goat, can sigh and mark the passing of an era. "Did male dominance exist? Of course it existed. But it seems to be gone now. And the era of the firstborn son is totally gone."

Ericsson's extended family is as good an illustration of the rapidly shifting landscape as any other. His 26-year-old granddaughter—"tall, slender, brighter than hell, with a take-no-prisoners personality"—is a biochemist and works on genetic sequencing. His niece studied civil engineering at the University of Southern California. His grandsons, he says, are bright and handsome, but in school "their eyes glaze over. I have to tell 'em: 'Just don't screw up and crash your pickup truck and get some girl pregnant and ruin your life.'" Recently Ericsson joked with the old boys at his elementary-school reunion that he was going to have a sex-change operation. "Women live longer than men. They do better in this economy. More of 'em graduate from college. They go into space and do everything men do, and sometimes they do it a whole lot better. I mean, hell, get out of the way—these females are going to leave us males in the dust."

Man has been the dominant sex since, well, the dawn of mankind. But for the first time in human history, that is changing—and with shocking speed. Cultural and economic changes always reinforce each other. And the global economy is evolving in a way that is eroding the historical preference for male children, worldwide. Over several centuries, South Korea, for instance, constructed one of the most rigid patriarchal societies in the world. Many wives who failed to produce male heirs were abused and treated as domestic servants; some families prayed to spirits to kill off girl children. Then, in the 1970s and '80s, the government embraced an industrial revolution and encouraged women to enter the labor force. Women moved to the city and went to college. They advanced rapidly, from industrial jobs to clerical jobs to professional work. The traditional order began to crumble soon after. In 1990, the country's laws were revised so that women could keep custody of their children after a divorce and inherit property. In 2005, the court ruled that women could register children under their own names. As recently as 1985, about half of all women in a national survey said they "must have a son." That percentage fell slowly until 1991 and then plummeted to just over 15 percent by 2003. Male preference in South Korea "is over," says Monica Das Gupta, a demographer and Asia expert at the World Bank. "It happened so fast. It's hard to believe it, but it is." The same shift is now beginning in other rapidly industrializing countries such as India and China.

Up to a point, the reasons behind this shift are obvious. As thinking and communicating have come to eclipse physical strength and stamina as the keys to economic success, those societies that take advantage of the talents of all their adults, not just half of them, have pulled away from the rest. And because geopolitics and global culture are, ultimately, Darwinian, other societies either follow suit or end up marginalized. In 2006, the Organization for Economic Cooperation and Development devised the Gender, Institutions and Development Database, which measures the economic and political power of women in 162 countries. With few exceptions, the greater the power of women, the greater the country's economic success. Aid agencies have started to recognize this relationship and have pushed to institute political quotas in about 100 countries, essentially forcing women into power in an effort to improve those countries' fortunes. In some war-torn states, women are stepping in as a sort of maternal rescue team. Liberia's president, Ellen Johnson Sirleaf, portrayed her country as a sick child in need of her care during her campaign five years ago. Postgenocide Rwanda elected to heal itself by becoming the first country with a majority of women in parliament.

In feminist circles, these social, political, and economic changes are always cast as a slow, arduous form of catch-up in a continuing struggle for female equality. But in the U.S., the world's most advanced economy, something much more remarkable seems to be happening. American parents are beginning to choose to have girls over boys. As they imagine the pride of watching a child grow and develop and succeed as an adult, it is more often a girl that they see in their mind's eye.

What if the modern, postindustrial economy is simply more congenial to women than to men? For a long time, evolutionary psychologists have claimed that we are all imprinted with adaptive imperatives from a distant past: men are faster and stronger and hardwired to fight for scarce resources, and that shows up now as a drive to win on Wall Street; women are programmed to find good providers and to care for their offspring, and that is manifested in more-nurturing and more-flexible behavior, ordaining them to domesticity. This kind of thinking frames our sense of the natural order. But what if men and women were fulfilling not biological imperatives but social roles, based on what was more efficient throughout a long era of human history? What if that era has now come to an end? More to the point, what if the economics of the new era are better suited to women?

Once you open your eyes to this possibility, the evidence is all around you. It can be found, most immediately, in the wreckage of the Great Recession, in which three-quarters of the 8 million jobs lost were lost by men. The worst-hit industries were overwhelmingly male and deeply identified with macho: construction, manufacturing, high finance. Some of these jobs will come back, but the overall pattern of dislocation is neither temporary nor random. The recession merely revealed—and accelerated—a profound economic shift that has been going on for at least 30 years, and in some respects even longer.

Earlier this year, for the first time in American history, the balance of the workforce tipped toward women, who now hold a majority of the nation's jobs. The working class, which has long defined our notions of masculinity, is slowly turning into a matriarchy, with men increasingly absent from the home and women making all the decisions. Women dominate today's colleges and professional schools—for every two men who will receive a B.A. this year, three women will do the same. Of the 15 job categories projected to grow the most in the next decade in the U.S., all but two are occupied primarily by women. Indeed, the U.S. economy is in some ways becoming a kind of traveling sisterhood: upper-class women leave home and enter the workforce, creating domestic jobs for other women to fill.

The postindustrial economy is indifferent to men's size and strength. The attributes that are most valuable today—social intelligence, open communication, the ability to sit still and focus—are, at a minimum, not predominantly male. In fact, the opposite may be true. Women in poor parts of India are learning English faster than men to meet the demands of new global call centers. Women own more than 40 percent of private businesses in China, where a red Ferrari is the new status symbol for female entrepreneurs. Last year, Iceland elected Prime Minister Johanna Sigurdardottir, the world's first openly lesbian head of state, who campaigned explicitly against the male elite she claimed had destroyed the nation's banking system, and who vowed to end the "age of testosterone."

Yes, the U.S. still has a wage gap, one that can be convincingly explained—at least in part—by discrimination. Yes, women still do most of the child care. And yes, the upper reaches of society are still dominated by men. But given the power of the forces pushing at the economy, this setup feels like the last gasp of a dying age rather than the permanent establishment. Dozens of college women I interviewed for this story assumed that they very well might be the ones working while their husbands stayed at home, either looking for work or minding the children. Guys, one senior remarked to me, "are the new ball and chain." It may be happening slowly and unevenly, but it's unmistakably happening: in the long view, the modern economy is becoming a place where women hold the cards.

> **Dozens of college women I interviewed assumed that they very well might be the ones working while their husbands stayed at home. Guys, one senior remarked to me, "are the new ball and chain."**

In his final book, *The Bachelors' Ball,* published in 2007, the sociologist Pierre Bourdieu describes the changing gender dynamics of Béarn, the region in southwestern France where he grew up. The eldest sons once held the privileges of patrimonial loyalty and filial inheritance in Béarn. But over the decades, changing economic forces turned those privileges into curses. Although the land no longer produced the impressive income it once had, the men felt obligated to tend it. Meanwhile, modern women shunned farm life, lured away by jobs and adventure in the city. They occasionally returned for the traditional balls, but the men who awaited them had lost their prestige and become unmarriageable. This is the image that keeps recurring to me, one that Bourdieu describes in his book: at the bachelors' ball, the men, self-conscious about their

diminished status, stand stiffly, their hands by their sides, as the women twirl away.

The role reversal that's under way between American men and women shows up most obviously and painfully in the working class. In recent years, male support groups have sprung up throughout the Rust Belt and in other places where the postindustrial economy has turned traditional family roles upside down. Some groups help men cope with unemployment, and others help them reconnect with their alienated families. Mustafaa El-Scari, a teacher and social worker, leads some of these groups in Kansas City. El-Scari has studied the sociology of men and boys set adrift, and he considers it his special gift to get them to open up and reflect on their new condition. The day I visited one of his classes, earlier this year, he was facing a particularly resistant crowd.

None of the 30 or so men sitting in a classroom at a downtown Kansas City school have come for voluntary adult enrichment. Having failed to pay their child support, they were given the choice by a judge to go to jail or attend a weekly class on fathering, which to them seemed the better deal. This week's lesson, from a workbook called *Quenching the Father Thirst*, was supposed to involve writing a letter to a hypothetical estranged 14-year-old daughter named Crystal, whose father left her when she was a baby. But El-Scari has his own idea about how to get through to this barely awake, skeptical crew, and letters to Crystal have nothing to do with it.

Like them, he explains, he grew up watching Bill Cosby living behind his metaphorical "white picket fence"—one man, one woman, and a bunch of happy kids. "Well, that check bounced a long time ago," he says. "Let's see," he continues, reading from a worksheet. What are the four kinds of paternal authority? Moral, emotional, social, and physical. "But you ain't none of those in that house. All you are is a paycheck, and now you ain't even that. And if you try to exercise your authority, she'll call 911. How does that make you feel? You're supposed to be the authority, and she says, 'Get out of the house, bitch.' She's calling you 'bitch'!"

The men are black and white, their ages ranging from about 20 to 40. A couple look like they might have spent a night or two on the streets, but the rest look like they work, or used to. Now they have put down their sodas, and El-Scari has their attention, so he gets a little more philosophical. "Who's doing what?" he asks them. "What is our role? Everyone's telling us we're supposed to be the head of a nuclear family, so you feel like you got robbed. It's toxic, and poisonous, and it's setting us up for failure." He writes on the board: $85,000. "This is her salary." Then: $12,000. "This is your salary. Who's the damn man? Who's the man now?" A murmur rises. "That's right. She's the man."

Judging by the men I spoke with afterward, El-Scari seemed to have pegged his audience perfectly. Darren Henderson was making $33 an hour laying sheet metal, until the real-estate crisis hit and he lost his job. Then he lost his duplex—"there's my little piece of the American dream"—then his car. And then he fell behind on his child-support payments. "They make it like I'm just sitting around," he said, "but I'm not." As proof of his efforts, he took out a new commercial driver's permit and a bartending license, and then threw them down on the ground like jokers, for all the use they'd been. His daughter's mother had a $50,000-a-year job and was getting her master's degree in social work. He'd just signed up for food stamps, which is just about the only social-welfare program a man can easily access. Recently she'd seen him waiting at the bus stop. "Looked me in the eye," he recalled, "and just drove on by."

The men in that room, almost without exception, were casualties of the end of the manufacturing era. Most of them had continued to work with their hands even as demand for manual labor was declining. Since 2000, manufacturing has lost almost 6 million jobs, more than a third of its total workforce, and has taken in few young workers. The housing bubble masked this new reality for a while, creating work in construction and related industries. Many of the men I spoke with had worked as electricians or builders; one had been a successful real-estate agent. Now those jobs are gone too. Henderson spent his days shuttling between unemployment offices and job interviews, wondering what his daughter might be doing at any given moment. In 1950, roughly one in 20 men of prime working age, like Henderson, was not working; today that ratio is about one in five, the highest ever recorded.

Men dominate just two of the 15 job categories projected to grow the most over the next decade: janitor and computer engineer. Women have everything else—nursing, home health assistance, child care, food preparation. Many of the new jobs, says Heather Boushey of the Center for American Progress, "replace the things that women used to do in the home for free." None is especially high-paying. But the steady accumulation of these jobs adds up to an economy that, for the working class, has become more amenable to women than to men.

The list of growing jobs is heavy on nurturing professions, in which women, ironically, seem to benefit from old stereotypes and habits. Theoretically, there is no reason men should not be qualified. But they have proved remarkably unable to adapt. Over the course of the past century, feminism has pushed women to do things once considered against their nature—first enter the workforce as singles, then continue to work while married, then work even with small children at home. Many professions that started out as the province of men are now filled mostly with women—secretary and teacher come to mind. Yet I'm not aware of any that have gone the opposite way. Nursing schools have tried hard to recruit men in the past few years, with minimal success. Teaching schools, eager to recruit male role models, are having a similarly hard time. The range of acceptable masculine roles has changed comparatively little, and has perhaps even narrowed as men have shied away from some careers women have entered. As Jessica Grose wrote in *Slate,* men seem "fixed in cultural aspic." And with each passing day, they lag further behind.

As we recover from the Great Recession, some traditionally male jobs will return—men are almost always harder-hit than women in economic downturns because construction and manufacturing are more cyclical than service industries—but that won't change the long-term trend. When we look back on this period, argues Jamie Ladge, a business professor at Northeastern University, we will see it as a "turning point for women in the workforce."

When we look back at this period, we will see it as a "turning point for women in the workforce."

The economic and cultural power shift from men to women would be hugely significant even if it never extended beyond working-class America. But women are also starting to dominate middle management, and a surprising number of professional careers as well. According to the Bureau of Labor Statistics, women now hold 51.4 percent of managerial and professional jobs—up from 26.1 percent in 1980. They make up 54 percent of all accountants and hold about half of all banking and insurance jobs. About a third of America's physicians are now women, as are 45 percent of associates in law firms—and both those percentages are rising fast. A white-collar economy values raw intellectual horsepower, which men and women have in equal amounts. It also requires communication skills and social intelligence, areas in which women, according to many studies, have a slight edge. Perhaps most important—for better or worse—it increasingly requires formal education credentials, which women are more prone to acquire, particularly early in adulthood. Just about the only professions in which women still make up a relatively small minority of newly minted workers are engineering and those calling on a hard-science background, and even in those areas, women have made strong gains since the 1970s.

Office work has been steadily adapting to women—and in turn being reshaped by them—for 30 years or more. Joel Garreau picks up on this phenomenon in his 1991 book, *Edge City,* which explores the rise of suburbs that are home to giant swaths of office space along with the usual houses and malls. Companies began moving out of the city in search not only of lower rent but also of the "best educated, most conscientious, most stable workers." They found their brightest prospects among "underemployed females living in middle-class communities on the fringe of the old urban areas." As Garreau chronicles the rise of suburban office parks, he places special emphasis on 1978, the peak year for women entering the workforce. When brawn was off the list of job requirements, women often measured up better than men. They were smart, dutiful, and, as long as employers could make the jobs more convenient for them, more reliable. The 1999 movie *Office Space* was maybe the first to capture how alien and dispiriting the office park can be for men. Disgusted by their jobs and their boss, Peter and his two friends embezzle money and start sleeping through their alarm clocks. At the movie's end, a male co-worker burns down the office park, and Peter abandons desk work for a job in construction.

Near the top of the jobs pyramid, of course, the upward march of women stalls. Prominent female CEOs, past and present, are so rare that they count as minor celebrities, and most of us can tick off their names just from occasionally reading the business pages: Meg Whitman at eBay, Carly Fiorina at Hewlett-Packard, Anne Mulcahy and Ursula Burns at Xerox, Indra Nooyi at PepsiCo; the accomplishment is considered so extraordinary that Whitman and Fiorina are using it as the basis for political campaigns. Only 3 percent of *Fortune* 500 CEOs are women, and the number has never risen much above that.

But even the way this issue is now framed reveals that men's hold on power in elite circles may be loosening. In business circles, the lack of women at the top is described as a "brain drain" and a crisis of "talent retention." And while female CEOs may be rare in America's largest companies, they are highly prized: last year, they outearned their male counterparts by 43 percent, on average, and received bigger raises.

Even around the delicate question of working mothers, the terms of the conversation are shifting. Last year, in a story about breastfeeding, I complained about how the early years of child rearing keep women out of power positions. But the term *mommy track* is slowly morphing into the gender-neutral *flex time,* reflecting changes in the workforce. For recent college graduates of both sexes, flexible arrangements are at the top of the list of workplace demands, according to a study published last year in the *Harvard Business Review.* And companies eager to attract and retain talented workers and managers are responding. The consulting firm Deloitte, for instance, started what's now considered the model program, called Mass Career Customization, which allows employees to adjust their hours depending on their life stage. The program, Deloitte's Web site explains, solves "a complex issue—one that can no longer be classified as a woman's issue."

"Women are knocking on the door of leadership at the very moment when their talents are especially well matched with the requirements of the day," writes David Gergen in the introduction to *Enlightened Power: How Women Are Transforming the Practice of Leadership.* What are these talents? Once it was thought that leaders should be aggressive and competitive, and that men are naturally more of both. But psychological research has complicated this picture. In lab studies that simulate negotiations, men and women are just about equally assertive and competitive, with slight variations. Men tend to assert themselves in a controlling manner, while women tend to take into account the rights of others, but both styles are equally effective, write the psychologists Alice Eagly and Linda Carli, in their 2007 book, *Through the Labyrinth.*

Over the years, researchers have sometimes exaggerated these differences and described the particular talents of women in crude gender stereotypes: women as more empathetic, as better consensus-seekers and better lateral thinkers; women as bringing a superior moral sensibility to bear on a cutthroat business world. In the '90s, this field of feminist business theory seemed to be forcing the point. But after the latest financial crisis, these ideas have more resonance. Researchers have started looking into the relationship between testosterone and excessive risk, and wondering if groups of men, in some basic hormonal way, spur each other to make reckless decisions. The picture emerging is a mirror image of the traditional gender map: men and markets on the side of the irrational and over-emotional, and women on the side of the cool and levelheaded.

We don't yet know with certainty whether testosterone strongly influences business decision-making. But the perception of the ideal business leader is starting to shift. The old model of command and control, with one leader holding all the decision-making power, is considered hidebound. The new model is sometimes called "post-heroic," or "transformational" in the words of the historian and leadership expert James Mac-Gregor Burns. The aim is to behave like a good coach, and channel your charisma to motivate others to be hardworking and creative. The model is not explicitly defined as feminist, but it echoes literature about male-female differences. A program at Columbia Business School, for example, teaches sensitive leadership and social intelligence, including better reading of facial expressions and body language. "We never explicitly say, 'Develop your feminine side,' but it's clear that's what we're advocating," says Jamie Ladge.

A 2008 study attempted to quantify the effect of this more-feminine management style. Researchers at Columbia Business School and the University of Maryland analyzed data on the top 1,500 U.S. companies from 1992 to 2006 to determine the relationship between firm performance and female participation in senior management. Firms that had women in top positions performed better, and this was especially true if the firm pursued what the researchers called an "innovation intensive strategy," in which, they argued, "creativity and collaboration may be especially important"—an apt description of the future economy.

It could be that women boost corporate performance, or it could be that better-performing firms have the luxury of recruiting and keeping high-potential women. But the association is clear: innovative, successful firms are the ones that promote women. The same Columbia-Maryland study ranked America's industries by the proportion of firms that employed female executives, and the bottom of the list reads like the ghosts of the economy past: shipbuilding, real estate, coal, steelworks, machinery.

If you really want to see where the world is headed, of course, looking at the current workforce can get you only so far. To see the future—of the workforce, the economy, and the culture—you need to spend some time at America's colleges and professional schools, where a quiet revolution is under way. More than ever, college is the gateway to economic success, a necessary precondition for moving into the upper-middle class—and increasingly even the middle class. It's this broad, striving middle class that defines our society. And demographically, we can see with absolute clarity that in the coming decades the middle class will be dominated by women.

We've all heard about the collegiate gender gap. But the implications of that gap have not yet been fully digested. Women now earn 60 percent of master's degrees, about half of all law and medical degrees, and 42 percent of all M.B.A.s. Most important, women earn almost 60 percent of all bachelor's degrees—the minimum requirement, in most cases, for an affluent life. In a stark reversal since the 1970s, men are now more likely than women to hold only a high-school diploma. "One would think that if men were acting in a rational way, they would be getting the education they need to get along out there," says Tom Mortenson, a senior scholar at the Pell Institute for the Study of Opportunity in Higher Education. "But they are just failing to adapt."

This spring, I visited a few schools around Kansas City to get a feel for the gender dynamics of higher education. I started at the downtown campus of Metropolitan Community College. Metropolitan is the kind of place where people go to learn practical job skills and keep current with the changing economy, and as in most community colleges these days, men were conspicuously absent. One afternoon, in the basement cafeteria of a nearly windowless brick building, several women were trying to keep their eyes on their biology textbook and ignore the text messages from their babysitters. Another crew was outside the ladies' room, braiding each other's hair. One woman, still in her medical-assistant scrubs, looked like she was about to fall asleep in the elevator between the first and fourth floors.

When Bernard Franklin took over as campus president in 2005, he looked around and told his staff early on that their new priority was to "recruit more boys." He set up mentoring programs and men-only study groups and student associations. He made a special effort to bond with male students, who liked to call him "Suit." "It upset some of my feminists," he recalls. Yet, a few years later, the tidal wave of women continues to wash through the school—they now make up about 70 percent of its students. They come to train to be nurses and teachers—African American women, usually a few years older than traditional college students, and lately, working-class white women from the suburbs seeking a cheap way to earn a credential. As for the men? Well, little has changed. "I recall one guy who was really smart," one of the school's counselors told me. "But he was reading at a sixth-grade level and felt embarrassed in front of the women. He had to hide his books from his friends, who would tease him when he studied. Then came the excuses. 'It's spring, gotta play ball.' 'It's winter, too cold.' He didn't make it."

It makes some economic sense that women attend community colleges—and in fact, all colleges—in greater numbers than men. Women ages 25 to 34 with only a high-school diploma currently have a median income of $25,474, while men in the same position earn $32,469. But it makes sense only up to a point. The well-paid lifetime union job has been disappearing for at least 30 years. Kansas City, for example, has shifted from steel manufacturing to pharmaceuticals and information technologies. "The economy isn't as friendly to men as it once was," says Jacqueline King, of the American Council on Education. "You would think men and women would go to these colleges at the same rate." But they don't.

In 2005, King's group conducted a survey of lower-income adults in college. Men, it turned out, had a harder time committing to school, even when they desperately needed to retool. They tended to start out behind academically, and many felt intimidated by the schoolwork. They reported feeling isolated and were much worse at seeking out fellow students, study groups, or counselors to help them adjust. Mothers going back to school described themselves as good role models for their children. Fathers worried that they were abrogating their responsibilities as breadwinner.

The student gender gap started to feel like a crisis to some people in higher-education circles in the mid-2000s, when it began showing up not just in community and liberal-arts colleges but in the flagship public universities—the UCs and the SUNYS and the UNCs. Like many of those schools, the University of Missouri at Kansas City, a full research university with more than 13,000 students, is now tipping toward 60 percent women, a level many admissions officers worry could permanently shift the atmosphere and reputation of a school. In February, I visited with Ashley Burress, UMKC's student-body president. (The other three student-government officers this school year were also women.) Burress, a cute, short, African American 24-year-old grad student who is getting a doctor-of-pharmacy degree, had many of the same complaints I heard from other young women. Guys high-five each other when they get a C, while girls beat themselves up over a B-minus. Guys play video games in each other's rooms, while girls crowd the study hall. Girls get their degrees with no drama, while guys seem always in danger of drifting away. "In 2012, I will be Dr. Burress," she said. "Will I have to deal with guys who don't even have a bachelor's degree? I would like to date, but I'm putting myself in a really small pool."

UMKC is a working- and middle-class school—the kind of place where traditional sex roles might not be anathema. Yet as I talked to students this spring, I realized how much the basic expectations for men and women had shifted. Many of the women's mothers had established their careers later in life, sometimes after a divorce, and they had urged their daughters to get to their own careers more quickly. They would be a campus of Tracy Flicks, except that they seemed neither especially brittle nor secretly falling apart.

Victoria, Michelle, and Erin are sorority sisters. Victoria's mom is a part-time bartender at a hotel. Victoria is a biology major and wants to be a surgeon; soon she'll apply to a bunch of medical schools. She doesn't want kids for a while, because she knows she'll "be at the hospital, like, 100 hours a week," and when she does have kids, well, she'll "be the hotshot surgeon, and he"—a nameless he—"will be at home playing with the kiddies."

Michelle, a self-described "perfectionist," also has her life mapped out. She's a psychology major and wants to be a family therapist. After college, she will apply to grad school and look for internships. She is well aware of the career-counseling resources on campus. And her fiancé?

Michelle: He's changed majors, like, 16 times. Last week he wanted to be a dentist. This week it's environmental science.

Erin: Did he switch again this week? When you guys have kids, he'll definitely stay home. Seriously, what does he want to do?

Michelle: It depends on the day of the week. Remember last year? It was bio. It really is a joke. But it's not. It's funny, but it's not.

Among traditional college students from the highest-income families, the gender gap pretty much disappears. But the story is not so simple. Wealthier students tend to go to elite private schools, and elite private schools live by their own rules. Quietly, they've been opening up a new frontier in affirmative action, with boys playing the role of the underprivileged applicants needing an extra boost. In 2003, a study by the economists Sandy Baum and Eban Goodstein found that among selective liberal-arts schools, being male raises the chance of college acceptance by 6.5 to 9 percentage points. Now the U.S. Commission on Civil Rights has voted to investigate what some academics have described as the "open secret" that private schools "are discriminating in admissions in order to maintain what they regard as an appropriate gender balance."

Jennifer Delahunty, the dean of admissions and financial aid at Kenyon College, in Ohio, let this secret out in a 2006 *New York Times* op-ed. Gender balance, she wrote back then, is the elephant in the room. And today, she told me, the problem hasn't gone away. A typical female applicant, she said, manages the process herself—lines up the interviews, sets up a campus visit, requests a visit with faculty members. But the college has seen more than one male applicant "sit back on the couch, sometimes with their eyes closed, while their mom tells them where to go and what to do. Sometimes we say, 'What a nice essay his mom wrote,'" she said, in that funny-but-not vein.

To avoid crossing the dreaded 60 percent threshold, admissions officers have created a language to explain away the boys' deficits: "Brain hasn't kicked in yet." "Slow to cook." "Hasn't quite peaked." "Holistic picture." At times Delahunty has become so worried about "overeducated females" and "undereducated males" that she jokes she is getting conspiratorial. She once called her sister, a pediatrician, to vet her latest theory: "Maybe these boys are genetically like canaries in a coal mine, absorbing so many toxins and bad things in the environment that their DNA is shifting. Maybe they're like those frogs—they're more vulnerable or something, so they've gotten deformed."

Clearly, some percentage of boys are just temperamentally unsuited to college, at least at age 18 or 20, but without it, they have a harder time finding their place these days. "Forty years ago, 30 years ago, if you were one of the fairly constant fraction of boys who wasn't ready to learn in high school, there were ways for you to enter the mainstream economy," says Henry Farber, an economist at Princeton. "When you woke up, there were jobs. There were good industrial jobs, so you could have a good industrial, blue-collar career. Now those jobs are gone."

Since the 1980s, as women have flooded colleges, male enrollment has grown far more slowly. And the disparities start before college. Throughout the '90s, various authors and researchers agonized over why boys seemed to be failing at every level of education, from elementary school on up, and identified various culprits: a misguided feminism that treated normal boys as incipient harassers (Christina Hoff Sommers); different brain chemistry (Michael Gurian); a demanding, verbally focused curriculum that ignored boys' interests (Richard Whitmire). But again, it's not all that clear that boys have

become more dysfunctional—or have changed in any way. What's clear is that schools, like the economy, now value the self-control, focus, and verbal aptitude that seem to come more easily to young girls.

Researchers have suggested any number of solutions. A movement is growing for more all-boys schools and classes, and for respecting the individual learning styles of boys. Some people think that boys should be able to walk around in class, or take more time on tests, or have tests and books that cater to their interests. In their desperation to reach out to boys, some colleges have formed football teams and started engineering programs. Most of these special accommodations sound very much like the kind of affirmative action proposed for women over the years—which in itself is an alarming flip.

Whether boys have changed or not, we are well past the time to start trying some experiments. It is fabulous to see girls and young women poised for success in the coming years. But allowing generations of boys to grow up feeling rootless and obsolete is not a recipe for a peaceful future. Men have few natural support groups and little access to social welfare; the men's-rights groups that do exist in the U.S. are taking on an angry, antiwoman edge. Marriages fall apart or never happen at all, and children are raised with no fathers. Far from being celebrated, women's rising power is perceived as a threat.

What would a society in which women are on top look like? We already have an inkling. This is the first time that the cohort of Americans ages 30 to 44 has more college-educated women than college-educated men, and the effects are upsetting the traditional Cleaver-family dynamics. In 1970, women contributed 2 to 6 percent of the family income. Now the typical working wife brings home 42.2 percent, and four in 10 mothers—many of them single mothers—are the primary breadwinners in their families. The whole question of whether mothers should work is moot, argues Heather Boushey of the Center for American Progress, "because they just do. This idealized family—he works, she stays home—hardly exists anymore."

The terms of marriage have changed radically since 1970. Typically, women's income has been the main factor in determining whether a family moves up the class ladder or stays stagnant. And increasing numbers of women—unable to find men with a similar income and education—are forgoing marriage altogether. In 1970, 84 percent of women ages 30 to 44 were married; now 60 percent are. In 2007, among American women without a high-school diploma, 43 percent were married. And yet, for all the hand-wringing over the lonely spinster, the real loser in society—the only one to have made just slight financial gains since the 1970s—is the single man, whether poor or rich, college-educated or not. Hens rejoice; it's the bachelor party that's over.

The sociologist Kathryn Edin spent five years talking with low-income mothers in the inner suburbs of Philadelphia. Many of these neighborhoods, she found, had turned into matriarchies, with women making all the decisions and dictating what the men should and should not do. "I think something feminists have missed," Edin told me, "is how much power women have" when they're not bound by marriage. The women, she explained, "make every important decision"—whether to have a baby, how to raise it, where to live. "It's definitely 'my way or the highway,' " she said. "Thirty years ago, cultural norms were such that the fathers might have said, 'Great, catch me if you can.' Now they are desperate to father, but they are pessimistic about whether they can meet her expectations." The women don't want them as husbands, and they have no steady income to provide. So what do they have?

"Nothing," Edin says. "They have nothing. The men were just annihilated in the recession of the '90s, and things never got better. Now it's just awful."

The situation today is not, as Edin likes to say, a "feminist nirvana." The phenomenon of children being born to unmarried parents "has spread to barrios and trailer parks and rural areas and small towns," Edin says, and it is creeping up the class ladder. After staying steady for a while, the portion of American children born to unmarried parents jumped to 40 percent in the past few years. Many of their mothers are struggling financially; the most successful are working and going to school and hustling to feed the children, and then falling asleep in the elevator of the community college.

Still, they are in charge. "The family changes over the past four decades have been bad for men and bad for kids, but it's not clear they are bad for women," says W. Bradford Wilcox, the head of the University of Virginia's National Marriage Project.

Over the years, researchers have proposed different theories to explain the erosion of marriage in the lower classes: the rise of welfare, or the disappearance of work and thus of marriageable men. But Edin thinks the most compelling theory is that marriage has disappeared because women are setting the terms—and setting them too high for the men around them to reach. "I want that white-picket-fence dream," one woman told Edin, and the men she knew just didn't measure up, so she had become her own one-woman mother/father/nurturer/provider. The whole country's future could look much as the present does for many lower-class African Americans: the mothers pull themselves up, but the men don't follow. First-generation college-educated white women may join their black counterparts in a new kind of middle class, where marriage is increasingly rare.

AS The traditional order has been upended, signs of the profound disruption have popped up in odd places. Japan is in a national panic over the rise of the "herbivores," the cohort of young men who are rejecting the hard-drinking salaryman life of their fathers and are instead gardening, organizing dessert parties, acting cartoonishly feminine, and declining to have sex. The generational young-women counterparts are known in Japan as the "carnivores," or sometimes the "hunters."

American pop culture keeps producing endless variations on the omega male, who ranks even below the beta in the wolf pack. This often-unemployed, romantically challenged loser can show up as a perpetual adolescent (in Judd Apatow's *Knocked Up* or *The 40-Year-Old Virgin*), or a charmless misanthrope (in Noah Baumbach's *Greenberg*), or a happy couch potato (in a Bud Light commercial). He can be sweet, bitter, nostalgic, or cynical, but he cannot figure out how to be a man. "We call each other 'man,' " says Ben Stiller's character in *Greenberg*, "but it's a joke. It's like imitating other people." The American male novelist, meanwhile, has lost his mojo and entirely given up on sex as a way for his characters to assert macho dominance, Katie Roiphe explains in her essay "The Naked and the Conflicted." Instead, she writes, "the current sexual style is more childlike; innocence is more fashionable than virility, the cuddle preferable to sex."

At the same time, a new kind of alpha female has appeared, stirring up anxiety and, occasionally, fear. The cougar trope started out as a joke about desperate older women. Now it's gone mainstream, even in Hollywood, home to the 50-something producer with a starlet on his arm. Susan Sarandon and Demi Moore have boy toys, and Aaron Johnson, the 19-year-old star of *Kick-Ass,* is a proud boy toy for a woman 24 years his senior. The *New York Times* columnist Gail Collins recently wrote that the cougar phenomenon is beginning to look like it's not about desperate women at all but about "desperate young American men who are latching on to an older woman who's a good earner." *Up in the Air,* a movie set against the backdrop of recession-era layoffs, hammers home its point about the shattered ego of the American man. A character played by George Clooney is called too old to be attractive by his younger female colleague and is later rejected by an older woman whom he falls in love with after she sleeps with him—and who turns out to be married. George Clooney! If the sexiest man alive can get twice rejected (and sexually played) in a movie, what hope is there for anyone else? The message to American men is summarized by the title of a recent offering from the romantic-comedy mill: *She's Out of My League.*

In fact, the more women dominate, the more they behave, fittingly, like the dominant sex. Rates of violence committed by middle-aged women have skyrocketed since the 1980s, and no one knows why. High-profile female killers have been showing up regularly in the news: Amy Bishop, the homicidal Alabama professor; Jihad Jane and her sidekick, Jihad Jamie; the latest generation of Black Widows, responsible for suicide bombings in Russia. In Roman Polanski's *The Ghost Writer,* the traditional political wife is rewritten as a cold-blooded killer at the heart of an evil conspiracy. In her recent video *Telephone,* Lady Gaga, with her infallible radar for the cultural edge, rewrites *Thelma and Louise* as a story not about elusive female empowerment but about sheer, ruthless power. Instead of killing themselves, she and her girlfriend (played by Beyoncé) kill a bad boyfriend and random others in a homicidal spree and then escape in their yellow pickup truck, Gaga bragging, "We did it, Honey B."

The Marlboro Man, meanwhile, master of wild beast and wild country, seems too farfetched and preposterous even for advertising. His modern equivalents are the stunted men in the Dodge Charger ad that ran during this year's Super Bowl in February. Of all the days in the year, one might think, Super

Bowl Sunday should be the one most dedicated to the cinematic celebration of macho. The men in Super Bowl ads should be throwing balls and racing motorcycles and doing whatever it is men imagine they could do all day if only women were not around to restrain them.

Instead, four men stare into the camera, unsmiling, not moving except for tiny blinks and sways. They look like they've been tranquilized, like they can barely hold themselves up against the breeze. Their lips do not move, but a voice-over explains their predicament—how they've been beaten silent by the demands of tedious employers and enviro-fascists and women. Especially women. "I will put the seat down, I will separate the recycling, I will carry your lip balm." This last one—lip balm—is expressed with the mildest spit of emotion, the only hint of the suppressed rage against the dominatrix. Then the commercial abruptly cuts to the fantasy, a Dodge Charger vrooming toward the camera punctuated by bold all caps: MAN'S LAST STAND. But the motto is unconvincing. After that display of muteness and passivity, you can only imagine a woman—one with shiny lips—steering the beast.

Critical Thinking

1. What are some of the factors leading to the erosion of the patriarchal principles in society?

HANNA ROSIN is an *Atlantic* contributing editor and the co-editor of *DoubleX*.

Gender Bender

New research suggests genes and prenatal hormones could have more sway in gender identity than previously thought.

SADIE F. DINGFELDER

"It's a boy!" announces the doctor to the exhausted mother, a determination the physician makes instantly. And most of the time, the observed sex of an infant does match the genetic sex—with two X chromosomes producing a girl, and an X plus a Y resulting in a boy.

But in the rare cases where they do not, when prenatal development goes awry and genetic boys are born looking more like girls or vice versa, physicians and parents generally assign the newborn a sex. Most often the child becomes female, because female genitals are easier to construct, says William G. Reiner, MD, a child psychiatrist and urologist at the University of Oklahoma health services center.

The prevailing theory behind this long-standing practice, says Reiner, has been that a person reared as a girl will eventually embrace that category. Now, however, new research by Reiner suggests that perhaps such assumptions ought not to be made. A study by Reiner and John Gearhart, MD, of Johns Hopkins University, finds that biology—in particular the hormonal influences on developing infants' brains—programs children to eventually identify as either male or female, almost regardless of social influences, at least in the case of the children he's studied.

"It's fair to say that some people in the world of psychology have held that [gender] is socially derived, learned behavior," says Reiner. "But our findings do not support that theory."

However, other researchers, such as Sheri Berenbaum, PhD, a psychologist at Pennsylvania State University, maintain that determinates of gender identity may be more complex than that.

"Genetic and hormonal factors are just two of the many influences on gender identity and gender-typical behavior—social influences are certainly very important as well," she says. "And all of these factors seem to interact throughout a child's development."

New Findings

This isn't the view of Reiner and Gearhart though, who point to the findings of their study, published in the Jan. 22 issue of the *New England Journal of Medicine* (Vol. 350, No. 4). The study found that some infants whose brains were exposed to male hormones in utero later identified as male even though they were raised as female and underwent early-childhood operations. Reiner says that indicates that prenatal sex differentiation can at least sometimes trump social influences.

The study followed 16 genetic males with a rare disorder called cloacal exstrophy. Children with this disorder are born without penises, or with very small ones, despite having normal male hormones, normal testes and XY-chromosome pairs. Fourteen of these children underwent early sex-reassignment surgery and were raised as girls by their parents, who were instructed not to inform them of their early medical histories.

The researchers assessed the gender identities and behaviors of these children when they were anywhere from 5 to 16 years old using a battery of measures including the Bates Child Behavior and Attitude Questionnaire and the Child Game Participation Questionnaire. Researchers also asked the children whether they categorized themselves as boys or girls.

> **"Obviously, gender is both a biological and social phenomenon," says Ruble. "Researchers now really need to look carefully at the unfolding of biologically driven processes in interaction with social influences during the first three years of life and beyond."**
>
> Diane Ruble
> New York University

Of the 14 children raised as females, three spontaneously declared they were male at the initial assessment. At the most recent follow-up, six identified as males, while three reported unclear gender identity or would not talk with researchers. The two participants raised as males from birth continued to identify as male throughout the study.

All of the participants exhibited male-typical behavior, such as rough-and-tumble play and having many male friends.

"If you are looking at the genetic and hormonal male, [sexual identity may be] not plastic at all," says Reiner. "And it appears to be primarily influenced by biology."

Some researchers, such as Kenneth J. Zucker, PhD, a psychologist and the head of the child and adolescent gender identity clinic at Toronto's Centre for Addiction and Mental Health, applaud Reiner's study for renewing interest in the biological determinants of gender and calling into question the notion of some that gender identity is mainly socially constructed and determined by socialization.

That's not to say, however, that socialization isn't still a major or important factor, Zucker emphasizes. "The debate is still up in the air because there are other centers who have studied kids with the same diagnosis, and the rate of changeover from female to male is nowhere near what Reiner is reporting," he explains. "It must be something about their social experience that is accounting for this difference."

Contradictory Evidence

Backing Zucker's belief that socialization still plays a major role—and biology is only part of the story—is research by Sheri Berenbaum, PhD, a psychologist at Pennsylvania State University, and J. Michael Bailey, PhD, a psychologist at Northwestern University.

In a study published in the March 2003 issue of the *Journal of Clinical Endocrinology & Metabolism* (Vol. 88, No. 3), they investigated the gender identity of genetic girls born with congenital adrenal hyperplasia (CAH). Girls with this disorder do not produce enough of the hormone cortisol, which causes their adrenal glands to produce an excess of male sex hormones. As a result, they develop in a hormonal environment that's between that of typical boys and typical girls. These girls tend to have ambiguous genitals, and like the infants with cloacal exstrophy, they generally undergo surgery to remake their bodies in the mold of typical females.

The researchers recruited 43 girls with CAH ages 3 to 18 and assessed their gender-typical behaviors and gender identities using a nine-item questionnaire. One question, for example, asks the child if she would take the opportunity to be magically turned into a boy.

In comparison with a control group of normal girls, those with CAH answered questions in a more masculine way. However, when compared with hormonally normal girls who identified as tomboys, they scored closer to typical girls. And few, says Berenbaum, actually identified as male.

"They behave in some ways more like boys, but they self-identify as girls," she explains.

According to Berenbaum, this shows that prenatal hormones, while important determinates of gendered behavior, aren't the only ones.

"Social influences are also pretty important," she says. "I think the interesting question is how biological predisposition affects our socialization experiences."

Diane Ruble, PhD, a New York University psychologist specializing in early childhood gender identity, agrees.

"In Sheri's work, the hormonal exposure has some masculinizing influence on their play behavior," says Ruble. "That may feed into difficulties that children have even if the hormonal exposure prenatally did not actually directly affect their identities as girls or boys."

For example, she says, a girl who discovers that her behavior is slightly masculine may feel more like a typical boy than girl. She may then primarily socialize with boys, leading to even more male-typical behavior.

"Obviously, gender is both a biological and social phenomenon," says Ruble. "Researchers now really need to look carefully at the unfolding of biologically driven processes in interaction with social influences during the first three years of life and beyond."

Further Readings

Berenbaum, S.A., & Bailey, J.M. (2003). Effects on gender identity of prenatal androgens and genital appearance: Evidence from girls with congenital adrenal hyperplasia. *Journal of Clinical Endocrinology and Metabolism, 88,* 1102–1106.

Martin, C.L., & Ruble, D.N. (in press). Children's search for gender cues: Cognitive perspectives on gender development. *Current Directions in Psychological Science.*

Martin, C.L., Ruble, D.N., & Szkrybalo, J. (2002). Cognitive theories of early gender development. *Psychological Bulletin, 128*(6), 903–933.

Reiner, W.G., & Gearhart, J.P. (2004). Discordant sexual identity in some genetic males with cloacal exstrophy assigned to female sex at birth. *The New England Journal of Medicine, 350*(4), 333–341.

Zucker, K. J. (1999). Intersexuality and gender identity differentiation. *Annual Review of Sex Research, 10,* 1–69.

Critical Thinking

1. What is the role of genes and hormones as prenatal influences on gendered behaviors?

2. According to scientists, what is the current understanding of the interplay between nature and nurture in boys' and girls' behaviors?

3. Can one's social identity (gender identity) be heavily influenced by biological processes? Explain your answer.

Goodbye to Girlhood

As pop culture targets ever younger girls, psychologists worry about a premature focus on sex and appearance.

STACY WEINER

Ten-year-old girls can slide their low-cut jeans over "eye-candy" panties. French maid costumes, garter belt included, are available in preteen sizes. Barbie now comes in a "bling-bling" style, replete with halter top and go-go boots. And it's not unusual for girls under 12 to sing, "Don't cha wish your girlfriend was hot like me?"

American girls, say experts, are increasingly being fed a cultural catnip of products and images that promote looking and acting sexy.

"Throughout U.S. culture, and particularly in mainstream media, women and girls are depicted in a sexualizing manner," declares the American Psychological Association's Task Force on the Sexualization of Girls, in a report issued Monday. The report authors, who reviewed dozens of studies, say such images are found in virtually every medium, from TV shows to magazines and from music videos to the Internet.

While little research to date has documented the effect of sexualized images specifically on *young* girls, the APA authors argue it is reasonable to infer harm similar to that shown for those 18 and older; for them, sexualization has been linked to "three of the most common mental health problems of girls and women: eating disorders, low self-esteem and depression."

Said report contributor and psychologist Sharon Lamb: "I don't think because we don't have the research yet on the younger girls that we can ignore that [sexualization is] of harm to them. Common sense would say that, and part of the reason we wrote the report is so we can get funding to prove that."

Boys, too, face sexualization, the authors acknowledge. Pubescent-looking males have posed provocatively in Calvin Klein ads, for example, and boys with impossibly sculpted abs hawk teen fashion lines. But the authors say they focused on girls because females are objectified more often. According to a 1997 study in the journal *Sexual Abuse,* 85 percent of ads that sexualized children depicted girls.

Even influences that are less explicitly erotic often tell girls who they are equals how they look and that beauty commands power and attention, contends Lamb, co-author of *Packaging Girlhood: Rescuing Our Daughters from Marketers' Schemes* (St. Martin's, 2006). One indicator that these influences are reaching girls earlier, she and others say: The average age for adoring the impossibly proportioned Barbie has slid from preteen to preschool.

When do little girls start wanting to look good for others? "A few years ago, it was 6 or 7," says Deborah Roffman, a Baltimore-based sex educator. "I think it begins by 4 now."

While some might argue that today's belly-baring tops are no more risque than hip huggers were in the '70s, Roffman disagrees. "Kids have always emulated adult things," she says. "But [years ago] it was, 'That's who I'm supposed to be as an adult.' It's very different today. The message to children is, 'You're already like an adult. It's okay for you to be interested in sex. It's okay for you to dress and act sexy, right now.' That's an entirely different frame of reference."

It's not just kids' exposure to sexuality that worries some experts; it's the kind of sexuality they're seeing. "The issue is that the way marketers and media present sexuality is in a very narrow way," says Lamb. "Being a sexual person isn't about being a pole dancer," she chides. "This is a sort of sex education girls are getting, and it's a misleading one."

Clothes Encounters

Liz Guay says she has trouble finding clothes she considers appropriate for her daughter Tanya, age 8. Often, they're too body-hugging. Or too low-cut. Or too short. Or too spangly.

Then there are the shoes: Guay says last time she visited six stores before finding a practical, basic flat. And don't get her started on earrings.

"Tanya would love to wear dangly earrings. She sees them on TV, she sees other girls at school wearing them, she sees them in the stores all the time. . . . I just say, 'You're too young.'"

"It's not so much a feminist thing," explains Guay, a Gaithersburg medical transcriptionist. "It's more that I want her to be comfortable with who she is and to make decisions based on what's right for her, not what everybody else is doing. I want her to develop the strength that when she gets to a point where kids are offering her alcohol or drugs, that she's got enough self-esteem to say, 'I don't want that.'"

Some stats back up Guay's sense of fashion's shrinking modesty. For example, in 2003, tweens—that highly coveted marketing segment ranging from 7 to 12—spent $1.6 million on thong underwear, *Time* magazine reported. But even more-innocent-seeming togs, toys and activities—like tiny "Beauty Queen" T-shirts, Hello Kitty press-on nails or preteen make-overs at Club Libby Lu—can be problematic, claim psychologists. The reason: They may lure young girls into an unhealthy focus on appearance.

Studies suggest that female college students distracted by concerns about their appearance score less well on tests than do others. Plus, some experts say, "looking good" is almost culturally inseparable for girls from looking sexy: Once a girl's bought in, she's hopped onto a consumer conveyor belt in which marketers move females from pastel tiaras to hot-pink push-up bras.

Where did this girly-girl consumerism start? Diane Levin, an education professor at Wheelock College in Boston who is writing an upcoming book, *So Sexy So Soon,* traces much of it to the deregulation of children's television in the mid-1980s. With the rules loosened, kids' shows suddenly could feature characters who moonlighted as products (think Power Rangers, Care Bears, My Little Pony). "There became a real awareness," says Levin, "of how to use gender and appearance and, increasingly, sex to market to children."

Kids are more vulnerable than adults to such messages, she argues.

The APA report echoes Levin's concern. It points to a 2004 study of adolescent girls in rural Fiji, linking their budding concerns about body image and weight control to the introduction of television there.

In the United States, TV's influence is incontestable. According to the Kaiser Family Foundation, for example, nearly half of American kids age 4 to 6 have a TV in their bedroom. Nearly a quarter of teens say televised sexual content affects their own behavior.

And that content is growing: In 2005, 77 percent of prime-time shows on the major broadcast networks included sexual material, according to Kaiser, up from 67 percent in 1998. In a separate Kaiser study of shows popular with teenage girls, women and girls were twice as likely as men and boys to have their appearance discussed. They also were three times more likely to appear in sleepwear or underwear than their male counterparts.

Preteen Preening

It can be tough for a parent to stanch the flood of media influences.

Ellen Goldstein calls her daughter Maya, a Rockville fifth-grader, a teen-mag maniac. "She has a year's worth" of Girls' *Life* magazine, says Goldstein. "When her friends come over, they pore over this magazine." What's Maya reading? There's "Get Gorgeous Skin by Tonight," "Crush Confidential: Seal the Deal with the Guy You Dig," and one of her mom's least faves: "Get a Fierce Body Fast."

"Why do you want to tell a kid to get a fierce body fast when they're 10? They're just developing," complains Goldstein. She

also bemoans the magazines' photos, which Maya has plastered on her ceiling.

"These are very glamorous-looking teenagers. They're wearing lots of makeup. They all have very glossy lips," she says. "They're generally wearing very slinky outfits. . . . I don't think those are the best role models," Goldstein says. "When so much emphasis is placed on the outside, it minimizes the importance of the person inside."

So why not just say no?

"She loves fashion," explains Goldstein. "I don't want to take away her joy from these magazines. It enhances her creative spirit. [Fashion] comes naturally to her. I want her to feel good about that. We just have to find a balance."

Experts say her concern is warranted. Pre-adolescents' propensity to try on different identities can make them particularly susceptible to media messages, notes the APA report. And for some girls, thinking about how one's body stacks up can be a real downer.

In a 2002 study, for example, seventh-grade girls who viewed idealized magazine images of women reported a drop in body satisfaction and a rise in depression.

Such results are disturbing, say observers, since eating disorders seem to strike younger today. A decade ago, new eating disorder patients at Children's National Medical Center tended to be around age 15, says Adelaide Robb, director of inpatient psychiatry. Today kids come in as young as 5 or 6.

Mirror Images

Not everyone is convinced of the uglier side of beauty messages.

Eight-year-old Maya Williams owns four bracelets, eight necklaces, about 20 pairs of earrings and six rings, an assortment of which she sprinkles on every day. "Sometimes, she'll stand in front of the mirror and ask, 'Are these pretty, Mommy?'"

Her mom, Gaithersburg tutor Leah Haworth, is fine with Maya's budding interest in beauty. In fact, when Maya "wasn't sure" about getting her ears pierced, says Haworth, "I talked her into it by showing her all the pretty earrings she could wear."

What about all these sexualization allegations? "I don't equate looking good with attracting the opposite sex," Haworth says. Besides, "Maya knows her worth is based on her personality. She knows we love her for who she is."

"Looking good just shows that you care about yourself, care about how you present yourself to the world. People are judged by their appearance. People get better service and are treated better when they look better. That's just the way it is," she says. "I think discouraging children from paying attention to their appearance does them a disservice."

Magazine editor Karen Bokram also adheres to the beauty school of thought. "Research has shown that having skin issues at [her readers'] age is traumatic for girls' self-esteem," says Bokram, founder of *Girls' Life.* "Do we think girls need to be gorgeous in order to be worthy? No. Do we think girls' feeling good about how they look has positive effects in other areas of their lives, meaning that they make positive choices academically, socially and in romantic relationships? Absolutely."

Some skeptics of the sexualization notion also argue that kids today are hardier and savvier than critics think. Isaac Larian, whose company makes the large-eyed, pouty-lipped Bratz dolls, says, "Kids are very smart and know right from wrong." What's more, his testing indicates that girls want Bratz "because they are fun, beautiful and inspirational," he wrote in an e-mail. "Not once have we ever heard one of our consumers call Bratz 'sexy.'" Some adults "have a twisted sense of what they see in the product," Larian says.

"It is the parents' responsibility to educate their children," he adds. "If you don't like something, don't buy it."

But Genevieve McGahey, 16, isn't buying marketers' messages. The National Cathedral School junior recalls that her first real focus on appearance began in fourth grade. That's when classmates taught her: To be cool, you needed ribbons. To be cool, you needed lip gloss.

Starting around sixth grade, though, "it took on a more sinister character," she says. "People would start wearing really short skirts and lower tops and putting on more makeup. There's a strong pressure to grow up at this point."

"It's a little scary being a young girl," McGahey says. "The image of sexuality has been a lot more trumpeted in this era. . . . If you're not interested in [sexuality] in middle school, it seems a little intimidating." And unrealistic body ideals pile on extra pressure, McGahey says. At a time when their bodies and their body images are still developing, "girls are not really seeing people [in the media] who are beautiful but aren't stick-thin," she notes. "That really has an effect."

Today, though, McGahey feels good about her body and her style.

For this, she credits her mom, who is "very secure with herself and with being smart and being a woman." She also points to a wellness course at school that made her conscious of how women were depicted. "Seeing a culture of degrading women really influenced me to look at things in a new way and to think how we as high school girls react to that," she says.

"A lot of girls still hold onto that media ideal. I think I've gotten past it. As I've gotten more comfortable with myself and my body, I'm happy not to be trashy," McGahey says. "But most girls are still not completely or even semi-comfortable with themselves physically. You definitely still feel the pressure of those images."

Critical Thinking

1. How are women and girls depicted in the media today?
2. How do media representations of women and girls affect their general health and well-being?

STACY WEINER writes frequently for *Health* about families and relationships. Comments: health@washpost.com.

(Rethinking) Gender

A growing number of Americans are taking their private struggles with their identities into the public realm. How those who believe they were born with the wrong bodies are forcing us to re-examine what it means to be male and female.

DEBRA ROSENBERG

Growing up in Corinth, Miss., J. T. Hayes had a legacy to attend to. His dad was a well-known race-car driver and Hayes spent much of his childhood tinkering in the family's greasy garage, learning how to design and build cars. By the age of 10, he had started racing in his own right. Eventually Hayes won more than 500 regional and national championships in go-kart, midget and sprint racing, even making it to the NASCAR Winston Cup in the early '90s. But behind the trophies and the swagger of the racing circuit, Hayes was harboring a painful secret: he had always believed he was a woman. He had feminine features and a slight frame—at 5 feet 6 and 118 pounds he was downright dainty—and had always felt, psychologically, like a girl. Only his anatomy got in the way. Since childhood he'd wrestled with what to do about it. He'd slip on "girl clothes" he hid under the mattress and try his hand with makeup. But he knew he'd find little support in his conservative hometown.

In 1991, Hayes had a moment of truth. He was driving a sprint car on a dirt track in Little Rock when the car flipped end over end. "I was trapped upside down, engine throttle stuck, fuel running all over the racetrack and me," Hayes recalls. "The accident didn't scare me, but the thought that I hadn't lived life to its full potential just ran chill bumps up and down my body." That night he vowed to complete the transition to womanhood. Hayes kept racing while he sought therapy and started hormone treatments, hiding his growing breasts under an Ace bandage and baggy T shirts.

Finally, in 1994, at 30, Hayes raced on a Saturday night in Memphis, then drove to Colorado the next day for sex-reassignment surgery, selling his prized race car to pay the tab. Hayes chose the name Terri O'Connell and began a new life as a woman who figured her racing days were over. But she had no idea what else to do. Eventually, O'Connell got a job at the mall selling women's handbags for $8 an hour. O'Connell still hopes to race again, but she knows the odds are long: "Transgendered and professional motor sports just don't go together."

To most of us, gender comes as naturally as breathing. We have no quarrel with the "M" or the "F" on our birth certificates. And, crash diets aside, we've made peace with how we want the world to see us—pants or skirt, boa or blazer, spiky heels or sneakers. But to those who consider themselves transgender, there's a disconnect between the sex they were assigned at birth and the way they see or express themselves. Though their numbers are relatively few—the most generous estimate from the National Center for Transgender Equality is between 750,000 and 3 million Americans (fewer than 1 percent)—many of them are taking their intimate struggles public for the first time. In April, *Los Aangeles Times* sportswriter Mike Penner announced in his column that when he returned from vacation, he would do so as a woman, Christine Daniels. Nine states plus Washington, D.C., have enacted antidiscrimination laws that protect transgender people—and an additional three states have legislation pending, according to the Human Rights Campaign. And this month the U.S. House of Representatives passed a hate-crimes prevention bill that included "gender identity." Today's transgender Americans go far beyond the old stereotypes (think "Rocky Horror Picture Show"). They are soccer moms, ministers, teachers, politicians, even young children. Their push for tolerance and acceptance is reshaping businesses, sports, schools and families. It's also raising new questions about just what makes us male or female.

Born female, he feels male. 'I challenge the idea that all men were born with male bodies.'

—Mykell Miller, age 20

What is gender anyway? It is certainly more than the physical details of what's between our legs. History and science suggest that gender is more subtle and more complicated than anatomy. (It's separate from sexual orientation, too, which determines which sex we're attracted to.) Gender helps us organize the world into two boxes, his and hers, and gives us a way of quickly sizing up every person we see on the street. "Gender is a way of making the world secure," says feminist scholar Judith Butler, a rhetoric professor at University of California, Berkeley. Though some scholars like Butler consider gender largely a social construct, others increasingly see it as a complex interplay of biology, genes, hormones and culture.

> ## She kept her job as a high-school teacher. 'Most people don't get this fortunate kind of ending.'
>
> —Karen Kopriva, age 49

Genesis set up the initial dichotomy: "Male and female he created them." And historically, the differences between men and women in this country were thought to be distinct. Men, fueled by testosterone, were the providers, the fighters, the strong and silent types who brought home dinner. Women, hopped up on estrogen (not to mention the mothering hormone oxytocin), were the nurturers, the communicators, the soft, emotional ones who got that dinner on the table. But as society changed, the stereotypes faded. Now even discussing gender differences can be fraught. (Just ask former Harvard president Larry Summers, who unleashed a wave of criticism when he suggested, in 2005, that women might have less natural aptitude for math and science.) Still, even the most diehard feminist would likely agree that, even apart from genitalia, we are not exactly alike. In many cases, our habits, our posture, and even cultural identifiers like the way we dress set us apart.

Now, as transgender people become more visible and challenge the old boundaries, they've given voice to another debate—whether gender comes in just two flavors. "The old categories that everybody's either biologically male or female, that there are two distinct categories and there's no overlap, that's beginning to break down," says Michael Kimmel, a sociology professor at SUNY-Stony Brook. "All of those old categories seem to be more fluid." Just the terminology can get confusing. "Transsexual" is an older term that usually refers to someone who wants to use hormones or surgery to change their sex. "Transvestites," now more politely called "cross-dressers," occasionally wear clothes of the opposite sex. "Transgender" is an umbrella term that includes anyone whose gender identity or expression differs from the sex of their birth—whether they have surgery or not.

Gender identity first becomes an issue in early childhood, as any parent who's watched a toddler lunge for a truck or a doll can tell you. That's also when some kids may become aware that their bodies and brains don't quite match up. Jona Rose, a 6-year-old kindergartner in northern California, seems like a girl in nearly every way—she wears dresses, loves pink and purple, and bestowed female names on all her stuffed animals.

But Jona, who was born Jonah, also has a penis. When she was 4, her mom, Pam, offered to buy Jona a dress, and she was so excited she nearly hyperventilated. She began wearing dresses every day to preschool and no one seemed to mind. It wasn't easy at first. "We wrung our hands about this every night," says her dad, Joel. But finally he and Pam decided to let their son live as a girl. They chose a private kindergarten where Jona wouldn't have to hide the fact that he was born a boy, but could comfortably dress like a girl and even use the girls' bathroom. "She has been pretty adamant from the get-go: 'I am a girl,'" says Joel.

Male or female, we all start life looking pretty much the same. Genes determine whether a particular human embryo will develop as male or female. But each individual embryo is equipped to be either one—each possesses the Mullerian ducts that become the female reproductive system as well as the Wolffian ducts that become the male one. Around eight weeks of development, through a complex genetic relay race, the X and the male's Y chromosomes kick into gear, directing the structures to become testes or ovaries. (In most cases, the unneeded extra structures simply break down.) The ovaries and the testes are soon pumping out estrogen and testosterone, bathing the developing fetus in hormones. Meanwhile, the brain begins to form, complete with receptors—wired differently in men and women—that will later determine how both estrogen and testosterone are used in the body.

After birth, the changes keep coming. In many species, male newborns experience a hormone surge that may "organize" sexual and behavioral traits, says Nirao Shah, a neuroscientist at UCSF. In rats, testosterone given in the first week of life can cause female babies to behave more like males once they reach adulthood. "These changes are thought to be irreversible," says Shah. Between 1 and 5 months, male human babies also experience a hormone surge. It's still unclear exactly what effect that surge has on the human brain, but it happens just when parents are oohing and aahing over their new arrivals.

Here's where culture comes in. Studies have shown that parents treat boys and girls very differently—breast-feeding boys longer but talking more to girls. That's going on while the baby's brain is engaged in a massive growth spurt. "The brain doubles in size in the first five years after birth, and the connectivity between the cells goes up hundreds of orders of magnitude," says Anne Fausto-Sterling, a biologist and feminist at Brown University who is currently investigating whether subtle differences in parental behavior could influence gender identity in very young children. "The brain is interacting with culture from day one."

So what's different in transgender people? Scientists don't know for certain. Though their hormone levels seem to be the same as non-trans levels, some scientists speculate that their brains react differently to the hormones, just as men's differ from women's. But that could take decades of further research to prove. One 1997 study tantalizingly suggested structural differences between male, female and transsexual brains, but it has yet to be successfully replicated. Some transgender people blame the environment, citing studies that show pollutants have disrupted reproduction in frogs and other animals. But those links are so far not proved in humans. For now, transgender issues are classified as "Gender Identity Disorder" in the psychiatric manual *DSM-IV.* That's controversial, too—gay-rights activists spent years campaigning to have homosexuality removed from the manual.

Gender fluidity hasn't always seemed shocking. Cross-dressing was common in ancient Greece and Rome, as well as among Native Americans and many other indigenous societies, according to Deborah Rudacille, author of *The Riddle of Gender.* Court records from the Jamestown settlement in 1629 describe the case of Thomas Hall, who claimed to be both a man and a woman. Of course, what's considered masculine or feminine has long been a moving target. Our Founding Fathers wouldn't be surprised to see men today with long hair or earrings, but they might be puzzled by women in pants.

Transgender opponents have often turned to the Bible for support. Deut. 22:5 says: "The woman shall not wear that which pertaineth unto a man, neither shall a man put on a woman's garment: for all that do so are abomination unto the Lord thy God." When word leaked in February that Steve Stanton, the Largo, Fla., city manager for 14 years, was planning to transition to life as a woman, the community erupted. At a public meeting over whether Stanton should be fired, one of many critics, Ron Sanders, pastor of the Lighthouse Baptist Church, insisted that Jesus would "want him terminated." (Stanton did lose his job and this week will appear as Susan Stanton on Capitol Hill to lobby for antidiscrimination laws.) Equating gender change with homosexuality, Sanders says that "it's an abomination, which means that it's utterly disgusting."

Not all people of faith would agree. Baptist minister John Nemecek, 56, was surfing the Web one weekend in 2003, when his wife was at a baby shower. Desperate for clues to his long-suppressed feelings of femininity, he stumbled across an article about gender-identity disorder on WebMD. The suggested remedy was sex-reassignment surgery—something Nemecek soon thought he had to do. Many families can be ripped apart by such drastic changes, but Nemecek's wife of 33 years stuck by him. His employer of 15 years, Spring Arbor University, a faith-based liberal-arts college in Michigan, did not. Nemecek says the school claimed that transgenderism violated its Christian principles, and when it renewed Nemecek's contract—by then she was taking hormones and using the name Julie—it barred her from dressing as a woman on campus or even wearing earrings. Her workload and pay were cut, too, she says. She filed a discrimination claim, which was later settled through mediation. (The university declined to comment on the case.) Nemecek says she has no trouble squaring her gender change and her faith. "Actively expressing the feminine in me has helped me grow closer to God," she says.

Others have had better luck transitioning. Karen Kopriva, now 49, kept her job teaching high school in Lake Forest, Ill., when she shaved her beard and made the switch from Ken. When Mark Stumpp, a vice president at Prudential Financial, returned to work as Margaret in 2002, she sent a memo to her colleagues (subject: Me) explaining the change. "We all joked about wearing panty hose and whether 'my condition' was contagious," she says. But "when the dust settled, everyone got back to work." Companies like IBM and Kodak now cover trans-related medical care. And 125 Fortune 500 companies now protect transgender employees from job discrimination, up from three in 2000. Discrimination may not be the worst worry for transgender people: they are also at high risk of violence and hate crimes.

Perhaps no field has wrestled more with the issue of gender than sports. There have long been accusations about male athletes' trying to pass as women, or women's taking testosterone to gain a competitive edge. In the 1960s, would-be female Olympians were required to undergo gender-screening tests. Essentially, that meant baring all before a panel of doctors who could verify that an athlete had girl parts. That method was soon scrapped in favor of a genetic test. But that quickly led to confusion over a handful of genetic disorders that give typical-looking women chromosomes other than the usual XX. Finally, the International Olympic Committee ditched mandatory lab-based screening, too. "We found there is no scientifically sound lab-based technique that can differentiate between man and woman," says Arne Ljungqvist, chair of the IOC's medical commission.

The IOC recently waded into controversy again: in 2004 it issued regulations allowing transsexual athletes to compete in the Olympics if they've had sex-reassignment surgery and have taken hormones for two years. After convening a panel of experts, the IOC decided that the surgery and hormones would compensate for any hormonal or muscular advantage a male-to-female transsexual would have. (Female-to-male athletes would be allowed to take testosterone, but only at levels that wouldn't give them a boost.) So far, Ljungqvist doesn't know of any transsexual athletes who've competed. Ironically, Renee Richards, who won a lawsuit in 1977 for the right to play tennis as a woman after her own sex-reassignment surgery, questions the fairness of the IOC rule. She thinks decisions should be made on a case-by-case basis.

'We all joked about wearing panty hose and whether my "condition" was contagious.'

—Margaret Stumpp, age 54

Richards and other pioneers reflect the huge cultural shift over a generation of gender change. Now 70, Richards rejects the term transgender along with all the fluidity it conveys. "God didn't put us on this earth to have gender diversity," she says. "I don't like the kids that are experimenting. I didn't want to be something in between. I didn't want to be trans anything. I wanted to be a man or a woman."

But more young people are embracing something we would traditionally consider in between. Because of the expense, invasiveness and mixed results (especially for women becoming men), only 1,000 to 2,000 Americans each year get sex-reassignment surgery—a number that's on the rise, says Mara Keisling of the National Center for Transgender Equality. Mykell Miller, a Northwestern University student born female who now considers himself male, hides his breasts under a special compression vest. Though he one day wants to take hormones and get a mastectomy, he can't yet afford it. But that doesn't affect his self-image. "I challenge the idea that all men were born with male bodies," he says. "I don't go out of my way to be the biggest, strongest guy."

Nowhere is the issue more pressing at the moment than a place that helped give rise to feminist movement a generation ago: Smith College in Northampton, Mass. Though Smith was one of the original Seven Sisters women's colleges, its students have now taken to calling it a "mostly women's college," in part because of a growing number of "transmen" who decide to become male after they've enrolled. In 2004, students voted to remove pronouns from the student government constitution as a gesture to transgender students who no longer identified with "she" or "her." (Smith is also one of 70 schools that have antidiscrimination policies protecting transgender students.) For now, anyone who is enrolled at Smith may graduate, but in order to be admitted in the first place, you must have been born a female. Tobias Davis, class of '03, entered Smith as a woman, but graduated as a "transman." When he first told friends over dinner, "I think I might be a boy," they were instantly behind him, saying "Great! Have you picked a name yet?" Davis passed as male for his junior year abroad in Italy even without taking hormones; he had a mastectomy last fall. Now 25, Davis works at Smith and writes plays about the transgender experience. (His work "The Naked I: Monologues From Beyond the Binary" is a trans take on "The Vagina Monologues.")

As kids at ever-younger ages grapple with issues of gender variance, doctors, psychologists and parents are weighing how to balance immediate desires and long-term ones. Like Jona Rose, many kids begin questioning gender as toddlers, identifying with the other gender's toys and clothes. Five times as many boys as girls say their gender doesn't match their biological sex, says Dr. Edgardo Menvielle, a psychiatrist who heads a gender-variance outreach program at Children's National Medical Center. (Perhaps that's because it's easier for girls to blend in as tomboys.) Many of these children eventually move on and accept their biological sex, says Menvielle, often when they're exposed to a disapproving larger world or when they're influenced by the hormone surges of puberty. Only about 15 percent continue to show signs of gender-identity problems into adult-

hood, says Ken Zucker, who heads the Gender Identity Service at the Centre for Addiction and Mental Health in Toronto.

In the past, doctors often advised parents to direct their kids into more gender-appropriate clothing and behavior. Zucker still tells parents of unhappy boys to try more-neutral activities— say chess club instead of football. But now the thinking is that kids should lead the way. If a child persists in wanting to be the other gender, doctors may prescribe hormone "blockers" to keep puberty at bay. (Blockers have no permanent effects.) But they're also increasingly willing to take more lasting steps: Isaak Brown (who started life as Liza) began taking male hormones at 16; at 17 he had a mastectomy.

For parents like Colleen Vincente, 44, following a child's lead seems only natural. Her second child, M. (Vincente asked to use an initial to protect the child's privacy), was born female. But as soon as she could talk, she insisted on wearing boy's clothes. Though M. had plenty of dolls, she gravitated toward "the boy things" and soon wanted to shave off all her hair. "We went along with that," says Vincente. "We figured it was a phase." One day, when she was 2½, M. overheard her parents talking about her using female pronouns. "He said, 'No—I'm a him. You need to call me him,'" Vincente recalls. "We were shocked." In his California preschool, M. continued to insist he was a boy and decided to change his name. Vincente and her husband, John, consulted a therapist, who confirmed their instincts to let M. guide them. Now 9, M. lives as a boy and most people have no idea he was born otherwise. "The most important thing is to realize this is who your child is," Vincente says. That's a big step for a family, but could be an even bigger one for the rest of the world.

Critical Thinking

1. What is the meaning of the term "transgendered"?
2. What is the process of transitioning from one sex to the other?
3. What impact have recent social shifts and changes had on people who are transgendered?

This story was written by **DEBRA ROSENBERG,** with reporting from Lorraine Ali, Mary Carmichael, Samantha Henig, Raina Kelley, Matthew Philips, Julie Scelfo, Kurt Soller, Karen Springen and Lynn Waddell.

Progress and Politics in the Intersex Rights Movement

Feminist Theory in Action

ALICE D. DREGER, AND APRIL M. HERNDON

Since 1990, when Suzanne Kessler published her ground-breaking feminist analysis of the understanding of gender among clinicians treating children with intersex, many academic feminists have produced important scholarly work on intersex and intersex rights.[1] A notable few have also lent their energies to actively working for intersex rights in medical and mainstream social arenas. Although the intersex rights movement and feminist scholarship on intersex have both progressed considerably since 1990, there remains theoretical and political irresolution on certain key issues, most notably those involving intersex identity and the constitution of gender.

This essay considers the progress made in intersex rights since 1990 and delineates important points of contention within feminist intersex scholarship and intersex politics. We argue that in the last fifteen years much progress has been made in improving medical and social attitudes toward people with intersex, but that significant work remains to be done to ensure that children born with sex anomalies will be treated in a way that privileges their long-term well-being over societal norms. We also argue that, while feminist scholars have been critically important in developing the theoretical underpinnings of the intersex rights movement and sometimes in carrying out the day-to-day political work of that movement, there have been intellectual and political problems with some feminists' approaches to intersex.

The authors have a foot in both camps considered here—academic feminism and intersex rights work. We are academic feminists who also worked as paid directors at the Intersex Society of North America (ISNA), the longest-running, best-funded, and historically most influential intersex advocacy group. Alice Dreger began working with ISNA in 1996 and volunteered as chair of its board of directors from 1998 to 2003 and 2004 to 2005, and as chair of the fund-raising committee in the 2003–4 interim. In 2005 she left the board to take on the paid, part-time position of director of medical education, which she completed in late 2005. April Herndon was employed full-time as director of programming for ISNA from June 2005 to May 2006, producing and updating educational and website materials, organizing speakers and volunteers, writing grants, and so forth.

Dreger's graduate training is in the history and philosophy of science; in academic practice she is an historian of medicine and a bioethicist. Herndon's graduate training is in American studies; in academic practice she is a women's studies and cultural studies scholar.

A word on terminology is in order here. In this essay we use the term *intersex* to refer to variations in congenital sex anatomy that are considered atypical for females or males. The definition of *intersex* is thus context specific. What counts as an intersex phallus, for example, depends on local standards for penises and clitorises. Similarly, as we elaborate below, a person with no obvious sex ambiguity but with "sex chromosomes" other than simply XX (female-typical) or XY (male-typical) is today considered an intersex person by some intersex advocates, medical researchers, and clinicians, but not by all.[2] Yet such a person could not have been considered intersex before the ability to diagnose "sex chromosomes." So the definition of intersex depends on the state of scientific knowledge as well as general cultural beliefs about sex.

For this reason, in practice we define a person as intersex if she or he was born with a body that someone decided isn't typical for males or females. (This is also ISNA's current definition—not a coincidence, since Dreger helped develop this definition at an ISNA board retreat around 2000.)[3] Delineating intersex ultimately depends on delineating males and females, and when you get into the nitty-gritty of biology, this is not a simple task; nature is messy and often surprising, as Vernon Rosario argues.[4] That said, there are some forms of intersex that make a person's body obviously different from what is usual—for example, when a child is born otherwise male but without a penis, or when a child is born otherwise female but with a very small vagina and a large clitoris. So when we say that intersex is context specific, we do not mean to imply that these biological variations are not real but that how many variations (and thus people) are included in the category intersex depends on time and place.

Several dozen known biological variations and conditions may be considered intersex. Some have their basis in genetic variations. Some result from nongenetically caused prenatal developmental anomalies. A few involve "ambiguous" genitalia, but not all do; some involve more subtle blends of female and male types—for example, when a person has the external appearance of one sex but internally most of the organs of the other sex. Making things rather confusing to the novice, the medical names for various intersex conditions may refer specifically to the genotype (genetic basis), or to the phenotype (body type), or to the etiology (causal pathway of the condition), or to some combination of these. So saying someone is "intersex" does not tell you anything specific about a person's genes, anatomy, physiology, developmental history, or psychology. *Intersex* functions as a blanket term for many different biological possibilities—and as we show, many different political possibilities too.

Background History of Intersex

Historical records in the West suggest that until well into the twentieth century intersex people tended simply to blend in with the general population, living their lives as unremarkable boys, girls, men, and women. Given that notable genital ambiguity shows up once in about every two thousand births, if genital ambiguity had been considered terribly disturbing throughout Western history, there would likely exist significantly more records of legal, religious, and medical reactions.[5] Indeed, although largely ignored by medical practitioners who treat intersex today, there is in fact a body of medical literature from the nineteenth and twentieth centuries that shows that people with "ambiguous" sex anatomies lived relatively uneventful lives psychologically and socially.[6] The only reason many of these people even show up in that medical literature is that they wandered into the medical systems for some other concern, and then the physician noted their sex anomalies. Doctors often seem to have been more concerned with sex anomalies than many of their patients.

Historically the tendency in the West—in legal, medical, and religious affairs—has been to try to keep people sorted into clear male and female roles, and people with intersex seem to have generally participated in that binary sorting.[7] Lorraine Daston and Katherine Park found that in early modern France people labeled hermaphrodites were strictly required to adhere to one gender (male or female) and to partner only with someone of the other gender, to avoid the appearance of homosexual or other "deviant" sexuality.[8] Dreger, Christine Matta, and Elizabeth Reis have shown that a similar system took hold in European and American medicine by the late nineteenth century.[9] The growing specter of homosexuality—*behavioral* sexual ambiguity—drove many late-nineteenth-century physicians to insist that *physical* ambiguity—hermaphroditism—must be illusory and solvable through careful diagnosis of "true" sex. Matta, for example, shows "the connection between physicians' increased interest in preventing 'abnormal' sexual behavior and their insistence that interventionist surgeries were the most appropriate means of treating cases of hermaphroditism."[10] Reis meanwhile notes that "nineteenth century doctors insisted on certainty rather than ambiguity in gender designation. . . .

Choosing an infrangible sex (despite indefinite and contradictory markers) was mandatory."[11]

By the mid-nineteenth century, some surgeons began offering "corrective" operations for large clitorises, short vaginas, and hypospadias (wherein the urinary meatus—the "pee hole"—appears somewhere other than the tip of the penis). Occasionally such operations were requested by patients or by parents of intersex children.[12] But surgical "normalization" did not become the standard of care for intersex children until the 1950s, when the psychologists John Money, Joan Hampson, John Hampson, and their colleagues at Johns Hopkins University developed what came to be known as the "optimum gender of rearing" model, which held that *all* sexually ambiguous children should—indeed *must*—be made into unambiguous-looking boys or girls to ensure unambiguous gender identities.[13]

The optimum gender of rearing (OGR) model was based on the assumption that children are born psychosexually neutral at birth—that gender is primarily a product of nurture (upbringing), not nature (genes and prenatal hormones)—and that having a sex anatomy that appeared to match one's gender identity is necessary to a stable gender identity. Money and the Hampsons believed that children could be steered one way or the other so long as the steering began before the age of two, give or take a few months.[14] After the 1950s, surgeons at Hopkins and then at other major U.S. medical centers operated early to make children's genitals more closely approximate the typical genitals of the gender assigned. They also removed gonads that did not match the assigned gender, even if those gonads were healthy and potentially fertile. When the child reached the age of puberty, endocrinologists administered hormones to push secondary-sex development in the direction of assigned gender if the hormones produced by the child's own endocrine glands were inadequate to the task. Most children were assigned female because of the belief that it was easier to make a convincing-looking girl than a convincing-looking boy. (At least one surgeon has summed it up, "You can make a hole but you can't build a pole.")[15] Boys were expected to have reasonably sized and reasonably functional penises; girls were primarily expected to be able to be on the receiving end of penile penetration.[16]

The team at Hopkins also provided intensive psychological gender coaching, though this last aspect of treatment was less common at other medical centers, even while everyone agreed intersex represented a psychosocial concern.[17] Although defenders of the Hopkins OGR team point out that their publications include suggestions that intersex children be told their medical histories in age-appropriate ways, in practice and in print many clinicians favored deception and withholding of medical records, lest patients become confused and depressed by their intersex states.[18] By the early 1990s it was common practice for medical students and residents to be taught that their ethical duty meant deceiving women born with XY chromosomes and testes, telling them, if anything, that they had "twisted ovaries" that had to be removed.[19] The pediatric endocrinologist Jorge Daaboul remembers telling women with XY chromosomes that they had one regular X chromosome and one X chromosome with a short arm, something he knew a Y chromosome is not.[20]

History of the Intersex Rights Movement

Kessler's 1990 *Signs* article, the first publication to provide a sustained feminist critique of the OGR model, explored the sexist and heterosexist assumptions made by clinicians working with intersex patients regarding what counts as normal for girls and boys.[21] Using published medical literature as well as original interviews with intersex clinicians, Kessler demonstrated that the medical treatment of intersex was directed primarily at obscuring, and when possible eliminating, apparent sex and gender ambiguity.

Anne Fausto-Sterling brought a feminist understanding of intersex to a wider audience in 1993 by simultaneously publishing "The Five Sexes" in *The Sciences* and an op-ed called "How Many Sexes Are There?" in *The New York Times*.[22] In these companion pieces Fausto-Sterling reiterated and thus publicized the existing medical taxonomy of five sex types, a division that had coalesced in the late nineteenth century.[23] These included males, females, true hermaphrodites (which Fausto-Sterling called "herms"), male pseudohermaphrodites ("merms"), and female pseudohermaphrodites ("ferms"). "Herms" were people with both ovarian and testicular tissues; "merms" were people with ambiguous or mixed-sex anatomy and testes; "ferms" were people with ambiguous or mixed sex anatomy and ovaries. Fausto-Sterling's purpose was to challenge the pervasive belief that sex (and thus, in many people's minds, gender) came in a simple dichotomy.

In response to Fausto-Sterling's article Cheryl Chase (now known as Bo Laurent) published a letter in *Sciences* announcing the formation of ISNA.[24] Cognizant of how people with intersex were treated as if they were shameful and in need of strict social discipline, Chase originally planned to call the organization "Intersex Is Not Criminal."[25] Around the time of Fausto-Sterling's articles, Chase and other intersex people, including Max Beck, Morgan Holmes, and Kiira Triea, had come to the realization that they had been wronged by the medical establishment and that they needed to agitate for the rights of children born like them.[26] Because intersex activists felt the harm that had come to them had occurred largely because of the medicalization and medical mismanagement of intersex, they focused their attentions on critiquing the OGR model. In doing so, these activists were informed by principles of feminism (particularly the right to speak for oneself and critiques of sexism), gay and lesbian rights (particularly critiques of heterosexism and homophobia), and patients' rights (especially regarding autonomy, informed consent, and truth telling).[27]

Slowly at first (from about 1993 to 1999) and more rapidly later, intersex activists found allies in academic feminism, medicine, law, and the media. Like the activists born intersex, the great majority of nonintersex allies focused their attentions on the contemporary medical standard of care for intersex. Among the problems noted with the OGR model were these: it treated children in a sexist, asymmetrical way, valuing aggressiveness and sexual potency for boys and passiveness and reproductive/sexual-receptive potential for girls; it presumed that homosexuality (apparent same-sex relations) and transgenderism (changing or blurring gender identities) constituted bad outcomes; it violated principles of informed consent by failing to tell decision-making parents about the poor evidentiary support for the approach; it violated the axioms of truth telling and "first, do no harm"; it forced children to have their bodies adapted to oppressive social norms, using surgeries and hormone treatments that sometimes resulted in irrevocable harm; it generally involved treating psychosocial issues without the active participation of psychosocial professionals such as psychologists, psychiatrists, and social workers.[28] A more recent critique questions whether there is any reason to believe nonstandard genitals constitute a psychological risk factor; in fact, the medical literature fails to support the medical establishment's foundational assumption that having intersex genitals significantly increases psychosocial risk.[29]

As intersex advocacy grew so did the number and prominence of activist and support organizations for people born with intersex. Partly to make up for the gap left by ISNA's move away from day-to-day support toward systematic medical reform, the Internet-based, U.S.-located Coalition for Intersex Support, Activism, and Education (CISAE), founded by Triea and Heike Boedeker, and Bodies Like Ours, founded by Janet Green and Betsy Driver, sought to provide active peer support for parents and affected adults. Emi Koyama conceived Intersex Initiative as a relatively local group, originally focused on Portland, Oregon, but she has since brought it to national prominence. Diagnosis-specific groups such as the international Androgen Insensitivity Syndrome Support Group (AISSG) thrived throughout the late 1990s and continue today. However, not all relevant patient advocacy groups agreed with ISNA, Bodies Like Ours, and Intersex Initiative that the OGR model had to go: for example, the CARES Foundation (for congenital adrenal hyperplasia) and the MAGIC Foundation (for conditions that affect children's growth, including some types of intersex), run mostly by parents and clinicians, tended to remain in agreement with the medical establishment.

Independent of advocacy organizations, some sex researchers and clinicians took a stand against the OGR, most notably Milton Diamond and his associates. Diamond and H. Keith Sigmundson reported what happened to David Reimer, the nonintersex boy whose transformation into a girl (following a circumcision accident) Money had directed.[30] Money had claimed Reimer's gender transformation worked—and that therefore the OGR system was likely to work for intersex children. But Money was lying; Money knew Reimer had not been happy as a girl, and indeed transitioned socially to a boy almost as soon as he learned of his past.[31] Knowing this and hearing the painful stories of many adults with intersex, Diamond called in 1998 for a moratorium on intersex genital surgeries while data was collected on outcomes.[32]

Initially the medical establishment mostly ignored critiques and calls for change, issuing only occasionally a restatement of the belief that the OGR model was necessary and effective.[33] These statements rarely answered the specific critiques noted above. When Dreger edited a 1998 special issue on intersex for the *Journal of Clinical Ethics* (which became the basis for the 1999 anthology *Intersex in the Age of Ethics*), she tried to find a clinician who would defend the OGR model, but could not. Notably, several were by that point willing to criticize it.[34] The one critique to which traditionalist clinicians did begin to respond was the lack of outcomes data in favor of the approach. The outcomes data that has recently emerged is mixed and tends to vary wildly in terms of implicit assumptions on the goal of intersex treatment.[35]

Since about 2004, there has been a marked increase in interest among clinicians to reform practice. For example, thanks to the initiative of the feminist academic sociologist Monica Casper, who served as ISNA's executive director in 2003, ISNA developed a medical advisory board of approximately twenty-five people, most of them clinicians, something that seemed a distant dream as late as 1998. In 2004, at the American Academy of Pediatrics Section on Urology meeting, many clinicians were clearly agonizing over the choice of treatment in intersex cases. Even surgeons who had historically been ardent defenders of the OGR model were publicly expressing serious reservations.[36] In October 2005 the highly influential Lawson Wilkins Pediatric Endocrine Society and the European Society for Paediatric Endocrinology held a consensus meeting in Chicago that resulted in a hopeful degree of movement toward providing more psychosocial care, peer support, truth telling, informed consent, and outcomes data.[37]

Also in 2005, a collective comprised mostly of the three stakeholder groups—intersex people, parents of intersex people, and clinicians—formed and issued new clinical guidelines and a handbook for parents based on a "patient-centered model of care," an explicit alternative to the OGR.[38] That group, known as the Consortium on the Management of Disorders of Sex Development (or DSD Consortium for short), was formed as a result of grants given to ISNA to complete, produce, and distribute drafts written several years earlier by the social workers Sallie Foley and Christine Feick. The DSD Consortium includes founders and leaders of many of the major diagnosis-specific intersex support groups as well as clinicians from all the specialties involved in intersex care. (We were members of the DSD Consortium, and Dreger led the project as coordinator and editor in chief.)

The DSD Consortium's *Clinical Guidelines* state:

Patient-centered care means remaining clearly focused on the well-being of individual patients. In the case of DSDs this specifically involves the following principles.

1. Provide *medical and surgical care when dealing with a complication that represents a real and present threat.* . . .
2. Recognize that what is normal for one individual may not be what is normal for others. . . .
3. Minimize the potential for the patient and family to feel ashamed, stigmatized, or overly obsessed with genital appearance; avoid the use of stigmatizing terminology (like "pseudo-hermaphroditism") and medical photography; *promote openness.* . . .
4. Delay elective surgical and hormonal treatments *until the patient can actively participate in decision-making.* . . .

5. *Respect parents by addressing their concerns and distress empathetically,* honestly, and directly. . . .
6. *Directly address the child's psychosocial distress* (if any) with the efforts of psychosocial professionals and peer support.
7. Always *tell the truth* to the family and the child.[39]

These principles may seem like common sense, but they are considered somewhat radical by clinicians who have long believed that the presence in a child of a trait that challenges social norms means the most basic tenets of medical ethics can (and indeed must) be set aside.[40]

The DSD Consortium's handbooks are drawing much interest and praise in medical centers around the United States and are being distributed by advocacy groups (such as the MAGIC Foundation) historically supportive of the medical establishment. Our own experience suggests that clinicians who until recently practiced the OGR model are quite receptive to the patient-centered alternative. We see this as clear evidence that the changes for which intersex activists first hoped in the early 1990s are finally happening. This is not to overlook continued delays in the implementation of a reformed model. In our experience many medical centers currently lack institutional resources—including adequately trained psychosocial professionals, leadership, cross-disciplinary relationships, and funding—needed to implement psychosocially attentive integrated team care. Some also suffer from disputes among clinicians over the best approach. But more and more are expressing interest in providing something like the patient-centered, multidisciplinary team approach recommended by the DSD Consortium.[41]

The success of the intersex rights movement is almost certainly due in part to concomitant success in the LGBT rights movement. As noted above, the treatment of intersex has historically been motivated by homophobia and transphobia—that is, fear of apparent same-sex relations and fear of people changing or blurring gender categories. Positive changes in social attitudes toward queer-identified people have thus led to positive changes in social attitudes toward people with what some have called "queer bodies."[42] Success can also be credited to the fact that intersex advocates have been extremely effective at using the power of the media to change minds.[43] Substantial Western media attention to intersex people and intersex medicine, as well as the publication in 2002 of Jeffrey Eugenides's Pulitzer Prize–winning *Middlesex: A Novel,* has helped make the existence of intersex known, believed, and understood by tens of millions more people. We should note that, although a few intersex people objected to Eugenides's portrayal of an intersex person because it was a fictional story by a nonintersex man, our experience has been that the learning engendered by his novel for doctors and laypeople alike has been generally progressive. (Both of us have been surprised at how many conservative older men and women have told us excitedly what they learned about intersex from reading *Middlesex* in book clubs, including Oprah Winfrey's.) The intersex rights movement has also benefited from several talented writers—including Martha Coventry, Esther Marguerite Morris Leidolf, and Triea—who have conveyed their personal histories with eloquence and power.[44] We see therefore many reasons to believe that the intersex rights movement will continue to make marked progress in the coming years, even while we are concerned that the skyrocketing marketing of genital cosmetic procedures—including penile enlargement and labia reduction surgeries—has the potential to produce a negative effect on intersex clinical reform, as norms for genital appearance become increasingly visible and rigid.[45]

Intersex Identity Politics

Although people sometimes refer to "the intersex community" as they do "the lesbian community," this is somewhat misleading. There are online virtual communities of people with intersex, but large numbers of intersex people do not live together in brick-and-mortar communities, and only occasionally do they come together for meetings that are primarily about political consciousness-raising rather than about sharing information about particular medical diagnoses (like hypospadias or congenital adrenal hyperplasia). ISNA has hosted a few small invitation-only retreats, and a number of intersex people have come together at the annual Creating Change conference of America's National Gay and Lesbian Task Force, and for one-time events such as the 2002 "Rated XXXY" San Francisco fundraiser produced by the intersex advocate, performer, and poet Thea Hillman, but such gatherings remain either irregular or infrequent.

There are sizable annual meetings of diagnosis-specific groups like the AISSG, the CARES Foundation, and the Hypospadias and Epispadias Association, but often the participants of these meetings do not consider themselves "intersex" and are in fact offended by the term being used in reference to them. Objections we have heard include that the term sexualizes them (or their children if the objector is a parent) by making the issue one of eroticism instead of biology; that it implies they have no clear sex or gender identity; and that it forces on them an identity, especially a queer identity, to which they do not relate.[46]

Historically the word *intersex* as we know it dates to the early twentieth century when it was coined by the biologist Richard Goldschmidt as a term for biological sex types that fell between male and female.[47] Throughout the twentieth century, members of the medical profession occasionally used the term to refer to what they would more typically call hermaphroditisms or pseudohermaphroditisms. Early intersex advocates chose the term because it was less confusing and stigmatizing than terms based on the root *hermaphrodite,* although occasionally they used those alternate terms for in-your-face self-empowerment. For example, ISNA's first newsletter was called *Hermaphrodites with Attitude,* and Chase's 1996 video of ten intersex people telling their own stories was called *Hermaphrodites Speak!* But today few intersex advocates call themselves "hermaphrodites" both because the irony is lost on most people and because the term makes intersex people sound like mythical figures who are simultaneously fully male and fully female—something physiologically impossible but a frequent fantasy of certain fetishists who e-mail support groups seeking "hermaphrodite" sex partners. (Such people are known contemptuously in intersex activist circles as "wannafucks.") Early in the intersex rights movement, activists, scholars, and journalists sometimes referred to

intersexuals, but this term has largely fallen out of favor because it can be essentializing and dehumanizing to equate people with one aspect of their physicality. Instead, many advocates and activists now prefer to use terms such as *person with intersex, intersex person,* or *person with an intersex condition,* taking a cue from the disability rights movement.[48]

As suggested above, the question of who counts as intersex remains contentious. The people who made up the early intersex rights movement tended to share a common experience: they were born with noted sexual ambiguity, surgically "corrected" as young children, subjected to continued medicalization and stigma inside and outside the clinic, and they eventually developed a queer political consciousness that allowed them to understand their plight as unjust. But as the intersex rights movement grew, the diversity of actual experiences became more obvious, and this led to internal questions of identity politics. Were people intersex who "just" had hypospadias? Were women intersex who had well-controlled congenital adrenal hyperplasia and very little genital "masculinization" (so little it was never medically "fixed")?

The movement tended to welcome all these people out of the generosity that typically marks early social movements looking for people who will help and be helped.[49] But the anxiety about who should belong is obvious in venues like *Hermaphrodites Speak!* where Tom, born with hypospadias, jokes, "I'm the real hermaphrodite here—these people are just imposters." The intersex activist David Iris Cameron took to carrying around a card that asked, "Is XXY intersex?"[50] Cameron has Klinefelter syndrome (XXY chromosomes), which the layperson prone to a simplistic algebraic understanding of "sex chromosomes" might think of as obviously intersex. But many physicians do not count Klinefelter syndrome as intersex, just as they do not count Turner's syndrome (one X with no second "sex chromosome"), because in many physicians' minds, neither results in enough external sex-atypical development to count.

In our experience some clinicians have played a sort of moving target game whereby their definition of intersex changes from venue to venue, or moment to moment. We end up spending a remarkable amount of time just trying to agree on which diagnoses (and thus which people) count in the conversation we're trying to have. This does not usually seem to be a purposeful attempt to stall or derail conversation (although that does sometimes result); rather it seems to stem from a lack of systematic consideration of what the term might mean. For example, some want to call intersex only those born with visibly ambiguous genitalia, or only those who have had a particularly unusual mix of prenatal sex hormones.

Two illustrations: the physician William Reiner, a longtime ISNA ally, has tended to insist that males born with cloacal exstrophy are not intersex because their brains are not subjected prenatally to a sex-atypical mix of hormones.[51] Yet in cases of cloacal exstrophy, because the gut wall does not form properly, males are born with no penis. Standard practice (challenged by Reiner's work) has been to assign these children as girls, castrate them, and give them feminizing hormones starting at the age of puberty. In other words, the children are *treated* as intersex. Indeed, in all other cases when a boy is born with very little or no penis, the child would fall under the category intersex. Yet Reiner—who has been a staunch advocate of both intersex rights and the well-being of children born with cloacal exstrophy—seems not to want to apply the intersex label to cloacal exstrophy males purely because they have male-typical prenatal brain development.

A second example: in a recent discussion with a clinician, the name of one particular intersex activist came up, and the clinician stopped conversation to say, "she isn't intersex, she was just progesterone-virilized." In other words, given her genotype the activist in question would have developed as a standard female, but because her mother was given progesterone during pregnancy (presumably to prevent miscarriage), the activist's genitals had been virilized to some degree in the womb. So this activist was born with ambiguous genitalia, and as a result she was sent through the OGR system. Yet because she had medically induced (rather than "naturally" occurring) genital virilization, the clinician did not think she counted as intersex.

To make matters even more confusing, sex development is complicated enough that two people who share nominally the same condition may have quite different genotypes (genetic codes) or phenotypes (body types). For example, just knowing a person has ovotestes (misleadingly called "true hermaphroditism" in the medical literature) won't reveal much about the person's chromosomes or even his or her genitalia; a person with ovotestes may appear fairly feminine, fairly masculine, or in-between in terms of genitalia and overall physique. The majority of people with ovotestes have XX (female-typical) sex chromosomes, but others have XY or some other combination. Moreover, genitals that start as "ambiguous" may become naturally less so, and vice versa. Sharon Preves notes the case of Sierra, a child born with a large clitoris. The doctors wanted to shorten the clitoris for psychosocial reasons. Her mother refused. Several weeks later Sierra's clitoris shrunk to a normal size.[52] She probably had genital engorgement—that is, blood had pooled in her genitals, causing them to temporarily swell, from her being squeezed through her mother's birth canal. Had Sierra had surgery she might now count as intersex. Because of her mother's good sense she now probably doesn't count by anyone's definition.

The definitional challenges encountered with physicians, combined with the rejection of the intersex label by many parents and affected adults, have led us to participate in a move toward using a new blanket term: *disorders of sex development* (DSDs). When we started working with the group that became the DSD Consortium, it became clear that we couldn't reach agreement on practice unless we came to agreement on terminology. Otherwise we couldn't say to whom our guidelines applied. Everyone recognized that it was critical to avoid all terms based on the misleading and stigmatizing "hermaphrodite."[53] Alternative available medical terms included *disorders of sex(ual) differentiation* and *disorders of sexual development*. Terms with *sexual* in them were rejected because of the implication that we were talking primarily about an issue of sexuality (eroticism, orientation) instead of sex (anatomy and physiology). "Differentiation" was rejected in favor of "development" because of disciplinary disagreement about what "differentiation" means.

(Endocrinologists mean one thing, geneticists another.) One participant, David Iris Cameron, suggested "variations of sex development," but this was rejected for discounting the health concerns that come with some intersex conditions—concerns like dangerous endocrine imbalances and an increased risk of gonadal cancers. Besides, "variations" would describe every human, not just the people we meant to describe, namely, those liable to be treated as problematically sex-atypical. In the end handbook contributors settled on "disorders of sex development," with many people in the group expressing enormous relief at this.

As noted above, the DSD Consortium's handbooks represented significant progress. The consortium included past and present leaders from many other critically important advocacy and support groups, including the AISSG, the CARES Foundation, ISNA, the MRKH Organization (for girls and women born with conditions including incomplete vaginal development), and Bodies Like Ours. In other words, we achieved buy-in on a clearly articulated patient-centered model of care among people who previously appeared not to agree. We know that this would have been impossible without the shift of nomenclature to DSD.

At the same time that the DSD Consortium was working in earnest, in October 2005 the Lawson Wilkins Pediatric Endocrine Society and the European Society for Paediatric Endocrinology held their consensus conference on intersex. One agreement reached at that meeting was to abandon the terms *intersex* and *(pseudo)hermaphroditism* in favor of *disorders of sex development,* defined as "congenital conditions in which development of chromosomal, gonadal, or anatomical sex is atypical."[54] This was not a coincidence; several clinicians from the DSD Consortium (notably the pediatric urologist and geneticist Eric Vilain, the pediatric psychiatrist and urologist Reiner, and the pediatric psychologist David Sandberg) called for the change in nomenclature. But it is worth noting that their call fell on receptive ears; clinicians were ready for this change.

Reception of the new terminology has been mixed among people with intersex. Several months after publication of the DSD Consortium's handbooks, three participating intersex adults—Cameron, Esther Morris Leidolf, and Peter Trinkl—asked that a one-sentence disclaimer be added noting that, though they support the documents, they do not support the term. Several adults with intersex also objected to the term at an October 2006 conference held by ISNA and in written responses to the Chicago consensus document.[55] It is obvious from the way we write that, as scholars and activists, we still prefer the term *intersex* even while we recognize the usefulness of using *DSD* in many contexts.[56] Understandably, many people dislike having the label of disorder applied to them. Ironically, after years of trying to demedicalize intersex to some extent, the term we're now using remedicalizes it. But we have found that the terminology accords with the experience of many intersex adults and parents; it gives them a term that feels right in that it seems simultaneously to name, scientize, and isolate what it is that has happened. It therefore makes the phenomenon seem more manageable by being less potentially all-encompassing of their identities. Moreover, the shift to this terminology clearly has allowed serious progress toward patient-centered care, in part because it has allowed alliance building across support and advocacy groups, and with clinicians. For that reason we have been pragmatists about the nomenclature change. We strongly suspect that as attitudes and behaviors among clinicians improve, it will become possible and indeed necessary to revisit the nomenclature issue. Reis's recent suggestion of "Divergence of Sex Development" might turn out to be a viable compromise.[57]

A number of transgender people who were not born with any apparent sex anomalies and were not subjected to intersex medical management believe they should count as intersex because something in their brains obviously makes them feel differently than average males and females. One transgender person wrote to us that unless one believes in a mind-brain dichotomy (which we don't), obviously there is something sex-atypical in the brains of transgender people. But it is not clear that that sex-atypicality (always) represents a neurological intersex comprising a female brain in a male body, or vice versa. Some transgendered persons' brains may be different from the average in some way other than a neurological sex inversion.

For transgender adults, there are definite advantages to counting as intersex. For one, people in the United States tend to be more accepting of identities that have a definitive (or at least implied) biological basis. The current *Diagnostic and Statistical Manual of Mental Disorders* (*DSM-IV*) provides another reason for transgender people to seek the intersex label. According to the *DSM-IV*, a person with atypical gender identity can be classed as having gender identity disorder only if the person is not intersex.[58] Thus being labeled with an intersex condition means avoiding the diagnosis of a "mental disorder" and possibly easier access to legal and medical sex reassignment.

Yet many intersex advocates have rejected the idea that transgender people are necessarily intersex. For one thing they (and we) have found that a few transgender adults claim specific intersex conditions (like 5-alpha-reductase deficiency or partial androgen insensitivity syndrome) they don't actually have. But even beyond that, some intersex activists argue that transgender persons have had radically different experiences from intersex persons who have been through the OGR mill. Of course many (though by no means all) transgender people have experienced significant stigma for being gender atypical since childhood. But Chase writes that some transgender advocates inappropriately imply that intersex often results in gender transition, an inaccurate implication that "facilitates the doctors' misguided perceptions that incorrect gender assignment is the only harm of OGR, and that studies documenting low transition rates are evidence of success."[59] While there is no singular intersex experience to which a singular transgender experience can be compared, we think it is important to acknowledge the concern that intersex experiences and advocacy may become muddied, co-opted, or misguided in the conflation of transgender and intersex.[60]

Still, even though there may be differences between intersex and transgender, there are also reasons for intersex and trans activists to unite. As Leslie Feinberg notes, the divisive behavior of territory marking over identities often weakens the movement for human rights. Feinberg states emphatically that "we

can never throw enough people overboard to win approval from our enemies."[61] Feinberg goes on to say that "people who don't experience common oppression *can* make history when they unite."[62] While there may be moments when intersex activists are justified in their demands that people understand the particulars of intersex and transgender, there is also reason to carefully consider whether these particulars are always important and why such lines are drawn in the first place. If the particulars of transgender and intersex are highlighted only in order to make intersex people more intelligible or acceptable, then the result might be that transgender people are made less intelligible or even pathologized. Thus intersex activists doing the work of cleaving intersex and transgender must diligently examine their motives and the possible outcomes of such work.

Finally, on the issue of intersex identity politics we might note for other scholars thinking about stepping into identity-centered activism that we have each been criticized and had our motives questioned for being nonintersex people working on intersex scholarship and activism. For example, we have both had our intentions interrogated in online forums, and Herndon has been attacked for daring to point out the similarities between what intersex people and fat people face in terms of stigma and medicalization.[63] But this has by no means been a frequent occurrence. In general, activists born intersex have welcomed our collaboration and have often acted as enthusiastic advisers to and supporters of our efforts.

Intersex and the Nature of Gender

Much scholarship in science and the humanities on intersex (including our own) has been motivated by attempts to ascertain the nature of gender. Historically, feminist intersex scholarship has aligned with other feminist theoretical scholarship in that it has taken gender to be a social construct distinct from sex (anatomy and physiology). For example, Kessler's 1990 intersex work aligned with her earlier work on gender by showing how social assumptions about what it means to be a male or a female are taught, learned, and reinforced. Dreger, Fausto-Sterling, Myra Hird, Holmes, Iain Morland, and many other feminist scholars working on intersex have similarly shown how social beliefs about gender are actively imposed on people whose bodies don't fit the simplistic assumptions that gender equals sex and that sex-gender formations come in only two flavors.[64]

Indeed, until relatively recently some feminists cited the alleged success of the OGR model as proof that gender is socially constructed.[65] But the concept of gender (as distinct from sex) as it developed in intersex clinical practice was hardly meant to be progressive. As Dreger has shown, the move in the early twentieth century to assigning a "workable" gender instead of a gender that aligned with a biological "true sex" was a conservative reaction to the unrelenting messiness of sex. Doctors dealing with intersex decided they had better resort to a system of gender assignment that would allow them to socially sort everyone into two types no matter how apparently in-between they were physically.[66] As Kessler and others have shown, the work of the Hopkins team continued in this tradition.[67] So even while Money and his allies supported the idea that gender is to a large degree socially constructed, in intersex care they maintained traditionalist, sexist, and heterosexist concepts.

Nevertheless, particularly in the early years of the intersex rights movement, many intersex people found feminist writings about the social construction of gender empowering and liberating. They could use this work to see how one particular construction had been forced on them and how their lives might have been better (and could yet be better) under different social constructions.[68] Social constructivism also gave solace to those who felt their gender identities did not fit into the simplistic male-female dichotomy promoted by Western popular culture. It was especially painful, therefore, for some intersex women (particularly women with AIS) to find their self-identities as women rejected by Germaine Greer in her book *The Whole Woman* because she insisted that "it is my considered position that femaleness is conferred by the final pair of XX chromosomes. Otherwise I don't know what it is."[69] As Morland has noted, when Greer was challenged by women with AIS and family members of girls with AIS, she was "dismissive; she then used the book's second edition not to retract the claims, but to publicly mock the AIS correspondents by referring to them too as men." Morland has persuasively argued that ironically "in trying to criticize the social construction of femaleness and intersex, Greer disenfranchised precisely those people who live at the intersection of the two categories."[70] Greer's simplistic and essentialist position seemed to represent something of a rearguard action against admitting anyone who might be a male-to-female transsexual into the ranks of real womanhood. Yet, we confess to never really understanding the intellectual balancing act performed by Greer and people like the leaders of the Michigan Womyn's Music Festival (who have tried hard to keep a "womyn born womyn only" policy of admission): they seem simultaneously to condemn and employ essentialist notions of womanhood.

In fact, neither a hard-line social constructivist nor a hard-line biological essentialist theory of gender seems supportable by the real-life experiences of people with intersex. On the one hand, if gender identity were purely a matter of social construction, it would not make sense that people with certain intersex conditions tend to revert to one particular gender identity despite monumental efforts aimed at making them the other. Consider, for example, the high percentage of males born with cloacal exstrophy, castrated and raised as girls, who declare themselves to be boys.[71] Similarly, many transgender people present gender identities in contradiction with the intensive gender training they've received—or indeed identities that confound any description in gendered terms.[72]

On the other hand, a simplistic biological explanation for gender identity also fails in the face of intersex. Not all males born with cloacal exstrophy or a micropenis and raised girls decide they are really boys or men. Of course, some who retain their female gender identities may be unaware of their medical histories or have plenty of reasons to decide to stay with the gender they were assigned. Gender transition comes at significant financial, physical, and emotional costs.

Ultimately it seems illogical to have so firm a belief in either the biological determination or social construction of gender that all of us with stable gender identities amount to either biologically programmed robots or victims of false consciousness. As Diana Fuss pointed out in *Essentially Speaking*, even hard-core constructivism amounts to an essentialism itself—in this case, actually a biological essentialism that presumes everyone is born with a blank slate for a brain where gender is concerned.[73]

Chase has argued that it is the very obsession with "the gender question" that has led to so much harm for people with intersex. According to Chase, while some people (like Money and some feminists) have used intersex to sit around debating nature versus nurture, real people with intersex have been hurt by these theories and their manifestations. Chase has therefore argued that "intersex [has been] primarily a problem of stigma and trauma, not gender."[74] Clearly, most OGR clinicians—from Money through today—have disagreed, arguing instead that "problems of gender identity development are *the core concern* in the psychosocial management of medical conditions involving ambiguous genitalia."[75] Yet a close reading of intersex autobiographical writing suggests that relatively few feel that getting the "wrong" gender assignment formed the central cause of their suffering. Indeed, this is a finding supported by outcome studies by OGR clinicians, . . . who then take this as proof that they've been on the right track all along![76] This failure to see why they're on the wrong track results from believing that "successful" gender identity means success in intersex patient care. Most intersex autobiographies support Chase's argument, showing how shame (including, but not limited to, shame about gender variation), secrecy, and medical mismanagement led to significant suffering.[77]

Nevertheless, contrary to Chase's simple formulation, clearly for a significant number of intersex people, gender—in the form of gender identity and gender role expectations—*is* a central concern in their lives. It is not uncommon for people with intersex to ponder how their gender identities and histories relate to their intersex. A few, like Mani Mitchell, feel that their intersex biology explains their feelings of being bigendered or intergendered.[78] Indeed, some have claimed that ISNA's message (that intersex is mostly about shame and trauma, not gender) fails to acknowledge their socially atypical genders. In fact, ISNA has never suggested people should not have the right to express their genders however they wish. ISNA (like the DSD Consortium, Bodies Like Ours, and all the diagnosis-specific support groups) has advocated raising all children as boys or girls, providing a best-guess gender assignment based on what can be surmised (after extensive tests) about the child's biology and future psychology, including how the parents are thinking about the child's gender. The reasoning behind this is twofold: (1) raising a child in a third or no gender is not a socially feasible way to reduce shame and stigma; (2) intersex is not a discrete biological category, so someone would always be deciding who to raise as male, female, or intersex: three categories don't solve the problem any more than two or five or ten do.

ISNA argued that gender assignment should not be reinforced with surgeries—that healthy tissue should be left in place for the patient to decide herself or himself what, if anything, to do with it. Although certain members of the medical establishment erroneously believed (and some still do believe) that ISNA advocated "raising children in a third gender," this was never the case. The cause of confusion seems to come from the fact that many clinicians can't understand what it would mean to raise a child with "ambiguous" genitalia as a boy or a girl, despite plenty of historical evidence that this has worked, no doubt because sex anomalies are largely hidden by clothing.[79]

We've been asked innumerable times why ISNA did not want to get rid of gender altogether. This question typically comes not from intersex adults but from scholars and students in gender studies. As Herndon noted while she was director of programming, ISNA privileged what is known from adults with intersex, and most adults with intersex don't have any problem with having a gender as men or women, nor do most reject the gender assignments given to them as children.[80] Many enjoy publicly "doing their gender," as Judith Butler would say.[81] This is true even for those who see themselves privately as third-gendered or ungendered. As noted above, most intersex adults agree that the problem with the medical management of intersex is not gender assignment but surgical and hormonal reinforcement of the assignment and other risky—and indeed physically and emotionally *costly*—manifestations of shame and secrecy.

A few critics have suggested that a better system than ISNA's would be more like what Feinberg, Kate Bornstein, and some other transgender activists promote. But our readings of Feinberg and Bornstein do not seem to be inconsistent with the message of ISNA—that people should ultimately be allowed to express their genders as they wish. Recounting a tense moment with a lesbian friend, Feinberg notes that many people believe that gender expression can only be oppressive. She writes of her friend, "She believes that once true equality is achieved in society humankind will be genderless. . . . If we can build a more just society, people like me will cease to exist. She assumes that I am simply a product of oppression."[82] Meanwhile, Bornstein notes that her own work is received in many different ways by members of the trans community, with some people agreeing with her and others being upset by her views. Trying to explain these disparate reactions, Bornstein writes, "Every transsexual I know went through a gender transformation for different reasons, and there are as many truthful experiences of gender as there are people who think they have a gender."[83] Thus several of the most visible leaders of the trans movement express views similar to those expressed by many intersex activists—that people's gender expressions need not be read only as oppressive and that the vast majority of people will have at least some positive investment in their gender expression.

The Future

Serious progress has been made in intersex rights in the last fifteen years, progress that we believe would have been much slower or even impossible without the philosophical and practical efforts of many academics who have devoted their energies to trying to end the oppression of intersex people. There remains much theoretical and practical work to be done in and around the intersex rights movement, and we fully expect that academic

feminists will continue to be an essential part of this work. We believe there are key insights feminists interested in helping can develop from the history we have presented here. For one, feminists should seek to listen carefully to intersex people in the same way they have listened to other marginalized groups, rather than assume they know what is true or right for intersex people.[84] Additionally, they should seek to write about intersex people on their own terms rather than just appropriate intersex for talking about other issues like the social construction of gender. They may also help by doing more than theorizing—by helping with the day-to-day fundraising and advocacy work that support the intersex rights movement. Finally, such feminist commentators should acknowledge that many intersex (and also transgender) people have suffered even more than biologically typical women from sexist and heterosexist oppression.

References

During the publication process of this essay, ISNA closed. Its website content remains available, and its assets have been transferred to a new nonprofit organization, Accord Alliance (www.accordalliance.org). We are grateful to Myra Hird, Emi Koyama, Bo Laurent, Esther Morris Leidolf, Kiira Triea, and especially Iain Morland for comments on earlier drafts of this essay.

1. Suzanne J. Kessler, "The Medical Construction of Gender: Case Management of Intersexed Infants," *Signs* 16 (1990): 3–26. For examples of subsequent work, see Alice Domurat Dreger, *Hermaphrodites and the Medical Invention of Sex* (Cambridge, MA: Harvard University Press, 1998); Dreger, ed., *Intersex in the Age of Ethics* (Hagerstown, MD: University Publishing Group, 1999); Anne Fausto-Sterling, *Sexing the Body: Gender Politics and the Construction of Sexuality* (New York: Basic, 2000); Michelle Morgan LeFay Holmes, "The Doctor Will Fix Everything: Intersexuality in Contemporary Culture" (PhD diss., Concordia University, 2000); Suzanne J. Kessler, *Lessons from the Intersexed* (New Brunswick: Rutgers University Press, 1998); Iain Morland, "Narrating Intersex: On the Ethical Critique of the Medical Management of Intersexuality, 1985–2005" (PhD diss., University of London, 2005); Sharon E. Preves, *Intersex and Identity: The Contested Self* (New Brunswick: Rutgers University Press, 2003).
2. "Sex chromosomes" is misleading; the X chromosome includes genes important to nonsex traits, and genes on chromosomes other than the X and Y are necessary for sex development. See Alice Domurat Dreger, "Sex beyond the Karyotype," in *Controversies in Science and Technology,* ed. Daniel Lee Kleinman and Jo Handelsman (New Rochelle, NY: Mary Ann Leibert, 2007), 467–78.
3. Intersex Society of North America, "What Is Intersex?" www.isna.org/faq/what_is_intersex (accessed July 29, 2008).
4. Vernon A. Rosario, "Quantum Sex: Intersex and the Molecular Deconstruction of Sex," GLQ: *A Journal of Lesbian and Gay Studies,* vol 15, no. 2.
5. Intersex Society of North America, "How Common Is Intersex?" www.isna.org/faq/frequency (accessed July 29, 2008).
6. Dreger, *Hermaphrodites;* Intersex Society of North America, "What Evidence Is There That You Can Grow Up Psychologically Healthy with Intersex Genitals?" www.isna.org/faq/healthy (accessed July 29, 2008); Christine Matta, "Ambiguous Bodies and Deviant Sexualities: Hermaphrodites, Homosexuality, and Surgery in the United States, 1850–1904," *Perspectives in Biology and Medicine* 48 (2005): 74–83;

John Money, "Hermaphroditism: An Inquiry into the Nature of a Human Paradox" (PhD diss., Harvard University, 1952); Elizabeth Reis, "Impossible Hermaphrodites: Intersex in America, 1620–1960," *Journal of American History* 92 (2005): 411–41; Elizabeth Reis, *Bodies in Doubt: An American History of Intersex* (Baltimore: Johns Hopkins University Press, 2009).

7. For an example of an exception, see the story of Thomas/ Thomasine Hall in Reis, "Impossible Hermaphrodites."

8. Lorraine Daston and Katherine Park, "The Hermaphrodite and the Order of Nature: Sexual Ambiguity in Early Modern France," *GLQ* 1 (1995): 419–38.

9. Dreger, *Hermaphrodites;* Matta, "Ambiguous Bodies"; Reis, "Impossible Hermaphrodites."

10. Matta, "Ambiguous Bodies," 74.

11. Reis, "Impossible Hermaphrodites," 412–13.

12. Dreger, *Hermaphrodites;* Matta, "Ambiguous Bodies"; Reis, "Impossible Hermaphrodites."

13. John Money, Joan G. Hampson, and John L. Hampson, "Imprinting and the Establishment of Gender Role," *Archives of Neurology and Psychiatry* 77 (1957): 333–36.

14. Money, Hampson, and Hampson, "Imprinting and the Establishment of Gender Role."

15. Melissa Hendricks, "Is It a Boy or a Girl?" *Johns Hopkins Magazine,* November 1993, 15.

16. Alice Domurat Dreger, "'Ambiguous Sex'—or Ambivalent Medicine? Ethical Problems in the Treatment of Intersexuality," *Hastings Center Report* 28, no. 3 (1998): 24–35.

17. For examples of Hopkins's gender coaching, see John Colapinto, *As Nature Made Him: The Boy Who Was Raised as a Girl* (New York: HarperCollins: 2000); and Kiira Triea, "Power, Orgasm, and the Psychohormonal Research Unit," in Dreger, *Intersex in the Age of Ethics,* 141–44.

18. For a recommendation of disclosure, see John Money, Joan G. Hampson, and John L. Hampson, "Hermaphroditism: Recommendations Concerning Assignment of Sex, Change of Sex, and Psychological Management," *Bulletin of the Johns Hopkins Hospital* 97 (1955): 284–300. On withholding, see Dreger, "Ambiguous Sex"; and Anita Natarajan, "Medical Ethics and Truth-Telling in the Case of Androgen Insensitivity Syndrome," *Canadian Medical Association Journal* 154 (1996): 568–70.

19. Sherri Groveman, "The Hanukkah Bush: Ethical Implications in the Clinical Management of Intersex," in Dreger, *Intersex in the Age of Ethics,* 23–28.

20. Jorge Daaboul, "Does the Study of History Affect Clinical Practice? Intersex as a Case Study: The Physician's View" (paper presented at the annual meeting of the American Association for the History of Medicine, Bethesda, May 2000).

21. Kessler, "Medical Construction of Gender."

22. Anne Fausto-Sterling, "The Five Sexes: Why Male and Female Are Not Enough," *Sciences* (March–April 1993): 20–25; Fausto-Sterling, "How Many Sexes Are There?" *New York Times,* March 12, 1993.

23. Dreger, *Hermaphrodites,* 139–66.

24. Cheryl Chase, letter to the editor, *Sciences* (July–August 1993): 3.

25. Cheryl Chase, pers. comm., July 9, 2004.

26. Kiira Triea, "Learning about Transsexuality from Transsexuals," Transkids, www.transkids.us/learning (accessed July 29, 2008).

27. Cheryl Chase, "Hermaphrodites with Attitude: Mapping the Emergence of Intersex Political Activism," *GLQ* 4 (1998): 189–211.

28. Kessler, "Medical Construction of Gender"; Dreger, "Ambiguous Sex"; Kessler, *Lessons from the Intersexed; Hermaphrodites Speak!* dir. Cheryl Chase, Intersex Society of North America, 1996; Julie Greenberg, "Legal Aspects of Gender Assignment," *Endocrinologist* 13 (2003): 277–86;

Groveman, "Hanukkah Bush"; Holmes, "Doctor Will Fix Everything."

29. Alice Domurat Dreger, "Intersex and Human Rights: The Long View," in *Ethics and Intersex,* ed. Sharon Sytsma (Dordrecht: Springer, 2006), 73–86; Intersex Society of North America, "What Evidence"; Peter A. Lee et al., "Consensus Statement on Management of Intersex Disorders," *Pediatrics* 118 (2006): 814–15.

30. Milton Diamond and H. Keith Sigmundson, "Sex Reassignment at Birth: A Long Term Review and Clinical Implications," *Archives of Pediatric and Adolescent Medicine* 150 (1997): 298–304.

31. Colapinto, *As Nature Made Him.*

32. Kenneth Kipnis and Milton Diamond, "Pediatric Ethics and the Surgical Assignment of Sex," *Journal of Clinical Ethics* 9 (1998): 398–410.

33. Alice Domurat Dreger, "Cultural History and Social Activism: Scholarship, Identities, and the Intersex Rights Movement," in *Locating Medical History: The Stories and Their Meaning,* ed. Frank Huisman and John Harley Warner (Baltimore: Johns Hopkins University Press, 2004), 390–409.

34. See, for example, Justine M. Schober, "A Surgeon's Response to the Intersex Controversy," in Dreger, *Intersex in the Age of Ethics,* 161–68; Bruce E. Wilson and William G. Reiner, "Management of Intersex: A Shifting Paradigm," in Dreger, *Intersex in the Age of Ethics,* 119–35.

35. See, for example, Dreger, "Cultural History and Social Activism"; Heino F. L. Meyer-Bahlburg et al., "Attitudes of Adult 46,XY Intersex Persons to Clinical Management Policies," *Journal of Urology* 171 (2004): 1615–19; Lee et al., "Consensus Statement"; Justine M. Schober, "Feminization (Surgical Aspects)," in *Pediatric Surgery and Urology: Long-Term Outcomes,* ed. Mark D. Stringer, Keith D. Oldham, and Peter D. E. Moriquand, 2nd ed. (Cambridge: Cambridge University Press, 2006), 595–610; and Schober, "Surgeon's Response."

36. Alice Domurat Dreger, "Agonize—Then Cut This Way" (2004), www.isna.org/articles/aap_urology_2004.

37. Lee et al., "Consensus Statement."

38. Consortium on the Management of Disorders of Sex Development, *Clinical Guidelines for the Management of Disorders of Sex Development in Childhood* (Rohnert Park, CA: Intersex Society of North America, 2006), and *Handbook for Parents* (Rohnert Park, CA: Intersex Society of North America, 2006). Both books can be read and downloaded from www.dsdguidelines.org.

39. Consortium, *Clinical Guidelines,* 2–3; emphases in original.

40. Dreger, "Ambiguous Sex"; Alice Domurat Dreger, *One of Us: Conjoined Twins and the Future of Normal* (Cambridge, MA: Harvard University Press, 2004).

41. See, for example, Lee et al., "Consensus Statement."

42. Morgan Holmes, "Queer Cut Bodies," in *Queer Frontiers: Millennial Geographies, Genders, and Generations,* ed. Joseph A. Boone et al., (Madison: University of Wisconsin Press, 2000), 84–110.

43. Chase, "Hermaphrodites with Attitude"; Dreger, "Cultural History and Social Activism"; Sharon E. Preves, "Out of the O.R. and into the Streets: Exploring the Impact of Intersex Media Activism," *Research in Political Sociology* 13 (2004): 179–223.

44. Martha Coventry, "Making the Cut," *Ms.,* October–November, 2000, 52–60; Esther Marguerite Morris Leidolf, "The Missing Vagina Monologue," *Sojourner* 27 (2001): 20–21, 28; Triea, "Power, Orgasm, and the Psychohormonal Research Unit."

45. Virginia Braun, "In Search of (Better) Sexual Pleasure: Female Genital 'Cosmetic' Surgery," *Sexualities* 8 (2005): 407–24.

46. April Herndon, "What Are Disorders of Sex Development?" (originally written for www.isna.org), www.alicedreger.com/herndon/DSDs (accessed June 5, 2007).

47. Elizabeth Reis, "Divergence or Disorder? The Politics of Naming Intersex," *Perspectives in Biology and Medicine* 50 (2007): 535–43.

48. Nowadays *intersex* is commonly used as both an adjective and as a noun. Previously *intersexed* had been the standard adjective.

49. Kiira Triea, pers. comm., August 31, 2006.

50. Alice Domurat Dreger, "Is XXY Intersex?" *ISNA News,* Fall 2002, 2.

51. William G. Reiner and John P. Gearhart, "Discordant Sexual Identity in Some Genetic Males with Cloacal Exstrophy Assigned to Female Sex at Birth," *New England Journal of Medicine* 350 (2004): 333–41.

52. Preves, *Intersex and Identity,* 148.

53. Alice Domurat Dreger et al., "Changing the Nomenclature/Taxonomy for Intersex: A Scientific and Clinical Rationale," *Journal of Pediatric Endocrinology and Metabolism* 18 (2005): 729–33.

54. Lee et al., "Consensus Statement."

55. Reis, "Divergence or Disorder?"

56. Herndon, "What Are Disorders?"

57. Reis, "Divergence or Disorder?"

58. For the reasoning behind this, see Heino F. L. Meyer-Bahlburg, "Intersexuality and the Diagnosis of Gender Identity Disorder," *Archives of Sexual Behavior* 23 (1994): 21–40.

59. Cheryl Chase, pers. comm., September 7, 2006.

60. Triea, "Learning about Transsexuality"; April Herndon, "What's the Difference between Being Transgender or Transsexual and Having an Intersex Condition?" Intersex Society of North America, www.isna.org/faq/transgender (accessed July 29, 2008).

61. Leslie Feinberg, *Transgender Warriors: Making History from Joan of Arc to Dennis Rodman* (New York: Beacon, 1997), 98.

62. Feinberg, *Transgender Warriors,* 99; emphasis in original.

63. April Herndon, "Fat and Intersex?" (2005), www.isna.org/node/961. This practice has also been extended to intersex people; Iain Morland, who was born intersex, has had his motives questioned online because he has also identified himself as a researcher (pers. comm., December 31, 2006).

64. Dreger, *Hermaphrodites;* Fausto-Sterling, "Five Sexes" and *Sexing the Body;* Myra J. Hird, "Gender's Nature: Intersexuals, Transsexuals, and the 'Sex'/'Gender' Binary," *Feminist Theory* 1 (2000): 347–64; Holmes, "Doctor Will Fix Everything"; Iain

Morland, "Is Intersexuality Real?" *Textual Practice* 15 (2001): 527–47.

65. Judith Butler, "Doing Justice to Someone: Sex Reassignment and Allegories of Trans-sexuality," *GLQ* 7 (2001): 624–25.

66. Dreger, *Hermaphrodites.*

67. See, for example, Kessler, "Medical Construction of Gender."

68. Dreger, "Cultural History and Social Activism."

69. Germaine Greer, "Greer Replies to the Father," www.medhelp.org/www/ais/debates/letters/father.htm (accessed July 29, 2008).

70. Iain Morland, "Postmodern Intersex," in *Ethics and Intersex,* ed. Sharon E. Sytsma (Dordrecht: Springer, 2006), 328.

71. Reiner and Gearhart, "Discordant Sexual Identity."

72. Kate Bornstein, *Gender Outlaw: On Men, Women, and the Rest of Us* (New York: Routledge, 1994).

73. Diana Fuss, *Essentially Speaking: Feminism, Nature, and Difference* (New York: Routledge, 1989).

74. Cheryl Chase, "What Is the Agenda of the Intersex Patient Advocacy Movement?" *Endocrinologist* 13 (2003): 240.

75. Meyer-Bahlburg, "Intersexuality," 21; emphasis added.

76. See, for example, Meyer-Bahlburg et al., "Attitudes of Adult 46, XY Intersex Persons."

77. See, for example, the narratives of people with intersex discussed in Kessler, *Lessons from the Intersexed* and Preves, *Intersex and Identity.*

78. *Yellow for Hermaphrodite: Mani's Story,* dir. John Keir, Greenstone Pictures, 2004.

79. Intersex Society of North America, "What Evidence Is There?"

80. Intersex Society of North America, "Why Doesn't ISNA Want to Eradicate Gender?" (2006), www.isna.org/faq/not_eradicating_gender.

81. Judith Butler, *Gender Trouble: Feminism and the Subversion of Identity* (New York: Routledge, 1990), 33.

82. Feinberg, *Transgender Warriors,* 83.

83. Bornstein, *Gender Outlaw,* 7–8.

84. April Herndon, ed., *Teaching Intersex Issues* (Rohnert Park, CA: Intersex Society of North America, 2006).

Critical Thinking

1. Discuss the extent to which the goals set by key activists in the intersex rights movement have been realized.

2. In what ways has the intersex rights movement been successful in North America and Europe?

From *GLQ: A Journal of Lesbian and Gay Studies,* vol 15, no. 2, pp. 199–224. Copyright © 2009 by Duke University Press. Reprinted by permission.

Finding the Switch

Homosexuality may persist because the associated genes convey surprising advantages on homosexuals' family members.

ROBERT KUNZIG

If there is one thing that has always seemed obvious about homosexuality, it's that it just doesn't make sense. Evolution favors traits that aid reproduction, and being gay clearly doesn't do that. The existence of homosexuality amounts to a profound evolutionary mystery, since failing to pass on your genes means that your genetic fitness is a resounding zero. "Homosexuality is effectively like sterilization," says psychobiologist Qazi Rahman of Queen Mary College in London. "You'd think evolution would get rid of it." Yet as far as historians can tell, homosexuality has always been with us. So the question remains: If it's such a disadvantage in the evolutionary rat race, why was it not selected into oblivion millennia ago?

Twentieth-century psychiatry had an answer for this Darwinian paradox: Homosexuality was not a biological trait at all but a psychological defect. It was a mistake, one that was always being created anew, in each generation, by bad parenting. Freud considered homosexuality a form of arrested development stamped on a child by a distant father or an overprotective mother. Homosexuality was even listed by the American Psychiatric Association as a mental disorder, and the idea that gays could and should be "cured" was widely accepted. But modern scientific research has not been kind to that idea. It turns out that parents of gay men are no better or worse than those of heterosexuals. And homosexual behavior is common in the animal kingdom, as well—among sheep, for instance. It arises naturally and does not seem to be a matter of aloof rams or overbearing ewes.

More is known about homosexuality in men than in women, whose sexuality appears more fluid. The consensus now is that people are "born gay," as the title of a recent book by Rahman and British psychologist Glenn Wilson puts it. But for decades, researchers have sought to identify the mechanism that *makes* a person gay.

Something seems to flip the sexuality switch before birth—but what? In many cases, homosexuality appears to be genetic. The best scientific surveys put the number of gays in the general population between 2 and 6 percent, with most estimates near the low end of that range—contrary to the 10 percent figure that is often reported in the popular media. But we know gayness is not entirely genetic, because in pairs of identical twins, it's often the case that one is gay and the other is not. Studies suggest there is a genetic basis for homosexuality in only 50 percent of gay men.

No one has yet identified a particular gay gene, but Brian Mustanski, a psychologist at the University of Illinois at Chicago, is examining a gene that helps time the release of testosterone from the testes of a male fetus. Testosterone masculinizes the fetal genitalia—and presumably also the brain. Without it, the fetus stays female. It may be that the brains of gay men don't feel the full effects of testosterone at the right time during fetal development, and so are insufficiently masculinized.

But if that gene does prove to be a gay gene, it's unlikely to be the only one. Whatever brain structures are responsible for sexual orientation must emerge from a complex chain of molecular events, one that can be disrupted at many links. Gay genes could be genes for hormones, enzymes that modify hormones, or receptors on the surface of brain cells that bind to those hormones. A mutation in any one of those genes might make a person gay.

Having some gay genes might promote feminine traits in straight men, making them kinder, gentler, more nurturing—and as a result, women may be more likely to choose them as mates.

More likely it will take mutations in more than one gene. And that, as Rahman and Wilson and other researchers have suggested, is one solution to the Darwinian paradox: Gay genes might survive because so long as a man doesn't have enough of them to make him gay, they increase the reproductive success of the woman he mates with. Biologists call it "sexually antagonistic selection," meaning a trait survives in one sex only because it is useful to the other. Nipples—useless to men, vital to women—are one example, and homosexuality maybe another. By interfering with the masculinization of the brain, gay genes might promote feminine behavior traits, making men who carry them kinder, gentler, more nurturing—"less aggressive and psychopathic than the typical male," as Rahman and Wilson put it. Such men may be more likely to help raise children rather than kill them—or each other—and as a result, women may be more likely to choose them as mates.

In this way, over thousands of generations of sexual selection, feminizing genes may have spread through the male population.

163

When the number of such genes exceeds a certain threshold in a man, they may flip the switch and make him want to have sex with other men. Evolutionarily speaking, that is bad for him. But for the women who are doing the selecting, the loss of a small number of potential mates may be a small price to pay for creating a much larger number of the kind of men they want.

Some gay genes may benefit women more directly—to the detriment of their own sons. The evidence comes from groundbreaking studies by Andrea Camperio-Ciani, a researcher at the University of Padua in Italy. Camperio was interested in understanding the evolutionary paradox and began by replicating a family-tree study done in the early 1990s by geneticist Dean Hamer of the National Institutes of Health. Hamer had concluded that some cases of homosexuality are passed down on the X chromosome, which a boy receives from his mother. Camperio and his colleagues compared the family trees of gay men to those of straight men, and confirmed that homosexuals had more gay male relatives on their mother's side than on their father's side—which suggests an X-linked trait. But the Italian researchers also found something more intriguing: Compared with the straight men, the gay men had more relatives, period.

Camperio did not quite know at first what to make of these results—or how they might help him understand the Darwinian paradox of homosexuality. Then one day, he was driving through the forest with his daughter, on the way to their country house. Their tradition was to play mathematical games to keep themselves entertained. This time, he began talking about a different puzzle. "I began explaining my research," Camperio recalls. "I explained to her that we found out that homosexuals come from large families. I told her that there is an inheritance from the mother—she's giving the homosexual genes to her son. I said, 'This is impossible—how can they be surviving?'"

His daughter, 15, replied, "But Dad, did you check if this factor that makes sons homosexual is not the same factor that makes the mother produce more children and have big families?"

Camperio stopped the car, looked her in the eyes, and said, "Shit! What is this? It's a great suggestion!"

The next day he left his daughter in the country and went back to the lab to investigate the idea. Sure enough, the mothers of homosexuals in the study did indeed have between a quarter and a third more children than the mothers of heterosexuals. Camperio also uncovered another dramatic finding: In families with gay sons, the aunts from the mother's side had many more children than the aunts on the father's side—the large families, in other words, were on the maternal side. Camperio realized his daughter was right. "There was something in the genes that, in the male, changed his sexual orientation, and in the female, increased her probability of having children," he says.

What could it be? Camperio spent the next few years going to gay men and begging them to let him interview their mothers and aunts—a daunting task in deeply Catholic Italy. In the end, it took him three years to get 30 subjects. When he interviewed the women, though, he found they had fewer miscarriages, fewer infections, and used fewer contraceptives than the mothers and aunts of heterosexuals, though the differences were only slight. One difference, though, was not slight at all: The homosexuals' mothers and aunts had had between *three and four times* as many sexual partners. They seemed to really like having sex with men.

Perhaps mothers of gays have a "man-loving" gene—that makes them more sexually active, and makes their sons gay.

Camperio's explanation for all this relies, like Rahman and Wilson's hypothesis, on sexually antagonistic selection. Perhaps, he suggests, the mothers of some homosexuals have a "man-loving" gene. In women, it would be adaptive, causing them to have more sex and more children. But in men, the "man-loving" gene would be expressed differently, causing homosexuality. To the gay sons, that would be an evolutionary disadvantage—but one outweighed by the advantage to the mothers, who would have more than enough other children to compensate. And so gayness in men would persist in these families—as a side effect of a trait that is beneficial to the women.

But even Camperio says his results can explain no more than 20 percent of the incidence of homosexuality. "The more we study, the more we find there will be other mechanisms," he says. His research confirms that there are many ways to become gay—including, perhaps, one way that is much stranger than the rest.

The gay men in Camperio's study didn't just have larger families than the straight men. They also had more older brothers—and not just because they came from larger families. It's true across the board: The more older brothers a man has, the more likely he is to be gay. The "fraternal birth order effect" was first uncovered by Ray Blanchard and Anthony Bogaert of the Center for Addiction and Mental Health in Toronto, and has since been replicated by a dozen other studies.

For every older brother a man has, his chances of being gay go up by around a third. In other words, if you have two older brothers, you're nearly twice as likely to be gay—regardless of whether the older brothers are themselves gay. It is not possible to explain that as an effect of genetics.

Some researchers have tried to explain it as an effect the older brothers have on their sibling's environment. Perhaps a boy grows up homosexual, one argument goes, because the presence of older brothers means more incestuous sex play early in life. Or perhaps their presence makes his parents treat him differently.

But in another study, Bogaert found that it was only *biological* older brothers that contributed to the effect. Men who grew up with older stepbrothers or adopted brothers—brothers born of different wombs—were no more likely to become gay. Meanwhile, men with biological older brothers who died in infancy or who were raised separately—including brothers they had never even met and sometimes didn't even know about—*did* manifest the effect. In other words, the effect could not be explained through upbringing.

If it wasn't genetic and it wasn't upbringing, then what could it possibly be? The answer is the prenatal environment—the result of something that occurs as the fetus develops in the womb.

So what happens in the womb to make a fetus gay? Researchers can only speculate, but Blanchard and Bogaert suggest the older-brother effect could result from a mother's immune reaction against her male fetuses. During her first male pregnancy, the mother's body reacts against some factor related to male fetal development. Her immune system detects male-specific proteins produced by the boy's Y chromosome—perhaps proteins located on the surface of his brain cells—and deems them foreign invaders. As a result, her body generates antibodies against them. Each successive male pregnancy strengthens this immune response. The next time she's pregnant, the anti-male antibodies cross through the placenta and influence the fetus's brain, interfering with the masculinization of his brain and making him gay.

It may even be that women with strong immune systems are more likely to produce gay sons. The reproductive advantages to her of having such a healthy constitution might outweigh the disadvantages of occasionally producing a son who will have no kids himself. Even if the immunization scenario is true, however, it explains only 15 to 30 percent of the cases of male homosexuality. "My theory is not meant to explain homosexuality in all males—obviously not in first-born males," says Blanchard. "And it does not explain homosexuality in women at all." It's really just a "working hypothesis," says Bogaert, for a strange and puzzling phenomenon.

Most recently, Bogaert, Blanchard, and their colleagues have found that older brothers increase the likelihood of homosexuality only in men who are right-handed—even though left-handed men are more likely to be gay in general. "We don't really know what that means," says Bogaert. It's one more piece of evidence, though, that homosexuality is determined biologically, before birth—just like handedness. As often happens with science, the mystery deepens and becomes more complicated before the ultimate pattern finally reveals itself.

So how do the pieces fit together? So far, they don't. Rather, they exist side by side. "There is no all-inclusive explanation for the variation in sexual orientation, at least none supported by actual evidence," says geneticist Alan Sanders of Northwestern University. It's one of the most consistent themes to emerge from the literature on homosexuality: the idea that there are many different mechanisms, not a single one, for producing homosexuality. Neither Camperio nor Bogaert sees much of a connection between the female-fecundity theory and the older-brother effect "They are somewhat disparate," Bogaert says. "But that is compatible with the idea that there are multiple biological pathways affecting sexual orientation."

The biggest gap in the science of homosexuality concerns lesbians: Much less research has been done on them than on men. That's because women's sexuality seems to be more complicated and fluid—women are much more likely to report fantasizing about both sexes, or to change how they report their sexual orientation over time—which makes it harder to study. "Maybe we're measuring sexual orientation totally wrong in women," says Mustanski. Rahman and Wilson suggest that lesbianism might result from "masculinizing" genes that, when not present to excess, make a woman a more aggressively protective and thus successful mother—just as feminizing genes might make a man a more caring father.

Right now, there is no one all-inclusive solution to the Darwinian mystery of why homosexuality survives, and no grand unified theory of how it arises in a given individual. Homosexuality seems to arise as a result of various perturbations in the flow from genes to hormones to brains to behavior—as the common end point of multiple

The Gay Science

Test your knowledge about breaking research on homosexuality.

True or False

1. 10 to 12 percent of men are gay.
2. Gay men have longer, thicker penises than straight men, on average.
3. As children, most gay men display gender-bending behavior, like dressing up in their sisters' clothes or playing with dolls.
4. In general, gay men are worse than straight men at certain cognitive skills, like reading maps, spatial orientation, finding missing objects, and packing trunks.
5. Lesbians are better than straight women at certain spatial, navigational, and language tasks.
6. Men with the most masculine voices tend to be straight.
7. Gay men often have distant fathers, suggesting that levels of childhood affection have an effect on sexual orientation.
8. The more older brothers you have, the more likely you are to be gay.
9. Sexual orientation correlates with whether you are right- or left-handed.
10. The ratio of the lengths of the second to fourth fingers predicts sexual orientation.

ANSWERS: 1. False: 2 to 6 percent of men are gay. **2.** True. **3.** True. **4.** True. **5.** True. **6.** False. The voices rated as most masculine are those of gay men (and the most feminine are those of lesbians). **7.** False, though some fathers may become distant in reaction to childhood gender nonconformity of boys who are born gay. **8.** True. **9.** True. Homosexuals are 39 percent more likely to be left-handed or ambidextrous. **10.** True.

biological paths, all of which seem to survive as side effects of various traits that help heterosexuals pass along their genes.

"It's the fundamental question for the next 10 years," says Mustanski. "How do these things interact? What is the model that explains all these things?"

Critical Thinking

1. What is meant by "sexual orientation"?
2. What role does nurture play in the development of sexual orientation?
3. Evaluate the idea that there are multiple developmental pathways to homosexual orientations, including multiple biological influences.

ROBERT KUNZIG is a freelance writer living in France and Alabama.

From *Psychology Today*, May/June 2008, pp. 89–93. Copyright © 2008 by Sussex Publishers, LLC. Reprinted by permission.

Children of Lesbian and Gay Parents

Does parental sexual orientation affect child development, and if so, how? Studies using convenience samples, studies using samples drawn from known populations, and studies based on samples that are representative of larger populations all converge on similar conclusions. More than two decades of research has failed to reveal important differences in the adjustment or development of children or adolescents reared by same-sex couples compared to those reared by other-sex couples. Results of the research suggest that qualities of family relationships are more tightly linked with child outcomes than is parental sexual orientation.

CHARLOTTE J. PATTERSON

Does parental sexual orientation affect child development, and if so, how? This question has often been raised in the context of legal and policy proceedings relevant to children, such as those involving adoption, child custody, or visitation. Divergent views have been offered by professionals from the fields of psychology, sociology, medicine, and law (Patterson, Fulcher, & Wainright, 2002). While this question has most often been raised in legal and policy contexts, it is also relevant to theoretical issues. For example, does healthy human development require that a child grow up with parents of each gender? And if not, what would that mean for our theoretical understanding of parent–child relations? (Patterson & Hastings, in press) In this article, I describe some research designed to address these questions.

Early Research

Research on children with lesbian and gay parents began with studies focused on cases in which children had been born in the context of a heterosexual marriage. After parental separation and divorce, many children in these families lived with divorced lesbian mothers. A number of researchers compared development among children of divorced lesbian mothers with that among children of divorced heterosexual mothers and found few significant differences (Patterson, 1997; Stacey & Biblarz, 2001).

These studies were valuable in addressing concerns of judges who were required to decide divorce and child custody cases, but they left many questions unanswered. In particular, because the children who participated in this research had been born into homes with married mothers and fathers, it was not obvious how to understand the reasons for their healthy development. The possibility that children's early exposure to apparently heterosexual male and female role models had contributed to healthy development could not be ruled out.

When lesbian or gay parents rear infants and children from birth, do their offspring grow up in typical ways and show healthy development? To address this question, it was important to study children who had never lived with heterosexual parents. In the 1990s, a number of investigators began research of this kind.

An early example was the Bay Area Families Study, in which I studied a group of 4- to 9-year-old children who had been born to or adopted early in life by lesbian mothers (Patterson, 1996, 1997). Data were collected during home visits. Results from in-home interviews and also from questionnaires showed that children had regular contact with a wide range of adults of both genders, both within and outside of their families. The children's self-concepts and preferences for same-gender playmates and activities were much like those of other children their ages. Moreover, standardized measures of social competence and of behavior problems, such as those from the Child Behavior Checklist (CBCL), showed that they scored within the range of normal variation for a representative sample of same-aged American children. It was clear from this study and others like it that it was quite possible for lesbian mothers to rear healthy children.

Studies Based on Samples Drawn from Known Populations

Interpretation of the results from the Bay Area Families Study was, however, affected by its sampling procedures. The study had been based on a convenience sample that had been assembled by word of mouth. It was therefore impossible to rule out the possibility that families who participated in the research were especially well adjusted. Would a more representative sample yield different results?

To find out, Ray Chan, Barbara Raboy, and I conducted research in collaboration with the Sperm Bank of California (Chan, Raboy, & Patterson, 1998; Fulcher, Sutfin, Chan,

Scheib, & Patterson, 2005). Over the more than 15 years of its existence, the Sperm Bank of California's clientele had included many lesbian as well as heterosexual women. For research purposes, this clientele was a finite population from which our sample could be drawn. The Sperm Bank of California also allowed a sample in which, both for lesbian and for heterosexual groups, one parent was biologically related to the child and one was not.

We invited all clients who had conceived children using the resources of the Sperm Bank of California and who had children 5 years old or older to participate in our research. The resulting sample was composed of 80 families, 55 headed by lesbian and 25 headed by heterosexual parents. Materials were mailed to participating families, with instructions to complete them privately and return them in self-addressed stamped envelopes we provided.

Results replicated and expanded upon those from earlier research. Children of lesbian and heterosexual parents showed similar, relatively high levels of social competence, as well as similar, relatively low levels of behavior problems on the parent form of the CBCL. We also asked the children's teachers to provide evaluations of children's adjustment on the Teacher Report Form of the CBCL, and their reports agreed with those of parents. Parental sexual orientation was not related to children's adaptation. Quite apart from parental sexual orientation, however, and consistent with findings from years of research on children of heterosexual parents, when parent–child relationships were marked by warmth and affection, children were more likely to be developing well. Thus, in this sample drawn from a known population, measures of children's adjustment were unrelated to parental sexual orientation (Chan et al., 1998; Fulcher et al., 2005).

Even as they provided information about children born to lesbian mothers, however, these new results also raised additional questions. Women who conceive children at sperm banks are generally both well educated and financially comfortable. It was possible that these relatively privileged women were able to protect children from many forms of discrimination. What if a more diverse group of families were to be studied? In addition, the children in this sample averaged 7 years of age, and some concerns focus on older children and adolescents. What if an older group of youngsters were to be studied? Would problems masked by youth and privilege in earlier studies emerge in an older, more diverse sample?

Studies Based on Representative Samples

An opportunity to address these questions was presented by the availability of data from the National Longitudinal Study of Adolescent Health (Add Health). The Add Health study involved a large, ethnically diverse, and essentially representative sample of American adolescents and their parents. Data for our research were drawn from surveys and interviews completed by more than 12,000 adolescents and their parents at home and from surveys completed by adolescents at school.

Parents were not queried directly about their sexual orientation but were asked if they were involved in a "marriage, or marriage-like relationship." If parents acknowledged such a relationship, they were also asked the gender of their partner. Thus, we identified a group of 44 12- to 18-year-olds who lived with parents involved in marriage or marriage-like relationships with same-sex partners. We compared them with a matched group of adolescents living with other-sex couples. Data from the archives of the Add Health study allowed us to address many questions about adolescent development.

Consistent with earlier findings, results of this work revealed few differences in adjustment between adolescents living with same-sex parents and those living with opposite-sex parents (Wainright, Russell, & Patterson, 2004; Wainright & Patterson, 2006). There were no significant differences between teenagers living with same-sex parents and those living with other-sex parents on self-reported assessments of psychological well-being, such as self-esteem and anxiety; measures of school outcomes, such as grade point averages and trouble in school; or measures of family relationships, such as parental warmth and care from adults and peers. Adolescents in the two groups were equally likely to say that they had been involved in a romantic relationship in the last 18 months, and they were equally likely to report having engaged in sexual intercourse. The only statistically reliable difference between the two groups—that those with same-sex parents felt a greater sense of connection to people at school—favored the youngsters living with same-sex couples. There were no significant differences in self-reported substance use, delinquency, or peer victimization between those reared by same- or other-sex couples (Wainright & Patterson, 2006).

Although the gender of parents' partners was not an important predictor of adolescent well-being, other aspects of family relationships were significantly associated with teenagers' adjustment. Consistent with other findings about adolescent development, the qualities of family relationships rather than the gender of parents' partners were consistently related to adolescent outcomes. Parents who reported having close relationships with their offspring had adolescents who reported more favorable adjustment. Not only is it possible for children and adolescents who are parented by same-sex couples to develop in healthy directions, but—even when studied in an extremely diverse, representative sample of American adolescents—they generally do.

These findings have been supported by results from many other studies, both in the United States and abroad. Susan Golombok and her colleagues have reported similar results with a near-representative sample of children in the United Kingdom (Golombok et al., 2003). Others, both in Europe and in the United States, have described similar findings (e.g., Brewaeys, Ponjaert, Van Hall, & Golombok, 1997).

The fact that children of lesbian mothers generally develop in healthy ways should not be taken to suggest that they encounter no challenges. Many investigators have remarked upon the fact that children of lesbian and gay parents may encounter anti-gay sentiments in their daily lives. For example, in a study of

10-year-old children born to lesbian mothers, Gartrell, Deck, Rodas, Peyser, and Banks (2005) reported that a substantial minority had encountered anti-gay sentiments among their peers. Those who had had such encounters were likely to report having felt angry, upset, or sad about these experiences. Children of lesbian and gay parents may be exposed to prejudice against their parents in some settings, and this may be painful for them, but evidence for the idea that such encounters affect children's overall adjustment is lacking.

Conclusions

Does parental sexual orientation have an important impact on child or adolescent development? Results of recent research provide no evidence that it does. In fact, the findings suggest that parental sexual orientation is less important than the qualities of family relationships. More important to youth than the gender of their parent's partner is the quality of daily interaction and the strength of relationships with the parents they have.

One possible approach to findings like the ones described above might be to shrug them off by reiterating the familiar adage that "one cannot prove the null hypothesis." To respond in this way, however, is to miss the central point of these studies. Whether or not any measurable impact of parental sexual orientation on children's development is ever demonstrated, the main conclusions from research to date remain clear: Whatever correlations between child outcomes and parental sexual orientation may exist, they are less important than those between child outcomes and the qualities of family relationships.

Although research to date has made important contributions, many issues relevant to children of lesbian and gay parents remain in need of study. Relatively few studies have examined the development of children adopted by lesbian or gay parents or of children born to gay fathers; further research in both areas would be welcome (Patterson, 2004). Some notable longitudinal studies have been reported, and they have found children of same-sex couples to be in good mental health. Greater understanding of family relationships and transitions over time would, however, be helpful, and longitudinal studies would be valuable. Future research could also benefit from the use of a variety of methodologies.

Meanwhile, the clarity of findings in this area has been acknowledged by a number of major professional organizations. For instance, the governing body of the American Psychological Association (APA) voted unanimously in favor of a statement that said, "Research has shown that the adjustment, development, and psychological well-being of children is unrelated to parental sexual orientation and that children of lesbian and gay parents are as likely as those of heterosexual parents to flourish" (APA, 2004). The American Bar Association, the American Medical Association, the American Academy of Pediatrics, the American Psychiatric Association, and other mainstream professional groups have issued similar statements.

The findings from research on children of lesbian and gay parents have been used to inform legal and public policy debates across the country (Patterson et al., 2002). The research literature on this subject has been cited in amicus briefs filed by the APA in cases dealing with adoption, child custody, and also in cases related to the legality of marriages between same-sex partners. Psychologists serving as expert witnesses have presented findings on these issues in many different courts (Patterson et al., 2002). Through these and other avenues, results of research on lesbian and gay parents and their children are finding their way into public discourse.

The findings are also beginning to address theoretical questions about critical issues in parenting. The importance of gender in parenting is one such issue. When children fare well in two-parent lesbian-mother or gay-father families, this suggests that the gender of one's parents cannot be a critical factor in child development. Results of research on children of lesbian and gay parents cast doubt upon the traditional assumption that gender is important in parenting. Our data suggest that it is the quality of parenting rather than the gender of parents that is significant for youngsters' development.

Research on children of lesbian and gay parents is thus located at the intersection of a number of classic and contemporary concerns. Studies of lesbian- and gay-parented families allow researchers to address theoretical questions that had previously remained difficult or impossible to answer. They also address oft-debated legal questions of fact about development of children with lesbian and gay parents. Thus, research on children of lesbian and gay parents contributes to public debate and legal decision making, as well as to theoretical understanding of human development.

References

American Psychological Association (2004). Resolution on sexual orientation, parents, and children. Retrieved September 25, 2006, from www.apa.org/pi/lgbc/policy/parentschildren.pdf

Brewaeys, A., Ponjaert, I., Van Hall, E.V., & Golombok, S. (1997). Donor insemination: Child development and family functioning in lesbian mother families. *Human Reproduction, 12,* 1349–1359.

Chan, R.W., Raboy, B., & Patterson, C.J. (1998). Psychosocial adjustment among children conceived via donor insemination by lesbian and heterosexual mothers. *Child Development, 69,* 443–457.

Fulcher, M., Sutfin, E.L., Chan, R.W., Scheib, J.E., & Patterson, C.J. (2005). Lesbian mothers and their children: Findings from the Contemporary Families Study. In A. Omoto & H. Kurtzman (Eds.), *Recent research on sexual orientation, mental health, and substance abuse* (pp. 281–299). Washington, DC: American Psychological Association.

Gartrell, N., Deck., A., Rodas, C., Peyser, H., & Banks, A. (2005). The National Lesbian Family Study: 4. Interviews with the 10-year-old children. *American Journal of Orthopsychiatry, 75,* 518–524.

Golombok, S., Perry, B., Burston, A., Murray, C., Mooney-Somers, J., Stevens, M., & Golding, J. (2003). Children with lesbian parents: A community study. *Developmental Psychology, 39,* 20–33.

Patterson, C.J. (1996). Lesbian mothers and their children: Findings from the Bay Area Families Study. In J. Laird & R.J. Green

(Eds.), *Lesbians and gays in couples and families: A handbook for therapists* (pp. 420–437). San Francisco: Jossey-Bass.

Patterson, C.J. (1997). Children of lesbian and gay parents. In T. Ollendick & R. Prinz (Eds.), *Advances in clinical child psychology* (vol. 19, pp. 235–282). New York: Plenum Press.

Patterson, C.J. (2004). Gay fathers. In M.E. Lamb (Ed.), *The role of the father in child development* (4th ed., pp. 397–416). New York: Wiley.

Patterson, C.J., Fulcher, M., & Wainright, J. (2002). Children of lesbian and gay parents: Research, law, and policy. In B.L. Bottoms, M.B. Kovera, & B.D. McAuliff (Eds.), *Children, social science and the law* (pp. 176–199). New York: Cambridge University Press.

Patterson, C.J., & Hastings, P. (in press). Socialization in context of family diversity. In J. Grusec & P. Hastings (Eds.), *Handbook of socialization.* New York: Guilford Press.

Stacey, J., & Biblarz, T.J. (2001). (How) Does sexual orientation of parents matter? *American Sociological Review, 65,* 159–183.

Wainright, J.L., & Patterson, C.J. (2006). Delinquency, victimization, and substance use among adolescents with female same-sex parents. *Journal of Family Psychology, 20,* 526–530.

Wainright, J.L., Russell, S.T., & Patterson, C.J. (2004). Psychosocial adjustment and school outcomes of adolescents with same-sex parents. *Child Development, 75,* 1886–1898.

Critical Thinking

1. What impact does parental sexual orientation have on child development?

2. What are the similarities and differences in children raised by heterosexual parents and children raised by homosexual parents?

Address correspondence to **CHARLOTTE J. PATTERSON,** Department of Psychology, P.O. Box 400400, University of Virginia, Charlottesville, VA 22904; e-mail: cjp@virginia.edu.

UNIT 6

Sexual Health and Well-Being

Unit Selections

Learning Outcomes

After reading this Unit, you will be able to:

- Describe the origin of the new mammogram guidelines.
- Describe the new mammogram guidelines and how they differ from the old guidelines.
- Identify the questions that are raised on the soundness of the new mammogram guidelines.
- Explain how gender, health, and illness intersect.
- Determine what impact the social construction of masculinity has on health.
- Evaluate the consequences of body dissatisfaction for boys and girls.
- Discuss the prevalence of condom use in the United States today.
- Discuss the concept of "hooking up" among college students.
- Identify the sexual risk-taking behaviors that are common among college students.
- Describe how boys and girls are different in body dissatisfaction.
- Discuss the availability of antiretroviral therapy in African countries.
- Describe the recommended approach to antiretroviral therapy.
- Describe the effectiveness of post-exposure prophylaxis treatment to prevent HIV.
- Evaluate the current challenges to broader access to post-exposure prophylaxis.
- Discuss the problems that HIV still presents in Western countries.
- Discuss HIV as a deadly disease, despite antiretroviral therapies.

Student Website

www.mhhe.com/cls

Internet References

The Body: The Complete HIV/AIDS Resource
www.thebody.com

The Johns Hopkins University HIV Guide
www.hopkins-aids.edu

National Cancer Institute: Breast Cancer
www.cancer.gov/cancertopics/types/breast

National Cancer Institute: Ovarian Cancer
www.cancer.gov/cancertopics/types/ovarian

National Cancer Institute: Testicular Cancer
www.cancer.gov/cancertopics/types/testicular

SexInfo: Sexually Transmitted Infections
www.soc.ucsb.edu/sexinfo/category/sexually-transmitted-infections

World Health Organization: Sexual Health
www.who.int/topics/sexual_health/en

The readings found in Unit 6 all focus on Sexual Health and Well-Being. Health, including sexual health, now receives a significant amount of attention in the mainstream media. Over the past two decades, the general public's awareness of, and interest and involvement in, their own health care has dramatically increased. We want to stay healthy and live longer, and we know that to do so, we must learn more about our bodies, including how to prevent problems, recognize danger signs, and find the most effective treatments. By the same token, if we want to stay sexually fit—from robust youth through a healthy, happy, sexy old age—we must be knowledgeable about sexual health care. This is one of the most important and fundamental topics covered in any human sexuality course. The urgency of this topic is demonstrated by the fact that this is one area of the sexuality curriculum in which all adult students seem highly interested.

Healthy sexualities are multifaceted and influenced by biological, psychological, and social factors. The World Health Organization (WHO) defines sexual health as follows:

> Sexual health is a state of physical, emotional, mental and social well-being in relation to sexuality; it is not merely the absence of disease, dysfunction, or infirmity. Sexual health requires a positive and respectful approach to sexuality and sexual relationships, as well as the possibility of having pleasurable and safe sexual experiences, free of coercion, discrimination, and violence. For sexual health to be attained and maintained, the sexual rights of all persons must be respected, protected, and fulfilled.

Many people seem to think of sexual health as simply "the absence of disease," but as the WHO definition indicates, it is so much more than that. Simply not having a sexually transmitted infection or a reproductive cancer is not enough. Cognitive, behavioral, and emotional components are important as well.

The meanings given to sexual behaviors and interactions will greatly influence the ways in which sexualities are experienced. Anxiety, fear, and shame are hardly conducive to healthy sexualities. The WHO definition makes mention of variables such as discrimination, violence, and sexual rights. Institutionalized discrimination and culturally validated violence are profoundly social in nature. The notion of sexual rights is hardly universal. Social and cultural processes play an important role in the sexual health of everyday people. To go back to a theme that has been present in readings throughout this book, we are simultaneously biological, psychological, and social beings. The area of sexual health is, in this way, no different from many other topics we have considered in this book.

The above discussion in no way minimizes the important and perhaps central role that disease (or lack thereof) plays in sexual health. In fact, many of the readings in this unit focus squarely on infections and disease; cancers and sexually transmitted infections being the primary interest. Even with physical disease states, there are often behavioral, psychological, and

© Steve Cole/Getty Images

sociocultural components that must be understood. This unit addresses all of this. There are many potential threats to our sexual health and well-being. Sexual or reproductive cancers, such as breast cancer, cervical cancer, ovarian cancer, male breast cancer, penile cancer, and testicular cancer, among many others, threaten the health of affected people around the world. In industrialized nations, many treatment options exist. Often, people in developing countries simply have no access to life-saving treatments that so many in Western countries take for granted. Some strains of the human papilloma virus (HPV), an extremely common infection, can lead to cancers. In addition to cancer, there are other life-threatening infections that can be sexually transmitted. Hepatitis B Virus, which can be transmitted through sexual activities, can be deadly. Untreated syphilis can lead to death, although with the common use of antibiotics, this has become quite uncommon in Western countries. However, there are still many thousands of people who die of syphilis infection throughout the world every year. HPV has killed over 25 million people worldwide over the past three decades. Over the years, HIV has certainly received much attention in the media. The fear of HIV has lessened somewhat since the 1980s, but among some people who are at high risk of infection through unprotected sexual behaviors, "HIV apathy" has taken hold. This is partly because HIV disease has gone from being almost always fatal to a long-term chronic infection for some, at least for those who have access to effective anti-retroviral medications and are highly compliant with their drug regimens. Sex educators are trying to find ways to fight the apathy among some people who are engaging in the highest risk sexual behaviors.

Because of the behavioral and social dimensions of sexually transmitted infections, educators and scientists have long been interested in understanding high-risk behaviors and situations. We have learned much from sexual risk-taking behavior research. Sex researchers Janice and John Baldwin at the University of California have found that knowing about the risks is simply not enough. Other components that may influence behavior include things like worry and perceptions of individual risk. Those who worry about becoming infected with an STI are more likely to be cautious in their behaviors. Also, those who perceive themselves to be potentially at risk may be less likely to engage in risky behaviors. Again, knowledge alone is not enough. On the other hand, too much worry can be paralyzing. This is the kind of research science that has immediate application and can provide the foundation for public health education efforts to prevent the spread of STIs and HIV. With no cure for HIV in sight, education and public health prevention efforts remain our very best hope.

In addition to cancers and STIs, other sexual health problems are explored in this unit, including erectile dysfunction, premature ejaculation, orgasm difficulties, lack of sexual desire, and painful intercourse. Some treatment options are also discussed in this unit. Whether we are talking about cancers, STIs, or other sexual health concerns, one of the biggest concerns we have in the field of human sexuality is the prevention and alleviation of pain and suffering. The ultimate goal is that we make this information our own. We need to go beyond knowledge alone to accepting personal responsibility, and accurately assessing personal risk. By taking responsibility, we help to create a world of possibilities, where sexualities may be expressed in healthy and satisfying ways. Ultimately, that is what this unit is all about.

New Mammogram Guidelines Raise Questions

Benefits of screening before age 50 don't outweigh risks, task force says.

JOCELYN NOVECK

For many women, getting a mammogram is already one of life's more stressful experiences.

Now, women in their 40s have the added anxiety of trying to figure out if they should even be getting one at all.

A government task force said Monday that most women don't need mammograms in their 40s and should get one every two years starting at 50—a stunning reversal and a break with the American Cancer Society's long-standing position. What's more, the panel said breast self-exams do no good, and women shouldn't be taught to do them.

The news seemed destined to leave many deeply confused about whose advice to follow.

"I've never had a scare, but isn't it better to be safe than sorry?" asked Beth Rosenthal, 41, sitting in a San Francisco cafe on Monday afternoon with her friend and their small children. "I've heard of a lot of women in their 40s, and even 30s, who've gotten breast cancer. It just doesn't seem right to wait until 50."

Her friend agreed. "I don't think I'll wait," said Leslie David-Jones, also 41, shaking her head.

For most of the past two decades, the American Cancer Society has been recommending annual mammograms beginning at 40, and it reiterated that position on Monday. "This is one screening test I recommend unequivocally, and would recommend to any woman 40 and over," the society's chief medical officer, Dr. Otis Brawley, said in a statement.

But the government panel of doctors and scientists concluded that getting screened for breast cancer so early and so often is harmful, causing too many false alarms and unneeded biopsies without substantially improving women's odds of surviving the disease.

"The benefits are less and the harms are greater when screening starts in the 40s," said Dr. Diana Petitti, vice chair of the panel.

The new guidelines were issued by the U.S. Preventive Services Task Force, whose stance influences coverage of screening tests by Medicare and many insurance companies. But Susan Pisano, a spokeswoman for America's Health Insurance Plans, an industry group, said insurance coverage isn't likely to change because of the new guidelines.

Experts expect the revisions to be hotly debated, and to cause confusion for women and their doctors.

"Our concern is that as a result of that confusion, women may elect not to get screened at all. And that, to me, would be a serious problem," said Dr. Len Lichtenfeld, the cancer society's deputy chief medical officer.

The guidelines are for the general population, not those at high risk of breast cancer because of family history or gene mutations that would justify having mammograms sooner or more often.

The new advice says:

Most women in their 40s should not routinely get mammograms.

Women 50 to 74 should get a mammogram every other year until they turn 75, after which the risks and benefits are unknown. (The task force's previous guidelines had no upper limit and called for exams every year or two.)

The value of breast exams by doctors is unknown. And breast self-exams are of no value.

Medical groups such as the cancer society have been backing off promoting breast self-exams in recent years because of scant evidence of their effectiveness. Decades ago, the practice was so heavily promoted that organizations distributed cards that could be hung in the shower demonstrating the circular motion women should use to feel for lumps in their breasts.

The guidelines and research supporting them were released Monday and are being published in Tuesday's issue of the Annals of Internal Medicine.

Sharp Criticism from Cancer Society

The new advice was sharply challenged by the cancer society.

"This is one screening test I recommend unequivocally, and would recommend to any woman 40 and over," the society's chief medical officer, Dr. Otis Brawley, said in a statement.

The task force advice is based on its conclusion that screening 1,300 women in their 50s to save one life is worth it, but that screening 1,900 women in their 40s to save a life is not, Brawley wrote.

That stance "is essentially telling women that mammography at age 40 to 49 saves lives, just not enough of them," he said. The cancer society feels the benefits outweigh the harms for women in both groups.

International guidelines also call for screening to start at age 50; the World Health Organization recommends the test every two years, Britain says every three years.

Breast cancer is the most common cancer and the second leading cause of cancer deaths in American women. More than 192,000 new cases and 40,000 deaths from the disease are expected in the U.S. this year.

Mammograms can find cancer early, and two-thirds of women over 40 report having had the test in the previous two years. But how much they cut the risk of dying of the disease, and at what cost in terms of unneeded biopsies, expense and worry, have been debated.

In most women, tumors are slow-growing, and that likelihood increases with age. So there is little risk by extending the time between mammograms, some researchers say. Even for the minority of women with aggressive, fast-growing tumors, annual screening will make little difference in survival odds.

The new guidelines balance these risks and benefits, scientists say.

The probability of dying of breast cancer after age 40 is 3 percent, they calculate. Getting a mammogram every other year from ages 50 to 69 lowers that risk by about 16 percent.

"It's an average of five lives saved per thousand women screened," said Georgetown University researcher Dr. Jeanne Mandelblatt.

False Alarms

Starting at age 40 would prevent one additional death but also lead to 470 false alarms for every 1,000 women screened. Continuing mammograms through age 79 prevents three additional deaths but raises the number of women treated for breast cancers that would not threaten their lives.

"You save more lives because breast cancer is more common, but you diagnose tumors in women who were destined to die of something else. The overdiagnosis increases in older women," Mandelblatt said.

She led six teams around the world who used federal data on cancer and mammography to develop mathematical models of what would happen if women were screened at different ages and time intervals. Their conclusions helped shape the new guidelines.

Several medical groups say they are sticking to their guidelines that call for routine screening starting at 40.

"Screening isn't perfect. But it's the best thing we have. And it works," said Dr. Carol Lee, a spokeswoman for the American College of Radiology. She suggested that cutting health care costs may have played a role in the decision, but Petitti said the task force does not consider cost or insurance in its review.

The American College of Obstetricians and Gynecologists also has qualms. The organization's Dr. Hal Lawrence said there is still significant benefit to women in their 40s, adding: "We think that women deserve that benefit."

But Dr. Amy Abernethy of the Duke Comprehensive Cancer Center agreed with the task force's changes.

"Overall, I think it really took courage for them to do this," she said. "It does ask us as doctors to change what we do and how we communicate with patients. That's no small undertaking."

Abernethy, who is 41, said she got her first mammogram the day after her 40th birthday, even though she wasn't convinced it was needed. Now she doesn't plan to have another mammogram until she is 50.

Barbara Brenner, executive director of the San Francisco-based Breast Cancer Action, said the group was "thrilled" with the revisions. The advocacy group doesn't support screening before menopause, and will be changing its suggested interval from yearly to every two years, she said.

Mammograms, like all medical interventions, have risks and benefits, she said.

"Women are entitled to know what they are and to make their best decisions," she said. "These guidelines will help that conversation."

Critical Thinking

1. Why did the panel publish changes in mammogram requirements?

2. What are some of the benefits and risks associated with early screening?

3. What are the key questions that remain concerning mammograms and health guidelines?

Health Behaviors, Prostate Cancer, and Masculinities
A Life Course Perspective

John Oliffe, RN, MEd, PhD

Statistical comparisons between men's and women's health outcomes have revealed that Australian men die younger than women and suffer higher rates of injury and most illnesses (Australian Institute of Health and Welfare 2004). Predominant men's health behaviors such as the adoption of activities that risk health, denial of illness, underuse of health care services, and poor uptake of health promoting strategies are strongly linked to men's poor health results (Gibson and Denner 2000; Huggins 1998; Lee and Owens 2002a; R. White 2002). Sociological theories of gender, especially masculinities, have been used to empirically and theoretically advance understandings about men's health behaviors with the ultimate goal of reducing men's high morbidity and mortality rates (Addis and Mahalik 2003; Courtenay 1998, 2000; International Longevity Center–USA [ILC] 2004; Lee and Owens 2002a, 2002b; O'Brien, Hunt, and Hart 2005; Sabo 2005; Watson 2000).

Influential works by Watson (2000) and Courtenay (1998, 2000), among others, have described five distinct connections between masculinity and men's health behaviors. First, men's perceived sense of role, place within society, and self-esteem are influenced by dominant ideals of masculinity, which make it difficult to promote their health (Courtenay 1998, 2000; Kilmartin 2000). This is especially true of Anglo-Australian cultures, which deem it "unmanly" to publicly maintain health and voluntarily seek regular medical "check-ups" (Connell 2000; Gibson and Denner 2000; Huggins 1998; Woods 2001). Men also take enormous health risks and perform heroic feats all because they want other men to grant them or acknowledge their manhood (Courtenay 1998; Kimmel 1994; Taylor, Stewart, and Parker 1998). Second, men's denial of illness or injury and suppression of affect, particularly in relation to pain, is informed by persistent myths of masculinity—such as the perception that it is tough to hold on to symptoms of ill health in the hope they will disappear and that only weak men respond to stress (O'Hehir, Scotney, and Anderson 1997; P. White, Young, and McTeer 1995). Reactive self-care, typically including the use of some form of self treatment and asking partners for advice before finally consulting a health care professional, is

a common behavior (A. White 2001; Ziguras 1998) and health only becomes a priority for men when they are under threat of illness or injury (Jones 1996; Mansfield, Addis, and Mahalik 2003). Third, when illness occurs—such as prostate cancer—a myriad of biographical disruptions (Bury 1982) can follow. Specifically, studies about information seeking (Broom 2005), diagnostic tests (Oliffe 2004), treatment-induced impotence (Gray, Fitch, Fergus, Mykhalovskiy, and Church 2002; Oliffe 2005), hormone therapy (Chapple and Ziebland 2002; Oliffe 2006), and spousal relationships (Fergus, Gray, and Fitch 2002) have indicated that many men are at odds with dominant ideals of masculinity as a result of being diagnosed and treated for prostate cancer but eventually reformulate or redefine their masculine identities.

Fourth, competence in health-related matters is commonly expressed through visible concern for one's health and caring for the health of others. Such practices are strongly linked to feminine ideals of fragility, gentleness, and nurturing, which are the antitheses of the robustness, stoicism, and self-reliance expected of men (Courtenay 2000, 2004; Lee and Owens 2002b; Robertson 2003; Watson 2000). Fifth, men and masculinity are puzzling concepts for medical professionals (Moynihan 1998; Seymour-Smith, Wetherell, and Phoenix 2002) and men's experiences of health care institutions and interactions with professionals can dissuade them from accessing services. Specifically, men's avoidance of health services has been linked to "male unfriendly" waiting rooms (Banks 2001); health care professionals' preoccupation with changing men's behaviors (Watson 2000); and the anonymity, loss of identity, and subsequent marginalized, subordinate masculinity that can occur when men enter health care institutions (Courtenay 2000).

It is important to note that these stereotypes do not reflect all men's health behaviors but rather represent a public discourse about men's health that men have to engage with (Hunt, Ford, Harkins, and Wyke 1999; Macintyre, Ford, and Hunt 1999; Macintyre, Hunt, and Sweeting 1996). Therefore, dominant ideals of masculinity such as power relations, physical prowess, stoicism, self-reliance, competitiveness, and independence, which underpin men's health behaviors, are descriptive rather than prescriptive (Lee and Owens 2002b). At the individual level, contextual insights to men's lives show diversity as well as commonality in the way men create their social realities and identities, including their gender (Lorber 2000). The plurality of masculinities has been used to describe differences in how closely men align to the aforementioned health and illness behaviors (Connell 1995, 1997, 2000).

Many factors influence individual decisions about health behaviors, and several theories have been developed to explain men's health behaviors—including the Health Belief Model, Transtheoretical (stages of change) Model, and Theory of Reasoned Action and Planned Behavior (Nutbeam and Harris 1999; Weiss and Lonnquist 2003). All of these theories are strongly influenced by the application of health psychology to behavior change and the relationship between the perception of potential risk and self-protective behavior (Nutbeam 1998). Most theories are based on the presumption that perceived risk is a primary motivator for the adoption of self-protective behavior (Nutbeam and Harris 1999). Many researchers have critically assessed such health behavior theories because they do not take into account the social and cultural contexts of men's lives (Buchbinder 1995; Gibbs and Oliffe 2004; Huggins 1998; ILC 2004; Lambevski et al., 2001; Thorogood 2002; Watson 2000; Woods 2001). Moreover, the espoused uniformity of men's health behaviors have been challenged because of the lack of empirical data about men's health care beliefs and practices (Fletcher, Higginbotham, and Dobson 2002; Lloyd 2001; Watson 2000). Increasingly, sociologically informed research, inclusive of the broader context of men's lives, cognizant of the dynamic interplay between microfactors (personal choices) and macrofactors (social-structural conditions), is suggested as the most constructive way to understand men's health behaviors (Watson 2000). From a theoretical perspective, social learning theory—a model where behavior and social environment are considered dynamic and reciprocal—is advocated as a way to develop strategies to engage men with their health based on empirical findings about men's lives (Blair 1995; Courtenay 2004; Gibbs and Oliffe 2004; Nutbeam and Harris 1999).

The current article responds to recommendations about the need for contextual understandings of men's health and illness behaviors by making available descriptions of participants' experiences over time and a gender analysis premised on the belief that "behavior" is influenced by age, history, social class, culture, and illness, all of which intersect with masculinity (Connell 2000; Courtenay 2000; Sabo 2005). Therefore, the following section, "Historical Perspectives of Australian Masculinities," is used to provide a brief background to some of the social contexts with which participants engaged throughout their lives.

Historical Perspectives of Australian Masculinities

Many Anglo-Australian men born in the 1920s and 1930s grew up with specific gender roles and expectations that defined men's primary focus as the family breadwinner (Crotty 2001;

Oliffe 2002). The gendered division of labor during this period was strongly influenced by government policy, which in the early 20th century, set women's wages at 54 percent of men's (Connell et al., 1999). The superior monetary worth, along with the physical demands associated with many jobs, resulted in masculine communities in industries such as mining, railway, shipping, and agriculture. Heavy manual labor and poor working conditions were common and to "keep a job," resilient, enduring male bodies were required (Donaldson 1991). A functional view of men's health was predominant—where health was measured by the ability to labor and therefore earn money and provide for one's family. Typically the female partner, as the "housewife," supported her husband by looking after the health of the men and children in her life and through the provision of meals and housework (Lee and Owens 2002b).

Working outside the home also provided men with freedom, and after the Second World War, high average wages and eight-hour working days ensured leisure time was accessible for most men (Connell et al., 1999). Sport (predominantly "Australian Rules" football) became an important arena for the display of masculinity and the yardstick by which most men were judged (Epstein 1998). Pub culture established a masculine pattern of high alcohol consumption and binge drinking, swapping yarns, laughing raucously, and literally wallowing in the rituals of Aussie mateship (Conway 1985). Men's sporting and recreational activities, as well as paid employment, were strongly linked to physical performance and prowess, thus perpetuating the superiority of a tough, durable male body (Donaldson 1991).

From the 1940s to 1970s, the therapeutic model of health care in Australia was dominant and traded on the belief "that all social problems were caused by illness and that disease had nothing to do with either working conditions or the health hazards associated with poverty" (O'Connor-Fleming and Parker 2001, 13). The focus was on individual pathology and therapies designed to cure disease, and the period saw marked weakening of departments of public health and a shift of power and resources to hospital-based services (O'Connor-Fleming and Parker 2001). In the 1970s Australian men felt the impact of feminism that challenged public and domestic patriarchy and changed work practices making men less economically autonomous (Moore 1998). Models of public health were also changing, and a shift from diagnosis and treatment to disease prevention occurred after the 1970s. Health promotion became and remains one of the key concepts in the contemporary vision of Australian public health (O'Connor-Fleming and Parker 2001) and embraces actions directed at strengthening the skills and capabilities of people and changing social, environmental, and economic conditions that create and sustain health (Nutbeam 1998). However, despite such public health policy and service changes, many men from this older generation continue to devote themselves to traditional gender roles, and previously established work, leisure, domestic, and health care behaviors often continue in later life (Lee and Owens 2002b). Although this overview relates directly to Australia, much of the information reflects similar happenings in other western countries in Europe, Canada, and the United States.

Method

Retrospective life course methods provide an effective way to develop contextual understandings about participants' health behaviors with time (Atchley and Barush 2004; Gambling and Carr 2004; Giele and Elder 1998; Jarviluoma, Moisala, and Vikko 2003; Lambevski et al., 2001; Morse and Field 1995; Watson 2000). As older men, participants' views about health and illness were particularly important because lifetimes of gendered experiences were embedded in their health practices (Buchbinder 1995; Courtenay 2000; Huggins 1998; Lee and Owens 2002b; Thorogood 2002; Woods 2001). The examination of an individual (microhistory) within a framework of time (macrohistory) enabled the exploration of participants' current attitudes and behaviors, while giving consideration to decisions that were made at an earlier point in time and potentially in another place (Morse and Field 1995).

Procedure

The three participants who were the focus of this article were recruited from prostate cancer support groups (PCSGs) and initially took part in a larger ethnographic study of thirty-five men that explored connections between prostate cancer and masculinity, the findings from which have been reported elsewhere (Oliffe 2004, 2005, 2006). The three men were invited to participate in the new arm of the research because of the rich stories that they shared during the original study and their willingness and general enjoyment of talking about the past, as well as the present and the future. Life course perspective emphasizes the importance of time, context, process, and meaning, and as such the small sample of three participants afforded the depth and sharing of details key to the method (Bengtson and Allen 1993). The data used for this study were drawn in part from the interviews for the original study. In addition, each of the men completed a second in-depth, semistructured interview and were observed at monthly PCSG meetings for six months.

Observations of the participants were conducted at PCSG meetings and focused on their interactions, and field notes and interpretations were documented to provide adjunct data. Participants were interviewed at their homes, and each interview averaged two hours in duration and were tape recorded and subsequently transcribed verbatim. Participants' interviews from the original study were reviewed to develop the questions, context, and focus for the second interview. The second interview began with the open-ended question, "What was it like growing up in Australia during the 1930s and 1940s?" This enabled participants to tell their stories and provide an oral history, with questions about experiences of health and illness being introduced as appropriate to the flow of the interview. Initially the interview focused on participants' experiences from childhood through to middle age and continued on chronologically to explore older age and their health behaviors since being diagnosed and treated for prostate cancer. Although specific interview questions were developed, a specialized form of dialogue in which one person asks the questions and the other gives the answers was avoided (Oakley 1981), and conversations determined how information was obtained (De Laine 1997). Occasional prompts used by the researcher in the interviews were guided by the overall research question, "How does masculinity inform and influence participants' health and illness behaviors over time?"

Data Analysis

The transcripts were managed using NVivo, and data were initially fractured using time-sensitive categories of "early formative years," "middle life," and "older age." An ipsative approach to data analysis was initially used in which each participant's data were studied and transcripts read multiple times by the researcher, highlighting key phrases and noting ideas and interpretations in the margins (Gambling and Carr 2004). Data were analyzed in the ethnographic style of coding, categorizing, and clustering themes (Morse and Field 1995), and were, then, coded, organized, and reorganized several times as subcategories were developed under each time-sensitive category. Exploration of the relationships between and within subcategories was conducted, and descriptive notes for each of the subcategories were developed. A subsequent review of all the data was completed, noting the commonalities and differences (Gambling and Carr 2004), and three themes resulted from the data analysis: (a) healthy "ill" boys; (b) intersection of work, wife, and family; and (c) health following illness. The term *theme* refers to coherent behavioral and belief patterns identified in participants' accounts (both within and across transcripts; Morse and Field 1995; Stenner 1993). Analysis continued during the writing up of the study, and themes were developed into storylines and the masculinities literature interwoven with the research findings (Morse and Field 1995). Participants read their interview transcripts and formative analyses and provided comments, feedback, and additional information (Acker, Barry, and Esseveld 1983). The use of a social constructionist gendered analysis provided a lens to interpret the connections between masculinity (as it intersected with age, history, social class, culture, and illness) and health behaviors and described the commonality as well as diversity that existed within and between participants' lives.

Participants

Participants had similar backgrounds; briefly, they were Anglo-Australian (defined as originating from a Welsh, English, Scottish, or Irish background, at least second-generation Australian-born), self-identified as working class, heterosexual, were diagnosed and treated for prostate cancer between 1995 and 2000, and attended PCSG meetings on a regular basis. The data were collected in 2001 and 2002, and participants had a female partner, were retired, and had lived in Melbourne, Australia, for at least forty-five years. The participants and their wives have been allocated pseudonyms and are introduced through the following vignettes.

Randwick grew up in a Victorian country town before moving to Melbourne, where he served an "eight-year apprenticeship as a baker." He later worked as a builder's laborer at a brewery and then as a truck driver. He "worked hard . . . twelve to fourteen hours a day . . . because we always seemed to need money." He and his wife had lived in the same house in a northern suburb of Melbourne for forty-five years, where they had reared their three children. He had always enjoyed "his glass of beer" and still had a couple of "great mates from the old days."

Kevin grew up in a small country town in Victoria and completed his schooling at a regional city boarding school. He moved to Melbourne and worked as "a clerk . . . at the steel works . . . and at a mill" until he "finally got a job at an oil refinery as an operator." Kevin married "early" after his partner "fell pregnant"; they had three children but later divorced. He remarried and had been with his current partner for twenty-eight years and stated that "it's the only relationship I've got and it's rat shit. . . . I sleep at one end of the house and she sleeps at the other end of the house." He "went through [his] whole working life not knowing what [he] wanted to do," and since taking an early retirement, he had been "as happy as I've ever been in my life."

Steve "knocked back a carpentry and joinery apprenticeship in [his] home town to join the railways" in the western suburbs of Melbourne. He worked for the railways for forty-three years and "was still doing night courses at fifty-five years of age"; when he retired, he "was the best in the painting field that the railways had." He married, had two children, and "lived in the same house for forty years." Being a "teetotaler," Steve was a "little bit out of it" socially and "not always invited to some social areas."

Results and Discussion

The research findings are presented chronologically across the life course continuum under the three key themes drawn from the analysis. Commentary is balanced with data, and participants' pseudonyms are used to label their quotations.

Early Formative Years: Healthy "Ill" Boys

The theme healthy "ill" boys refers to social and self-expectations described by participants about embodying health despite experiencing episodic illnesses in childhood and adolescence.

Randwick was six years old when his father died. He was brought up by his grandmother in country Victoria while his mother lived and worked 200 kilometers away in Melbourne. Although his mother was a qualified schoolteacher, "they wouldn't let her teach so she had to wash and iron" because after the war "in special areas . . . they kept them [women] out of work." Randwick's grandmother discovered his hearing and sight difficulties in 1941, when he was fourteen years old. During a Sunday lunch at a hotel, he asked his grandmother what the notice on the table said. She told him to use his eyes to "look at it" and "read it." Randwick recalled,

I'd squint my eyes, which I found out from school . . . you could get them to focus . . . and just through that one particular day, saying that, she [Randwick's grandmother] suddenly woke up that I couldn't see properly. Well, I'd gone through umpteen years of school, of getting up and walking down nearer to the board and then back again to do sums and things like that. In the early stages, they said it was me being lazy and the same with hearing. I had the same problem that I wasn't hearing people, and

I'd say "I didn't hear." Well, they said I was imagining it. And I began to think myself, I must be imagining that I can't hear properly and I can't see properly. Well, once it was determined that it wasn't imagination, both things were rectified. I've been using glasses and a hearing aid ever since.

Randwick's grandmother recognized and validated his sensory impairment and arranged a consultation with a Melbourne based doctor who successfully treated both his hearing and sight problems. However, for many years prior, Randwick had been uncertain about the legitimacy of what he experienced and harbored increasing self-doubt about his ability to differentiate between imaginary and real symptoms. During this time, he minimized the impact of his disabilities through trial and error problem solving that included squinting and moving closer to an object to focus.

Kevin's father fell off a lamppost in 1943 while he was working for the Electricity Commission, after which he "went on an invalid pension" and "basically never worked again." His mother went out to work, but the wages she received were "barely enough to keep the family going and what he [Kevin's father] got went on smokes and booze." Kevin had "bedwetting" (enuresis) for the first fourteen years of his life. He recalled that when it was first discovered, his mother took him to the doctor:

I was told [by the doctor] "you'll have to eat mice if you continue wetting the bed, because that's the treatment." I didn't know at the time, but this was basically a threat. Well, I don't want to eat mice, so I'll stop wetting the bed, as if I had any control over it.

The doctor's prescribed treatment, to "eat mice," inferred Kevin's bedwetting was voluntary, which he would control with the appropriate deterrent. However, Kevin was unable to stop wetting the bed. This became particularly problematic when he was "sent to a Catholic boarding school" in a regional Victorian city, after the money "was put up by a rich uncle." At boarding school, Kevin slept in a dormitory that housed hundreds of other boys. He was wetting the bed each night and had to choose between sleeping in the smell and discomfort of his urine-soaked mattress and admitting his lack of urinary control. He initially minimized his "embarrassment about wetting the bed" by attempting to conceal it:

I used to just pull the bed up and try and hide it, so that each night I climbed into a wet bed . . . well, it was either that or have the whole bed stripped and the sheets hung out . . . the second storey window to dry, for the whole school to see.

Christian Brothers supervised the boys in the boarding school dormitory. When they eventually discovered Kevin's soiled bed linen and mattress, they gave him "six of the best . . . for hiding it." Consequently the urine-stained sheets hung from the window each morning, and Kevin rated the four years at boarding school as the "most miserable time of my [his] life." He was unable to control or conceal his bed-wetting, and social isolation and low self-esteem followed.

Steve's mother died from cancer when he was twelve years old, and he and his three brothers were raised by his father's parents in a small Victorian country town. Steve's father was an absent provider who "spent his life as a laboring type" and although he "neglected his health" had "good innings" before dying at age eighty-four. The entire family were "apprenticeship-orientated" and didn't worry about health "because blokes, let's be honest, we all do neglect that sort of thing." Steve recalled that he was fit, healthy, and played Australian Rules football and cricket competitively "like my [his] uncles and brothers." On the rare occasion that he was unwell or felt "debilitated . . . the family doctor was responsible for my [his] health."

Participants' experiences showed how social expectations can implicitly and explicitly influence actions and illuminated the genesis of three commonly cited men's health behaviors. First, participant reliance on females as primary health providers was evident. This gendered practice—as has been well established by Lee and Owens (2002b)—in which females were responsible for the health of the men in their lives was established during the participant's formative years. Second, professional health services were accessed for medical problems that required the expertise of a doctor, who subsequently diagnosed and treated the ailment. This practice was reflective of the "therapeutic age" (O'Connor-Fleming and Parker 2001) in which the focus of health services was treatment rather than prevention. Third, participants were expected to be healthy and, when dysfunction or illness occurred, denial, stoicism, concealment, and private problem solving were acceptable, if not compulsory behaviors. Although economic policy preserved a gendered division of labor in which the male body was privileged, there was also pressure for those bodies to perform. The ideals of a functional, resilient, "hard" masculine body were also reinforced by the social worth ascribed to the participants' fathers, based on their ability to work. Therefore, political, social, and economic structures influenced how men lived in their bodies, which may have contributed to the labeling of imaginative or naughty rather than "disabled" or "ill" boys.

Middle Life: Intersection of Work, Wife, and Family

Participants identified themselves as working class, and the centrality of work, wife, and family were strongly represented in discussions about their middle life. Manual labor was traded for money, which in turn enabled men to financially support their wife and family. Ownership of a family home and car were important signifiers of provider status commensurate with, and representative of, successful working-class masculinity.

Steve left home when he was fourteen years old to begin a railway apprenticeship in Melbourne. He "married a local girl" and "built locally" in the working class west of Melbourne. The family weatherboard (clapboard) home was convenient to the railways where he worked for forty-three years. Steve described the work and conditions he experienced as a painter in the railways:

You were sort of railway fodder . . . lugging trestles and planks. In painting it was always full of fumes, oh, bloody turps and thinners . . . there was no air extrusion. In a

workshop situation, you caught everything that was going . . . hygiene was nonexistent in the railway workshops. There'd be ten or a dozen of you . . . washing with Solvol [heavy duty soap], hands all in the one bucket. When I went over there [the railway workshop] last time and saw the extruders and extraction fans and water baths . . . I said to the young people . . . you people don't know you're alive . . . in that regard.

Steve knew that as long as he kept his "nose clean" and "head down," he had a "job for life." Job security was important; Steve was newly married, had two young children and a mortgage, and was the sole breadwinner. He "had a lot of bronchial problems through spray painting" and knew "the workshop conditions weren't good but we did it that way." Steve suspected but had no proof of a connection between his persistent wheeze and the workplace, nor was there legislation to support the pursuit of improved work conditions. There was a "lot of politicking . . . like union bashing or union joining," but occupational health and safety was not legislated during the 1950s, 1960s, and 1970s at his workplace. Indeed, Steve felt fortunate to have a "permanent job, superannuation"; he was "blue collar working class . . . just above the ruck" and took pride in his physical and intellectual abilities. By his mid-forties Steve's physical prowess at work had begun to deteriorate, and he "realized those young blokes are as good, or better than me." However, he proudly recalled that, until then, he was able to do the physical work, and "all through," he had the respect of his coworkers. When Steve was unwell during his working years, he would go to the family doctor. He described a typical consultation during that period:

What bugged me a bit, his [Doctor] actual treating surgery was only [small] . . . and my problems then were bronchial [breathing]. As soon as you got in to talk to him, he wanted to have a bloody smoke. It was just cough, cough, cough . . . that was the early 80s.

The scenario Steve described was difficult to imagine in light of current understandings of the connections between tobacco and disease. However, prior to the 1980s, tobacco was marketed in shrewd, often gendered ways, and little public health information was available to inform people about the health risks associated with smoking. Randwick smoked to be with his mates, and similarly, the work break "smoko" connected Steve with his fellow workers:

I didn't enjoy tobacco but because my mates were smoking, to be with them . . . you had it. . . . I would wait for the first opportunity to just drop it behind me. (Randwick)

At smoko . . . you would gather together to share a smoke and a yarn. (Steve)

For Randwick and Steve, smoking tobacco was a short-lived practice. However, Kevin began smoking at ten years of age and became addicted to cigarettes. After boarding school, he used smoking and other behaviors to express his masculinity:

Here I am at 15 suddenly let loose. . . . I've gone from being super disciplined and whacked every day, to now . . . I've got real money in me pocket and these fancy clothes

. . . and women. Smokes, booze. Like the pubs never bothered about under age. They couldn't give a damn. . . . I was like a dog that was let off the leash. I just went mad. A series of girlfriends and finished up getting married to this woman that somehow or another fell pregnant.

Kevin distanced himself from the Christian Brothers who "wore frocks" and "were all hung-up in one way or another." He did this by modeling himself on men who had "an axe in their hand, and a cross-cut saw" or were "truck drivers." He did what "real" Australian men did—as Kevin described, "he drank in the pub, swapped yarns with his mates, he smoked, talked about sheilas [women], didn't act on it much, and that was it." Kevin grew up with his "old man down the pub," and after leaving boarding school, he replicated his father's drinking and smoking because "it was the fast track to being a man."

Randwick and Bess married in 1948 and soon after Randwick began working as a truck driver. Eventually they saved enough money to purchase a property in an outer northern Melbourne suburb that was "a big block of land with houses built higgledy-piggledy along the way." He explained that:

There were no roads or footpaths, and we were told that a freeway was on the plans, but we wouldn't see it in our lifetime. Well, apparently we've lived too long because in 1969 they put a freeway through . . . we're about five houses from it.

Initially the noise of the freeway traffic "jumped over the wooden fence" that separated cars and houses, but in the last few years, "Citylink [the freeway construction and maintenance company] built a concrete wall, which . . . quietened it down." Randwick walked the stark iron and concrete overpass that stretched across the freeway to get his daily newspaper, but in winter "it was too cold to cross" so he would go the "long way around the creek." The eight-lane freeway, which ran underneath, connected Melbourne's major airports to the city center and carried thousands of vehicles each day. Randwick and his family endured noise and air pollution from vehicles that drove by and aircraft that flew over their house. The once serene outer suburban home of the 1950s had become a busy, almost inner-city suburb as Melbourne had grown in all directions in the past fifty years.

Randwick could not afford to sell the family home and purchase in another location after the freeway was built. He and his family had little choice but to adapt to the changing environment. Furthermore, he was proud to have "built the house" and "felt lucky . . . not to lose the house" when the freeway was built. Their home, regardless of environmental changes and potential health hazards, was important to Randwick and his family. Symbolically, the house confirmed Randwick's craftsmanship and breadwinner status. Within the walls, a lifetime of family memories and artifacts resided and responded. Randwick and Bess would never choose to leave their home, for many challenges had been overcome in achieving the "great Australian dream"—to own your own home:

We had the car on time payment and we sold that to buy the block of land, and then we struggled to get the house

done and finished . . . we only had the flooring in one room, and a small fire, we used to sit in that room with an overcoat . . . one of the kiddies got a bad flu, and the doctor said we had to line a room or she had to go to hospital. . . . I was particularly busy with the truck [working] at the time . . . Bess got a neighbor over the road . . . to line it.

Randwick explained that he subsequently "pulled out all the thin masonite [building material]" used by his neighbor to line the room in his absence so that he could rightfully claim the entire building of their family home. His late model Ford Falcon resided in the adjoining carport. Side-by-side, Randwick's two biggest investments, house and car, signified the success of a lifetime of hard work. To abandon such achievements in search of a quieter, cleaner environment would potentially negate the years of hard work. The visual representation would be lost, and the history, as well as the future, would be submerged and perhaps questioned.

The connections between social class and gender were particularly evident during middle life. Participants embodied multiple masculinities both within and between their accounts, yet the stratification in terms of class closely aligned to the ideals of working-class masculinity. Therefore these accounts reflect only certain versions of Australian masculinity, in which participants traded labor for money to establish and sustain their breadwinner role. The findings also illustrated how brief childhood could be during the 1930s and 1940s because of the imperative to take up paid employment. Health was evidenced by functionality and physical performance, and heavy manual labor and poor work conditions demanded self-sacrifice but also offered men freedom to indulge in behaviors such as smoking and binge drinking. Marriage signified a union in which the economic continuum "for richer and for poorer" was the responsibility of the working man, while the housewife assumed the primary role for the concept "in sickness and in health." Ownership of the family home and car were important signifiers of provider status. Environmental factors such as air and noise pollution were not known to have detrimental effects on health, and tobacco and alcohol consumption were marketed as valid pursuits to embody dominant ideals of Australian masculinity. The middle life was a period when participants delivered the promise of hard work but did not necessarily take control or have knowledge of factors that potentially affected their health. Furthermore "rationality" as a unified stable identity to minimize or avoid potential health risks was challenged when the material conditions, structural constraints, and human emotions in participants' lives were analyzed, as previously described by Lambevski et al., (2001) and Watson (2000).

Older Age: Health Following Illness

The theme "health following illness" refers to participants' health behaviors in older age following prostate cancer. The diagnosis and treatment of prostate cancer provided reason to take pause, and some health behaviors were reformulated while other established practices were continued. Therefore, these thematic findings relate specifically to prostate cancer and are limited in what they can say about "older age" in other men's lives in regard to health behaviors where "health following illness" may not be relevant.

Randwick had a prostatectomy in 1995, but the cancer metastasized and he was subsequently treated with Androgen Deprivation Therapy (ADT). Bess interrupted both research interviews to give Randwick his twelve o'clock medications. I observed Randwick and Bess smiling at each other as they exchanged the pill cup and glass of water. They were content in their established roles: Randwick the "patient," taking his pills, and Bess the "caregiver," administering medications following the doctor's instructions. Randwick explained as he pointed to the medications strategically positioned on the dining room table:

It's an area of the table which [Bess] has partitioned off . . . she laid out all my pills to be taken every day, and it was a little bit of a mind-boggling thing for [Bess] to work out when and how for me to take them. . . . I wasn't any help to her. I just took what she gave me.

Randwick described the integral role Bess played in complex issues of stock control, monitoring, and administration of his medications. The designated space on the table for his medications reflected the presence of illness and treatment in their lives. Historically, the table was a site of social gatherings and family dinners at which Bess would coordinate the cooking and serve the family meals. Her role in the domestic sphere continued as a caregiver and conduit between the doctor's orders and patient's treatment. Bess continued female health care roles similar to those provided by Randwick's grandmother. Randwick proudly acknowledged the parallels "when I was growing up my grandmother saw to it that I had medication or whatever." Although cognitively and physically capable of taking his own medications, Randwick and Bess continued culturally informed gendered roles through more than forty years of marriage.

Kevin had been on ADT since his radiation therapy in 1998 because the doctor suspected the cancer had spread from the prostate gland to other parts of the body. Although the exact location of the spread was unknown, Kevin rated his prognosis as poor. He accepted that he had been responsible for his health as a younger man and regretted his subscription to what men typically did to express and prove their masculinity. Kevin's retrospective summation suggested that his understandings of health had shifted significantly over time:

My diet was the pits. Smoking and drinking, which was what you did anyhow, was all part of the deal . . . no regular exercise. You got exercise when you built something or dug the garden. So there was me in charge of me health. I made a botch of it.

Kevin described how, since being diagnosed and treated for prostate cancer, he had tried to maintain and improve his health. He took "herbal medications and alternative treatments" as "a bit of insurance" and although "you expect it's a waste of money . . . you never know." He had changed his diet and proclaimed, as he pointed to the simmering saucepan on the stove:

Eat more beans! . . . from what I've read diet has a fair bit to do with whether you cop it [prostate cancer] or not . . . to optimize your chances, the diet is . . . more beans . . . less red meat.

Kevin had established new health care practices but was determined to continue a lifelong practice of drinking beer each evening, which he perceived as contentious and perhaps contradictory to the positive lifestyle changes he had made:

I'm going to keep drinking me two bottles, because the best part of the day for me is when I'm half charged and enjoying meself with me hi-fi. If I'm gonna deny myself that, what's the point?

Although Steve had not required any further treatment since completing radiation therapy in 1999, he did not believe he was necessarily cured of cancer. He continued to meet up with "a dozen retired men" he had worked with at the railways. Five of them had been diagnosed and treated for prostate cancer. He pondered the high incidence and tentatively suggested it may have something to do with "all the manual labor." Steve described a dialogue of coded numbers shared between the men in the group who had prostate cancer. He explained,

You say "how're you managing?" "No, no, she's down on the one." You don't need to ask any more, that's the PSA readings [numerical predictive blood test for prostate gland pathology], you know. "Oh, she's up to about seven . . . I'm not doing too well at the moment I better go back again" and that's it, you don't push 'em any further.

Steve explained that numbers were used because "blokes don't talk about it" even though "we're in the same area sort of thing." The conversations were confidential because the numbers could not be understood by men who did not have prostate cancer:

. . . that's [the numbers] the secret, and the guys who don't know what you're talking about, they just look and stay quiet for a moment and then you go on to something else . . . the wife and family and footy [football] teams.

Although prostate cancer was acknowledged and discussed, it occurred only in relative privacy and with the permission of other men. Similarly, PCSG meetings provided an environment conducive to talking about prostate cancer and its treatments, as well as health-promoting activities, such as diet and exercise. Steve suggested that prior to prostate cancer "I wouldn't have talked to anyone like I do now," but at the PCSG "I can talk more openly to people, particularly in my own age group." Kevin initially went to the PCSG "hoping someone might have some sort of magical cure," and although "no one has," he continued to go because:

I can do my bit to facilitate that continuance of the group . . . where other guys can get emotional support or whatever.

Randwick had never spoken with other men about health or illness; however, the "sharing of information" at PCSGs helped him solve a posttreatment side-effect of urinary incontinence, so he continued to attend and "say your [his] little piece" as a way of helping the "different chaps that come in." Participants broke with the ideals of what men talk about and discussed their illness experiences and shared health and prostate cancer information at the support group meetings.

Speaking about illness and health with other men was new, and each of the participants interacted in specific ways and took up particular roles at the PCSG meetings. For example, many men spoke simultaneously at group meetings, and the high ceilings and echoing multivocality often isolated Randwick audibly to the buzz of the feedback from his "hearing aid." However, Randwick fulfilled a "helper" role in the quieter moments by talking one to one with men about their urinary incontinence and sharing information about how he had overcome such problems. Steve would sit forward in his chair looking over the rims of his glasses listening intensely to whoever was speaking before actively joining in with the "give' em hell," "let's beat this cancer" catch cries that emerged from various group members. Steve was an "encourager" of other men, especially quick to reassure newly diagnosed men that they would survive. When I first spoke with Kevin at a PCSG meeting, he talked about a particular prostate cancer drug trial and asked me to search for and send him any information or results that I could find. During the meetings, Kevin's arms were generally on the fold, but occasionally his right hand would extend to his face where his thumb and forefinger would pensively massage his chin. His role was that of the "critical thinker," and he consistently discussed and critiqued specific prostate cancer research and media articles with other group members.

Interaction styles and roles varied, but all the participants discussed health and illness as a means to supporting their own as well as other men's health. As older retired men diagnosed and treated for prostate cancer, illness provided the context for health, and health was actively pursued. As Lee and Owens (2002b) predicted, participants continued some established health behaviors in later life. However, increased awareness and willingness to talk and learn about health and illness and the adoption of some "new" health-promoting behaviors were evident, especially at PCSGs. In addition, at group meetings, a process of "illness demotion" was achieved through normalizing prostate cancer and collectively hypothesizing causes, cures, and symptom controls while simultaneously sharing strategies to promote health.

Discussion and Conclusion

This study contributes in three distinct ways to men's health research. First, empirically the findings illustrate how deeply problematic it is to think of men's health behaviors as a purely natural phenomenon, outside the influences of society and culture. Clearly health and illness behaviors are contextually bound, subject to change, and strongly influenced by individual experiences and beliefs as well as historical, political, social, and economic factors. At the individual or microlevel, diverse behaviors within, between, and across participants' lives

were described. For example, risk taking, reactive self-care, denial of illness, and the situating of females as primary health providers—all typical men's health behaviors—were taken up by the participants at various times. However, some such behaviors were abandoned and atypical practices adapted when participants actively promoted their own and other men's health while trying to understand and address the diagnosis, treatment, and recovery from their prostate cancer. The straightforward, unitary, rational perceptions about what constitutes or underpins health-enhancing or risk-taking behaviors were also consistently disrupted by the details of "what else" was occurring in and around the men's lives. For example, participants' "middle life" relationships to work, wife, and family were influenced by government policy, and the economic value ascribed to their labor strongly influenced dominant social constructions about men's breadwinner roles (despite the risk of injury and illness) at particular points in history.

Macrostructures also intersected with health and illness behaviors. For example, some health behaviors can be reasonably claimed as artifacts from the therapeutic era that spanned the 1940s through to the 1970s, however participant interactions at PCSG meetings showed how they could also engage with activities synonymous with health promotion on their own terms. The study findings did not indicate that participants were uniformly unknowing, let down by health systems, or disadvantaged by gender roles, and therefore not responsible for their health. Instead the insights and understandings about their lives revealed dynamic interplays between agency and structure and provided contextual information, the details of which could reliably inform the design of men's health services as previously suggested by Watson (2000) and Lambevski et al., (2001). That said, a significant challenge remains to raise men's awareness of the benefits of actively maintaining their health before illness occurs.

Second, theoretically this study illustrates the value of using the masculinities frameworks to provide an "act-by-act" analysis and description of how men can refashion their identities. Masculinities and health behaviors connect in unique and often contradictory ways across history and within individual lifetimes, and the study findings showed how masculine ideals are contextual and fluid across history, as are men's alliances to them. Such recognition is theoretically important because there has been a propensity to describe men's deviation from, and alignment to, a "one-size-fits-all" concept of hegemonic masculinity. In this study, reciprocity between the empirical data and the masculinities frameworks highlighted the plurality of hegemonic masculinities and the value of contextually locating gender analyses in and across specific points in history. This approach offers the opportunity for fine-grained analyses by explicitly avoiding delinked static versions of hegemonic masculinity to generate the study findings, as has previously been suggested by Connell and Messerschmidt (2006).

Third, from a methodological perspective, life course made overt the connections between health behaviors and age, history, social class, culture, and illness—all of which intersect with masculinity. The method is premised on the belief that it is helpful to remember and embed individual lives in complex and ambiguous societal and cultural relations. Epistemologically and ontologically, the capture of one truth and/or generalizability of the findings were not espoused. Instead the commitment to contextual understandings of participants' lives was the central motivation for using this method (Buchbinder 1995; Courtenay 2000; Huggins 1998; Lambevski et al., 2001; Thorogood 2002; Tierney 2000; Watson 2000; R. White 2002; Woods 2001). By making audible the experiences of individual men, the potential to empirically interrogate unitary and/or essentialized versions of what are commonly collectivized as men's health behaviors were possible. Life course methods provided a way to unearth the beliefs and experiences that inform men's health behaviors, and such information can provide the foundations for working with some rather than to change all men's health behaviors.

In summary, the lives of Randwick, Steve, and Kevin provided powerful insights about the intersections of gender and health across time. Without such approaches, there is great potential for reworking analyses that perpetuate dominant commentaries rather than inductively derive understandings about masculinity and men's health. Only by first describing behaviors and thoughtfully considering the experiences and beliefs that underpin them can the timing and content of targeted health services be effective in promoting men's health.

References

Acker, J., K. Barry, and J. Esseveld. 1983. Objectivity and truth: Problems in doing feminist research. *Women's Studies International Forum* 6 (4): 423–89.

Addis, M., and J. Mahalik. 2003. Men, masculinity, and the contexts of help seeking. *American Psychologist* 58 (1): 5–14.

Atchley, R., and A. Barush. 2004. *Social forces and aging—An introduction to social gerontology,* 10th ed. Belmont, CA: Wadsworth/Thompson Learning.

Australian Institute of Health and Welfare. 2004. *Australia's health 2004.* Canberra, Australia: AIHW Cat. No. AUS–44.

Banks I. 2001. No man's land: men illness and the NHS. *British Medical Journal* 323: 1058–60.

Bengtson, V. L., and K. R. Allen. 1993. The life course perspective applied to families over time. In *Sourcebook of family theories and methods: A contextual approach,* edited by P. G. Boss, W. J. Doherty, R. LaRossa, W. R. Schumm, and S. K. Steinmetz, 469–504. New York: Plenum.

Blair, J. E. 1995. Social marketing: Consumer focused health promotion. *American Association of Occupational Health Nurses* 43: 527–31.

Broom, A. 2005. Virtually healthy: The impact of Internet use on disease experience and the doctor-patient relationship. *Qualitative Health Research* 15 (3): 325–45.

Buchbinder, D. 1995, August 10–11. Men's troubles: The social construction of masculinity and men's health. In *Proceedings of the National Men's Health Conference,* 39–41. Melbourne, Australia: Commonwealth Department of Human Services and Health.

Bury, M. 1982. Chronic illness as biographical disruption. *Sociology of Health and Illness* 4 (2): 167–82.

Chapple, A., and S. Ziebland. 2002. Prostate cancer: Embodied experience and perceptions of masculinity. *Sociology of Health & Illness* 24 (6): 820–41.

Connell, R. 1995. *Masculinities.* Oxford, UK: Polity.

Connell, R. 1997. Australian masculinities, health and social change. In *Proceedings of the Second National Men's Health Conference,* 1–12, in Fremantle, Western Australia.

Connell, R. 2000. *The men and the boys.* St. Leonards, New South Wales, Australia: Allen & Unwin.

Connell, R., and J. W. Messerschmidt. 2006. Hegemonic masculinity: Rethinking the concept. *Gender & Society* 19 (6): 829–59.

Connell, R., T. Schofield, L. Walker, J. Wood, D. L. Butland, J. Fisher, and J. Bowyer. 1999. *Men's health: A research agenda and background report.* Canberra, Australia: Department of Health and Aged Care.

Conway, R. 1985. *The great Australian stupor.* South Melbourne, Australia: Sun Books.

Courtenay, W. H. 1998. College men's health: An overview and a call to action. *Journal of American College Health* 46: 279–90.

Courtenay, W. H. 2000. Constructions of masculinity and their influence on men's well-being: A theory of gender and health. *Social Science and Medicine* 50: 1385–1401.

Courtenay, W. H. 2004. Making health manly: Social marketing and men's health. *The Journal of Men's Health & Gender* 1: 275–6.

Crotty, M. 2001. *Making the Australian male: Middle-class masculinity 1870–1920.* Carlton Victoria, Australia: University Press.

De Laine, M. 1997. *Ethnography theory and applications in health research.* Sydney, Australia: MacLennan and Petty.

Donaldson, M. 1991. *Time of our lives: Labour and love in the working class.* North Sydney, Australia: Allen & Unwin.

Epstein, D. 1998, August. *Stranger in the mirror: Gender, ethnicity, sexuality and nation in schooling.* Paper presented at the Multiple Marginalities: Gender Citizenship and Nationality in Education Conference at the Nordic-Baltic Research Symposium in Helsinki, Finland.

Fergus, K., R. Gray, and M. Fitch. 2002. Active consideration: Conceptualizing patient-provided support for spouse caregivers in the context of prostate cancer. *Qualitative Health Research* 12: 492–514.

Fletcher, R., N. Higginbotham, and A. Dobson. 2002. Men's perceived health needs. *Journal of Health Psychology* 7 (3): 233–41.

Gambling, L. F., and R. L. Carr. 2004. Lifelines: A life history methodology. *Nursing Research* 53 (3):207–10.

Gibbs, L., and J. L. Oliffe. 2004. Promoting men's health. In *Hands-on health promotion,* edited by R. Moodie and A. Hulme, 356–62. Melbourne, Australia: IP Communications.

Gibson, M., and B. J. Denner. 2000. *Men's health report 2000. The MAN model: Pathways to men's health.* Daylesford, Victoria, Australia: Centre for Advancement of Men's Health.

Giele, J., and G. Elder. 1998. Life course research: Development of a field. In *Methods of life course research: Qualitative and quantitative approaches,* edited by J. Giele and G. Elder, 5–28. Thousand Oaks, CA: Sage.

Gray, R., M. Fitch, K. Fergus, E. Mykhalovskiy, and K. Church. 2002. Hegemonic masculinity and the experience of prostate cancer: A narrative approach. *Journal of Aging and Identity* 7 (1): 43–62.

Huggins, A. 1998. Masculinity and self-care. In *Promoting men's health—An essential book for nurses,* edited by T. Laws, 3–14. Melbourne, Australia: Ausmed Publications.

Hunt, K., G. Ford, L. Harkins, and S. Wyke. 1999. Are women more ready to consult than men? Gender differences in family practitioner consultation for common chronic conditions. *Journal of Health Services Research & Policy* 4 (2): 96–100.

International Longevity Center–USA. 2004. *Promoting men's health: Addressing barriers to healthy lifestyle and preventative health care.* Retrieved May 22, 2005, from www.ilcusa.org/pub/books.htm.

Jarviluoma, H., P. Moisala, and A. Vikko. 2003. *Gender and qualitative methods.* London: Sage.

Jones, J. 1996, August. *Understanding of health: The background to a study of rural men's perceptions of health.* Paper presented at the 3rd Biennial Australian Rural and Remote Health Science Conference, Toowoomba, Queensland, Australia.

Kilmartin, C. 2000. *The masculine self,* 2nd ed. Boston: McGraw-Hill.

Kimmel, M. 1994. Masculinities as homophobia: Fear, shame, and silence in the construction of gender identity. In *Theorizing masculinities,* edited by H. Brod and M. Kaufman, 119–41. Thousand Oaks, CA: Sage.

Lambevski, S., S. Kippax, J. Crawford, J. Abelson, M. Bartos, and A. Mischewski. 2001. *Living as men "it's like being in a washing machine": Masculinities in contemporary urban Australia.* Sydney, Australia: National Centre in HIV Social Research Faculty of Arts and Social Sciences, University of New South Wales, Australia.

Lee, C., and R. Owens. 2002a. Issues for a psychology of men's health. *Journal of Health Psychology* 7 (3): 209–17.

Lee, C., and R. Owens. 2002b. *The psychology of men's health series.* Philadelphia: Open University Press.

Lloyd, T. 2001. Men and health: The context for practice. In *Promoting men's health: A guide for practitioners,* edited by N. Davidson and T. Lloyd, 3–34. Edinburgh, UK: Harcourt.

Lorber, J. 2000. *Using gender to undo gender: A feminist degendering movement, feminist theory.* Retrieved June 23, 2003, from www.sagepub.co.uk/journals/details/issue/sample/a012013.pdf.

Macintyre, S., G. Ford, and K. Hunt. 1999. Do women "over-report" morbidity? Men's and women's responses to structured prompting on a standard question on long standing illness. *Social Science and Medicine* 48 (1): 89–98.

Macintyre, S., K. Hunt, and H. Sweeting. 1996. Gender differences in health: Are things really as simple as they seem? *Social Science and Medicine* 42 (4): 617–24.

Mansfield, A., M. Addis, and J. Mahalik. 2003. "Why won't he go to the doctor?" The psychology of men's help seeking. *International Journal of Men's Health* 2 (2): 93–110.

Moore, C. 1998. Australian masculinities. *Journal of Australian Studies* 56: 1–17.

Morse, J. M., and P. A. Field. 1995. *Qualitative research methods for health professionals,* 2nd ed. Thousand Oaks, CA: Sage.

Moynihan, C. 1998. Theories in health care and research. Theories of masculinity. *British Medical Journal* 317: 1072–75.

Nutbeam, D. 1998. Promoting the health of Australians—How strong is our infrastructure support? *Australian and New Zealand Journal of Public Health* 22(Suppl. 3): 301.

Nutbeam, D., and E. Harris. 1999. *Theory in a nutshell: A guide to health promotion theory.* New York: McGraw-Hill.

Oakley, A. 1981. Interviewing women. In *Doing feminist research,* edited by H. Roberts, 30–61. London: Routledge & Kegan Paul.

O'Brien, R., K. Hunt, and G. Hart. 2005. "It's caveman stuff, but that is to a certain extent how guys still operate": Men's accounts of masculinity and help seeking. *Social Science and Medicine* 61: 503–16.

O'Connor-Fleming, M. L., and E. Parker. 2001. *Health promotion: Principles and practice in the Australian context,* 2nd ed. Crows Nest, New South Wales, Australia: Allen & Unwin.

O'Hehir, B., E. Scotney, and G. Anderson. 1997, June. *Healthy lifestyles—Are rural men getting the message?* Paper presented at the National Rural Public Health Forum: Rural Public Health in Australia, Adelaide, Australia.

Oliffe, J. L. 2002. In search of a social model of prostate cancer: Finding out about Bronch. In *Manning the next millennium: Studies in masculinities,* edited by S. Pearce & V. Muller, 69–84. Perth, Western Australia: Black Swan Press.

Oliffe, J. L. 2004. Transrectal Ultrasound Prostate Biopsy (TRUS-Bx): Patient perspectives. *Urologic Nursing* 24 (5): 395–400.

Oliffe, J. L. 2005. Constructions of masculinity following prostatectomy-induced impotence. *Social Science and Medicine* 60 (10): 2240–59.

Oliffe, J. L. 2006. Embodied masculinity and androgen deprivation therapy. *Sociology of Health and Illness* 28 (4): 410–32.

Robertson, S. 2003. Men managing health. *Men's Health Journal* 2 (4): 111–13.

Sabo, D. 2005. The study of masculinities and men's health. In *Handbook of studies on men and masculinities,* edited by M. Kimmel, J. Hearn, and R.W. Connell, 326–52. London: Sage.

Seymour-Smith, S., M. Wetherell, and A. Phoenix. 2002. "My wife ordered me to come!": A discursive analysis of doctors' and nurses' accounts of men's use of general practitioners. *Journal of Health Psychology* 7: 253–67.

Stenner, P. 1993. Discoursing jealousy. In *Discourse analytic research: Repertoires and readings of texts in action,* edited by E. Burman and I. Parker, 114–32. London: Routledge.

Taylor, C., A. Stewart, and R. Parker. 1998. "Machismo" as the barrier to health promotion in Australian males. In *Promoting men's health—An essential book for nurses,* edited by T. Laws, 15–30. Melbourne, Australia: Ausmed Publications.

Thorogood, N. 2002. What is the relevance of sociology for health promotion? In *Health promotion: Disciplines, diversity, and developments,* 2nd ed., edited by R. Bunton and G. Macdonald, 53–79. London: Routledge.

Tierney, W. 2000. Undaunted courage, life history and the postmodern challenge. In *Handbook of qualitative research,* 2nd ed., edited by N. K. Denzin and Y. S. Lincoln, 537–53. Thousand Oaks, CA: Sage.

Watson, J. 2000. *Male bodies health, culture and identity.* Philadelphia: Open Press.

Weiss, G. L., and L. E. Lonnquist. 2003. *The sociology of health, healing, and illness.* London: Prentice Hall.

White, A. 2001. How men respond to illness. *Men's Health Journal* 1 (1): 18–19.

White, P., K. Young, and W. McTeer. 1995. Sports, masculinity, and the injured body. In *Men's health and illness: Gender, power and the body,* edited by D. Sabo and F. Gordon, 158–82. Thousand Oaks, CA: Sage.

White, R. 2002. Social and political aspects of men's health. *Health: An Interdisciplinary Journal for the Social Study of Health, Illness and Medicine* 6 (3): 267–85.

Woods, M. 2001. Men's use of general practitioner services. *NSW Public Health Bulletin* 12 (12): 334–35.

Ziguras, C. 1998. Masculinity and self-care. In *Promoting men's health—An essential book for nurses,* edited by T. Laws, 45–61. Melbourne, Australia: Ausmed Publications.

Critical Thinking

1. What is the influence of gender on health and illness?

2. What impact does the social construction on masculinity have on physical health?

JOHN OLIFFE, RN, MEd, PhD, is an assistant professor at the school of nursing, University of British Columbia, Vancouver, Canada. His research program is supported by the Canadian Institutes of Health Research new investigator and the Michael Smith Foundation for Health Research scholar awards. His current research projects explore the connections between masculinity and men's health and illness in the areas of prostate cancer, immigrant health, smoking and fatherhood, and the mental health of college-age men.

Author's Note—Special thanks to Randwick, Steve, and Kevin, who gave so freely of their time to share the details about ordinarily private health and illness issues. This study and article were made possible through career support by the Canadian Institutes of Health Research new investigator and the Michael Smith Foundation for Health Research scholar awards. Many thanks to Joy Johnson, Michael Halpin, Maria PallottaChiarolli, and Tina Thornton for their feedback and editorial assistance on the earlier drafts of this article.

Body Dissatisfaction in Adolescent Females and Males: Risk and Resilience

KATHERINE PRESNELL, PHD, SARAH KATE BEARMAN, PHD, AND MARY CLARE MADELEY, BA

One of the most remarkable and consistent research findings is the overwhelming prevalence of weight and shape-related concerns among adolescents. Estimates from community samples of adolescents suggest that as many as 46% of girls and 26% of boys report significant distress about their body size and shape, while only 12% of girls and 17% of boys indicate that they are satisfied with their body shape (Neumark-Sztainer, Story, Hannan, Perry, & Irving, 2002; Ricciardelli & McCabe, 2001). In fact, body dissatisfaction has become so commonplace in Western culture that it has been termed a "normative discontent" (Rodin, Silberstein, & Striegel-Moore, 1985). This is especially troubling because, at the upper end of the continuum, body dissatisfaction is associated with high levels of subjective distress, unhealthy weight control behaviors, and extreme methods of altering appearance, such as cosmetic surgery and steroid use (Neumark-Sztainer, Paxton, Hannan, Haines, & Story, 2006).

> **As many as 46% of girls and 26% of boys report significant distress about their body size and shape.**

Body image is a broad term comprised of an individual's internal perceptions, thoughts, and evaluation of their outward physical appearance. Body dissatisfaction is one component of body image, and refers to the subjective negative evaluation of some aspect of one's physical appearance (Thompson, Heinberg, Altabe, & Tantleff-Dunn, 1999). Body dissatisfaction has been consistently shown to place adolescents at increased risk for the development and maintenance of disordered eating (Stice & Shaw, 2002), since strategies such as extreme dietary restriction or compensatory measures may be used in an attempt to alter weight and shape. Moreover, body image concerns are often resistant to change during treatment for eating disorders, and persistent body image disturbances are associated with relapse in anorexia and bulimia nervosa (Keel, Dorer, Franko, Jackson, & Herzog, 2005). Body dissatisfaction is also a strong predictor of depressed mood and low self-esteem among adolescents (Paxton, Neumark-Sztainer, Hannan, & Eisenberg, 2006). The negative impact of body dissatisfaction on a range of psychological problems underscores the need to explore factors that contribute to its development. Recent research also suggests that reducing body dissatisfaction may be successful in preventing the onset of depression and eating pathology (Bearman, Stice, & Chase, 2003).

Adolescence is a critical developmental period, bringing numerous physical changes, social challenges, and role transitions that increase vulnerability to body dissatisfaction. Theories of the development of body dissatisfaction highlight multiple contributing factors, including individual, familial, peer, and sociocultural influences. This article will highlight factors that influence the development of body dissatisfaction during adolescence, and consider protective factors that may decrease adolescents' risk of body image concerns. Understanding the mechanisms that link these factors to body dissatisfaction can help guide the development of effective prevention interventions.

Sociocultural Influences
Ideal-Body Internalization

Beauty standards that are sanctioned by an individual's culture are hypothesized to influence how individuals perceive and evaluate their bodies. Western culture currently endorses an ultra-thin figure for women and a lean, muscular one for men. Pressure to conform to these ideals is evident in messages from the media, parents, and peers. As these ideals become increasingly difficult to attain, a sense of dissatisfaction often develops in those who place high importance on achieving them. Historically, there has been greater sociocultural emphasis on appearance and thinness for females, and research indicates consistently higher rates of body dissatisfaction among females in relation to males (Thompson et al., 1999). However, body dissatisfaction is also a substantial concern among adolescent boys. Adolescent boys are more likely than girls to engage in behaviors to increase weight and musculature, and there is evidence that boys are divided between those who desire to lose weight and those who wish to gain weight and musculature (e.g., Neumark-Sztainer et al, 1999). Thus, there may be two pathways to body dissatisfaction among boys—weight concerns and muscularity concerns—whereas girls consistently report a desire to be thinner. Regardless of gender, however, failure to attain a highly-valued ideal has been shown to lead to body dissatisfaction (Jones, 2004).

Differences in Ideals across Cultures

There is some evidence that beauty ideals and body dissatisfaction vary among cultural or ethnic groups. Ethnic groups that place greater emphasis on thinness tend to have higher levels of body dissatisfaction, particularly as obesity rates rise. For example, African American girls generally endorse a larger body ideal and report greater body satisfaction than Caucasian girls (Perez & Joiner, 2003). However, recent research indicates that this gap in body dissatisfaction may be decreasing, and that the most pronounced disparity occurs during the college-age years (Roberts, Cash, Feingold, & Johnson, 2006). Other research also suggests few differences in body dissatisfaction among African American, Asian American, and Hispanic women (Grabe & Hyde, 2006). Moreover, ethnic status failed to moderate the relation between body dissatisfaction and depression for girls, suggesting that regardless of ethnic identity, dissatisfaction with one's body increases the risk of depression (Siegel, 2002).

Media Influences

Use of media that conveys messages about body ideals is consistently associated with greater body dissatisfaction, and experimental exposure to images portraying the thin-ideal result in moderate decreases in self-esteem and increases in body dissatisfaction among females (e.g., Stice & Shaw, 1994). Some evidence suggests that media and peer influences are more influential during adolescence than parental influences for girls (Shroff & Thompson, 2006), but that the effect of media may be less pronounced among boys (McCabe & Ricciardelli, 2001).

Parent and Peer Influences

Although societal norms regarding ideal body shape and weight are transmitted in a variety of ways, messages from one's immediate subculture may be particularly salient in communicating these values. These may be transmitted through parental modeling of eating and body-related attitudes and behaviors, as well as through direct comments about weight and encouragement of weight loss. Adolescent girls perceive greater feedback from their mothers to lose weight and increase muscle tone than do boys, and this perception is greater for girls who are heavier (McCabe & Ricciardelli, 2001). Direct messages from parents encouraging their children to lose weight predict higher drive for thinness and body dissatisfaction among daughters, and appear to have a greater influence than parental modeling of dieting behaviors (Wertheim, Martin, Prior, Sanson, & Smart, 2002).

Relatedly, criticism and teasing about appearance have been associated with greater body dissatisfaction, although this may differ by gender. Boys tend to receive more messages from family and friends regarding increasing muscles and these messages decrease over time, whereas girls receive more messages regarding weight loss, and these messages increase over time (McCabe & Ricciardelli, 2005). For both adolescent boys and girls, messages from their parents and closest same-sex friend resulted in attempts to change physical size and shape.

In addition to direct pressure, lack of social support or support that is perceived as conditional on meeting appearance expectations, may promote body dissatisfaction. Indeed, deficits in social support from parents and peers predicted body dissatisfaction for both adolescent girls and boys (Bearman, Presnell, Martinez, & Stice, 2006).

Biological Factors
Body Mass and Pubertal Status

Biological factors may play a role in the development of body dissatisfaction when they deviate from culturally-sanctioned attractiveness ideals. Pubertal changes, including increased body fat, move girls farther from the thin-ideal. Increasing body mass is consistently associated with greater body dissatisfaction among girls, although dissatisfaction is not always associated with being objectively overweight, as many normal-weight females also express displeasure with their bodies (Presnell, Bearman, & Stice, 2004). Boys, however, may have a more complex relationship between body mass and body dissatisfaction. Overweight boys report lower self-esteem and greater self-consciousness than normal-weight boys, yet adolescent boys report nearly equal rates of wanting to lose versus gain weight, suggesting the optimal weight range may fall in the middle (Blyth et al., 1981). Indeed, research suggests that body dissatisfaction is greatest for boys who are over- or underweight, with those of average weight being the most satisfied with their appearance (Presnell, Bearman, & Stice, 2004). Both types of concerns have been associated with elevated body dissatisfaction among boys, although they may employ different strategies to achieve this ideal weight, including dieting to reduce body mass, or excessive exercise and steroid use to increase size and muscularity (Ricciardelli & McCabe, 2003).

Pubertal timing may also be associated with body dissatisfaction. McCabe and Ricciardelli (2004) noted that early-maturing and on-time girls reported higher levels of body dissatisfaction than girls whose pubertal development was delayed relative to peers. Again, this may be because pubertal increases in body size move girls farther from the ideal. In contrast, boys who physically matured earlier than their same-sex peers had the highest levels of body satisfaction. However, other research suggests that pubertal status may interact with other variables, such as initiating dating, to place adolescents at risk for body dissatisfaction (Cauffman & Steinberg, 1996).

Individual Risk Factors

Negative Mood

Mood disturbances have also been implicated in the development of body dissatisfaction because depressed mood induces selective attention to negative information about oneself and the world. This may result in a focus on displeasing aspects of one's body and foster negative comparisons to others. Experimental studies indicate that temporary increases in negative mood result in temporary increases in body dissatisfaction in girls, suggesting at least a short-term relation (Baker, Williamson, & Sylve, 1995).

However, prospective studies have failed to demonstrate this relationship, perhaps because the experimental studies may not represent the types of mood disturbances experienced outside of the laboratory. There is some evidence that this relation may differ by gender, with boys showing a stronger relation between negative affect and body dissatisfaction than girls (Presnell et al., 2004). Additionally, negative affect also predicted body change strategies in a sample of adolescent boys (Ricciardelli & McCabe, 2003).

Dieting

Adolescents who believe that being thin will result in psychosocial benefits may turn to dieting as a means of altering their physique. Adolescent girls in particular may attempt to counter pubertal weight gain by restricting their caloric intake. However, research suggests that self-reported attempts to restrict caloric intake predict weight gain, rather than weight loss (Stice et al., 1999). Thus, dieting may increase frustration and reduce feelings of self-efficacy for producing weight change. Indeed, self-reported dieting attempts predict increases in body dissatisfaction among both girls and boys (Bearman et al., 2006). Despite the suggestion that boys may be more likely to strive to achieve bulk in the form of muscle rather than to lose weight, boys who express concern about weight loss and dieting are also more likely to express body dissatisfaction (Jones & Crawford, 2005). Additionally, boys with lower levels of body satisfaction are more likely to diet, and less likely to engage in activities that might increase muscle, such as physical activity (Neumark-Sztainer et al., 2006).

Self-reported attempts to restrict caloric intake predict weight gain, rather than weight loss.

Potential Protective Factors

Few studies have identified factors that either enhance body image or buffer the negative effects of risk factors for body dissatisfaction. To date, this work has primarily focused on positive parental relationships. Feeling supported by one's immediate social network may serve as a protective factor from the myriad pressures that are hypothesized to foster body dissatisfaction. One prospective study found that a supportive maternal relationship was associated with increased body satisfaction (Barker & Galambos, 2003). Another found that feeling close to either parent was associated with fewer concurrent weight and eating concerns among girls, but the prospective association between parental closeness and weight concerns was not significant (Swarr & Richards, 1996). Several studies have demonstrated no impact of parental relationships or acceptance on body dissatisfaction for boys (e.g. Barker & Galambos, 2003).

It will be important for future research to consider other variables that may mitigate the impact of body dissatisfaction. Theoretically, cognitive factors such as attributional style or perceived control, which have been linked to disorders such as depression and anxiety, may be associated with body dissatisfaction. Control-related beliefs play a role in the impact of life stressors on depressed mood and perceived helplessness regarding the future (Weisz, Southam-Gerow & McCarty, 2001). It is possible that individuals who have control-related beliefs regarding their weight and shape may face less risk of body dissatisfaction because they believe they are capable of changing their appearance or adapting to those displeasing aspects. Higher levels of perceived control have been shown to act as protective factors for depression among youth (Weisz, Sweeney, Proffitt, & Carr, 1993); future research should examine the role control related beliefs play in the development of body dissatisfaction, as well as other potential buffering factors that have been implicated in research of other related disorders.

Conclusions

Body dissatisfaction has been identified as one of the most potent and consistent risk factors for eating disorders, and contributes significantly to poor self-esteem and depression among adolescents. An understanding of the factors that increase the risk for body dissatisfaction can help guide prevention efforts for these outcomes. This article has highlighted internalization of socially-prescribed body ideals, body mass, media influences, and messages from parents and peers as key risk factors for the development of body dissatisfaction, whereas others have received less consistent support. Given the complexity of the development of body image concerns, interventions aimed at reducing body dissatisfaction will likely need to target multiple factors, including individual, familial, and sociocultural factors. Interventions that reduce sociocultural pressures to be thin and educate adolescents to more critically evaluate messages from the media hold promise in reducing body dissatisfaction. Unfortunately, there is relatively little research on protective factors that may aid youth in developing a positive body image. Additional research is needed to determine how best to foster greater body satisfaction or mitigate the effects of established risk factors.

References

Baker, J.D., Williamson, D.A., & Sylve, C. (1995). Body image disturbance, memory bias, and body dysphoria: Effects of negative mood induction. *Behavior Therapy, 26,* 747–759.

Barker, E.T., & Galambos, N.L. (2003). Body dissatisfaction of adolescent girls and boys: Risk and resource factors. *Journal of Early Adolescence, 23,* 141–165.

Bearman, S.K., Presnell, K., Martinez, E., & Stice, E. (2006). The skinny on body dissatisfaction: A longitudinal study of adolescent girls and boys. *Journal of Youth and Adolescence, 35,* 229–241.

Bearman, S.K., Stice, E., & Chase, A. (2003). Evaluation of an intervention targeting both depressive and bulimic pathology: A randomized prevention trial. *Behavior Therapy, 34*(3), 277–293.

Blyth, D.A., Simmons, R.G., Bulcroft, R., Felt, D., Van Cleave, E.F., & Bush, D.M. (1981). The effects of physical development in self-image and satisfaction with body image for early adolescent males. *Research in Community and Mental Health, 2,* 43–73.

Cauffman, E., & Steinberg, L. (1996). Interactive effects of menarcheal status and dating on dieting and disordered eating among adolescent girls. *Developmental Psychology, 32,* 631–635.

Grabe, S. & Hyde, J.S. (2006). Ethnicity and body dissatisfaction among women in the United States: A meta-analysis. *Psychological Bulletin, 132*(4), 622–640.

Jones, D.C. (2004). Body image among adolescent girls and boys: A longitudinal study. *Developmental Psychology, 40,* 823–835.

Jones, D.C., & Crawford, J.K. (2005). Adolescent boys and body image: Weight and muscularity concerns as dual pathways to body dissatisfaction. *Journal of Youth and Adolescence, 34*(6), 629–636.

Keel, P.K., Dorer, D.J., Franko, D.L., Jackson, S.C., & Herzog, D.B. (2005). Postremission predictors of relapse in women with eating disorders. *American Journal of Psychiatry, 162,* 2,263–2,268.

McCabe, M.P., & Ricciardelli, L.A. (2001). Parent, peer, and media influences on body image and strategies to both increase and decrease body size among adolescent boys and girls. *Adolescence, 36,* 225–240.

McCabe, M.P., & Ricciardelli, L.A. (2004). A longitudinal study of pubertal timing and extreme body change behaviors among adolescent boys and girls. *Adolescence, 39,* 145–166.

McCabe, M.P., & Ricciardelli, L.A., (2005). A prospective study of pressures from parents, peers, and the media on extreme weight change behaviors among adolescent boys and girls. *Behaviour Research and Therapy, 43,* 653–668.

Neumark-Sztainer, D., Paxton, S.J., Hannan, P.J., Haines, J., & Story, M. (2006). Does body satisfaction matter? Five-year longitudinal associations between body satisfaction and health behaviors in adolescent females and males. *Journal of Adolescent Health, 39,* 244–251.

Neumark-Sztainer, D., Story, M., Falkner, N.H., Beuhring, T., & Resnick, M.D. (1999). Sociodemographic and personal characteristics of adolescents engaged in weight loss and weight/muscle gain behaviors: Who is doing what? *Preventive Medicine, 28,* 40–50.

Neumark-Sztainer, D., Story, M., Hannan, P.J., Perry, C.L., & Irving, L.M. (2002). Weight-related concerns and behaviors among overweight and nonoverweight adolescents: Implications for preventing weight-related disorders. *Archives of Pediatric Adolescent Medicine, 156,* 171–178.

Paxton, S.J., Neumark-Sztainer, D., Hannan, P.J., & Eisenberg, M.E. (2006). Body dissatisfaction prospectively predicts depressive mood and low self-esteem in adolescent girls and boys. *Journal of Clinical Child and Adolescent Psychology, 35,* 539–549.

Perez, M., & Joiner, T.E. (2003). Body image dissatisfaction and disordered eating in black and white women. *International Journal of Eating Disorders, 33,* 342–350.

Presnell, K., Bearman, S.K., & Slice, E. (2004). Risk factors for body dissatisfaction in adolescent boys and girls: A prospective study. *International Journal of Eating Disorders, 36,* 389–401.

Ricciardelli, L.A., & McCabe, M.P. (2001). Dietary restraint and negative affect as mediators of body dissatisfaction and bulimic behavior in adolescent girls and boys. *Behaviour Research and Therapy, 39,* 1,317–1,328.

Ricciardelli, L.A. & McCabe, M.P. (2003). Sociocultural influences on body image and body changes among adolescent boys and girls. *Journal of Social Psychology, 143,* 5–26.

Roberts, A., Cash, T.F., Feingold, A., & Johnson, B.T. (2006). Are black-white differences in females' body dissatisfaction decreasing? A meta-analytic review. *Journal of Consulting and Clinical Psychology, 74,* 1,121–1,131.

Rodin, J., Silberstein, L., & Striegel-Moore, R. (1985). *Women and Weight: A Normative Discontent.* Nebraska Symposium on Motivation, Lincoln, Nebraska: University of Nebraska Press, 267–307.

Shroff, H., & Thompson, J.K. (2006). The tripartite influence model of body image and eating disturbance: A replication with adolescent girls. *Body Image, 3,* 17–23.

Siegel, J.M. (2002). Body image change and adolescent depressive symptoms. *Journal of Adolescent Research, 17,* 27–41.

Stice, E., Cameron, R.P., Killen, J.D. & Taylor, C.B. (1999). Naturalistic weight-reduction efforts prospectively predict growth in relative weight and onset of obesity among female adolescents. *Journal of Consulting & Clinical Psychology, 67,* 967–974.

Stice, E., & Shaw, H.E. (1994). Adverse effects of the media portrayed thin-ideal on women and linkages to bulimic symptomatology. *Journal of Social and Clinical Psychology, 13,* 288–308.

Stice, E., & Shaw, H.E. (2002). Role of body dissatisfaction in the onset and maintenance of eating pathology: A synthesis of research findings. *Journal of Psychosomatic Research, 53,* 985–993.

Swarr, A.E., & Richards, M.H. (1996). Longitudinal effects of adolescent girls' pubertal development, perceptions of pubertal timing, and parental relations on eating problems. *Developmental Psychology, 32,* 636–646.

Thompson, J.K., Heinberg, L.J., Altabe, M., & Tantleff-Dunn, S. (1999) *Exacting Beauty: Theory, Assessment, and Treatment of Body Image Disturbance.* Washington, D.C.: American Psychological Association.

Weisz, J.R., Sweeney, L., Proffitt, V. & Carr, T. (1993). Control-related beliefs and self-reported depressive symptoms in late childhood. *Journal of Abnormal Psychology, 102,* 411–418.

Weisz, J., Southam-Gerow, M.A., & McCarty, C.A. (2001). Control-related beliefs and depressive symptoms in clinic-referred children and adolescents: Developmental differences and model specificity. *Journal of Abnormal Psychology, 110,* 97–109.

Wertheim, E.H., Martin, G., Prior, M., Sanson, A., & Smart, D. (2002). Parent influences in the transmission of eating and weight-related values and behaviors. *Eating Disorders, 10,* 321–334.

Critical Thinking

1. What are the key differences between boys and girls in the area of body satisfaction/dissatisfaction?

2. What are the outcomes of body dissatisfaction in boys and girls?

KATHERINE PRESNELL, PhD, is an Assistant Professor in the Department of Psychology at Southern Methodist University (SMU) and Director of the Weight and Eating Disorders Research Program at SMU. Her research focuses on understanding sociocultural, psychological, and behavioral risk factors that contribute to eating disorders and obesity, as well as developing effective prevention interventions for these disorders. **SARAH KATE BEARMAN,** PhD, is a postdoctoral fellow at the Judge Baker Children's Center, Harvard Medical School. Her research interests include the etiology and prevention of youth depression and body image concerns, as well as the effectiveness of evidence-based interventions for children in real-world settings. **MARY CLARE MADELEY,** BA, is a graduate student in the Department of Psychology at Southern Methodist University. Her research interests focus on risk factors for eating disorders.

Condom Use Rates in a National Probability Sample of Males and Females Ages 14 to 94 in the United States

MICHAEL REECE, PHD, MPH ET AL.

Introduction

The male condom is one of the oldest methods of contraception and offers significant advantages because it is not made with hormones, is available without a prescription, can be used directly by men, is widely available in the United States and in many parts of the world, and its use can be visibly validated by both sex partners. The condom is the only current contraceptive method (other than abstinence) that protects against most sexually transmissible infections (STI), and its efficacy for the prevention of human immunodeficiency virus (HIV) transmission, unintended pregnancy, and the reduction of risk for most STI has been well documented [1,2].

Sexual health practitioners have long promoted condom use for prevention of STI and unintended pregnancy [3,4]. However, it was the recognition of the serious threat posed by the HIV epidemic that propelled extensive research agendas related to condom use and condom education, promotion, and distribution programs. As correct and consistent condom use remains one of the most cost-effective STI/HIV and contraceptive methods, their promotion continues to be a major component of STI/HIV interventions worldwide [5–7].

Prior studies have indicated increasing rates of condom use for HIV/STI and pregnancy prevention purposes among both adolescents [8–13] and adults [14–19] in the general population of the United States. Unfortunately, surveillance of condom use across expansive segments of the U.S. population is less routine as the collection of such data is methodologically complex, time-consuming, and costly [20,21].

Most national studies providing rates of condom use among adolescents and adults in the general U.S. population were conducted and published in the mid- to late-1990s to early 2000s [5–11,14,15,22–24], with the most recent data focused on sexual health among aging adults, collected in 2005–2006 [25]. However, given constant shifts in social attitudes and policies about condoms, changes in sexual relationship structures and behaviors, and changes in the epidemiology of STI and HIV, there is a need for the ongoing surveillance of condom use behaviors across the general U.S. population. The availability of contemporary condom use data will help to inform and guide accurate and appropriately targeted sexual health interventions

Aims

The purpose of this study was to establish contemporary condom use rates in a probability sample of the U.S. population aged 14 to 94 years.

Methods
Data Collection

Data presented are from the National Survey of Sexual Health and Behavior (NSSHB), conducted during early 2009. NSSHB data were collected using a population-based cross-sectional survey of adolescents and adults in the United States via research panels of Knowledge Networks (Menlo Park, CA, USA). Research panels accessed through Knowledge Networks are based on a national probability sample established using both random digit dialing (RDD) and an address-based sampling (ABS) frame. ABS involves the probability sampling of a frame of residential addresses in the United States derived from the U.S. Postal Service's Delivery Sequence File, which contains detailed information on every mail deliverable address in the United States. Collectively, the sampling frame from which participants are recruited covers approximately 98% of all U.S. households. Randomly selected households are recruited to panels through a series of mailings and subsequently by telephone follow-ups to nonresponders when possible. Once an individual agrees to be in a panel of Knowledge Networks, they are provided with access to the Internet and computer hardware if needed, and data collection by Knowledge Networks occurs via the Internet. Multiple health-related studies have substantiated the validity of such methods for obtaining data from nationally representative samples of the U.S. population [26–31].

To further correct sources of sampling and non-sampling error, study samples were corrected with post-stratification adjustments using demographic distributions from the most recent data available (at the time of the study) from the Current Population Survey (CPS), the monthly population survey conducted by the U.S. Bureau of the Census considered to be the standard for measuring demographic and other trends in the United States. These adjustments result in a panel base weight that was employed in a probability-proportional-to-size selection method for establishing the samples for this study. Population specific distributions for this study were based upon data from the December 2008 CPS [32].

Once the sample frame for this study was established, all adult individuals within that frame received a recruitment message from Knowledge Networks that provided a brief description of the NSSHB and invited them to participate. Of 6,182 adults (≥ 18 years), 5,045 (82%) consented to and participated in the study. Adolescent (14–17 years) recruitment included obtaining consent from a parent (or guardian) and subsequently from the adolescent. A total of 2,172 parents reviewed the study description and 62% (N = 1,347) consented for their child to be recruited. Of 1,347 adolescents who were contacted, 831 responded, with 98.7% (N = 820) consenting to and completing the study.

All study protocols were approved by the Institutional Review Board of the primary authors' academic institution.

Main Outcome Measures

Measures included those related to participant characteristics, sexual behaviors, and condom use. Participant characteristics were previously collected by Knowledge

Networks and form the foundation for establishing stratified samples and establishing post-stratification weights. For adolescents and adults, these included gender, age, race (black, Hispanic, white, other), U.S. geographic region (Midwest, North, South, West), and sexual orientation. Household income was based upon an adult's reported household income; for adolescents, these data represent income reported by their parent or guardian. Additionally, educational attainment and marital status were collected from adults.

Sexual behaviors were collected using two different measures, one related to participants' most recent partnered sexual event for those who had indicated partnered sexual interactions within the past year, and the other to their lifetime and recent (past month, past 3 months, past year, ever) sexual behaviors (both solo and partnered), consistent with other nationally representative studies of sexual behaviors [26,27]. For most recent event and lifetime assessments presented in this article, behaviors included vaginal intercourse, being the receptive partner in anal intercourse (defined as having a man insert his penis into one's anus), and being the insertive partner in penile-anal intercourse (males only).

For the most recent partnered sexual event, participants were asked to indicate the occurrence (yes/no) of each specific sexual behavior, the partner's gender, and their relationship with that partner. Relationship to partner was dichotomized in order to compare relationship partners (including spouse or domestic partner, girlfriend/boyfriend or significant other, or dating partner) to casual partners (friend, recent or new acquaintance, or transactional sex partner). Participants also reported their participation in these sexual behaviors during specific periods of life (lifetime, within the past month, within the past 6 months, within the past year, more than 1 year ago). All sexual behavior measures were pretested with a group of 10 adolescents who agreed upon clarifying language to be added to items presented to adolescent participants.

Condom use measures included one specific to the most recent vaginal or anal intercourse event and one specific to condom use over the past 10 vaginal and anal intercourse events. Condom use during the most recent intercourse event was collected to facilitate comparisons with condom use rates from other nationally representative studies, across which the most uniform measure has been condom use during the last or most recent event (e.g., General Social Survey, National Household Survey of Drug Abuse, National Survey of Family Growth [NSFG], Youth Risk Behavior Surveillance Survey [YRBS], The National Longitudinal Study of Adolescent Health [Add Health]) [5–11,14,15,22–24]. A last or most recent event-specific measure has also been found to be a fairly good proxy of condom use over time [33].

Considering that a sexual encounter and the behaviors that occur within it are influenced by contextual and situational factors that may be missed by assessing only one single event, condom use was also assessed for intercourse across time. Measures estimating the proportion of past events including condom use have been utilized in past national studies of condom use (e.g., National AIDS Behavioral Survey, National Household Survey of Drug Abuse, National Social Life, Health, and Aging Project, NSFG, National Sexual Health Survey) [14,15,19,25,34,35]. To reduce the potential for participant error possible when asking individuals to calculate a condom use rate [21], individuals reporting intercourse within the past year were asked to estimate the number of events of the past 10 that involved condom use for each specific type of intercourse. Each item included the response option "I have not had (anal or vaginal) intercourse at least 10 times;" those choosing this response did not provide estimates.

Analyses

During analyses, post-stratification data weights were used to reduce variance and minimize bias caused by nonsampling error, including distributions for age, race, gender, Hispanic ethnicity, education, and U.S. census region. Mean rates of condom use, with corresponding 95% confidence intervals using Adjusted Wald methods [36,37], were calculated for vaginal and anal intercourse during the most recent partnered sexual event and for the past 10 vaginal and anal intercourse events. Chi-square tests, independent samples t-tests, and one-way analyses of variance (ANOVA) were also conducted to assess the statistical significance of specific trends across age ranges and between race groups. Level of significance was set at $\alpha = 0.05$.

To assess whether sociodemographic variables (relationship status, race/ethnicity, income, geographical region, sexual orientation, and education) predicted condom use during the last 10 intercourse events, analysis of covariance was used with age entered as a covariate. Participants were categorized into one of four models based upon gender and age (adolescent females, adolescent males, adult females, adult males). Post hoc comparisons were considered to be significant if P values were under 0.05 after using Bonferroni's adjustment for multiple comparisons.

Results

A total of 5,865 participants completed the NSSHB. Of the adolescents (14–17 years), 50.5% (N = 414) were males and 49.5% (N = 406) were females. Of adults (≥ 18 years), 49.9% (N = 2,522) were men and 50.1% (N = 2,523) were women.

Condom Use Rates during Past 10 Vaginal Intercourse Events

Among adults reporting vaginal intercourse within the past year (N = 3,146, 62.4%), condoms were reported for an average of 20.0% of past 10 vaginal events, with use slightly higher among men (21.5% of events) than women (18.4% of events). Among adolescents reporting past year vaginal intercourse (N = 125, 15.2%), condoms were reported by men for 79.1% and by women for 58.1% of past 10 vaginal intercourse events.

Condom use during the past 10 vaginal intercourse events among adults varied by relationship status. Condom use was highest among single adults (46.7% of past 10 events), followed by those who were single but in a relationship (24.1%), and married adults (11.1%,) [F (2 , 3146) = 228.45, $P = 0.000$]. Among unmarried adults (N = 1,260), condoms were used during one-third of vaginal intercourse events (33.3%). The highest proportions of condom use over past 10 vaginal events were by those who identified as black (30.9%), followed by Hispanic (25.4%), other (22.9%) and white (17.1%) (F [3, 3146] = 17.9, $P < 0.001$).

Condom Use Rates during Most Recent Vaginal Intercourse Event

Among adults whose most recent sexual event included vaginal intercourse, condoms were reported by men (N = 992) for 24.7% of events, and by women (N = 870) for 21.8% of events. Condoms were reported for 79.6% of events reported by adolescent men (N = 57) and 70.2% events reported by adolescent women (N = 58). Condoms were used more often at last event with casual sexual partners than with relationship partners, a trend that is apparent among men and women across all cohorts, although rates were slightly more similar between these two types of partners among adolescents.

Condom use rates for most recent vaginal intercourse event also varied by race/ethnicity among different age cohorts. Rates of condom use at most recent vaginal intercourse event were higher for black (36.9%) and Hispanic (37.8%) males than white (22.4%) or "other" (25.0%) males (X^2 [3, 846] = 17.8, $P < 0.001$). Rates for white and Hispanic females (20.5% and 20.0%, respectively) were lower than for black females (39.5%,) and those of other ethnicities (30.1%) (X^2 [3, 733] = 15.9, $P = 0.001$). These differences are more striking when considered at specific points along the lifespan, with rates among black and Hispanic individuals being approximately twice that of white individuals, a trend that is sustained throughout much of the first three decades of adulthood.

Condom Use Rates during Anal Intercourse

Anal intercourse during both the past year and at most recent event was rare among adolescents (<5%) and therefore rates for anal intercourse are presented only for adults, among whom anal intercourse was also uncommonly practiced and infrequent. Within the past year, 12.7% of adult women (N = 304) and 3.6% of adult men (N = 86) reported being receptive in anal intercourse and 15.9% of men (N = 385) were insertive in anal intercourse. Condom use was reported for 20.3% of the past 10 anal intercourse events (of both types combined). Men reported more frequent condom use (25.8%) than women (13.2%) (t = 4.67, d.f. = 675, $P < 0.001$).

During their most recent sexual events, 6.5% (N = 77) of males were anally insertive, with 26.5% of events including condoms. Of these men, 100% of heterosexual men (N = 56) indicated a female partner and used condoms for 37.5% of events. Of gay men, 100% (N = 13) indicated a male partner and used condoms for 61.5% of events. For bisexual men (N = 6), 66.7% of insertive anal partners were men, with condoms used for 40.0% of events, and 33.3% were women with which condoms were used for 0% of events. Only 2.4% of men (N = 34) and 3.1% of women (N = 36) reporting being receptive in anal intercourse, with condom use being reported for 44.1% of events described by men and 10.8% of events described by women.

Predictors of Condom Use during Past 10 Vaginal Intercourse Events

Predictors of condom use were assessed across four different multivariate models (adolescent males, adolescent females, adult males, and adult females). In the model for adolescent males (accounting for 21.9% of the variance), race/ethnicity emerged as a significant predictor of condom use with Hispanic men reporting more consistent condom use than white men ($P = 0.01$). The model for adolescent females accounted for 39.3% of the variance in condom use, with predictors of more consistent use including education (10–11th graders reported less consistent use than 8th–9th graders) ($P < 0.05$); race/ethnicity (those with "other" race/ethnicity reporting less consistent use than white (P < 0.01) and black ($P = 0.001$) females); and sexual orientation (heterosexual females reported more consistent use than bisexuals) ($P < 0.01$).

In the model for adult men (accounting for 24.3% of the variance), significant predictors of condom use included education (men with a bachelor's degree reported more consistent use than those with less education) ($P < 0.001$);

relationship status (partnered participants reported less condom use than singles) ($P < 0.001$); and race/ethnicity (Hispanic men reported more consistent use than white men ($P < 0.001$) and men of black or of other race/emnicity) ($P < 0.01$).

In the model for adult women (accounting for 12.9% of the variance), significant predictors of condom use included education (more consistent use by women with a bachelor's degree or higher than participants with less education) ($P < 0.01$); relationship (partnered women used condoms less consistently than single women) ($P < 0.001$); and race/ethnicity (black women used condoms more consistently than white or Hispanic women) ($P < 0.001$).

Predictors of Condom Use during Past 10 Anal Intercourse Events

Because of the low occurrence of anal intercourse during the most recent sexual event, the multivariate model was only replicated to predict condom use during adults' past 10 anal intercourse events. In the adult male model (accounting for 23.8% of the variance), significant predictors of condom use included education (participants with a bachelor's degree reported more consistent use than men with a high school or less education) ($P < 0.01$); relationship status (use was less consistent among men in partnered relationships) ($P < 0.01$); and sexual orientation (gay or bisexually identified men reported more consistent use than heterosexual men) ($P < 0.01$). In the model for adult women (accounting for 3.8% of the variance), the only significant predictor was relationship status, with partnered women reporting less consistent condom use than single women ($P < 0.01$).

Predictors of Condom Use during Most Recent Vaginal Intercourse Event

The NSSHB collected an extensive range of variables related to the characteristics of the most recent sexual event. These included those related to the characteristics of a participant's sexual partner, contraceptive use, and intentions related to pregnancy, alcohol, and marijuana use, STI status of self and knowledge of partner's STI status, sexual history with the partner, one's own and knowledge of partner's recent sexual activities with others, and a range of situational characteristics related to the event (e.g., place) and other evaluations of the sexual event (e.g., pleasure, orgasm, pain). Given this, specific and more extensive analyses of the predictors of condom use during the most recent vaginal intercourse event have been presented in other reports from the NSSHB [38–41].

Discussion

These data provide a valuable snapshot of contemporary condom use rates for sexually active Americans. Of particular importance is that these data provide for population-based assessments of condom use across ages that represent a range of sexually active participants from middle adolescence to advanced age. Consistencies between this and other studies in terms of the measures used for assessing condom use allow for some comparisons of the rates of condom use established by these collective studies, particularly those conducted within the past two decades. However, differences in the methods used for the collection of data (particularly that this study used Internet-based data collection) and the social and generational shifts that are inherent in studies conducted among different groups of people at different points in time, should be considered when rates from this and other studies are being compared. Regardless, these data do add to the collective body of data related to condom use rates in the United States and therefore some consideration of the consistencies between this and other studies is important.

These data document higher rates of condom use when compared with those available from other studies made available in recent years among adults for most recent sexual intercourse, with 24.7% of men and 21.8% of women reporting condom use for most recent vaginal intercourse, compared with rates from the General Social Survey that stayed reasonably stable at 19.5% from 1996 to 2000 [14]. However, adult rates of condom use in this sample for past 10 vaginal events (20.0%) are highly consistent with these previously reported rates.

Also consistent with other studies was that condoms continue to be used more with casual sexual partners than with relationship partners; usage rates among casual sex partners are at least 100% higher than among relationship partners; a trend that holds steady across age groups that span 50 years for both men and women. However, rates of condom use among casual partners are lowest among men over age 50, suggesting the need to ensure that condom use with casual partners can be maintained as individuals age and have sexual interactions with non-relational partners.

These data are consistent with a trend suggested by other reports that have described condom use among adolescents as increasing over studies conducted since 1991 [9,10,12,14]. Compared with data from the YRBS over the period 1991–2001, which have shown increases in condom use over time, these data provide condom use rates that are slightly higher among both adolescent males and females. YRBS data in 2001 suggested a rate of 65.1% for males and 51.3% for females at last intercourse compared with rates from this study of 79.1% and 58.1%, respectively.

Collectively, rates from this study, when considered among the body of literature documenting condom use rates among adolescents over the past two decades, document a trend in adolescent condom use that might suggest that public health efforts to encourage the use of condoms from the onset of sexual activity have been effective.

However, rates of condom use are significantly lower among the early age categories of adulthood than in adolescence. This suggests that sexual health promotion efforts should focus on the maintenance of condom use as individuals transition from adolescence to adulthood and as they enter into a range of both short- and long-term relationships. The data related to less condom use among individuals in relationships is consistent with other studies that have documented this as being related to the desire to conceive among some, and more generally both factors related to relationship maintenance and the use of other contraceptives [14,42–44]. However, public health efforts to ensure that sexually active individuals have the knowledge and skills necessary to make informed decisions about both pregnancy and STI prevention remain important. This is particularly true for those who are involved in romantic or sexual relationships and who may use other non-condom contraceptives to avoid pregnancy, but for whom the relative risk for STI or HIV infection is unknown. The sampling and data collection methods used for this study could be applied to studies that are longitudinal in nature, resulting in the ability to better understand the factors that influence condom use as individuals move from adolescence to adulthood and across evolving relationships and sexual partners.

There was a great deal of consistency between the condom use rates for past 10 intercourse events and rates of condom use during intercourse reported at most recent event. Among adolescents, 82.8% of those who reported using a condom during their most recent vaginal intercourse event were those who reported condom use for ≥ 70% of their past 10 vaginal intercourse events. Among adults, there was greater condom use consistency between past 10 and most recent vaginal intercourse events among those who were single; of single adults aged 18–44, those using a condom at most recent vaginal event were also those whose condom use rate across past 10 vaginal events was >80%. Among all adults however these rates were also consistent. The lowest level of consistency was among those over age 60, with those using a condom at most recent vaginal event being those whose rate for past 10 events of the same behavior was 66.7%; the highest consistency was among those aged 25–34, for which this rate was 85.1%.

It is impossible to accurately assess the extent to which the rates of condom use provided for the past 10 vaginal and anal intercourse events reflect those that could be considered to present some risk in terms of the likelihood for unintended pregnancy or for HIV or STI transmission. A more appropriate assessment of such risk is possible with an analysis of condom use during the most recent sexual event. In more detailed reports from the NSSHB for the general population [38] and for specific groups such as those of black or Hispanic race [39], adolescents [40], and the aging [41], we present analyses of condom use within the context of variables that help to determine the level of risk present in a particular sexual encounter. However, a limitation of our study, as with all self-report condom and STI studies, is that largely unknown is the prevalence of pathogens present in any sexual interaction for which condom use is assessed. Valid assessments of condom use in relation to infection status are possible with daily diary studies that incorporate clinical STI tests within the study protocols [45,46].

These data also document differences in condom use rates when individuals are compared by race and gender. Men (both adolescent and adult) consistently reported more condom use over their past 10 vaginal intercourse events than women. However, in the NSSHB single men in particular reported a more diverse range of sexual partner types within the past year than did women and also reported more frequent vaginal intercourse, which could be among the factors that influence more consistent condom use by men. For both past 10 and most recent intercourse events, black and Hispanic men on the whole reported more condom use than white men, and black women and women of "other" races, across all ages, reported more condom use than white and Hispanic women. Major sexual health disparities continue to exist between black and Hispanic individuals and their white counterparts in the United States, most notably in terms of HIV infection. Particularly over the past decade, significant public health efforts (including those that encourage more consistent condom use) have been focused on black and Hispanic communities; these efforts may be related to the higher condom use rates observed among these racial groups for both adolescents and adults. Additionally in the NSSHB data, black or Hispanic adults were generally more likely to describe themselves as single and accordingly to report that their partner at most recent sexual event was a casual partner when compared with white adults. The differences in condom use rates by partnership status and nature of sexual partner at most recent event observed across the total sample may also help to explain these increased condom use rates among black and Hispanic adults.

One limitation of population-based sampling is that it does not provide for a comprehensive analysis of condom use trends among groups who have been prioritized by public health given disproportionate rates of infections like HIV. For example, these data do not allow for analyses of data within the population of men who identify as gay or bisexual given that, as is consistent with other population-based studies, these men represent less than 5% of the total sample of men. Additionally, 62% of parents or guardians consented to their child being contacted during recruitment, yet 99% of those adolescents subsequently consented to participate in the study. Although the sampling methods helped to control for differences between those who consented and those who did not (in terms of sociodemographic characteristics), it could be that those parents who allowed their child to participate, and their children, could be different on other important variables that could influence sexual behaviors and condom use. Lastly, the purpose of this study was to provide baseline condom use rates for the United States. Comparisons between the results of this study with those establishing rates of condom use in other countries might be helpful for those considering sexual health policies on a global scale. However, such comparisons should attend carefully to not only methodological differences between these studies but also to differences related to culture, geography, and language, and condom use considered within a particular culture's or country's societal attitudes toward sexuality and sexuality-related education.

Conclusions

These data document that condom use rates are highest among adolescents, higher among black and Hispanic individuals, and higher among men than women. Although analyses presented in this article do not consider the risk for infection or pregnancy (nor desire for pregnancy) during the sexual events considered, they do contribute to the foundation of data available to those in clinical, educational, and other settings who are on the frontline of efforts in the United States to improve sexual health yet who need updated data to substantiate and evaluate efforts to promote condom use among individuals at risk for sexually transmitted infections or who desire to prevent pregnancy.

References

1. Gallo MF, Steiner MJ, Warner L, Hylton-Kong T, Figueroa JP, Hobbs MM, Behets FM. Self-reported condom use is associated with reduced risk of chlamydia, gonorrhea, and trichomoniasis. Sex Transm Dis 2007;34:829–33.

2. Rietmeijer CA, Krebs JW, Feorino PM, Judson FN. Condoms as physical and chemical barriers against human immunodeficiency virus. JAMA 1988;259:1851–53.

3. Valdiserri RO. Cum hastis sic clypeatis: The turbulent history of the condom. Bull NY Acad Med 1988;64:237–45.

4. Guyotjeannin C. The history of the contraceptive sheath. Contracept Fertil Sex 1984;12:847–51.

5. Albarracin D, Durantini MR, Earl A. Empirical and theoretical conclusions of an analysis of outcomes of HIV-prevention interventions. Curr Dir Psychol Sci 2006;15:73–8.

6. Koyama A, Corliss HL, Santelli JS. Global lessons on healthy adolescent sexual development. Curr Opin Pediatr 2009; 21:444–9.

7. CDC. Male latex condoms and sexually transmitted diseases. 2010. Available at: www.cdc.gov/condomeffectiveness/condoms.pdf (accessed January 25, 2010).

8. Everett SA, Warren CW, Santelli JS, Kann L, Collins JL, Kolbe LJ. Use of birth control pills, condoms, and withdrawal among U.S. high school students. J Adolesc Health 2000; 27:112–8.

9. Santelli JS, Lindberg LD, Abma J, McNeely CS, Resnick M. Adolescent sexual behavior: Estimates and trends from four nationally representative surveys. Fam Plann Perspect 2000;32:156–94.

10. Anderson JE, Santelli J, Gilbert BC. Adolescent dual use of condoms and hormonal contraception. Sex Transm Dis 2003;30:719–22.

11. Santelli J, Carter M, Orr M, Dittus P. Trends in sexual risk behaviors, by nonsexual risk behavior involvement, U.S. high school students, 1991–2007. J Adolesc Health 2009;44:372–79.

12. Anderson JE, Santelli JS, Morrow B. Trends in adolescent contraceptive use, unprotected and poorly protected sex, 1991–2003. J Adolesc Health 2006;38:734–39.

13. Santelli JS, Morrow B, Anderson JE, Lindberg LD. Contraceptive use and pregnancy risk among U.S. high school students, 1991–2003. Perspect Sex Reprod Health 2006; 38:106–11.

14. Anderson JE. Condom use and HIV risk among US adults. Am J Public Health 2003;93:912–4.

15. Catania JA, Canchola J, Binson D, Dolcini MM, Paul JP, Fisher L, Choi KH, Pollack L, Chang J, Yarber WL, Heiman JR, Coates T. National trends in condom use among at-risk heterosexuals in the United States. J Acquir Immune Defic Syndr 2001;27:176.

16. Piccinino LJ, Mosher WD. Trends in contraceptive use in the United States: 1982–1995. Fam Plann Perspect 1998; 30:4–46.

17. Anderson JE, Wilson R, Doll L, Jones TS, Barker P. Condom use and HIV risk behaviors among U.S. adults: Data from a national survey. Fam Plann Perspect 1999;31:24–8.

18. Anderson JE, Santelli J, Mugalla C. Changes in HIV-related preventive behavior in the US population. J Acquir Immune Defic Syndr 2003;34:195–202.

19. Catania JA, Coates TJ, Stall R, Turner H, Peterson J, Hearst N, Dolcini MM, Hudes E, Gagnon J, Wiley J, Groves R. Prevalence of AIDS-related risk factors and condom use in the United States. Science 1992;258:1101–6.

20. Laumann EO, Michael RT, Gagnon JH. A political history of the national sex survey of adults. Fam Plann Perspect 1994;26:34–8.

21. Noar SM, Cole C, Carlyle K. Condom use measurement in 56 studies of sexual risk behavior: Review and recommendations. Arch Sex Behav 2006;35:327–45.

22. Anderson JE, Mosher WD, Chandra A. Measuring HIV risk in the U.S. population aged 15–44: Results from Cycle 6 of the National Survey of Family Growth. Adv Data 2006;377:1–27.

23. Sieving RE, Beuhring T, Resnick MD, Bearinger LH, Shew M, Ireland M, Blum RW. Development of adolescent self-report measures from the National Longitudinal Study of Adolescent Heath. J Adolesc Health 2001;28:73–81.

24. Kann L, Kinchen SA, Williams BI, Ross JG, Lowry R, Grunbaum JA, Kolbe LJ; State and Local YRBSS Coodinators. Youth Risk Behavior Surveillance System. Youth risk behavior surveillance—United States, 1999. MMWR CDC Surveill Summ 2000;49:1–32.

25. Waite LJ, Laumann EO, Das A, Schumm LP. Sexuality: Measures of partnerships, practices, attitudes, and problems in the National Social Life, Health, and Aging Study. J Gerontol B Psychol Sci Soc Sci 2009;64(1 suppl);i56–i66.

26. Herbenick D, Reece M, Sanders SA, Dodge B, Ghassemi A, Fortenberry JD. Prevalence and characteristics of vibrator use by women in the United States: Results from a nationally representative study. J Sex Med 2009;6:1857–66.

27. Reece M, Herbenick D, Sanders SA, Dodge B, Ghassemi A, Fortenberry JD. Prevalence and characteristics of vibrator use by men in the United States. J Sex Med 2009;6:1867–74.

28. Baker L, Wagner TH, Singer S, Bundorf MK. Use of the Internet and e-mail for health care information: Results from a national survey. JAMA 2003;289:2400-6.

29. Heiss F, McFadden D, Winter J. Who failed to enroll in Medicare Part D, and why? Early results. Health Aff 2006;25:344–54.

30. Holman EA, Silver RC, Poulin M, Andersen J, Gil-Rivas V, McIntosh DN. Terrorism, acute stress, and cardiovascular health: A 3-year national study following the September 11th attacks. Arch Gen Psychiatry 2008;65:73–80.

31. Silver RC, Holman EA, McIntosh DN, Poulin M, Gil-Rivas V. Nationwide longitudinal study of psychological responses to September 11. JAMA 2002;288:1235.

32. Current Population Survey December 2008. U.S. Census Bureau. 1994—[cited June 9, 2010]. Available from: www.bls.census.gov/ferretftp.htm.

33. Younge SN, Salazar LF, Crosby RF, DiClemente RJ, Wingood GM. Rose condom use at last sex as a proxy for other measures of condom use: Is it good enough? Adolescence 2008;43:927–31.

34. Manlove M, Ikramullah E, Terry-Humen E. Condom use and consistency among male adolescents in the United States. J Adolesc Health 2008;43:325–33.

35. Choi KH, Catania JA, Dolcini MM. Extramarital sex and HIV risk behavior among US adults: Results from the national AIDS behavioral survey. Am J Public Health 1994; 84:2003–7.

36. Fleiss JL, Levin B, Paik MC. Statistical methods for rates and proportions. 3rd edition. New York: John Wiley; 2003.

37. Agresti A, Coull B. Approximate is better than exact for interval estimation of binomial proportions. Am Stat 1998;52:119–26.

38. Sanders SA, Reece M, Herbenick D, Schick V, Dodge B, Fortenberry JD. Condom use during most recent vaginal intercourse event among a probability sample of adults in the United States. J Sex Med 2010;7(suppl 5):362–73.

39. Dodge B, Reece M, Herbenick D, Schick V, Sanders SA, Fortenberry JD. Sexual health among U.S. Black and Hispanic Men and Women: A Nationally Representative Study. J Sex Med 2010;7(suppl 5):330–45.

40. Fortenberry JD, Schick V, Herbenick D, Sanders SA, Reece M. Sexual behaviors and condom use at last vaginal intercourse: A national sample of adolescents ages 14 to 17 years. J Sex Med 2010;7(suppl 5):305–14.

41. Schick V, Herbenick D, Reece M, Sanders SA, Dodge B, Middlestadt SE, Fortenberry JD. Sexual behaviors, condom use, and sexual health of Americans over 50: Implications for sexual health promotion among aging adults. J Sex Med 2010;7(suppl 5):315–29.

42. Misovich SJ, Fisher JD, Fisher WA. Close relationships and elevated HIV risk behavior: Evidence and possible underlying psychological processes. Rev Gen Psychol 1997;1:72–107.

43. Fortenberry JD, Tu W, Harezlak J, Katz BP, Orr DP. Condom use as a function of time in new and established adolescent sexual relationships. Am J Public Health 2002;92:211–3.

44. Sayegh MA, Fortenberry JD, Shew M, Orr DP. The developmental association of relationship quality, hormonal contraceptive choice and condom non-use among adolescent women. J Adolescent Health 2006;39:388–95.

45. Batteiger BE, Tu W, Ofner S, Van Der Pol B, Stothard DR, Orr DP, Katz BP, Fortenberry JD. Repeated Chlamydia trachomatis genital infections in adolescent women. J Infect Dis 2010;201:42–51.

46. Ott MA, Ofner S, Fortenberry JD. Beyond douching: Use of feminine hygiene products and STI risk among young women. J Sex Med 2009;6:1335–40.

Critical Thinking

1. Can sociodemographic variables predict condom usage.

2. How can health professionals use statistics from this study to promote condom use.

Hooking Up and Sexual Risk Taking among College Students: A Health Belief Model Perspective

TERESA M. DOWNING-MATIBAG, PhD, AND BRANDI GEISINGER, BS

In today's efficiency-oriented society, many college students are choosing an alternative to old-fashioned dating, which some claim ties them down and constrains their time. Rather, they are having casual sexual relationships and saving their time and money for other pursuits (Gilmartin, 2006; Glen & Marquardt, 2001). These sexual encounters, known as "hookups," involve a range of intimate behaviors, from kissing and fondling to sexual intercourse, between partners who do not have relational commitments (Flack et al., 2007; Manning, Giordano, & Longmore, 2006). Because hookups commonly involve alcohol consumption and binge drinking, they are associated with high levels of sexual risk taking (Lambert, Kahn, & Apple, 2003; Paul & Hayes, 2002) or, in cases where students are too inebriated to give consent, involuntary risk exposure (Flack et al., 2007).

According to the Task Force of the National Advisory Council on Alcohol Abuse and Alcoholism (2002) and the Centers for Disease Control and Prevention ([CDC],1995b), in addition to having sex while under the influence of alcohol, sexual risk taking among college students involves having unprotected sex and multiple sex partners. Consequently, those who hook up might experience unwanted pregnancies, sexually transmitted infections (STIs), and sexual violence (Flack et al., 2007; CDC, 1995b). As hooking up threatens the sexual, physical, and psychological health of college-age youth, understanding sexual risk taking within the context of this popular practice is important.

In this study we explored college students' rationales for sexual risk taking during hooking up using the theoretical framework of the Health Belief Model (HBM; Lin, Simoni, & Zemon, 2005; Rosenstock, 1974; Rosenstock, Strecher, & Becker 1988). In doing so, we explored and now demonstrate how this model can be applied through qualitative research to identify the factors that contribute to sexual risk taking in hookup relationships. Although casual sexual intimacy is generally risky, some behaviors are riskier than others; it is hookups during which condoms or some form of protection against STIs (including HIV/AIDS) are needed but not used that are our focus. The study is based on semistructured interviews with 71 college students about their hooking-up experiences.

Theory

The HBM is a cognitive model for understanding health risk behavior (Conner & Norman, 1996; National Cancer Institute, 2005), including sexual risk behavior among various age (Brown, DiClemente, & Reynolds, 1991) and cultural (Lin et al., 2005) groups. Developed in the 1950s by social psychologists working for the U.S. Public Health Services and since elaborated on (Rosenstock, 1974; Rosenstock et al., 1988), this model has provided the basis for prevention-focused interventions and research in areas such as substance abuse, smoking, obesity, sexual risk taking, and HIV/AIDS (Conner & Norman, 1996). One of the shortcomings of the current research is that the general model's capacity to lend insight into the health beliefs of specific populations, such as college students participating in high-risk sexual encounters (Zak-Place & Stern, 2004), mid-life diabetics struggling with obesity, or even teenagers considering their first cigarette, has not been fully articulated. Qualitative research that uses the HBM as a framework for understanding health-related risk taking among diverse groups and their "socio-sexual environment" (Morrison, 2004, p. 328), however, could inform our understanding of how to better serve their needs. In a related manner, it could help us improve the degree to which HBM-related scales accurately reflect the psychosocial contexts in which various risk behaviors occur.

The original HBM suggested that whether individuals undertook preventive health behaviors was contingent on four factors: (a) their perceived susceptibility to an adverse health outcome; (b) their perceptions of the level of severity of the adverse health outcome and related consequential outcomes; (c) their perceptions of the benefits of given preventive behaviors, in terms of helping them avoid the adverse health outcome; and (d) the perceived barriers to (or costs of) implementing given preventive behaviors (Rosenstock, 1974). A fifth factor, their level of perceived self-efficacy (Bandura, 1977) in implementing preventive behaviors, was later added to the model (Rosenstock et al., 1988). Self-efficacy refers to the degree to which individuals believe that they are capable of implementing preventive actions (Rosenstock, Strecher, & Becker, 1994). Here, we draw on the five-factor HBM model to explore college students' beliefs regarding sexual risk taking during hooking up.

Adolescent Sexual Risk Taking and the Health Belief Model

Numerous studies have examined the capacity of the HBM to predict whether sexually active adolescents and young adults will use protection against STIs during sexual or oral intercourse (Brown et al., 1991; Laraque, McLean, Brown-Peterside, Ashton, & Diamond, 1997; Lin et al., 2005; Steers, Elliott, Nemiro, Ditman, & Oskamp, 1996). Although these studies found support for particular components of the HBM, the results varied widely and the model as a whole has not been fully validated (Brown et al., 1991, Zak-Place & Stern, 2004). In a multiethnic study of undergraduate college students attending six schools, for example, Steers et al., (1996) found that HIV-preventive behaviors were predicted by perceived susceptibility and self-efficacy. The authors determined that social support predicted safe-sex practices, as well. Another study of HIV-preventive behavior among 573 urban women, 65% of whom were under 25 years of age, demonstrated that beliefs about susceptibility and barriers were associated with less frequent sex or abstinence, and that perceived susceptibility, severity, and barriers were related to condom use (Gielen, Faden, Ocampo, Kass, & Anderson, 1994). Finally, in a study of preventive behaviors among college students, Zac-Place and Stern (2004) found that self-efficacy, but not the other components of the HBM, predicted students' intentions to use condoms and get tested for STIs and HIV. Their study is not alone in casting doubt on the cognitive core of the HBM. Other studies that examined the use of protection against STIs among adolescents or college-age young adults also questioned the validity of the HBM as a framework for understanding

sexual risk taking among these groups (Newcomb et al., 1998; Scandell & Wlazelek, 2002).

Perhaps one reason for the mixed findings in the literature is that researchers in previously conducted studies relied on quantitative survey data and were limited in their understanding of young adults' own perceptions of why they hooked up or did not use protection against STIs during hookups (Brown et al., 1991). Most researchers relied on scaled survey questions that operationalized the basic components of the HBM, yet were not generally informed by the social and cultural environments that frame young adults' perceptions of hooking up and its consequences (Lin et al., 2005; Roye & Hudson, 2003). If young adults' culturally informed cognitions are not taken into account in quantitative measures of their health beliefs regarding sexual risk taking, it is doubtful that these measures will yield meaningful data. It is also doubtful that studies based on these measures will show support for the cognitive core of the HBM. One exception is a study by Neff and Crawford (1998), the findings from which suggest that a key barrier to individuals' use of protection is their expectation that the disinhibitory effects of alcohol will prevent them from doing so. Neff and Crawford's exploration of alcohol's influence in sexual encounters among young adults demonstrates sensitivity to this group's perspective.

To address the need for a more contextualized or culturally informed understanding of hooking up in the literature, we engaged in a qualitative study of hooking up and used our analysis to clarify the applicability of the HBM for understanding sexual risk taking among college students. Using Lofland, Snow, Anderson, and Lofland's (2005) approach to qualitative research, we applied the theoretical framework of the HBM to a thematic analysis of our interview data. Approval for the study was granted by the institutional review board of the university where the study took place.

Methods
Participants
We completed semistructured interviews with 71 college students at a large midwestern university. The students were enrolled in an introductory sociology class and had the option of participating in our research or completing an alternate assignment. The requirements for participation in the study were announced during class. Students were told that they needed to have participated in at least one hookup, namely a sexual activity (kissing and fondling of the breasts or genitals, or oral, anal, or vaginal sex) with someone to whom they had no relational commitments (Flack et al., 2007; Glen & Marquardt, 2001; Lambert et al., 2003). Interested students were told to send an e-mail to one of the researchers to schedule an

interview. On arrival at their interviews, students reestablished their eligibility for participation in the interview. Only one of the participants was ineligible and withdrew from the study.

The final sample of 71 respondents reflected the predominately White, Christian, heterosexual demographics of the midwestern region of the United States, although the sample was slightly less diverse. The sample included 62 (87.32%) non-Hispanic Whites, 2 (2.82%) African Americans, 3 (4.22%) Hispanics, 1 (1.4%) Asian, and 3 (4.22%) students of mixed racial and ethnic status. According to the U.S. Census for the year 2000, the racial and ethnic population distribution for all persons age 18 and older for the midwestern United States was 85.42% non-Hispanic White, 9.09% African American, 4.12% Hispanic or Latino, 1.82% Asian, and less than 1% of mixed racial status (U.S. Census Bureau, 2000).

Thirty-nine (54.94%) of the respondents were women and 32 (45.07%) were men. Thirty-five students were Protestant Christians, 25 were Catholic Christians, 8 were agnostics, 1 was atheist, and 2 were undeclared. The ages of the participants ranged from 18 to 24 years, with the average being about 19.5 years. Only 1 participant self-identified as homosexual (gay), and 2 identified as bisexual; all of the others identified as heterosexual. Finally, the respondents included 6 seniors, 9 juniors, 17 sophomores, and 39 freshmen. Of the 69 students who indicated the highest level of sexual intimacy that occurred during their last hookup before the interview, 37 (53.6%) indicated that they had vaginal intercourse, 21 (30.4%) that they had either given or received oral sex, and 11 (15.9%) that they had experienced either sexual touching or masturbation. Of the 69 students who indicated how far they went during their last hookup, more than 80 percent experienced a level of sexual intimacy that required protection against STIs.

Data Collection

Four researchers, including one professor and three students, conducted the interviews. The interviews averaged 45 minutes in length, took place in two private rooms on campus, and were tape recorded with the interviewees' consent. On arrival, participants filled out a questionnaire requesting their general demographics and sexual orientation. Then the four-part interview began. Part one of the interview assessed the students' perceptions of sex and dating norms on campus, and what they thought their peers and friends believed about the pros, cons, and acceptability of hooking up. Part two assessed the events that occurred during students' most recent hookup, and part three assessed their evaluations of their hooking-up experiences as a whole.

Part four of the interview, of greater relevance here, assessed students' perceptions of sexual risk taking during hooking up, with respect to STIs.[1] They were asked about their perceived risks regarding and what type of precautions they took against STIs during their most recent hookup and when hooking up in general. They were asked how often they used a condom during hookups that involved sexual intercourse, how often they used a condom or dental dam during hookups that involved fellatio or cunnilingus, and whether they had ever been concerned about having an STI or had ever received testing for STIs. If they had ever engaged in a hookup that involved vaginal, anal, or oral sex and did not use protection, they were asked to explain why. Likewise, if they had ever engaged in unprotected vaginal, anal, or oral sex and had not been tested for STIs, they were asked why they had not been tested, if they planned to get tested, and how comfortable they would be going for testing.

Data Analysis

We used microanalytic content analysis to identify the key factors associated with students' use of protective barriers against STIs during hooking up, followed by the use of global content analysis to link the patterns that emerged across the interviews to the key components of the HBM (Lofland et al., 2005). Initially, the first and second authors separately analyzed all of the data by highlighting and coding examples of students' sexual health-related beliefs. We then considered whether and how these beliefs corresponded to the components of the HBM. All of the data was coded, thematically, by hand, and a word processing search function was also used to identify key concepts that related to students' sexual risk taking. The primary researcher (the first author) reviewed the second author's coded examples to assure correspondence in the interpretation of the data. In the few cases where we disagreed as to how an example should be coded, we discussed the example and eventually achieved consensus. We noted instances in which the correspondence between our data and the HBM were not clear, and used them as a basis for suggesting ways to better ground the HBM within the situational and phenomenological contingencies of life on campus.

In short, the analysis involved a thorough reading of all of the collected and transcribed data and coding the data within a specific domain of interest. This approach demanded that we become intimately familiar with all of the data, and allowed us to ask specific questions about our data. Our primary domain of interest was sexual risk taking during hooking up, and we explored this issue through the theoretical lens of the HBM.

Results

The HBM states that for people to take preventive actions, they must believe that (a) they are susceptible to an adverse health outcome, (b) the cost of incurring the adverse health outcome would be severe, (c) the benefits of protection outweigh the costs, and (d) they can undertake the necessary actions to protect themselves from the outcome (Brown et al., 1991). Each of these components was represented in the data, as well as one self-efficacy-related factor often overlooked in quantitative HBM research: disinhibition. This concept refers to the idea that people who under normal circumstances would take the necessary precautions against STIs might make poor judgments because of high levels of sexual arousal or, more commonly, alcohol use (Aguinaldo & Myers, 2008).[2] Furthermore, our analysis suggested that students' perceptions of their self-efficacy in using protection against STIs varied across situational contexts, another issue that is underexplored in quantitative HBM studies of adolescent sexual risk behavior.

Each aspect of the HBM was examined relative to our findings. Qualitative data analysis was used to identify the specific factors that underlie each aspect of the HBM within the context of hooking up among college students. In a subsequent study, we will draw on this analysis to recommend adaptations to the scalar measures that are traditionally used in (quantitative) HBM-related research on sexual risk behavior. We believe that our results can be used to improve the relevance of the items that are included in such scales to the actual experiences and perceptions of college students involved in hooking up.

Perceived Susceptibility to Adverse Outcomes

Many of the students interviewed were unaware of their own vulnerability to STIs. Only about 50% of the students were concerned about contracting an STI during a hookup that involved sexual intercourse, and the majority of students were not concerned about contracting an STI during a hookup that went only as far as fellatio or cunnilingus. We identified three common reasons students underestimated their vulnerability to STIs: (a) they placed too much trust in their partners, with respect to STIs in general, (b) they placed too much trust in their community, especially with respect to HIV/AIDS, in that they believed that the low prevalence of HIV/AIDS in their midwestern state warranted their not concerning themselves about it, and (c) they were inadequately informed of the risk of STIs, especially with respect to oral sex.

Partner Trust

Having a high degree of partner trust was one of the most commonly occurring themes in our interviews. About 74% of the students had some level of acquaintance with their partners prior to the hookup, which influenced the degree to which they believed they were at risk for STIs. Students acquainted with their partners often indicated that they felt safe around them because of their personal characteristics. For instance, when asked whether he thought his partner could have had an STI, Hayden stated,

> I hope not, but I don't think she does. Just she doesn't; she's not someone that does. She's just recently started drinking, too, so she's not someone who goes out all the time and gets wasted and does stuff like that.

Another student, Tim, replied, "No, because most of the time [that I hooked up], it's been like a friend of a friend, so you hope they're clean." Laura, explaining why she was not worried that her partner might have had an STI, replied,

> Um just, just because I, I had gone to school with that kid and we all . . . everybody kind of knew each other at my high school. I had a very large high school but . . . I knew that he really hadn't had that many girlfriends; he was just kind of the shy kid.

Finally, Ryan, explaining why he was not concerned, commented,

> I knew them because I went to high school with them, and I just knew who they were and who they'd been with, and I guess it wasn't a big worry at the time, I guess, so.

Community Trust

In addition to giving misplaced trust to their specific partners, students gave misplaced trust to the community of students at large in terms of HIV/AIDS. Much of this community-based trust was because of the students' (correct) perception that there was a lower instance of HIV in their predominantly rural, midwestern state than in other regions of the country (CDC, 2005). Ron exemplified how students used their perceptions of regional rates of HIV/AIDS to justify not using protection:

> Like I don't know what she could have, anything. But I never really thought about HIV because we're in [midwest state] and I feel like [it's my] own little [midwest] because we're so far away from everything. You know, like it's hard to imagine. Like I think [midwest state] has maybe as low as 2% population-wise of people with HIV compared to

the nation. Of course that doesn't mean I can't get it. But I feel like it's a risk that's not nearly as high as if I lived somewhere else. So I don't think about HIV.

Ron, like many of his classmates, created an illusion of safety through his belief that he was not going to contract HIV through sex in his Midwestern state because the state is relatively small and is isolated from the worst of the STIs. Only about 25% of the students indicated that HIV was of concern to them.

Lack of Knowledge

Oral intercourse was problematic for a different reason. Even though almost half of the students reported engaging in oral sex during their last hookup, the majority, at best, seemed confused about how to protect themselves against oral STIs. At worst, they were appalled at the idea of using protection with oral sex and at the discovery that STIs could be transmitted through this venue. The majority of the students' perceptions of the risks of oral sex are reflected in the following interview excerpt between Jackie and the interviewer:

Interviewer (I): Did you use protection?

Jackie (J): No, 'cuz we didn't have sex.

I: So, even with oral sex, you didn't use protection?

J: Right.

Other examples include Andy, who said that he had never been "concerned [about] oral sex," and Veronica, who had given oral sex to several men, who stated, "I consider myself pretty much like not experienced enough to think about that [STDs]." In fact, of the 71 students interviewed, not one reported that they had ever used or would consider using protective barriers against STIs when giving or receiving oral intercourse. Furthermore, less than 5% of the students stated that they had been concerned about STIs following oral sex.

Perceptions of the Level of Severity or Costs of Adverse Outcomes

The second component of the HBM states that, for a person to take preventive measures, he or she must believe that the consequences of contracting that illness would be severe. As Boone and Lefkowitz (2004) suggested, the majority of students believed that the costs of contracting an STI would be high. In fact, many stated that the worst possible outcome of a hookup would be contracting an STI. In response to the question, "Have you ever been worried about a sexually transmitted disease?" Cara replied, "Of course. I mean, they talk about it all the time. When I watch TV, that's all they talk about anymore: 'Get tested,' and all that stuff. So yeah, I'm very worried about

it." Joe, who consistently used protection during vaginal intercourse said, "I've had a lot of friends contract STDs and it just started scaring me a lot." Unfortunately, we did not probe for details regarding students' perceptions of the consequences of contracting STIs, so our analysis regarding this aspect of the HBM is limited.

Perceptions That the Benefits Associated with Prevention Are Higher (or Lower) than the Costs

The third component of the HBM proposes that if people are to engage in preventive behavior, they need to believe that the benefits are greater than the costs. This was problematic for many of the students we interviewed. Although most believed that protective methods such as condoms would effectively prevent STIs, some feared that insistence on using protection might thwart their chances for having sex, or compromise their pleasure.

Loss of Opportunity

When Michael was asked why he chose not to use protection, he explained, "Basically, during the time of things actually happening, I would know if I actually stopped and went to go get something, when I got back, time would have passed and nothing would happen at all." Shelley replied, "Well, I usually like to use condoms as well as birth control, but I mean, I guess, I just, I wasn't really thinking at the time of doing it because it kind of interferes with the mood."

Pleasure Interference

Another reason the costs of protection were perceived to be too high was that some students believed it would interfere with sexual pleasure, especially in the case of oral sex. Aaron stated,

> They really haven't made protection that is appealing during oral sex. I mean, yes they have what, the little cloth blankets or latex blankets and I guess some people just prefer you just use a condom, but I don't know, I guess it's just not appealing to me.

Mike explained:

> I guess I have never really concerned [myself about] protected oral sex. I mean, I know you hear about it but it's just, one, I know girls don't like, I know there's flavored condoms, but I mean I know girls don't like to do that.

Perceptions of Self-Efficacy in Performing Preventive Behaviors

The last component of the HBM is self-efficacy, or individuals' perceptions that they can perform the necessary behaviors to avoid an adverse health outcome (Rosen-stock et al., 1988). A critical issue among students who failed to use protection for oral intercourse was a sense of confusion regarding how to obtain or use the necessary materials. A critical issue among students who failed to use protection for vaginal or anal sexual intercourse was that although they expressed high levels of perceived self-efficacy in terms of their knowledge about and ability to use protection, they demonstrated a lack of efficacy in terms of their preparedness for the type of unexpected sexual intercourse that occurs during hooking up. Furthermore, they portrayed themselves as inefficacious in terms of their ability to discuss STIs and the use of protection with their partners. Finally, regardless of students' expressions of confidence in terms of understanding how to protect themselves against STIs during sexual intercourse, their sexual encounters occurred in situational contexts which sometimes undermined or facilitated their efficacy levels. We therefore examined how self-efficacy is affected by situational and social contingencies, factors often overlooked in HMB research (Boone & Lefkowitz, 2004).

Efficacy in Knowledge

Without exception, students stated that they knew how to prevent STIs during sexual intercourse. They knew where they could obtain or purchase protective barriers, such as condoms, and understood how to use them. However, students were often unaware of how they could protect themselves, or that protection was necessary, during oral sex. As stated earlier, not one of the students interviewed reported using a protective barrier during oral sex. Additionally, only a small minority of students queried were familiar with the possibility of using dental dams for protection against STIs during cunnilingus. Adam, for example, was confused about using barrier protection for oral sex, and did not feel confident that he would be able to do so:

> I don't even know where the hell to buy a dental dam or whatever the hell, so I just never really contemplated doing it, it just kind of, I don't know. Maybe that'll be another lapse of judgment on my part when, I just I've never done it, period, even in high school, doing stuff just. I guess condoms would be more, I guess, I don't know. I mean I know what you're talking about with dams and the little, I know what you're talking about with that, but I just never seen one or even thought about buying 'em.

As in similar cases, Adam's feelings of inefficacy were manifest by a lack of knowledge regarding where to obtain or how to use a dental dam. Another reason for students' lack of efficacy in protecting themselves against STIs dur-

ing oral sex was that they did not believe such behavior was normative. As John suggested, both peer-based norms and the media can reinforce students' views of appropriate behaviors:

> About the females giving me head without protection, I guess that's just a mental thing, that I'm like you know, you see in any pornos [pornographic movies], you know stuff like that. It's not the norm for a guy to use protection or anything like that during that, but I mean even during pornos and stuff like that, they do wear protection while having sex and stuff like that, so.

From John's perspective, it wasn't "normal" to use protection when "getting head" in his own community, although it might be in the lives of "porn" stars.

Efficacy in Planning

With respect to vaginal intercourse, whether or not the students felt comfortable enough to obtain, keep on hand, and be willing to use the necessary protective barriers were all of concern. Those who did not use protection emphasized the difficulty of being prepared for their casual sexual encounters. Brad said,

> For me to have a condom in my wallet all the time, or something like that . . . it's not very efficient. Plus I hear if it's in your wallet then they wear out anyway, so there's really no good either way. I usually never have one on me.

James, when asked why he didn't use any protection, simply replied, "Ah, didn't have any." Joy, however, who expressed confidence in her ability to plan for protection, portrayed the opposite perception. She explained, "I was on birth control, and I always keep an extra thing of emergency contraceptives just in case something happens. I wasn't planning on it to, but you can never be too safe." Joy was not representative of her peers who experienced sexual intercourse during hooking up, as less than 5% indicated that they were always prepared for this level of sexual intimacy.

In some cases, it wasn't so much students' planning for sexual intercourse that mattered as much as it was their being in situations in which they had access to adequate protection. Mary said she would not normally have had condoms on hand, yet one of her friends had recently given her a box of them as a joke. She used a condom because a peer had made them available, not because she had efficaciously planned for safe sex. Regardless of their perceived self-efficacy in protecting themselves against STIs, then, students' actual use of protection varied according to the situational contingencies that cohered within their more immediate social environments.

Efficacy in Discussion

The final area in which efficacy was problematic was when students needed to discuss the risk of STIs and the use of protection with their partners. Many students expressed a lack of efficacy in this area when they assumed or hoped that their partners would tell them if they had an STI, and were uncomfortable directly addressing the issue. Only one student indicated that he was comfortable talking openly with his partners about STIs and protection use prior to engaging in sexual behavior. The rest of the students used clues about their partners and their backgrounds to assess the potential that they could have an STI. One man stated that he was "hopefully assuming" everything was okay with his partner, and that he didn't talk to her because he was uncomfortable. Many students alleviated such discomfort by deciding to trust their partners, and underestimating their susceptibility to risk, as discussed above. They assumed that their partners were STI-free because they did not mention that they were not. In addition to situations in which students had clearer choices as to whether or not to use protection against STIs, there were some situations, involving a loss of control because of sexual coercion or disinhibition, in which their levels of self-efficacy did not seem to matter at all.

Sexual Coercion

When students experienced an actual or perceived lack of control[3] over the level of sexual intimacy they experienced during a hookup, their perceptions of self-efficacy regarding their use of protective barriers against STIs were severely compromised. In all of the cases in our sample, a loss of control over the level of sexual activity that occurred during the hookup, because of sexual coercion, occurred among women. Although none of the women in our study identified their experiences as rape or sexual assault, a few indicated that they had not wanted to have sexual intercourse during the hookup, but that it happened because of their partners' verbal coercion, physical forcefulness, or both.

Ana, for example, lamented, "So I didn't even say, 'Well, put a condom on,' because I was just like, 'We shouldn't do this,' you know." Ana described her hookup partner as having badgered her for sexual intercourse over a period of weeks and then forcing himself on her one evening when she was drunk, yet he remained sober. Even though she felt betrayed by his insensitivity to her telling him she didn't want to have intercourse, she claimed that she couldn't have done anything different (to prevent him from having sex with her), and blamed herself for letting things go too far. In another example, Kim said,

I was already completely drunk and we decided to go out. His truck got stuck in the mud and then he called his friend to come and get us. Then his friend's truck got stuck in the mud. And so, while we tried to figure out what to do, we drank some whiskey. And then, by the time like they decided that they were going to walk, I was too drunk to move and so then I wound up staying in his truck and he just started [having sex with me] and I was too scared to say, "No," because I was really scared of the kid.

Both Ana and Kim were in situations in which they were at risk for STIs, yet could not draw on their perceived self-efficacy in terms of using protection in voluntary sexual relationships to protect themselves.

Disinhibition

Finally, our analysis suggested that sexual risk taking among college students often occurs because of psychological disinhibition. This concept refers to the idea that, to use protection, individuals need to be mentally capable of making informed decisions or fully cognizant of their choices when hookups occur. In this study, the degree to which students experienced psychological disinhibition was impacted by two factors: (a) the usage of alcohol, and (b) being "swept away" by sexual arousal.

Alcohol

Almost 80% of the students said there was alcohol involved prior to or during the hookup, and most of these students (about 81% of those who reported using alcohol) stated that the alcohol played a role in the occurrence and evolution of the hookup. These students suggested that had they been sober, the sexual activity would not have progressed as far, or might not have happened at all. Sheena, in explaining how she felt after hooking up while intoxicated, said,

I lost some respect for myself, like, "Why did you do this?" I don't know. It's not something I ever envisioned myself doing and I hoped I never would. You know, I didn't want to be one of those people who just randomly hooked up with someone that they just met. Like I want to get to know people more and, I don't know, I just lost a little respect for myself because, "Why did you do that?"

Sheena's shock at her own behavior suggested that, had she been thinking clearly, she would have limited her sexual involvement. Other students similarly attributed their failure to use protection to alcohol. Haley stated, "In my sober mind I would never, ever, have sex without a condom. So, yeah, I think alcohol definitely had a role in that." Alcohol use, when it affected students' decision-making abilities, impacted both the likelihood that a hookup would occur and, if so, whether protection would be used.

Being Swept Away

The sense of being "swept away" by the intensity of the moment also played an important role in how far about 50% of the students decided to go during their hook-ups, and whether they chose to use protection. Many of these students were shocked at their own behavior. The phrase, "It just happened," came up repeatedly—as if the students themselves did not understand how they had become so sexually involved. Others indicated that they never thought they would have sexual intercourse without protection, or even have casual sex at all, but that they experienced a "lapse of judgment" because of being caught up in the heat of the moment. Justin told the interviewer that he was so caught up in the moment that when he "came to the realization" that he was having sex yet not wearing a condom, he "threw one on" and continued. Others indicated that they were disgusted by their own behavior, their lack of self-control, and their failure to use protection. For example, Sabrina said, "It just happened. . . . He was gorgeous; that's what did it, probably. I mean he was like the epitome; he was like god in man form he was so hot." She said that she later cried because she was so upset about what she had done.

Discussion

After interviewing just a few students, it was apparent that there were aspects of hooking up that had not been addressed in the current literature (Lambert et al., 2003; Paul, McManus, & Hayes, 2000). Discussing hooking up one-on-one with the students yielded insight into the phenomenology of hooking up and the reasons students often fail to protect themselves against STIs (Paul & Hayes, 2002). This phenomenological perspective gave us insight into how the cognitive core of the HBM can be contextualized by recognizing the culturally informed meanings that students bring to their hookup experiences. As recommended by Lin et al., (2005) in their HBM-based study on HIV risk behaviors among Taiwanese student immigrants to the United States, it helped us to understand how the HBM can be adapted to reflect students' culturally relevant health beliefs. In a related manner, it clarified our understanding of how the components of the HBM specifically relate to sexual risk behavior among college students, and how prevention programs might be adapted to better address their needs. In the following discussion, we concurrently address the implications of our findings for prevention programs and for future research, as these topics are related.

The HBM poses that for individuals to engage in preventive behaviors, they must perceive that they are susceptible to an adverse health outcome (Rosenstock et al., 1988). Therefore, survey-based studies of sexual risk behavior that rely on the HBM model generally include a number of items regarding respondents' perceptions of their own susceptibility (Lin et al., 2005). Our findings suggest, however, that such studies would be improved by taking into account not only students' estimates of their own susceptibility, but also the criteria they use to assess their partners' susceptibility. This is because students who did not use protection often trusted that their hookup partners were STI-free based on appearance or informal character assessments. They also tended to rationalize that because there were low rates of HIV/AIDS in the region where they lived, they did not have to protect themselves against it. Finally, they underestimated their susceptibility to STIs because of not knowing that their partners could transmit STIs to them via oral intercourse. Students' failure to accurately assess their own or their partners' susceptibility to STIs, then, was largely because the vast majority had serious, if not predictable, gaps in their knowledge of sexual health. These gaps need to be specified in future HBM-based models that assess students' sexual risk-related cognitions.

In relation to prevention programming, our findings suggest a need to challenge students' taken-for-granted assumptions regarding their own and their partners' susceptibility to STIs. Programs that emphasize that approximately one in three individuals age 24 years and younger who have been sexually active contracts an STI (Cates, 1999), and that most STI-infected individuals are initially asymptomatic, might encourage students to make more realistic assessments of STI prevalence among young adults in their age group. Students also need to be exposed to documented evidence of STI outbreaks on college campuses, such as the outbreak of 56 HIV cases that occurred among college students in North Carolina between 2000 and 2003 (CDC, 2004), which resulted in college students representing more than 1 in 5 of the new HIV infections among 18- to 30-year-olds in that state (Yates, 2004). Few students are aware, furthermore, that the CDC has estimated that 1 in 500 college students in the United States are infected with HIV (CDC, 1995a). Programs also need to challenge students' assumptions regarding the oral transmission of STIs. Students must consider, for example, that the individual with whom they are having oral sex during a given hookup might have recently had unprotected oral, vaginal, or anal sex with an STI-infected partner, and that participating in fellatio or cunnilingus with this person could expose them to the infection (Halpern-Felsher, Cornell, Kropp, & Tschann, 2005).

Related to students' misperceptions of their vulnerabilty to STIs is the question as to whether they are willing to consider the costs of STIs when they believe their partners are STI-free. We found that, among those students who failed to use prophylactics for sexual intercourse, even high perceived costs of STIs were not taken into account in situations where hookup partners were deemed trustworthy or "clean." Similarly, most of the students in our sample who failed to use prophylactics when necessary declared the benefits (or pleasures) of unprotected sex to be greater than the costs of using protection. They also associated costs more with compromised pleasure than with the risk of contracting an STI. Students' beliefs that STIs are problematic, but do not necessarily apply to them, might explain why quantitative studies of sexual risk behavior that rely on the HBM do not consistently find an association between perceived costs and condom use (Brown et al., 1991; Maes & Louis, 2003). We therefore recommend that quantitative studies based on the HBM account for the fact that compromised sexual pleasure, for some students, is a very real barrier to using condoms. Similarly, HBM-based studies should account for the fact that, for some students, the risk of contracting HIV through unprotected sexual intercourse is of much lesser concern than the possibility of experiencing compromised pleasure from using condoms. We need to quantitatively assess the degree to which factors such as compromised pleasure or the risk of HIV/AIDS impact students' decisions regarding the use of condoms. Given the degree to which students emphasize sexual pleasure as an objective of hooking up (Bogle, 2008; Paul & Hayes, 2002), prevention educators also need to openly discuss with them safe alternatives to coitus and oral sex (McPhillips, Braun, & Gavey, 2001).

We also recommend that STI-prevention programs emphasize to students the health-related consequences of STIs and encourage them to understand the implications of having STIs for their well-being. Roye and Hudson (2003), for example, demonstrated that when young women watched videos of other young women like themselves who had contracted HIV talking about their experiences, they were more likely to believe that they themselves were susceptible, and more likely to use precautions against infection. Roye and Hudson's (2003) research findings suggest that when young people understand how the costs of contracting STIs can impact their lives, they are more likely to take them into account before and during sexually intimate situations.

Students' understanding of how STIs could negatively impact their lives must be paired with a sense of self-efficacy regarding the use of protection against them. However, we found a mismatch between students' general sense of confidence regarding accessing and using protection against STIs (during vaginal intercourse) and their use of protection during the spontaneous sexual encounters that were involved in many of their hookups. Contextualizing the HBM, then, involves not only taking students' culturally informed risk perceptions into account, but also accounting for situational characteristics, such as spontaneity and the use of alcohol, that compromise their sexual self-efficacy. Given Bandura's (1977) emphasis that self-efficacy is better understood not as a global, but rather a situational, construct, developing ways to enhance students' self-efficacy in situations in which they are more vulnerable to sexual risk taking is a worthy goal (see also Brown et al., 1991).

The level of spontaneity involved in hooking up encourages us to consider efficacy in planning for the unexpected, negotiating the use of protection with relatively unfamiliar or nonromantic partners, and avoiding situations in which it might be difficult to make protective decisions (Corbin & Fromme, 2002). These factors must be taken into account in both HBM-related research, including HBM-based measures of sexual self-efficacy and programming.

As for the spontaneous nature of hooking up, our findings suggest that if students were able to access condoms and dental dams in their living quarters or the places where they recreate, even those with relatively low levels of perceived self-efficacy in the area of sexual protection might be more likely to use them. A student who does not see him- or herself as generally prepared to use prophylactics against STIs might, in fact, wear a condom if one were immediately available. Such was the case with one of the young women we interviewed, whose friend had given her a box of condoms as a present. Because she hadn't planned to hook up and was a relative newcomer to the hookup culture, she said she would not have otherwise used a condom for the intercourse that occurred. There is evidence that high school and college students' access to condoms through student health clinics increases their use of protection during sexual intercourse (Peterson & Gabany, 2001; Schuster, Bell, Berry, & Kanouse, 1997). Our study findings suggest that expanding college students' access to condoms beyond health clinics to their living quarters and places of entertainment would further promote their use. As students at the University of South Carolina noted in their campus newspaper, *The Daily Gamecock,* it is important for university administrators to realize that students are sexually active, and that placing condom machines in campus restrooms and dormitories would help them keep safe (Stevens, 2008).

As for the negotiations that might occur during a hookup, there is evidence that students' sexually efficacious behavior could be promoted by programs that involve role-playing videos or activities that teach them how to effectively negotiate the use of protection (Roye & Hudson, 2003; Sikkema, Winett, & Lombard, 1995; see also Boone & Lefkowitz, 2004). Roye and Hudson (2003), for example, demonstrated that showing young women videos of other young women discussing condom use with their male partners gave them confidence to successfully negotiate condom use with their own partners—even when they believed their partners were trustworthy—and reduced their incidence of STIs. Furthermore, Handler (1990) showed that engaging at-risk youth in role playing that involved negotiating safe sex enhanced their confidence that they would make health protective decisions during future sexual encounters. An apparent advantage of role-playing activities, to supplement the use of informational materials, is that such activities can promote educative dialogue and interaction among students themselves and between students and health professionals regarding safer sex practices (Handler, 1990; Roye & Hudson, 2003). We advocate for interventions that engage students in role playing because most of the students in our study demonstrated considerable barriers to translating their perceived sexual self-efficacy into protective behaviors when necessary. There is evidence that interventions involving role playing can facilitate the translation process and avert students from harm.

Our findings also suggest that students' self-efficacy in the use of protection against STIs would be enhanced by alcohol-abuse prevention programs that promote the responsible use of alcohol and alert students to the dangers of being alone with hookup partners when they are intoxicated. The Neff and Crawford (1998) study cited earlier examined how students' expectations regarding the disinhibitory effects of alcohol impacted their sexual behavior, by utilizing the framework of the HBM. Other researchers have examined the relationship between alcohol use and sexual risk using separate scalar measures of condom use self-efficacy (Mahoney, Thombs, & Ford, 1995). We specifically recommend that alcohol use be considered a barrier to self-efficacy in the use of prophylactics and that HBM-related survey items measure students' levels of confidence that they will use protection against STIs while under the influence of alcohol. Such items should ask students about their level of actual success in accessing protection when they have been drinking alcohol, as well as about their confidence that they will be able to access protection in the future. Because responsible alcohol consumption is a preventive behavior, researchers should develop survey items that assess students' willingness to avoid alcohol over-consumption as a means of preventing risky sex.

Finally, students' self-efficacy in the use of prophylactics against STIs can be compromised in situations in which they are coerced into having sexual intercourse (Flack et al., 2007). Women appear to be particularly vulnerable to such situations, and the fact that the hookup culture so often involves alcohol use and a playful, commitment-free attitude toward sex seems to heighten their vulnerability. According to many of the students inter-

viewed, one of the advantages of hooking up is that one is not responsible for the emotional well-being of his or her hookup partners (Glen & Marquardt, 2001; Paul & Hayes, 2002). It is possible that the affective disengagement many students associate with hooking up is associated with a greater willingness to coerce one's partner into having some type of sexual intercourse, and a lack of conscience regarding the psychological harm that such behavior can inflict.

Although the HBM is not designed to address the issue of sexual coercion, we recommend that sexual risk-prevention programs emphasize to students the importance of consensual sexual intimacy. Such programs should involve students in activities that facilitate their understanding of sexual consent and enhance their ability to discuss their preferences with their hookup partners. Furthermore, programs must teach students how to avoid situations, such as those described in this study, in which young women find themselves alone with sexually aggressive men to whom they are afraid to refuse sex.

Given what we have garnered from the literature and the present study regarding the prevalence of hooking up among college students, we recommend the development of mandatory and nationwide sexual risk-prevention programs that provide incoming students with accurate information regarding STIs and how to protect themselves against them. Furthermore, because hooking up is a cultural phenomenon to which students are exposed throughout their college careers, prevention programs and resources need to be available and promoted to students from their first to last days on campus, through a variety of venues. Although our findings apply to college campuses in the Midwest in particular, we surmise from the extant literature that hooking up is a national phenomenon and that many of the risk behaviors identified here are national in scope, as well (Bogle, 2008; Paul & Hayes, 2002; Weiss & Bullough, 2004). Furthermore, given the prevalence of abstinence-only education in the United States, we can guarantee that many young people are transitioning to college life while being fairly naïve about the risks of STIs. Santelli, Ott, Rogers, Summers, and Schleifer (2006) go so far as to link young people's lack of knowledge about sexual health to abstinence-only education, which they claim violates their rights to health by making them vulnerable to poor decision making. Even if indirectly, we believe our study provides support for their concern.

Future research could address the issue of the limited sample that was used in our study in several ways. First, it could involve studies of hooking up among college students from diverse racial, ethnic, or religious groups, or with nonheterosexual orientations. Winfield and Whaley's (2002) research on whether the HBM predicts condom use among African American college students is a good example of how to incorporate diversity into our research. Future research could also examine hooking up at various types of colleges and universities located within specific regions of the country, or in urban or rural communities. Research across diverse populations and contexts can yield insight into the complexities of human health and well-being (Morse, 2002). Understanding such complexities is necessary to better inform our efforts to prevent STIs, and we recommend that multiple methodologies, including qualitative and mixed-methods approaches, be used for identifying the nuances of sexual risk taking during hooking up among specific subpopulations.

We also recommend that future research examine whether our findings are supported by quantitative surveys of larger, more representative samples. We strongly recommend, however, that the scale items utilized in such research be adapted to better reflect the realities of hooking up on campus. As discussed previously, scale items must account for the fact that students' decisions regarding sexual intimacy are based on the culturally informed beliefs they bring to their understanding of sexual risk and by situational characteristics that are not currently accounted for by the HBM. For example, the current HBM does not account for the fact that students' evaluations of their risks of contracting an STI are informed by their evaluations of whether or not any given partner has an STI, not merely by a generalized estimation of their personal vulnerability. It also does not account for the roles of alcohol, sexual coercion, or condom accessibility in students' ability to translate their sense of self-efficacy in using condoms into protective behaviors. We have offered suggestions for addressing these and other limitations in future research.

To conclude, we emphasize the importance of studying hooking up as a unique phenomenon that is different from what we have traditionally called "casual sex." Hooking up is a cultural phenomenon that is legitimizing "relationship-free" sexual intimacy among many adolescents and young adults, and it is taking the hush out of surreptitious sexual encounters with relative strangers, classmates, online acquaintances, and even longtime friends. Going to college has always been an important period of transition for young adults, as it involves moving away from the family nest and living in a peer-dominated culture where the individual must assume primary responsibility for managing their lives, from their classes and career trajectories to their interpersonal and sexual relationships (Pascarella & Terenzini, 2005). Understanding the rules and practices of this cultural landscape and their implications for sexual risk prevention is integral to our ability to promote the well-being of this and future generations.

Notes

1. When we refer to STIs, we include HIV/AIDS, and we emphasized this during the student interviews.

2. Again, in the Neff and Crawford (1998) study, individuals' expectations that the disinhibitory effects of alcohol would prevent them from practicing safe sex were conceptualized as a barrier to using protection against STIs, within the five-factor HBM. Even though we agree that individuals' alcohol-related expectations are important to address, we propose that the direct impact of alcohol on individuals' decision-making capacities, not to mention the direct impact of sexual arousal itself on such capacities, is not fully accounted for by the HBM.

3. According to Ajzen (2002), perceived behavioral control can serve as a proxy for actual behavioral control, and is thus predictive of whether or not individuals will implement intended behaviors. Although we did not measure perceived or actual behavioral control in this study, the data suggest that women in situations that involve having sexual intercourse against their will believe they have no choice regarding the use of protection against STIs.

References

Aguinaldo, J. P., & Myers, T. (2008). A discursive approach to disinhibition theory: The normalization of unsafe sex among gay men. *Qualitative Health Research, 18,* 167–181.

Ajzen, I. (2002). Perceived behavioral control, self-efficacy, locus of control, and the theory of planned behavior. *Journal of Applied Social Psychology, 32,* 665–683.

Bandura, A. (1977). Self-efficacy: Toward a unifying theory of behavioral change. *Psychological Review, 84,* 191–215.

Bogle, K. A. (2008). *Hooking up: Sex, dating, and relationships on campus.* New York: New York University Press.

Boone, T. L., & Lefkowitz, E. S. (2004). Safer sex and the health belief model: Considering the contributions of peer norms and socialization factors. *Journal of Psychology & Human Sexuality, 16*(1), 66–83.

Brown, L. K., DiClemente, R. J., & Reynolds, L. A. (1991). HIV prevention for adolescents: Utility of the health belief model. *AIDS Education and Prevention, 3,* 50–59.

Cates, W. (1999). Estimates of the incidence and prevalence of sexually transmitted diseases in the United States. *Sexually Transmitted Diseases, 26*(Suppl. 4), 2–7.

Centers for Disease Control and Prevention. (1995a). *HIV/AIDS and college students.* Retrieved June 28, 2008, from www.aegis.com/default.asp?req=www.aegis.com/pubs/Cdc_Fact_Sheets/1995/CPATH003.html.

Centers for Disease Control and Prevention. (1995b). *Youth risk behavior surveillance: National college health risk behavior survey.* Atlanta, GA: U.S. Department of Health and Human Services.

Centers for Disease Control and Prevention. (2004). *HIV transmission among Black college student and non-student men who have sex with men—North Carolina, 2003.* Retrieved June 28, 2008, from www.cdc.gov/mmwr/preview/mmwrhtml/mm5332a1.htm.

Centers for Disease Control and Prevention. (2005). Trends in HIV diagnoses: 33 states, 2001–2004. *Morbidity and Mortality Weekly Report, 54,* 1149–1153.

Conner, M., & Norman, P. (1996). *Predicting health behavior: Research and practice with social cognition models.* Berkshire, UK: Open University Press.

Corbin, W. R., & Fromme, K. (2002). Alcohol use and serial monogamy as risks for sexually transmitted diseases in young adults. *Health Psychology, 21,* 229–236.

Flack, W. F., Daubman, K. A., Caron, M. L., Asadorian, J. A., D'Aureli, N. R., Gigliotti, S. N., (2007). Risk factors and consequences of unwanted sex among university students: Hooking up, alcohol, and stress response. *Journal of Interpersonal Violence, 22*(2), 139–157.

Gielen, A. C., Faden, R. R., Ocampo, P., Kass, N., & Anderson, J. (1994). Women's protective sexual behaviors: A test of the health belief model. *Aids Education and Prevention, 6,* 1–11.

Gilmartin, S. K. (2006). Changes in college women's attitudes toward sexual intimacy. *Journal of Research on Adolescence, 16,* 429–454.

Glen, N., & Marquardt, E. (2001). *Hooking up, hanging out, and hoping for Mr. Right: College women on dating and mating today.* New York: Institute for American Values. Retrieved August, 5, 2008, from www.americanvalues.org/Hooking_Up.pdf.

Halpern-Felsher, B. L., Cornell, J. L., Kropp, R. Y., & Tschann, J. M. (2005). Oral versus vaginal sex among adolescents: Perceptions, attitudes, and behavior. *Pediatrics, 115,* 845–851.

Handler, A. (1990, June). *The role of negotiation skills in safer sex practice when educating at-risk youth.* Paper presented at the International Conference on AIDS, Los Angeles, CA. Abstract retrieved July 8, 2009, from http://gateway.nlm.nih.gov/MeetingAbstracts/ma?f=102196561.html.

Lambert, T., Kahn, A. S., & Apple, K. J. (2003). Pluralistic ignorance and hooking up. *Journal of Sex Research, 40,* 129–133.

Laraque, D., McLean, D. E., Brown-Peterside, P., Ashton, D., & Diamond, B. (1997). Predictors of reported condom use in Central Harlem youth as conceptualized by the health belief model. *Journal of Adolescent Health, 21,* 318–327.

Lin, P., Simoni, J. M., & Zemon, V. (2005). The health belief model, sexual behaviors, and HIV risk among Taiwanese immigrants. *AIDS Education and Prevention, 17,* 469–483.

Lofland, J., Snow, D., Anderson, L., & Lofland, L. (2005). *Analyzing social settings: A guide to qualitative observation and analysis.* New York: Barnes & Noble.

Maes, C. A., & Louis, M. (2003). Knowledge of AIDS, perceived risk of AIDS, and at-risk sexual behaviors among older adults. *Journal of the American Academy of Nurse Practitioners, 15,* 509–516.

Mahoney, C. A., Thombs, D. L., & Ford, O. J. (1995). Health belief and self-efficacy models: Their utility in explaining college student condom use. *AIDS Education and Prevention, 7*(1), 32–49.

Manning, W. D., Giordano, P. C., & Longmore, M. A. (2006). Hooking up: The relationship contexts of "nonrelationship" sex. *Journal of Adolescent Research, 21,* 459–483.

McPhillips, K., Braun, V., & Gavey, N. (2001). Defining (hetero) sex: How imperative is the "coital imperative"? *Women's Studies International Forum, 24,* 229–240.

Morrison, L. (2004). Traditions in transition: Young people's risk for HIV in Chiang Mai, Thailand. *Qualitative Health Research, 14,* 328–344.

Morse, J. M. (2002). Qualitative health research: Challenges for the 21st century. *Qualitative Health Research, 12,* 116–129.

National Cancer Institute. (2005). *Theory at a glance: A guide for health promotion practice* (2nd ed.). Washington, DC: Author. Retrieved May 15, 2007, from www.nci.nih.gov/PDF/481f5d53-63df-41bc-bfaf-5aa48ee1da4d/TAAG3.pdf.

Neff, J. A., & Crawford, S. L. (1998). The health belief model and HIV risk behaviors: A causal model analysis among Anglos, African-Americans, and Mexican-Americans. *Ethnicity & Health, 3,* 283–299.

Newcomb, M. D., Wyatt, G. E., Romero, G. J., Tucker, M. B., Wayment, H. A., Carmona, J. V., et al., (1998). Acculturation, sexual risk taking, and HIV health promotion among Latinas. *Journal of Counseling Psychology, 45,* 454–467.

Pascarella, E. T., & Terenzini, P. T. (2005). *How college affects students: A third decade of research.* (vol. 2). Indianapolis, IN: Jossey-Bass.

Paul, E. L., & Hayes, K. A. (2002). The casualties of "casual" sex: A qualitative exploration of the phenomenology of college students' hookups. *Journal of Social and Personal Relationships, 19,* 639–661.

Paul, E. L., McManus, B., & Hayes, A. (2000). "Hookups": Characteristics and correlates of college students' spontaneous and anonymous sexual experiences. *Journal of Sex Research, 37,* 76–88.

Peterson, Y., & Gabany, S. G. (2001). Applying the NIMH multi-site condom use self-efficacy scale to college students. *American Journal of Health Studies, 17,* 1–15.

Rosenstock, I. (1974). Historical origins of the health belief model. *Health Education Monographs, 2,* 328–335.

Rosenstock, I. M., Strecher, V. J., & Becker, M. H. (1988). Social learning theory and the health belief model. *Health Education & Behavior, 15,* 175–183.

Rosenstock, I. M., Strecher, V. J., & Becker, M. H. (1994). The health belief model and HIV risk behavior change. In R. J. DiClemente & J. L. Peterson (Eds.), *Preventing AIDS: Theories and methods of behavioral interventions* (pp. 5–24). New York: Plenum.

Roye, C. F., & Hudson, M. (2003). Developing a culturally appropriate video to promote dual-method use by urban teens: Rationale and methodology. *AIDS Education & Prevention, 15,* 148–158.

Santelli, J. S., Ott, M., Rogers, J., Summers, D., & Schleifer, R. (2006). Abstinence and abstinence-only education: A review of U.S. policies and programs. *Journal of Adolescent Health, 38,* 83–87.

Scandell, D., & Wlazelek, B. (2002). A validation study of the AIDS health belief scale. *Canadian Journal of College Health, 11,* 41–49.

Schuster, M. A., Bell, R. M., Berry, S. H., & Kanouse, D. E. (1997). Students' acquisition and use of school condoms in high school condom availability program. *Pediatrics, 100,* 689–694.

Sikkema, K. J., Winett, R. A., & Lombard, D. N. (1995). Development and evaluation of an HIV-risk reduction program for female college students. *AIDS Education and Prevention, 7,* 145–159.

Steers, W. N., Elliot, E., Nemiro, J., Ditman, D., & Oskamp, S. (1996). Health beliefs as predictors of HIV-preventive behavior and ethnic differences in prediction. *Journal of Social Psychology, 136,* 99–110.

Stevens, C. (2008, December 5). Condom access challenged: Vending machines could tarnish Gamecock image, aim to promote safer sex. *The Daily Gamecock.* Retrieved June 28, 2008, from http://media.www.dailygamecock.com/media/storage/paper247/

news/2008/01/29/News/Condom.Access.Challenged 3173104
.shtml.

Task Force of the National Advisory Council on Alcohol Abuse and
Alcoholism. (2002). *A call to action: Changing the culture
of drinking at U.S. colleges* (NIH publication no. 02-5010).
Bethesda, MD: National Institute on Alcohol Abuse and
Alcoholism. Retrieved August 10, 2007, from www
.collegedrinkingprevention.gov/NIAAACollegeMaterials/
TaskForce/ TaskForce_TOC.aspx.

U.S. Census Bureau. (2000). *Race for the population 18 years
and over.* Census Summary File 1. Retrieved August
10, 2007, from http://factfinder.census.gov/servlet/
DatasetMainPageServlet?_ds_name=DEC_2000_SF4_U&
_program=DEC&_lang=en.

Weiss, D., & Bullough, V. L. (2004). Adolescent American sex.
Journal of Psychology & Human Sexuality, 16, 43–53.

Winfield, E. B., & Whaley, A. L. (2002). A comprehensive test of
the health belief model in the prediction of condom use among
African American college students. *Journal of Black Psychology,
28,* 330–346.

Yates, E. L, (2004, April 22). N. C. students, faculty, address HIV
outbreak. *Black Issues in Higher Education.* Retrieved January
8, 2009, from http://findarticles.com/p/articles/mi_m0DXK/is_/
ai_n6145040.

Zak-Place, J., & Stern, M. (2004). Health belief factors and
dispositional optimism as predictors of STD and HIV preventive
behavior. *Journal of American College Health, 52,* 229–236.

Critical Thinking

1. Describe the social phenomenon of hooking up among
   college students.

2. In what ways are hooking up and sexual risk taking
   interrelated?

TERESA M. DOWNING-MATIBAG, PhD, is an assistant professor in
the Department of Sociology at Iowa State University in Ames, Iowa,
USA. BRANDI GEISINGER, BS, is a recent graduate from the Iowa
State University Department of Psychology in Ames, Iowa, USA.

Authors' Note—We acknowledge the Iowa State University Department of Sociology and the Institute for Social and Behavioral Research
for supporting this study.

Rationing Antiretroviral Therapy in Africa—Treating Too Few, Too Late

Nathan Ford, DHA, Edward Mills, PhD, and Alexandra Calmy, MD

The past 6 years have seen striking advances in access to antiretroviral therapy in Africa. From 2002 onward, the international drive to scale up antiretroviral treatment gained considerable momentum, most notably with the establishment of the Global Fund to Fight AIDS, Tuberculosis, and Malaria, the "3 by 5" Initiative of the World Health Organization (WHO), and the U.S. President's Emergency Plan for AIDS Relief (PEPFAR). Today, an estimated 3 million people in the developing world are receiving antiretroviral therapy.

The momentum has now begun to wane, with various groups arguing that the focus on AIDS has had its day and that health care funding should now be redirected to other areas, such as maternal and child health and primary care. But before the international community gives up on prioritizing care for patients with HIV infection, we believe that on-the-ground discussions must address not only whether enough has been done to scale up treatment but also whether the treatment that patients are receiving is good enough.

The standard approach to HIV treatment in Africa is to wait until people are visibly sick, treat them with effective but poorly tolerated drugs, and then wait until they are sick again before switching regimens. There are several problems with this approach.

The first is that too few people are receiving treatment. The 3 million people receiving antiretroviral therapy are usually said to account for about 30% of the need for such treatment, but even this rate reflects the use of stringent eligibility criteria that have been abandoned in wealthier countries.

Second, we are waiting until people are symptomatic before they are treated. In most African countries, patients begin receiving treatment when the CD4+ count falls below 200 cells per cubic millimeter, at which point most patients already have symptomatic and severe (WHO stage 3 or 4) infection. In the United States and Europe, treatment is initiated earlier—as soon as the CD4+ count reaches 350 cells per cubic millimeter—and increasingly, experts are arguing that even that is too late.

In many patients in Africa, the CD4+ count takes only about a year to decline from the cutoff for such early initiation to that for the later initiation now practiced in developing countries.[1] Although delaying therapy may mean saving money on drugs during this period, the long-term cost of such delays is increased substantially by the need for more intensive clinical care, decreased income, and likely regimen switches. Cost is thus no longer a tenable justification for delaying therapy. More important, recent observational data presented by Kitahata et al., show that the risk of death increases by 69% when the initiation of therapy is delayed until the CD4+ count drops below 350 cells per cubic millimeter. Patients' immunologic nadir—how low their CD4+ count is allowed to drop—is predictive of the degree of benefit they will obtain from future antiretroviral therapy. Although guidelines for low-income settings recommend initiating treatment when a patient's CD4+ count drops below 200 cells per cubic millimeter, patients frequently begin receiving therapy even later, on average when the CD4+ count is just over 100 cells per cubic millimeter. Enrolling patients in treatment programs earlier is a priority.[2]

There are also important public health costs. For one thing, a policy of late initiation encourages the spread of tuberculosis. One recent study estimated that patients starting antiretroviral therapy at a CD4+ count below 200 cells per cubic millimeter have more than three times the risk of tuberculosis of those who begin therapy earlier.[3] Moreover, late initiation compromises the potential effect of antiretroviral therapy on HIV transmission by allowing patients to remain viremic longer. One study estimated that starting treatment earlier would reduce HIV transmission by 56%.[4] However, if the current guidelines for the initiation of therapy in the West were adopted in developing countries, several million more people would be eligible for care, and the treatment gap would widen even further.

Another concern is that in most developing countries, patients are receiving drugs with major tolerability issues. The majority of treatment programs in Africa use an antiretroviral regimen based on stavudine. There are a number of sound reasons for using this drug, including the fact that it forms part of a simple, affordable, fixed-dose combination. However, the drug's severe side effects have rendered it all but obsolete in the West. A tenofovir-based regimen would be preferable, but the use of tenofovir has largely been limited by its cost.

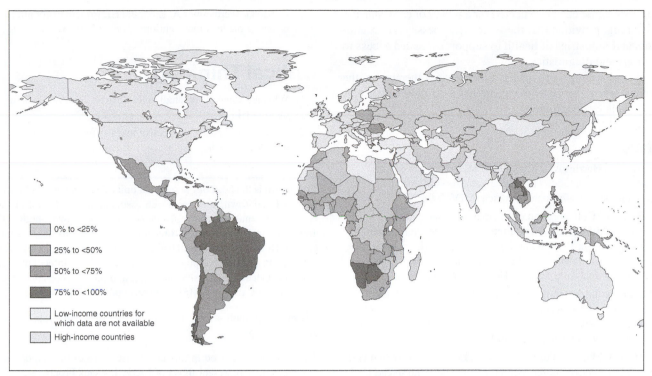

Estimated Proportion of Persons with HIV Infection Receiving Antiretroviral Therapy in Low-Income and Middle-Income Countries as of December 2007. No coverage proportion was calculated for countries in which the estimated number of persons requiring therapy was less than 500. Data are from the World Health Organization.

Furthermore, not only should initial treatment begin earlier in developing countries, but when the first-line regimen fails, patients should also be switched earlier to another regimen. In the Western world, evaluations of viral load and genotyping are performed regularly, and the drug regimen is altered at the first sign of virologic resistance. In Africa, access to viral-load assessment is extremely limited, and patients must wait until immunologic or clinical deterioration is manifested before being switched to new drugs, which reduces future treatment options and increases the risk of transmission.

It should be acknowledged that although there are outstanding clinical questions regarding the optimal time for initiating and switching treatments, the overriding rationale behind current guidelines for antiretroviral therapy is rationing—limiting the number of people who must be treated, providing the cheapest available drugs, and delaying shifts to more expensive drugs for as long as possible. But as other experts have argued, rationing on the basis of clinical criteria alone is an inherently flawed way of prioritizing the needs competing for scarce resources.[5]

The drive to scale up antiretroviral treatment in Africa has encouraged a public health approach that promotes reaching the greatest number of patients with the simplest, most affordable regimens. We would argue that treating people when they are less sick with drugs that are less toxic and providing a simple tool for monitoring adherence and detecting treatment failure would be entirely consistent with this approach and would improve access to care by facilitating the decentralization of services from the hospital level to the clinic. Newer, more potent drugs should be considered for inclusion in treatment

guidelines, rather than being reserved for use in salvage regimens for a minority of patients in the West. The better the drug, the simpler the treatment, and the fewer treatment switches will be necessary. Viral-load monitoring should be expanded to reinforce adherence and ensure that treatment failure is detected as early as possible.

Taking this new approach will require a reorientation of the organization and support of HIV care programs. A policy of earlier initiation of therapy could help to streamline services that are currently overwhelmed, by prioritizing clinic care according to patients' health needs. Clinic services could be primarily used by patients who are clinically sick, whereas patients with stronger immunity could, after initial consultation, receive follow-up medication and care in the community. In this way, a policy of earlier initiation of therapy could help to streamline services that are already overwhelmed by the competing needs of patients with various levels of illness.

Earlier treatment and regimen switching would initially require additional investment by national governments and the international community (in particular, PEPFAR and the Global Fund), but it might well turn out to be cheaper in the long run, as the need for managing clinical complications is reduced and the rate of new infections falls. The initial provision of antiretroviral therapy in the late 1990s ultimately led to massive cost savings, thanks to the avoidance of hospitalizations and opportunistic infections; in this way, Brazil alone is estimated to have saved more than $1 billion in 4 years. At the same time, increased demand forced the cost of medicines down considerably, from more than $10,000 per patient per year to less than $100.

213

The same dynamic can be expected for a policy of early starting and switching, provided that there are clear messages to manufacturers and ministries of health to support expanded access to better drugs and diagnostics.

The battle to start providing antiretroviral therapy in the developing world has been won. The battle to provide the best care we can is just beginning.

Notes

1. Lawn SD, Harries AD, Anglaret X, Myer L, Wood R. Early mortality among adults accessing antiretroviral treatment programmes in sub-Saharan Africa. AIDS 2008;22:1897–908.

2. ART-LINC Collaboration of International Databases to Evaluate AIDS (IeDEA). Antiretroviral therapy in resource-limited settings 1996 to 2006: patient characteristics, treatment regimens and monitoring in sub-Saharan Africa, Asia and Latin America. Trop Med Int Health 2008;13:870–9.

3. Moreno S, Jarrin I, Iribarren JA, et al., Incidence and risk factors for tuberculosis in HIV-positive subjects by HAART status. *Int J Tuberc Lung Dis* 2008;12:1393–400. [Erratum, *Int J Tuberc Lung Dis* 2009;13:150.]

4. Auvert B, Males S, Puren A, Taljaard D, Caraël M, Williams B. Can highly active antiretroviral therapy reduce the spread of HIV? A study in a township of South Africa. *J Acquir Immune Defic Syndr* 2004;36:613–21.

5. Persad G, Wertheimer A, Emanuel EJ. Principles for allocation of scarce medical interventions. *Lancet* 2009;373:423–31.

Critical Thinking

1. What are some of the challenges African countries face in treating HIV infection?

2. Compare and contrast effective and ineffective approaches to HIV treatment.

MR. FORD is the head of the medical unit of Médecins sans Frontières (MSF), Cape Town, and a research associate at the School of Public Health and Family Medicine, University of Cape Town—both in Cape Town, South Africa. **DR. MILLS** holds a Canada Research Chair in Global Health, Faculty of Health Sciences, University of Ottawa, Ottawa. **DR. CALMY** is a physician in the HIV Unit, Infectious Disease Services, Geneva University Hospital, and an HIV consultant for the MSF Access Campaign, MSF International—both in Geneva.

Acknowledgments—No potential conflict of interest relevant to this article was reported.

The opinions expressed in this article are those of the authors and do not necessarily represent those of Médecins sans Frontières, the University of Cape Town, the University of Ottawa, or Geneva University Hospital.

Silent Treatment

HIV Plan B

JUSTINE SHARROCK

One winter night in 2000, Danny, who was 21 at the time, went home with a guy he met at a crowded bar in San Francisco. Random hookups weren't out of the ordinary for Danny, but this one ended badly: As he was buttoning up to go home, his new friend mentioned he was HIV positive. Usually conscientious about safe sex, Danny hadn't been, and he panicked. "I was in shock," he says. "I just couldn't believe it." He vaguely remembered reading about an emergency treatment that could prevent infection, so when he got home he called the California AIDS hotline. Memory served. A monthlong regimen known as post-exposure prophylaxis treatment (PEP)—usually given to health care workers who have been stuck with needles—was available at local clinics and emergency rooms to people who had recently been exposed to HIV. The side effects of debilitating nausea and fatigue were a small price to pay for its potential benefits: A study of health care workers published in the *New England Journal of Medicine* linked the rapid administration of the drug to an 81 percent decrease in the risk of contracting the virus.

Danny went to a city clinic, where after a consultation, he was given a prescription for two antiretroviral drugs—the same kind that HIV-positive patients have taken since the '80s. As preventative medicine, the drugs work with a one-two punch: The first intercepts the virus' initial attachment to DNA, and the second stops infected cells from spreading the virus.

Danny was lucky that California is one of the few states (along with New York, Massachusetts, New Mexico, and Rhode Island) where policies ensure that the general public—not just hospital workers who have been exposed on the job—can access the drugs. Elsewhere, the decision is up to individual hospitals, clinics, and doctors. Surveying all 50 state health departments and more than 50 ERs nationwide, I encountered STD clinicians and workers at AIDS hotlines and Planned Parenthoods who did not know PEP could be prescribed to the public. An Alabama health department official told me, "It's not available." A nurse at a North Dakota clinic said he all but encouraged patients to fly to San Francisco.

Since the virus must be intercepted before it attaches to cells and reaches the lymph nodes, it is crucial that PEP be administered immediately—each passing hour means decreased effectiveness.

"It needs to be treated like a gunshot wound or a stabbing," says Antonio Urbina, a medical director at St. Vincent Catholic Medical Center's HIV clinic in New York City. Yet of the largest hospitals in each state, only a quarter offer PEP in their emergency rooms. In a 2005–06 CDC survey taken at gay pride parades around the country, less than 20 percent of HIV-negative respondents knew about PEP. "When I tell people that I used it, they say they've never heard of it," says Danny. "You see signs about crystal meth or syphilis, but even in the gay publications, you never see ads for PEP."

PEP is FDA approved, commercially available, and even often covered by insurance (though for the uninsured the drugs run upward of $1,000). In 2005, the CDC recommended that PEP be administered to all patients on a case-by-case basis within 72 hours of a high-risk exposure, followed up by testing and counseling. But for reasons that are more political than scientific, there is no federal funding for the treatment. Some public health officials claim that public availability of PEP will encourage risky behavior—the same argument used against RU-486, abortions, and condom distribution. Robert Janssen, director of the Division of HIV/AIDS Prevention at the CDC, explains, "Biomedical interventions raise concerns that people would feel, 'Oh, I have these pills, they will keep me from getting it.'"

Yet 73 percent of non-hospital-worker PEP recipients in a San Francisco study decreased high-risk sex over the following year. And since PEP drugs are so toxic, most doctors would be careful about overprescribing. "I'm concerned with two things," says Urbina. "Is the person that exposed them either HIV positive or at high risk for HIV, and is there potential contact with infectious body fluid? If both are yes, in my equation, you give PEP." Peter Leone, medical director of North Carolina's HIV department, who hasn't received the necessary support to institute a public PEP program in his state, believes the benefits of PEP outweigh the risks. "Nationally, there is a 'Don't Ask, Don't Tell' policy," he says. "We're okay to say it's a good idea, as long as we don't know about it and don't do anything to support it. We don't deny care to smokers or people who didn't buckle their seat belts. It says a lot about the political climate around sexuality and homophobia." For the 40,000 people infected with HIV in the United States each year, the knowledge of a lost opportunity for prevention is devastating. In Britain, an HIV-positive couple has filed suit against the government for withholding lifesaving information.

Two months after he finished his treatment, Danny tested negative for HIV—whether because he hadn't contracted the virus from the encounter or because the PEP worked, he'll never know. Since a randomized clinical trial is unethical, researchers have to rely on observational and tangential research. "At least if you test positive after PEP, you'll know you did everything you could," says Danny. He keeps his medication label as a token of how a little bottle may have saved his life.

Critical Thinking

1. Present an overview of existing challenges to universal access to timely post-exposure prophylaxis.

2. Discuss the relationship of knowledge to access in relation to post-exposure prophylaxis.

3. What are the costs versus the benefits to widening access to post-exposure prophylaxis?

Who Still Dies of AIDS, and Why

In the age of HAART, the virus can still outwit modern medicine.

GARY TAUBES

In the video, filmed last November, Mel Cheren appears understandably dismayed. He's being interviewed by a reporter for CBS News on *Logo,* a gay-themed news program; he's sitting in a wheelchair, and he's talking about the indignity and the irony of dying from AIDS at a time when AIDS should be a chronic disease, not a fatal one. Cheren, a music producer and founder of West End Records, had been an AIDS activist since the earliest days of the epidemic. It was Cheren, in 1982, who gave the Gay Men's Health Crisis its first home, providing a floor of his brownstone on West 22nd Street. In the interview, Cheren talks about what it's like to lose more than 300 friends to the AIDS epidemic, outlive them all, and then get diagnosed yourself at age 74.

Indeed, the fact that Cheren had plenty of sex through the height of the epidemic, had been tested regularly, and had apparently emerged uninfected had led him to believe that testing was no longer necessary, or at least so one doctor had told him half a dozen years earlier. He's only learned the truth after he began losing weight, had trouble walking, and was finally referred to a specialist who didn't consider AIDS an unreasonable diagnosis for a man of Cheren's experience and advanced years and so ordered up the requisite blood test. "There was one guy," Cheren says in the interview, explaining how he might have been infected. A male escort. "We really hit it off, sexually . . . "

By the time Cheren learned he had AIDS, he was already suffering from a rare, drug-resistant pneumonia, what infectious-disease specialists refer to as an opportunistic infection, and he had lymphoma, an AIDS-related cancer that had spread to his bones.

Within a month of his diagnosis, Cheren was dead. The official cause was pneumonia, although, as his cousin Mark Cheren points out, cause of death in these cases is a moot point. "Infection from pneumonia was probably the culprit," he says, "but only because that acts quickest when you don't stop it."

Dying from AIDS, or dying with an HIV infection, which may not be the same thing, is a significantly less common event than it was a decade ago, but it's not nearly as uncommon as anyone would like. Bob Hattoy, for instance, died last year as well. Hattoy, 56, was "the first gay man with AIDS many Americans had knowingly laid eyes on," as *The New York Times* described him after Hattoy announced his condition to the world in a speech at the 1992 Democratic National Convention. Hattoy went on to work in the Clinton White House as an advocate for gay and lesbian issues. In the summer of 1993, he told *The New York Times,* "I don't make real long-term plans." But the advent of an anti-retroviral drug known as a protease inhibitor, in 1995, and then, a year later multidrug cocktails called HAART—for

highly active anti-retroviral therapy—gave Hattoy and a few hundred thousand HIV-infected Americans like him the opportunity to do just that.

If the pharmaceutical industry ever needed an icon for evidence of its good works, HAART would be it. Between 1995 and 1997, annual AIDS deaths in New York City dropped from 8,309 to 3,426, and that number has continued to decline ever since. The success of HAART has been so remarkable that it now tends to take us by surprise when anybody does succumb, although 2,076 New Yorkers died in 2006 (2007 figures are not yet available). Though many of the most prominent deaths, like Cheren's and Hattoy's, tend to be of gay men, the percentage of the dead who contracted the disease through gay sex is now reportedly as low as 15 percent (with a large proportion still reported as unknown). Intravenous-drug users make up the biggest group, 38.5 percent, and women account for almost one in three of total AIDS deaths.

One of the ironies of the success of HAART is that it has fostered the myth that the AIDS epidemic has come to an end, and that living with HIV is only marginally more problematic than living with herpes or genital warts. This is one obvious explanation for why HIV infection is once again on the rise among young men—specifically, MSMs, as they're now known in the public-health jargon, for men who have sex with men—increasing by a third between 2001 and 2006. Among those 30 and over, the infection rate is still decreasing, notes Thomas Frieden, commissioner of the city's Department of Health and Mental Hygiene, suggesting that the increased rate of infection among men under 30 is due in part to decreased awareness of the disease or the toll it can take.

"If you do the mathematics," Frieden says, "HAART became available in 1996. If you were of age before then, sexually active, and you saw a lot of people dying or sick or disfigured from AIDS, maybe you're more careful than if you came of age after 1996 and didn't see that. When we've done focus groups, what young men have told us is that the only thing they hear about HIV these days is that if you get it, you can climb mountains, like Magic Johnson. Certainly it's true that the treatment for HIV is very effective and it's possible to live a long and productive life with an HIV infection. It's also true that it remains an incurable infection. That the treatment is very arduous and sometimes unsuccessful. It remains a disease often fatal, and frequently disabling."

At the moment some 100,000 New Yorkers are infected with the HIV virus, and AIDS remains the third leading cause of death in men under 65, exceeded only by heart disease and cancer. The question of who will die from AIDS in the HAART era—or who dies with an HIV infection but not technically from AIDS—and what kills them is worth asking now that such deaths have become relatively infrequent.

Frieden's department of Health and Mental Hygiene tried to answer this question with a study it published in the summer of 2006. The newsworthy conclusions were that deaths among New Yorkers with AIDS were still dropping, thanks to HAART, and that one in four of these individuals was now living long enough to die of the same chronic diseases that are likely to kill the uninfected—particularly cancer or heart disease—although most of these non-HIV-related deaths were from the side effects of drug abuse. HIV-related illnesses were still responsible for the remaining three out of four deaths. Or at least "HIV disease," in these cases, was recorded as a cause of death on the death certificates.

What the Health Department study couldn't do is say precisely what these HIV-related deaths were. For the answer to this question, you have to go to physicians who specialize in treating HIV-infected patients. Michael Mullen, clinical director of infectious diseases at Mount Sinai School of Medicine, for instance, says the best way to think about AIDS deaths is to divide HIV-infected individuals into three groups.

The bulk of these deaths occur within the first group, those who either never started HAART to begin with or didn't stay on it once they did. For these patients, "it might as well still be the eighties," says Mullen, and they die from the same AIDS-defining illnesses that were the common causes of death twenty years ago—pneumocystis pneumonia, central-nervous system opportunistic infections (such as toxoplasmosis), lymphoma, Kaposi's sarcoma, etc.

A large proportion of these victims are indigent; many are intravenous-drug users—IVDUs, as they're known in the official jargon, accounted for 21 percent of HIV-positive New Yorkers in 2006, but, as noted above, 38.5 percent of the city's AIDS deaths. The virus is not more aggressive or virulent in these cases. Rather, these are the people who either don't or can't do what it takes to fight it. "These individuals are repeatedly admitted to the hospital," says Mullen, "sometimes for opportunistic infections, sometimes for drug-related issues, often for HIV-related lymphomas and malignancies. They will not take the medication, nine times out of ten, because of drug use." Often these individuals are co-infected with hepatitis, which increases the risk that the more toxic side effects of the anti-retroviral drugs will lead to permanent liver or kidney damage.

By far the highest death rates in this group are in what the authorities now refer to as concurrent HIV/AIDS diagnoses. These patients never get diagnosed with HIV infection until they already have active AIDS. (Cheren, because of his age and his AIDS awareness, is an extreme case.) These constituted more than a quarter of the 3,745 new cases of HIV infections diagnosed in New York in 2006. "Those people have never been tested before," says Mullen. "Believe it or not, people like this still exist." Typically, they've had the infection for ten years—the average time between HIV infection and the emergence of AIDS—but won't know it or acknowledge it until admitted to the emergency room with pneumonia or some other opportunistic infection. These individuals are twice as likely to die in the three to four years after their diagnosis as someone who was just diagnosed with HIV alone. Half of these deaths will occur in the first four months after diagnosis, often from whatever AIDS-related ailment led them to the emergency room in the first place.

It's because of these concurrent HIV/AIDS diagnoses that the Centers for Disease Control and Prevention and the city's Department of Health and Mental Hygiene have been lobbying for HIV tests to be given routinely to anyone who visits an emergency room for any reason. In one recent study from South Carolina, almost three out of four of those people with concurrent HIV/AIDS diagnoses had visited a medical facility after their infection and prior to getting their blood tested for the virus—averaging six visits each before they were finally tested and diagnosed. "By remaining untested during their routine contacts with the health-care system," said Frieden, in testimony to the New York State Assembly Committee on Health, "they have missed the high-quality treatment that could improve their health and extend their lives. Many may have unknowingly infected their partners—and these partners may not learn that they are infected until they too are sick with AIDS. And so this cycle of death continues."

The second group of HIV-infected patients consists of those at the other extreme, the ones who are least likely to die from AIDS or its complications. These individuals were diagnosed with HIV after the advent of HAART and have taken their medications religiously ever since. In these cases, HAART is likely to suppress their virus for decades, and they're now significantly more likely to die of heart disease or cancer than of anything related to AIDS. To get an idea of the mortality rate among these patients, consider Alexander McMeeking's practice, on East 40th Street. McMeeking ran the HIV clinic at Bellevue from 1987 to 1989 and then left to start a private practice. To the best of his knowledge, only three of his 300-odd Bellevue patients survived long enough to get on HAART. They are still alive today. "Fortunately, thank God, all three are doing great," says McMeeking. "I tell them they will essentially die of old age."

McMeeking's practice now includes 600 HIV-infected patients, and last year he lost only two of those—one to lung cancer, another to liver cancer.

Now the question is whether these patients doing well with HAART are actually more susceptible to the kind of chronic diseases that kill the uninfected. Are they more likely to die from heart disease, cancers, liver and kidney failure, and other chronic diseases either because of the HIV itself or the anti-retroviral regimen keeping it under control? One observation made repeatedly in studies—including the 2006 report from the Department of Health and Mental Hygiene—is that these HIV-infected individuals appear to have higher rates of several different cancers, in particular lung cancer among smokers, non-Hodgkins lymphoma, and cancers of the rectal area. These cancers appear both more precocious and more aggressive in HIV-infected patients—they strike earlier and kill quicker. The reason is not yet clear, although a likely explanation is that the ability of the immune system to search out and destroy incipient malignancies is sufficiently compromised from either the anti-retroviral drugs, the virus, or the coexistence of several viruses—squamous-cell cancers of the rectal area are caused by the same human papilloma virus that causes cervical cancer in woman—that the cancers get a foothold they don't get in non-HIV-infected individuals.

One finding that's considered indisputable is that HAART, and particularly the protease inhibitors that are a critical part of the anti-retroviral cocktail, can play havoc with risk factors for heart disease. They raise cholesterol and triglyceride levels; they lower HDL, and they can cause increased resistance to the hormone insulin. These changes often accompany a condition known as HIV-related lipodystrophy, which afflicts maybe half of all individuals who go on HAART. Subcutaneous fat is lost on the face, arms, legs, and buttocks, while fat accumulates in the gut, upper back (a condition known as a buffalo hump), and breasts. The question is whether these metabolic disturbances actually increase the likelihood of having a heart attack. It's certainly reasonable to think they would, but it's remarkably difficult to demonstrate that the drugs or the virus itself is responsible: The fact that a relatively young man or woman with AIDS has a heart attack does not mean that the heart attack was caused by HIV or the disturbance in cholesterol and lipid levels induced by the therapy.

"If it's 1988, 1989," says one doctor, "and I have a patient with HIV disease and hypertension, he's not going to live long enough to die of hypertension. I want to treat the disease."

Any difference in disease incidence between HIV-infected and uninfected individuals, explains John Brooks, leader of the clinical-epidemiology team within the CDC's Division of HIV/AIDS Prevention, can be due to the infection itself, to the therapy—HAART—or to "the host, the person who has HIV infection, both physiologically and socioculturally." It's the last factor—the host—that complicates the science. Until recently, for instance, physicians saw little reason to worry about heart-disease risk factors in their HIV-infected patients and so didn't bother to aggressively treat risk factors in those patients, as they did the HIV-negative. "Think about it," says Brooks, "if it's 1988, 1989, and I have a patient with HIV disease and hypertension, he's not going to live long enough to die of hypertension. I want to treat the disease."

The rate of cigarette smoking among HIV-infected individuals is also twice as high as the national average. The rate of intravenous drug use is far higher, as is the rate of infection with hepatitis B or C, because intravenous drug use is a common route to getting both HIV and hepatitis. So the fact that an HIV-infected patient may seem to be suffering premature heart disease, diabetes, or liver or kidney disease earlier than seems normal for the population as a whole—or the fact that a study reports such a finding about a population of HIV-infected individuals—only raises the issue of whether the population as a whole is the relevant comparison group. "Since one of the major risk factors for HIV is intravenous drug use," says Brooks, "you have to ask, what's the contribution of heroin to somebody's kidney disease versus the HIV versus untreated high blood pressure versus smoking?"

I still expect most of my patients to live a normal life expectancy," says an AIDS doctor, "but they may do so with a bit more nips and scrapes.

From his own clinical experience, McMeeking agrees that heart disease, certain cancers, and liver and kidney disease do seem to pose a greater threat to his HIV-infected patients than might otherwise be expected in a comparable uninfected population. "I still expect most of my patients to live a normal life expectancy," he says, "but they may do so with a bit more nips and scrapes."

The third group of HIV-infected individuals consists of those in the middle of the two extremes. HAART, in these cases, has literally been a life saver, but has not guaranteed a normal life expectancy. These are the patients, like Bob Hattoy, who were diagnosed with AIDS in the late eighties or early nineties, before the advent of HAART. They began on one drug (AZT, for instance) and then stayed alive long enough to get on protease inhibitors and the HAART cocktails. These patients were on the cusp of the HIV transformation from a deadly to a chronic-disease epidemic; they were infected late enough to survive but too early to derive all the benefits from HAART.

The anti-retroviral drugs of HAART work by attacking the life cycle of the virus. The earliest generation of HAART drugs attacked the enzymes that the virus uses to reproduce in the cells. (Protease inhibitors, for instance, go after an enzyme called HIV-1 protease, which the virus uses to assemble itself during reproduction.) The latest drugs go after the methods that the virus uses to enter cells in which it will replicate. The key to the effectiveness of HAART, as researchers discovered in the mid-nineties, was to include at least three drugs in the cocktail to which the patient's specific virus had no resistance. This would suppress viral replication sufficiently so that the virus wouldn't be able to mutate fast enough to evolve resistance to any of the drugs. But patients who began on one or two anti-AIDS drugs and only then moved to HAART already had time to evolve resistance to a few of the drugs in the cocktail. This made the entire package less effective and increased the likelihood that they would evolve resistance to the other drugs as well.

"We call it 'sins of the past,'" says Mullen. "We gave these patients sequential monotherapy; it was state-of-the-art at the time, and a lot of those people are alive today because of that. It got them through until HAART came along, but their HAART is not highly active, only fairly active. Their virus has baseline mutations that interfere with the response." This group of patients also includes those who were infected initially with a strain of HIV already resistant to one or several of the components of HAART, or those patients who were less than 99 percent faithful in taking the regimen of pills that constitute HAART. Anything less than that and the virus has the opportunity to evolve resistance.

Perhaps a quarter of all new cases, says Mullen, are infected with a strain of the virus resistant to one or more drugs in the HAART cocktail. "You can't use the frontline regimen, because the virus has already seen those drugs," he says. "You have to go to more complicated regimens. This is why we do resistance testing before we start a person on medication. We see what drugs the virus has seen or is resistant to and can take that into account."

Sins-of-the-past patients have to have faith that the pharmaceutical industry can stay one step ahead of their disease. The prognosis, at the moment, is promising. There are several entirely new classes of AIDS drugs, including one by Merck, called an integrase inhibitor, that was just approved by the FDA last October. A recent report of the discovery of 270 new human proteins employed by the AIDS virus to hijack cells and start replicating—the definition of a successful infection—means the pharmaceutical industry will not run out of new targets to block the infection in the near future.

Still, some sins-of-the-past patients simply do worse than others, and the occasional patient will lose the battle before new drugs come along or simply give up. "I had a friend who died last week," one sins-of-the-past patient told me recently. "He just lost faith. He would get sick a lot, would get better, then sick again. Finally he decided to try Eastern medicine, and stopped taking his [HAART] medications entirely. It killed him. It's not a good example, other than to show that people can reach their breaking point."

Critical Thinking

1. What are the lifestyle changes that you can make to reduce your risk of developing cardiovascular disease, cancer, diabetes, and AIDS?

2. Why do people continue to die from HIV-related illness despite effective antiviral treatments?

3. What population groups are most likely to die from AIDS and why?

UNIT 7

Sexualities and Social Issues

Unit Selections

Learning Outcomes

After reading this Unit, you will be able to:

- Discuss the consequences of illegal abortions.

- Explain how illegal abortions impact the lives of those who seek them, as well as the lives of family and friends.

- Describe the main challenges faced by the porn industry today.

- Discuss current market trends that are reshaping the adult entertainment industry as we know it.

- Summarize what we currently know about the effectiveness of residency restrictions on registered sex offenders.

- Explain the implications of recent research findings on re-offense rates for sex offenders by location/proximity to potential victims.

- Summarize the most common myths and assumptions about domestic violence.

- Discuss how myths and faulty assumptions on domestic violence can influence both an abuser as well as a victim.

- Discuss common myths and misperceptions of domestic abuse and violence.

- Explain how males and females differ or are similar in their acceptance of rape myths.

- Summarize the factors that influence people's acceptance of common rape myths.

- Describe the physical and mental consequences of sexual assaults on men.

- Describe the sexual consequences of sexual assaults on men.

Student Website
www.mhhe.com/cls

Internet References

Child Exploitation and Obscenity Section (CEOS)/U.S. Department of Justice
www.usdoj.gov/criminal/ceos/trafficking.html

The Child Rights Information Network (CRIN)
www.crin.org

Planned Parenthood
www.plannedparenthood.org

Rape, Abuse, and Incest National Network (RAINN)
www.rainn.org

This final unit deals with several topics that are of interest for different reasons. These topics have a common denominator—they have all taken positions of prominence in the public's awareness. Some of the topics explored in this unit are much less controversial than others. Yet even with the least controversial among them, there are debates and significant disagreement in how we, as a society, should deal with these issues. Controversies abound around almost anything to do with topics such as sex, sexuality, sex education, contraception, and abortion. Indeed, sex in one way or another has very much been at the heart of the "culture wars" in the United States.

Clearly, many people are having sex. This regularly leads to unplanned pregnancies. In our age of supposed sexual enlightenment, some individuals, possibly in the heat of the moment, fail to understand the likelihood of pregnancy with unprotected intercourse. Even with our astounding medical technologies, there is no 100 percent effective, safe, or aesthetically acceptable method of birth control. Before sex can become safe as well as enjoyable, people must receive thorough and accurate information regarding conception and contraception, birth, and birth control. However, we have learned that information about, or even access to, birth control is not enough. We still have some distance to go to make every child one who is planned and wanted.

Despite the relative simplicity of the above assertion, abortion and birth control remain emotionally charged issues in American society. While opinion surveys indicate that most of the public supports family planning and abortion, at least in some circumstances, there are certain individuals and groups strongly opposed to some forms of birth control and abortion. Voices for and against birth control and abortion—traditional and newer methods—remain passionate, and face-offs range from academic debates and legislative hearings to work stoppages by pharmacists and protests with or without violence. The Supreme Court's, the legislative's, and the medical community's efforts are at times at odds; some seek to restrict the right or access to abortion or the availability of birth control methods, while others seek to mandate freer access to contraceptive and reproductive choice options. Voices on both sides are raised in emotionally and politically charged debate between "we must never go back to the old days" (of illegal and unsafe back-alley abortions) and "the baby has no choice." Abortion remains a fiercely debated topic. Because of that, legislative efforts for and against it abound. This is likely to continue for a very long time to come.

This unit explores other emotionally charged and difficult topics as well. We know that sexual abuse and violence permeate our society. For centuries, a strong code of silence surrounded sexual abuse and violence. Many now agree that the silence has increased not only the likelihood of sexual abuse and violence, but the harm to the victims of these acts.

Beginning in the middle of the twentieth century, two societal movements helped to begin eroding this code of silence. The child welfare/child rights movement exposed child abuse and mistreatment. This movement sought to improve the lives of children and families. Soon after, and to a large extent fueled by

© Ingram Publishing

the emerging women's movement, primarily grass-roots organizations that became known as "rape crisis" groups or centers became catalysts for altering the way we looked at (or avoided looking at) rape and sexual abuse.

Research today suggests that these movements have accomplished many of their initial goals and brought about significant social change. The existence and prevalence of rape and other sexual abuse is much more accurately known today than ever before. Many of the myths previously believed (rapists are strangers that jump out of bushes, sexual abuse only occurs in poor families, all rapists are male and all victims are female, and so on) have been replaced with more accurate information. The code of silence has been recognized for the harm it can cause, and millions of friends, parents, teachers, counselors, and others have learned how to be approachable, supportive listeners to victims disclosing their abuse experiences. Also, we have come to recognize the role that power, especially unequal power, plays in rape, sexual abuse, sexual violence, and sexual harassment. However, as current events have shown, the battle is far from over, and sexual abuse continues to have serious devastating consequences for victims, and those who love them, as well as society as a whole.

As we, as a society, have sought to expose and reduce abusive sex, it has become increasingly clear that all of society and each of us as individuals and potential partners must grapple with the broader issue of what constitutes consent. What is nonabusive sexual interaction? How can people communicate interest, arousal, desire, and/or propose sexual interaction, when remnants of unequal power, ignorance, misinformation, fear, adversarial sex roles, and inadequate communication skills still exist?

Finally, another layer of perplexing questions that confront the proactive/reactive dilemma: What is, or should be, the role of employers, school personnel, or simply any of us who may be seen as contributing on some level due to lack of awareness or complicity to an environment that allows uncomfortable, abusive, or inappropriate sexual interactions? Conversely, is it possible that we could become so "sensitive" to the potential for abuse that combined with our discomfort, anger, and fear we could become hysterical vigilantes pushing an eager legal system to indict "offenders" who have not committed abuse or harassment?

These are just some of the many issues that you may grapple with as you process the information included in this unit.

As we have seen throughout this book, human sexuality is biology, behavior, society, culture and much, much more. Our sexual beliefs, behaviors, choices, even feelings and comfort levels are profoundly affected by what our culture prescribes and proscribes, which has been transmitted to us by the full range of social institutions with which we interact. We are biological organisms living in many complex social worlds. We each have a long road ahead of us as we try to understand human sexualities.

This book has been part of your journey for sexual knowledge. It is important to continue on that journey, always asking questions, and seeking answers and accurate knowledge. This is a journey that will truly take a lifetime.

Flower Grandma's Secret

Physician Susan Wicklund had never told her grandmother about her medical specialty: reproductive health and abortion. She finally decided to divulge the truth just before appearing on a national television program that would reveal the constant harassment and danger she faced from anti-abortion fanatics. Before Wicklund could say much, Grandma offered her own heartbreaking disclosure. Here, from Wicklund's new memoir.

SUSAN WICKLUND

When I drove into Grandma's driveway all I could think about was how she would react. I had started out to tell her many times over the last years. On so many visits I had meant to have that conversation, but had never found a way. Something had always intervened. Some other errand had always come up. I had found a way not to face her judgment.

It didn't matter that I was rock solid in my resolve and in my chosen profession. This was my grandma. My Flower Grandma. What she thought of me mattered a lot, and I had no idea how she'd take it.

It was February of 1992, a Saturday afternoon. The next day the *60 Minutes* segment I'd done with Leslie Stahl would air. Grandma never missed *60 Minutes*. I had to tell her before she saw it—before she saw her oldest granddaughter talking about the death threats and stalking and personal harassment my family and I were enduring.

The harassment wasn't the issue that mattered now. It was the fact that I was, as a physician, traveling to five clinics in three states to provide abortion services for as many as one hundred women every week, and that I had been doing this work for four years already.

I wasn't at all ashamed of my career. In fact, I always considered it an honor to be involved in reproductive choices, this most personal and intimate realm for women. I just never felt the need to make it public. Very few of my family and friends were aware of what I did.

Within a day, however, everyone I had grown up with, everyone who knew my family, and every member of my family would know the truth. Would I be isolated and ostracized? Would I get support or condemnation?

I pulled off the highway and into the drive leading to the house I'd grown up in. Mom and Dad still lived in the white, two-story wood-frame home.

Dad had worked as a precision machinist in the town of Grantsburg, 10 miles away. His love had been the gunsmithing, hunting and fishing he did in his free time. My three siblings and I had always been included. We were as competent with firearms, field dressing a deer or catching a batch of sunfish as anyone in the area. Dad was retired now and not feeling well. It was painful to watch him, the strong man who starred in my memories, struggling with simple tasks.

Mom was retired too, from her elected position as Clerk of Court for our county. She was the one everyone—especially women—turned to for advice and support. Mom had been instrumental, many years earlier, in starting a shelter for victims of domestic abuse. In her job she had seen so many situations where women and children had nowhere to go for help. It was just like Mom to tackle a need that everyone else ignored.

I grew up in the unincorporated village of Trade Lake, Wis., a small gathering of about six houses, several of which were the homes of my relatives. The only business left was one small gas station/grocery store. When I was a kid there had been a feed store and creamery and a meat market, but those had been gone for better than 30 years. Only rotten shells of buildings remained.

Even now, Trade Lake is a very rural place. People still raise chickens in backyards, drive tractors to the little grocery store. Chimneys puff wood smoke in the winter.

The small river that wound its way through our yard came into view. Behind it, the woods where I'd built forts and climbed oak trees with my sister. She and I each had a horse and spent the bulk of our summers out of doors. Grandma and Grandpa had lived just down the road. We picked mayflowers every spring with Grandma. In the summer we fished with Grandpa for sunfish and crappies with cane poles baited with worms dug out of the garden.

Mine had been a good childhood. This was a safe place. Turning in the driveway had always been a good thing—a coming home. This time was different.

I felt myself sweating under my coat. My racing heart pushed against my throat. I had to reveal something to my dear grandma that could change everything she believed and loved about me.

Grandma had moved into a trailer house in the backyard of the family home. Grandpa died 15 years earlier and Mom wanted her mother even closer—just steps across the yard. I saw the clothesline filled with rugs, the twine still strung up on the porch to hold the morning glories that filled the railings in the summer.

Flower Grandma. My daughter, Sonja, gave her the name when she was 3 and there were too many grandmas to keep track of. Sonja spent many days baking cookies with her great-grandmother and playing outside, just as I had as a young girl. She ran back and forth constantly between the houses of her two grandmothers. This grandma always had flowers growing in every nook and cranny, inside and out.

Flower Grandma she became, and Flower Grandma she stayed. Before long my entire extended family called her Flower Grandma, and even her friends at the local senior center fell into the habit.

I coasted to a stop at the bottom of the slope. I sat there long enough to take a deep breath and fight back a few unexpected tears. I didn't know where the sadness came from. The car engine ticked. I was alone, vulnerable, aching. Was I longing for those simple childhood days, whipping down the hill on my sled? How far I'd come from that.

I peeled myself out of the car, shed my coat and left it on the seat. It was unusually warm for February in Wisconsin. The hardwood forest was all bare sticks and hard lines. I knew it would soon be time to tap the maple trees and cook the wonderful syrup we all loved on Grandma's Swedish pancakes.

I turned and deliberately moved up the steps to the trailer house. I was terrified of what Grandma would say, but there was no avoiding this moment.

The big door was already open by the time I got to the top step. Out peeked her welcoming smile. She was giggling.

"Hi, Grandma!"

"Oh my goodness! What a surprise! What a sweet, sweet surprise! Did I know you were coming today?"

I hugged her in the doorway, held her tight, stepped inside.

"Did you somehow know I was making ginger snaps?" she teased as she set a plate full on the kitchen table. She poured me a glass of milk and I sat down on the wooden chair next to hers. I tried to bury myself in the smell of her place, a mixture of ginger cookies, Estée Lauder perfume (the one in the blue, hourglass bottle always on her dresser), and home permanents. She and Mom always gave each other perms, trying to get just the right curl in their hair. The smell never left the place.

I think she sensed that I had come to talk about something important. I started talking a few times about other, inconsequential things, then, finally, I plunged in.

"Grandma, you know I work as a doctor."

"Of course. And we are all so proud of you."

"Yes, but I don't think you know the whole story. I'm a doctor who works mostly for women, helping women with pregnancy problems."

Flower Grandma hesitated just a second, pushed back her chair, stood and held out her hand for me to follow. She went to sit in her rocker, the same one sitting in my living room today. The rocker I have sat in so many hours since. The rocker I sit in right now, writing this down and trembling as I do.

She seemed distant. I moved to the old leather hassock beside her. She took my hand and placed it on top of one of hers, then covered it with her other one. Our hands made a stack on the arm of the rocker—old skin, young skin. We sat in silence a minute. She turned to look directly at me. Her eyes, framed by gentle wrinkles, were full of some deep trouble.

After a moment, she stared straight ahead and started to speak. Slowly. Deliberately. In a very quiet voice. At the same time she began stroking my hand. It was as if the gentle stroking was pushing her to talk.

"When I was 16 years old my best friend got pregnant," she said. A chill went through me.

"I always believed it was her father that was using her," she went on, "but I never knew for sure. She came to my sister, Violet, and me, and asked us to help her."

While I listened, my thoughts whirled through my head. Stories I had read of women self-aborting and dying of infections when a safe, legal option was not available. The many women who came to the clinics where I worked, many of whom still had to overcome huge difficulties to end an unwanted pregnancy.

It isn't uncommon to have patients confide in me that prior to coming in for an abortion, they had used combinations of herbs to try to force a miscarriage. These home remedies can be extremely dangerous and have caused the deaths of many women.

I felt myself tighten and withdraw, anticipating what Flower Grandma was going to tell me. I wanted to see her eyes, but she kept them straight ahead. And she kept stroking my hand. So soft. I only wanted to think about those hands. Hands embracing and caressing mine—strong, gentle, soft.

"The three of us were so naive. We knew very little about these things, but we had heard that if you put something long and sharp 'up there,' in the private place, sometimes it would end the pregnancy."

In spite of myself I conjured the modest room: a dresser in the corner with a kerosene lamp and maybe a hairbrush or hand mirror beside it. I saw three young, scared girls, still children, acting on old wives' tales and whispered instructions.

My stomach turned. Was this my Grandma? Was I really here in her trailer house hearing this? I could barely breathe. She kept talking, all the while stroking the top of my hand, her eyes looking off into space, traveling back in time. Occasionally a pat-pat with her hand would break the rhythm of the stroking. Such old skin, full of brown age spots and paper thin. Stroking my hand in perfect measure with her words.

Please just stop, Grandma. Don't tell me anymore. Just hold my hand and let's talk about what you'll plant in the spring. Tell me about the oatmeal bread you baked yesterday. Are there many birds coming to the birdfeeder? I was flushed all over. And still she stroked while she talked. Pat-pat, stroke.

"We closed ourselves, the three of us, in one of the bedrooms late one morning. We didn't talk much, and she didn't ever cry out in pain. It took a few tries to make the blood come. None of us spoke. We didn't know what to expect next, or what to do when the blood kept coming. It was all over the sheets. All over us. So bright red. It was awful. It just wouldn't stop."

She was still stroking my hand. I was shaking uncontrollably. I stared at the African violets under the plant light, trying to make them the focus of my attention. Her voice was a monotone, never a pause.

"We put rags inside of her to try to stop the bleeding, but they soaked full. We all three stayed in her bed. We just didn't know what to do."

My hand was trembling so hard it was all I could do to keep it on top of hers. She grasped it briefly, held it tight, patted it a few times and then went on.

"We stayed there together, unable to move, even after she was dead. Her father found us, all three of us, in the bed. He stood in the doorway, staring. No words for a long time. When he did speak, he told my sister and me to leave and that we were never, ever to speak of this. We were not to tell anyone, ever. Ever."

She stopped stroking my hand and sat still before turning to look directly at me. "That was 72 years ago. You are the first person I have ever told that story. I am still so ashamed of what happened. We were just so young and scared. We didn't know anything."

Terrible sadness welled up inside me. And anger. I couldn't picture my Grandma as someone responsible for the death of anything, much less her best friend at the age of 16. She had carried this secret all her life, kept it inside, festering with guilt and shame.

I wondered if the pregnancy was indeed the result of incest. Would it have made a difference? What were friends and family told about the death? What had they actually used to start the bleeding? What had the doctor put on the death certificate as the cause of death?

I knew, through the patients I had met, that no one has to look very far into their family history to find these stories tucked away, hidden from view. But it didn't lessen the shock of finding it here, so close, in the heart of my own family.

Flower Grandma sighed and held my hand tight. Tears welled in her eyes.

"I know exactly what kind of work you do, and it is a good thing. People like you do it safely so that people like me don't murder their best friends. I told you how proud I am of what you do, and I meant it."

Critical Thinking

1. What are the major concerns regarding illegal abortions?

2. How do the negative consequences of illegal abortions impact not only the victim who sought such services but also family members and those who love her?

3. Discuss the social stigma associated with legal abortion services. In what ways does this stigma impact the providers of abortion services?

SUSAN WICKLUND has worked in the field of women's reproductive health for more than 20 years. For much of that time she has been on the front lines of the abortion war, both as a doctor and as a spokesperson for women's rights.

From *Ms.*, by Susan Wicklund, Fall 2007, pp. 67–69. Copyright © 2007 by Ms. Magazine. Reprinted by permission of Ms. Magazine and Susan Wicklund.

Porn Panic!

The recession has dealt knockout blows to the auto and financial industries, and now adult entertainment could be the next to drop to its knees.

C. Brian Smith

It's a rainy Monday and I am crouched in the corner of Jet Set Men's modest one-room studio in North Hollywood, Calif. I'm careful not to make a sound because Kyle, one of the two models in this scene, has been trying, and failing, to climax for 20 minutes. Kyle stares at a portable DVD player—concealed offstage—for inspiration.

The camera is on standby. Kyle's costar, Tyler Saint, gently caresses Kyle's forehead and whispers inaudible words of encouragement—in stark contrast to the last 45 minutes, during which Tyler's demeanor was more maniacally commanding.

"How about a different lube?" suggests director John Tegan. Kyle politely refuses. Tegan leans over to me and whispers, "Once I had a guy take four hours." I sink back into the couch, thinking that if we're going to be here for another three hours, I may need a sandwich.

Kyle motions that he is nearly ready to resume filming, reassuming his previous position on a stack of tires. Tyler seamlessly slips back into character as the angry rapist, and Tegan calls out "action." Moments later the scene has wrapped. I'm more relieved than Kyle.

I compliment Ross Cannon, the cameraman, on expertly maneuvering the high-definition camera in one hand while operating a plastic dome light in the other. He smiles proudly. "Oh, that's the C light. Without it, you miss all the good stuff. It's normally much bigger and heavier, but you need to hire another guy to work it. I found this one at a church bazaar—works great."

Chris Steele, head of production for Jet Set Men, explains, "We've had to adapt in order to continue shooting high production value on a budget that can still turn a profit. Everybody on the crew has learned to adjust. If we don't, we're sure to go broke."

Steele and his Jet Set Men aren't alone. There are very few businesses in the world that aren't performing somersaults in an effort to survive today's economic tumult. But Jet Set and others in the adult industry are facing a double whammy: the worst recession in decades coupled with nothing less than a tectonic shift in the way people are consuming their products. Much as Napster did to the record industry 10 years ago, websites like XTube are shaking traditional porn businesses to their core. And now an industry that is perhaps best known for going for broke could go, well, broke.

In January, Larry Flynt asked Congress for a $5 billion bailout to help "rejuvenate the sexual appetite of America." But it's unrealistic to expect that the government will rush to save porn companies in the same way it's done for the auto and financial industries—after all, pornography is something that is seldom spoken of in polite society, something that's hidden in a closet or under the bed. But it's equally unrealistic to expect that the failure of the gay porn industry—a business model that has employed so many, entertained so many more, and donated millions of dollars to gay rights and HIV organizations—won't change life as we know it.

Recession-Proof?

If there's one thing that's always comforted people in the porn biz, it's that, good times or bad, sin sells. Americans, they say, have traditionally been more willing to cut back their spending on just about anything—other than cigarettes, alcohol, and pornography. Phil Harvey, the 71-year-old cofounder of Adam & Eve, one the largest erotica retail companies in the world, dusted off this conventional wisdom recently in an address to the annual XBiz State of the Industry Conference in Woodland Hills, Calif. "As far as I can tell," he said, "over a period of some 35 years, we're recession-proof. . . . Our sales, while not booming, don't appear to have been impacted by the downturn in the economy at all."

But Harvey's words did little to calm the nerves of some of the giants in the gay porn industry. "The recession is very noticeable and is cutting into sales," says Chi Chi LaRue, drag queen, porn director, and owner of Channel 1 Releasing. "Anybody who says it's not is either not telling the truth or is not smart enough to see it." Adds Michael Lucas, director, performer, and CEO of Lucas Entertainment: "I don't know what Mr. Harvey is smoking. People in the adult world often like to flex their muscles and speak with wishful thinking, even when it's absolutely ridiculous."

Depending on whom you talk to, DVD sales are down by between 25% and 45%. Model fees have been cut by about 20%. Several webmasters report that February was the worst month for new memberships—ever. And the credit crunch has made it more difficult than ever to retain those Web-based customers. "Declined credit cards on recurring billings have increased from one or two per week to seven to 10 per day," says Alex Sulaco, owner of ManifestMen.com. Ten declined cards a day at a $30 membership level comes out to nearly $10,000 a month in losses.

Midsize studio PZP Productions announced in February that it was suspending production for the rest of the year. "The recession is strangling us," explains owner Peter Z. Pan. "A lot of little companies are going out of business. I'm just barely hanging on. If I don't produce any new content [now], and if the economy begins to turn around in a few months, I think I can survive. And that's because I have very little overhead. Other small companies will just disappear."

A Saturated Market

Over the last decade, the gay porn market has been inundated with massive amounts of new product. Self-proclaimed producers from all walks flocked to adult entertainment, operating under the correct assumption that sex sells and the sort-of-correct assumption that there's an endless supply of customers. "What most failed to consider is that there is also an endless supply of content," says veteran porn analyst Tom Hymes.

"I got into the industry at a really amazing time," says porn commentator and online talk-show host Jason Sechrest. "It was 1998, Jenna Jameson was just becoming a household name, and the adult entertainment industry was on the cover of *Time* and *Newsweek*. We started telling CNN that we were a multimillion-dollar industry! We may as well have just taken a gun and put it to our head. Everyone with a camcorder picked it up and said, 'Hey! I'm going to do that!'"

The gay porn world comprises an ever-growing field of players. There are traditional companies (Falcon Studios, Titan Media, Channel 1 Releasing, Jet Set Men, Lucas Entertainment, Raging Stallion Studios, Hot House Entertainment); Web-based video-on-demand sites (SeanCody.com, RandyBlue.com, CorbinFisher.com, CockyBoys.com, StraightBoysFucking.com); DIY-porn "tube" sites (XTube.com, GayTube.com, YouPorn.com, RedTube.com); BitTorrent and peer-to-peer file-sharing networks (ThePirateBay.org); online distribution and pay-per-view sites (AEBN.net); fetish sites (BoundGods.com); live webcam sites (Flirt4Free.com, Cam4.com); reality sites (Fratpad.com); porn star sites (BrentCorriganInc.com); porn star fan sites (KruezerAtNight.com); hookup sites (Manhunt.net); and there are still one or two mom-and-pop video stores down the street. For the time being, at least.

For every name above, there are hundreds of similar companies and websites. The straight-guys-having-gay-sex-for-money genre, one of the most profitable, is also the most saturated. "Google-search 'straight men gay porn' and you're sure to get thousands of hits," says Jet Set Men's Steele. "Sean Cody has a business model that works—he got in it early, made a name for himself, and has the momentum. But for every one Sean Cody, there are maybe 5,000 sites that will fail."

Raging Stallion Studios/Pistol Media merged with AEBN/NakedSword in February to create one of the largest gay adult entertainment companies in the world. Steve Johnson, CEO of Falcon Entertainment, says this is just the beginning of a much-needed consolidation in the industry. "There's a lot of redundancy and competitiveness," he says. "We're all creating accounting systems and distribution systems and making websites and having warehouses and maintaining studios and factories, and we all walk around being paranoid of each other when we ought to be embracing each other."

Giving It Away

I recently asked a group of college students how they felt about pornography, and they unanimously agreed that porn is terrific—and that it is and should be free. In a *Wall Street Journal* article titled "The Economics of Giving It Away," Chris Anderson noted that members of the Google generation are "saving their money and playing free online games, listening to free music on Pandora, canceling basic cable and watching free video on Hulu, and killing their landlines in favor of Skype. It's a consumer's paradise: The Web has become the biggest store in history and everything is 100% off."

That's where tube sites come in. Essentially YouTube for porn, tube sites are largely composed of user-generated content provided to other users for free. Whereas traditional porn studios' revenue comes from the sale of DVDs, and websites make money from monthly memberships, tube sites sell ad space and make revenue by generating as much traffic as possible. "Picture a bug zapper you put in your backyard," Steele says. "Bugs from all over the neighborhood fly in. That's all a tube site is, a bug zapper."

Lights attract bugs; free porn attracts people—lots and lots and lots of people. Roughly 15% of the 100 most-visited websites offer free porn. XTube, which features approximately 75% gay content, receives more than 5 million hits a day and has 7 million members—up from 4 million a year ago. "We changed the whole adult industry," says XTube operations director Kurtis Potec. "We took what was an analog world based around a physical product and changed it to a digital world. We understand a lot of people wouldn't be happy with that."

Cash-strapped consumers, however, are very happy with the site. Dean Berkeley, who sells online porn memberships for a living, says bluntly, "I don't have any friends who would subscribe to a porn site now. Not one. They all say, 'Why would I buy porn when I have XTube?'"

Still, major studios insist that high quality will always ensure a loyal consumer base, regardless of free alternatives. Titan founder Bruce Cam, who classifies XTube's content as "faceless jerk-offs and mystery holes," says, "The problem is not tube sites. The problem is when someone steals our copyrighted content and posts it on a tube site. Then, all of a sudden, we're competing against our own stuff." That's when a tube site becomes an illegal tube site.

Stealing It Away—Illegal Tube Sites

It's 1:30 p.m. at the State of the Industry Conference in Woodland Hills, and straight-porn producer Jay Quinlan has just been asked about illegal tube sites. He slams back what's left of his third Miller Lite, leans into the microphone, and points to no one in particular. "I have one video that showed up on Pornhub, went to number 1 [on the site], got 250,000 views, and here's the kicker—the video hadn't even appeared on my *own* site yet! That's thievery! How do you sell something that's been watched a quarter of a million times? The people who own [the illegal tube sites] are thieves, liars, and scumbags. They should be brought out to the backroom and shot!"

Some of the larger tube sites, like XTube, are vigilant in their prohibition of pirated material. But because these sites' revenue comes from generating traffic, many tacitly permit users to upload copyrighted content. When contacted by angry porn producers, the response from illegal tube site owners is very similar to what I heard from LifeOut.com's Jason Ward when I asked if he was responsible for the conduct of his site's visitors: "We cannot stop members from uploading copyrighted content. What do you mean by 'conduct'? Does that mean sites should approve every message that is sent through their mail? Does that mean every photo uploaded to a site should be reviewed? If that's the case, then every site from MySpace to Facebook to Gay.com would be spending incredible resources to ensure everything is completely compliant." Instead, it's the larger porn studios that are spending those incredible resources—to ensure pirate sites are sued. "We have a full in-house legal team, and basically all they do is piracy work," Titan's Keith Webb says. "We've won over 30 cases and settled over 100 more out of court in our favor."

In November 2008, New York–based gay porn studio Pitbull Productions was awarded damages in excess of $2.85 million when it sued WhatsTea.com, a video-on-demand website, for copyright infringement. "At the end of the day, your library, your intellectual property, your copyrights and trademarks—that's your business asset," says Pitbull's CEO Jalin Fuentes.

For the most part, though, the mice are eluding the cat. Even if the majority of porn companies could afford drawn-out legal battles (they can't), finding a person—or an entity—to sue is often impossible since most tube sites are based outside of the United States. Many producers are resigned to the reality that all porn will be stolen eventually and are making the best of a bad situation. "All of our content is watermarked with our name and website," says Lea Busick, director of sales and marketing for TopBucks, which operates MaleSpectrum.com. "So when [a clip] does end up on a tube site we still get the exposure for the brand. You can bitch and moan about [piracy] or you can work within it and play the game."

Competing with the Homemade Porn Star

"I can't believe *The Advocate* is calling me," says 25-year-old Mike Rizzo of Belmar, N.J., who is also known as "oboymikee." "Everybody wants to be famous somehow, I guess."

Online, Rizzo is best known for his XTube videos (there were 11 of them at press time), which have been viewed more than 3 million times. The videos, most of which feature Rizzo by himself, are simple in content and far from professional in production value. But they're not horrible. The scenes are well edited, generally shot with two cameras, and include foot-tapping music.

"There's no money in it. I shoot them all at my house. It's an ego boost," Rizzo says. "I put a new video up a few weeks ago and it already has 700,000 hits. The other day someone at the grocery store recognized me from XTube. I'm a plumber. I'm not going to get famous being a plumber."

Ten years ago, "amateur" was just a tab in online thumbnail photo galleries. Today, it's one of the most commonly used keywords when searching for porn. "People like amateur work because it seems so close to you," says "LordBenthefirst," a college student who shoots XTube videos between classes. "It feels like you could have sex with this person if they lived in your town."

The rise of amateur porn began about nine years ago when sites like SeanCody.com, RandyBlue.com, and CorbinFisher .com began filming young, nervous, and generally straight men having sex with each other. These companies are now some of the most lucrative in the business and offer top dollar for the right model. But the success of the genre these sites created could destroy them in the end. "I think [sites like SeanCody.com] are really getting hurt by all of the real, free amateur stuff on XTube," says Titan Media's Webb. "If you're just looking for a hot guy who is jerking off on the couch, why pay for it when you can get it for free?"

And now amateur content is being offered in real time, for free. I signed on to the live webcam site Cam4.com and moments later was watching, along with 2,000 others, two relatively attractive young men having sex. I could even offer the men suggestions and critiques using a chat room on the site. Skeptical and pretty certain I was watching a prerecorded scene, I typed, "Hey, can you move that pillow?" Seconds later, it was hurled across the room, out of the frame. Everyone's a director, I suppose.

Many people in the business believe that the popularity of amateur videos will bring about the demise of the traditional porn star. "Models were asking for and getting $3,000 to $4,000 per scene one year ago. Now they have to really negotiate to get $2,000," says gay-porn reporter Damon Kruezer, publisher of KruezerAtNight.com. "Well-known twink performer Aaron Tyler was doing video work full-time nine months ago, but now he's an office temp. And Brodie Sinclair, who is a CockyBoys exclusive model, says he has to work part-time at a burger joint and part-time as a personal trainer in Miami to pay the bills. Both men are escorting as well."

"When amateurism is celebrated and anyone with an opinion can publish a blog, post a video on YouTube, or change an entry on Wikipedia, the distinction between expert and amateur becomes dangerously blurred," writes Andrew Keen in his book *The Cult of the Amateur*. According to Keen, the Web 2.0 phenomenon is not just strangling the economy but killing culture. "We are facing the law of digital Darwinism, the survival of the loudest and most opinionated," he says.

But is pornography an art form or simply a masturbation tool? Should we really worry if the beloved skin flick is being sullied by the ever-growing attraction to the gratis, do-it-yourself variety?

"In the early days of the industry, porn filmmakers came out of film schools. They were trained in Hollywood and brought a level of professionalism," says J.C. Adams, editor of the industry news site the Gay Porn Times. "The rapid growth of the amateur has pushed out the actual filmmakers. Now, with the economic condition, it's harder for these guys to make the kind of films they want to make since everything is reduced to a seven-minute scene on XTube. There aren't too many of them left."

That's music to the ears of plumbers like Rizzo. "I think it's about time," he says. "We could never compete with [porn studios] because they have all the money. I'm doing this out of my paycheck. I'm glad we're giving them a run for their money, because I love doing it."

A Hard-Core Industry Forced to Get Harder

As consumers turn away from traditional porn, professional content producers are increasingly catering to niche audiences with edgier, kinkier product. Michael Lucas, whose recently released titles include *Piss!* and *Farts!* says, "There are literally hundreds of thousands of vanilla gay movies that have been produced over the past 40 years. People are definitely getting bored with the same action."

The demand for hard-core content has widespread effects, many of them negative. Studios have a hard time competing with the raunchiest amateurs because many of their billing providers, like CCBill and Visa, prohibit certain content. "I don't know how Michael Lucas is getting away with [water sports]," says Bill Gardner, cofounder of Hot Desert Knights. "If Visa finds out, they'll shut his site down in a heartbeat."

The demand for extreme fetish also has caused models to have to choose between participating in undesirable sexual scenarios or going without work altogether. Nowhere is this more evident—and more controversial—than in the world of bareback porn.

"Bareback? I don't even consider that a fetish anymore, it's become so big," says the owner of one Los Angeles gay video rental store.

Many in the industry, like Chi Chi LaRue, believe they have a moral obligation to produce videos that depict only safe sex. But others say there are economic drawbacks to featuring only safe-sex scenes. "As a small company, I am forced by distributors to shoot bareback content," says Tyler Reed, who owns the one-man operation USA Jock Studio. "Unless you have extremely high-quality models, sets, and so forth, distributors won't even touch the safe content anymore."

But haven't the majority of studios publicly stated that they shoot only safe-sex porn? Tyler sighs. "Don't think for a second that these huge companies promoting safe product lines don't also have their hands in the bareback action somewhere—a hidden wing of a conglomerate or some bareback website," he says. "Bareback sells two-to-one, guaranteed. And if you put the word 'bareback' in the title, you're looking at three-to-one."

The Murky Crystal Ball

I concluded each interview by asking people to predict what the gay porn industry would look like in three years. After a deep, collective sigh, most everyone agreed on two things: First, the convergence of Internet and television will effectively kill the DVD. Second, the marketplace will be much, much smaller. "In 1930 there were over 200 American car companies," says Jesse Kiehl, CEO of Fierce Dog Media. "Now there are barely three. Expect a similar thing to happen to porn."

Many in the industry believe that new technologies will shape the orgasmic wave of the future, and their companies are racing to provide mobile content so people can take their porn on the road.

To compete with the reality of amateurs, more and more porn stars are following the lead of Brent Corrigan and Michael Lucas by offering fans minute-by-minute updates about every (excruciating) detail of their private lives. "Look at Paris Hilton," Lucas says. "She's an open book. People have seen everything from her vagina to her dumb-ass behavior, and I don't see any other reason why she's become so famous."

Diane Duke, executive director of the Free Speech Coalition, which lobbies for the adult entertainment business, insists that cooperation from lawmakers is essential. "In California, the legislature just approved a budget that provides a tax credit to mainstream Hollywood because of difficulties it's having with everything from the economy to piracy. Our industry is suffering from the exact same issues, and yet the legislature is constantly trying to impose additional burdens on our industry. It's going to be up to your readers who are consumers of adult entertainment to speak up."

And while it's perhaps unrealistic to expect anyone to come rushing to the aid of the adult entertainment industry, these companies' failure will likely affect more than just your libido. Gay porn studios have been very generous in their support of LGBT and HIV service organizations. Last year Titan Media alone donated more than $100,000 to such groups, and though many companies are reticent to discuss specific figures regarding charitable donations, Titan is not alone in its support of gay organizations. And of course, porn has a specific place in our collective development. "[Gay pornography] is a huge part of our culture," J.C. Adams says. "For many of us, porn was our first exposure to male intimacy and porn stars were the only openly gay or bi men that we saw or heard of."

But for the gays of the Google generation—some of whom brought their boyfriends to the prom—pornography serves a singular purpose, and in so doing, neither evokes nostalgia nor warrants respect. As the next crop of teenagers becomes old enough to buy porn, it seems less and less likely that they will be interested in doing so.

Critical Thinking

1. How are current market trends impacting the porn industry?
2. What is the potential future landscape of the porn industry? What possible future challenges might the porn industry face?

Does Proximity to Schools Tempt Former Sex Offenders?

CYNTHIA CALKINS MERCADO, PHD, AND BRIAN H. BORNSTEIN, PHD

Last November, the Supreme Court of Georgia considered the constitutionality of sex offender residency restrictions, one of the more recent policies to gain popularity in the criminal justice arena. Residency restrictions prohibit sex offenders from living or working within a certain distance (typically between 500 and 2,500 feet) of places such as schools, day-care facilities or parks. At least 30 states and many local jurisdictions have residency restrictions in place. Some states, such as Alabama, have exceptions that allow offenders with already established residences to remain when a school or other youth-serving institution later establishes itself in the area. Georgia, however, had no such statutory exception, leaving Anthony Mann in violation of his probation when a child-care facility moved within 1,000 feet of the home that he owned with his wife and a barbeque restaurant he co-owned.

Applying a Fifth Amendment takings analysis, the Georgia Supreme Court noted that "there is no place in Georgia where a registered sex offender can live without being at continual risk of being ejected," (*Mann v. Department of Georgia Corrections et al,* 282 Ga. 754, 755, 2007). The court found the statute to be unconstitutional with regard to Mann's home, but not his work, given that much of the work in running the restaurant could be done off-site.

Other Court Rulings

In another case, Keith Seering and his family left their home and moved into a fold-down camper on rural farmland to comply with Iowa's 2,000-foot residency restriction. However, after the farm owner demanded that they leave the property, Seering challenged the statute's constitutionality. In upholding the residency restriction, the Iowa Supreme Court found no deprivation of Seering's substantive or due process rights (*State v. Seering,* 701 N.W.2d 655, 2005).

Other courts have similarly upheld residency restriction legislation. In 2005, the Eighth Circuit Court of Appeals upheld the same statute at issue in *Seering,* with the court finding that no fundamental right exists to choose where one lives (*Doe v. Miller,* 418 F.3d 950, 2005). The Association for the Treatment of Sexual Abusers (ATSA) petitioned for writ of *certiorari,* noting the national significance of *Doe v. Miller* and arguing that residency restrictions "actually harm the innocent children they are intended to protect" by increasing offender transience (ATSA, 2005). The U.S. Supreme Court, however, declined to hear the case.

What the Research Shows

Although many challenges to residency restriction legislation have survived constitutional scrutiny, some argue that residency restrictions lead to housing instability and housing shortages. Research can inform several issues that may be relevant to these cases. For instance, in Orange County, Fla., research shows that more than 95 percent of residential properties are within 1,000 feet of designated child-dense areas, while 2,500-foot restrictions encompass nearly 100 percent of residential space.

To date, there is still little research on the utility of residency restriction statutes. However, a recent study failed to show that sex offenders who re-offend live closer to schools and parks than those who do not re-offend. Further, research has found that "social or relationship proximity" to children, rather than residential proximity, affects sexual recidivism. Notably, after considering studies on the impact of residency restrictions, both the Colorado and Minnesota legislatures opted not to enact such legislation.

Some evidence suggests that offenders (regardless of the crime they have committed) who become more integrated in the community and lead more stable lives are less likely to re-offend than those who experience change and turmoil. Indeed, it is possible that being able to remain in the same house would provide a source of stability that would reduce re-offending, in much the same way that job stability reduces likelihood of recidivism. Though existing research indicates that residency restrictions limit housing options and that geographical proximity to child-dense community structures may have little effect on recidivism generally, further research might address whether residential instability impacts sexual re-offense patterns. Psychologists and other social scientists can contribute valuable data to this policy debate by studying such questions. It is possible that the benefit produced by residency-restriction statutes is offset by the risks they create.

Critical Thinking

1. Summarize the effort to restrict where registered sex offenders can live.
2. How effective are residency restrictions with regard to registered sex offenders?
3. How do location and proximity to victims impact re-offense rates for registered sex offenders?

Acknowledgments—"Judicial Notebook" is a project of APA's Div. 9 (Society for the Psychological Study of Social Issues).

The Face of Domestic Violence

How could Amanda White have stayed with a husband who beat her over and over again? A young mom opens up about what she went through and why she believed it would all get better.

Sᴀʀᴀʜ Eʟɪᴢᴀʙᴇᴛʜ Rɪᴄʜᴀʀᴅs, ᴀs ᴛᴏʟᴅ ᴛᴏ ʜᴇʀ ʙʏ Aᴍᴀɴᴅᴀ Wʜɪᴛᴇ

First Signs of Trouble

I sat in my mom's house not knowing what to do.

My body still ached from being beaten by my husband a day earlier. But he kept pleading through the door: "I was drunk. I'm sorry. I'll never do that to you again. I know I need help." I had a 2-week-old baby. I wanted to believe him. I opened the door.

I had a crush on Dietrich White back in junior high. When I ran into him almost a decade later in 1997, I was 21 and even more attracted to his sexy smile and blue eyes. I was thrilled when he asked me out. I was living with my mom in Hot Springs, Arkansas, while I took time off from college to heal from complications of endometriosis surgery. I tried to fill my time by running a booth-rental business in a crafts mall, but many of my friends were away at school and I was lonely.

Dietrich and I became a couple and spent nearly every day together. He said we were soul mates, brought me flowers, and took me on a trip to Florida. Two months later we were engaged. We moved in together in Little Rock (about an hour away from my mom), where Dietrich owned a carpet-cleaning business. I intended to return to school, but Dietrich said he earned enough to support us, so I could spend my time decorating our home and planning my dream wedding.

Dietrich and I rarely argued, but sometimes he got jealous and claimed I looked at other men. I was flattered that he was so in love with me that he couldn't stand the idea of me being with someone else. I wish I had known then that jealousy is often a warning sign of an abusive personality.

Our idyllic life didn't last long. Within a few months Dietrich had lost many of his customers and became distant. We had our first fight when I couldn't find him at his jobsite one afternoon; I smelled beer on his breath when he came home. "Where the hell have you been?" I demanded. He lied that he had been working and headed for the shower. I got so mad I threw a glass-covered candle at the bathtub. Dietrich stormed over and slapped me hard across the face. No one had ever hit me before, and I was stunned. "Did you just hit me?" I screamed.

"You made me do it!" I remember him shouting back. "You have no right to attack me when I've been working."

Later I apologized, and he said, "We never need to do that again." I tried to forget about the incident, but the next day my mother saw my black eye. "He was drinking, and I started it," I tried to explain. She exploded. "I don't care about the circumstances," she said. "No man can do that!"

Dietrich's irrational jealousy erupted again a month later when he accused me of sleeping with a friend of his. He canceled our wedding, which was just two weeks away, and asked me to move out. My parents lost thousands of dollars, but my mother was relieved. I was devastated.

On what would have been our wedding day I found out I was pregnant. After my endometriosis surgery, my doctor had told me I was infertile, so we hadn't been using birth control. The timing was terrible, but I was thrilled to learn I could have kids. My mom urged me to have the baby on my own, but I didn't want to be a single mother. Besides, I believed that a child would complete our little family and make things better.

Pain and Denial

When I was eight months pregnant we finally got married—in a judge's office. Then, after our son was born, Dietrich's business tanked and we had to move in with my mom. After she left for work one morning he said he had overheard us talking about my high school boyfriend and accused me of planning to see him. When I denied it he called me a liar and punched me several times in the face. I fell and the baby started screaming. I had never seen Dietrich this enraged. "Please stop!" I begged hysterically as I tried to reach the baby. He'd calm down and let me nurse the baby, but then he'd explode and come at me again.

At first I had white flashes in front of my eyes and a pounding pressure in my head, but my adrenaline kicked in and I felt dazed and couldn't tell where I'd been hit. Seven long hours later he told me to wash the blood off my face. I thought the nightmare was over, but as soon as I climbed into the tub he came into the bathroom and started choking me under the water until I passed out. I was sure I was going to die. He must have pulled my head out of the water in time because I came to, stumbled out of the bathroom and discovered that he'd taken the baby. By the time I called my sister-in-law to come get me, Dietrich had returned. He had calmed down, told me the baby was at his mother's house and took me to the hospital.

My mom found me in the ER, where they examined my black eyes and bruises. When the doctor asked what happened, I said I fell down a flight of stairs. He didn't ask any more questions and I was released. When we got home, Dietrich had brought back the baby, but my mom made him leave. She called the police the next day, but they said you have to call within four hours of a domestic-violence incident in order for them to make an arrest (the state law has since been changed to 12 hours). That evening Dietrich came over to apologize. He said he'd been drunk the night before. He swore he'd go to Alcoholics Anonymous. He promised we'd go to couples counseling. Three days later I let him back in.

My mom was furious. It's hard to explain how anyone could stay with someone after being hurt like that, but I had convinced myself it was because of the alcohol and that this one incident had gotten out of control. I knew that Dietrich loved me. I wanted to believe he was truly sorry and would never harm me again.

A Fresh Start?

I felt reassured when Dietrich made good on his pledge to attend a couple of AA meetings. He thought we needed a clean slate, so in the fall of 1998 we moved almost 1,000 miles away to Tampa, Florida. Those days were the best of our marriage. He found work laying down tile; I helped out while the baby slept. We took our son swimming in the ocean, and Dietrich toted him around in a baby carrier. He also fussed over me and bought me a beautiful silk bathrobe and diamond bracelet. I really thought he had changed.

But six months later Dietrich couldn't get any more work. That's when he started to abuse me again. During an argument he pushed me and broke my arm. Again I lied to doctors at the hospital and said I had fallen down the stairs. And to my surprise I found out I was pregnant. We eventually ran out of money and moved back to Arkansas. After our second son was born, in November 1999, Dietrich attacked my mom when she tried to stop him from driving drunk with the baby in the car.

In 2001, three years into our marriage, I finally got up the courage to leave. My parents were so relieved and rented me a house. Dietrich begged me to come back, but even though I learned I was pregnant for the third time, I stayed strong and filed for divorce. He said there was no way I could care for three kids on my own, and that scared me. So by the time I delivered a third son, Dietrich and I were back together.

Hitting Rock Bottom

I know it sounds crazy now, but I really didn't think I was a battered woman—at least not yet. Then one May night in 2002 Dietrich beat me so badly with a child's chair that he broke my nose, shattered my knuckles, and fractured several bones in my face. My mom called the police. My hair was full of blood and my body was covered in gashes and bruises. I needed 65 stitches; Dietrich was arrested and charged with domestic battery in the first degree. The court added child endangerment charges since he had attacked me with the kids around. While he spent some time in jail, he was released on bond.

You'd think the severity of that beating would have been the last straw. This time, though, I thought jail had really scared him. During Thanksgiving at his parents' house that year he acted as if he had really missed me and the boys. I was moved by his sincerity and, during a weak moment, yes, we had sex. As luck would have it, since Dietrich would never let me use birth control, I got pregnant for the fourth time.

As the Arkansas trial drew closer, Dietrich started to unravel under the pressure and, afraid of jail time, fled to Ohio. He threatened that if I didn't join him, he would kill my family. Now that I knew what he was capable of, I was terrified he would do it. So I told my parents I was taking the kids to see friends but instead left for Ohio. They frantically called Dietrich's relatives and hired a private investigator but couldn't find me for more than a year. I wasn't surprised that the beatings continued in Ohio, but I was shocked when one night in 2004 someone called the police, and they arrested Dietrich *and* me. We had a fourth son by then, and I was charged with child endangerment for allowing the kids to witness the violence.

A New Life

The threat of losing my kids was the turning point. I had no idea how much they had suffered. I was devastated when I looked through their coloring books and saw they had scratched out all the faces. I thought I had protected them by making sure they were in another room or sleeping. But who was I kidding? Of course they heard the fighting and saw the bruises. Of course they lived in constant fear, too.

I knew I had to make it up to them and prove myself as a mom. So I completed all the court's required parenting classes and attended a domestic-violence support group. Dietrich begged me to drop the charges from the beating in Arkansas, which would increase his sentence. But I wouldn't do it. My mom was so proud. In the end he was sentenced to serve 18 years in prison. After seven years of marriage, our divorce became final in 2005.

At age 30 I returned to Arkansas to start over. Now I work for the Saline County Safe Haven, a local domestic-violence shelter. I've testified before the state legislature to raise money, and I speak to women to help them recognize the signs of abuse. I was proudest, though, when I completed my training to be a police officer. I was recruited to handle domestic-violence calls, and it feels great to help women find a shelter or get legal help. More than anything, I try to make them understand that they're choosing to continue the cycle of abuse every time they go back. I wish I had learned that lesson sooner.

The boys know their father is in jail and isn't allowed to contact them. They don't talk about him much, but occasionally one might say, "I wish our dad wasn't so mean so he could be with us." I put them each in counseling for about a year, and except for some minor anger issues they all seem to have recovered. I'm proud of them. They're all so loving, get good grades, and play school sports. I spend as much time as possible with them and organize my schedule so I can be home when they get out of school.

Dietrich will be eligible for parole in June, and I know he'll get out eventually. He may try to find me and get me to come back as he did before, but I'm a different person now. I won't let anyone hurt us ever again.

Critical Thinking

1. Is it sometimes OK for a woman to hit a man, especially if he has provoked her?
2. Should the wife in Ohio in 2004 have been arrested?
3. Is there anything more doctors should have done?

Options for Reporting Sexual Violence: Developments over the Past Decade

SABRINA GARCIA, MA, AND MARGARET HENDERSON, MPA

"Blind reporting can give victims of sexual violence, and other sensitive crimes, a safe haven to file a report at the same time that it removes that refuge from their assailants."[1] For the victim, the benefit of such a system lies in having time to build trust with the law enforcement officer and to consider all of the implications of participating in reporting, investigating, or prosecuting the case *before* making a decision whether to proceed. For the law enforcement agency, this type of reporting can help gain intelligence about the local incidence and perpetration of all sexual violence in the community, as well as build trust and credibility with populations vulnerable to assault.

Developments in the field and changing social expectations have made law enforcement agencies reconsider and refine their processes for working with victims of sexual violence. Careful thought, clear direction, and institutional commitment are required to set up graduated reporting systems that respect the circumstances and challenges of victims, provide consistent response by investigators over time, and gather intelligence and evidence that will ultimately achieve law enforcement's primary goal: to protect and serve.

Major Changes

Since 1999, these developments have affected the terms used to describe this practice and applied the concept to parallel processes. The two major changes involved the U.S. Department of Defense establishing a graduated reporting system (confidential, restricted, and unrestricted) in all branches of the military in 2004. Then, in 2005, Violence Against Women legislation (VAWA 2005) mandated that states afford forensic medical examinations to victims of sexual assault *without* 1) requiring cooperation with law enforcement or participation in the criminal justice system and 2) incurring any out-of-pocket expenses.[2]

U.S. Military Process

By 2004, the Department of Defense implemented landmark policies to address the incidence of sexual violence taking place within the military. They originally distinguished three levels of reporting.[3]

1. Confidential reporting: The service member reports the victimization to specified officials and gains access to supportive services. The service providers are not required to automatically report the incident to law enforcement or initiate an official investigation.
2. Restricted reporting: The service member reports the victimization to specified officials and gains access to supportive services. The service providers will not inform law enforcement unless the victim consents or an established exception is exercised under DoD Directive 6495.01.
3. Unrestricted reporting: The service member reports the victimization and gains access to supportive services. Both the report and any details from the service providers are reportable to law enforcement and may be used to initiate the official investigative process.

VAWA 2005 Mandate

States that do not comply with the VAWA 2005 requirement regarding forensic examinations will not be eligible to receive STOP Violence Against Women Formula Grant Program funds. According to the Office on Violence Against Women (OVW), "In fiscal year 2009, the STOP Program awarded almost $116 million in grant funds. Since 1995, OVW has made approximately 353 awards to states and territories, totaling more than $750 million, to address domestic violence, dating violence, sexual assault, and stalking."[4] This funding enables states to introduce innovations and improvements to their client services, law enforcement, and judicial systems.

Of importance, VAWA 2005 emphasizes health care and evidence collection, *not* reporting to law enforcement. It requires states to meet these forensic requirements but does not mandate a particular strategy for compliance. States, therefore, vary in their approaches.[5] Moreover, states also are not required to implement restricted reporting processes, but many are doing so voluntarily.[6]

. . . VAWA 2005 emphasizes health care and evidence collection, *not* reporting to law enforcement.

OVW's Web site offers some frequently asked questions, including one concerning the effect of the VAWA 2005 forensic examination requirement on law enforcement. "Many victims refuse to undergo examinations because they are not ready to report the sexual assault to the police. Advocates for sexual assault victims maintain that the VAWA 2005 forensic examination requirement will encourage more victims to undergo examinations directly following the crime, thereby preserving forensic evidence for future prosecutions when victims are ready to cooperate with law enforcement. Jurisdictions that have implemented anonymous reporting, including the U.S. Military, have found this to be true."[7]

Term Usage

Law enforcement officials and other professionals who work with victims of sexual violence might be unclear about the distinguishing characteristics among the terms *blind, restricted, confidential, Jane Doe,* or *anonymous* reporting processes and might use them differently. To aid the law enforcement community, the authors offer a clarification of these terms and provide general guidance on setting up these systems of reporting. They use the term *restricted reporting* to refer to processes in which victims contact law enforcement for assistance and the term *anonymous reporting* for those in which victims seek medical intervention and evidence collection but not necessarily investigation as set forth in VAWA 2005.[8]

In anonymous reporting processes, the victims are given a code number at the hospital that they can use to identify themselves if they choose to report at a later time. They are not required to cooperate with law enforcement or criminal justice authorities. Generally speaking, no direct connection is made between the victim and law enforcement officials unless the victim is willing to request their involvement. An advantage to anonymous reporting is that the integrity of the evidence is maintained while the victims have time to heal, consider their options, and make decisions. A disadvantage concerns hospitals and law enforcement investing resources in collecting and storing evidence that might not be used.

Twofold Benefits

For Victims

In addition to dealing with the ordeal of the violence itself, victims also might be traumatized by the reactions of family, friends, or the professionals from whom they seek help. Historically, too many survivors experienced revictimization through the law enforcement and criminal justice processes. Reporting systems that force—or are *perceived* to force—immediate all-or-nothing decisions whether to pursue investigation understandably scare off some victims. In contrast, allowing time to create dialogue between the victim and the law enforcement

officer has the added benefit of building trust between them as well. A victim who trusts the integrity of the investigator is more likely to withstand the potential challenges, intrusions, or disappointments of the investigative process.

For Law Enforcement

Law enforcement officers might initially experience frustration in spending time with a victim who is uncertain about following through or in their being held back from a compelling investigation. However, victim-friendly reporting processes constitute an investment in both building positive community relationships and in gathering intelligence related to the commission of sexually violent crimes.

Agencies that implement some form of graduated reporting options likely will experience an increase in the initial reports that develop into formal investigations. For example, in 2005, the first year of the Department of Defense's graduated reporting system, 108 (24.8 percent) of the 435 victims who initially used the confidential reporting mechanism later chose to file formal reports.[9] And, for the Chapel Hill, North Carolina, Police Department, 22 percent of these types of reports developed into formal investigations over a period of 10 years.[10]

An advantage to anonymous reporting is that the integrity of the evidence is maintained while the victims have time to heal, consider their options, and make decisions.

Untapped Potential

These graduated reporting options represent an innovation from over a decade ago that some in law enforcement have yet to fully embrace. Room for expansion in terms of both philosophy and implementation could prove beneficial for both victims and the law enforcement community. Where such systems exist, one learning opportunity now relates to how best to use the information while maintaining any promised expectations of confidentiality.

Using the Data

The initial report acts as a foundation document, offering the first account presented by the victim that can link to a suspect's method of operation, description, crime location, or identity. The information also might inform other existing investigations of the same or related types of crime or patterns of perpetration. The information presented to law enforcement by the victim of sexual violence is potentially unavailable by any other means or through any other person. Similarly, narcotics and vice operations commonly practice receiving, but not acting upon, such information to make the best strategic use of the data.

Specific information for any crime is primarily gained from two distinct sources, the victim and the offender. As law enforcement is aware, gaining access to a crime through the "eyes of a victim" lends unique insight to an offender's behavior and motivation. It also can provide links to other crimes that

Basic Steps in Establishing a Restricted Reporting System

1. Clarify the goal of setting up a flexible system of reporting. Is the law enforcement agency interested in strengthening its service to victims, reacting to negative publicity, or responding to emerging trends in the field? If the ultimate goal is to investigate and enable the successful prosecution of more cases of sexual violence, the agency must understand that it might take a long time to gain the trust of the community.

2. Identify the resources available to support the system. Which staff will be trained and involved in receiving reports from victims? What kind of private office space is available for the interviews?

3. Designate who will receive, document, store, or have access to the information. Create a secure location for storing this information, preferably away from other records.

4. Determine the circumstances or processes in which information might be shared across types of investigations within the agency. For example, consider a situation in which a rape victim discloses significant information about a drug dealer. When does the victim of sexual violence hold all authority over the information shared? When might information related to the drug supply, storage, or sales be shared, anonymously or not, with another investigator?

5. Set forth the circumstances or processes in which information might be shared with other helping professionals outside the agency, such as the rape crisis center, sexual assault nurse examiner, or sexual assault response team. The victim should be informed of and preferably have the opportunity to clarify how much information must or could be shared with which other people.

6. Consider creating an information sheet that describes the reporting system for others so that they will understand the intention, the process, the involved staff, and any limitations victims should consider. Decide how best to share this information within the agency, directly with victims, or throughout the community.

7. Create a standardized intake form that, along with the details of the sexual offense, clarifies the victim's preferences for sharing or receiving information, conditions for future contact, and expected next steps. Similarly, standardized categorization of the information will aid in analyzing the report, retrieving data, and matching specific characteristics across investigations.

8. Institute training for and reinforcement of the following basic principles for working with victims of sexual violence:

- Establish and uphold a policy of confidentiality. It is the basis of trust.
- Accept as little or as much information as the victim is willing to provide. Putting pressure on the victim for immediate and full disclosure can threaten the sense of trust placed in the officer and sense of safety with the process.
- Take information whenever the victim might offer it. A delay in disclosure might reflect more on the victim's sense of support than on the validity of the statement.
- Allow information from third parties. Some victims might feel so threatened that they will only share information through other parties, such as the rape crisis center.
- Clarify options for future contact. Specify the means (phone, e-mail, in person), the content (first name or professional title, code phrase, full disclosure), and the circumstances (if another victim comes forth, if more evidence is discovered).
- Maintain these reports in separate files unless the victim decides to file a formal report.
- Consistently categorize the information within each report.
- Compare the information with that in other formal investigative reports to provide an ongoing analysis of sexual assault reports.

might not seem connected due to their nonsexualized presentation. Related crimes that can easily be overlooked are property crimes, such as breaking and entering, burglary, carjacking, or robbery. Perpetrators might employ these strategies to gain access to potential victims for the purpose of sexual assault.

However, data collection and analysis must be grounded in the specific dynamics of sexual violence perpetration and victimization. The relationship between law enforcement and a confidential informant who provides drug or vice intelligence, for example, will not parallel the one between law enforcement and a victim of sexual violence.

Relating to Victims

For victims to risk talking at all, law enforcement officers should demonstrate a basic knowledge about the potential emotional and behavioral reactions to the violence and convey an understanding of the negative personal impact of working through the justice system. Affirming the challenges of both experiences (the violence and the reporting) does not mean the officers accept the victims' accounts with unquestioning belief but simply that they convey a basic understanding of some part of the experience.[11] It is appropriate to share legal definitions or potential interpretations of behavior, recognizing that sex offenders are effective in using these myths and misunderstandings to convince victims that their actions contributed to the sexually violent outcome of the encounter. Too often and too accurately, victims delay or avoid reporting the crime because the perpetrator has convinced them that no one else will believe or care.

Linking Cases

Once a victim talks with an officer, another challenge lies in taking the initiative to consistently code and study the report.

Comparison of Anonymous and Restricted Reporting Systems

	Anonymous Reporting to Hospitals	Restricted or Blind Reporting
Authority behind the system	VAWA 2005 requires states to provide victims medical intervention and evidence collection at no charge and with no obligation to report to law enforcement.	established at the discretion of individual law enforcement agencies.
The evidence or information is collected by	the hospital.	an investigator or specialist designated by the agency.
The evidence or information is stored by	a central repository for the state.	the designated investigator or specialist.
The victim has the option to	report to law enforcement or take no action.	file a blind report (share information) or file a full report (request an investigation).
The evidence or information	is stored until the victim files a report with law enforcement, who retrieves and processes the medical evidence.	the victim specifies how the agency might use the information contained within a blind report. If a full report is filed, the evidence or information is processed for the investigation.

The end goal is to achieve case linkage through comparative analysis.

To structure reported information into a usable format, developing a restricted reporting form and using it consistently prove critical. The structure of the form should enable easy review with other formally submitted police reports. Assigning responsibility to one person, such as the department's crime analyst, investigation commander, or sex crime specialist, is a preferred way to consistently maintain and analyze the reports. In addition to asking traditional questions about the perpetrator, weapons, vehicle, and crime, this form also can be used to track custody of evidence kits or other collected evidence, as well as the strategies employed to identify, groom, isolate, intimidate, or control the victim. As a beginning, expectations of the information contained within the reports should be considered from four perspectives.

1. Collection: Designate space on the report form to document how the information and evidence were obtained, as well as from whom, where, and when.
2. Collation: Sort the information into specific categories, such as the time frame when crimes were committed, locations, and victimology.
3. Analysis: Note the specific behaviors, features, controls, or dialogue/monologue by offender and victim. These characteristics can demonstrate ritualized behaviors or scripted language required by the perpetrator to complete the offense.
4. Dissemination: Clarify how, when, what, and with whom the information is shared, with the victim's permission. This includes internal and external sharing with professional peers or multidisciplinary teams.

If the victim decides to proceed with a full investigation, the original restricted report and the official incident report should be cross-coded by number. This will allow for easy retrieval of the information.

Agencies that implement some form of graduated reporting options likely will experience an increase in the initial reports that develop into formal investigations.

Conclusion

Setting up restricted reporting systems helps ensure that law enforcement agencies receive a more accurate account of the crimes committed within their jurisdictions. These endeavors provide a venue for victims to satisfy their need to notify others of the potential for harm, gain faith in a complex process unknown to them, and receive the response that they deserve.

As with most innovative techniques that address specialized crimes, law enforcement organizations should take time up front to clarify their goals for implementing the system and the resources they are willing to direct toward sustaining it. Planning and providing training for both the process of reporting and the dynamics of sexual violence also is critical for successful implementation. In the end, agencies should remember that the lack of confidential reporting can create a picture-perfect community but not always a safe one.

Notes

1. Sabrina Garcia and Margaret Henderson, "Blind Reporting of Sexual Violence," *FBI Law Enforcement Bulletin,* June 1999, 12–16.
2. Access http://frwebgate.access.gpo.gov/cgi-bin/getdoc. cgi?dbname=109_cong_bills&docid=f:h3402enr.txt.pdf for the complete text of VAWA 2005.
3. The Web site for the U.S. Department of Defense Sexual Assault Prevention and Response, www.sapr.mil, now lists only two options for reporting—restricted and unrestricted—and refers to the policy on confidentiality for specific personnel.

4. See, the Office on Violence Against Women website at www.ovw.usdoj.gov/stop_grant_desc.htm.

5. States needing technical assistance in reaching compliance should contact the Maryland Coalition Against Sexual Assault (MCASA), which was designated by the Office on Violence Against Women as the national technical assistance provider on this issue. Information regarding this project can be found at www.mcasa.org.

6. See the Office on Violence Against Women website at www.ovw.usdoj.gov.

7. For further information on forensic examination requirements and other STOP Program requirements, please visit www.ovw.usdoj.gov/docs/FAQ_FINAL_nov_21_07.pdf or contact the Office on Violence Against Women at 800 K Street, NW, Washington, DC 20530, Phone: (202) 307-6026 and Fax: (202) 305-2589.

8. One disadvantage of using the term *Jane Doe* in relation to sexual assault forensic exams is that law enforcement often uses this phrase to refer to unidentified victims for whom investigations are initiated. In the circumstances addressed by VAWA 2005, investigation will not begin until or unless the victim decides to do so.

9. See Department of Defense Report of Sexual Assaults in CY 2005 at www.sapr.mil/contents/references/2005%20RTC%20Sexual%20Assaults.pdf.

10. Statistics provided by Sabrina Garcia, Chapel Hill, North Carolina, Police Department.

11. Local rape crisis centers and state sexual assault coalitions are sources for training about the victim's perspective.

Critical Thinking

1. What are the benefits of the various options for reporting victimization, to the victims and to law enforcement?

2. Are there any disadvantages to any of these options?

Ms. Garcia is the domestic violence/sexual assault specialist for the Chapel Hill, North Carolina, Police Department. **Ms. Henderson** is the associate director of the Public Intersection Project at the School of Government, University of North Carolina at Chapel Hill.

From *FBI Law Enforcement Bulletin* by Sabrina Garcia and Margaret Henderson, May 2010, pp. 1–8. Published by Federal Bureau of Investigation, www.fbi.gov.

Domestic Abuse Myths

Five mistakes we make when we talk about Rihanna and Chris Brown's relationship.

RAINA KELLEY

Last week, R&B singer Chris Brown was formally charged with two felonies, assault and making criminal threats, in connection with the alleged beating of his pop-star girlfriend Rihanna on Feb. 8. Though we will never know exactly what happened that night, many of us have seen Rihanna's bruised and bloodied face on the front pages and read horrific details of the alleged attack from the affidavit of a LAPD detective in which he describes contusions on the singer's body. At the same time, rumors are that the 21-year-old singer is back in a relationship with Brown, whom she has accused, according to the affidavit, of biting, choking and punching her until her mouth filled with blood.

While we can argue about how much of all that is true, it really doesn't matter. This sad story doesn't have to be verifiable for it to potentially warp how Rihanna's hundreds of thousands of tween fans think about intimate relationships. We've all heard that this should be a "teachable moment"—a chance to talk about domestic violence with our kids. But children and teens aren't just listening to your lectures, they're listening to the way you speculate about the case with other adults; they're absorbing how the media describes it; they're reading gossip websites. When you tune in to all the talk about Rihanna and Chris Brown, it's scary how the same persistent domestic-violence myths continue to be perpetuated. Celebrity scandals may have a short shelf life, but what we teach kids about domestic violence will last forever. So rather than "raise awareness," here are five myths that anyone with a child should take time to debunk:

Myth No. 1: It Was a Domestic Argument, and She Provoked Him

We need to remember that any discussion of domestic violence should not revolve around what the couple may have been arguing about, or as one CNN anchor put it: "the incident that sparked the fight." Nor should we be using the word "provoked" when describing this case, as in the Associated Press account that said the "argument" was "provoked" by Rihanna's "discovery of a text message from another woman." Domestic violence has to do with, well, physical violence, not arguments.

There isn't a verbal argument that should "spark" or "provoke" an attack of the kind that leaves one person with wounds that require medical attention.

Cable news has to stop referring to this incident as a "violent fight." A "fight" involves two people hitting each other, not—as is alleged in this case—a woman cowering in a car while a man punches and bites her. If Rihanna had called the police beaten and bloodied and alleging an attack of this nature by a stranger, no one would be calling it a "fight." They'd say that a man was being accused of severely beating and choking a young woman half his size.

Myth No. 2: Evolution Makes Us Do It

Steven Stosny, a counselor and founder of an organization that treats anger-management issues believes that the tragic tendency of women to return to the men who hurt them (battered-woman syndrome) is a product of evolution. Stosny was quoted on CNN.com as saying "To leave an attachment relationship—a relationship where there's an emotional bond—meant certain death by starvation or saber-tooth tiger."

Apologies to Mr. Stosny, but that is the most ridiculous thing I have ever heard. This is the kind of argument that really boils my blood because it seems to naturalize the torture of women. Very little is known about the emotional attachments of early humans. And trust me, after 50,000 years, our fear of saber-tooth tigers has abated. In most domestic-abuse cases, we're talking about a situation where one person is wielding power over an individual through pain, fear, and domination. It's not about being scared to leave because of the dangers that await you in the world, it's about being too scared of what's at home to leave.

Myth No. 3: People Make Mistakes. Give the Guy a Break

When singer Kanye West talked about the Rihanna-Brown case with his VH1 audience recently, he asked: "Can't we give Chris a break? . . . I know I make mistakes in life." Kanye's not the only one saying this kind of thing, so let's get something straight: People leave the oven on or fry turkeys in the garage and burn their house down. One may even accidentally step on the gas instead of the brake and run over the family cat. Mistakes resulting in tragic consequences happen all the time. But one cannot mistakenly beat someone up. You do not accidentally give someone black eyes, a broken nose, and a split lip.

Myth No. 4: Brown Said He Was Sorry and They're Working It Out

Experts will tell you that domestic violence is an escalating series of attacks (not fights) designed to increase a victim's dependence on her abuser. According to the police documents released last week, Rihanna told police that Brown had hit her before and it was getting worse. Sorry means you don't do it again. In discussions about abuse, we need to make it clear that sorry is not enough.

Myth No. 5: She's Young, Rich and Beautiful. If It Was Really as Bad as the Media Says, She'd Leave

The secret to the abuser's power is not only making his victim dependent on him, but convincing her that she is to blame for the attack. No amount of money or fame can protect someone from the terrible cycle of emotional dependence, shame and fear that keeps them with abusive partners. Women who are abused look for ways they may have "provoked" an attack, finding fault with their own behavior to explain the unexplainable—why would someone they love hurt them? And it doesn't help when people outside the relationship blame the victim. In this case, Phylicia Thompson, a cousin of Brown's, told "Extra TV" that, *"Chris was not brought up to beat on a woman. So it had to be something to provoke him for Chris to do it."* As the rumors swirl about whether Rihanna is back with Brown, understand that those who are abused do not stay with their abusers because they want to be beaten again, or because they are really at fault; it's usually because they feel trapped and guilty.

You may have noticed the words *power, control,* and *domination* running through my rant. That was purposeful. What we need to remember, and what we need to teach our children, is that yes, you should never hit anybody and you should never let anybody hit you. But, we also need to tell them that love does not guarantee respect and that any relationship they find themselves involved in should be based on both equally.

Critical Thinking

1. What are some of the most common myths about domestic violence?
2. What impact do domestic violence myths have on abusers? On victims? On relationships?

Male Rape Myths
The Role of Gender, Violence, and Sexism

KRISTINE M. CHAPLEAU, MS, DEBRA L. OSWALD, PhD, AND BRENDA L. RUSSELL, PhD

More than 247,000 women and men in the United States were estimated as being raped or sexually assaulted in 2002 (U.S. Department of Justice, 2003). Most research has focused on female victims; however, 13% (31,640) of reported rape and sexual assault victims were male (U.S. Department of Justice, 2003). Although women are victimized far more often than men, the proportion of male victims compared to female victims may be skewed because of gender differences in reporting rates. While the reporting rate for women is low (e.g., Koss, Gidycz, & Wisniewski, 1987), preliminary results suggest that men are 1.5 times less likely to report a rape by a male perpetrator to the police than are women (Pino & Meier, 1999). This rate may be even lower when accounting for sexual assaults committed by women, although little is known about the effects of perpetrator gender on the likelihood that male victims will report sexual assault to the police.

Unfortunately, even when rape victims do report, the legal system often fails to punish the perpetrators. Justice for female sexual assault victims is often derailed by unsympathetic police officers (Campbell & Johnson, 1997), district attorneys (Frohmann, 1991), and juries (Koss, 2000). Similar data are not reported for male victims, which, given the lower reporting rate, suggests that perpetrators of male rape are also seldom prosecuted. Sexual assault is often emotionally devastating to men. Like female victims, men can experience vulnerability, depression, suicidal thoughts, sleep disturbances, social isolation, sexual dysfunction, and confusion about their sexual orientation if the perpetrator was male (Goyer & Eddleman, 1984; Groth & Burgess, 1980; Mezey & King, 1989). Furthermore, there is correlational evidence that male victims sexually coerce others as well. Russell and Oswald (2002) found that of college-aged men who reported using coercion to obtain sex, almost 63% reported having at least one experience of being sexually coerced themselves by a female partner. Thus, sexual coercion against men has serious consequences for the victims as well as for others.

In sum, male rape is problematic and currently understudied. Because male and female victims experience similar social sanctions and negative sequelae, it follows that similar social forces and ideologies work against rape victims of both genders. In this study, we investigate the extent to which people believe rape myths about male victims. Rape myths about female victims have been found to play a central role in the misperceptions and treatment of female rape victims. Similarly, we argue that there are myths about male victims of rape that need to be explored and understood. Given the limited research on male rape myths, we first examine the research on female rape victims to direct our study of biases toward male rape victims.

Rape Myths about Female Victims

For female victims, past research has shown that a primary social force in their maltreatment is rape myths (e.g., Brownmiller, 1975; Burt, 1980; Campbell & Johnson, 1997; Du Mont, Miller, & Myhr, 2003). Rape myths are stereotypical or false beliefs about the culpability of victims, the innocence of rapists, and the illegitimacy of rape as a serious crime (Lonsway & Fitzgerald, 1994). For example, in the development of the Illinois Rape Myth Acceptance Scale, Payne, Lonsway, and Fitzgerald (1999) identified seven types of female rape myths: (a) "she asked for it"; (b) "it wasn't really rape"; (c) "he didn't mean to"; (d) "she wanted it"; (e) "she lied"; (f) "rape is a trivial event"; and (g) "rape is a deviant event" (p. 37). Although there seems to be agreement on the identification of rape myths (Lonsway & Fitzgerald, 1994), pinpointing the underlying ideologies that facilitate female rape myth acceptance has been more challenging.

With roots in feminist theory, most of the proposed attitudinal variables relate to sexism (for a review, see Lonsway & Fitzgerald, 1994). One of the earliest studies on this topic found that the best attitudinal predictor of rape myth acceptance was acceptance of interpersonal violence (Burt, 1980). This is the belief that "force and coercion are legitimate ways to gain compliance and specifically that they are legitimate in intimate and sexual relationships" (Burt, 1980, p. 218). Other strong predictors in Burt's study were sex role stereotyping and adversarial sexual beliefs. So participants who judged others based on rigid sex roles, thought that men and women naturally struggle for dominance, and that men should ultimately win this struggle, even if by force, were more likely to denounce female rape victims.

Updating Burt's (1980) construct of sex role stereotyping, Glick and Fiske (1996) proposed that sexism consists of two components reflecting hostile and benevolent attitudes toward women. Hostile sexism is denigrating attitudes that punish women who defy traditional gender roles (Glick, Diebold, Bailey-Werner, & Zhu, 1997). Conversely, benevolent sexism is reverent attitudes that reward women who are traditionally feminine (Glick et al., 1997). Although hostile and benevolent sexism are both stereotypical beliefs about women, they differ in prejudicial evaluations (i.e., bad and good) (Glick & Fiske, 1996). Those who have these conflicting feelings toward women resolve this conflict by categorizing individual women as either "good girls" or "bad girls" (Glick & Fiske, 1996). "Good girls" are venerated and thus worthy of chivalry; "bad girls" are denigrated and denied patriarchal protection. Glick and Fiske (1997) found that for both male and female participants, hostile sexism (but not benevolent sexism) significantly correlated with Burt's (1980) Rape Myth Acceptance Scale (using partial correlations controlling for benevolent sexism scores).

Viki and Abrams (2002), however, suggested that individuals who score higher in benevolent sexism may be more likely to blame victims of acquaintance rape for falling short of the "ladylike" standard. Consistent with this hypothesis, benevolent sexism, but not hostile sexism, was associated with blaming victims of acquaintance rape (but not stranger rape) (Abrams, Viki, Masser, & Bohner, 2003; Viki & Abrams, 2002) and recommendations for shorter prison sentences for acquaintance rapists (Viki, Abrams, & Masser, 2004). Viki and colleagues concluded that individuals who are high in benevolent sexism may blame acquaintance rape victims to protect their belief in a just world.

A consistent finding is that heterosexual men are more accepting of rape myths than are women (Lonsway & Fitzgerald, 1994). To explain this gender difference, Lonsway and Fitzgerald (1995) examined the role of hostility toward women in rape myth acceptance. They hypothesized that Burt's (1980) Acceptance of Interpersonal Violence Scale and Adversarial Sexual Beliefs Scale share a common ideology: hostility toward women. Using revised scales that were gender neutral, they found that hostility toward women accounted for almost twice the variance in rape myth acceptance scores for men than it did for women. Lonsway and Fitzgerald (1995) concluded that rape myths serve different purposes for men and women. For men, rape myths about female victims justify men's sexual domination of women; for women, rape myths mitigate fear and feelings of vulnerability.

Rape Myths about Male Victims

Less is known about rape myths concerning male victims, but previous research has identified the following beliefs: (a) Being raped by a male attacker is synonymous with the loss of masculinity (Groth & Burgess, 1980), (b) "men who are sexually assaulted by men must be gay" (Stermac, Del Bove, & Addison, 2004, p. 901), (c) "men are incapable of functioning sexually unless they are sexually aroused" (Smith, Pine, & Hawley, 1988, p. 103), (d) "men cannot be forced to have sex against their will" (Stermac et al., 2004, p. 901), (e) "men are less affected by sexual assault than women" (Stermac et al., 2004, p. 901), (f) "men are in a constant state of readiness to accept any sexual opportunity" (Clements-Schreiber & Rempel, 1995, p. 199), and (g) "a man is expected to be able to defend himself against sexual assault" (Groth & Burgess, 1980, p. 808). For example, in Smith et al.'s (1988) study, participants perceived a male victim of a female-perpetrated assault as more likely to have encouraged the assault, enjoyed the encounter, and thus experienced little trauma. Male participants endorsed these perceptions more than women did, but this gender difference disappeared when the perpetrator was another man.

Struckman-Johnson and Struckman-Johnson (1992) first attempted to measure these myths by focusing on three general beliefs: (a) Male rape does not happen (e.g., "it is impossible to rape a man"), (b) rape is the victim's fault (e.g., "men are to blame for not escaping"), and (c) men would not be traumatized by rape (e.g., "men do not need counseling after being raped"). Each of these beliefs was presented twice to manipulate the gender of the perpetrator. Consistent with research on female rape myths, they found that men were more accepting of male rape myths than were women. Furthermore, with the exception of the myth that denies the existence of male rape, male and female participants endorsed male rape myths to a greater extent when the perpetrator was a woman instead of a man. Despite these interesting initial results, little additional research has been conducted to further understand male rape myths. Thus, it is not clear how these rape myths develop, who believes these myths, and the function these myths have in determining attitudes toward male victims of rape.

We speculate that the same attitudes that function to support rape myths about female victims may also function to support rape myths about male victims. Specifically, adversarial sexual beliefs and acceptance of interpersonal violence correlates with participants' support of female rape myths (Lonsway & Fitzgerald, 1995). It may be that individuals who accept interpersonal aggression will accept aggressive behavior in general, regardless of the victim's gender. Furthermore, many of the items on the Acceptance of Interpersonal Violence Scale depict men as the sexual aggressor. Participants who believe that men should assert themselves through violence may also be less sympathetic to male victims.

Furthermore, just as ambivalent sexism toward women is related to rape myth acceptance concerning female victims (e.g., Chapleau, Oswald, & Russell, 2007; Glick & Fiske, 1997; Viki et al., 2004), we hypothesize that Glick and Fiske's (1999) corresponding ambivalent sexism toward men (including the components of hostile and benevolent sexism toward men) will be related to support of male rape myths. Glick and Fiske state that just as sexist attitudes about women can be positive and negative, there are also ambivalent sexist attitudes toward men. Specifically, women resent men for their greater social power and aggressiveness while also admiring and needing them for these same qualities. For example, women may characterize men as being arrogant, sex starved, and domineering (hostile sexism) but also strong, resourceful, and stoic (benevolent sexism). Male participants also can hold these dual stereotypes toward men, but they typically score higher on benevolent sexism and lower on hostile sexism than do women. We expect that participants who are higher in benevolent sexism toward men will be more supportive of male rape myths, such that they will judge male rape victims harshly for not being "man enough" to escape a sexual assault and, if assaulted, expect male victims to quickly reclaim their manhood and deny that the assault was traumatic. We also expect that hostile sexism toward men will be associated with rape myth acceptance because the belief that men often use unscrupulous means to obtain sex and power may be incompatible with the idea that a man could be sexually victimized.

Study Summary

The overall purpose of this study is to further investigate male rape myths using Struckman-Johnson and Struckman-Johnson's (1992) measure. Currently, this is the only measure of male rape myth acceptance that distinguishes between male and female assailants; however, it has not yet been examined for its psychometric properties. Therefore, the first goal is to use confirmatory factor analysis to examine the underlying structure the male rape myth measures. In their study, Struckman-Johnson and Struckman-Johnson calculated one total score for male rape myth acceptance suggesting a general, one-factor model. Yet they created their measure using three of the most prevalent male rape myths in research literature (i.e., denial, blame, and trauma) suggesting a three-factor model. They also expected that the acceptance of each myth would differ depending on the gender of the perpetrator, suggesting a two-factor structure. In sum, we test three possible models of male rape myths: a three-factor solution by myth, a two-factor solution by gender of the perpetrator, or a one-factor solution of general male rape myths.

The second goal of this study is to explore the variables that might be associated with increased support of male rape myths. Specifically, we examine how acceptance of interpersonal violence, adversarial sex beliefs, and ambivalent sexism toward men relate to male rape myth acceptance, as these

variables are similar to factors that support female rape myths. We also examine gender differences in the acceptance of male rape myths and compare the level of support for male rape myths versus female rape myths. We expect to replicate previous findings (Struckman-Johnson & Struckman-Johnson, 1992) that men are more supportive of male rape myths than are women.

Method
Participants

The participants were 423 college students from a medium-sized Midwestern, private, Catholic university (57.7%; $n = 246$) and a small Eastern public college ($n = 180$). The demographics of the combined sample were 65% female ($n = 276$), 85.2% White/Caucasian ($n = 363$), with a mean age of 19.6 ($SD = 2.74$).

Procedure

The participants completed measures of male rape myth acceptance, female rape myth acceptance, ambivalent sexism toward men, adversarial sexual beliefs, and acceptance of interpersonal violence, as part of a larger study on sexual aggression (see Oswald & Russell, 2006). All participants received extra credit in an introductory psychology course.

Measures
Male Rape Myths

Using Struckman-Johnson and Struckman-Johnson's (1992) measure, participants indicated how much they agreed with 12 items that reflect misconceptions about men as victims of rape. Six items refer to men victimized by another man (e.g., "it is impossible for a man to rape a man"), and six items refer to women as perpetrators (e.g., "it is impossible for a man to be raped by a woman"). This measure uses a 6-point Likert-type scale (1 = *strongly disagree,* 6 = *strongly agree*), with higher scores indicating more endorsement of these rape myths.

Illinois Rape Myth Acceptance Scale, Short Form

Participants completed Payne et al.'s (1999) scale, which uses a 5-point Likert-type scale (1 = *strongly disagree,* 5 = *strongly agree*) to assess agreement with myths about women as victims of rape (e.g., "many women secretly desire to be raped"). Higher scores signify more agreement with rape myths. The coefficient alpha was .85.

Adversarial Sexual Beliefs

Burt's (1980) measure contains nine items that assess participants' belief that men and women's romantic relationships with each other are, by nature, adversarial and exploitative. This measure uses a 7-point Likert-type scale (1 = *strongly disagree,* 7 = *strongly agree*), with higher scores denoting greater endorsement of this viewpoint. The coefficient alpha was .83, and the overall mean was used in the analyses.

Acceptance of Interpersonal Violence

Participants completed five items from Burt's (1980) measure (e.g., "sometimes women need to be forced to have sex"). Participants responded using a 7-point Likert-type scale (1 = *strongly disagree, 7 = strongly agree*). The coefficient alpha was .51, and the overall mean was used in the analyses. Although the reliability is lower than desired, it is similar to what was reported by Burt. Despite the low reliability, this scale was used because previous research has found it to be one of the best predictors of rape myth acceptance (Burt, 1980).

Ambivalence toward Men Inventory

Employing Glick and Fiske's (1999) measure, participants expressed how much they agreed with items advocating hostile and benevolent stereotypes and prejudices about men (e.g., men are unwilling to share power with women; men should provide for women) using a 6-point Likert-type scale (0 = *disagree strongly, 5 = agree strongly*). Two means were extracted for analysis to assess benevolent sexism and hostile sexism (Glick & Fiske, 1999). The coefficient alphas for benevolent and hostile sexism were .85 and .81, respectively.

Results

Confirmatory Factor Analysis

To examine the factor structure of the male rape myth measure, we computed three alternative confirmatory factor models using EQS 5.7b (Bentler, 1998). The first model had each myth (denial, blame, and trauma) as a latent factor with four items as indicator variables. The three latent factors were allowed to covary. The second model was a two-factor model where each factor represented the myths by the gender of the perpetrator. There were six items as indicator variables to each latent factor, and the factors were allowed to covary. The third model was a general factor model in which all 12 items represented the single latent variable of male rape myth.

For identification purposes, the variance for each latent variable was set to 1. Maximum likelihood with Satorra-Bentler estimation was used to estimate the parameters and model chi-square. In interpreting the models, we examined the path estimates, standardized root mean residuals (SRMR), root mean square error of approximation (RMSEA), χ^2, and several fit indices. Because the χ^2 is influenced by the sample size, we also looked at the χ^2 to degrees of freedom ratio, where a ratio of 2 or less indicates a good fit (Ullman, 1996). We considered the following general "rules of thumb" that an RMSEA less than .05 indicates a "good fit" and less than .08 indicates an "acceptable fit" (Hu & Bentler, 1999; McDonald

& Ho, 2002 suggest .06 for a "good fit"), the SRMR should be close to .08 or less (Hu & Bentler, 1999), and goodness of fit statistics should generally be larger than .90 (Hu & Bentler, 1999; McDonald & Ho, 2002).

The three-factor model with each latent variable representing a type of myth resulted in a Satorra-Bentler Scaled χ^2 (51) = 154.53, $p < .01$ (χ^2/df ratio = 3.03, Goodness of Fit Index [GFI] = .89, Comparative Fit Index [CFI] = .83, SRMR = .07, and RMSEA = .10). All the items had statistically significant parameters on the designated factor, indicating that the items were loaded onto the correct factors. The chi-square was significant, and the fit indices were weaker than desired according to traditional "rules of thumb." However, the SRMR and relatively small residuals suggest an adequate first approximation of the data. Factor analyses for the two-factor model by gender, $\chi^2(53) = 200.42, p < .01$ (χ^2/df ratio = 3.78, GFI = .87, CFI = .80, SRMR = .08, and RMSEA = .11) and general model, $\chi^2(54) = 233.09$, $p < .01$ (χ^2/df ratio = 4.32, GFI = .85, CFI = .74, SRMR = .09, and RMSEA = .12) each demonstrated worse fit indices and model statistics.

Of the models tested, the three-factor model was the best fit and indicates that the myths should be examined as separate factors. The three subscales were labeled Denial (alpha = .60), Blame (alpha = .82), and Trauma (alpha = .50). The intercorrelations between the three subscales were significant. Denial positively correlated with Blame ($r = .44, p < .01$) and Trauma ($r = .50, p < .01$). Blame positively correlated with Trauma ($r = .44, p < .01$). Although the three-factor model was the best fit of the tested models, the less than ideal fit statistics, significant chi-square, and low coefficient alphas for two of the subscales suggest that this confirmatory factor model does not meet most of the traditional standards of a good scale structure. Additional scale development is needed. Thus, although we use the subscales in subsequent analyses to examine gender differences and the ideologies associated with male rape myth acceptance, these results should be considered exploratory until additional scale validation and replication of the results occur.

Comparisons of Rape Myth Acceptance by Participant Gender

The mean for each subscale was computed and used in a 2 (Gender) × 3 (Myth) mixed model ANOVA, with myth as the within-subjects variable. The goal was to determine gender differences in male rape myth acceptance and across myth type. There was a main effect of myth type, $F(2, 416) = 32.07$, $p < .01$, $\eta^2 = .13$, such that participants were most supportive of the Blame myth ($M = 2.01, SD = 1.09$) followed by the Trauma myth ($M = 1.86, SD = .83$), and the Denial myth ($M = 1.71, SD = .79$). Post hoc analysis revealed that all mean differences were significant ($ps < .01$). Collapsing across myth type, men ($M = 2.14$) demonstrated more overall male rape myth acceptance than did women ($M = 1.71$),

$F(1, 417) = 35.51, p < .01, \eta^2 = .08$. These main effects were qualified by the Myth Type × Gender interaction, $F(2, 416) \times 18.15, p < .01, \eta^2 = .08$, such that men were more supportive of male rape myths than were women, but the magnitude of these differences depended on the type of myth. For men, there were significant differences between all three rape myths ($ps < .01$). Men had the highest mean on the Blame subscale ($M = 2.49, SD = 1.23$), followed by the Trauma subscale ($M = 2.13, SD = .85$), and the lowest mean for the Denial subscale ($M = 1.80, SD = .84$). For women, the differences between the three rape myths (Blame: $M = 1.76, SD = .92$; Trauma: $M = 1.71, SD = .77$; Denial: $M = 1.66, SD = .76$) were nonsignificant ($ps < .10$).

Comparisons of Male Rape Acceptance with Female Rape Acceptance

A total score on the male rape myth measure significantly correlated with the Illinois Rape Myth Acceptance Scale ($r = .58, p < .01$). Not surprisingly, men ($M = 2.01, SD = .61$), compared to women ($M = 1.72, SD = .50$), were more supportive of female rape myths, $t(247.3) = 4.89, p < .01$. To determine if there were differences in the acceptance of male versus female rape myths within genders, the raw scores on the male and female rape myth scales were transformed into z scores for analysis (because they were measured using different Likert-type scales). For men, there was no difference in the level of support for male ($M = .38, SD = 1.06$) and female rape myths ($M = .34, SD = 1.10$), $t(144) = .51, p > .10$. Similarly, for women, there was also no significant difference between the acceptance of male ($M = -.21, SD = .90$) and female rape myths ($M = -.19, SD = .89$), $t(273) = -.44, p > .10$. Thus, support for rape myths did not vary by gender of the victim and, overall, men were more supportive of all rape myths than were women.

Regression Models for Male Rape Myth Acceptance

Separate regression models were conducted for men and women to see if the underlying ideologies supporting male rape myths differed by participant gender. All predictors were entered into regression equations simultaneously.

For the Denial myth, acceptance of interpersonal violence was the only significant predictor ($\beta = .31, t = 3.17, p < .01$) for men, $F(4, 140) = 6.76, p < .01, R^2 = .14$. For women, $F(4, 268) = 16.01, p < .01, R^2 = .18$, benevolent sexism toward men ($\beta = .30, t = 4.37, p < .01$) and acceptance of interpersonal violence ($\beta = .13, t = 2.08, p < .05$) were significant predictors, and hostile sexism was marginally significant ($\beta = .13, t = 1.78, p = .08$).

For the Blame myth, benevolent sexism toward men was the only predictor ($\beta = .35, t = 3.71, p < .01$), $F(4, 140) = 15.09, p < .01, R^2 = .28$, and acceptance of interpersonal

violence was marginally significant ($\beta = .16, t = 1.77, p = .08$) for men. For women, $F(4, 268) = 19.75, p < .01, R^2 = .22$, benevolent sexism ($\beta = .29, t = 4.36, p < .01$) and acceptance of interpersonal violence ($\beta = .15, t = 2.55, p < .05$) were significant predictors.

For the Trauma myth, acceptance of interpersonal violence was a significant predictor for men, $F(4, 140) = 5.14, p < .01, R^2 = .10$ ($\beta = .27, t = 2.65, p < .01$). For women, $F(4, 268) = 14.48, p < .01, R^2 = .16$, benevolent sexism ($\beta = .24, t = 3.51, p < .01$) and acceptance of interpersonal violence ($\beta = .22, t = 3.63, p < .01$) were significant predictors.

Discussion

The goal of this study was to develop a better understanding of rape myths about male victims. To date, the only measure of male rape myth acceptance that distinguishes between male and female perpetrators (Struckman-Johnson & Struckman-Johnson, 1992) has received little psychometric investigation. We found that subscales by myth type (Denial, Blame, and Trauma), rather than by the perpetrator's gender or a general model of male rape myth acceptance, was the best fit for the data. This suggests that it is beneficial to examine male rape myths separately rather than to use an overall rape myth score. Indeed, all three myths are unique and it would be important for theoretical reasons to examine them separately.

However, although breaking down the scale by myth type resulted in the best fit of the three tested models, the scale fit statistics and model chi-square did not meet the traditional standards of a good fit. Furthermore, the Denial and Trauma subscales had reliability coefficients that were lower than desired. Thus, the results suggest that the current Male Rape Myth Scale needs to be improved, and we recommend two specific changes. First, we suggest that a six-factor model that examines the three myths separated by gender of the perpetrator should be tested in future research. Research has shown that people are more likely to agree with the myths when the perpetrator is a woman than a man (Struckman-Johnson & Struckman-Johnson, 1992), and this is a potentially important theoretical distinction. Furthermore, collapsing across gender of perpetrator may have resulted in the weak fit statistics and low reliability coefficients for the subscales. Second, we suggest developing and including additional items. There were not enough scale items to allow a test of a six-factor model in the current study, and additional items would allow for this test. The additional items relevant to each of the myths should also help to increase the scale reliability. In sum, we conclude that although the Struckman-Johnson and Struckman-Johnson Male Rape Myth Scale was an important step for research on male rape myths, efforts for additional scale development and improvements are warranted. We hope that this study raises the awareness of other researchers who use this scale as well as prompts future validation efforts.

The second goal of this study was to investigate the factors associated with support of male rape myths. Given the concern about the rape myth subscales, these findings should be interpreted with caution. Nonetheless, these preliminary results provide tentative insights into the ideologies associated with acceptance of male rape myths. Similar to previous research, we found that men were more supportive of the rape myths than were women. Men were most accepting of the myth that male rape victims are responsible for being raped. Men were less accepting of the myth that men would not be upset after a sexual assault and the least accepting of the idea that men simply do not get raped. Overall, acceptance of male and female rape myths was highly correlated. Consistent with previous research, men were more accepting of rape myths against both male and female victims. Past literature on female rape myths has argued that men are more accepting of female rape myths because of adversarial, antiwoman attitudes (e.g., Lonsway & Fitzgerald, 1995). If hostility toward women is the only contributing ideology, we would expect that men would endorse female rape myths to a greater extent than they endorse male rape myths. However, men's acceptance of rape myths did not significantly differ based on the gender of the victim. Women's acceptance of rape myths also did not vary based on the gender of the victim. This supports Struckman-Johnson and Struckman-Johnson's (1992) conclusion that men are more accepting of rape myths in general, not just against female victims.

In exploring the ideologies associated with each of the rape myths, we find that benevolent sexism toward men is associated with male rape myths. This is consistent with the research that benevolent sexism toward women is associated with blaming female victims of acquaintance rape (Abrams et al., 2003; Chapleau et al., 2007; Viki et al., 2004). Viki et al., (2004) concluded that benevolent sexism is associated with victim blaming to protect one's belief in a just world. Similarly, individuals high in benevolent sexism toward men may believe that men are supposed to be invincible and, if a man is raped, he must have showed some unmanly weakness to provoke or permit the assault. For female participants, agreement with benevolent sexism toward men was associated with support for all three myths; however, for men, benevolent sexism was associated with only the blame myth. Perhaps future research can shed light on this gender difference.

Surprisingly, hostile sexism toward men was not significantly associated with support for any of the male rape myths. Hostile sexism toward men is the belief that men exploit women for sex and power. It might be that hostile sexist beliefs are relevant only in the cases of heterosexual interactions and may not apply when the aggressor is male. Alternatively, Abrams et al., (2003) found that hostile sexism against women was associated with men's rape proclivity, not rape myth acceptance. Similarly, hostile sexism toward

men may also predict rape proclivity against male victims. For example, Clements-Schreiber and Rempel (1995) found that women who endorsed stereotypes that men are sexually weak were more likely to coerce men into having sex. This is an interesting issue for future research.

Consistent with research on female rape myths, acceptance of interpersonal violence was a strong predictor for support of male rape myths for both male and female participants. Men and women who normalize sexual violence may not think of such acts as "real rape" (e.g., Du Mont et al., 2003). However, this finding is tentative given the low reliability coefficient for the Acceptance of Interpersonal Violence Scale. Contrary to expectations, adversarial sexual beliefs were not a predictor of male rape myths. In hindsight, this is not surprising as this scale assesses the belief that men and women are competing for dominance in a relationship (Burt, 1980), whereas the Male Rape Myth Scale includes aggressors of both genders. Future research should explore this association when the rape myth scales are broken down by perpetrator gender.

In sum, we find preliminary support that the ideologies associated with rape myths about female victims are also associated with rape myths about male victims. Because this is the first study to examine the ideologies underlying male rape myths, there may be other important attitudinal variables that were not part of this study. Continued examination of other attitudinal variables is warranted.

Although this study provides a first step toward understanding male rape myths, there are limitations to consider. The first limitation is that our findings show the Male Rape Myth Scale is in need of additional development. Thus, the subsequent analyses must be interpreted with caution until replicated. Similarly, the Acceptance of Interpersonal Violence Scale, despite being commonly used in research, displays poor internal reliability, and future research would be wise to revise this measure. The second limitation is that the attitudes of college students may not generalize to other populations. However, rape and sexual coercion is a serious problem on college campuses, and these findings are important to consider within that context. We also had a relatively small number of men compared to women, so research with additional samples is needed. A third limitation is that the mean level of support for the rape myths was below the midpoint, suggesting that people do not believe in rape myths. Struckman-Johnson and Struckman-Johnson (1992) had a similar finding and posited that by providing a definition of male rape in the instructions, they had "educated" their participants and dissipated the associated myths. Nonetheless, we found sizable proportions of men and women who agreed with the myths. Most notably, 26% of men and 16% of women agreed that a man would not be very upset after being raped by a woman, and 25% of men and nearly 10% of women agreed that a man is blameworthy for not escaping a woman. Thus, low mean values on this scale do not necessarily suggest that rape myth acceptance is not a significant problem.

This research takes a first step at systematically understanding myths about male rape and the ideologies that support these beliefs. Our results suggest that the ideologies that support male rape myths are similar to those that support female rape myths. Brownmiller (1975) discussed "rape culture" to describe how rape and the threat of rape are used to intimidate women. Although we do not disagree with her view that rape is used as a tool to keep women "in their place," we believe that this is only half of the story. We propose that rape is a weapon used to keep both women and men from straying too far from their prescribed gender roles. Although the call to study male rape sounded not long after researchers began examining female rape, this area of research is still understudied. By mapping the largely uncharted territory of male rape myths, we can refine our current understanding of sexual aggression to better serve everyone.

References

Abrams, D., Viki, G. T., Masser, B., & Bohner, G. (2003). Perceptions of stranger and acquaintance rape: The role of benevolent and hostile sexism in victim blame and rape proclivity. *Journal of Personality and Social Psychology, 84,* 111–125.

Bentler, P. (1998). *EQS 5.7b* (Multivariate Software, Inc.). Hillsdale, NJ: Lawrence Erlbaum.

Brownmiller, S. (1975). *Against our will: Men, women, and rape.* New York: Simon & Schuster.

Burt, M. R. (1980). Cultural myths and supports for rape. *Journal of Personality and Social Psychology, 38,* 217–230.

Campbell, R., & Johnson, C. R. (1997). Police officers' perceptions of rape: Is there consistency between state law and individual beliefs? *Journal of Interpersonal Violence, 12,* 255–274.

Chapleau, K. M., Oswald, D. L., & Russell, B. L. (2007). How ambivalent sexism toward women and men support rape myth acceptance. *Sex Roles, 57,* 131–136.

Clements-Schreiber, M. E., & Rempel, J. K. (1995). Women's acceptance of stereotypes about male sexuality: Correlations with strategies to influence reluctant partners. *Canadian Journal of Human Sexuality, 4,* 223–231.

Du Mont, J., Miller, K., & Myhr, T. L. (2003). The role of "real rape" and "real victim" stereotypes in the police reporting practices of sexually assaulted women. *Violence Against Women, 9,* 466–486.

Frohmann, L. (1991). Discrediting victims' allegations of sexual assault: Prosecutorial accounts of case rejections. *Social Problems, 38,* 213–226.

Glick, P., Diebold, J., Bailey-Werner, B., & Zhu, L. (1997). The two faces of Adam: Ambivalent sexism and polarized attitudes toward women. *Personality and Social Psychology Bulletin, 23,* 1323–1334.

Glick, P., & Fiske, S. (1996). The ambivalent sexism inventory: Differentiating hostile and benevolent sexism. *Journal of Personality and Social Psychology, 70,* 491–512.

Glick, P., & Fiske, S. (1997). Hostile and benevolent sexism: Measuring ambivalent sexist attitudes toward women. *Psychology of Women Quarterly, 21,* 119–136.

Glick, P., & Fiske, S. (1999). The Ambivalence toward Men Inventory: Differentiating hostile and benevolent beliefs about men. *Psychology of Women Quarterly, 23,* 519–536.

Goyer, P. F., & Eddleman, H. C. (1984). Same-sex rape of nonincarcerated men. *American Journal of Psychiatry, 141,* 576–579.

Groth, A. N., & Burgess, A. W. (1980). Male rape: Offenders and victims. *American Journal of Psychiatry, 137,* 806–810.

Hu, L., & Bentler, P. M. (1999). Cutoff criteria for fit indexes in covariance structure analysis: Conventional criteria versus new alternatives. *Structural Equation Modeling, 6,* 1–55.

Koss, M. P. (2000). Shame, blame, and community: Justice responses to violence against women. *American Psychologist, 55,* 1332–1343.

Koss, M. P., Gidycz, C. A., & Wisniewski, N. (1987). The scope of rape: Incidence and prevalence of sexual aggression and victimization on a national sample of students in higher education. *Journal of Consulting and Clinical Psychology, 55,* 162–170.

Lonsway, K. A., & Fitzgerald, L. F. (1994). Rape myths: In review. *Psychology of Women Quarterly, 18,* 133–164.

Lonsway, K. A., & Fitzgerald, L. F. (1995). Attitudinal antecedents of rape myth acceptance: A theoretical and empirical reexamination. *Journal of Personality and Social Psychology, 68,* 704–711.

McDonald, R., & Ho, M. R. (2002). Principles and practices in reporting structural equation analyses. *Psychological Methods, 7,* 64–82.

Mezey, G., & King, M. (1989). The effects of sexual assault on men: A survey of 22 victims. *Psychological Medicine, 19,* 205–209.

Oswald, D. L., & Russell, B. L. (2006). Perceptions of sexual coercion in heterosexual dating relationships: The role of initiator gender and tactics. *Journal of Sex Research, 43,* 87–95.

Payne, D. L., Lonsway, K. A., & Fitzgerald, L. F. (1999). Rape myth acceptance: Exploration of its structure and its measurement using the Illinois rape myth acceptance scale. *Journal of Research in Personality, 33,* 27–68.

Pino, N. W., & Meier, R. F. (1999). Gender differences in rape reporting. *Sex Roles, 40,* 979–990.

Russell, B. L., & Oswald, D. L. (2002). Sexual coercion and victimization of college men: The role of love styles. *Journal of Interpersonal Violence, 17,* 273–285.

Smith, R. E., Pine, C. J., & Hawley, M. E. (1988). Social cognitions about adult male victims of female sexual assault. *Journal of Sex Research, 24,* 101–112.

Stermac, L., Del Bove, G., & Addison, M. (2004). Stranger and acquaintance sexual assault of adult males. *Journal of Interpersonal Violence, 19,* 901–915.

Struckman-Johnson, C., & Struckman-Johnson, D. (1992). Acceptance of male rape myths among college men and women. *Sex Roles, 27,* 85–100.

Ullman, J. B. (1996). Structural equation modeling. In B. Tabachnick & L. Fidell (Eds.), *Using multivariate statistics* (3rd ed., pp. 709–812). New York: HarperCollins.

U.S. Department of Justice. (2003). *2002 national crime victimization statistics.* Retrieved October 28, 2004, from www.ojp.usdoj.gov/abstract/cvus/index.htm.

Viki, G. T., & Abrams, D. (2002). But she was unfaithful: Benevolent sexism and reactions to rape victims who violate traditional gender role expectations. *Sex Roles, 47,* 289–293.

Viki, G. T., Abrams, D., & Masser, B. (2004). Evaluating stranger and acquaintance rape: The role of benevolent sexism in perpetrator blame and recommended sentence length. *Law and Human Behavior, 28,* 295–303.

Critical Thinking

1. How do men and women differ in their acceptance of rape myths?

2. What factors impact the acceptance of rape myths?

3. What is the impact of rape myths on men and women today?

KRISTINE M. CHAPLEAU, MS, is a doctoral student in clinical psychology at Marquette University. Her research interests include sexual coercion and rape as well as gender and racial stereotyping and prejudice. DEBRA L. OSWALD, PhD, completed her doctorate in social psychology and a postdoctoral fellowship in quantitative psychology. She is currently an assistant professor at Marquette University. Her research examines social stigma, gender issues, and interpersonal relationships. BRENDA L. RUSSELL, PhD, completed her doctorate in social psychology. She is currently an associate professor at Pennsylvania State University—Berks. Her research interests include legal psychology, sexual coercion and rape, and program evaluation.

Authors' Note—This study was conducted as a first-year project for the clinical psychology graduate program at Marquette University. The results of this study were presented in a poster at the annual meeting of the Midwestern Psychological Association (May 2005). The authors would like to thank Kara Lindstedt, Angela Pirlott, and Sara Thimsen for their assistance with data collection.

Effects of Sexual Assaults on Men: Physical, Mental, and Sexual Consequences

Richard Tewksbury

This paper presents an overview and summary of the consequences of male sexual assault. At present there are few discussions of the physical, mental health and sexual consequences for men who are sexually assaulted (however, see Davies, 2002 for a "selective review of the . . . prevalence and effects of male sexual assault victims" [p. 203]). The present discussion presents an update to the existing literature and a more focused discussion of the health consequences than is presently available. The intent is to provide both scholars and practitioners with a concise resource for guidance on what to expect in cases of reported male sexual assault so as to facilitate formulating effective, efficient and sensitive systems for receiving and responding to reports of men's sexual victimization.

Research addressing sexual assault/rape of men did not appear until less than 30 years ago (and, most of the early literature focuses on male children rather than adults [e.g., Josephson, 1979]). Although a few studies addressing sexual assault in correctional facilities were available prior to 1980, it was not until the early 1980s that any research specifically addressing the consequences of "male rape" in the community appeared. Most of the sexual assault/rape literature that is available focuses on female victims/survivors.

The existing literature encompasses both documentation and estimates of rates of men's victimization and clinical assessments of consequences of victimization. However, public perceptions of, and education about, male sexual assault in the free community continue to lag behind that which is known about sexual assault victimization of females.

To date the most comprehensive discussion of the consequences of sexual assault for men is that provided by Davies (2002). In this overview, drawing on the research published prior to and including the year 2000, the author shows that community and service providers' reactions to male sexual assault victims are often dependent on the victim's sexual orientation and the perpetrator's gender. Also included are discussions of the difficulties such victims may experience in (and in deciding to) reporting their victimization, stigmas service providers may apply to reporting victims, and the importance of service providers to be cognizant of such experiences and to work to overcome or alleviate such obstacles. Davies' discussion is organized around identifying the ways such reactions are constructed and the effects of such on service provision. What Davies does not provide is a discussion organized around the varieties of consequences for male victims, specifically the physical, mental health and sexual consequences that may be experienced by victims.

In pursuit of providing both scholars and service providers with a concise overview of the diverse consequences male victims of sexual assault experience, the discussion that follows draws from a diverse body of literatures, informed by medical, health care, forensic, psychological, sociological and criminological research. This discussion is intended to provide scholars and practitioners with a comprehensive overview of the physical, mental health and sexual consequences of the sexual assault of males. Discussion begins with a review of what is known about the prevalence of male sexual assault and an overview of the likelihood of men to report their victimization (and reasons for not reporting).

Prevalence of Male Sexual Assault

The currently available research literature on male sexual assault has a primary focus on documenting the existence of such events. The research literature suggests that a significant number of men do report at least one instance of sexual assault. One community-wide epidemiological study in Los Angeles reported 7.2 percent of men were sexually assaulted (after age 15) at least one time (Sorenson, Stein, Siegel, Golding & Burnam, 1988). Elliott, Mok, and Briere (2004) report that among a stratified random sample of the American population 3.8 percent of men report sexual assault victimization during adulthood (with 61% of these men also reporting a sexual victimization during childhood). An Australian study using data from a representative sample of more than 10,000 men shows a sexual victimization rate of 4.8 percent for adulthood and 2.8 percent for childhood. In the United States, data from the National Violence Against Women Survey showed three percent of men had experienced some form of sexual victimization (Desai, Arias, & Thompson, 2002; Pimlott-Kubiak & Cortina, 2003). Martin and colleagues (1998) report a 6.7 percent sexual victimization rate among male members of the U.S. Army. Three clinic based studies in the United Kingdom report rates of 6.6 percent adult victimization (Keane, Young, Boyle, & Curry, 1995), 8 percent victimization during adulthood and 12 percent during childhood (Coxell, King, Mezey, & Kell, 2000) and 2.89 percent and 5.35 percent adult and childhood victimization rates (Coxell, King, Mezey, & Gordon, 1999). Also from the United Kingdom, Plant, Plant, and Miller (2005) report a sexual abuse rate of 3.2 percent for men post age 16 and 11.7 percent for victimization prior to age 16. Other research, reviewing cases in hospital emergency rooms or rape crisis centers suggests between four percent and 12 percent of sexual assault victims are male (Forman, 1983; Frazier, 1993; Grossin, Sibille, Grandmaison, Banasr, Brion, & Durigon, 2003; Kaufman, Divasto, Jackson, Voorhees, & Christy, 1980; Pesola, Westfal, & Kuffner, 1999; Riggs, Houry, Long, Markovchick, & Feldhaus, 2000; Scarce, 1997; Stermac, Sheridan, Davidson, & Dunn, 1996).

Research with college student samples has reported rates of victimization suggesting between one in five and one in eleven males being victims of some form of sexual victimization. Struckman-Johnson (1988) reported 16 percent of a sample of male undergraduates had been pressured or forced to have sex at some point in life. Tewksbury and Mustaine (2001) reported 22.2 percent of male undergraduates at 12 universities had been victimized by some form of sexual assault and 8.3 percent had been a victim of a "serious sexual assault" at some point in time. Similar results (14%) have also been reported with a British sample of college students (Davies, Pollard, & Archer, 2001).

Others (Hickson, Davies, Hunt Weatherburn, McManus, & Coxon, 1994; Island & Letellier, 1991; Krahe, Schutze, Fritscher, & Waizenhofer, 2000; Waterman, Dawson, & Bologna, 1989) have reported sexual assault victimizations among gay/bisexual men dating or in relationships with other men. These studies have reported rates of victimization ranging from 12 percent to 27.6 percent.

It is important to acknowledge, however, that most researchers believe that male sexual assault (perpetrated by any variety of assailant) is severely under-reported, perhaps even more so than sexual assaults of women (see discussion below).

Stermac, del Bove, and Addison (2004) report that few differences are seen between men sexually assaulted by a stranger and those assaulted by an acquaintance, with the exception that those who are victimized by strangers are more likely to be single, to be assaulted in an outdoor location, and, if the assault is reported, it is so in a shorter period of time (Stermac et al., 1996). Some scholars (and other observers), however, believe that male sexual assault is primarily an occurrence between homosexual men, similar to either heterosexual date rape or marital rape. Support for this view comes from the research that suggests that gay and bisexual men are over-represented among male victims (Keane et al., 1995; Mezey & King, 1989) and others who also report that either current or former intimate partners are responsible for 65 percent of sexual assaults on gay/bisexual men (Hickson et al., 1994).

One commonly reported correlate of men's sexual victimization as adults is the high rate of these men to have also been sexually victimized during childhood. Two major studies, drawing on data from both the United Kingdom (Coxell et al., 1999) and the United States (Desai et al., 2002) have shown a strong correlation between childhood sexual victimization and subsequent adult sexual victimization. Coxell et al., (1999) report that consensual childhood sexual experiences are also statistically related to men's adult sexual victimization. Additionally, Elliott et al., (2004) report that among a representative community sample, 61 percent of men who report a sexual victimization during adulthood also report having been sexually victimized as a child.

Reporting and Seeking of Services

Throughout the literature there is both frequent discussion of what scholars believe to be under-reporting of male sexual assault victimization and documentation of research subjects that have never reported their victimization (to law enforcement, health care, mental health, or social services providers). Numerous reports suggest that male sexual assault victims (both adult and child) are far less likely to report their victimization than are female victims (Calderwood, 1987; Hodge & Cantor, 1998; Kaufman et al., 1980; McLean, Balding, & White, 2005). However, this differential rate of reporting may be dissipating or disappearing (McLean et al., 2005). Individuals sexually assaulted during childhood, however, are more likely than those assaulted as adults to subsequently seek mental health services (Golding, Stein, Siegel, Burnam, & Sorenson, 1988). Often, but not universally, implicit is the belief that victims anticipate rejection and authorities not to believe them if they should report. Central to the discouragement to report are issues of stigma, shame, fear, and a belief victims may have their sexuality questioned (Anderson, 1982; Scarce, 1997).

Several sets of researchers (King & Woollett, 1997; Lacey & Roberts, 1991; Walker, Archer, & Davies, 2005) have reported that men who are sexually assaulted and seek mental health services frequently do not do so for lengthy periods of time. King and Woollett (1997), drawing on data from 115 men sexually assaulted in the community, show a mean of 16.4 years between victimization and seeking of mental health services. Lacey and Roberts (1991) report fewer than one-half of victims reported the incident or sought services within 6 months, and an average of approximately 2.5 years passed between occurrence and seeking of services. Walker et al., (2005) reported that 12.5 percent of victimized men never disclosed their victimization to anyone, and among those who did disclose, 54 percent did not do so for at least one year. However, Pesola et al., (1999) report that among male sexual assault victims seeking services in a New York City (Greenwich Village) hospital emergency department, 94 percent do so within 36 hours.

It is not uncommon, especially for victims who do not have serious physical injuries, for male sexual assault victims to deny victimization (Kaufman et al., 1980; Scarce, 1997). Denial directly links to a low likelihood of reporting or seeking services (medical and/or mental health) following victimization. Or, when seeking medical or mental health services victims may do so by claiming an alternative reason or need, or will do so and be very vague in explaining injuries and requests for services.

One major problem identified in the research literature, however, is that many rape crisis centers either explicitly refuse services to male victims, or are highly insensitive to male victims needs (Donnelly & Kenyon, 1996). Furthermore, when services are offered for men they are rarely designed specifically for men; one study of service availability reports that only five percent of programs that serve male victims have any programs or services specifically designed for men (Washington, 1999). It is not surprising, then, that male sexual assault may be severely under-reported.

Physical Consequences of the Sexual Assault of Men

At the baseline level, men who report having been sexually assaulted as adults (post age 16) report poorer physical health statuses than men who do not report adult sexual victimization (Plant et al., 2005).

Most research suggests that the sexual assault of men is more likely to be violent, and accompanied by more and greater corollary injuries, than sexual assaults of women (however, also see Kimberling, Rellini, Kelly, Judson, & Learman, 2002; and McLean et al., 2005). Here it is important to acknowledge that not all sexual assaults are violent, and often center on coercion of victims. However, "rapes" in the traditional sense of the word have been shown to be more violent when perpetrated against male victims. King (1995) reported that when men are raped in almost all instances some form of physical force is used against the victim, and weapons are commonly involved. Weapons are most likely to be involved when men are sexually assaulted by a stranger (Stermac et al., 2004). Kaufman et al., (1980), describing data drawn from male rape survivors seen in hospital emergency rooms, report men who are sexually assaulted are more likely than women to have nongenital injuries (see also Hillman, Tomlinson, McMillan, French, & Harris, 1990). However, they also conclude that men who are sexually assaulted are not likely to seek medical attention, unless they suffer significant physical injuries.

Only one study to date (Lipscomb, Muram, Speck, & Mercer, 1992) compares the experiences and consequences of men sexually assaulted in the community ($n = 19$) with those sexually assaulted while incarcerated ($n = 80$). This study suggests that men sexually assaulted while incarcerated are less likely to be assaulted with a weapon (67.5% vs. 31.6% report no weapon involved), and to have their assault be either only oral or a combination of oral and anal penetration (62.5% vs. 52.6%). And, although not a statistically significant difference, men sexually assaulted while incarcerated may be more likely to exhibit an absence of physical trauma resulting from their assault (75% vs. 58% having no physical trauma observed by examining health care professionals). Hodge and Canter (1998) reporting on cases in the community report that gay male sexual assault victims are more likely than heterosexual male victims to sustain serious injuries.

Studies of the incidence of physical trauma or injuries of male sexual assault victims suggest that while some victims do experience significant physical injuries, a majority of victims do not. Five studies in hospital emergency rooms report disparate results for the presence of injuries. Genital or rectal trauma is reported in 35 percent of male victims in a Denver-based study (Riggs et al., 2000). However, "general body trauma occurred more often than genital trauma" (p. 360) with approximately two-thirds of victims having some form of general injury. A second study, in a NYC hospital emergency room reports 25 percent of male sexual assault victims have some form of "documented trauma or physical injury" (Pesola et al., 1999). Stermac et al., (2004) report that 45 percent of male sexual assault victims seen in a large, urban Canadian hospital-based sexual assault care center present with some type of physical injuries. The most common type of injury was some form of soft tissue injury (approximately 25% of male victims), most frequently seen in the perineal and anal areas. Also, 20 percent present with lacerations. Grossin et al., (2003), however, report that only 5.6 percent of male sexual assault victims seen in a French medical clinic suffered any type of genital trauma. And, McLean, Balding, and White (2004) report that 66 percent of a sample of 376 cases of male sexual assault victimizations in Manchester, UK are rapes, with 18 percent of the sample presenting with anal injuries. However, these researchers also report that fewer male than female sexual assault victims present with non-genital injuries.

Among men who are anally penetrated during sexual assault, a majority (63%) who present to health care professionals do exhibit at least one form of rectal injury (Ernst, Green, Ferguson, Weiss, & Green, 2000; Hillman et al., 1990; however, also see McLean et al., 2004). The types of injuries seen include tears of the anus, abrasions, bleeding, erythema, hematoma, discoloration with tenderness, fissures, the presence of dirt, vegetation or hair in the anus, engorgement, and friability. It is important to note that no male victim had "gross active bleeding on examination of the external genitalia" (p. 434), although fully 18 percent of victims reported such had occurred prior to seeking medical care (Ernst et al., 2000).

Injuries to victims may also come as a result of assailants' means of controlling victims. One-third of victims in Struckman-Johnson et al.'s (1996) Nebraska study reported having been restrained during their assault. Not infrequently the act of restraint itself can lead to injuries. Also, abrasions to the throat and abdomen may be common, as these are consequences of victims being held down and attempting to resist (Schiff, 1980). Bruises, broken bones and black eyes may be found, as these can be indications of "submissive injuries" (striking the victim in a way that will quickly and effectively subdue them) (Schiff, p. 1499). Stermac et al., (2004) reported that in addition to perineal/anal area injuries, other common locations for injuries are head/neck/face (16% of victims), leg/knee/feet (10%), and arm/hands (15%).

Male sexual assault victims also report somatic symptoms, including tension headaches, nausea, ulcers, and colitis (Anderson, 1982; Rentoul & Appleboom, 1997). In some cases male sexual assault victims have also been identified as hypochondriacal (Anderson, 1982).

A number of symptoms have been reported by male sexual assault victims, although few are unique to this population, and no constellation of symptoms has yet to be identified as indicative of sexual assault victimization. Included among the symptoms reported have been decreased appetite and weight loss (Anderson, 1982; Huckle, 1995; Mezey & King, 1989), nausea and vomiting (Huckle, 1995; Mezey & King, 1989), constipation and abdominal pain (Goyer & Eddleman, 1984; Mezey & King, 1989) and fecal incontinence (Schiff, 1980). One study of long-term consequences of sexual victimization among adolescents suggests that for boys there is a relationship between sexual assault victimization and sleep difficulties, depression, somatic complaints, alcohol, drug and tobacco use, suicide attempts, and violence (Choquet, Darves-Bornoz, Ledoux, Manfredi, & Hassler, 1997).

There is also evidence in the literature of the transmission of sexually transmitted diseases as a result of male rape (Hillman et al., 1990, 1991). However, while instances of STDs being transmitted during a sexual assault have been documented, they are also infrequent and involved only a very small proportion of sexually assaulted men (Lacey & Roberts, 1991). Others have documented that men with a history of sexual victimization are more likely to (at some point in time) acquire a sexually transmitted disease (deVisser et al., 2003).

While some identification of symptoms and physical markers/consequences have been identified, there is very little guidance provided in the research literature regarding prevalence of encountered injuries, what clinicians can/should expect to encounter with "typical" male sexual assault victims or other consequences that may be reported. Similarly, while some medical literature (Josephson, 1979; Schiff, 1980; Wiwanitkit, 2005) purports to present guidance on how to conduct examinations of male victims, and where examinations should focus, these discussions are brief and lacking in specifics and details. Finally, readers are cautioned that the findings of studies conducted in clinical settings need to be viewed as representing only a subset of the population of male sexual assault victims; as reported above, most male sexual assault victims do not seek services, therefore studies based on those who do seek services need to be viewed and generalized with caution.

Mental Health Consequences of the Sexual Assault of Men

Scarce (1997) reports that in his review of the available research on male rape there is no "typical" emotional/psychological response. Rather, responses range from apparent calm and composure to near complete emotional breakdown. However, men who are sexually victimized are more likely than non-victimized men to display psychological disturbances. Male children who are sexually victimized are more likely than victimized adults to report mental health problems. King, Coxell, and Mezey (2002) report that men victimized during childhood have a 2.4

times greater likelihood of reporting psychological disturbance and men victimized as adults have a 1.7 times greater likelihood of psychological disturbance than non-victimized men. Similarly, Burnam et al., (1988) report that among a cross-sectional probability sample of more than 3,000 adults in two Los Angeles communities, not only is sexual assault victimization related to later onset of depression, anxiety disorders and substance abuse, but the likelihood of such consequences are greater for men victimized as children, rather than for those first victimized as adults. And, the presences of such consequences are also statistically significant predictors of subsequent sexual assault victimization.

More specifically, drawing on a stratified random sample of the American population, Elliott et al., (2004) report higher scores on the Trauma Symptom Inventory for sexually assaulted men than women. On eight of the ten scales of the Inventory, sexually assaulted men report higher levels of distress than sexually assaulted women. Depression also frequently leads to attempts to self-medicate (Burnam et al., 1988; Choquet et al., 1997; Coxell et al., 1999; Iseley & Gehrenbeck-Shim, 1997; Plant, Miller, & Plant, 2004; Ratner et al., 2002; Walker et al., 2005) in efforts to block out memories or overcome feelings of low self-worth (Scarce, 1997). Self-medication includes use/abuse of alcohol, illicit drugs and licit (both prescription and over-the-counter) medications. Male sexual assault victims are more likely than female sexual assault victims to report subsequent alcohol abuse problems, although abuse of illicit drugs does not show a gender difference (Burnam et al., 1988). Additionally, researchers in both England (Plant et al., 2004) and Australia (deVisser et al., 2003) report that sexually assaulted men are more likely than other men to smoke tobacco.

The most common emotional response of men to sexual assault victimization is a sense of stigma, shame, and embarrassment, and, at least in part, because of such perceptions male sexual assault victims more often than not "cope" while displaying a "calm, composed and subdued demeanor" (Rentoul & Appleboom, 1997, p. 270). King et al., (2002) also report that subsequent self-harming behaviors are more likely for males victimized as children (as compared with adult victims). Compared with non-victimized men, rates of self-harm are 3.7 times higher for men sexually victimized as children and more than twice as likely to be seen in men victimized as adults. Clearly, shame is directly tied to frequent expressions of self-blame from victims and importantly serves to inhibit reporting or seeking of medical or mental health services.

Men who are sexually assaulted commonly present a high degree of depression and hostility (Iseley & Gehrenbeck-Shim, 1997; Walker et al., 2005). Several community-based studies have shown that male sexual assault victims are, in the short run at least, more likely than female victims to present with greater degrees of depression and hostility (Carmen, Ricker, & Mills, 1984; Frazier, 1993; Goyer & Eddleman, 1984). Depression often includes shame, questions of one's efficacy in general, sexually and in regards to constructions/presentation of masculinity, and changes toward a more negative body image. Not infrequently sleep disturbances (Anderson, 1982; Goyer & Eddleman, 1984), and/or thoughts and attempts at suicide may result (Choquet et al., 1997; Isely & Gehrenbeck-Shim, 1997; Lockwood, 1980; Ratner et al., 2002; Scarce, 1997; Struckman-Johnson et al., 1996; Walker et al., 2005). Suicidal attempts are most likely among adolescent and young adult victims (Calderwood, 1987). And, as reported in numerous studies (see Rentoul & Appleboom, 1997) male rape victims also frequently report heightened levels of anxiety, both related to fears of re-victimization and free-floating. Decreased levels of self esteem among male sexual assault victims is common (Ratner et al., 2002; Walker et al., 2005). Some observers (Calderwood, 1987) have suggested that men's emotional reactions are at least in part a result of shock as men are not socialized (as are women) to fear and be aware of the risk of rape.

Male sexual assault victims have also been shown to be more ready to acknowledge and express anger and hostility following victimization than female victims (Groth & Burgess, 1980). Expressions of anger and hostility may be directed/focused on nearly any others in the immediate environment, including one's assailant, support system members or caretakers (Anderson, 1982). Withdrawal from social settings and social contacts also commonly occur among male sexual assault victims (Walker et al., 2005).

Victims may also experience rape trauma syndrome (a form of posttraumatic stress disorder). Rape trauma syndrome (RTS) is conceptualized as composed of two phases: acute and long term (however, others [Calderwood, 1987] have conceptualized RTS as a three stage process: acute, re-organization, and latent phases). The acute phase is characterized by a period of extreme disorganization and chaos in the victim's life. The acute phase also is frequently accompanied by physical symptoms, including skeletal muscular tension and pain, gastrointestinal irritability, genitourinary disturbances, impotence and extreme emotional expressions. The long term phase is typically characterized by efforts to re-organize one's life and some form of avoidance/withdrawal behaviors. Long term symptoms of RTS also include nightmares/flashbacks, fear of places similar to where victimization occurred, fear of crowds, and fear/avoidance of consensual sexual activities. Additionally, while RTS is not a universally accepted diagnosis (especially in the judicial system), there are also multiple researchers who have reported male sexual assault survivors near-universally experience some form of post-traumatic stress disorder (Huckle, 1995; Isely & Gehrenbeck-Shim, 1997; Mezey, 1992; Mezey & King, 1989; Myers, 1989; Rogers, 1997).

Effects on Sexuality and Identity

In addition to physical and mental health consequences many sexually assaulted men also report effects on their sexuality and sexual activities. These effects include consequences for how sexually assaulted men think of themselves sexually, as gendered beings and how men construct and manage a sexual identity.

The most common sexual consequence reported in the literature for sexually assaulted men are questions about one's "true" sexuality (Forman, 1983; Huckle, 1995; Iseley & Gehrenbeck-Shim, 1997; King & Woollett, 1997; Mezey & King, 1989; Scarce, 1997; Struckman-Johnson & Struckman-Johnson, 1994; Walker et al., 2005). Victims often question whether being raped "makes" them gay and may question whether there is something about them that leads others to perceive them as gay. Perhaps the most serious and significant questions and concerns arise related to sexually assaulted men questioning their "true" sexuality if and when during the course of being assaulted men experience any form of sexual arousal. However, erections are a common involuntary response for many men in times of intense pain, anxiety, panic and/or fear (see Redmond, Kosten, & Reiser, 1983).

Relatedly, men who are sexually victimized (especially those perpetrated against by males) may be expected to question their gender and gender role presentations. Walker et al., (2005) report that 70 percent of a sample of male sexual assault victims report long-term crises with their sexual orientation and 68 percent with their sense of masculinity. These reactions may be most acute for men who hold traditional or stereotypical views about sexuality and gender; to be put into a "homosexual" or "feminine" role may lead to questions about whether one is "sufficiently" masculine. This type of reaction is found among both heterosexual and gay/bisexual men (Garnets & Herek, 1990). Similarly (see Struckman-Johnson & Struckman-Johnson, 1994) men who are victimized by female assailants may question how they could be victimized by a "weaker" female. This too may contribute to questions about gender role fulfillment.

Male sexual assault victims also are likely to report sexual anxieties (deVisser et al., 2003), sexual dysfunction, and possibly impotence, following victimization (Huckle, 1995; Lacey & Roberts, 1991; Walker et al., 2005). For other men periods of frequent sexual activity, including with a number of different partners, is common following victimization (Plant et al., 2005; Walker). Some heterosexual men may also begin to engage in consensual same-sex sexual behaviors following victimization (Walker). Plant et al., (2005) report that male sexual assault victims (whether victimized as children or adults) are more likely than their non-victimized peers to report that sexual activity has "interfered with" their everyday lives.

Sexual identity questions and sexual dysfunction are commonly reported consequences of sexual assault for victimized men. While often overlooked, or not recognized for extended periods of time, they may, in fact, be among the most severe and longest lasting consequences for victimized men.

Summary

In sum, the existing literature suggests that men who are sexually assaulted are highly unlikely to report their victimization or to seek medical or mental health services. Among those who do seek services, it is frequently a long time (perhaps one year or longer) after victimization when medical or mental health services are accessed, except in cases where significant injuries are suffered during the assault and immediate care is necessary. When services are sought, those presenting with health care needs often present either due to suffering significant injuries that cannot be ignored or with myriad different symptoms or problems, most of which will either be non-sexual/non-genital in nature or vague and difficult to initially connect to sexual victimization. Because many sexual assaults on men do not involve anal penetration (Hickson et al., 1994; Lacey & Roberts, 1991; Lipscomb et al., 1992; Ratner et al., 2002; Stermac et al., 2004) it may be extremely difficult to identify physical markers of an assault. The mental health status of men who are sexual assault victims can vary quite widely, ranging from highly emotional responses that inhibit normal functioning to very calm and subdued approaches where victims are highly introspective and would not likely be perceived to have suffered trauma. However, depression, anxiety, anger/hostility and on occasional suicidal ideations/attempts are common. Sexually assaulted men also commonly suffer from sexual dysfunction and questions about their sexuality.

There are no universal signs, symptoms, consequences or markers of sexual assault victimization for men. Some sexually assaulted men will experience some forms of physical injuries, some will experience some forms of psychological/emotional disturbance, and some may experience sexual dysfunction or identity questions. Many sexually assaulted men, however, will not exhibit physical or mental health indications, or will present themselves to service providers under false pretenses or so long after being victimized that connecting symptoms/injuries to sexual assault victimization may not be likely/possible.

In the end, it is important to understand that some sexually assaulted men may not exhibit any visible or identifiable consequences of sexual assault victimization, and that men reporting (or suspected of having experienced) a victimization need to be viewed with an eye toward questioning the cause of any physical or mental health issues that are presented. Because of the nature of many male sexual assaults and the socialized expectations for how men manage and cope with victimization(s), this may continue to be both one of the most under-reported and misunderstood forms of violence and health problems in our society.

References

Anderson, C. L. (1982). Males as sexual assault victims: Multiple levels of trauma. *Journal of Homosexuality, 7,* 145–162.

Burnam, M. A., Stein, J. A., Golding, J. M, Siegel, J. M., Sorenson, S. B., Forsythe, A. B., (1988). Sexual assault and mental disorders in a community population. *Journal of Consulting and Clinical Psychology, 56,* 843–850.

Calderwood, D. (1987). The male rape victim. *Medical Aspects of Human Sexuality, 21*(5), 53–55.

Carmen, E., Ricker, P. R., & Mills, T. (1984). Victims of violence and psychiatric illness. *American Journal of Psychiatry, 141,* 378–383.

Choquet, M., Darves-Bornoz, J. M., Ledoux, S., Manfredi, R., & Hassler, C. (1997). Self-reported health and behavioral problems among adolescent victims of rape in France: Results of a cross-sectional survey. *Child Abuse and Neglect, 21,* 823–832.

Coxell, A., King, M. B., Mezey, G. C., & Gordon, D. (1999). Lifetime prevalence, characteristics, and associated problems of non-consensual sex in men: Cross sectional survey. *British Medical Journal, 318,* 846–850.

Coxell, A., King, M. B., Mezey, G. C., & Kell, P. (2000). Sexual molestation of men: Interviews with 224 men attending a genitourinary medicine service. *International Journal of STD and AIDS, 11,* 574–578.

Davies, M. (2002). Male sexual assault victims: A selective review of the literature and implications for support services. *Aggression and Violent Behavior, 7,* 203–214.

Davies, M,, Pollard, P., & Archer, J. (2001). The influence of victim gender and sexual orientation on blame towards the victim in a depicted stranger rape. *Violence and Victims, 16,* 607–619.

Desai, S., Arias, I., & Thompson, M. P. (2002). Childhood victimization and subsequent adult revictimization assessed in a nationally-representative sample of women and men. *Violence and Victims, 17,* 639–653.

deVisser, R. O., Smith, A. M., Rissel, C. E., Richters, J., & Grulich, A. E. (2003). Sex in Australia: Experiences of sexual coercion among a representative sample of adults. *Australian and New Zealand Journal of Public Health, 27,* 198–203.

Donnelly, D., & Kenyon, S. (1996). "Honey, we don't do men." Gender stereotypes and the provision of services to sexually assaulted males. *Journal of Interpersonal Violence, 11,* 441–448.

Elliott, D. M., Mok, D. S., & Briere, J. (2004). Adult sexual assault: prevalence, symptomatology, and sex differences in the general population. *Journal of Traumatic Stress, 17,* 203–211.

Ernst, A. A., Green, E., Ferguson, M. T., Weiss, S. J., & Green, W. M. (2000). The utility of anoscopy and colposcopy in the evaluation of male sexual assault victims. *Annals of Emergency Medicine, 36,* 432–437.

Forman, B. D. (1983). Reported male rape. *Victimology, 7,* 235–236.

Frazier, P. (1993). A comparative study of male and female rape victims seen at a hospital based rape crisis program. *Journal of Interpersonal Violence, 8,* 65–76.

Garnets, L., & Herek, G. (1990). Violence and victimization of lesbians and gay men: Mental health consequences. *Journal of Interpersonal Violence, 5,* 366–383.

Golding, J. M., Stein, J. A., Siegel, J. M., Burnam, M. A., & Sorenson, S. B. (1988). Sexual assault history and use of health and mental health services. *American Journal of Community Psychology, 16,* 625–644.

Goyer, P., & Eddleman, H. (1984). Same-sex rape of nonincarcerated men. *American Journal of Psychiatry, 141,* 576–579.

Grossin, C., Sibille, I., de la Grandmaison, G. L., Banasr, A., Brion, F., & Durigon, M. (2003). Analysis of 418 cases of sexual assault. *Forensic Science International, 131,* 125–130.

Groth, N., & Burgess, A. W. (1980). Male rape: Offenders and victims. *American Journal of Psychiatry, 137,* 806–810.

Hickson, F. C. I., Davies, P. M., Hunt, A. J., Weatherburn, P., McManus, T. J., & Coxon, A. P. M. (1994). Gay men as victims of non-consensual sex. *Archives of Sexual Behavior, 23,* 281–294.

Hillman, R., O'Mara, N., Tomlinson, D., & Harris, J. R. W. (1991). Adult male victims of sexual assault: An underdiagnosed condition. *International Journal of STD and AIDS, 2,* 22–24.

Hillman, R., Tomlinson, D., McMillan, A., French P. D., & Harris, J. R. (1990). Sexual assault of men: A series. *Genitourinary Medicine, 66,* 247–250.

Hodge, S., & Cantor, D. (1998). Victims and perpetrators of male sexual assault. *Journal of Interpersonal Violence, 13,* 222–239.

Huckle, P. L. (1995). Male rape victims referred to a forensic psychiatric service. *Medicine, Science, and the Law, 35*(3), 187–192.

Iseley, P. J., & Gehrenbeck-Shim, D. (1997). Sexual assault of men in the community. *Journal of Community Psychology, 25,* 159–166.

Island, D., & Letellier, P. (1991). *Men who beat the men who love them.* New York: Harrington Park Press.

Josephson, G. W. (1979) The male rape victim: Evaluation and treatment. *Journal of the American College of Emergency Physicians, 8,* 13–15.

Kaufman, A., Divasto, P. Jackson, R, Voorhees, R., & Christy, J. (1980). Male rape victims: Non-institutionalized assault. *American Journal of Psychiatry, 137,* 221–223.

Keane, F. E., Young, S. M., Boyle, H. M., & Curry, K. M. (1995). Prior sexual assault reported by male attenders at a department of genitourinary medicine. *International Journal of STD and AIDS, 6,* 95–100.

Kimberling, R., Rellini, A., Kelly, V., Judson, P. L., & Learnman, L. A. (2002). Gender differences in victim and crime characteristics of sexual assaults. *Journal of Interpersonal Violence, 17,* 526–532.

King, M. (1995). Sexual assaults on men: Assessment and management. *British Journal of Hospital Medicine, 53,* 245–246.

King, M., Coxell, A., & Mezey, G. (2002). Sexual molestation of males: Associations with psychological disturbance. *British Journal of Psychiatry, 181,* 153–157.

King, M., & Woollett, E. (1997). Sexually assaulted males: 115 men consulting a counseling service. *Archives of Sexual Behavior, 26,* 579–588.

Krahe, B., Schutze, S., Fritscher, I., & Waizenhofer, E. (2000). The prevalence of sexual aggression and victimization among homosexual men. *Journal of Sex Research, 37*(2), 142–150.

Lacey, H. G., & Roberts, R. (1991). Sexual assault on men. *International Journal of STD and AIDS, 2,* 258–260.

Lipscomb, G. H., Muram, D., Speck, P. M., & Mercer, B. M. (1992). Male victims of sexual assault. *Journal of the American Medical Association, 267,* 3064–3066.

Lockwood, D. (1980). *Prison sexual violence.* New York: Elsevier.

Martin, L., Rosen, L. N., Durand, D. B., Stretch, R. H., & Knudson, K. H. (1998). Prevalence and timing of sexual assaults in a sample of male and female U.S. Army soldiers. *Military Medicine, 163,* 213–216.

McLean, I. A., Balding, V., & White, C. (2004). Forensic medical aspects of male-on-male rape and sexual assault in greater Manchester. *Medicine, Science and the Law, 44,* 165–169.

McLean, I. A., Balding, V., & White, C. (2005). Further aspects of male-on-male rape and sexual assault in greater Manchester. *Medicine, Science and the Law, 45,* 225–232.

Mezey, G. C. (1992). Treatment for male victims of rape. In G. C. Mezey & M. B. King (Eds.), *Male victims of sexual assault* (pp. 131–144). Oxford: Oxford University Press.

Mezey, G. C., & King, M. (1989).The effects of sexual assault on men: A survey of 22 victims. *Psychological Medicine, 19,* 205–209.

Myers, M. F. (1989). Men sexually assaulted as adults and sexually abused as boys. *Archives of Sexual Behavior, 18,* 203–215.

Pesola, G. R., Westfal, R. E., & Kuffner, C. A. (1999). Emergency department characteristics of male sexual assault. *Academic Emergency Medicine, 6,* 792–798.

Pimlott-Kubiak, S., & Cortina, L. M. (2003). Gender, victimization and outcomes: Reconceptualizing risk. *Journal of Consulting and Clinical Psychology, 71,* 528–539.

Plant, M., Miller, P., & Plant, M. (2004). Childhood and adult sexual abuse: Relationships with alcohol and other psychoactive drug use. *Child Abuse Review, 13,* 200–214.

Plant, M., Plant, M., & Miller, P. (2005). Childhood and adult sexual abuse: Relationships with "addictive" or "problem" behaviours and health. *Journal of Addictive Diseases, 21,* 25–38.

Ratner, P. A., Johnson, J. L., Shoveller, J. A., Chan, K., Martindale, S. L., Schilder, A. J., (2002). Non-consensual sex experienced by men who have sex with men: Prevalence and association with mental health. *Patient Education and Counseling, 49,* 67–74.

Redmond, D. E. Jr., Kosten, T. R., & Reiser, M. F. (1983). Spontaneous ejaculation associated with anxiety: Psychophysiological considerations. *American Journal of Psychiatry, 140,* 1163–1166.

Rentoul, L., & Appleboom, N. (1997). Understanding the psychological impact of rape and serious sexual assault of men: A literature review. *Journal of Psychiatric and Mental Health Nursing, 4,* 267–274.

Riggs, N., Houry, D., Long, G., Markovchick, V., & Feldhaus, K. M. (2000). Analysis of 1,076 cases of sexual assault. *Annals of Emergency Medicine, 35,* 358–360.

Rogers, P. (1997). Post traumatic stress disorder following male rape. *Journal of Mental Health, 6,* 5–10.

Scarce, M. (1997). *Male on male rape: The hidden toll of stigma and shame.* New York: Insight Books.

Schiff, A. (1980). Examination and treatment of the male rape victim. *Southern Medical Journal, 73,* 1498–1502.

Sorenson, S. B., Stein, J. A., Siegel, J. M., Golding, J., & Burnam, M. (1988). The prevalence of adult sexual assault. *Journal of Sex Research, 24,* 101–112.

Stermac, L., del Bove, G., & Addison, M. (2004). Stranger and acquaintance sexual assault of adult males. *Journal of Interpersonal Violence, 19,* 901–915.

Stermac, L., Sheridan, P., Davidson, A., & Dunn, S. (1996). Sexual assault of adult males. *Journal of Interpersonal Violence, 11,* 52–64.

Struckman-Johnson, C. (1988). Forced sex on dates: It happens to men too. *Journal of Sex Research, 24,* 234–241.

Struckman-Johnson, C., & Struckman-Johnson, D. (1994). Men pressured and forced into sexual experience. *Archives of Sexual Behavior, 23,* 93–114.

Struckman-Johnson, C., Struckman-Johnson, D., Rucker, L., Bumby, K., & Donaldson, S. (1996). Sexual coercion reported by men and women in prison. *Journal of Sex Research, 33,* 67–76.

Tewksbury, R., & Mustaine, E. E. (2001). Lifestyle factors associated with the sexual assault of men: A routine activity theory analysis. *The Journal of Men's Studies, 9,* 153–182.

Walker, J., Archer, J., & Davies, M. (2005). Effects of rape on men: A descriptive analysis. *Archives of Sexual Behavior, 34,* 69–80.

Washington, P. A. (1999). Second assault of male survivors of sexual violence. *Journal of Interpersonal Violence, 14,* 713–730.

Waterman, C. K., Dawson, L. J., & Bologna, M. J. (1989). Sexual coercion in gay male and lesbian relationships: Predictors and implications for support services. *Journal of Sex Research, 26,* 118–124.

Wiwanitkit, V. (2005). Male rape, some notes on the laboratory investigation. *Sexuality and Disability, 23*(1), 41–46.

Critical Thinking

1. What are the physical, mental, and sexual consequences of sexual assaults on men?

RICHARD TEWKSBURY, Department of Justice Administration, University of Louisville. Correspondence concerning this article should be addressed to Richard Tewksbury, Department of Justice Administration, University of Louisville, Louisville, KY 40292. Electronic mail: tewks@louisville.edu.

From *International Journal of Men's Health*, Spring 2007, pp. 22–35. Copyright © 2007 by Men's Studies Press. Reprinted by permission.

Test-Your-Knowledge Form

We encourage you to photocopy and use this page as a tool to assess how the articles in *Annual Editions* expand on the information in your textbook. By reflecting on the articles you will gain enhanced text information. You can also access this useful form on a product's book support website at www.mhhe.com/cls.

NAME: DATE:

_____

TITLE AND NUMBER OF ARTICLE:

_____

BRIEFLY STATE THE MAIN IDEA OF THIS ARTICLE:

_____

LIST THREE IMPORTANT FACTS THAT THE AUTHOR USES TO SUPPORT THE MAIN IDEA:

_____

WHAT INFORMATION OR IDEAS DISCUSSED IN THIS ARTICLE ARE ALSO DISCUSSED IN YOUR TEXTBOOK OR OTHER READINGS THAT YOU HAVE DONE? LIST THE TEXTBOOK CHAPTERS AND PAGE NUMBERS:

_____

LIST ANY EXAMPLES OF BIAS OR FAULTY REASONING THAT YOU FOUND IN THE ARTICLE:

_____

LIST ANY NEW TERMS/CONCEPTS THAT WERE DISCUSSED IN THE ARTICLE, AND WRITE A SHORT DEFINITION:

NOTES

NOTES

NOTES

NOTES

NOTES

NOTES

NOTES

NOTES